# PLAYS
## for the
# THEATRE

*A Drama Anthology*

# PLAYS
## for the
# THEATRE

## A *Drama Anthology*

### FIFTH EDITION

# Edited by Oscar G. Brockett

HOLT, RINEHART AND WINSTON, INC.

New York   Chicago   San Francisco
Philadelphia   Montreal   Toronto
London   Sydney   Tokyo

Cover Photograph by Steve Sharp

The editor of *Plays for the Theatre* is grateful to the following publishers, playwrights, and translators for permission to reprint the plays in this volume:

*The Oedipus Rex of Sophocles:* An English version by Dudley Fitts and Robert Fitzgerald, copyright 1949 by Harcourt Brace Jovanovich, Inc.; renewed 1977 by Cornelis Fitts and Robert Fitzgerald. Reprinted by permission of the publisher. CAUTION: All rights, including professional, amateur, motion picture, recitation, lecturing, public reading, radio broadcasting, and television are strictly reserved. Inquiries on all rights should be addressed to Harcourt Brace Jovanovich, Inc., Orlando, FL 32887.

*The Menaechmi* by Plautus, reprinted by permission of the publishers from *The Menaechmi of Plautus*, translated into English prose and verse by Richard W. Hyde and Edward C. Weist, Cambridge, Mass.: Harvard University Press, Copyright © 1930 by the President and Fellows of Harvard College: © 1958 by Richard W. Hyde and Edward C. Weist.

*The Second Shepherds' Play*, reprinted from *An Anthology of English Drama Before Shakespeare* by permission of the editor, Robert B. Heilman.

*The Shrine in the Fields (Nonomiya)*, translated by H. Paul Varley in *Twenty Plays of the Nō Theatre*, edited by Donald Keene. Copyright © 1970 Columbia University Press. By permission.

*Tartuffe*, translated and copyright © 1961, 1962, 1963 by Richard Wilbur, is reprinted by permission of Harcourt Brace Jovanovich, Inc.; CAUTION: Professional and amateurs are hereby warned that this translation, being fully protected under the copyright laws of the United States, the British Commonwealth, including the Dominion of Canada, and all other countries which are signatories of the Universal Copyright Convention and the International Copyright Union, is subject to royalty. All rights, including professional, amateur, motion picture, recitation, lecturing, public reading, radio broadcasting, and television are strictly reserved. Inquiries on professional and amateur rights should be addressed to Mr. Gilbert Parker, Curtis Brown Ltd., Ten Astor Place, New York, NY 10003. Inquiries on translation rights should be addressed to Harcourt Brace Jovanovich, Inc., Orlando, FL 32887.

*(continued on p. vi)*

**Library of Congress Cataloging-in-Publication Data**

Plays for the theatre.

1. Drama—Collections.     I. Brockett, Oscar Gross,
1923–      .
PN6112.P57   1988        808.82        87-299

**ISBN 0-03-012803-X**

8 9 090 9 8 7 6 5 4 3 2 1

Holt, Rinehart and Winston, Inc.
The Dryden Press
Saunders College Publishing

*To the Memory of my Wife: Lenyth Brockett*

# Contents

# Introduction

Selecting the plays for an anthology is a task accompanied by both anguish and risk — anguish at the realization of how many excellent plays must be left out, and risk because it is always uncertain whether plays long regarded as masterpieces will still speak to the contemporary reader. Any selection is arbitrary to a degree but I have chosen plays that have stood the test of long performance in the theatre or, in the case of recent dramas, those that seem to have the likelihood of doing so. I have also selected plays that are representative of various periods, countries, and genres. Obviously, the impression of drama gained by knowing only some of its finest examples is incomplete. Nevertheless, a useful if limited view of past drama can be obtained by reading some outstanding plays, much as one might get acquainted with a new terrain by noting its highest mountain peaks. This collection, then, offers a rough map of drama as revealed by significant plays ranging from the classic to the contemporary.

**Oedipus Rex** [c. 430 B.C.]    The world's oldest surviving dramas are the tragedies that were presented during the fifth century B.C. at the religious and civic festivals held in Athens to honor the god Dionysus. *Oedipus Rex* is considered by many critics to be the greatest of these works, and in modern times it has been one of the most frequently produced Greek plays. Aristotle, in his celebrated discussion of tragedy (written in the fourth century B.C.) refers to it often as an ideal example of the tragic form.

The most striking feature of Greek tragedy is the alternation of dramatic episodes (or scenes) with choral passages. Little is known for certain about the Greek tragic chorus, but in Sophocles' day it probably included fifteen performers who sang (or recited) and danced the choral passages to musical accompaniment. The Chorus (in *Oedipus Rex* composed of Elders from the City of Thebes) acts as a group, gives advice to the leading characters, expresses the community's point of view (and sometimes the playwright's), and functions as an "ideal spectator." Other typical features of Greek tragedy are the small number of individualized characters, the restriction of the action to a single place, the tightly unified plot, the serious and philosophic tone, and the poetic language.

The action of *Oedipus Rex* is extremely concentrated, for a complete reversal of the hero's position takes place in a single day. The story follows Oedipus, King of Thebes, as he attempts to discover the murderer of Laius, the former king, after an oracle has declared that the plague now destroying the people will not be lifted until the guilty one is cast out. Oedipus' search gradually uncovers terrible truths about the past and his own origins. The initial suspicion that Oedipus himself may

*1*

be the slayer of Laius is a moment of high dramatic tension; it is followed by other electrifying moments (such as Jocasta's recognition that she is both Oedipus' wife and his mother) and the ultimate outcome: blindness, exile, and anguish for the once mighty king.

Sophocles is particularly admired for his skillful management of extensive plot materials: he accomplishes the gradual unveiling of mystery after mystery and a steady increase in dramatic tension, with the utmost economy of means. Although, like many great plays, *Oedipus Rex* is open to many interpretations, most critics have agreed that its central concern is the uncertainty of fate and man's helplessness in the face of destiny.

**The Menaechmi** [c. 184 B.C.]    Of the few Roman plays that survive, the majority are comedies. Indeed, rollicking farces (exemplified by Plautus' *The Menaechmi*) designed solely for entertainment are a peculiarly Roman contribution to the development of drama. The subject matter of surviving Roman comedies is drawn from everyday domestic life and features intrigues that turn on mistaken identity, misunderstood motives, and deliberate deception. The characters are familiar, if sometimes exaggerated types: the old man obsessed with his money or children, the young man who rebels against parental authority, the clever slave, the parasite who lives by flattery and trickery, the courtesan or mistress, the shrewish wife, the unscrupulous slave dealer, and the cowardly soldier. Latin comedy has no chorus, but the action is sometimes interrupted by songs. Thus, it often resembles modern musical comedy.

Plautus opens *The Menaechmi* with a prologue designed to put the audience at ease and to set forth humorously all the information needed to understand what is to come. The opening scenes introduce the characters and situation, the comical possibilities of which are then fully exploited as the twins are in turn mistaken for each other. Plautus' inventiveness is everywhere evident, but especially in the reunion, for its potential sentimentality is subverted by good-natured cynicism when Menaechmus I offers all his property for sale — including his wife.

Although wholly different in tone, Latin comedy shares with Greek tragedy many structural conventions: a story is taken up near the climactic moment; action and time are restricted in scope; and there is no intermingling of serious and comic elements. In the Renaissance, when dramatists turned to antiquity for guidance, it was the Latin writers, above all, from whom they learned. Thus Roman comedy is important not only in its own right but also for its influence on later practices.

**The Second Shepherds' Play** [1425–1450 A.D.]    After Rome was overrun by invaders in the fifth century A.D., public performances financed by the state ceased, and thereafter for approximately five hundred years theatrical activity in Western Europe was at best sporadic. Then drama was revived by the Catholic Church, although in a form radically different from that seen in Greece or Rome. Beginning in the tenth century, short playlets dramatizing Biblical events were performed in Latin in connection with church services. Around 1200, plays began to be presented out of doors, and eventually they were elaborated into lengthy series, or cycles, of plays dramatizing events ranging from the Creation to the Last Judgment. Productions of cycles were usually financed by trade guilds or religious societies;

written in the vernacular language, the cycles often required several days to perform in their entirety. *The Second Shepherds' Play* is the thirteenth segment (out of a total of thirty-two) from the cycle performed at Wakefield, England. Thus it is only one part of a much larger whole.

The major portion of *The Second Shepherds' Play* is an elaboration of a single sentence in the New Testament (Luke 2:8): "And there were in the same country shepherds abiding in the field, keeping watch over their flock by night." This hint has been transformed into a short play rich in contemporary medieval detail and farcical humor. The anonymous author opens his story with a scene in which each of three shepherds complains of his hardships; thus, characters and situation are introduced in a leisurely fashion. Forward movement of the action does not begin until Mak appears, but thereafter it progresses swiftly as Mak steals a sheep, takes it home, and attempts to pass it off as a newborn baby when the suspicious shepherds arrive looking for the missing animal; the ruse is discovered and Mak is punished. Then, in a manner not unusual in medieval literature, the tone of the play alters suddenly, an angel appears to announce the birth of Christ, and the shepherds go to Bethlehem to worship him. The Biblical text thus is the basis for a short, entertaining farce that has been linked to a wholly serious and devotional playlet celebrating the birth of Christ. The mingling of such diverse elements and the rapid shift in tone and locale, typical of medieval practice, clearly distinguishes the drama of this age from that of the classical era.

**The Shrine in the Fields (Nonomiya)** [Fifteenth Century]   While the religious cycles were flourishing in Europe, a markedly different kind of drama was developing half way round the world in Japan. There, Noh drama and its performance were so codified that they remain today much as they were 500 years ago.

Each Noh script is very short. The dialogue serves principally to outline the circumstances which lead up to and culminate in a dance. A musical dance-drama, Noh is sung or intoned. Furthermore, many of the protagonist's lines are delivered by a chorus of six to ten members who sit immobile at one side of the stage. An orchestra, composed of two or three drums and a flute, accompanies the action.

Noh is performed on a stage whose features have long been standardized. The main stage is about 18 feet square. Behind it, backed by a wall on which a stylized pine tree is painted, is a shallow space where the musicians sit. An area to the left of the stage is reserved for the chorus. The actors make their entrances along a bridge, about six feet wide and about 40 feet long. There is no scenery. Stage properties are sometimes used, but these are bamboo skeletal outlines of the things they represent (boats, huts, shrines, etc.). They are set in place and removed by stage attendants, who remain on stage throughout but are considered to be invisible.

Actors are divided into two main categories: those who play the *waki* (the secondary character whose function it is to introduce the drama and lead the main character to reveal the secret which will culminate in a climactic dance) and his followers; and those who play the *shite* (the main character) and his followers. The *shite* characters wear carved and painted masks. All the actors are male, and all wear embroidered silk costumes, with one garment layered on top of another. Headdresses and fans are important accessories.

The conventions of Noh drama are fixed and precise. Although the scripts are short, they usually require more than an hour to perform. A Noh program is made up of from three to five plays rather than a single work.

The major influence on Noh is Zen Buddhism, which teaches that ultimate peace comes from overcoming individual desire to achieve union with all being. The protagonists of Noh are ghosts, demons, or obsessed humans whose souls cannot find rest because in life they became too devoted to love, honor, or other goals that pull them back into the physical world.

*The Shrine in the Fields* represents one of the five basic types of Noh plays. A "woman play," it is based on episodes from a famous Japanese novel, *The Tale of Genji*, in which Lord Genji is the lover of Lady Rokujo (the protagonist of *The Shrine in the Fields*) but after a time he neglects her. At a festival, attendants on Lord Genji's wife publicly humiliate Lady Rokujo by pushing her carriage out of the procession and disabling it. She then leaves the capital and goes to Nonomiya, where her daughter is being prepared to become priestess of Ise (the Sun Goddess). While at Nonomiya, Lady Rokujo is visited by Lord Genji, who begs her to return to him. Although she refuses, her love and humiliation keep drawing her back to Nonomiya even after her death.

In Noh, each play occurs in a specific season of the year and the mood throughout must be in keeping with that season. In *The Shrine in the Fields*, the season is Autumn and the mood is one of melancholy and bittersweet longing. The introductory scene drastically compresses time and place: the itinerant priest (the *waki*) travels almost instantaneously from the capital to Nonomiya. The ghost of Lady Rokujo (in the guise of a village girl) appears and, as the priest questions her, it becomes apparent that she is protecting some secret. Later she returns as herself, the Miyasudokoro (Lady Rokujo) of long ago. As she tells her story, the emotion builds until, as in all Noh plays, it finds expression in a dance. The script does not indicate its length, but in performance the dance lasts for 20 or more minutes. In the final scene, the pulls between this and the next world are fully symbolized by passing back and forth through the gate of the shrine. At the end, the freeing of the soul is indicated by Miyasudokoro rushing out of the "burning house," an image for the world, which in Buddhist teaching enlightened persons are counseled to flee as willingly as they would a burning building. Thus, at the end we are asked to believe that Miyasudo-koro has at last broken her attachment to the world.

A number of devices are used to distance the spectator from the action. The language is stylized throughout; there are numerous quotations from earlier literary works; most of the passages are intoned or sung; the lines of dialogue are divided between the characters and the chorus; and the climactic scene is danced. In addition, the stage remains bare except for the addition of the outline of a shrine gate and brushwood fence.

Overall, *The Shrine in the Fields* does not seek to tell a story or to develop character so much as to capture a particular mood, to distill a powerful emotion, and to express an attitude about the physical world and human existence. Although its message may resemble that of western Medieval religious drama, its means are quite different.

**Hamlet** [c. 1600]    For many reasons, but primarily because of religious controversies, the production of medieval cycles was forbidden or abandoned in the sixteenth century. This separation of drama from the church stimulated the development of a wholly secular theatre. The first country to produce a drama of lasting excellence was England during the years between 1580 and 1640. Indeed, the plays of William Shakespeare, which date from this period, often are said to be the finest ever written.

The plays of the English Renaissance were still sufficiently close to their medieval predecessors to retain many practices from the earlier era: a sprawling, often episodic plot; scenes set in many times and places; and intermingled comic and serious elements. Before the end of the sixteenth century, however, renewed interest in classical drama had modified and refined medieval practices cosiderably to create more complex conceptions of dramatic form and characterization. A synthesis of medieval and classical inheritances can be noted in Shakespeare's works, which are both numerous and varied in dramatic type. Shakespeare's genius is probably seen at its best, however, in the tragedies, of which Hamlet is an outstanding example.

Like *Oedipus Rex*, *Hamlet* has as its protagonist a man who is charged with punishing the murderer of a king. But Shakespeare uses a much broader canvas than Sophocles does and includes within his drama more facets of his story, more characters, and a wider sweep of time and place. *Hamlet* is rich in implications, of which the most important is the pervasiveness of betrayal — brother of brother, wife of husband, parent of child, friend of friend — which almost overpowers Hamlet as he learns that his father has been murdered by his uncle, that his mother has been unfaithful to his father, that his mother has accepted his uncle's usurpation of the throne that is rightfully his, and that his supposed friends have become his uncle's spies. A second set of implications is related to the opposing demands made on Hamlet — that he right the injustices occasioned by his father's death (seemingly requiring him to murder his uncle) and that he adhere to Christian teachings (under which that murder would be a deadly sin). Another group of implications concerns the nature of kingship and the need to rule oneself before attempting to rule others. This motif is seen especially in the conduct of Claudius and is suggested through the contrast between Claudius and his dead brother and between Hamlet and Fortinbras (who is left to return order to the state). Shakespeare's dramatic poetry is generally conceded to be the finest in the English language. The basic medium is blank verse, which allows the flexibility of ordinary speech while elevating it through imagery and rhythm.

Because of its compelling story, powerful characters, and great poetry, *Hamlet* is one of the world's finest achievements in drama. Although it embodies many ideas typical of its time, it transcends the limitations of a particular era. It continues to move spectators in the theatre as it has since its first presentation around 1600.

**Tartuffe** [1669]    While English drama retained many medieval traditions, continental dramatists were more inclined to follow Greek and Roman practices. This conscious imitation of the classics led to a set of literary standards summed up in the term *neoclassicism*; these included the unities of time, place, and action; strict distinction between tragedy and comedy, with no intermingling of serious and comic elements; the use of universalized character types; and the demand that drama teach moral lessons. Most of the plays written in compliance with these rules now seem lifeless, but the tragedies of Racine and the comedies of Molière, written in France during the seventeenth century, reached a peak of artistry in the neoclassical mode.

Molière is one of the most skillful and inventive comic dramatists of all times, and *Tartuffe* is one of his best plays. Here, within the restricted frame of one room, one day, and one main story, using a limited number of characters and little physical action, Molière has created an excellent comedy of character in the neoclassic style.

The plot of *Tartuffe* can be divided into five stages: the demonstration of Tartuffe's complete hold over Orgon, the unmasking of Tartuffe, Tartuffe's attempted revenge, the foiling of Tartuffe's plan, and the happy resolution. Each scene of the play, with the possible exception of the young lovers' quarrel, contributes to the main action and hence to the play's unity. The scene in which Orgon hides under the table while Tartuffe attempts to seduce Elmire, Orgon's wife, is one of the most amusing in all comic drama. Molière has been criticized for delaying Tartuffe's appearance until the third act, but he makes skillful use of this delay by having other characters discuss Tartuffe at length, thereby establishing clearly his hypocrisy and Orgon's gullibility in trusting him. The final resolution, in which Tartuffe is suddenly discovered to be a notorious criminal, has also been criticized as overly contrived but it is emotionally satisfying since it punishes Tartuffe and reestablishes the norm.

In *Tartuffe*, Molière uses the verse form which by that time had become standard in tragedy — the alexandrine (twelve-syllable lines, with each pair of adjacent lines rhyming). Critics agree that Richard Wilbur's translation is the most satisfactory one now available, both for accuracy and for its rendition of Molière's verse. *Tartuffe* was first presented in its five-act form in 1669 and has since remained in the repertory almost continuously. It is still performed more often than any other play by Molière.

**The Servant of Two Masters** [1745]    One of the most popular of all theatrical forms between 1575 and 1775 was *commedia dell'arte*. Originating in Italy, it spread throughout Europe and became a favorite with audiences ranging from rulers to peasants. It influenced many European dramatists, among them Molière, who wrote a number of comedies around *commedia* characters. Originally, a *commedia* script was merely a scenario that outlined the situation, complications, and outcome. In performance, the actors improvised the dialogue and fleshed out the action. The plots were most often comic, revolving around love affairs and comic misunderstandings and deliberate deceptions. The actors developed a number of surefire bits of comic business *(lazzi)* which could be brought in if the audience appeared to be losing interest.

*Commedia* scripts utilized a number of fixed characters. There were usually two pairs of young lovers. Unlike the other roles, these did not make use of masks and they dressed in the latest fashions. They were usually the children of other stock characters, especially Pantalone (a Venetian merchant) and Dottore (a lawyer or doctor who loved to show off his spurious learning). These characters had their fixed costumes and masks. The most varied of the *commedia* types were the servants *(zanni)*, of whom the most popular was Arlecchino (Harlequin), a mixture of cunning and stupidity and usually at the center of every intrigue and mix-up. His costume of diamond-shaped red, green, and blue pattern is the most familiar of all the *commedia* traditions. His mask was black. Sometimes this character was called by other names (in *The Servant of Two Masters* he is called Truffaldino). Among the other servants, a rather coarse, somewhat bawdy maid figured prominently. She carried on her own love intrigues with one or more male servants. In *The Servant of Two Masters* she is called Smeraldina.

By the 1730's, *commedia* had lost much of its vitality, in part because it had become repetitious and predictable. Carlo Goldoni, a Venetian playwright, sought to revive it by reforming some of its conventions. Among his reforms, perhaps the most important was achieved when acting companies permitted him to write out all the dialogue, while leaving room for the actors to improvise *lazzi*. *The Servant of Two Masters* is among the most successful plays of this type. Through it, we can recapture much of the flavor and spirit of *commedia*, even though the element of improvisation has largely disappeared.

*The Servant of Two Masters* incorporates the stock characters of *commedia*. There are two pairs of lovers (Clarice and Silvio; Beatrice and Florindo), two masters (Pantalone and Dottore), and three servants (Truffaldino, Smeraldina, and Brighella — although Brighella has been transformed into an innkeeper). By far the most important character is Truffaldino, for, though the story revolves around the lovers, it is Truffaldino's stupidity which creates most of the difficulties and his cleverness which resolves them. He is also offered several opportunities to improvise *lazzi*, the most extended being his attempt to serve dinner to two groups simultaneously.

Goldoni is a master of plot development. Everything is carefully set up in the opening scenes, although much of the subsequent action is facilitated by coincidence — especially that of Beatrice (disguised as her brother) and Florindo (her lover) taking up residence in the same inn and each hiring Truffaldino as a servant.

In *The Servant of Two Masters*, Goldoni is concerned primarily with providing entertainment for a popular audience and with reworking the conventions of a long-familiar form. That he succeeded is indicated by the continuing popularity of the play.

**The Wild Duck** [1884]   During the nineteenth century a revolt against absolute values and sentimentality gave rise to Modernism, of which the first important manifestation was Realism. Many influences contributed to the realist vision, among them deepening interest in the emerging sciences of sociology and psychology and emphasis on environment as a determinant of human behavior. The result was a drama based on contemporary events closely observed and carefully rendered through lifelike dialogue and detailed settings. Henrik Ibsen's plays epitomize the new trend so well that he is often called the founder of modern drama. *The Wild Duck* illustrates many of the techniques Ibsen used; it reproduces the speech and actions of ordinary people of the middle and lower classes in a fully detailed environment that plays an essential part in the story. In his dialogue Ibsen abandoned the older devices of the aside and soliloquy; instead, his characters reveal themselves as they would in real life, through indirection rather than explicit statement.

In *The Wild Duck*, the idealistic Gregers Werle returns home after an absence of fifteen years, decides that the lives of all his acquaintances are based on lies, and determines to make them face the truth. His efforts lead to catastrophe: in forcing some unwelcome truths on his former schoolmate, Hjalmar Ekdal, he sets in train a series of events that end with a child's suicide. Opposed to Gregers in this tug of war between truth and illusion is Dr. Relling, who believes that people need a "saving lie" in order to endure life. Hjalmar illustrates this principle, for he enjoys a lazy, happy and self-centered life under the illusion that he will someday discover a great invention. Because of Ibsen's ironic treatment of Hjalmar, the play has many passages of genuine humor that relieve the generally somber tone.

Ibsen's themes are related to the central motif of the wild duck, which seems to symbolize various stages in human experience: the unfettered freedom of youth, the wounds of experiences, the effort to escape, and the necessity of going on living, though wounded and in an environment of illusions (symbolized by the Ekdals' attic). An engrossing play because of its tightly woven story, believable characters, and skillful balance of the serious and the satiric, *The Wild Duck* is significant from a historical viewpoint both as one of the works that helped to establish a new realistic drama and as a forerunner of Symbolist drama which was to become important in the next decade.

**"The Hairy Ape"** [1921]    Of the several revolts against Realism in the late nineteenth and early twentieth centuries, the earliest was Symbolism. Rejecting the Realists' belief that truth is discovered by close observation of the environment, the Symbolists held that external appearances were merely the mask of inner spiritual realities that could only be communicated through the use of symbols. Although the appeal of this drama was limited, it foreshadowed other antirealistic movements, including Expressionism, which emerged in Germany around 1912 and which spread to other countries after 1918. The Expressionists proclaimed the supreme importance of the human spirit, which they believed was being crushed or distorted by materialism and industrialization; like the Symbolists, they regarded appearance as the mask of significant inner truths. Therefore, to comprehend Expressionist drama the reader must be prepared to look behind its deliberate distortions for deeper significance.

*"The Hairy Ape"* shows the influence of Expressionism on American drama. The unity of the play derives from a central theme: man's frustrated search for identity in a hostile environment. In the first scene, Yank is confident that he and his fellow stokers are the only ones who "belong" because it is they who make the ship go (and, by extension, the factories and machines of modern industrialized society). But when the shipowner's pampered, anemic daughter (who represents the power of money and influence) calls Yank a "filthy beast" (a "hairy ape"), his confidence is shattered. Seeking to reestablish his identity, he first visits Fifth Avenue, the home territory of the rich and powerful, where he proclaims his superiority by physically attacking the men only to have his very existence go unacknowledged. Thrown into jail, he decides that the answer lies in destroying the steel and machinery over which he originally thought he had power. In jail he learns that the IWW opposes the owners of factories and ships and, when he is released, he offers to blow up the IWW's enemies. Rejected there too, Yank decides that the answer may lie with the apes at the zoo. When he releases a gorilla, it crushes him, and he dies still without a sense of belonging.

Yank is symbolic of modern man in an industrialized society — cut off from a past when human beings had an integral relationship with the natural environment and now little better than cogs in the industrial machine — he feels alienated from his world and lacks all sense of belonging. As Yank says to the gorilla, "I ain't got no past to tink in, nor nothin' dat's comin', on'y what's now — and dat don't belong."

*"The Hairy Ape"* is representative of the outlook and techniques of Expressionism. The episodic structure and distorted visual elements are typical of the movement, as is the longing for fulfillment, which suggests a need to change society so that the individual can find a coherent, satisfying relationship between himself and his world.

### The Good Woman of Setzuan [1940]

The Expressionists' idealistic dream of transforming mankind foundered in disillusionment during the 1920's. Some writers came to believe that society could be improved only by adopting a program of concrete political action, and in the theatre they sought to focus attention on the great difference between human needs and existing conditions. Attempts to use the theatre as a weapon of social action took several forms, but the most significant and fruitful from an aesthetic viewpoint was Epic Theatre, exemplified in the plays of Bertolt Brecht. Brecht used many of the devices of Expressionist drama, such as episodic structure, unity derived from theme or thesis, and nonillusionistic visual elements. But Brecht, unlike the Expressionists, did not suggest that external appearance is untruthful or insignificant; rather, he wished to provoke audiences to reflect on the immediate world and its injustices, and he believed that he could do so most effectively if his audience remained fully conscious that it was in a theatre. Rejecting the theatre of illusion on the basis that it merely lulls the spectator's critical faculties, Brecht devised several techniques (such as inserted songs, projected captions, and presentational acting) to interrupt the empathetic response and intensify the spectator's awareness of social, economic, and political injustices. It was his hope that the spectator would become aware of the need to work for change outside the theatre.

*The Good Woman of Setzuan* is a parable about the difficulties of remaining good under existing social and economic conditions. The "good woman," Shen Te, is generous and well-intentioned, but she soon finds herself exploited and betrayed. Her solution is to disguise herself as her cousin Shui Ta—that is, to let the exploitative side of her character determine her actions. As time passes, she finds herself more and more frequently forced into taking on the role of the ruthless "cousin." Brecht uses this device to suggest the progressive deterioration of morality. The play ends in a stalemate, for the Gods leave Shen Te with the same simplistic message they delivered in the prologue — "Be good" — and she is no nearer to knowing how to accomplish this.

The play alternates short and long scenes. The short scenes serve the purposes of breaking up and commenting on the action. They contribute to Brecht's aim of forcing the audience to think by giving it clues about the significance of what it has seen and time in which to reflect upon it. The long scenes are broken up by the insertion of songs and speeches delivered directly to the audience. While not all the songs are closely related to the plot, they do serve to underscore Brecht's main ideas about society. Throughout the play Brecht skillfully and persistently reminds the audience that Shen Te's predicament is a universal human situation — and one that might be solved by taking the right social and political action.

### Death of a Salesman [1949]

Symbolism, Expressionism, Epic Theatre, and other antirealistic styles by no means replaced Realism in the modern theatre, but they unquestionably altered it. Realistic plays written since World War II are radically different in tone and technique from the works of Ibsen and earlier Realists. In general outlook, they differ from earlier drama principally by portraying human personality as more complex, and by being less optimistic about the likelihood of improving society. At the same time, dramatic techniques have been taken over from nonrealistic drama.

Many of these results are seen to good effect in Arthur Miller's *Death of a Salesman*. The play's structure, with its fluid handling of time and place to follow the shifting thoughts of the protagonist, is so unlike the drama of Ibsen that on first acquaintance it may seem an entirely different style. Yet, like Ibsen, Miller evokes a specific social milieu, carefully observed and rendered, and creates a highly individualized protagonist, the vivid and memorable Willy Loman.

*Death of a Salesman* develops a primary conflict in the American consciousness: its tendency to measure success in wholly material terms even though it upholds love and family cohesiveness as major values. As a result, the play suggests, Americans often unconsciously mingle these goals in such a way that love and approval are withheld from those who have not succeeded materially. Miller has embodied this conflict in Willy Loman's obsessive desire to succeed and his confusion of success with the right to be loved. Miller has used two characters to represent the poles between which Willy is pulled. Uncle Ben, Willy's brother, epitomizes material success, while Linda, Willy's wife, represents love given without question or conditions.

It is interesting to compare Miller's play with works from earlier periods. Both *Death of a Salesman* and *Oedipus Rex* involve a search into the past to find the roots of present evils. The scenes in *Oedipus Rex*, however, all take place in the present, and the past is revealed only through narration. *Death of a Salesman*, on the other hand, uses "flashbacks" to transport the audience backward in time to witness various scenes. The play shares with *The Good Woman of Setzuan* a concern for the destructiveness of materialistic values.

In *Death of a Salesman* Miller has combined believable characters and a plausible environment with technical devices taken over from nonrealistic styles. When first produced, the play seemed startlingly novel because of this mixture of elements, but subsequent developments have served to define it more clearly as modified Realism. After more than 35 years it is still one of the most effective and moving of all American plays.

**Happy Days** [1961]   In the 1950's a new style, now usually called Absurdism, emerged. *Absurdism* is a term coined by the critic Martin Esslin to describe the work of Samuel Beckett, Eugene Ionesco, and several other dramatists. Esslin concludes the Absurdism grew out of a "sense that the certitudes and unshakable basic assumptions of former ages have been swept away, that they have been . . . discredited as cheap and somewhat childish illusions." Or, as Ionesco put it, "cut off from his religious, metaphysical, and transcendental roots, man is lost; all his actions become senseless, absurd and useless." Most Absurdist plays, rather than telling a story, explore this condition, in which the characters are depicted as seeking to insulate themselves against the void with meaningless activities or abortive attempts at communication.

*Happy Days* embodies most of the traits of Absurdism. It has virtually abandoned action. The first act shows a woman trapped up to her waist in a mound of earth. She does not struggle against her physical entrapment but fills her days with a routine built around objects which she keeps in a shopping bag; she speaks often to her husband, who for the most part remains unseen behind the mound and who responds only rarely. In the second act, she is buried up to her neck and can only move her eyes and mouth; at first she is not even sure that her husband is still alive, but eventually he crawls up the mound into her view. Despite her situation, the woman remains determinedly cheerful; she speaks often of her blessings and the small things that will make this "another happy day." She never questions why she is in this situation, nor does she wonder at her isolation. She apparently accepts her lot as something no more to be questioned than human existence itself.

As in others of his plays, in *Happy Days* Beckett uses visual imagery to sum up his vision of human situation. Here, as in other plays, he shows human beings trapped in a symbolic wasteland, cut off from all but the most minimal contact, passing time as best they can while waiting doggedly or hoping desperately for something that will give meaning to the moment or to life itself. Occasionally they reveal flashes of anxiety, but they quickly divert themselves with games, memories, and speculations.

The form, structure, and mood of *Happy Days* cannot be separated from its meaning. Beckett has said that his plays formulate as clearly as he can what he is trying to convey. In them, there is little progression and there is no resolution in the usual sense. The plays end much as they started; they explore a state of being rather than show a developing action.

**A Raisin in the Sun** [1959]    A fruitful development of the late 1950's, and particularly of the 1960's, was the emergence of plays written by blacks and other minority playwrights. One of the best examples of this drama is A *Raisin in the Sun* by Lorraine Hansberry, the first play by a black woman to appear on Broadway and to be the winner of both the New York Drama Critics Circle and Best Play of the Year Awards.

In many respects it is a traditional play: it focuses on a family and its dreams, and in structure it is a play of impeccable craftsmanship. It concerns the Younger family: the tenacious Lena, or Mama; Beneatha, her daughter, who wants to become a doctor; Walter, Lena's son, a chauffeur; his wife Ruth, a cleaning woman; and Travis, the young son of Walter and Ruth. Poor but proud, they dream of bettering their position in a world where they have been held back because they are black. When they receive the insurance on Mama's recently deceased husband, their dreams seem within reach, but circumstances thwart them. Nevertheless, all come to a better understanding of themselves and, as the play ends, they courageously move into an all-white neighborhood, determined to continue their struggle.

Despite its traditional form, the play introduces almost every theme that has since been developed by black playwrights. The opposition of the white community to the intrusion of the Youngers explores the problem of integration. The contrast between the opportunistic Walter and the idealistic Beneatha dramatizes the difference between materialism and altruism. The issue of the blacks' loss of their heritage is developed through one of Beneatha's suitors, a Nigerian student who arouses the girl's interest in her African "roots." The theme of growth and maturity is touchingly shown by Mama's nurturing of a spindly plant in a tenement window. The final moment, when she takes the plant with her to their new home, implies that the family will not "dry up like a raisin in the sun," but will survive and flourish. In a play of universal appeal, Hansberry makes clear the injustice American society had done to blacks.

**Fool for Love** [1983]    The period since the 1960's has been a time of near-frenetic theatrical experimentation. Much of the drama of this period has employed a surface realism to illuminate ideas or behavior indicative of a much larger pattern. *Fool for Love* by Sam Shepard is an excellent example of this type of drama. Its basic outline is simple: Eddie returns to May after an unexplained absence, swears he loves her and will never leave again; then, after a brief stay, he slips away without warning. It is this pattern — apparently endlessly repetitive — that the play explores. It is the pattern not only of Eddie's and May's relationship but also that of their father and his wives — a compulsive, seemingly-uncontrollable attraction, so intense and overpowering that it cannot be long endured, leading to unannounced departures, long absences, and unpredictable returns. In *Fool for Love*, this pattern is embedded in a gradually-revealed and somewhat sensational story of multiple families and incest.

As are most of Shepard's plays, *Fool for Love* is grounded in myths about America. The myth of the American West, for example, has encouraged the idea that problems can be dealt with best by leaving them behind and moving on. While this myth has its positive side, it also suggests rootlessness, temporariness, and the substitution of fantasy for reality. All of these are evident in *Fool for Love*. The motel room in which the action occurs is a visual embodiment of rootlessness, and all of the characters' possessions apparently can be moved at a moment's notice.

As the title suggests, the play also deals with attitudes about love. Both Eddie and the Old Man have believed that their women will wait happily at home while they themselves go away without warning and return when ready. But the characters cannot merely accept love; they demand it and feel cheated if they believe that what is owed them is given to another. May threatens violence to both Eddie and the Countess; the unseen Countess vents her rage through violence; and Eddie projects an aura of suppressed violence toward Martin. Throughout the play, Eddie and May express frustration, guilt, and resentment at their own inability to fulfill others' expectations, and it is implied that the Old Man finally gave up both his families because of the same feelings. Love, then, makes fools of those who wish to own and control loved ones. It becomes a sado-masochistic game which no one wins, simultaneously obsessive and destructive. Martin, the only character who does not fit this pattern, seems incapable of deep feeling, either for himself or others.

That Shepard is not attempting to write a wholly realistic play is indicated in several ways. The Old Man is both present and absent, a visual reminder of the ongoing pattern that the play treats. Furthermore, the incestuous relationship of May and Eddie is symbolic as well as actual: their compulsions are a form of inbreeding that perpetuates a pattern.

Overall, both the realism and symbolism in *Fool for Love* are important only as they support or reflect these underlying patterns.

# Sophocles

# Oedipus Rex

## English Version by Dudley Fitts and Robert Fitzgerald

PERSONS REPRESENTED

OEDIPUS
A PRIEST
CREON
TEIRESIAS
IOCASTE [JOCASTA]
MESSENGER
SHEPHERD OF LAÏOS
SECOND MESSENGER
CHORUS OF THEBAN ELDERS

THE SCENE———*Before the palace of* OEDIPUS, *King of Thebes. A central door and two lateral doors open onto a platform which runs the length of the façade. On the platform, right and left, are altars; and three steps lead down into the "orchestra," or chorus-ground. At the beginning of the action these steps are crowded by suppliants who have brought branches and chaplets of olive leaves and who lie in various attitudes of despair.* OEDIPUS *enters.*

## PROLOGUE

OEDIPUS:  My children, generations of the living
    In the line of Kadmos, nursed at his ancient hearth:
    Why have you strewn yourselves before these altars
    In supplication, with your boughs and garlands?
    The breath of incense rises from the city
    With a sound of prayer and lamentation.
                       Children,
    I would not have you speak through messengers,
    And therefore I have come myself to hear you—
    I, Oedipus, who bear the famous name.
       [*To a* PRIEST.]
    You, there, since you are eldest in the company,
    Speak for them all, tell me what preys upon you,
    Whether you come in dread, or crave some blessing:
    Tell me, and never doubt that I will help you

13

In every way I can; I should be heartless
Were I not moved to find you suppliant here.
PRIEST: Great Oedipus, O powerful King of Thebes!
You see how all the ages of our people
Cling to your altar steps: here are boys
Who can barely stand alone, and here are priests
By weight of age, as I am a priest of God,
And young men chosen from those yet unmarried;
As for the others, all that multitude,
They wait with olive chaplets in the squares,
At the two shrines of Pallas, and where Apollo
Speaks in the glowing embers.
                                        Your own eyes
Must tell you: Thebes is tossed on a murdering sea
And can not lift her head from the death surge.
A rust consumes the buds and fruits of the earth;
The herds are sick; children die unborn,
And labor is vain. The god of plague and pyre
Raids like detestable lightning through the city,
And all the house of Kadmos is laid waste,
All emptied, and all darkened; Death alone
Battens upon the misery of Thebes.

You are not one of the immortal gods, we know;
Yet we have come to you to make our prayer
As to the man surest in mortal ways
And wisest in the ways of God. You saved us
From the Sphinx, that flinty singer, and the tribute
We paid to her so long; yet you were never
Better informed than we, nor could we teach you:
It was some god breathed in you to set us free.

Therefore, O mighty King, we turn to you:
Find us our safety, find us a remedy,
Whether by counsel of the gods or men.
A king of wisdom tested in the past
Can act in a time of troubles, and act well.
Noblest of men, restore
Life to your city! Think how all men call you
Liberator for your triumph long ago;
Ah, when your years of kingship are remembered,
Let them not say *We rose, but later fell*—
Keep the State from going down in the storm!
Once, years ago, with happy augury,
You brought us fortune; be the same again!
No man questions your power to rule the land:
But rule over men, not over a dead city!
Ships are only hulls, citadels are nothing,

When no life moves in the empty passageways.
OEDIPUS: Poor children! You may be sure I know
All that you longed for in your coming here.
I know that you are deathly sick; and yet,
Sick as you are, not one is as sick as I.
Each of you suffers in himself alone
His anguish, not another's; but my spirit
Groans for the city, for myself, for you.

I was not sleeping, you are not waking me.
No, I have been in tears for a long while
And in my restless thought walked many ways.
In all my search, I found one helpful course,
And that I have taken: I have sent Creon,
Son of Menoikeus, brother of the Queen,
To Delphi, Apollo's place of revelation,
To learn there, if he can,
What act or pledge of mine may save the city.
I have counted the days, and now, this very day,
I am troubled, for he has overstayed his time.
What is he doing? He has been gone too long.
Yet whenever he comes back, I should do ill
To scant whatever duty God reveals.
PRIEST: It is a timely promise. At this instant
They tell me Creon is here.
OEDIPUS:                              O Lord Apollo!
May his news be fair as his face is radiant!
PRIEST: It could not be otherwise: he is crowned with bay,
The chaplet is thick with berries.
OEDIPUS:                              We shall soon know;
He is near enough to hear us now.
          [*Enter* CREON.]
                              O Prince:
Brother: son of Menoikeus:
What answer do you bring us from the god?
CREON: A strong one. I can tell you, great afflictions
Will turn out well, if they are taken well.
OEDIPUS: What was the oracle? These vague words
Leave me still hanging between hope and fear.
CREON: Is it your pleasure to hear me with all these
Gathered around us? I am prepared to speak,
But should we not go in?
OEDIPUS:                              Let them all hear it.
It is for them I suffer, more than for myself.
CREON: Then I will tell you what I heard at Delphi.

In plain words
The god commands us to expel from the land of Thebes

An old difilement we are sheltering.
It is a deathly thing, beyond cure;
We must not let it feed upon us longer.
OEDIPUS: What defilement? How shall we rid ourselves of it?
CREON: By exile or death, blood for blood. It was
Murder that brought the plague-wind on the city.
OEDIPUS: Murder of whom? Surely the god has named him?
CREON: My lord: long ago Laïos was our king,
Before you came to govern us.
OEDIPUS:                                        I know;
I learned of him from others; I never saw him.
CREON: He was murdered; and Apollo commands us now
To take revenge upon whoever killed him.
OEDIPUS: Upon whom? Where are they? Where shall we find a clue
To solve that crime, after so many years?
CREON: Here in this land, he said
                              If we make enquiry,
We may touch things that otherwise escape us.
OEDIPUS: Tell me: Was Laïos murdered in his house,
Or in the fields, or in some foreign country?
CREON: He said he planned to make a pilgrimage.
He did not come home again.
OEDIPUS:                                        And was there no one,
No witness, no companion, to tell what happened?
CREON: They were all killed but one, and he got away
So frightened that he could remember one thing only.
OEDIPUS: What was that one thing? One may be the key
To everything, if we resolve to use it.
CREON: He said that a band of highwaymen attacked them,
Outnumbered them, and overwhelmed the King.
OEDIPUS: Strange, that a highwayman should be so daring—
Unless some faction here bribed him to do it.
CREON: We thought of that. But after Laïos' death
New troubles arose and we had no avenger.
OEDIPUS: What troubles could prevent your hunting down the killers?
CREON: The riddling Sphinx's song
Made us deaf to all mysteries but her own.
OEDIPUS: Then once more I must bring what is dark to light.
It is most fitting that Apollo shows,
As you do, this compunction for the dead.
You shall see how I stand by you, as I should,
To avenge the city and the city's god,
And not as though it were for some distant friend,
But for my own sake, to be rid of evil.
Whoever killed King Laïos might—who knows?—
Decide at any moment to kill me as well.
By avenging the murdered king I protect myself.

Come, then, my children: leave the altar steps,
Lift up your olive boughs!
                                    One of you go
And summon the people of Kadmos to gather here.
I will do all that I can; you may tell them that.
        [*Exit a* PAGE.]
So, with the help of God,
We shall be saved—or else indeed we are lost.
PRIEST: Let us rise, children. It was for this we came,
And now the King has promised it himself.
Phoibos has sent us an oracle; may he descend
Himself to save us and drive out the plague.
        [*Exeunt* OEDIPUS *and* CREON *into the palace by the central door. The*
        PRIEST *and the* SUPPLIANTS *disperse R and L. After a short pause the*
        CHORUS *enters the orchestra.*]

## PARODOS

CHORUS: What is God singing in his profound                    [STROPHE 1]
        Delphi of gold and shadow?
        What oracle for Thebes, the sunwhipped city?

        Fear unjoints me, the roots of my heart tremble.

        Now I remember, O Healer, your power, and wonder:
        Will you send doom like a sudden cloud, or weave it
        Like nightfall of the past?

        Speak, speak to us, issue a holy sound:
        Dearest to our expectancy: be tender!

        Let me pray to Athenê, the immortal daughter of Zeus,    [ANTISTROPHE 1]
        And to Artemis her sister
        Who keeps her famous throne in the market ring,
        And to Apollo, bowman at the far butts of heaven—

        O gods, descend! Like three streams leap against
        The fires of our grief, the fires of darkness;
        Be swift to bring us rest!

        As in the old time from the brilliant house
        Of air you stepped to save us, come again!

        Now our afflictions have no end,                         [STROPHE 2]
        Now all our stricken host lies down
        And no man fights off death with his mind;

        The noble plowland bears no grain,
        And groaning mothers can not bear—

See, how our lives like birds take wing,
Like sparks that fly when a fire soars,
To the shore of the god of evening.

The plague burns on, it is pitiless,                    [ANTISTROPHE 2]
Though pallid children laden with death
Lie unwept in the stony ways,

And old gray women by every path
Flock to the strand about the altars

There to strike their breasts and cry
Worship of Phoibos in wailing prayers:
Be kind, God's golden child!

There are no swords in this attack by fire,             [STROPHE 3]
No shields, but we are ringed with cries.
Send the besieger plunging from our homes
Into the vast sea-room of the Atlantic
Or into the waves that foam eastward of Thrace —

For the day ravages what the night spares —

Destroy our enemy, lord of the thunder!
Let him be riven by lightning from heaven!

Phoibos Apollo, stretch the sun's bowstring,            [ANTISTROPHE 3]
That golden cord, until it sing for us,
Flashing arrows in heaven!
                              Artemis, Huntress,
Race with flaring lights upon our mountains!

O scarlet god, O golden-banded brow,
O Theban Bacchos in a storm of Maenads,
      [*Enter* OEDIPUS, *C.*]
Whirl upon Death, that all the Undying hate.
Come with blinding torches, come in joy!


## SCENE I

OEDIPUS: Is this your prayer? It may be answered. Come,
        Listen to me, act as the crisis demands,
        And you shall have relief from all these evils.

        Until now I was a stranger to this tale,
        As I had been a stranger to the crime.
        Could I track down the murderer without a clue?
        But now, friends,

As one who became a citizen after the murder,
I make this proclamation to all Thebans:
If any man knows by whose hand Laïos, son of Labdakos,
Met his death, I direct that man to tell me everything,
No matter what he fears for having so long withheld it.
Let it stand as promised that no further trouble
Will come to him, but he may leave the land in safety.

Moreover: If anyone knows the murderer to be foreign,
Let him not keep silent: he shall have his reward from me.
However, if he does conceal it; if any man
Fearing for his friend or for himself disobeys this edict,
Hear what I propose to do:

I solemnly forbid the people of this country,
Where power and throne are mine, ever to receive that man
Or speak to him, no matter who he is, or let him
Join in sacrifice, lustration, or in prayer.
I decree that he be driven from every house,
Being, as he is, corruption itself to us: the Delphic
Voice of Zeus has pronounced this revelation.
Thus I associate myself with the oracle
And take the side of the murdered king.

As for the criminal, I pray to God—
Whether it be a lurking thief, or one of a number—
I pray that that man's life be consumed in evil and wretchedness.
And as for me, this curse applies no less
If it should turn out that the culprit is my guest here,
Sharing my hearth.
                    You have heard the penalty.
I lay it on you now to attend to this
For my sake, for Apollo's, for the sick
Sterile city that heaven has abandoned.
Suppose the oracle had given you no command:
Should this defilement go uncleansed for ever?
You should have found the murderer: your king,
A noble king, had been destroyed!
                                    Now I,
Having the power that he held for me,
Having his bed, begetting children there
Upon his wife, as he would have, had he lived—
Their son would have been my children's brother.
If Laïos had had luck in fatherhood!
(But surely ill luck rushed upon his reign)—
I say I take the son's part, just as though
I were his son, to press the fight for him
And see it won! I'll find the hand that brought

Death to Labdakos' and Polydoros' child,
Heir of Kadmos' and Agenor's line.
And as for those who fail me,
May the gods deny them the fruit of the earth,
Fruit of the womb, and may they rot utterly!
Let them be wretched as we are wretched, and worse!


For you, for loyal Thebans, and for all
Who find my actions right, I pray the favor
Of justice, and of all the immortal gods.
CHORAGOS: Since I am under oath, my lord, I swear
    I did not do the murder, I can not name
    The murderer. Might not the oracle
    That has ordained the search tell where to find him?
OEDIPUS: An honest question. But no man in the world
    Can make the gods do more than the gods will.
CHORAGOS: There is one last expedient—
OEDIPUS:                                     Tell me what it is.
    Though it seem slight, you must not hold it back.
CHORAGOS: A lord claivoyant to the lord Apollo,
    As we all know, is the skilled Teiresias.
    One might learn much about this from him, Oedipus.
OEDIPUS: I am not wasting time:
    Creon spoke of this, and I have sent for him—
    Twice, in fact; it is strange that he is not here.
CHORAGOS: The other matter—that old report—seems useless.
OEDIPUS: Tell me. I am interested in all reports.
CHORAGOS: The King was said to have been killed by highwaymen.
OEDIPUS: I know. But we have no witnesses to that.
CHORAGOS: If the killer can feel a particle of dread,
    Your curse will bring him out of hiding!
OEDIPUS:                                     No.
    The man who dared that act will fear no curse.
    [*Enter the blind seer* TEIRESIAS, *led by a* PAGE.]
CHORAGOS: But there is one man who may detect the criminal.
    This is Teiresias, this is the holy prophet
    In whom, alone of all men, truth was born.
OEDIPUS: Teiresias: seer: student of mysteries,
    Of all that's taught and all that no man tells,
    Secrets of Heaven and secrets of the earth:
    Blind though you are, you know the city lies
    Sick with plague; and from this plague, my lord,
    We find that you alone can guard or save us.


Possibly you did not hear the messengers?
Apollo, when we sent to him,
Sent us back word that this great pestilence
Would lift, but only if we established clearly

The identity of those who murdered Laïos.
They must be killed or exiled.
                          Can you use
Birdflight or any art of divination
To purify yourself, and Thebes, and me
From this contagion? We are in your hands.
There is no fairer duty
Than that of helping others in distress.

TEIRESIAS: How dreadful knowledge of the truth can be
  When there's no help in truth! I knew this well,
  But made myself forget. I should not have come.

OEDIPUS: What is troubling you? Why are your eyes so cold?

TEIRESIAS: Let me go home. Bear your own fate, and I'll
  Bear mine. It is better so: trust what I say.

OEDIPUS: What you say is ungracious and unhelpful
  To your native country. Do not refuse to speak.

TEIRESIAS: When it comes to speech, your own is neither temperate
  Nor opportune. I wish to be more prudent.

OEDIPUS: In God's name, we all beg you—

THEIRESIAS:                     You are all ignorant.
  No; I will never tell you what I know.
  Now it is my misery; then, it would be yours.

OEDIPUS: What! You do know something, and will not tell us?
  You would betray us all and wreck the State?

TEIRESIAS: I do not intend to torture myself, or you.
  Why persist in asking? You will not persuade me.

OEDIPUS: What a wicked old man you are! You'd try a stone's
  Patience! Out with it! Have you no feeling at all?

TEIRESIAS: You call me unfeeling. If you could only see
  The nature of your own feelings . . .

OEDIPUS:                       Why,
  Who would not feel as I do? Who could endure
  Your arrogance toward the city?

TEIRESIAS:               What does it matter!
  Whether I speak or not, it is bound to come.

OEDIPUS: Then, if "it" is bound to come, you are bound to tell me.

TEIRESIAS: No, I will not go on. Rage as you please.

OEDIPUS: Rage? Why not!
                    And I'll tell you what I think:
  You planned it, you had it done, you all but
  Killed him with your own hands: if you had eyes,
  I'd say the crime was yours, and yours alone.

TEIRESIAS: So? I charge you, then,
  Abide by the proclamation you have made:
  From this day forth
  Never speak again to these men or to me;
  You yourself are the pollution of this country.

OEDIPUS: You dare say that! Can you possibly think you have
  Some way of going free, after such insolence?

TEIRESIAS: I have gone free. It is the truth sustains me.
OEDIPUS: Who taught you shamelessness? It was not your craft.
TEIRESIAS: You did. You made me speak. I did not want to.
OEDIPUS: Speak what? Let me hear it again more clearly.
TEIRESIAS: Was it not clear before? Are you tempting me?
OEDIPUS: I did not understand it. Say it again.
TEIRESIAS: I say that you are the murderer whom you seek.
OEDIPUS: Now twice you have spat out infamy. You'll pay for it!
TEIRESIAS: Would you care for more? Do you wish to be really angry?
OEDIPUS: Say what you will. Whatever you say is worthless.
TEIRESIAS: I say you live in hideous shame with those
    Most dear to you. You can not see the evil.
OEDIPUS: It seems you can go on mouthing like this for ever.
TEIRESIAS: I can, if there is power in truth.
OEDIPUS:                           There is:
    But not for you, not for you,
    You sightless, witless, senseless, mad old man!
TEIRESIAS: You are the madman. There is no one here
    Who will not curse you soon, as you curse me.
OEDIPUS: You child of endless night! You can not hurt me
    Or any other man who sees the sun.
TEIRESIAS: True: it is not from me your fate will come.
    That lies within Apollo's competence.
    As it is his concern.
OEDIPUS:                Tell me.
    Are you speaking for Creon, or for yourself?
TEIRESIAS: Creon is no threat. You weave your own doom.
OEDIPUS: Wealth, power, craft of staesmanship!
    Kingly position, everywhere admired!
    What savage envy is stored up against these,
    If Creon, whom I trusted, Creon my friend,
    For this great office which the city once
    Put in my hands unsought — if for this power
    Creon desires in secret to destroy me!

    He has bought this decrepit fortune-teller, this
    Collector of dirty pennies, this prophet fraud—
    Why, he is no more clairvoyant than I am!
                          Tell us.
    Has your mystic mummery ever approached the truth?
    When that hellcat the Sphinx was performing here,
    What help were you to these people?
    Her magic was not for the first man who came along:
    It demanded a real exorcist. Your birds—
    What good were they? or the gods, for the matter of that?
    But I came by,
    Oedipus, the simple man, who knows nothing—
    I thought it out for myself, no birds helped me!

And this is the man you think you can destroy,
That you may be close to Creon when he's king!
Well, you and your friend Creon, it seems to me,
Will suffer most. If you were not an old man,
You would have paid already for your plot.
CHORAGOS: We can not see that his words or yours
Have been spoken except in anger, Oedipus,
And of anger we have no need. How can God's will
Be accomplished best? That is what most concerns us.
TEIRESIAS: You are a king. But where argument's concerned
I am your man, as much a king as you.
I am not your servant, but Apollo's.
I have no need of Creon to speak for me.

Listen to me. You mock my blindness, do you?
But I say that you, with both your eyes, are blind:
You can not see the wretchedness of your life,
Nor in whose house you live, no, nor with whom.
Who are your father and mother? Can you tell me?
You do not even know the blind wrongs
That you have done them, on earth and in the world below.
But the double lash of your parents' curse will whip you
Out of this land some day, with only night
Upon your precious eyes.
Your cries then — where will they not be heard?
What fastness of Kithairon will not echo them?
And that bridal-descant of yours — you'll know it then,
The song they sang when you came here to Thebes
And found your misguided berthing.
All this, and more, that you can not guess at now,
Will bring you to yourself among your children.

Be angry, then. Curse Creon. Curse my words.
I tell you, no man that walks upon the earth
Shall be rooted out more horribly than you.
OEDIPUS: Am I to bear this from him? — Damnation
Take you! Out of this place! Out of my sight!
TEIRESIAS: I would not have come at all if you had not asked me.
OEDIPUS: Could I have told that you'd talk nonsense, that
You'd come here to make a fool of yourself, and of me?
TEIRESIAS: A fool? Your parents thought me sane enough.
OEDIPUS: My parents again! — Wait: who were my parents?
TEIRESIAS: This day will give you a father, and break your heart.
OEDIPUS: Your infantile riddles! Your damned abracadabra!
TEIRESIAS: You were a great man once at solving riddles.
OEDIPUS: Mock me with that if you like; you will find it true.
TEIRESIAS: It was true enough. It brought about your ruin.
OEDIPUS: But if it saved this town?

TEIRESIAS: [*to the* PAGE] Boy, give me your hand.
OEDIPUS:  Yes, boy; lead him away.
                          —While you are here
    We can do nothing. Go; leave us in peace.
TEIRESIAS:  I will go when I have said what I have to say.
    How can you hurt me? And I tell you again:
    The man you have been looking for all this time,
    The damned man, the murderer of Laïos,
    That man is in Thebes. To your mind he is foreign-born,
    But is will soon be shown that he is Theban,
    A revelation that will fail to please.
                           A blind man,
    Who has his eyes now; a penniless man, who is rich now;
    And he will go tapping the strange earth with his staff
    To the children with whom he lives now he will be
    Brother and father—the very same; to her
    Who bore him, son and husband—the very same
    Who came to his father's bed, wet with his father's blood.

    Enough. Go think that over.
    If later you find error in what I have said,
    You may say that I have no skill in prophecy.
        [*Exit* TEIRESIAS, *led by his* PAGE. OEDIPUS *goes into the palace.*]


## ODE I

CHORUS:  The Delphic stone of prophecies                 [STROPHE 1]
    Remembers ancient regicide
    And a still bloody hand.
    That killer's hour of flight has come.
    He must be stronger than riderless
    Coursers of untiring wind,
    For the son of Zeus armed with his father's thunder
    Leaps in lightning after him;
    And the Furies follow him, the sad Furies.

    Holy Parnassos' peak of snow               [ANTISTROPHE 1]
    Flashes and blinds that secret man,
    That all shall hunt him down:
    Though he may roam the forest shade
    Like a bull wild from pasture
    To rage through glooms of stone.
    Doom comes down on him; flight will not avail him;
    For the world's heart calls him desolate,
    And the immortal Furies follow, for ever follow.

    But now a wilder thing is heard              [STROPHE 2]
    From the old man skilled at hearing Fate in the wingbeat of a bird.

Bewildered as a blown bird, my soul hovers and can not find
Foothold in this debate, or any reason or rest of mind.
But no man ever brought — none can bring
Proof of strife between Thebes' royal house,
Labdakos' line, and the son of Polybos;
And never until now has any man brought word
Of Laïos' dark death staining Oedipus the King.

Divine Zeus and Apollo hold                                        [ANTISTROPHE 2]
Perfect intelligence alone of all tales ever told;
And well though this diviner works, he works in his own night;
No man can judge that rough unknown or trust in second sight,
For wisdom changes hands among the wise.
Shall I believe my great lord criminal
At a raging word that a blind old man let fall?
I saw him, when the carrion woman faced him of old,
Prove his heroic mind! These evil words are lies.

## SCENE II

CREON: Men of Thebes:
   I am told that heavy accusations
   Have been brought against me by King Oedipus.

   I am not the kind of man to bear this tamely.

   If in these present difficulties
   He holds me accountable for any harm to him
   Through anything I have said or done — why, then,
   I do not value life in this dishonor.
   It is not as though this rumor touched upon
   Some private indiscretion. The matter is grave.
   The fact is that I am being called disloyal
   To the State, to my fellow citizens, to my friends.
CHORAGOS: He may have spoken in anger, not from his mind.
CREON: But did you not hear him say I was the one
   Who seduced the old prophet into lying?
CHORAGOS: The thing was said; I do not know how seriously.
CREON: But you were watching him! Were his eyes steady?
   Did he look like a man in his right mind?
CHORAGOS:                                         I do not know.
   I can not judge the behavior of great men.
   But here is the King himself.
      [*Enter* OEDIPUS.]
OEDIPUS:                                  So you dared come back.
   Why? How brazen of you to come to my house,
   You murderer!
             Do you think I do not know
   That you plotted to kill me, plotted to steal my throne?

Tell me, in God's name: am I coward, a fool,
That you should dream you could accomplish this?
A fool who could not see your slippery game?
A coward, not to fight back when I saw it?
You are the fool, Creon, are you not? hoping
Without support or friends to get a throne?
Thrones may be won or bought: you could do neither.
CREON: Now listen to me. You have talked; let me talk, too.
  You can not judge unless you know the facts.
OEDIPUS: You speak well: there is one fact; but I find it hard
  To learn from the deadliest enemy I have.
CREON: That above all I must dispute with you.
OEDIPUS: That above all I will not hear you deny.
CREON: If you think there is anything good in being stubborn
  Against all reason, then I say you are wrong.
OEDIPUS: If you think a man can sin against his own kind
  And not be punished for it, I say you are mad.
CREON: I agree. But tell me: what have I done to you?
OEDIPUS: You advised me to send for that wizard, did you not?
CREON: I did. I should do it again.
OEDIPUS:                              Very well. Now tell me:
  How long has it been since Laïos —
CREON:                                    What of Laïos?
OEDIPUS: Since he vanished in that onset by the road?
CREON: It was long ago, a long time.
OEDIPUS:                                And this prophet,
  Was he practicing here then?
CREON:                              He was; and with honor, as now.
OEDIPUS: Did he speak of me at that time?
CREON:                                        He never did:
  At least, not when I was present.
OEDIPUS:                                        But . . . the enquiry?
  I suppose you held one?
CREON:                              We did, but we learned nothing.
OEDIPUS: Why did the prophet not speak against me then?
CREON: I do not know; and I am the kind of man
  Who holds his tongue when he has no facts to go on.
OEDIPUS: There's one fact that you know, and you could tell it.
CREON: What fact is that? If I know it, you shall have it.
OEDIPUS: If he were not involved with you, he could not say
  That it was I who murdered Laïos.
CREON: If he says that, you are the one that knows it! —
  But now it is my turn to question you.
OEDIPUS: Put your questions. I am no murderer.
CREON: First, then: You married my sister?
OEDIPUS:                                        I married your sister.
CREON: And you rule the kingdom equally with her?
OEDIPUS: Everything that she wants she has from me.

CREON: And I am the third, equal to both of you?
OEDIPUS: That is why I call you a bad friend.
CREON: No. Reason it out, as I have done.
　　　Think of this first: Would any sane man prefer
　　　Power, with all a king's anxieties,
　　　To that same power and the grace of sleep?
　　　Certainly not I.
　　　I have never longed for the king's power—only his rights.
　　　Would any wise man differ from me in this?
　　　As matters stand, I have my way in everything
　　　With your consent, and no responsibilities.
　　　If I were king, I should be a slave to policy.

　　　How could I desire a scepter more
　　　Than what is now mine—untroubled influence?
　　　No, I have not gone mad; I need no honors,
　　　Except those with the perquisites I have now.
　　　I am welcome everywhere; every man salutes me,
　　　And those who want your favor seek my ear,
　　　Since I know how to manage what they ask.
　　　Should I exchange this ease for that anxiety?
　　　Besides, no sober mind is treasonable.
　　　I hate anarchy
　　　And never would deal with any man who likes it.

　　　Test what I have said. Go to the priestess
　　　At Delphi, ask if I quoted her correctly.
　　　And as for this other thing: if I am found
　　　Guilty of treason with Teiresias,
　　　Then sentence me to death! You have my word
　　　It is a sentence I should cast my vote for—
　　　But not without evidence!
　　　　　　　　　　　　　You do wrong
　　　When you take good men for bad, bad men for good.
　　　A true friend thrown aside—why, life itself
　　　Is not more precious!
　　　　　　　　　　　　In time you will know this well:
　　　For time, and time alone, will show the just man,
　　　Though scoundrels are discovered in a day.
CHORAGOS: This is well said, and a prudent man would ponder it.
　　　Judgments too quickly formed are dangerous.
OEDIPUS: But is he not quick in his duplicity?
　　　And shall I not be quick to parry him?
　　　Would you have me stand still, hold my peace, and let
　　　This man win everything, through my inaction?
CREON: And you want—what is it, then? To banish me?
OEDIPUS: No, not exile. It is your death I want,
　　　So that all the world may see what treason means.

CREON: You will persist, then? You will not believe me?
OEDIPUS: How can I believe you?
CREON:                                 Then you are a fool.
OEDIPUS: To save myself?
CREON:                             In justice, think of me.
OEDIPUS: You are evil incarnate.
CREON:                                   But suppose that you are wrong?
OEDIPUS: Still I must rule.
CREON:                         But not if you rule badly.
OEDIPUS: O city, city!
CREON:                 It is my city, too!
CHORAGOS: Now, my lords, be still, I see the Queen,
    Iocastê, coming from her palace chambers;
    And it is time she came, for the sake of you both.
    This dreadful quarrel can be resolved through her.
        [*Enter* IOCASTE.]
IOCASTE: Poor foolish men, what wicked din is this?
    With Thebes sick to death, is it not shameful
    That you should rake some private quarrel up?
        [*To* OEDIPUS:]
    Come into the house.

                        —And you, Creon, go now:
    Let us have no more of this tumult over nothing.
CREON: Nothing? No, sister: what your husband plans for me
    Is one of two great evils: exile or death.
OEDIPUS: He is right.
                    Why, woman I have caught him squarely
    Plotting against my life.
CREON:                             No! Let me die
    Accurst if ever I have wished you harm!
IOCASTE: Ah, believe it, Oedipus!
    In the name of the gods, respect this oath of his
    For my sake, for the sake of these people here!

                                                                [STROPHE 1]
CHORAGOS: Open your mind to her, my lord. Be ruled by her, I beg you!
OEDIPUS: What would you have me do?
CHORAGOS: Respect Creon's word. He has never spoken like a fool,
    And now he has sworn an oath.
OEDIPUS:                             You know what you ask?
CHORAGOS:                                             I do.
OEDIPUS:                                             Speak on, then.
CHORAGOS: A friend so sworn should not be baited so,
    In blind malice, and without final proof.
OEDIPUS: You are aware, I hope, that what you say
    Means death for me, or exile at the least.
CHORAGOS: No, I swear by Helios, first in Heaven!                [STROPHE 2]
    May I die friendless and accurst,

The worst of deaths, if ever I meant that!
    It is the withering fields
        That hurt my sick heart:
    Must we bear all these ills,
        And now your bad blood as well?
OEDIPUS: Then let him go. And let me die, if I must,
    Or be driven by him in shame from the land of Thebes.
    It is your unhappiness, and not his talk,
    That touches me.
           As for him—
    Wherever he goes, hatred will follow him.
CREON: Ugly in yielding, as you were ugly in rage!
    Natures like yours chiefly torment themselves.
OEDIPUS: Can you not go? Can you not leave me?
CREON:                         I can.
    You do not know me; but the city knows me,
    And in its eyes, I am just, if not in yours.
       [*Exit* CREON.]

                                        [ANTISTROPHE 1]

CHORAGOS: Lady Iocastê, did you not ask the King to go to his chambers?
IOCASTE: First tell me what has happened.
CHORAGOS: There was suspicion without evidence: yet it rankled
    As even false charges will.
IOCASTE:                        On both side?
CHORAGOS:                       On both.
IOCASTE:                             But what was said?
CHORAGOS: Oh let it rest, let it be done with!
    Have we not suffered enough?
OEDIPUS: You see to what your decency has brought you:
    You have made difficulties where my heart saw none.
CHORAGOS: Oedipus, it is not once only I have told you—       [ANTISTROPHE 2]
      You must know I should count myself unwise
    To the point of madness, should I now forsake you—
        You, under whose hand,
           In the storm of another time,
        Our dear land sailed out free.
        But now stand fast at the helm!
IOCASTE: In God's name, Oedipus, inform your wife as well:
    Why are you so set in this hard anger?
OEDIPUS: I will tell you, for none of these men deserves
    My confidence as you do. It is Creon's work,
    His treachery, his plotting against me.
IOCASTE: Go on, if you can make this clear to me.
OEDIPUS: He charges me with the murder of Laïos.
IOCASTE: Has he some knowledge? Or does he speak from hearsay?
OEDIPUS: He would not commit himself to such a charge,
    But he has brought in that damnable soothsayer
    To tell his story.

IOCASTE:                     Set your mind at rest.
If it is a question of soothsayers, I tell you
That you will find no man whose craft gives knowledge
Of the unknowable.

                    Here is my proof:

An oracle was reported to Laïos once
(I will not say from Phoibos himself, but from
His appointed ministers, at any rate)
That his doom would be death at the hands of his own son—
His son, born of his flesh and of mine!

Now, you remember the story: Laïos was killed
By marauding strangers where three highways meet.
But his child had not been three days in this world
Before the King had pierced the baby's ankles
And left him to die on a lonely mountainside.

Thus, Apollo never caused that child
To kill his father, and it was not Laïos' fate
To die at the hands of his son, as he had feared.
This is what prophets and prophecies are worth!
Have no dread of them.
                    It is God himself
Who can show us what he wills, in his own way.
OEDIPUS:  How strange a shadowy memory crossed my mind,
      Just now while you were speaking; it chilled my heart.
IOCASTE:  What do you mean? What memory do you speak of?
OEDIPUS:  If I understand you, Laïos was killed
      At a place where three roads meet.
IOCASTE:                                So it was said;
      We have no later story.
OEDIPUS:                        Where did it happen?
IOCASTE:  Phokis, it is called: at a place where the Theban Way
      Divides into the roads toward Delphi and Daulia.
OEDIPUS:  When?
IOCASTE:  We had the news not long before you came
      And proved the right to your succession here.
OEDIPUS:  Ah, what net has God been weaving for me?
IOCASTE:  Oedipus! Why does this trouble you?
OEDIPUS:                                Do not ask me yet.
      First, tell me how Laïos looked, and tell me
      How old he was.
IOCASTE:              He was tall, his hair just touched
      With white; his form was not unlike your own.
OEDIPUS:  I think that I myself may be accurst
      By my own ignorant edict.

IOCASTE:                    You speak strangely.
    It makes me tremble to look at you, my King.
OEDIPUS: I am not sure that the blind man can not see.
    But I should know better if you were to tell me —
IOCASTE: Anything — though I dread to hear you ask it.
OEDIPUS: Was the King lightly escorted, or did he ride
    With a large company, as a ruler should?
IOCASTE: There were five men with him in all: one was a herald,
    And a single chariot, which he was driving.
OEDIPUS: Alas, that makes it plain enough!
                         But who —
    Who told you how it happened?
IOCASTE:                    A household servant,
    The only one to escape.
OEDIPUS:                    And is he still
    A servant of ours?
IOCASTE:                    No; for when he came back at last
    And found you enthroned in the place of the dead king,
    He came to me, touched my hand with his, and begged
    That I would send him away to the frontier district
    Where only the shepherds go —
    As far away from the city as I could send him.
    I granted his prayer; for although the man was a slave,
    He had earned more than this favor at my hands.
OEDIPUS: Can he be called back quickly?
IOCASTE:                    Easily.
    But why?
OEDIPUS:        I have taken too much upon myself
    Without enquiry; therefore I wish to consult him.
IOCASTE: Then he shall come.
               But am I not one also
    To whom you might confide these fears of yours?
OEDIPUS: That is your right; it will not be denied you,
    Now least of all; for I have reached a pitch
    Of wild foreboding. Is there anyone
    To whom I should sooner speak?

    Polybos of Corinth is my father.
    My mother is a Dorian: Meropê.
    I grew up chief among the men of Corinth
    Until a strange thing happened —
    Not worth my passion, it may be, but strange.

    At a feast, a drunken man maundering in his cups
    Cries out that I am not my father's son!

    I contained myself that night, though I felt anger
    And a sinking heart. The next day I visited

My father and mother, and questioned them. They stormed,
Calling it all the slanderous rant of a fool;
And this relieved me. Yet the suspicion
Remained always aching in my mind;
I know there was talk; I could not rest;
And finally, saying nothing to my parents,
I went to the shrine at Delphi.
The god dismissed my question without reply;
He spoke of other things.
                                    Some were clear,
Full of wretchedness, dreadful, unbearable:
As, that I should lie with my own mother, breed
Children from whom all men would turn their eyes;
And that I should be my father's murderer.

I heard all this, and fled. And from that day
Corinth to me was only in the stars
Descending in that quarter of the sky,
As I wandered farther and farther on my way
To a land where I should never see the evil
Sung by the oracle. And I came to this country
Where, so you say, King Laïos was killed.

I will tell you all that happened there, my lady.
There were three highways
Coming together at a place I passed;
And there a herald came towards me, and a chariot
Drawn by horses, with a man such as you describe
Seated in it. The groom leading the horses
Forced me off the road at his lord's command;
But as this charioteer lurched over towards me
I struck him in my rage. The old man saw me
And brought his double goad down upon my head
As I came abreast.
                            He was paid back, and more!
Swinging my club in this right hand I knocked him
Out of his car, and he rolled on the ground.
                                                    I killed him.

I killed them all.
Now if that stranger and Laïos were — kin,
Where is a man more miserable than I?
More hated by the gods? Citizen and alien alike
Must never shelter me or speak to me —
I must be shunned by all.
                                    And I myself
Pronounced this malediction upon myself!

Think of it: I have touched you with these hands,
These hands that killed your husband. What defilement!

Am I all evil, then? It must be so,
Since I must flee from Thebes, yet never again
See my own countrymen, my own country,
For fear of joining my mother in marriage
And killing Polybos, my father.
                                        Ah,
If I was created so, born to this fate,
Who could deny the savagery of God?

O holy majesty of heavenly powers!
May I never see that day! Never!
Rather let me vanish from the race of men
Than know the abomination destined me!
CHORAGOS: We too, my lord, have felt dismay at this.
     But there is hope: you have yet to hear the shepherd.
OEDIPUS: Indeed, I fear no other hope is left me.
IOCASTE: What do you hope from him when he comes?
OEDIPUS:                                        This much:
     If his account of the murder tallies with yours,
     Then I am cleared.
IOCASTE:                    What was it that I said
     Of such importance?
OEDIPUS:                    Why, "marauders," you said,
     Killed the King, according to this man's story.
     If he maintains that still, if there were several,
     Clearly the guilt is not mine: I was alone.
     But if he says one man, singlehanded, did it,
     Then the evidence all points to me.
IOCASTE: You may be sure that he said there were several;
     And can he call back that story now? He cán not.
     The whole city heard it as plainly as I.
     But suppose he alters some detail of it:
     He can not ever show that Laïos' death
     Fulfilled the oracle: for Apollo said
     My child was doomed to kill him; and my child—
     Poor baby! — it was my child that died first.

     No. From now on, where oracles are concerned,
     I would not waste a second thought on any.
OEDIPUS: You may be right.
                              But come: let someone go
     For the shepherd at once. This matter must be settled.
IOCASTE: I will send for him.
     I would not wish to cross you in anything,
     And surely not in this. — Let us go in.
          [*Exeunt into the palace.*]

## ODE II

CHORUS:  Let me be reverent in the ways of right,                          [STROPHE 1]
Lowly the paths I journey on;
Let all my words and actions keep
The laws of the pure universe
From highest Heaven handed down.
For Heaven is their bright nurse,
Those generations of the realms of light;
Ah, never of mortal kind were they begot,
Nor are they slaves of memory, lost in sleep;
Their Father is greater than Time, and ages not.

The tyrant is a child of Pride                                             [ANTISTROPHE 1]
Who drinks from his great sickening cup
Recklessness and vanity,
Until from his high crest headlong
He plummets to the dust of hope.
That strong man is not strong.
But let no fair ambition be denied;
May God protect the wrestler for the State
In government, in comely policy,
Who will fear God, and on His ordinance wait.

Haughtiness and the high hand of disdain                                   [STROPHE 2]
Tempt and outrage God's holy law;
And any mortal who dares hold
No immortal Power in awe
Will be caught up in a net of pain:
The price for which his levity is sold.
Let each man take due earnings, then,
And keep his hands from holy things,
And from blasphemy stand apart—
Else the crackling blast of heaven
Blows on his head, and on his desperate heart;
Though fools will honor impious men,
In their cities no tragic poet sings.

Shall we lose faith in Delphi's obscurities,                              [ANTISTROPHE 2]
We who have heard the world's core
Discredited, and the sacred wood
Of Zeus at Elis praised no more?
The deeds and the strange prophecies
Must make a pattern yet to be understood.
Zeus, if indeed you are lord of all,
Throned in light over night and day,
Mirror this in your endless mind:
Our masters call the oracle

Words on the wind, and the Delphic vision blind!
Their hearts no longer know Apollo,
And reverence for the gods has died away.


SCENE III

[*Enter* IOCASTE.]

IOCASTE: Princes of Thebes, it has occurred to me
To visit the altars of the gods, bearing
These branches as a suppliant, and this incense.
Our King is not himself: his noble soul
Is overwrought with fantasies of dread,
Else he would consider
The new prophecies in the light of the old.
He will listen to any voice that speaks disaster,
And my advice goes for nothing.
[*She approaches the altar, R.*]
To you, then, Apollo,
Lycean lord, since you are nearest, I turn in prayer.
Receive these offerings, and grant us deliverance
From defilement. Our hearts are heavy with fear
When we see our leader distracted, as helpless sailors
Are terrified by the confusion of their helmsman.
[*Enter* MESSENGER.]

MESSENGER: Friends, no doubt you can direct me:
Where shall I find the house of Oedipus,
Or, better still, where is the King himself?

CHORAGOS: It is this very place, stranger; he is inside.
This is his wife and mother of his children.

MESSENGER: I wish her happiness in a happy house,
Blest in all the fulfillment of her marriage.

IOCASTE: I wish as much for you: your courtesy
Deserves a like good fortune. But now, tell me:
Why have you come? What have you to say to us?

MESSENGER: Good news, my lady, for your house and your husband.

IOCASTE: What news? Who sent you here?

MESSENGER: I am from Corinth.
The news I bring ought to mean joy for you,
Though it may be you will find some grief in it.

IOCASTE: What is it? How can it touch us in both ways?

MESSENGER: The word is that the people of the Isthmus
Intend to call Oedipus to be their king.

IOCASTE: But old King Polybos — is he not reigning still?

MESSENGER: No. Death holds him in his sepulchre.

IOCASTE: What are you saying? Polybos is dead?

MESSENGER: If I am not telling the truth, may I die myself.

IOCASTE: [*to a* MAIDSERVANT:] Go in, go quickly; tell this to your master.

O riddlers of God's will, where are you now!
This was the man whom Oedipus, long ago,
Feared so, fled so, in dread of destroying him —
But it was another fate by which he died.
      [*Enter* OEDIPUS, *C.*]
OEDIPUS:  Dearest Iocastê, why have you sent for me?
IOCASTE:  Listen to what this man says, and then tell me
    What has become of the solemn prophecies.
OEDIPUS:  Who is this man? What is his news for me?
IOCASTE:  He has come from Corinth to announce your father's death!
OEDIPUS:  Is it true, stranger? Tell me in your own words.
MESSENGER:  I can not say it more clearly: the King is dead.
OEDIPUS:  Was it by treason? Or by an attack of illness?
MESSENGER:  A little thing brings old men to their rest.
OEDIPUS:  It was sickness, then?
MESSENGER:                                      Yes, and his many years.
OEDIPUS:  Ah!
    Why should a man respect the Pythian hearth, or
    Give heed to the birds that jangle above his head?
    They prophesied that I should kill Polybos,
    Kill my own father; but he is dead and buried,
    And I am here — I never touched him, never,
    Unless he died of grief for my departure,
    And thus, in a sense, through me. No. Polybos
    Has packed the oracles off with him underground.
    They are empty words.
IOCASTE:                              Had I not told you so?
OEDIPUS:  You had; it was my faint heart that betrayed me.
IOCASTE:  From now on never think of those things again.
OEDIPUS:  And yet — must I not fear my mother's bed?
IOCASTE:  Why should anyone in this world be afraid,
    Since Fate rules us and nothing can be foreseen?
    A man should live only for the present day.


    Have no more fear of sleeping with your mother:
    How many men, in dreams, have lain with their mothers!
    No resaonable man is troubled by such things.
OEDIPUS:  That is true; only —
    If only my mother were not still alive!
    But she is alive. I can not help my dread.
IOCASTE:  Yet this news of your father's death is wonderful.
OEDIPUS:  Wonderful. But I fear the living woman.
MESSENGER:  Tell me, who is this woman that you fear?
OEDIPUS:  It is Meropê, man; the wife of King Polybos.
MESSENGER:  Meropê? Why should you be afraid of her?
OEDIPUS:  An oracle of the gods, a dreadful saying.
MESSENGER:  Can you tell me about it or are you sworn to silence?

OEDIPUS: I can tell you, and I will.
  Apollo said through his prophet that I was the man
  Who should marry his own mother, shed his father's blood
  With his own hands. And so, for all these years
  I have kept clear of Corinth, and no harm has come —
  Though it would have been sweet to see my parents again.
MESSENGER: And is this the fear that drove you out of Corinth?
OEDIPUS: Would you have me kill my father?
MESSENGER:                                  As for that
  You must be reassured by the news I gave you.
OEDIPUS: If you could reassure me, I would reward you.
MESSENGER: I had that in mind, I will confess: I thought
  I could count on you when you returned to Corinth.
OEDIPUS: No: I will never go near my parents again.
MESSENGER: Ah, son, you still do not know what you are doing —
OEDIPUS: What do you mean? In the name of God tell me!
MESSENGER:  — If these are your reasons for not going home.
OEDIPUS: I tell you, I fear the oracle may come true.
MESSENGER: And guilt may come upon you through your parents?
OEDIPUS: That is the dread that is always in my heart.
MESSENGER: Can you not see that all your fears are groundless?
OEDIPUS: How can you say that? They are my parents, surely?
MESSENGER: Polybos was not your father.
OEDIPUS:                                  Not my father?
MESSENGER: No more your father than the man speaking to you.
OEDIPUS: But you are nothing to me!
MESSENGER:                                  Neither was he.
OEDIPUS: Then why did he call me son?
MESSENGER:                                  I will tell you:
  Long ago he had you from my hands, as a gift.
OEDIPUS: Then how could he love me so, if I was not his?
MESSENGER: He had no children, and his heart turned to you.
OEDIPUS: What of you? Did you buy me? Did you find me by chance?
MESSENGER: I came upon you in the crooked pass of Kithairon.
OEDIPUS: And what were you doing there?
MESSENGER:                                  Tending my flocks.
OEDIPUS: A wandering shepherd?
MESSENGER:                        But your savior, son, that day.
OEDIPUS: From what did you save me?
MESSENGER:                                Your ankles should tell you that.
OEDIPUS: Ah, stranger, why do you speak of that childhood pain?
MESSENGER: I cut the bonds that tied your ankles together.
OEDIPUS: I have had the mark as long as I can remember.
MESSENGER: That was why you were given the name you bear.
OEDIPUS: God! Was it my father or my mother who did it?
  Tell me!
MESSENGER: I do not know. The man who gave you to me
  Can tell you better than I.

OEDIPUS: It was not you that found me, but another?
MESSENGER: It was another shepherd gave you to me.
OEDIPUS: Who was he? Can you tell me who he was?
MESSENGER: I think he was said to be one of Laïos' people.
OEDIPUS: You mean the Laïos who was king here years ago?
MESSENGER: Yes; King Laïos; and the man was one of his herdsmen.
OEDIPUS: Is he still alive? Can I see him?
MESSENGER:                                    These men here
    Know best about such things.
OEDIPUS:                                    Does anyone here
    Know this shepherd that he is talking about?
    Have you seen him in the fields, or in the town?
    If you have, tell me. It is time things were made plain.
CHORAGOS: I think the man he means is that same shepherd
    You have already asked to see. Iocastê perhaps
    Could tell you something.
OEDIPUS:                                    Do you know anything
    About him, Lady? Is he the man we have summoned?
    Is that the man this shepherd means?
IOCASTE:                                    Why think of him?
    Forget this herdsman. Forget it all.
    This talk is a waste of time.
OEDIPUS:                                    How can you say that?
IOCASTE: For God's love, let us have no more questioning!
    Is your life nothing to you?
    My own is pain enough for me to bear.
OEDIPUS: You need not worry. Suppose my mother a slave,
    And born of slaves: no baseness can touch you.
IOCASTE: Listen to me, I beg you: do not do this thing!
OEDIPUS: I will not listen; the truth must be made known.
IOCASTE: Everything that I say is for your own good!
OEDIPUS:                                    My own good
    Snaps my patience, then; I want none of it.
IOCASTE: You are fatally wrong! May you never learn who you are!
OEDIPUS: Go, one of you, and bring the shepherd here.
    Let us leave this woman to brag of her royal name.
IOCASTE: Ah, miserable!
    That is the only word I have for you now.
    That is the only word I can ever have.
        [*Exit into the palace.*]
CHORAGOS: Why has she left us, Oedipus? Why has she gone
    In such a passion of sorrow? I fear this silence:
    Something dreadful may come of it.
OEDIPUS:                                    Let it come!
    However base my birth, I must know about it.
    The Queen, like a woman, is perhaps ashamed
    To think of my low origin. But I
    Am a child of Luck; I can not be dishonored.

Luck is my mother; the passing months, my brothers,
Have seen me rich and poor.
                    If this is so,
How could I wish that I were someone else?
How could I not be glad to know my birth?


## ODE III

CHORUS: If ever the coming time were known                    [STROPHE]
        To my heart's pondering,
        Kithairon, now by Heaven I see the torches
        At the festival of the next full moon,
        And see the dance, and hear the choir sing
        A grace to your gentle shade:
        Mountain where Oedipus was found,
        O mountain guard of a noble race!
        May the god who heals us lend his aid,
        And let that glory come to pass
        For our king's cradling-ground.

        Of the nymphs that flower beyond the years,          [ANTISTROPHE]
        Who bore you, royal child,
        To Pan of the hills or the timberline Apollo,
        Cold in delight where the upland clears,
        Or Hermês for whom Kyllenê's heights are piled?
        Or flushed as evening cloud,
        Great Dionysos, roamer of mountains,
        He — was it he who found you there,
        And caught you up in his own proud
        Arms from the sweet god-ravisher
        Who laughed by the Muses' fountains?


## SCENE IV

OEDIPUS:  Sirs: though I do not know the man,
        I think I see him coming, this shepherd we want:
        He is old, like our friend here, and the men
        Bringing him seem to be servants of my house.
        But you can tell, if you have ever seen him.
            [*Enter* SHEPHERD *escorted by servants.*]
CHORAGOS:  I know him, he was Laïos' man. You can trust him.
OEDIPUS:  Tell me first, you from Corinth: is this the shepherd
        We were discussing?
MESSENGER:                    This is the very man.
OEDIPUS:  [*to* SHEPHERD] Come here. No, look at me. You must answer
        Everything I ask.— You belonged to Laïos?
SHEPHERD:  Yes: born his slave, brought up in his house.
OEDIPUS:  Tell me: what kind of work did you do for him?

SHEPHERD: I was a shepherd of his, most of my life.

OEDIPUS: Where mainly did you go for pasturage?

SHEPHERD: Sometimes Kithairon, sometimes the hills near-by.

OEDIPUS: Do you remember ever seeing this man out there?

SHEPHERD: What would he be doing there? This man?

OEDIPUS: This man standing here. Have you ever seen him before?

SHEPHERD: No. At least, not to my recollection.

MESSENGER: And that is not strange, my lord. But I'll refresh
   His memory: he must remember when we two
   Spent three whole seasons together, March to September,
   On Kithairon or thereabouts. He had two flocks;
   I had one. Each autumn I'd drive mine home
   And he would go back with his to Laïos' sheepfold. —
   Is this not true, just as I have described it?

SHEPHERD: True, yes; but it was all so long ago.

MESSENGER: Well, then: do you remember, back in those days,
   That you gave me a baby boy to bring up as my own?

SHEPHERD: What if I did? What are you trying to say?

MESSENGER: King Oedipus was once that little child.

SHEPHERD: Damn you, hold your tongue!

OEDIPUS:                                             No more of that!
   It is your tongue needs watching, not this man's.

SHEPHERD: My King, my Master, what is it I have done wrong?

OEDIPUS: You have not answered his question about the boy.

SHEPHERD: He does not know . . . He is only making trouble . . .

OEDIPUS: Come, speak plainly, or it will go hard with you.

SHEPHERD: In God's name, do not torture an old man!

OEDIPUS: Come here, one of you; bind his arms behind him.

SHEPHERD: Unhappy king! What more do you wish to learn?

OEDIPUS: Did you give this man the child he speaks of?

SHEPHERD:                                             I did.
   And I would to God I had died that very day.

OEDIPUS: You will die now unless you speak the truth.

SHEPHERD: Yet if I speak the truth, I am worse than dead.

OEDIPUS: Very well; since you insist upon delaying —

SHEPHERD: No! I have told you already that I gave him the boy.

OEDIPUS: Where did you get him? From your house? From somewhere else?

SHEPHERD: Not from mine, no. A man gave him to me.

OEDIPUS: Is that man here? Do you know whose slave he was?

SHEPHERD: For God's love, my King, do not ask me any more!

OEDIPUS: You are a dead man if I have to ask you again.

SHEPHERD: Then . . . Then the child was from the palace of Laïos.

OEDIPUS: A slave child? or a child of his own line?

SHEPHERD: Ah, I am on the brink of dreadful speech!

OEDIPUS: And I of dreadful hearing. Yet I must hear.

SHEPHERD: If you must be told, then . . .
                           They said it was Laïos' child;
   But it is your wife who can tell you about that.

OEDIPUS: My wife! — Did she give it to you?

SHEPHERD: My lord, she did.
OEDIPUS: Do you know why?
SHEPHERD: I was told to get rid of it.
OEDIPUS: An unspeakable mother!
SHEPHERD: There had been prophecies . . .
OEDIPUS: Tell me.
SHEPHERD: It was said that the boy would kill his own father.
OEDIPUS: Then why did you give him over to this old man?
SHEPHERD: I pitied the baby, my King,
　　　And I thought that this man would take him far away
　　　To his own country.
　　　　　　　　　　　He saved him — but for what a fate!
　　　For if you are what this man says you are,
　　　No man living is more wretched than Oedipus.
OEDIPUS: Ah God!
　　　It was true!
　　　　　　All the prophecies!
　　　　　　　　　　　— Now,
　　　O Light, may I look on you for the last time!
　　　I, Oedipus,
　　　Oedipus, damned in his birth, in his marriage damned,
　　　Damned in the blood he shed with his own hand!
　　　　　*[He rushes into the palace.]*


## ODE IV

CHORUS: Alas for the seed of men. [STROPHE 1]

　　　What measure shall I give these generations
　　　That breathe on the void and are void
　　　And exist and do not exist?

　　　Who bears more weight of joy
　　　Than mass of sunlight shifting in images,
　　　Or who shall make his thought stay on
　　　That down time drifts away?

　　　Your splendor is all fallen.

　　　O naked brow of wrath and tears,
　　　O change of Oedipus!
　　　I who saw your days call no man blest —
　　　Your great days like ghósts góne.

　　　That mind was a strong bow. [ANTISTROPHE 1]

　　　Deep, how deep you drew it then, hard archer,
　　　At a dim fearful range,
　　　And brought dear glory down!

You overcame the stranger —
The virgin with her hooking lion claws —
And though death sang, stood like a tower
To make pale Thebes take heart.


Fortress against our sorrow!


True king, giver of laws,
Majestic Oedipus!
No prince in Thebes had ever such renown,
No prince won such grace of power.


And now of all men ever known                          [STROPHE 2]
Most pitiful is this man's story:
His fortunes are most changed, his state
Fallen to a low slave's
Ground under bitter fate.


O Oedipus, most royal one!
The great door that expelled you to the light
Gave at night — ah, gave night to your glory:
As to the father, to the fathering son.


All understood too late.


How could that queen whom Laïos won,
The garden that he harrowed at his height,
Be silent when that act was done?


But all eyes fail before time's eye,                   [ANTISTROPHE 2]
All actions come to justice there.
Though never willed, though far down the deep past,
Your bed, your dread sirings,
Are brought to book at last.
Child by Laïos doomed to die,
Then doomed to lose that fortunate little death,
Would God you never took breath in this air
That with my wailing lips I take to cry:


For I weep the world's outcast.


I was blind, and now I can tell why:
Asleep, for you had given ease of breath
To Thebes, while the false years went by.

ÉXODOS

[*Enter, from the palace,* SECOND MESSENGER.]
SECOND MESSENGER: Elders of Thebes, most honored in this land,
    What horrors are yours to see and hear, what weight
    Of sorrow to be endured, if, true to your birth,
    You venerate the line of Labdakos!
    I think neither Istros nor Phasis, those great rivers,
    Could purify this place of the corruption
    It shelters now, or soon must bring to light —
    Evil not done unconsciously, but willed.

    The greatest griefs are those we cause ourselves.
CHORAGOS:  Surely, friend, we have grief enough already;
    What new sorrow do you mean?
SECOND MESSENGER:                         The Queen is dead.
CHORAGOS: Iocastê? Dead? But at whose hand?
SECOND MESSENGER:                                 Her own.
    The full horror of what happened you can not know,
    For you did not see it; but I, who did, will tell you
    As clearly as I can how she met her death.

    When she had left us,
    In passionate silence, passing through the court,
    She ran to her apartment in the house,
    Her hair clutched by the fingers of both hands.
    She closed the doors behind her; then, by that bed
    Where long ago the fatal son was conceived —
    That son who should bring about his father's death —
    We hear her call upon Laïos, dead so many years,
    And heard her wail for the double fruit of her marriage,
    A husband by her husband, children by her child.

    Exactly how she died I do not know:
    For Oedipus burst in moaning and would not let us
    Keep vigil to the end: it was by him
    As he stormed about the room that our eyes were caught.
    From one to another of us he went, begging a sword,
    Cursing the wife who was not his wife, the mother
    Whose womb had carried his own children and himself.
    I do not know: it was none of us aided him,
    But surely one of the gods was in control!
    For with a dreadful cry
    He hurled his weight, as though wrenched out of himself,
    At the twin doors: the bolts gave, and he rushed in.
    And there we saw her hanging, her body swaying
    From the cruel cord she had noosed about her neck.

A great sob broke from him, heartbreaking to hear,
As he loosed the rope and lowered her to the ground.

I would blot out from my mind what happened next!
For the King ripped from her gown the golden brooches
That were her ornament, and raised them, and lunged them down
Straight into his own eyeballs, crying, "No more,
No more shall you look on the misery about me,
The horrors of my own doing! Too long you have known
The faces of those whom I should never have seen,
Too long been blind to those for whom I was searching!
From this hour, go in darkness!;" And as he spoke,
He struck at his eyes—not once, but many times;
And the blood spattered his beard,
Bursting from his ruined sockets like red hail.
So from the unhappiness of two this evil has sprung,
A curse on the man and woman alike. The old
Happiness of the house of Labdakos
Was happiness enough: where is it today?
It is all wailing and ruin, disgrace, death—all
The misery of mankind that has a name—
And it is wholly and for ever theirs.

CHORAGOS: Is he in agony still? Is there no rest for him?

SECOND MESSENGER: He is calling for someone to lead him to the gates
So that all the children of Kadmos may look upon
His father's murderer, his mother's—no,
I can not say it?
                                And then he will leave Thebes,
Self-exiled, in order that the curse
Which he himself pronounced may depart from the house.
He is weak, and there is none to lead him,
So terrible is his suffering.
                                But you will see:
Look, the doors are opening; in a moment
You will see a thing that would crush a heart of stone.

[*The central door is opened;* OEDIPUS, *blinded, is led in.*]

CHORAGOS: Dreadful indeed for men to see.
Never have my own eyes
Looked on a sight so full of fear.

Oedipus!
What madness came upon you, what daemon
Leaped on your life with heavier
Punishment than a mortal man can bear?
No: I can not even
Look at you, poor ruined one.
And I would speak, question, ponder,

If I were able. No.
You make me shudder.
OEDIPUS: God.     God.
      Is there a sorrow greater?
      Where shall I find harbor in this world?
      My voice is hurled far on a dark wind.
      What has God done to me?
CHORAGOS: Too terrible to think of, or to see.
OEDIPUS: O cloud of night,                                    [STROPHE 1]
      Never to be turned away: night coming on,
      I can not tell how: night like a shroud!


      My fair winds brought me here.
                              O God. Again
      The pain of the spikes where I had sight,
      The flooding pain
      Of memory, never to be gouged out.
CHORAGOS: This is not strange.
      You suffer it all twice over, remorse in pain,
      Pain in remorse.
OEDIPUS: Ah dear friend                                    [ANTISTROPHE 1]
      Are you faithful even yet, you alone?
      Are you still standing near me, will you stay here,
      Patient, to care for the blind?
                              The blind man!
      Yet even blind I know who it is attends me,
      By the voice's tone —
      Though my new darkness hide the comforter.
CHORAGOS: Oh fearful act!
      What god was it drove you to rake black
      Night across your eyes?
OEDIPUS: Apollo. Apollo. Dear                                    [STROPHE 2]
      Children, the god was Apollo.
      He brought my sick, sick fate upon me.
      But the blinding hand was my own!
      How could I bear to see
      When all my sight was horror everywhere?
CHORAGOS: Everywhere; that is true.
OEDIPUS: And now what is left?
      Images? Love? A greeting even,
      Sweet to the senses? Is there anything?
      Ah, no, friends: lead me away.
      Lead me away from Thebes.
                              Lead the great wreck
      And hell of Oedipus, whom the gods hate.
CHORAGOS: Your fate is clear, you are not blind to that.
      Would God you had never found it out!

OEDIPUS: Death take the man who unbound                    [ANTISTROPHE 2]
　　　My feet on that hillside
　　　And delivered me from death to life! What life?
　　　If only I had died,
　　　This weight of monstrous doom
　　　Could not have dragged me and my darlings down.
CHORAGOS: I would have wished the same.
OEDIPUS: Oh never to have come here
　　　With my father's blood upon me! Never
　　　To have been the man they call his mother's husband!
　　　Oh accurst! Oh child of evil,
　　　To have entered that wretched bed—
　　　　　　　　　　　　　　　　　　the selfsame one!
　　　More primal than sin itself, this fell to me.


CHORAGOS: I do not know how I can answer you.
　　　You were better dead than alive and blind.
OEDIPUS: Do not counsel me any more. This punishment
　　　That I have laid upon myself is just.
　　　If I had eyes,
　　　I do not know how I could bear the sight
　　　Of my father, when I came to the house of Death,
　　　Or my mother: for I have sinned against them both
　　　So vilely that I could not make my peace
　　　By strangling my own life.
　　　　　　　　　　　　Or do you think my children,
　　　Born as they were born, would be sweet to my eyes?
　　　Ah never, never! Nor this town with its high walls,
　　　Nor the holy images of the gods.
　　　　　　　　　　　　　For I,
　　　Thrice miserable!—Oedipus, noblest of all the line
　　　Of Kadmos, have condemned myself to enjoy
　　　These things no more, by my own malediction
　　　Expelling that man whom the gods declared
　　　To be a defilement in the house of Laïos.
　　　After exposing the rankness of my own guilt,
　　　How could I look men frankly in the eyes?
　　　No, I swear it,
　　　If I could have stifled my hearing at its source,
　　　I would have done it and made all this body
　　　A tight cell of misery, blank to light and sound:
　　　So I should have been safe in a dark agony
　　　Beyond all recollection.
　　　　　　　　　　Ah Kithairon!
　　　Why did you shelter me? When I was cast upon you,
　　　Why did I not die? Then I should never
　　　Have shown the world my execrable birth.

Ah Polybos! Corinth, city that I believed
The ancient seat of my ancestors: how fair
I seemed, your child! And all the while this evil
Was cancerous within me!
                              For I am sick
In my daily life, sick in my origin.

O three roads, dark ravine, woodland and way
Where three roads met: you, drinking my father's blood,
My own blood, spilled by my own hand: can you remember
The unspeakable things I did there, and the things
I went on from there to do?
                              O marriage, marriage!
The act that engendered me, and again the act
Performed by the son in the same bed—
                              Ah, the net
Of incest, mingling fathers, brothers, sons,
With brides, wives, mothers: the last evil
That can be known by men: no tongue can say
How evil!
            No. For the love of God, conceal me
Somewhere far from Thebes; or kill me; or hurl me
Into the sea, away from men's eyes for ever.

Come, lead me. You need not fear to touch me.
Of all men, I alone can bear this guilt.
        [*Enter* CREON.]
CHORAGOS:  We are not the ones to decide; but Creon here
        May fitly judge of what you ask. He only
        Is left to protect the city in your place.
OEDIPUS:  Alas, how can I speak to him? What right have I
        To beg his courtesy whom I have deeply wronged?
CREON:  I have not come to mock you, Oedipus,
        Or to reproach you either.

            [*To* ATTENDANTS:]—You, standing there:
        If you have lost all respect for man's dignity,
        At least respect the flame of Lord Helios:
        Do not allow this pollution to show itself
        Openly here, an affront to the earth
        And Heaven's rain and the light of day. No, take him
        Into the house as quickly as you can.
        For it is proper
        That only the close kindred see his grief.
OEDIPUS:  I pray you in God's name, since your courtesy
        Ignores my dark expectation, visiting
        With mercy this man of all men most execrable:
        Give me what I ask—for your good, not for mine.

CREON: And what is it that you would have me do?

OEDIPUS: Drive me out of this country as quickly as may be
    To a place where no human voice can ever greet me.

CREON: I should have done that before now — only,
    God's will had not been wholly revealed to me.

OEDIPUS: But his command is plain: the parricide
    Must be destroyed. I am that evil man.

CREON: That is the sense of it, yes; but as things are,
    We had best discover clearly what is to be done.

OEDIPUS: You would learn more about a man like me?

CREON: You are ready now to listen to the god.

OEDIPUS: I will listen. But it is to you
    That I must turn for help. I beg you, hear me.
    The woman in there —
    Give her whatever funeral you think proper:
    She is your sister.
                        —But let me go, Creon!
    Let me purge my father's Thebes of the pollution
    Of my living here, and go out to the wild hills,
    To Kithairon, that has won such fame with me,
    The tomb my mother and father appointed for me,
    And let me die there, as they willed I should.
    And yet I know
    Death will not ever come to me through sickness
    Or in any natural way: I have been preserved
    For some unthinkable fate. But let that be.

    As for my sons, you need not care for them.
    They are men, they will find some way to live.
    But my poor daughters, who have shared my table,
    Who never before have been parted from their father —
    Take care of them. Creon; do this for me.
    And will you let me touch them with my hands
    A last time, and let us weep together?
    Be kind, my lord.
    Great prince, be kind!
                        Could I but touch them.
    They would be mine again, as when I had my eyes.
        [*Enter* ANTIGONE *and* ISMENE, *attended.*]
    Ah, God!
    Is it my dearest children I hear weeping?
    Has Creon pitied me and sent my daughters?

CREON: Yes, Oedipus: I knew that they were dear to you
    In the old days, and know you must love them still.

OEDIPUS: May God bless you for this — and be a friendlier
    Guardian to you than he has been to me!

    Children, where are you?
    Come quickly to my hands: they are your brother's —

Hands that have brought your father's once clear eyes
To this way of seeing —
                              Ah dearest ones,
I had neither sight nor knowledge then, your father
By the woman who was the source of his own life!
And I weep for you — having no strength to see you —,
I weep for you when I think of the bitterness
That men will visit upon you all your lives.
What homes, what festivals can you attend
Without being forced to depart again in tears?
And when you come to marriageable age,
Where is the man, my daughters, who would dare
Risk the bane that lies on all my children?
Is there any evil wanting? Your father killed
His father; sowed the womb of her who bore him;
Engendered you at the fount of his own existence!
That is what they will say of you

                              Then, whom
Can you ever marry? There are no bridegrooms for you,
And your lives must wither away in sterile dreaming.

O Creon, son of Menoikeus!
You are the only father my daughters have,
Since we, their parents, are both of us gone for ever.
They are your own blood: you will not let them
Fall into beggary and loneliness;
You will keep them from the miseries that are mine!
Take pity on them; see, they are only children,
Friendless except for you. Promise me this,
Great Prince, and give me your hand in token of it.
        [CREON *claps his right hand.*]
Children:
I could say much, if you could understand me,
But as it is, I have only this prayer for you:
Live where you can, be as happy as you can —
Happier, please God, than God has made your father!
CREON: Enough. You have wept enough. Now go within.
OEDIPUS: I must; but it is hard.
CREON:                              Time eases all things.
OEDIPUS: But you must promise —
CREON:                              Say what you desire.
OEDIPUS: Send me from Thebes!
CREON:                              God grant that I may!
OEDIPUS: But since God hates me . . .
CREON:                              No, he will grant your wish.
OEDIPUS: You promise?
CREON:              I can not speak beyond my knowledge.
OEDIPUS: Then lead me in.

CREON:                                Come now, and leave your children.
OEDIPUS:  No! Do not take them from me!
CREON:                                              Think no longer
     That you are in command here, but rather think
     How, when you were, you served your own distruction.
          [*Exeunt into the house all but the* CHORUS; *the* CHORAGOS *chants directly
          to the audience:*]
CHORAGOS:  Men of Thebes: look upon Oedipus.
     This is the king who solved the famous riddle
     And towered up, most powerful of men.
     No mortal eyes but looked on him with envy,
     Yet in the end ruin swept over him.

     Let every man in mankind's frailty
     Consider his last day; and let none
     Presume on his good fortune until he find
     Life, at his death, a memory without pain.

# Plautus

# The Menaechmi

C. 184 B.C.

## Translated by Richard W. Hyde and Edward C. Weist

*DRAMATIS PERSONAE*

PROLOGUS
PENICULUS (SPONGE), *a parasite*
MENAECHMUS I, *of Epidamnus*
EROTIUM, *a courtesan*
CULINDRUS, *cook of Erotium*
MENAECHMUS II (SOSICLES), *of Syracuse*
MESSENIO, *slave of Menaechmus II*
MAID *of Erotium*
WIFE *of Menaechmus I*
FATHER-IN-LAW *of Menaechmus I*
DOCTOR
*Sailors;* DECIO *and other slaves*

SCENE——*Epidamnus: a street, on which stand the houses of* MENAECHMUS I (L.) *and* EROTIUM (R.).

## PROLOGUE

PROLOGUS:  Now first and above all, spectators, I'm bringing a few
    Of the best of good wishes to me — and then also to you;
    I'm bringing you Plautus — by mouth, of course, not in his person,
    And therefore I pray you receive him with kindliest ears.
    To the argument gird up your minds, as I babble my verse on,
    And I shall explain it — in briefest of terms, have no fears.
        Now, once an old merchant was living in Syracuse city,
    And he by some chance had a couple of twin sons, — yes, two of 'em —
    And they looked so alike that the nurse couldn't tell (more's the pity)
    Which one she gave suck to; no more could their mother, in lieu of whom
    The nurse was called in, no, not even their mother who'd borne 'em.
        Much later, the boys being now about seven years old,
    Their father filled up a big ship with a lot of his goods
    And, putting one twin in safe-keeping with them in the hold,
    Betook himself off to Tarentum to market, to turn 'em
    To cash; and the other twin, having been naughty in moods,
    Stayed home with his mother. Tarentum was holding some games

When they got there, and people were flocking to town, as they ever
Will do for the games; and the little boy strayed, as one never
Should do, from his father among all the crowds, and got lost.
He was found by a rich Epidamnian merchant (whose fame's
The worse for the story) who grabbed him and took him off home.
The father, however, by such a deep blow so star-crossed,
(That is, after the boy disappeared) was dejected at heart,
And only a little while later he died of despair.
Syracuse at last heard the bad news that the father was dead
And that some one had picked up the twin who had gone off to roam;
So the grandfather changed the remaining twin's name then and there,
Since the other had been so beloved (*he* could tell 'em apart);
The other one's name he bestowed on the twin safe at home,
And called him Menaechmus, the same as the one I have said.
And lest you get muddled, as I am, I'm free to confess,
I'll tell you both twins are the same in their name. What a mess!
    But now on the poet's rude feet I must seek Epidamnus,
To speed on my tale, or the *Transcript* critic will be slammin' us
For being so dull. The old merchant I told you about
Had no children whatever, unless you may count all his money.
He adopted the stolen young twin, so that neither made out
Much worse on the deal, for the man got a son, and the youth
At length got a wife and a dowry, and (this strikes me funny)
Came into the property after the old wretch's death.
For, wandering into the country — to tell you the truth —
Where torrents of rain had been falling, not far from the town, the
Epidamnian stepped in a freshet, and thought himself still able
To cross as of old. None the less, as he got out of breath,
The current caught quickly the kidnapper's feet, and pulled down the
Epidamnian — down to the place where they act his third syllable.
So from him the young man inherits a whale of a fortune,
And there is the house where the rich kidnapped twin is now dwelling.
    The other twin, living in Syracuse — pray don't importune,
For I've not forgotten it — comes with his slave now today
To seek out his twin brother here, as you've just heard me telling.
This town's Epidamnus in the present play,
In other plays the city's changed straightway;
So with the families in these two houses,
Where now Menaechmus dwells and now he souses.
The next incumbent may be beggar, thief,
Procurer, doctor, thug, or Indian chief.


### ACT I

[*Enter* PENICULUS, *L. He looks at houses, and finally notices audience.*]
PENICULUS:  My nickname's Sponge [Peniculus], because when I eat I wipe the table
clean.
        Men who bind prisoners with chains and put shackles on runaway slaves

are very foolish, if you ask me. You see, if you add insult to injury, a poor fellow is going to want all the more to escape and go wrong. They'll get out of their chains somehow, you can be sure, — file away a link, or knock out a nail with a stone. — That way's ridiculous.

  If you really want to keep hold on somebody so he won't get away, you want to tie him with food and drink; first hitch his beak to a full dinnerpail. Give him all he wants to eat and drink every day, and he'll never try to run away, not even if he's committed murder; you'll keep him all right if you bind him this way. The bonds of food and drink are very elastic, you know; the farther you stretch them, the tighter they hold you. [*crosses towards house of* MENAECHMUS I]

  I'm just going over to see my friend Menaechmus, with whom I've been serving a long term: I'm going to let him bind me. He does more than feed a man, you see; he reforms you and builds you up; there isn't a better doctor alive. Just to show you what kind of man he is — he gives wonderful feasts, regular Thanksgiving dinners: he builds such skyscrapers of dishes that you have to stand on your couch to get anything off the top. But I haven't been there for quite a few days; I've been confined at home with my dear ones (I don't eat or buy anything but what is dear). But my army of dear ones is deserting, and I must go see him. [*Approaches door. Enter* MENAECHMUS I, *projected from doorway; the impulse evidently comes from his wife. He wears cloak under his pallium.*] But the door is opening. There's Menaechmus — he's coming out. [*Withdraws U.C.*]

MENAECHMUS I: [*Song*]

   If you were not
    Stubborn, bad,
   Stupid, and a
    Little mad,
   What your husband hates, you'd see
   And behave accordingly.
   Mind your manners — do you hear —
   Or home you go to "father dear." —
   When I say I'm going out,
   You're on hand to ask about
   Where I'm going,
    What to do,
   What's my business,
    What's for you.
   I can't get out anywhere,
   But you want me to declare
   All I've done and all I do,
   Customs officer — that's you!
   I've handled you with too much care;
   Listen what I'm going to do:
   Food I give you,
    Maids, indeed,
   Gold and dresses —
    All you need;

Now you'll keep your spying eyes
Off your husband, if you're wise.

And besides that, so you won't have your watching for nothing, I'm going to invite a courtesan out to dinner somewhere, to spite you. [*Looks back into house.*]

PENICULUS: [*aside*] The man pretends he's cursing his wife, but he's really cursing me. It's me that he hurts by dining out, not his wife.

MENAECHMUS I:  Can you beat it? I've finally scolded my wife away from the door. [*to audience*] Where are you philandering husbands? Why don't you come up and congratulate me, and reward me for my brave fight? [*shows cloak*] I've just stolen this cloak from my wife inside, and I'm going to take it to my mistress. This is a fine way to cheat my clever watchdog. Its

An excellent job,
An honest job,
A gentleman's job,
A workmanlike job.

I stole it from that shrew at my expense, and it's going to be a total loss. [*indicating house of* EROTIUM] But I got the spoils from the enemy without losing a man.

PENICULUS: [*accosting him*] Here, sir, is any of that haul for me?

MENAECHMUS I: [*retreating left and covering his head with his cloak*] The game's up. I've fallen into a trap.

PENICULUS: O no, sir, into a body guard, rather; don't be afraid.

MENAECHMUS I:  Who are you?

PENICULUS:  It's me.

MENAECHMUS I: [*grasping his hand*] O, my period of light-heartedness, my psychological moment, good morning!

PENICULUS:  Good morning.

MENAECHMUS I:  What are you up to?

PENICULUS:  Why, holding my friend-in-need by the hand.

MENAECHMUS I:  You couldn't have met me at a better time.

PENICULUS:  That's my way: I am an expert in fitting occasions.

MENAECHMUS I:  Want to see a rich treat?

PENICULUS:  What cook cooked it? I'll know if the pan slipped when I see the leavings.

MENAECHMUS I:  Say, did you ever see the painting in the temple where the eagle steals Ganymede, or Venus Adonis?

PENICULUS:  Plenty of times. But what's that got to do with me?

MENAECHMUS I: [*revealing cloak*] Well, look at me. Do I look like that picture?

PENICULUS:  What's that rig?

MENAECHMUS I:  Say that I'm a gallant soul.

PENICULUS:  When do we eat?

MENAECHMUS I:  Say what I tell you.

PENICULUS: [*listlessly*] All right; gallant soul.

MENAECHMUS I:  Won't you add anything of your own?

PENICULUS: [*with a sigh*] Well, gay dog.

MENAECHMUS I:  Go on, go on.

PENICULUS:  I will not go on until I know what I'm going to get. You've had a squabble with your wife and so I've got to be careful.

MENAECHMUS I: Suppose we find a place where we can have a funeral without my wife's knowing it—and then burn up the day?

PENICULUS: [*enthusiastically*] Wonderful, but go on—how soon can I light the pyre? The day's already dead up to the waist.

MENAECHMUS I: You'll wait, if you're going to contradict me.

PENICULUS: Knock my eye out, Menaechmus, if I say anything you don't tell me to.

MENAECHMUS I: Move over here away from the door. [*Pulls* PENICULUS *R., and twirls him around.*]

PENICULUS: Yes.

MENAECHMUS I: [*cautiously*] Come farther away. [*Twirling him around again.*]

PENICULUS: All right.

MENAECHMUS I: Come boldly away from the lion's den. [*Twirling him a third time.*]

PENICULUS: See here, I have an idea you'd make a good charioteer.

MENAECHMUS I: Why?

PENICULUS: Because you're always looking around to see that your wife is not following you.

MENAECHMUS I: But what do you say—

PENICULUS: What do I say? Any thing you want, sir.

MENAECHMUS I: Can you make a good guess from the odor of something if you smell it?

PENICULUS: Why, if you got the board of augurs,—

MENAECHMUS I: [*interrupting*] Come on, smell this cloak I've got. [*holds up the hem of the cloak*] What does it smell of? [PENICULUS *sniffs and draws back*] Why do you hang back?

PENICULUS: You ought to smell the top of a woman's dress, because the smell here is unforgettable.

MENAECHMUS I: Then smell here, Peniculus. [*holding up another part.*] How dainty you are!

PENICULUS: [*smelling cautiously*] It smells.

MENAECHMUS I: Of what? What does it smell of?

PENICULUS: [*triumphantly*] A theft, a courtesan, and luncheon! And you—

MENAECHMUS I: You've said it. Now I'm going to take this to the courtesan Erotium here, and I'll have lunch prepared for us three.

PENICULUS: Great!

MENAECHMUS I: And after that we'll drink till tomorrow's morning star.

PENICULUS: You've said a mouthful! Shall I knock now?

MENAECHMUS I: Yes. [PENICULUS *crosses, and standing with his back to* EROTIUM'S *door, raises one leg to knock*] But wait a minute.

PENICULUS: You've held up the drinking a mile.

MENAECHMUS I: Knock gently.

PENICULUS: I think you're afraid the door is made of Samian ware.

[*Enter* EROTIUM *from her house. Music.*]

MENAECHMUS I: [*dragging* PENICULUS *to C.*] Wait, wait, please. She's coming out herself. See how the sun is blinded beside her body's splendor.

EROTIUM: Menaechmus, sweetheart, good morning.

PENICULUS: [*interrupting*] What about me?

EROTIUM: [*pushing* PENICULUS *away*] You don't count.

PENICULUS: That's what usually happens to the reserves in a regiment.

MENAECHMUS I: I'd like you to get ready for him and me today—a battle.

EROTIUM: So it shall be.

PENICULUS: [*pushing in*] Yes, and we'll drink in this battle, and the better fighter will be found by the bottle. You're at the head of the regiment, and you'll decide which of us shall spend the night with you.

MENAECHMUS I: [*pulling* PENICULUS *away from* EROTIUM] My heart's delight, how I hate my wife when I see you!

EROTIUM: [*spying the cloak*] Incidentally you can't keep from wearing her clothes. What's this? [*Examining the edge of the cloak.*]

MENAECHMUS I: Clothes for you from my wife, rosebud.

EROTIUM: You're an easy winner over every one of my other lovers. [*Crossing to her door and posing before it.*]

PENICULUS: [*aside*] The courtesan is flattering him now that she sees what he's stolen. [*looking towards* EROTIUM] If you really loved him, you should have bitten his nose off with your kisses.

MENAECHMUS I: Take this, Peniculus. I want to make the offering I have vowed.

PENICULUS: Yes, [*holding* MENAECHMUS' *pallium*] but please, dance with that cloak on.

MENAECHMUS I: I dance? You must be mad.

PENICULUS: Either I or you. If you won't dance, take that thing off.

MENAECHMUS I: [*removing cloak*] I ran a great risk getting this.

PENICULUS: Yes, I think you ran a greater risk than Hercules when he stole the girdle of Hippolyta.

MENAECHMUS I: [*beckoning to* EROTIUM] Take this. [*He hands her the cloak.*] You are the only person who really understands me.

EROTIUM: That's the spirit that should inspire honest lovers.

PENICULUS: [*aside*] At least the ones that are on their way to the poorhouse.

MENAECHMUS I: [*taking cloak and holding it up*] I paid four minae for that last year for my wife. [*He teases* EROTIUM *by drawing away the cloak as she reaches for it, but finally hands it to her.*]

PENICULUS: [*aside*] Four minae gone up in smoke, as I foot up the account.

MENAECHMUS I: Do you know what I want you to do?

EROTIUM: Name it; I'll do anything you want.

MENAECHMUS I: Have a luncheon prepared for us at your house —

PENICULUS: [*Pushing him aside;* MENAECHMUS I *listens approvingly.*] And dainties bought at the market:

> The son of a glandule of pork,
>> Or the son of a fattened ham,
> Or the jowl of a hog —
>> Some food of that sort,
> Which set on the table,
> Will tickle my palate
> And give me the gorge of a kite.

And hurry up.

EROTIUM: Very good.

MENAECHMUS I: We'll go on to the forum but we'll be back soon. We'll pass the time when the lunch is being cooked in drinking.

EROTIUM: Come when you will. [*crossing to her door*] Things will be ready.

MENAECHMUS I: Hurry now. [*to* PENICULUS] You follow me.

PENICULUS: By Hercules, I'll watch over you and follow you, and I wouldn't take the wealth of heaven if I had to lose you. [*Exeunt* MENAECHMUS I *and* PENICULUS *at his heels, L.*]

EROTIUM: [*calling inside*]: Call out my cook Culindrus in there at once. [*Enter* CULINDRUS.] Take a basket [*Exit* CULINDRUS, *who returns immediately with a market basket*] and some money [*giving him coins*]. There's three nummi.

CULINDRUS: Yes.

EROTIUM: Go and get some provisions, enough for three people — not too little, and not too much.

CULINDRUS: What sort of men will they be?

EROTIUM: I and Menaechmus and his parasite.

CULINDRUS: There's ten already, because a parasite easily does the work of eight men.

EROTIUM: I've told you the guests. You take care of the rest.

CULINDRUS: Yes indeed. [*running off, L.*] Everything's cooked. Tell them dinner is served.

EROTIUM: Hurry back. [*Exit into her house.*]

CULINDRUS: I'm back already. [*Exit, L.*]


## ACT II

[*Enter* MENAECHMUS II, R., *and his slave* MESSENIO *carrying a bag, followed at a distance by sailors with baggage. Sailors cross to extreme L., where they deposit baggage and loll.*]

MENAECHMUS II: I think, Messenio, that there is no greater joy for sea travellers than sighting the distant land while still far out at sea.

MESSENIO: Frankly, it's a greater pleasure if it is your native land you're coming to. But, pray, why is it that we have now come to Epidamnus? Are we to be like the ocean, and go round all the islands?

MENAECHMUS II: [*sadly*] We are searching for my twin brother.

MESSENIO: Is there never to be an end to this search? This is the sixth year that we have spent on it: we have knocked about Histria, Spain, Massilia, Illyria, the whole Adriatic, all the Italian coast — every place that the sea touches; if you had been hunting a needle you'd have found it long ago, if there had been one. We're trying to find a dead man among the living; for if he were alive, we should have found him long ago.

MENAECHMUS II: Then, if you please, I am looking for some one who says he knows my brother is dead. Assured of this, I shall seek no further. But otherwise I shall never give up the search as long as I live; I know how dear he is to my heart.

MESSENIO: You might as well try to find a knot in a bulrush. Let's leave this place and go home. — Or are we, perhaps, going to write a book of travels?

MENAECHMUS II: [*angrily*] You had better stop making these witty remarks, unless you want to get into trouble. Don't provoke me; I am not carrying on this affair to suit you.

MESSENIO: [*aside*] Hey, now! That remark puts me in my place; he couldn't have put it more neatly and completely! But just the same I can't help talking. [*aloud*] Harkee, Menaechmus: when I look into the purse, it seems as though we were lightly clad for a summer journey! By heaven, if you don't go back home now, you'll be searching for that blessed brother of yours without a penny to bless *yourself* with. For Epidamnus is full of rakes and tremendous drinkers; a tremendous lot of swindlers and spongers live here, and their courtesans are called the most seductive in the whole world. That's why the place is called Epidamnus: scarcely anybody can come here without getting damned.

MENAECHMUS II: I'll be on my guard against that; just hand the purse over to me.

MESSENIO: What do you want with it?

MENAECHMUS II: I am worried about you, from what you have said.

MESSENIO: And why?

MENAECHMUS II: I am afraid you might get me damned in Epidamnus. You are very fond of the ladies, Messenio, and I am an irascible man of the most unmanageable disposition; with the money in my possession I shall be able to protect you doubly, both from any mishap and also from my anger.

MESSENIO: [*hands him purse*] Take it and keep it; I'm agreeable. [*Enter* CULINDRUS, *the cook, L. with his market basket of provisions.*]

CULINDRUS: [*to audience*] I have done a good job of marketing — just what I like myself! I'll set a fine lunch before the company. — Glory, there I see Menaechmus. Woe to my back! Here are the guests walking about at the door before I am back with the provisions. I'll go and speak to him. [*to* MENAECHMUS II] Good day, Menaechmus.

MENAECHMUS II: The lord love you, whoever you are. [*to* MESSENIO] This fellow seems to know my name. Do you know who he is?

MESSENIO: Not I, by heaven.

CULINDRUS: Where are the other guests?

MENAECHMUS II: What guests?

CULINDRUS: Why, your parasite?

MENAECHMUS II: My parasite? [*to* MESSENIO] Why, the man is mad.

MESSENIO: [*to* MENAECHMUS II] Didn't I tell you this place was full of swindlers?

MENAECHMUS II: What parasite of mine are you looking for, young man?

CULINDRUS: 'Sponge.'

MESSENIO: Nonsense, I have the sponge safe in the bag.

CULINDRUS: [*paying no attention to him*] You come too early for lunch, Menaechmus; I've just got back from the marketing.

MENAECHMUS II: [*gently*] Young man, tell me: what is the price of pigs in this town — unblemished ones, for sacrifice?

CULINDRUS: [*puzzled*] A drachma each.

MENAECHMUS II: Well, I'll give you a drachma; [*holds it out, but takes it back*] go get yourself purified of your insanity at my expense. For really, you must be perfectly mad, to be bothering a perfect stranger like me, — whoever you are.

CULINDRUS: I am Culindrus. Don't you know my name?

MENAECHMUS II: The devil take you, whether your name is Cylinder or Collander; I don't know you and I don't want to.

CULINDRUS: Your name is Menaechmus, I am sure of that much.

MENAECHMUS II: Now you're talking sense, since you call me by my right name. But where have you known me?

CULINDRUS: Where have I known *you*, who keep my mistress Erotium as your lady?

MENAECHMUS II: By heaven, I keep no such person, and I don't know you, either.

CULINDRUS: You don't know me, who have so often filled your cup for you here, when you have been drinking?

MESSENIO: O miserable me, not to have anything to break this fellow's head with!

MENAECHMUS II: You used to be cup-bearer for me, who have never before today been in Epidamnus or even seen it?

CULINDRUS: You deny it?

MENAECHMUS II: By heaven, I most certainly do deny it.

CULINDRUS: Don't you live in that house over there?

MENAECHMUS II: May the devil fly away with those that do!

CULINDRUS: [*aside*] Why, then, this man is mad too, calling the devil on his own head. [*aloud*] Harkee, Menaechmus.

MENAECHMUS II: Well, what do you want?

CULINDRUS: If you should ask me, I should advise you to take that drachma you promised me a minute ago and get a pig for yourself, because you are most certainly mad if you bedevil yourself this way.

MENAECHMUS II: Gad, what a chatterer this man is; he makes me tired.

CULINDRUS: [*to audience*] He often jokes with me like this. How droll he is, so long as his wife is not about! [*to* MENAECHMUS II, *showing his basket of provisions*] What do you say to that?

MENAECHMUS II: What do you want now, you good for nothing?

CULINDRUS: Is what you see here enough provision for the three of you, or should I go buy some more for yourself, the parasite, and the lady?

MENAECHMUS II: What ladies, what parasites are you talking about?

MESSENIO: What's the matter with you? Why are you badgering the gentleman?

CULINDRUS: [*to* MESSENIO] What business is it of yours? I never saw you before. I am just having a talk with this gentleman, whom I know.

MENAECHMUS II: By the lord, you're no sane man, I'm sure of that.

CULINDRUS: These things shall be cooked, I promise you, and without delay. [*crossing to* EROTIUM's *door*] Don't go too far from the house! Do you wish anything more?

MENAECHMUS II: Yes. I wish you to go utterly and completely to the devil!

CULINDRUS: It would be better if you were to go — inside and take your place at table while I [*grandly*] am exposing these morsels to the violence of Vulcan! I'll go in and tell Erotium that you are out here, so that she can bring you in instead of your having to cool your heels outside. [*Exit into house.*]

MENAECHMUS II: Has he gone away? He has. Oh, Messenio, I see that your warning was far from being false.

MESSENIO: Yes, but watch out; I am sure that a courtesan lives here, just as that madman said who just went away.

MENAECHMUS II: All the same, I wonder how he knew my name.

MESSENIO: Nothing strange in that; it's just a way these courtesans have. They send their serving-boys and serving-girls down to the harbor; if a foreign ship comes in, they ask where it comes from and what the owner's name is, and then they immediately glue themselves to him. If he is taken in by them, he is sent home a ruined man. [*grandly*] Now in the harbor there [*pointing to* EROTIUM's *house*] rides a pirate craft, of which we must be wary.

MENAECHMUS II: By heaven, that is good advice.

MESSENIO: I'll soon know how good it is, if you'll only take it.

MENAECHMUS II: Be quiet a minute; I heard the door creak. Let's see who comes out.

MESSENIO: I'll set this bag down, then. [*to sailors*] Keep a sharp eye on those bundles, you toilers of the sea!

[*Enter* EROTIUM *from her house.*]

EROTIUM: [*Song*] — [*to the slaves within*]
>                    Go in, and do not close the door,
>                         I want it left just so.
>                    See what there is to do inside
>                         And do it all — now go.

The couches must be spread, and perfumes burned:
Neatness entices lovers, I have learned.
Splendor to lovers' loss, to our gain is turned. [*coming forward and looking about her*]
But where is the man they said was before my door? [*catching sight of* MENAECHMUS II] Ah, there he is: he's been of use before,
Yet is, as he deserves, my governor.
I'll go and speak to him myself. — My dear,
I am amazed to see you standing here;
Less wide your door than mine when you appear.
>                    Now all you ordered is prepared,
>                         The doors are open wide,
>                    Your lunch is cooked, and when you like,
>                         Come take your place inside.

MENAECHMUS II: [*to* MESSENIO] Whom is this woman talking to?

EROTIUM: [*surprised*] Why, to whom but yourself?

MENAECHMUS II: What have you had to do with me, now or ever? Why do you speak to me?

EROTIUM: Because, in truth, it is the will of Love that I should exalt you of all others, and not beyond your desert, for it is you alone who make me flourish, by your kindness.

MENAECHMUS II: [*aside to* MESSENIO] Surely this woman is either insane or drunk, Messenio, to address an unknown man like me so familiarly.

MESSENIO: Didn't I tell you that was the way here? Why, these are just falling leaves compared to what will happen if we stay here a couple of days more: then it will be trees falling on you. All the courtesans here are just wheedlers of money. But let me speak to her a bit. [*to* EROTIUM, *who is looking into her house*] Harkee, my lady, I'm speaking to you.

EROTIUM: What is it?

MESSENIO: [*escaping her advances*] Where have you known this gentleman before?

EROTIUM: In the same place where he has known me for this long time, in Epidamnus.

MESSENIO: [*sarcastically*] In Epidamnus! A man who before this day has never set foot in this place?

EROTIUM: Ha, ha, you are joking. — Menaechmus, why don't you be a dear and come in? It will be nicer for you there.

MENAECHMUS II: [*aside to* MESSENIO] Great Scott, the woman has called me by my own name! I'd like very much to know the meaning of it all.

MESSENIO: She has got scent of that purse you have there.

MENAECHMUS II: That's a sound warning. Here, take it [*gives him purse*]; I'll soon find out which she loves better, me or my purse.

EROTIUM: [*attempting to draw* MENAECHMUS II *into her house*] Let us go inside to lunch.

MENAECHMUS II: You are very kind, but [*backing away*] no, thank you.

EROTIUM: But then why did you tell me just a little while ago to prepare a lunch for you?

MENAECHMUS II: I told you to prepare a lunch?

EROTIUM: Why of course, for you and your parasite.

MENAECHMUS II: Plague take it, what parasite? [*to* MESSENIO] Certainly this woman is not quite sane.

EROTIUM: 'Sponge.'

MENAECHMUS II: What is this sponge you all keep talking about? The kind you rub your shoes with?

EROTIUM: The one who came here with you a little while ago when you brought me the cloak you had stolen from your wife.

MENAECHMUS II: What? I gave you a cloak that I had stolen from my wife? Are you in your right senses? [*to* MESSENIO] Why, this woman dreams standing up, like a horse.

EROTIUM: Why do you enjoy making fun of me and denying what you have done?

MENAECHMUS II: Tell me what I have done, that I deny.

EROTIUM: That you gave me your wife's cloak today.

MENAECHMUS II: [*angrily*] I still deny it. I haven't a wife, never had one, and I have never in my life set foot in this place before. I had breakfast on board my ship, and from there I came by here and met you.

EROTIUM: Alack, I am a lost woman! What ship?

MENAECHMUS II: [*grandiloquently*] A wooden one is she, often bruised and often busted, often smitten with sledge; like the furrier's furniture, — peg is paired with peg.

EROTIUM: Oh, my love, stop this joking and come inside with me at once.

MENAECHMUS II: [*beginning to weaken*] But, madam, you are looking for some other man, not me.

EROTIUM: Don't I know you, — Menaechmus, son of Moschus, who was born in Sicily, the story goes, at Syracuse where King Agathocles reigned, and after him Pintia, and then Liparo, who at his death left the kingdom to Hiero, who now is king?

MENAECHMUS II: What you say is quite true.

MESSENIO: By heaven, the woman isn't from there herself, is she, to know you so well?

MENAECHMUS II: [*capitulating*] I don't think I can refuse. [*Moves toward* EROTIUM'S *house.*]

MESSENIO: [*seizing his arm*] You are a lost man if you cross that threshold.

MENAECHMUS II: Be quiet. The affair goes well. I shall assent to anything she says, so long as it means entertainment. [*confidentially to* EROTIUM] I have been contradicting you for a purpose: I was afraid that this fellow might tell my wife about the cloak and the breakfast. Now, whenever you please, let us go indoors.

EROTIUM: Are you going to wait for the parasite any longer?

MENAECHMUS II: Certainly not. I don't care a straw about him, and if he comes, I don't want to have him let in.

EROTIUM: Goodness, that's quite agreeable to me. — But do you know what I should like to have you do for me?

MENAECHMUS II: Command me.

EROTIUM: I wish you would take that cloak you gave me just now to the embroiderer's to be repaired, and get them to add some new trimming that I want.

MENAECHMUS II: [*scenting booty*] By heaven, that's a good idea. It shall be so disguised that my wife wouldn't recognize it if she saw you wearing it in the street.

EROTIUM: You can take it with you presently, when you go.

MENAECHMUS II: Yes, certainly.

EROTIUM: Let us go inside.

MENAECHMUS II: I'll follow you; I just want to speak to this fellow. [*Exit* EROTIUM *into the house.* MENAECHMUS II *crosses* MESSENIO *to bag, R.*] Hi there, Messenio, come here.

MESSENIO: What for?

MENAECHMUS II: Pick up that bag.

MESSENIO: What for?

MENAECHMUS II: Never mind what for. [*shamefacedly*] I know what you are going to call me.

MESSENIO: So much the worse.

MENAECHMUS II: Hold your accursed tongue, you knave. I have the booty practically in my hands, such a siegework I have begun! You go as quickly as you can and take these porters immediately to an inn; then do you be sure to come back for me before sundown. [*Crosses to* EROTIUM's *door.*]

MESSENIO: Master, you don't know what these courtesans are!

MENAECHMUS II: Be quiet, I tell you, and go. It is my loss, not yours, if I do anything foolish. This woman is silly and inexperienced; and as far as I can judge, there is plunder for us here. [*Exit into* EROTIUM's *house.*]

MESSENIO: I am lost! Are you going? He is surely lost too. The pirate craft is leading the yacht straight to destruction. But I'm a fool to expect to rule my master. He brought me to obey, not to give him orders. [*to sailors*] You, follow me, so that I can come back in time to meet my master, as he ordered. [*Exeunt.*]

[*Enter* PENICULUS, *exasperated.*]

PENICULUS: More than thirty years old I am, but in all that time I have never done anything more mischievous or evil than I did to-day when, miserable me, I pushed into the middle of the assembly. While I stood there gaping, Menaechmus sneaked off from me and went away to see his lady friend, I suppose, and didn't want to take me. — May the devil take the men who invented the scurvy practice of holding assemblies to take up the time of busy men! Wouldn't it be better, now, to pick on unengaged people for that, and if they didn't appear when the roll was called, let *them* pay the fine on the spot? There are plenty of men who eat only once a day, who have nothing to do, who are never invited out to dine or give a dinner themselves; that's the sort of people who should have the job of sitting in the assembly and the law courts. If things were run that way, I shouldn't have missed my breakfast to-day; on my life, he was willing enough to give it to me. — I'll just go anyhow. I may still get some scraps, and the hope whets my appetite. [*Door opens, revealing* MENAECHMUS II *very drunk, with a garland on his head and wearing the cloak.*] But what's this? Menaechmus coming out of the house with a garland on? The dinner's over; I've just come in time to fetch him away, egad! I'll see what he's about, and then I'll go speak to him. [*Withdraws.*]

MENAECHMUS II: [*to* EROTIUM *within*] It will be so changed that you won't recognize it.

PENICULUS: [*to audience*] He is taking the mantle to an embroiderer's; the breakfast eaten, the wine drunk, and the parasite shut outside. By heaven, I'll revenge myself handsomely for this trick, or my name's not Peniculus. Just watch how you'll catch it!

MENAECHMUS II: [*not seeing* PENICULUS] Ye gods! to whom did you ever in one day give more blessings, beyond all expectation? I've wined and dined with a courtesan, I've got me this [*indicating the cloak*], and she'll never have it again.

PENICULUS: [*aside*] From my hiding place I can't hear what he says. Now that he is full of dinner he is talking about me and my share.

MENAECHMUS II: [*still not noticing* PENICULUS] She says I stole this cloak from my wife and gave it to her. As soon as I saw she was mistaken, I began to assent, as though there had been something between us; whatever she said, I said too. Why waste words? — I have never had a better time at less expense.

PENICULUS: I'll go up to him. I'm just aching for a row.

MENAECHMUS II: Who is this coming towards me?

PENICULUS: [*violently*] What's that you say, you fellow lighter than a feather, you villain, you knave, you disgrace of humanity, you trickster, you cheap clown? What have I done to deserve ill of you? Sneak away from me in the forum a while ago and celebrate the funeral of the breakfast in my absence, would you? How did you dare do that, when I was entitled to it just as much as you were?

MENAECHMUS II: I beg you, young man, what have you to do with me, that you should ignorantly berate a stranger this way? Do you want to get a whipping for your insolence?

PENICULUS: Ha! you've given me that already.

MENAECHMUS II: Answer me, young man. What is your name?

PENICULUS: Are you mocking me too, pretending not to know my name?

MENAECHMUS II: As far as I can tell, I have never either seen or known you before this day. But, whoever you are, if you behave decently, we may get on together.

PENICULUS: You don't know me?

MENAECHMUS II: If I did, I should not deny it.

PENICULUS: Menaechmus, wake up! [*shakes him*]

MENAECHMUS II: By heaven, I *am* awake, I should think.

PENICULUS: Don't you know your own parasite?

MENAECHMUS II: I see that your head isn't sound, young man.

PENICULUS: Answer me: Did you not filch that cloak today from your wife and give it to Erotium?

MENAECHMUS II: Good Lord, I haven't any wife, I didn't give any mantle to Erotium, and I never stole it!

PENICULUS:  Are *you* sane? [*aside*] This affair is done for. [*to* MENAECHMUS] Didn't I
see you come out of that house with a woman's cloak on?

MENAECHMUS II:  [*angry*] Plague take ou! Do you think everybody is an effeminate
rogue simply because you are one? You declare that I had on a woman's cloak?

PENICULUS:  I certainly do.

MENAECHMUS II:  Go to the devil where you belong, or get yourself purified, you utter
madman.

PENICULUS:  [*furious*] By heaven, no one shall persuade me not to tell this whole
affair, just as it happened, to your wife at once. All your abuse will fall back on
your own head. I'll make you pay for hogging that breakfast.

    [*Exit into house of* MENAECHMUS I.]

MENAECHMUS II:  What sort of business is this? Is everybody going to make fun of me
this way as soon as I meet them? — But I heard the door creak.

    [*Enter a servant-girl from house of* EROTIUM, *with a bracelet in her hand.*]

MAID:  Menaechmus, Erotium says she would love to have you take this bracelet
along to the goldsmith's and have an ounce of gold added and have it done
over.

MENAECHMUS II:  I promise to take care of this and anything else she wants attended
to, anything at all. [*Takes it.*]

MAID:  Do you know what bracelet this is?

MENAECHMUS II:  Only that it's a gold one.

MAID:  It is the one which you said you once stole from your wife's cupboard on the
sly.

MENAECHMUS II:  By all that's holy, I never did!

MAID:  Don't you remember, pray? Give it back if you don't. [*Reaches for it.*]

MENAECHMUS II:  [*keeping it out of reach*] Wait a moment. I do indeed remember it.
[*lamely*] Why, it's the — one I gave her.

MAID:  The very same.

MENAECHMUS II:  Where are the armlets I gave her along with it?

MAID:  You never gave her any.

MENAECHMUS II:  I certainly did, along with the bracelet.

MAID:  I'll say you will look after it?

MENAECHMUS II:  Do. It shall be taken care of. I'll see that it's brought back — as soon
as the cloak.

MAID:  [*coaxingly*] Menaechmus, I'd love to have you give me some earrings. Have
them made to weigh two drachmas each! Then I'd be glad to see you when you
come here.

MENAECHMUS II:  Certainly! Give me the gold, and I'll pay for working.

MAID:  Oh, please, *you* give the gold. I'll repay you later.

MENAECHMUS II:  No, you give it. Later I'll repay you double!

MAID:  I haven't any.

MENAECHMUS II:  [*no longer interested*] Well, when you get some, you can give it to
me then.

MAID:  [*turning to go*] Is there anything else, please? [*Exit.*]

MENAECHMUS II:  Say I will take good care to sell these things for what they will bring!
Has she gone inside? [*examines door to make sure*] Yes; the door is shut. The
gods certainly aid me, prosper me, and love me. But why do I linger when now
is the time and the chance to escape from these courtesan liars? Hasten,

Menaechmus! Right foot forward, march! [*starts reeling off stage*] I'll take off this garland and throw it away over to the left [*throws it beyond house of* MENAECHMUS I], and then if they follow me they'll think I went that way. I'm off to find my slave, if I can, to tell himself about the blessings that the gods are sending me.

[*Exit, R.*]

## ACT III

[*Enter* WIFE *from house of* MENAECHMUS I, *followed by* PENICULUS.]

WIFE: [*coming C.*] How can I put up with married life when my husband sneaks out of the house with anything he can lay his hands on and carries it off to his mistress?

PENICULUS: Keep quiet a minute. You'll catch him in the act — I'll warrant you that. Come here a minute. He was wearing a wreath, he was reeling drunk, he was taking the cloak he stole from you today to the dyers'. [*seeing wreath*] But look, here's the wreath he had on. Now am I a liar? See, this is the way he went, if you want to hunt him down. [*Looking off L. Enter* MENAECHMUS I, *L.*] For heaven's sake, there's the fellow himself coming back. What a piece of luck! But he hasn't got the cloak with him.

WIFE: What'll I do to him?

PENICULUS: The same as usual — treat him rough.

WIFE: All right.

PENICULUS: Let's step aside and catch him from ambush. [*Drawing her back between houses. Pantomine during* MENAECHMUS I'*s song: they listen in vain for something that will betray him.* WIFE *gives up in disgust, and exits haughtily.* PENICULUS *sits dejected.* WIFE *returns in time to hear* MENAECHMUS I *tell of stealing of cloak.*]

MENAECHMUS I: [*Song*]
It's very silly fashion and an awful nuisance, too,
That all of us obey, especially the titled few.
We want a lot of hangers-on — who may be good or bad:
Reputation doesn't matter when there's money to be had.
You may be poor and honest — as a fool you're sent away;
But if you're rich and wicked, you're a worthy protégé.
The lawless man, who when he's trusted with a thing, will swear
He never saw it — that's the man for whom we patrons care —
The contentious man, the trickster, who by means of perjury
Or bribes supports a life of law-suits, greed, and luxury.
But the patron has no holiday when the law-days are decreed;
He must defend the guilty man and see that he is freed.
In just this way was I detained today by some poor sinner,
And now I've missed my mistress, to say nothing of the dinner.
I spoke before the aediles to allay their just suspicions,
And proposed a set of intricate and tortuous conditions,
Which, if we could have proved them, would have surely won the case.
But then this brainless fellow brought a bondsman to the place!
I'm sure I never saw a man more clearly caught than he:

Three witnesses were there, who swore to all his deviltry.
May heaven destroy the man who's made a ruin so complete
Of all my day — and me, who in the law-courts set my feet!
As soon as it was possible, I came directly here.
I've ordered lunch; I know she's waiting for me; yet I fear —
>             She's mad at me now;
>                 But the cloak ought to move her,
>             That I stole from my wife,
>                 And took to my lover.

PENICULUS: [*aside to wife*] What do you say to that?

WIFE: I'm blessed with a bad marriage and a bad husband.

PENICULUS: Can you hear what he's saying all right?

WIFE: I should say I could.

MENAECHMUS I: Now the best thing for me to do is to go in here, [*starting towards* EROTIUM's *door*] where I can have a good time.

PENICULUS: [*suddenly blocking his way;* WIFE *steps forward on other side.*] Wait a minute; there's a bad time coming first.

MENAECHMUS I: [*to audience*] Who's this? What do I see? My wife and my parasite standing together in front of my house? She doesn't seem to be in good humor; I don't like it. I'll go up and speak to her, though. [*approaching* WIFE] Tell me, my dear, what's wrong with you?

PENICULUS: Soft soap!

MENAECHMUS I: [*pushing* PENICULUS *away*] Stop making a nuisance of yourself. Am I talking to you? [*He goes to* WIFE *and attempts to fondle her.*]

WIFE: [*resisting*] Take away your arm; cut out your pawing!

PENICULUS: Keep at him, madam!

MENAECHMUS I: Why are you so disagreeable to me?

WIFE: You ought to know.

PENICULUS: He does, the villain, but he's making out he doesn't.

MENAECHMUS I: Has one of the slaves been cutting up? Have the maids or menservants answered you back? Tell me; they'll be punished.

WIFE: Nonsense!

MENAECHMUS I: You must be angry with one of the servants.

WIFE: Nonsense!

MENAECHMUS I: Well, are you angry with me?

WIFE: Now that is not nonsense.

MENAECHMUS I: What the deuce! I haven't done anything.

WIFE: There you are — back where you started. Nonsense!

MENAECHMUS I: What is the trouble, wife?

WIFE: A fine question to ask me!

MENAECHMUS I: Do you want me to ask *him*, then? What's the trouble?

WIFE: [*emphatically*] A cloak.

MENAECHMUS I: [*taken back*] A cloak? What about a cloak?

PENICULUS: What are you trembling for?

MENAECHMUS I: I'm not trembling —

PENICULUS: Except for one thing: the cloak's no joke. You won't sneak away from me again and eat dinner! [*to* WIFE] Go at the fellow!

MENAECHMUS I: Will you shut up?

PENICULUS: No, by George, I will not shut up. [*tattling to* WIFE] He's shaking his head at me to keep me from talking.

MENAECHMUS I: I am not, or winking either.

PENICULUS: That beats all: he says he's not doing a thing when you can see he's doing it.

MENAECHMUS I: [*loudly invoking*] By Jupiter and all the gods — is that enough for you, my dear? — I swear I did not shake my head at him.

PENICULUS: She'll believe that of you; get back to business.

MENAECHMUS I: What business?

PENICULUS: Oh, the dyers', I suppose. Come on now, give the cloak back.

MENAECHMUS I: What cloak are you talking about?

PENICULUS: I give up, if he can't remember his own affairs.

WIFE: So you thought you could get away with all this underhand business and me not know it, did you? You'll pay interest on what you stole, I'm sure of that. Take that! [*Slapping him down.*]

PENICULUS: [*echoing the triumph*] Take that! Now will you go and eat dinner behind my back? Now will you come out drunk and make fun of me in front of the house with a garland on your head?

MENAECHMUS I: I haven't had dinner or set foot in that house to-day.

PENICULUS: Do you mean to say that?

MENAECHMUS I: I guess I do!

PENICULUS: This fellow takes the cake! Didn't I see you standing here in front of the door just now, wearing a garland, and you said I was crazy and you didn't know me, and you insisted you were a foreigner?

MENAECHMUS I: Listen here, since I left you, this is the first time I've been home.

PENICULUS: Oh, I know you. You thought I didn't have any way of getting even with you. Now I've told everything to your wife.

MENAECHMUS I: What did you tell her?

PENICULUS: I don't know; ask her.

MENAECHMUS I: [*crossing to* WIFE] What is it, my dear? What stories has he been telling you? What is it? Why don't you say something? Why don't you tell me what it is?

WIFE: As if you didn't know! Oh dear, I am an unlucky woman!

MENAECHMUS I: Why unlucky? Explain yourself.

WIFE: What a thing for you to ask me!

MENAECHMUS I: Well, I wouldn't ask you if I knew, would I?

PENICULUS: What a man! Look how he makes believe. You can't hide it; she knows all about it. I told her everything.

MENAECHMUS I: What is it?

WIFE: Well, if you aren't ashamed and won't own up yourself, listen to me and keep your ears open. A cloak has been stolen from me out of the house.

MENAECHMUS I: A cloak stolen from me?

PENICULUS: See how the fellow is trying to catch you. It was stolen from her, not from you. If it had been stolen from you, it would be safe now.

MENAECHMUS I: [*pushing* PENICULUS *aside*] I'm not doing business with you. [*to* WIFE] What is it you're saying, madam?

WIFE: A cloak has disappeared from the house, I tell you.

MENAECHMUS I: Who stole it?

WIFE: I suppose the man that took it knows that.

MENAECHMUS I: Who is this man?

WIFE: A certain Menaechmus.

MENAECHMUS I: A rotten thing to do! But what Menaechmus do you mean? [*searching the stage*]

WIFE: You, I say!

MENAECHMUS I: Me?

WIFE: Yes, you, you!

MENAECHMUS I: Who accuses me?

WIFE: *I* do.

PENICULUS: I do, too; and you took the cloak over here to your mistress Erotium's.

MENAECHMUS I: What? I gave it to her?

WIFE: Yes, you — you [*like an owl*], I say!

PENICULUS: Do you want me to go and get an owl to say, "You, you!" to you? [*mocking her*] You see, we're tired of saying it.

MENAECHMUS I: By Jupiter and all the gods — is that enough for you, my dear? — I swear I didn't give —

PENICULUS: And we swear we're telling nothing but the truth.

MENAECHMUS I: But I didn't give it to her; I only lent it.

WIFE: Maybe you did, but I don't ever lend your dress-suit or your top-coat to anybody. [*By degrees she drives* MENAECHMUS I *and incidentally* PENICULUS, *R.*] It's the wife's business to lend her clothes, and the husband's to lend his. Now go and bring that cloak back home.

MENAECHMUS I: I'll see it's brought home.

WIFE: Well, you'd better, because you won't get into my house again unless you bring that cloak with you. [*marching to her door*] I'm going home.

PENICULUS: [*following* WIFE] What's to become of me after taking so much trouble for you?

WIFE: The trouble will be repaid when something is stolen from your house. [*Exit into house.*]

PENICULUS: That'll never be, because I haven't got anything at home to lose. Curse the husband and the wife, too! I'll go down to town; I can see I'm through with this family. [*Exit, L.*]

MENAECHMUS I: [*runs to door, peeks in, then turns laughing to audience*] My wife thinks she's punished me by shutting me out — as if I didn't have a better place where they'll let me in. If you don't like me, you've got to put up with me; Erotium here likes me. She won't shut me out from her: she'll shut me in *with* her. Well, I'll go and ask her to give me back the cloak I gave her this morning. I'll buy her a better one. [*knocking at* EROTIUM's *door*] Here, where's the doorman? Open up, and call Erotium out, somebody.
[*Enter* EROTIUM *from her house.*]

EROTIUM: Who wants me?

MENAECHMUS I: A greater enemy to himself than to your tender years.

EROTIUM: Menaechmus, my love, why do you stand out there? Come in.

MENAECHMUS I: By and by. Do you know why I've come to see you?

EROTIUM: Of course: to enjoy yourself with me.

MENAECHMUS I: No, it's that cloak I gave you a little while ago: give it back to me, that's a dear. My wife has found out about the whole thing. I'll buy you any cloak you want, worth twice as much.

EROTIUM: Why, I just gave it to you to take to the dyer's, and the bracelet, too, to take to the jeweler's to be done over.

MENAECHMUS I: You gave me the cloak and the bracelet? How could you, when I've just got back and seen you for the first time since I gave it to you and went to town?

EROTIUM: Oh, I get your idea. You're trying to cheat me out of what I let you take.

MENAECHMUS I: No, no, I don't want the cloak to cheat you; I tell you, my wife's found out about it.

EROTIUM: [*with mounting fury*] No, no, I didn't go out of my way to ask you to give it to me in the first place. You brought it to me yourself, and you gave it to me for a present. Now you want it back. All right. Have it. Take the old thing. Wear it yourself, or let your wife wear it, or lock it up in your trunk if you want to. After this you won't set foot inside this house again, you trifler with the affections of an innocent woman. [*changing her mood momentarily*] Unless you bring me money, you haven't got a chance. Go and find some other poor girl you can deceive. [*Exit into her house, slamming door.*]

MENAECHMUS I: By George, her temper's up! [*rushing to her door*] Here, woman, stop, say! Come back! Won't you wait? Won't you please come back for my sake? She's gone and closed the door. Now I'm the shut-outenest of men! They don't believe me at home or at my mistress's. I'll have to go and see what my friends advise me to do. [*Exit, L.*]

## ACT IV

[*Enter* MENAECHMUS SOSICLES, *R.*]

MENAECHMUS II: That was a foolish thing I did a while ago when I handed over my purse and money to Messenio. He has got himself into a chop-house somewhere, I suppose.

[*Enter* WIFE, *from her house.*]

WIFE: I'll watch and see how soon my husband will get home. Ah ha, there he is. I'm saved! He is bringing back the cloak.

MENAECHUMS II: [*to himself*] I wonder where Messenio can be rambling now.

WIFE: I'll go up to the fellow and welcome him as he deserves. [*to* MENAECHMUS II] You scoundrel, aren't you ashamed to come into my sight with that garment?

MENAECHMUS II: [*surprised*] What's this? What is troubling you, madam?

WIFE: You shameless wretch, do you dare say a single word to me? Do you dare to speak?

MENAECHMUS II: Pray, what have I done, that I shouldn't dare to speak to you?

WIFE: You ask me? Oh, the shameless impudence of the man!

MENAECHMUS II: [*mockingly*] I supose you know, madam, why it was that the Greeks used to call Hecuba a bitch?

WIFE: No. I do *not*.

MENAECHMUS II: Because Hecuba used to act just the way you do now: she used to heap abuse on everybody that she saw. That's how she got to be called a bitch, and she deserved it, too.

WIFE: It's impossible to put up with such outrages. I'd rather be husbandless all my life than stand for such outrages!

MENAECHMUS II: Is it any of *my* business whether you can put up with the state of marriage or whether you are going to leave your husband? Or is it the custom here to babble to perfect strangers?

WIFE: Babble, you say? I swear I'll remain married not an instant longer — to put up with your ways!

MENAECHMUS II: For all of me, by heaven, you can be a widow as long as Jove sits on his throne.

WIFE: For that, by goodness, I'll call my father and tell him about your outrages. [*calls within the house to* SLAVE, *who comes at once*] Here, Decio, go find my father, and ask him to come with you to me. [SLAVE *runs off L.*] Tell him it's absolutely necessary. [*to* MENAECHMUS II] I'll tell him of all your outrages!

MENAECHMUS II: Are you mad? What outrages? [*mocking her*]

WIFE: You steal cloaks and money from your wife and take them to your mistress. Is that straight enough?

MENAECHMUS II: [*applauding*] Bravo, woman! You certainly are a bad one, and a bold one, too! Do you dare say that I stole this when I got it from another woman, who wanted me to have it repaired?

WIFE: A few minutes ago you didn't deny stealing it; and are you going to hold it now before my very eyes? Aren't you ashamed?

MENAECHMUS II: I beg of you, woman, tell me, if you can, what potion I can drink that will make me able to put up with your bad humor. I don't know whom you take me for. As for you, I don't know you any more than I know the man in the moon.

WIFE: You may make fun of me, but you won't be able to make fun of my father. He's coming now. [*pointing off L. where* FATHER *appears hobbling towards them*] Back there. Do you know *him?*

MENAECHMUS II: [*facetiously*] Yes, I knew him when I knew Methuselah. I met him the same day I met you.

WIFE: You deny that you know me? that you know my father?

MENAECHMUS II: Yes, and your grandfather too, if you want to lug *him* in.
[*Stalks to extreme R.*]

WIFE: By heaven, that's the way you always are about everything.
[*Enter* FATHER.]

FATHER: [*Song*]
I'm getting along just as fast as my age will permit and this business requires.
But if some of you say that that's easy for me — very briefly I'll show that you're liars:
My body's a burden, my nimbleness gone, and of strength I've a notable lack,
I am quite overgrown with my years — oh, confounded old age is a curse on the back!
Why, if I were to tell all the terrible evils that age, when it comes, brings along,
I'm certain as certain can be that past suitable limits I'd lengthen this song.

However my mind is a little disturbed at this thing, for it seems a bit queer
That my daughter should suddenly send to my house with directions for me to come here.
And how the affair is related to me, she has not let me know up to now;

But I'm a good guesser, and feel pretty sure that her husband and she've
    had a row.
That's what usually happens when men are enslaved by their wives and
    must come when they call;
And then it's the wives who are mostly to blame, while the husbands aren't
    guilty at all.

And yet there are bounds, which we all must observe, to the things that a
    wife can endure,
And a woman won't call in her father unless the offense of her husband is sure.
But I think very soon the suspense will be over, and then I'll know what is
    the matter—
But look, there's my daughter in front of the door, and her husband; he's
    not looking at her.
        It's just as I suspected.

I'll speak to her.

WIFE: I'll go meet him [*meeting him* C.] I hope you are well, father.

FATHER: I hope you are well. Do I find you well? Are you well, that you summoned
me? Why are you sad? Why does he [*pointing with staff*] stand apart from
you, in anger? You have been quarreling about something. Tell me which of
you is at fault, and be brief about it; no rigmarole.

WIFE: I am guilty of nothing on my part; I'll ease you on this point first, father. But I
can't live here, and I can't stand it another minute. Take me away.

FATHER: Why, what's the matter?

WIFE: I'm made fun of, father.

FATHER: By whom?

WIFE: By *him*, to whom you gave me: my husband.

FATHER: [*to audience*] Look at that now! A squabble! [*to wife*] How many times have
I told you to see to it that neither of you come to me with your complaints?

WIFE: [*tearfully*] But father, how could I help it? I think you could understand—
unless you don't want to.

FATHER: How many times have I told you to humor your husband? Pay no attention
to what he does, or where he goes, or what he is about.

WIFE: Why, he has been making love to a courtesan who lives right next door.

FATHER: That's sensible enough. And I'll warrant he'll make love to her all the more,
with you spying on him this way.

WIFE: And he drinks there, too.

FATHER: Well, will he drink any the less on your account, here or anywhere else that
he chooses? Devil take it, why will you be so foolish? You might as well expect
to forbid him to accept dinner invitations or to entertain guests at his own
house. Do you want husbands to be slaves? You might as well expect to give
him a stint of work, and have him sit among the slave-girls and card wool.

WIFE: [*resentfully*] Apparently I had you come here to defend my husband's case,
father, not mine! You're *my* attorney, but you plead *his* case.

FATHER: If he has been delinquent in any way, I'll be even more severe with him
than I was with you. But since he keeps you well supplied with gold trinkets
and clothes and gives you servants and provisions as he should it is better for
you, girl, to take a sane view of things.

WIFE: But he steals my gold and my cloaks from the cupboard. He robs me and takes my trinkets to courtesans on the sly.

FATHER: He does wrong if he does; you do wrong if he doesn't: that's accusing an innocent man.

WIFE: But he has the cloak right now, father, and the bracelet that he took to the woman. He is bringing them back now because I have found out about it.

FATHER: I'll find out from him just what has happened. I'll go speak to him. [*goes over to* MENAECHMUS II *and taps him with staff*] Menaechmus, for my enlightenment tell me what you are quarreling about. Why are you sad? Why does she stand apart from you, in anger?

MENAECHMUS II: Whoever you are, whatever your name is, old man, I call as my witnesses great Jupiter and the gods—

FATHER: Why? Wherefore? And for what?

MENAECHMUS II: That I have neither wronged this woman, who accuses me of stealing this cloak from her house—

WIFE: Perjury, eh?

MENAECHMUS II: If I have ever set my foot inside the house in which she lives, may I be the most accursedly accursed!

FATHER: Are you in your right mind, to make such a wish? Do you deny that you have ever set foot in the house you live in, you utter madman?

MENAECHMUS II: Old man, do you say I live in that house?

FATHER: Do you deny it?

MENAECHMUS II: I' faith, I do deny it.

FATHER: No; you deny not "in faith" but in joke—unless, of course, you have moved out overnight. [*motions* WIFE *to* C.]—Come here, please, daughter. What do you say? You haven't moved from the house, have you?

WIFE: Why should we, or where should we move *to*, I ask you?

FATHER: By heaven, I don't know.

WIFE: It's clear that he is making fun of you. Don't you get that?

FATHER: Menaechmus, you have joked long enough; now attend to business.

MENAECHMUS II: I ask you, what business have I with you? Or who are you? Are you sane? And this woman, who has been plaguing me this way and that—is she sane? [*tears his hair in exasperation*]

WIFE: [*to* FATHER, *frightened*] Do you see the color of his eyes? See how a green color is coming over his temples and forehead! How his eyes shine!

MENAECHMUS II: [*to audience*] Alack, they say I'm crazy, whereas it is they who are really that way themselves. What could be better for me, since they say I am mad than to pretend to be insane, to scare them off? [*begins to jump about madly*]

WIFE: How he stretches and gapes! What shall I do, father?

FATHER: Come over here, my child, as far as you can from him. [*Retreating L.*]

MENAECHMUS II: [*pretending madness*] Ho, Bacchus! Ho, Bromius! Where in this forest do you bid me to the hunt? I hear, but cannot leave this place, so closely am I guarded by that rabid bitch upon my left. And behind there is that bald goat, who often in his time has ruined innocent citizens by his false testimony.

FATHER: Curse you!

MENAECHMUS II: Lo, Apollo from his oracle bids me to burn out the eyes of that woman with flaming torches. [*Charges at* WIFE, *then immediately retreats*]

WIFE: I am lost, father! He threatens to burn out my eyes.

FATHER: [*to* WIFE, *aside*] Hist, daughter!

WIFE: What? What shall we do?

FATHER: Suppose I summon the slaves? I'll go bring some people to take this man away and chain him up indoors before he makes any more disturbance.

MENAECHMUS II: [*aside*] I'm stuck; if I don't hit upon a scheme, they'll take me into the house with them. [*aloud*] Apollo, you forbid me to spare her face with my fists unless she leaves my sight and goes utterly to the devil? [*advances threateningly*] I'll do your bidding, Apollo!

FATHER: Run home as fast as you can, before he thumps you.

WIFE: I am running. Watch him father; don't let him get away! Oh! am I not a miserable woman to have to listen to such things! [*Exit into her house.*]

MENAECHMUS II: [*aside*] I got rid of her rather well. [*aloud, threatening* FATHER] Now, Apollo, as for this most filthy wretch, this bearded tremulous Tithonus, who is called the son of Cygnus, you bid me break his limbs and bones and joints with that staff which he holds?

FATHER: [*retreats, shaking his staff*] You'll get a beating if you touch me or come any closer.

MENAECHMUS II: I'll do your bidding! I'll take a double-edged axe and chop the flesh of this old man to mince meat, down to the very bones!

FATHER: [*aside*] Well then, I must beware and take care of myself. Really, I am afraid, from the way he threatens, that he may do me harm. [MENAECHMUS *retreats C.*]

MENAECHMUS II: You give me many commands, Apollo! Now you bid me take my fierce untamed yoked horses and mount my chariot, to crush this old stinking toothless lion. Now I've mounted! [*business*] Now I hold the reins! Now the goad is in my hand! Forward, my steeds, make loud the clatter of your hooves! And in swift flight make undiminished the fleetness of your feet. [*Gallops about the stage.*]

FATHER: Do you threaten me with yoked horses?

MENAECHMUS II: Lo, Apollo, again you bid me make a charge at him, this fellow who stands here, and slay him. [*rushes forward, then suddenly stops*] But who is this, who drags me from my chariot by the hair? He alters your commands, even the commands of Apollo! [*pretends to fall senseless to the ground*]

FATHER: [*advances cautiously*] Alas, by heaven, it is a severe disease! O gods, by your faith, what sudden changes do ye work! Take this madman — how strong he was a little while before. This disease has smitten him all of a sudden. I'll go get a doctor as quick as I can. [*Exit, L.*]

MENAECHMUS II: [*getting up*] Lord! These idiots who compel me, a sane man, to act like a madman! Have they got out of my sight now, I wonder? Why don't I go straight back to the ship while the going is good? [*as he starts to go, R., to audience*] I beg all of you, if the old man comes back don't tell him what street I've taken. [*Exit, R.*]

## ACT V

[*Enter* FATHER.]

FATHER: I've waited on the doctor's leisure until my limbs ache from sitting and my eyes from looking! I had a hard time persuading him to leave his patients. He

says he set the broken leg of Aesculapius and the arm of Apollo, so that now I
wonder whether I should say I am bringing a doctor or a joiner! [*glancing off
L.*] Here he comes. Hurry up that ant's pace, will you!
    [*Enter* DOCTOR.]

DOCTOR: What did you say was his disease? Tell me about it, sir. Has he a demonia-
cal affliction, or hallucinations? Explain. Is he lethargic, or has he a dropsical
propensity?

FATHER: That's why I'm bringing you here; I want you to tell me just that and make
him sound again.

DOCTOR: Ah, that is quite simple. He shall be sound as a nut, upon my honor.

FATHER: I want him cared for very carefully.

DOCTOR: I shall contrive a cure that will last a century; that is how carefully I shall
care for him for you.

FATHER: There's the man himself.

DOCTOR: Let us observe what he does. [*They withdraw C.*]
    [*Enter* MENAECHMUS I.]

MENAECHMUS I: [*to audience, while* DOCTOR *observes*] Good Lord, this has certainly
been a perverse and adverse day for me! I thought I was acting on the sly, but
that parasite has let everything out. He has filled me with fear and covered me
with disgrace; he's my Ulysses, stirring up trouble for his master! As sure as I'm
alive, I'll rid him of his life! But I'm a fool to call it *his*. It's mine; it was my food
and money that gave him life. Well then, I'll take the breath out of him! — The
courtesan acted true to form, in the regular courtesan way: because I asked for
the cloak so that I could take it back to my wife, she said she had given it to me!
[*sighs*] By heaven, I certainly lead a miserable life!

FATHER: Do you hear what he says?

DOCTOR: He says that he is miserable.

FATHER: I wish you'd go up to him.

DOCTOR: [*going up to* MENAECHMUS I] How do you do, Menaechmus. Please, why
do you leave your arm uncovered? Do you not know how injurious that is to
your present indisposition?

MENAECHMUS I: Go hang yourself!

FATHER: [*to* DOCTOR] Do you notice anything?

DOCTOR: Notice anything? This case cannot be cured with an acre of hellebore! But,
Menaechmus,—

MENAECHMUS I: Well?

DOCTOR: Answer me this question: is it white or red wine that you drink?

MENAECHMUS I: And what is it to you? Go to the devil!

DOCTOR: Ah, the first symptoms of insanity.

MENAECHMUS I: Why not ask whether the bread I eat is crimson or purple or
orange-colored? or whether I eat scaly birds and feathered fish?

FATHER: Dear me! Do you hear how he raves? Why don't you give him some kind of
a potion before complete madness sets in?

DOCTOR: One moment. I wish to continue my diagnosis.

FATHER: You're killing me with your talk!

DOCTOR: [*to* MENAECHMUS I] Tell me this: do you ever notice a hardening of your
eyes?

MENAECHMUS I: What! Do you take me for a lobster, you good-for-nothing?

DOCTOR: Tell me, are you subject to rumbling of the bowels — as far as you know?

MENAECHMUS I: When I've a full stomach, no. But when I go hungry, then there is a rumbling.

DOCTOR: [to FATHER] Dear me, that is no madman's answer! [to MENAECHMUS I] Do you sleep soundly at night? Do you go to sleep readily on retiring?

MENAECHMUS I: Yes, if I have paid my bills. [angrily] Jupiter and all the gods destroy you, you confounded busybody!

DOCTOR: The madness begins again. [to FATHER] You hear what he says; be on your guard.

FATHER: On the contrary, he talks like a perfect Nestor now, compared to what he was a while ago. Why, a few minutes ago he called his wife a rabid bitch.

MENAECHMUS I: I said what?

FATHER: You were raving, I say.

MENAECHMUS I: I raving?

FATHER: Yes, you. You threatened to trample me to death with a four-horse chariot. I myself saw you do it. I myself accuse you of it.

MENAECHMUS I: [to FATHER, furiously, pushing DOCTOR aside] Yes, and I know that you stole the sacred chaplet from the statue of Jupiter, and that you were clapped into jail for it; also that after you got out of prison you were strung up and flogged; also that you killed your father and sold your mother! Isn't that a sane man's retort? One flock of abuse deserves another.

FATHER: For God's sake, doctor, I beg of you; hurry! Whatever you are going to do, do it! Can't you see the man is raving?

DOCTOR: [aside to FATHER] It would be best if he were to be conveyed to my house.

FATHER: You think so?

DOCTOR: By all means. I shall be able to care for him there according to my own prescriptions.

FATHER: Just as you say.

DOCTOR: [rubbing his hands, to MENAECHMUS I] I shall set you to drinking hellebore for some twenty days!

MENAECHMUS I: [savagely] Yes, and I'll string you up and jab you with oxgoads for thirty days!

DOCTOR: [aside to FATHER] Go, fetch men to take him to my house.

FATHER: How many do we need?

DOCTOR: As I judge the extent of his madness, four; no less.

FATHER: They shall be here directly. [starts to go] Guard him, doctor!

DOCTOR: No, no! I shall go to my house and make the necessary preparations. Have the slaves bring him to me.

FATHER: I'll have him there immediately.

DOCTOR: Good. I leave you [Exit L.]

FATHER: [calling after him] Good-bye. [Exit R. to get slaves.]

MENAECHMUS I: [watching them off] Father-in-law gone; doctor gone; I'm alone. Great Jupiter! what makes all these people say that I'm insane? Since I was born I've never had a day's illness. I'm not mad; I don't brawl or pick fights in court. I'm sane, and I realize that others are, too. I recognize people, talk to them. These people who say falsely that I'm mad, perhaps they're mad themselves. — What shall I do? I want to go home, but my wife won't have it. Nobody will let me in here [looking at EROTIUM's house] either. What cursed luck! I'll be standing here forever! Well perhaps they'll let me into my house by evening. [*Withdraws U. C. to wait, where he sits and dozes.*]

[*Enter* MESSENIO *L., does not observe* MENAECHMUS]

MESSENIO: [*Song*]

It's a proof of an excellent slave,
If, his master's belongings to save,
    He'll use as much care
    When his master's not there
As when master is watching the slave.

For his back and his shins he must fear,
The demands of his stomach not hear,
    And the punishment know
    Of the slothful and slow —
This servant whose conscience is clear.

There are beatings, and chains, and the mills,
Hunger, weariness, terrible chills —
    The reward of the lazy;
    But since I'm not crazy,
I'm good, and avoid all these ills.

I'm good at taking a tongue-lashing but a whip-lashing I don't like, and I very much prefer to eat the meal to turning the mill. Therefore I follow my master's orders properly and gravely. My principle is to consider my back; it's worth my while. Let others behave the way they think best suits them; I'll be what I should. If that's my rule, if I keep out of trouble so I can serve my master at all times, I've little to fear. The day's near when my master will reward me for my good services. I've left the baggage and the slaves at the inn, as he ordered, and now I've come to meet him. I'll knock on the door to let him know I'm here, and to get him safely out of this place of ruin. But I'm afraid that I'll be too late and get there after the battle is over. [*Goes to* EROTIUM's *door, but seeing slaves approach, withdraws to extreme R. to watch.*]

[*Enter* FATHER *with a corporal's guard of four burly slaves.*]

FATHER: By all the gods and men I bid you take wise heed to my orders past and present. Pick up that man [*pointing to* MENAECHMUS] and fetch him to the doctor's at once, unless you care nothing for your shanks and sides. A straw for his threats, do you hear? Why do you stand there? Why do you hesitate? He should have been shoulder-high and hustled off already. I go to the doctor's; I'll be waiting there when you come. [*Exit L.*]

[*Slaves advance towards* MENAECHMUS I.]

MENAECHMUS I: [*awakening and seeing himself surrounded*] I'm lost! What is this? Why do these men run at me? What do you want? What are you after? Why do you surround me? [*They raise him on their shoulders.*] Where are you taking me? Where are you carrying me? Murder! Help! Good folk of Epidamnus, help! Let me go!

MESSENIO: [*coming forward*] By the immortal gods, what's this I see? A gang of thugs carrying off my master bodily!

MENAECHMUS I: [*shouting*] Doesn't anybody dare to help me?

MESSENIO: [*dramatically*] I do, master. I dare most daringly! [*to audience, singing*]:
> Oh! what an outrageous crime I see!
> Epidamnians, this man was free,
> My master, when he came today:
> And now they're carrying him away,
> While you're at peace, by light of day!

[*cuffs one of the slaves*] Let go of him, you.

MENAECHMUS I: I implore you, whoever you are, help me: protect me from this outrage.

MESSENIO: [*acting the faithful slave*] Yes, yes, I'll help and defend and stand by you. I'll never let you be murdered. Sooner myself than you! [*general scuffle, in time with music*] Gouge the eye out of that fellow who has you by the shoulder. I'll plow these faces for the sowing of my fists! You shall smart to-day for trying to carry him off! Let go!

MENAECHMUS I: I've got him by the eye!

MESSENIO: Good; make us see the socket! You villains! You robbers! You bandits!

SLAVES: Murder! Stop, for God's sake!

MESSENIO: Let go then! [*They drop* MENAECHMUS I.]

MENAECHMUS I: [*to slaves*] Lay hands on me, will you? [*to* MESSENIO] Give 'em your fists!

MESSENIO: [*to slaves*] Go on, get out! Get out of here, devil take you! There's one for you [*gives a final kick to last slave*]; take it as a prize for being the last to go! [*Exeunt slaves; to* MENAECHMUS I:] I measured those faces pretty well, all right, and just to my taste. I came to your help in the nick of time then, master!

MENAECHMUS I: May the gods bless you forever, young man, whoever you may be: If it hadn't been for you, I should never have seen the sun set this day!

MESSENIO: Well then, by George, if you did the right thing you'd set me free.

MENAECHMUS I: *I* set you free?

MESSENIO: To be sure, master; because I saved your life.

MENAECHMUS I: What's this? There's some mistake, young man.

MESSENIO: [*worried*] What do you mean?

MENAECHMUS I: By father Jupiter I swear that I am not your master.

MESSENIO: What!

MENAECHMUS I: That's the truth. No slave of mine ever served me as you have.

MESSENIO: Well then, if you say I'm not your slave, let me go free.

MENAECHMUS I: By heaven, as far as I am concerned you can be free to go wherever you please.

MESSENIO: [*eagerly*] Those are really your orders?

MENAECHMUS I: Why yes, if I have any power over you.

MESSENIO: Hail, my patron! How happy I am that you have freed me!

MENAECHMUS I: [*dryly*] I can believe it!

MESSENIO: But, my patron, please do not command me any less now than when I was your slave. I shall live with you and go with you when you go back home.

MENAECHMUS I: [*aside*] I guess not!

MESSENIO: Wait for me. I'm off to the inn to bring the baggage and the money. The journey-money is safely sealed up in your bag. I'll have it here directly.

MENAECHMUS I: [*much interested*] Do, by all means.

MESSENIO: I'll give it back to you all safe, just as you gave it to me. Wait for me here. [*Exit L.*]

MENAECHMUS I: [*alone*] There certainly have been strange things happening to me today, and in strange ways! People denying that I am I, and that fellow whom I just freed, who said he was my slave! He says he will bring me a purse with money in it. If he does, I'll tell him he is free to go away wherever he wishes, so that when he comes to his senses he won't try to get the money back. — My father-in-law and the doctor said I was insane. Heaven only knows what it all means! It seems just like a dream. — Now I'll go in here to the courtesan, even though she is angry with me, and see if I can't get her to give me back the cloak, so I can take it home. [*Exit into the house of* EROTIUM.]

[MENAECHMUS II *enters L. looking about stage for* MESSENIO. *Exit L., but returns immediately with him.*]

MENAECHMUS II: [*angrily*] You brazen rascal, do you dare tell me that you have been with me to-day since the time I ordered you to meet me here?

MESSENIO: [*angrily, thinking that his master is trying to cheat him*] Why, I rescued you just a few minutes ago when four men were carrying you off bodily, before this very house. You were yelling for help to all of heaven and earth when I ran up and rescued you with my fists, in spite of them. Therefore, because I had saved your life, you set me free. When I said I was going to get the money and the luggage, you ran ahead to meet me, so you could deny what you had done!

MENAECHMUS II: I set you free?

MESSENIO: Yes.

MENAECHMUS II: [*emphatically*] I'd turn slave myself sooner than free you, and that's that!

[*Enter* MENAECHMUS I *from the house of* EROTIUM.]

MENAECHMUS I: [*shouting into the house*] Swear by your eyes if you want to, but you can't make out that I took away the cloak and the armlet, you wantons!

MESSENIO: [*crossing towards* MENAECHMUS I] Immortal gods! what do I see!

MENAECHMUS II: What do you see?

MESSENIO: Your mirror.

MENAECHMUS II: What do you mean?

MESSENIO: He's your very image, as like you as can be.

MENAECHMUS II: [*comparing himself with the stranger*] Well! He's certainly not unlike me, now that I look at myself.

MENAECHMUS I: [*seeing* MESSENIO] The young man who saved me! Hail, whoever you are.

MESSENIO: Saving your presence, sir, tell me your name, for heaven's sake!

MENAECHMUS I: Well, by Apollo, you have not deserved so of me that I should object to your question. Menaechmus is my name.

MENAECHMUS II: [*surprised*] No, by Apollo, it's *mine!*

MENAECHMUS I: I'm a Sicilian, from Syracuse.

MENAECHMUS II: That's just where I came from!

MENAECHMUS I: What's that you say?

MENAECHMUS II: The truth.

MESSENIO: [*standing between them, indicating* MENAECHMUS I] This is the man I know, of course; *this* is my master. I'm *his* slave, though I thought I was that fellow's. I thought he was you, and made a nuisance of myself to him. [*to* MENAECHMUS II] I beg your pardon, sir, if I said anything indiscreet to you.

MENAECHMUS II: [*angrily, to* MESSENIO] Why you're raving! Don't you remember coming off the ship with me today?

MESSENIO: [*hurriedly changing sides*] Yes, yes, you're quite right. You are my master. [*to* MENAECHMUS I] You can hunt for another slave. [*to* MENAECHMUS II] Good-day to you. [*to* MENAECHMUS I] Good-bye to you. I say that this man is Menaechmus.

MENAECHMUS I: Well, I say *I* am.

MENAECHMUS II: What's this nonsense! *You* Menaechmus?

MENAECHMUS I: Yes; Menaechmus, Son of Moschus.

MENAECHMUS II: *My* father's son?

MENAECHMUS I: No indeed, young man, not yours. [*dryly*] I've no wish to appropriate your father and tear him away from you.

MESSENIO: [*steps forward to audience*] Immortal gods! Fulfil this unhoped-for hope of mine! For unless my mind is playing tricks, these two are the twin brothers! They both recall the same father and country. I'll speak to my master. [*aloud*] Menaechmus!

MENAECHMUS I *and* II: [*together*] What is it?

MESSENIO: I don't want both of you; just my master. Which of you came here in the ship with me?

MENAECHMUS I: Not I.

MENAECHMUS II: I did.

MESSENIO: [*aside to* MENAECHMUS II] This man is either a sycophant or your own twin brother. I've never seen anyone who looked so like you; water is not more like water, or milk like milk, than he is like you and you like him. Also, he says his father and his country are the same as yours. We'd better go up to him and investigate.

MENAECHMUS II: By heaven, that's good advice, and I'm grateful. Keep on helping me, for goodness' sake. If you prove he is my brother, you shall be free.

MESSENIO: I hope so.

MENAECHMUS II: And I hope so, too.

MESSENIO: [*between them again; he assumes the dignity of a cross-questioner*]Let's see now. [*to* MENAECHMUS I] Menaechmus is your name, I believe you said?

MENAECHMUS I: Indeed it is.

MESSENIO: This man's name is Menaechmus, too. You are a Sicilian, from Syracuse. That's where he comes from. Moschus was your father, you said. His father, too. Now, both of you can help me, and yourselves as well.

MENAECHMUS II: You deserve to receive from me anything you ask. I'm your humble servant, as though you had bought me with money.

MESSENIO: [*dramatically*] I hope that I'll find you two to be twin brothers, born on the same day to the same mother and father.

MENAECHMUS I: This is a strange tale. I wish you could make your hope come true.

MESSENIO: I can. Come now, each of you, answer me some questions.

MENAECHMUS II: Ask whenever you wish. I'll answer. I'll keep back nothing that I know.

MESSENIO: [*interrogating each in turn*] Is your name Menaechmus?

MENAECHMUS I: It is.

MESSENIO: And it is yours too?

MENAECHMUS II: It is.

MESSENIO: Moschus, you say, was your father?

MENAECHMUS I: He was.

MENAECHMUS II: And mine too.

MESSENIO: Are you from Syracuse?

MENAECHMUS I: Yes.

MESSENIO: And you?

MENAECHMUS II: Yes, of course.

MESSENIO: So far the evidence agrees without a flaw. Give me your attention further. [to MENAECHMUS I] Tell me, what is the earliest thing that you remember in your native land?

MENAECHMUS I: I can remember going away with my father to the market at Tarentum. Then, in the crowd I strayed off from him, and after that I was carried off.

MENAECHMUS II: God save us!

MESSENIO: [to MENAECHMUS II] What are you shouting about? Won't you be still? [to MENAECHMUS I] How old were you when your father took you away from home?

MENAECHMUS I: I was seven at the time, for I was just beginning to lose my teeth. And from that time I never saw my father again.

MESSENIO: So. How many sons were there in the family at that time?

MENAECHMUS I: Two, if I am not mistaken.

MESSENIO: Which was the elder, you or your brother?

MENAECHMUS I: We were both the same age.

MESSENIO: How can that be so?

MENAECHMUS I: We were twins.

MENAECHMUS II: [breaking in] Thank Heaven!

MESSENIO: [with finality] If you interrupt again, I'll be still.

MENAECHMUS II: [contritely] No, I'll be still.

MESSENIO: Tell me, did you both have the same name?

MENAECHMUS I: Of course not. My name was Menaechmus, as it is now. My brother was called Sosicles.

MENAECHMUS II: That's enough proof. I can't keep from embracing him. My own twin brother, come to my arms! I am Sosicles. [crosses and tries to embrace MENAECHMUS I]

MENAECHMUS I: [doubting] Then how did your name become Menaechmus?

MENAECHMUS II: After we heard that you had been carried away and father was dead, grandfather changed my name and gave me yours.

MENAECHMUS I: [still doubting] I believe it happened just as you say. But answer me this.

MENAECHMUS II: What?

MENAECHMUS I: What was our mother's name?

MENAECHMUS II: Teuximarcha.

MENAECHMUS I: Everything fits together. — Let me embrace you, brother, unexpected sight after so many years. [They embrace warmly.]

MENAECHMUS II: And you, too, for whom till now I have been searching with so many trials and troubles, and at whose discovery I now rejoice.

MESSENIO: And this was why the courtesan called you by his name: she mistook you for him, I suppose, when she invited you to lunch.

MENAECHMUS I: Why, of course. I ordered luncheon here (my wife didn't know) and gave her a cloak that I'd stolen from home.

MENAECHMUS II: Do you mean the cloak I have in my hand, brother?

MENAECHMUS I: How did you get it?

MENAECHMUS II: The courtesan who took me in to lunch here said I'd given it to her. I dined well, wined well, and had a glorious time with her. She gave me this cloak and jewelry.

MENAECHMUS I: I'm certainly glad if you've had any fun because of me. I think she thought you were I when she invited you in.

MESSENIO: [*hopefully*] Is there anything to prevent me from being free, as you promised?

MENAECHMUS I: A very good and fair request, brother. Grant it, for my sake.

MENAECHMUS II: Have your freedom. [MESSENIO *cuts a caper.*]

MENAECHMUS I: Congratulations on your freedom, Messenio.

MESSENIO: There ought to be a formal ceremony, so I'll be free forever.

MENAECHMUS II: Since we've had so much good fortune, brother, let's both return to our native land. [*They start R.*]

MENAECHMUS I: I'll do as you wish, brother, and I'll have an auction and sell all my property. But meanwhile, let's go in.

MENAECHMUS II: Very well.

[*They cross towards* MENAECHMUS' *house.*]

MESSENIO: [*to* MENAECHMUS I] Will you do me a favor?

MENAECHMUS I: What is it?

MESSENIO: Give me the job of auctioneer.

MENAECHMUS I: Certainly.

MESSENIO: Do you want the auction cried at once?

MENAECHMUS I: Yes, for a week from today.

[*Exeunt* MENAECHMUS I *and* II *into house of* MENAECHMUS I]

MESSENIO:

EXTRAORDINARY AUC — TION

WEEK — FROM TODAY

MENAECHMUS SELLS HIS PROPERTY

CASH AND NO DELAY

ALL MUST GO — HOUSE AND LOT

SLAVES AND FURNITURE

WIFE GOES TOO IF ANY ONE

TAKES A FANCY TO HER

[*aside*] I scarcely think he'll make a million out of the whole auction. [*to audience*] Now, spectators, fare you well, and lustily applaud us all. [*Exit R.*]

The Wakefield Cycle

# The Second Shepherds' Play[1]

## [Anonymous] Editing and notes by Robert B. Heilman

### CHARACTERS

FIRST SHEPHERD
SECOND SHEPHERD
THIRD SHEPHERD
MAK
GILL, *his wife*
ANGEL
JESUS
MARY

> [*Enter the* FIRST SHEPHERD.]

FIRST SHEPHERD: Lord! What these weathers are cold, and I am ill wrapped.
My hands nearly numb, so long have I napped.
My legs they fold, my fingers are chapped;
It is not as I would, for I am all lapped
   In sorrow
In storms and tempest,
Now in the east, now in the west,
Woe is him has never rest
   Midday nor morrow!

But we poor shepherds that walk on the moor,
In faith, we are near-hands out of the door;
No wonder, as it stands, if we be poor,
For the tilth of our lands lies fallow as the floor,
   As ye ken.
We are so hamyd,
For-taxed and ramyd,[2]
We are made hand-tamed
   By these gentlery-men.
Thus they rob us of our rest. Our Lady them curse!
These men that are lord-fast, they make the plough tarry.

[1] C. 1425-1450
[2] Crippled, taxed to death, ruined

That, men say, is for the best; we find it contrary.
Thus are husbandmen oppressed, in point to miscarry,
  In life.
Thus hold they us under;
Thus they bring us in blunder.
It were great wonder
  If ever should we thrive.

For may he get a painted sleeve, or a brooch, now-a-days,
Woe to him that him grieves, or one word gainsays!
Dare no man him reprove, what mastery he has.
And yet may no man believe one word that he says,
  No letter.
He can make purveyance,[3]
With boast and arrogance;
And all is through maintenance
  Of men that are greater.

There shall come a swain as proud as a peacock,
He must borrow my wagon, my plough also,
That I am full fain to grant ere he go.
Thus live we in pain, anger, and woe
  By night and day.
He must have if he longéd;
If I should forgang[4] it,
I were better be hanged
  Than once say him nay.

It does me good, as I walk thus by mine own,
Of this world for to talk in manner of moan.
To my sheep will I stalk and hearken anon;
There abide on a ridge, or sit on a stone,
  Full soon.
For I trow, pardie,
True men if they be,
We get more company
  Ere it be noon. [*Moves aside.*]
    [*Enter the* SECOND SHEPHERD.]
SECOND SHEPHERD: Ben'c'te[5] and Dominus! What may this bemean?
  Why, fares this world thus, oft have we not seen?
  Lord, these weathers are spiteful, and the winds full keen,
  And the frosts so hideous, they water my eyes,
    No lie.
  Now in dry, now in wet,
  Now in snow, now in sleet,

[3] Provision
[4] Do without
[5] Benedicite

When my shoes freeze to my feet,
  It is not all easy.
But as far as I ken, or yet as I go,
We poor wedded men endure much woe;
We have sorrow then and then, it falls oft so.
Silly Capel, our hen, both to and fro
  She cackles;
But begin she to croak,
To groan or to cluck,
Woe is him, is our cock,
  For he is in the shackles.


These men that are wed have not all their will.
When they are full hard bestead, they sigh full still.
God knows they are led full hard and full ill;
In bower nor in bed they say naught theretill,
  This tide.
My part have I found,
I know my lesson.
Woe is him that is bound,
  For he must abide.


But now late in our lives — a marvel to me,
That I think my heart rives such wonders to see,
What that destiny drives, it should so be —
Some men will have two wives, and some men three
  In store.
Some are woe that has any;
But so far ken I,
Woe is him that has many,
  For he feels sore.


But, young men, of wooing, for God that you bought,
Be well ware of wedding, and think in your thought,
"Had I known" is a thing it serves of naught.
Mickle still mourning has wedding home brought,
  And griefs,
With many a sharp shower;
For thou may catch in an hour
What shall seem full sour
  As long as thou lives.


For, as ever read I epistle,[6] I have one to my fere,[7]
As sharp as a thistle, as rough as a briar;
She is browed like a bristle, with a sour-laden cheer;

[6] In the Bible
[7] Mate

Had she once wet her whistle, she could sing full clear
    Her paternoster.
She is as great as a whale;
She has a gallon of gall;
By him that died for us all,[8]
    I would I had run till I had lost her!

FIRST SHEPHERD: God, look over the row! Full deafly ye stand.
SECOND SHEPHERD: Yea, the devil in thy maw — so tarrying!
    Sawest thou anywhere Daw?
FIRST SHEPHERD:                  Yea, on a lea-land
    Heard I him blow. He comes here at hand,
        Not far.
    Stand still.
SECOND SHEPHERD: Why?
FIRST SHEPHERD: For he comes, hope I.
SECOND SHEPHERD: He will make us both a lie
    Unless we beware.
        [*Enter* THIRD SHEPHERD, *a boy.*]
THIRD SHEPHERD: Christ's cross me speed, and Saint Nicholas!
    Thereof had I need; it is worse than it was.
    Whoso could, take heed and let the world pass;
    It is ever in dread and brittle as glass,
        And slides.
    This world fared never so,
    With marvels more and moe,
    Now in weal, now in woe,
        And all things writhes.

    Was never since Noah's flood such floods seen,
    Winds and rains so rude, and storms so keen;
    Some stammered, some stood in doubt, as I ween.
    Now God turn all to good! I say as I mean,
        For ponder.
    These floods so they drown,
    Both in fields and in town,
    And bear all down,
        And that is a wonder.

    We that walk in the nights our cattle to keep,
    We see sudden sights when other men sleep.
    Yet methinks my heart lightens; I see shrews[9] peep.
    Ye are two tall wights! I will give my sheep
        A turn.
    But full ill have I meant;
    As I walk on this land,

[8] Note the many anachronisms in the play
[9] Rogues

I may lightly repent,
My toes if I spurn.
    [*To the other two.*]
Ah, sir, God you save, and master mine!
A drink fain would I have, and somewhat to dine.
FIRST SHEPHERD: Christ's curse, my knave, thou art an evil hind!
SECOND SHEPHERD: What! the boy likes to rave! Abide until syne[10]
    We have made it.
Ill thrift on thy pate!
Though the fellow came late,
Yet is he in state
    To dine — if he had it.

THIRD SHEPHERD: Such servants as I, that sweats and swinks,[11]
    Eat our bread full dry. and that me forthinks.[12]
    We are oft wet and weary when master men winks;
    Yet come full late both dinners and drinks.
        But neatly
    Both our dame and our sire,
    When we have run in the mire,
    They can nip at our hire,
        And pay us full lately.

    But hear my truth, master, for the fare that ye make:
    I shall do, hereafter, work as I take;[13]
    I shall do a little, sir, and between times play,
    For yet lay my supper never on my stomach
        In fields.
    Whereto should I threap?[14]
    With my staff can I leap;
    And men say "Light cheap
        Badly for-yields."[15]

FIRST SHEPHERD: Thou were an ill lad, to ride a-wooing
    With a man that had but little of spending.
SECOND SHEPHERD: Peace, boy! I bade; no more jangling,
    Or I shall make thee a-feared, by the Heaven's King,
        With thy gawds.[16]
    Where are our sheep, boy? We scorn.
THIRD SHEPHERD: Sir, this same day at morn
    I left in the corn,
        When they rang lauds.[17]
    They have pasture good; they cannot go wrong.
FIRST SHEPHERD: That is right. By the rood, these nights are long!

[10] After
[11] Labors
[12] I regret
[13] As I am paid

[14] Talk back
[15] An easy bargain badly pays back
[16] Tricks
[17] Early church service

      Yet I would, ere we go, one gave us a song.

SECOND SHEPHERD: So I thought as I stood, for mirth us among.

THIRD SHEPHERD: I grant.

FIRST SHEPHERD: Let me sing the tenory.

SECOND SHEPHERD: And I the treble so high.

THIRD SHEPHERD: Then the mean falls to me.
      Let see how ye chant.
      [*Enter* MAK *with a cloak thrown over his smock.*]

MAK: Now, Lord, for thy names seven, that made both moon and stars,
    Well more than I can name; thy will, Lord, of me tharns.[18]
    I am all uneven; that moves oft my brains.
    Now would God I were in heaven, for there weep no bairns
      So still.

FIRST SHEPHERD: Who is that pipes so poor?

MAK: Would God ye knew how I fare!
    Lo, a man that walks on the moor,
      And has not all his will!

SECOND SHEPHERD: Mak, where hast thou gone? Tell us tidings.

THIRD SHEPHERD: Is he come? Then everyone take heed to his things.
      [*Takes the cloak from* MAK]

MAK: What! Ich be[19] a yeoman, I tell you, of the king;
    The self and the same, sent from a great lording,
      And such.
    Fie on you! Go hence,
    Out of my presence!
    I must have reverence.
      Why, who be ich?

FIRST SHEPHERD: Why make ye it so quaint? Mak, ye do wrong.

SECOND SHEPHERD: But Mak, list ye saint?[20] I trow for that you long.

THIRD SHEPHERD: I trow the shrew can paint! The devil might him hang!

MAK: Ich shall make complaint, and give you all a whang˙
      At a word,
    And tell even how ye doth.

FIRST SHEPHERD: But, Mak, is that truth?
    Now take out that southern tooth,
      And set in a turd.

SECOND SHEPHERD: Mak, the devil in your eye! A stroke would I lend you.

THIRD SHEPHERD: Mak, know ye not me? By God, I could 'tend to you.

MAK: God, look you all three! Methought I had seen you.
    Ye are a fair company.

FIRST SHEPHERD:              Can ye now mean you?[21]

SECOND SHEPHERD: Rascal, jape!
    Thus late as thou goes,

---

[18] Finds me wanting               [20] Do you like to show off?

[19] Mak affects southern accent     [21] Identify yourself

What will men suppose?
And thou hast an ill noise[22]
   Of stealing of sheep.


MAK: And I am true as steel, all men wot,
   But a sickness I feel that holds me full hot;
   My belly fares not well, it is out of state.
THIRD SHEPHERD: Seldom lies the devil dead by the gate.
MAK: Therefore
   Full sore am I and ill;
   If I stand stone still,
   I eat not a needle
      This month and more.


FIRST SHEPHERD: How fares thy wife? By my hood, how fares she?
MAK: Lies weltering, by the rood, by the fire, lo!
   And a house full of brood. She drinks well, too;
   Ill speed other good that she will do!
      But so,
   Eats as fast as she can;
   And every year that comes to man
   She brings forth a lakan,[23]
      And some years two.


Although I were more gracious and richer by far,
I were eaten out of house and of harbor.
Yet she is a foul dowse[24] if ye come near;
There is none that trows nor knows a worse
      Than ken I.
Now will ye see what I proffer —
To give all in my coffer
Tomorrow at next to offer
      Her head-mass penny.[25]
SECOND SHEPHERD: I wot so for-wakéd[26] is none in this shire.
   I would sleep, if I takéd less to my hire.
THIRD SHEPHERD: I am cold and naked, and would have a fire.
FIRST SHEPHERD: I am weary, for-rakéd,[27] and run in the mire.
   Stay awake, thou!
SECOND SHEPHERD: Nay, I will lie down by,
   For I must sleep, truly.
THIRD SHEPHERD: As good a man's son was I
      As any of you.
   But, Mak, come hither! Between shalt thou lie down.

---

[22] Bad reputation
[23] Plaything; i.e., child
[24] Whore
[25] He will gladly pay for her requiem mass

[26] Worn out with watching
[27] Worn out with walking

MAK: Then might I stop you, certain, of that ye would rown.[28]
   No dread.
From my top to my toe,
*Manus tuas commendo,*
*Pontio Pilato,*
   Christ's cross me speed! [*Then he rises, the shepherds being asleep,
   and says:*]
Now were time for a man that lacks what he would
To stalk privily then unto a fold,
And nimbly to work then, and be not too bold,
For he might pay for the bargain, if it were told,
   At the ending.
Now were time for to begin,
But he needs good counsel
That fain would fare well,
   And has but little spending.

But about you a circle as round as a moon,
Till I have done that I will, till that it be noon,
That ye lie stone still till that I have done,
And I shall say thereto of good words a few.
   On height
Over your heads my hand I lift:
Out go your eyes, foredo your sight!
But yet I must make better shift
   If it be right.

Lord, how they sleep hard! That may ye all hear.
I never was a shepherd, but now will I learn.
If the flock be scared, yet shall I nip near.
How! Draw hitherward! Now mends our cheer
   From sorrow.
A fat sheep, I dare say;
A good fleece, dare I lay!
Pay back when I may,
   But this will I borrow.
      [MAK *crosses the stage to his house.*]
How, Gill, art thou in? Get us some light.
WIFE: Who makes such din this time of the night?
I am set for to spin; I hope[29] not I might
Rise a penny to win. I curse them on height.
   So fares
A housewife that has been
To be rushed thus between;
Here may no work be seen,
   Because of such chores.

[28] Whisper
[29] Expect

MAK: Good wife, open the hek![30] Seest thou not what I bring?
WIFE: I may let thee draw the snek.[31] Ah, come in, my sweeting!
MAK: Yea, thou dost not reck of my long standing.
WIFE: By thy naked neck art thou like for to hang.
MAK:               Go way:
            I am worthy of my meat,
            For in a pinch can I get
            More than they that swink and sweat
                All the long day.

            Thus it fell to my lot, Gill, I had such grace.
WIFE: It were a foul blot to be hanged for the case.
MAK: I have escaped, Gillot, often as hard a place.
WIFE: But so long goes the pot to the water, men say,
                At last
            Comes it home broken.
MAK: Well know I the token,
            But let it never be spoken;
                But come and help fast.

            I would he were slain; I like well to eat.
            This twelvemonth was I not so fain of one sheep's meat.
WIFE: Should they come ere he be slain, and hear the sheep bleat—
MAK: Then might I be ta'en! That were a cold sweat!
                Go bar
            The gate door.
WIFE:                          Yes, Mak,
            For if they come at thy back—
MAK: Then might I pay for all the pack!
                The devil of them warn.

WIFE: A good trick have I spied, since thou ken none.
            Here shall we him hide till they be gone—
            In my cradle abide. Let me alone,
            And I shall lie beside in childbed, and groan.
MAK: Thou hast said:
            And I shall say thou was light
            Of a male child this night.
WIFE: Now well is the day bright,
                That ever was I bred.

            This is a good disguise and a far cast;
            Yet a woman's advice helps at the last!
            I wot never who spies. Again go thou fast.
MAK: Unless I come ere they rise, there blows a cold blast!

[30] Hatch
[31] Latch

I will go sleep.
  [MAK *returns to the shepherds and resumes his place.*]
Yet sleeps all this company;
And I shall go stalk privily,
As it never had been I
    That carried their sheep.

FIRST SHEPHERD: *Resurrex a mortruis!* Take hold of my hand.
  *Judas carnas dominus!* I may not well stand;
  My foot sleeps, by Jesus; and I walter fastand.[32]
  I thought that we laid us full near England.
SECOND SHEPHERD: Ah, yea!
  Lord, but I have slept well.
  As fresh as an eel,
  As light I me feel
    As leaf on a tree.

THIRD SHEPHERD: Ben'c'te be herein! So my body shakes,
  My heart is out of skin, what so it quakes.
  Who makes all this din? So my brows blacks[33]
  To the door will I win. Hark, fellows, wake!
    We were four:
  See ye aught of Mak now?
FIRST SHEPHERD: We were up ere thou.
SECOND SHEPHERD: Man, I give God a vow,

    Yet went he nowhere.
THIRD SHEPHERD: Methought he was lapped in a wolf's skin.
FIRST SHEPHERD: So are many wrapped now — namely, within.
THIRD SHEPHERD: When we had long napped, methought with a gin[34]
  A fat sheep he trapped; but he made no din.
SECOND SHEPHERD: Be still!
  Thy dream makes thee mad;
  It is but phantom, by the rood.
FIRST SHEPHERD: Now God turn all to good,
    If it be his will!

SECOND SHEPHERD: Rise, Mak! For shame! Thou liest right long.
MAK: Now Christ's holy name be us among!
  What is this? By Saint James, I may not well gang!
  I think I be the same. Ah! my neck has lain wrong
    Enough.
    [*They help* MAK *up.*]
  Mickle thank! Since yester even,
  Now, by Saint Stephen,

[32] Roll about famishing; cf. *wallow, welter*
[33] Head aches (?)
[34] Trick

I was flayed with a dream
    That my heart of slough.[35]
I thought Gill began to croak and travail full sad,
Well nigh at the first cock, of a young lad
For to mend our flock. Then be I never glad;
I have tow on my rock[36] more than ever I had.
    Ah, my head!
A house full of young tharnes![37]
The devil knock out their brains!
Woe is him has many bairns,
    And thereto little bread!

I must go home, by your leave, to Gill, as I thought.
I pray you look in my sleeve that I steal naught;
I am loath you to grieve or from you take aught.
THIRD SHEPHERD: Go forth; ill might thou live! Now would I we sought,
    This morn.
That we had all our store.
FIRST SHEPHERD: But I will go before;
    Let us meet.
SECOND SHEPHERD: Where?
THIRD SHEPHERD:           At the crooked thorn.
    [MAK *crosses to his cottage.*]
MAK: Undo this door! Who is here? How long shall I stand?
WIFE: Who makes such a stir? Now walk in the wenyand![38]
MAK: Ah, Gill, what cheer? It is I, Mak, your husband.
WIFE: Then may we see here the devil in a band,
    Sir Guile.
Lo, he comes with a lote[39]
As he were holden in the throat.
I may not sit at my note[40]
    A hand-long while.

MAK: Will ye hear what to-do she makes to get her a gloze?[41]
She does naught but plays, and wiggles her toes.
WIFE: Why, who wanders? Who wakes? Who comes? Who goes?
Who brews? Who bakes? What makes me thus do?
    And then,
It is ruth to behold,
Now in hot, now in cold,
Full woeful is the household
    That wants a woman.

But what end has thou made with the shepherds, Mak?
MAK: The last word that they said, when I turned my back,

---

35 Slew my heart
36 Distaff
37 Bellies
38 Waning (of the moon) — supposedly unlucky

39 Noise, i.e., as if he were being hanged
40 Work
41 Lie, excuse

They would look that they had their sheep, all the pack.
I expect they will not be well paid when they their sheep lack,
    Perdie.
But how so the game goes,
To me they will suppose,
And make a foul noise,
    And cry out upon me.


But thou must do as thou hight.[42]

WIFE:                        I accord me theretill;
    I shall swaddle him right in my cradle.
    If it were a greater plight, yet could I help till.
    I will lie down straight. Come, cover me.

MAK:                          I will.

WIFE: Behind!
    Come Coll and his maroo,[43]
    They will nip us full narrow.

MAK: But I may cry "Out, harrow!"
    The sheep if they find.


WIFE: Hearken aye when they call; they will come anon.
    Come and make ready all, and sing by thine own;
    Sing lullaby thou shall, for I must groan
    And cry out by the wall on Mary and John,
        For sore.
    Sing lullaby fast
    When thou hears at the last;
    Unless I play a false cast,
        Trust me no more!

        [*The* SHEPHERDS *meet at the crooked hawthorne.*]

THIRD SHEPHERD: Ah, Coll, good morn! Why sleep thou not?

FIRST SHEPHERD: Alas, that ever was I born! We have a foul blot.
    A fat wether have we lorn.

THIRD SHEPHERD:              Marry, God forbid!

SECOND SHEPHERD: Who should do us that scorn? That were a foul spot.

FIRST SHEPHERD: Some shrew.
    I have sought with my dogs
    All Horbury Shrogs,
    And of fifteen hogs[44]
        Found I but one ewe.


THIRD SHEPHERD: Now trust me if ye will; by Saint Thomas of Kent,
    Either Mak or Gill was at that assent.

FIRST SHEPHERD: Peace, man, be still! I saw when he went.

[42] Promised
[43] Mate
[44] Year-old sheep

Thou slanders him ill. Thou ought to repent,
    Good speed.
SECOND SHEPHERD: Now as ever might I thrive,
    If I should even here die,
    I would say it were he
      That did that same deed.
THIRD SHEPHERD: Go we thither, I rede, and run on our feet.
    I shall never eat bread the truth till I wit.
FIRST SHEPHERD: Nor drink, in my heed, with him I meet.
SECOND SHEPHERD: I will rest in no stead till that I him greet,
    My brother!
    One thing I will plight:
    Till I see him in sight
    Shall I never sleep one night
      Where I do another.
      [At MAK'S *house they hear* GILL *groan and* MAK *sing a lullaby.*]
THIRD SHEPHERD: Will ye hear how they hack? Our sir likes to croon.
FIRST SHEPHERD: Heard I never one crack so clear out of tune!
    Call on him.
SECOND SHEPHERD: Mak! Undo your door soon.
MAK: Who is it that spake as it were noon
      On loft?
    Who is that, I say?
THIRD SHEPHERD: Good fellows, were it day —
MAK: As far as ye may,
      Good, speak soft,

Over a sick woman's head that is at malaise;
I had liefer be dead e'er she had any dis-ease.
WIFE: Go to another place! I may not well wheeze.
    Each foot that ye tread goes through my nose,
      So high!
FIRST SHEPHERD: Tell us, Mak, if ye may,
    How fare ye, I say?
MAK: But are ye in this town today?
      How fare ye, I say?
    Ye have run in the mire, and are wet yet
    I shall make you a fire if ye will sit.
    A nurse would I hire, think ye on it.
    Well paid is my hire; my dream — this is it,
      In season.
    I have bairns, if ye knew,
    Well more than enow.
    But we must drink as we brew,
      And that is but reason.

I would have ye dine ere ye go. Methinks that ye sweat.
SECOND SHEPHERD: Nay, neither mends our mood, drink nor meat.

MAK: Why, sir, ails you aught but good?

THIRD SHEPHERD:                                 Yea, our sheep that we get
    Are stolen as they go. Our loss is great.

MAK: Sirs, drink!
    Had I been there,
    Some should have paid full sore.

FIRST SHEPHERD: Marry, some men think that ye were;
      And that makes us think.


SECOND SHEPHERD: Mak, some men trows that it should be ye.

THIRD SHEPHERD: Either ye or your spouse, so say we.

MAK: Now, if ye have suspicion of Gill or me,
    Come and rip our house, and then ye may see
      Who had her.
    If I any sheep got,
    Any cow or stott,[45]
    And Gill, my wife, rose not
      Since here she laid her,
    As I am true and leal, to God here I pray
    That this be the first meal that I shall eat this day.

FIRST SHEPHERD: Mak, as have I weal, advise thee, I say:
    He learned timely to steal that could not say nay.

WIFE: I swelt![46]
    Out, thieves, from my house!
    Ye come to rob us, for the nonce.

MAK: Hear ye not how she groans?
      Your hearts should melt.


WIFE: Out, thieves, from my bairn! Approach him not there!

MAK: Knew ye what she had borne, your hearts would be sore.
    Ye do wrong, I you warn, that thus come before
    To a woman that has farne.[47] But I say no more.

WIFE: Ah, my middle!
    I pray to God so mild,
    If ever I you beguiled,
    That I eat this child
      That lies in this cradle.


MAK: Peace, woman, for God's pain, and cry not so!
    Thou hurts thy brain, and makes me full of woe.

SECOND SHEPHERD: I think our sheep be slain. What find ye two?

THIRD SHEPHERD: All work we in vain; as well may we go.
      But, hatters,[48]
    I can find no flesh,
    Hard nor nesh,[49]

---

[45] Young steer
[46] Faint
[47] Fared; i. e., had a child

[48] Confound it
[49] Soft

Salt nor fresh,
> But two empty platters.
Live cattle but this, tame nor wild,
None, as have I bliss, so loud as he smelled.
WIFE: No, so God me bless, and give me joy of my child!
FIRST SHEPHERD: We have marked amiss; I hold us beguiled.
SECOND SHEPHERD: Sir, done.
> Sir, Our Lady him save!
> Is your child a knave?[50]
MAK: Any lord might him have,
> This child as his son.

When he wakens he skips, that joy is to see.
THIRD SHEPHERD: In good time to his hips, and in glee.
> Who were his godfathers, so soon ready?
MAK: So fair fall their lips!
FIRST SHEPHERD:                    Hark now, a lie!
MAK: So God them thank,
> Parkin and Gibbon Waller, I say,
> And gentle John Horn, in good faith,
> He made all the garray[51]
> > With his great shank.

SECOND SHEPHERD: Mak, friends will we be, for we are all one.
MAK: We! Now I hold for me, for amends get I none.
> Farewell, all three! All glad were ye gone! [*Shepherds go out.*]
THIRD SHEPHERD: Fair words may there be, but love there is none
> This year.
FIRST SHEPHERD: Gave ye the child anything?
SECOND SHEPHERD: I trow, not one farthing!
THIRD SHEPHERD: Fast back will I fling;
> Abide ye me here.
> [SHEPHERDS *re-enter.*]
Mak, take it to no grief, if I come to thy bairn.
MAK: Nay, thou does me great reproof; and foul has thou fared.
THIRD SHEPHERD: The child will it not grieve, that little daystar.
> Mak, with your leave, let me give your bairn
> But sixpence.
MAK: Nay, go 'way; he sleeps.
THIRD SHEPHERD: Methinks he peeps.
MAK: When he wakens he weeps;
> I pray you, go hence!

THIRD SHEPHERD: Give me leave him to kiss, and lift up the clout.
> What the devil is this? He has a long snout!
FIRST SHEPHERD: He is marked amiss. We wait ill about.

[50] Boy
[51] Commotion

SECOND SHEPHERD: "Ill spun weft," ywis, "aye comes foul out."
     Aye, so!
  He is like to our sheep!
THIRD SHEPHERD: How, Gib, may I peep?
FIRST SHEPHERD: I trow, nature will creep
     Where it may not go!

SECOND SHEPHERD: This was a quaint gawd[52] and a far cast!
  It was a high fraud!
THIRD SHEPHERD:         Yea, sirs, was't.
  Let's burn this bawd, and bind her fast.
  Ah, false scold, hang at the last,
     So shall thou.
  Will ye see how they swaddle
  His four feet in the middle?
  Saw I never in a cradle
     A hornéd lad ere now.

MAK: Peace, bid I! What! Let be your fare!
  I am he that him begot, and yon woman him bare.
FIRST SHEPHERD: After what devil shall he be hatt?[53] "Mak"?
  Lo, God, Mak's heir!
SECOND SHEPHERD: Let be all that. Now God give him care, I say.
WIFE: A pretty child is he
  As sits on a woman's knee;
  A dilly-downe, perdie,
     To make a man laugh.

THIRD SHEPHERD: I know him by the ear-mark; that is a good token.
MAK: I tell you, sirs, hark! His nose was broken;
  Later told me a clerk that he was forespoken.[54]
FIRST SHEPHERD: This is a false work; I would fain be wroken.[55]
     Get a weapon.
WIFE: He was taken by an elf,
  I saw it myself;
  When the clock struck twelve
     Was he misshapen.

SECOND SHEPHERD: Ye two are well gifted, same in a stead.
THIRD SHEPHERD: Since they maintain their theft, let's do them to death.
MAK: If I trespass eft, gird off my head!
  With you will I be left.
FIRST SHEPHERD:         Sirs, take my lead:
     For this trespass
  We will neither curse nor fight,
     Quarrel nor chide,

[52] Trick                 [54] Enchanted
[53] Named              [55] Avenged

But have done as tight,[56]
    And cast him in canvas.
    *[They toss him and go back to the fields.]*
FIRST SHEPHERD: Lord, what! I am sore in point for to burst.
    In faith, I may no more; therefore will I rest.
SECOND SHEPHERD: As a sheep of seven score he weighed in my fist.
    For to sleep anywhere methinks that I list.
THIRD SHEPHERD: Now I pray you,
    Lie down on this green.
FIRST SHEPHERD: On these thieves yet I mind.
THIRD SHEPHERD: Whereto should ye strain
    So, I say you? *[They sleep.]*
    *[An* ANGEL *sings "Gloria in excelsis"; then let him say:]*
ANGEL: Rise, herd-men kind! For now is he born
    That shall take from the fiend what Adam had lorn:
    That devil to sheynd[57] this night is he born;
    God is made your friend now at this morn.
      He behests
    At Bethlehem go see,
    Where lies the Free
    In a crib full poorly
      Between two beasts.

FIRST SHEPHERD: This was a wise voice that ever yet I heard.
    It is a marvel to name, thus to be scared.
SECOND SHEPHERD: Of God's son of heaven he spake upward
    All the wood in a levin[58] methought that he made
      To appear.
THIRD SHEPHERD: He spake of a bairn
    In Bethlehem, I you warn.
FIRST SHEPHERD: That betokens yon star;
    Let us seek him there.

SECOND SHEPHERD: Say, what was his song? Heard ye not how he cracked it,
    Three briefs to a long?
THIRD SHEPHERD:           Yea, marry, he hacked it;
    Was no crotchet wrong, nor nothing that lacked it.
FIRST SHEPHERD: For to sing us among, right as he knacked it, I can.
SECOND SHEPHERD: Let's see how ye croon.
    Can ye bark at the moon?
THIRD SHEPHERD: Hold your tongues, have done!
FIRST SHEPHERD: Hark after, then!
SECOND SHEPHERD: To Bethlehem he bade that we should gang;
    I am full afeared that we tarry too long.

[56] Quickly
[57] Destroy
[58] Lightning

THIRD SHEPHERD: Be merry and not sad; o mirth is our song;
    Everlasting glad our reward may we fang[59]
      Without noise.
FIRST SHEPHERD: Therefore thither hie we,
    If we be wet and weary,
    To that child and that lady.
    We have it not to lose.
SECOND SHEPHERD: We find by the prophecy — let be your din —
    Of David and Isaiah and more than I mind,
    They prophesied by clergy that in a virgin
    Should he light and lie, to slacken our sin
      And slake it,
    Our Race from woe.
    For Isaiah said so:
    "*Ecce virgo*
      *Concipiet*" a child that is naked.

THIRD SHEPHERD: Full glad may we be, and abide that day
    That lovely to see, that all mights may.
    Lord, well were me, for once and for aye,
    Might I kneel on my knee some word for to say
      To that child.
    But the angel said,
    In a crib was he laid;
    He was poorly arrayed,
      Both humble and mild.

FIRST SHEPHERD: Patriarchs that have been, and prophets before,
    They desired to have seen this child that is born.
    They are gone full clean; that have they lorn.
    We shall see him, I ween, ere it be morn,
      To token.
    When I see him and feel,
    Then know I full well
    It is true as steel
      That prophets have spoken:

    To so poor as we are that he would appear,
    First find, and declare by his messenger.
SECOND SHEPHERD: Go we now, let us fare; the place is us near.
THIRD SHEPHERD: I am ready, prepared; go we together
      To that bright.
    Lord, if thy will be —
    We are simple all three —

[59] Take

Grant us some kind of glee
    To comfort thy wight.
      [*They enter the stable.*]
FIRST SHEPHERD: Hail, comely and clean! Hail, young child!
    Hail, maker, as I mean, from a maiden so mild!
    Thou has cursed, I ween, the devil so wild;
    The false guiler of teen,[60] now goes he beguiled.
      Lo, he merry is!
    Lo, he laughs, my sweeting!
    A welfare meeting
    I have holden my heting.[61]
      Have a bob of cherries!

SECOND SHEPHERD: Hail, sovereign Savior, for thou hast us sought!
    Hail! noble child and flower, that all things has wrought!
    Hail, full of favor, that made all of naught!
    Hail! I kneel and I cower. A bird have I brought
      To my bairn.
    Hail, little tiny mop!
    Of our creed thou art crop.
    I would drink of thy cup,
      Little day-star.

THIRD SHEPHERD: Hail, darling dear, full of godhead!
    I pray thee be near when that I have need.
    Hail! Sweet is thy cheer! My heart would bleed
    To see thee sit here in so poor weed,
      With no pennies.
    Hail! Put forth thy dall[62]
    I bring thee but a ball:
    Have and play thee withal,
      And go to the tennis.

MARY: The Father of Heaven, God omnipotent,
    That set all in seven days, his Son has sent.
    My name could he neven[63] and descend ere he went.
    I conceived him full even, through might as he meant;
      And now he is born.
    Keep ye you from woe!
    I shall pray him so.
    Tell it forth as ye go,
      And mind on this morn.

FIRST SHEPHERD: Farewell, lady, so fair to behold,
    With thy child on thy knee!

---

[60] Contriver of evil
[61] Held to my promise
[62] Hand
[63] Call

SECOND SHEPHERD:                    But he lies full cold.
    Lord, well is me. Now we go, thou behold.
THIRD SHEPHERD:  Forsooth, already it seems to be told
      Full oft.
FIRST SHEPHERD:  What grace we have found!
SECOND SHEPHERD:  Come forth; now are we won!
THIRD SHEPHERD:  To sing are we bound:
    Let take aloft!
                  EXPLICIT PAGINA PASTORUM

# Author Uncertain but Attributed to Zeami Motokiyo

# The Shrine in the Fields (Nonomiya)

## Translated by H. Paul Varley

*Persons:*  A Traveling Priest (*waki*)[1]
A Village Girl, later Miyasudokoro (*shite*)[2]
*Place:*  Sagano in Yamashiro Province
*Time:*  Late Autumn, the Seventh Day of the Ninth Month

> [*The stage assistant places a* torii[3] *at the front of the stage. To either upright of the* torii *are attached short sections of fence made of brushwood twigs.*
>
> THE PRIEST *enters. He carries a rosary in his hand. He stands at the naming-place.*]

PRIEST:  I am an itinerant priest. Recently I have been staying in the Capital, where I have visited all the famous sites and relics of the past. Autumn is nearing its close and Sagano will be lovely now. I think I shall go there for a visit. [*He turns towards the* torii, *indicating that he has already arrived in Sagano.*] When I asked the people about this wood they told me it is the ancient site of the Shrine in the Fields. I would like to visit the place, though I am no more than a passing stranger. [*He advances to stage center, still facing the* torii.]
I enter the wood and I see
A rustic log *torii*
And a fence of brushwood twigs.
Surely nothing has changed from the past!
But why should time have spared this place?
Be that as it may, how lucky I am
To have come at this lovely time of year
And to be able to worship at such a place.
> [*He kneels and presses his palms together.*]
The Great Shrine at Ise
Makes no distinction
Between gods and Buddhas:
The teachings of the Buddhist Law
Have guided me straight along the path,
And I have arrived at the Shrine.

[1] Secondary role
[2] Principal character
[3] Gate to a shrine; here it stands for the shrine, which is not represented on stage

My heart is pure in the evening light,
Pure in the clear evening light!

> [THE GIRL *enters. She carries a branch of* sakaki.[4] *She stands at the* shite-*position and faces the musicians.*]

GIRL: Shrine in the Fields
Where I have lived with flowers;
Shrine in the Fields
Where I have lived with flowers—
What will be left when autumn has passed?

> [*She faces front.*]

Now lonely autumn ends,
But still my sleeves
Wilt in a dew of tears;
The dusk racks my body,
And my heart of itself
Takes on the fading colors
Of the thousand flowers;
It withers, as all things, with neglect.

Each year on this day,
Unknown to anyone else,
I return to the old remains.
In the wood at the Shrine in the Fields
Autumn has drawn to a close
And the harsh winds blow;
Autumn has drawn to a close
And the harsh winds blow;
Colors so brilliant
They pierced the senses
Have faded and vanished;
What remains now to recall
The memories of the past?
What use was it to come here?

> [*She takes a few steps to her right, then faces front.*]

Ahh—how I loathe the attachment
That makes me go back and forth,
Again and again on my journey
To this meaningless, fugitive world.

> [THE PRIEST *rises and faces her.*]

PRIEST: As I was resting in the shade of the trees, thinking about the past and refreshing my mind, a charming young lady has suddenly appeared. Please tell me who you are.

GIRL: It would be more appropriate if I asked who you are. This
is Nonomiya, the Shrine in the Fields,
where in ancient days the virgin
designated as the Priestess of Ise was

---

[4] Evergreen associated with enduring love and devotion

temporarily lodged. The custom has
fallen into disuse, but today, the
seventh day of the ninth month, is
still a time for recalling the past. Each year, unknown to anyone else, I come to
sweep the shrine and to perform a service. I do not know where you have come
from, but your presence here is an intrusion. Please leave at once.

[*She takes two steps towards* THE PRIEST.]

PRIEST: No, no. There can be no objection to my being here. I am only a wandering
priest who has renounced the uncertain world. But tell me, why should you
return here, to these old ruins, on this particular day each year in search of the
past?

GIRL: This is the day when Genji the Shining One visited this place, the seventh day
of the ninth month. He brought with him a twig of *sakaki* and pushed it
through the sacred fence. Miyasudokoro at once composed the poem:
"This sacred enclosure
Has no cypress to mark the spot;
By some error you have picked
A twig of *sakaki* wood."
It happened on this day!

PRIEST: That was truly a worthy poem.
—And the *sakaki* branch
You hold in your hand
Is the same color it was in the past.

GIRL: The same color as in the past?
How clever to put it that way!
Only the *sakaki* stays green forever,
And in its unvarying shade,

PRIEST: On the pathways through the wood,
The autumn deepens

GIRL: And leaves turn crimson only to scatter.

PRIEST: In the weed-grown fields.

[*She goes to the* torii *and places the* sakaki *branch there.* THE PRIEST
*kneels.*]

CHORUS: The stalks and leaf tips wither;
Nonomiya, the Shrine in the Fields,
Stands amidst the desolation
Of withered stalks and leaves.
The seventh day of the ninth month
Has returned again today
To this place of memories.

[*She moves to stage center.*]

How fragile it seemed at the time,
This little fence of brushwood twigs.

[*She gazes at the fence.*]

And the house that looked so temporary
Has now become the guardian's hut.

[*She turns towards the gazing-pillar.*]

A dim glow shines from inside:
I wonder if the longing within me
Reveals itself outwardly?
How lonely a place is this shrine,
How lonely a place is this palace!
[*She gazes across the front of the stage.*]
PRIEST: Please tell me more of the story of Miyasudokoro.
[THE GIRL *kneels at stage center.*]
CHORUS: The lady known as Miyasudokoro
Became the wife of the former Crown Prince,
The brother of Kiritsubo's Emperor,[5]
A man at the height of his glory;
They were like the color and perfume
Of the same flower, indissolubly bound.
GIRL: They knew, of course, the truth
That those who meet must part —
CHORUS: Why should it have surprised them?
But it came so soon — like a nightmare —
His death that left her alone.
GIRL: She could not remain in that state,
Helpless and given to tears;
CHORUS: Soon Genji the Shining One
Imposed his love and began
Their clandestine meetings.
GIRL: How did their love affair end?
CHORUS: And why, after they separated,
Did his love never turn to hate?
With customary tenderness
He made his way through the fields
To distant Nonomiya.
The autumn flowers had all withered,
The voices of insects were sparse.
Oh, the loneliness of that journey!
Even the wind echoing in the pines
Reminded him there is no end
To the sadness of autumn.
So the Prince visited her,
And with the deepest affection
Spoke his love in many ways;
How noble and sensitive a man!
GIRL: Later, by the Katsura River,
She performed the cleansing rite,
CHORUS: Setting the white-wrapped branches[6]

---

[5] Kiritsubo was Genji's mother
[6] Streamers of paper or mulberry bark inscribed with prayers and attached to *sakaki* branches, then tossed into the stream

Adrift on the river waves;
Herself like a drifting weed,
No roots or destination,
She moved at the water's will.
"Through the waves of the eighty rapids
Of Suzuka River to Ise,
Who will worry if the waves wet me or no?"
She wrote this poem to describe her journey.
Never before had a mother
Escorted her daughter, the Virgin,
All the way to the Také Palace.[7]
Mother and daughter on the way
Felt only the bitterness of regret.
　　　[*for* PRIEST]
Now that I have heard your tale,
I am sure you are no ordinary woman.
Please tell me your name.

GIRL: Revealing my name
Would serve no purpose;
In my helplessness
I am ashamed of myself.
Sooner or later
My name will be known,
It can't be helped;
But now say a prayer for one nameless,
And not of this world.

CHORUS: [*for* PRIEST] Not of this world?
What strange words to hear!
Then, have you died and departed

GIRL: This world, long ago,
A name my only monument:

CHORUS: Miyasudokoro

GIRL: Is myself.

CHORUS: Autumn winds rise at dusk;
　　　[*She stands.*]
Through the forest branches
The evening moonlight shines
　　　[*She goes to the* shite-*position.*]
Dimly illuminating,
Under the trees,
　　　[*She looks at the* torii.]
The rustic logs of the *torii.*
She passes between the two pillars
And vanishes without a trace;
She has vanished without a trace.
　　　[*She slowly exits.*]

---

[7] Residence of the virgin priestess following her temporary stay at Nonomiya

* * *

PRIEST: Alone I lie on the forest moss,
      A sleeve of my robe spread beneath me —
      Under forest trees, a mossy robe:
      My mat is grass of the same color.
      Unfolding my memories
      I shall offer prayers all night long;
      I shall pray for her repose.
            [THE GIRL, *now revealed as* MIYASUDOKORO, *enters and stands at the*
            shite-*position.*]
MIYASUDOKORO: In this carriage,
      Lovely as the autumn flowers
      At Nonomiya,
      I too have returned to the past,
      To long ago.
PRIEST: How strange!
      In the faint moonlight
      The soft sounds
      Of an approaching carriage,
      A courtly carriage
      With reed blinds hanging —
      A sight of unimagined beauty!
      It must be you, Miyasudokoro!
      But what is the carriage you ride in?
MIYASUDOKORO: You ask about my carriage?
      I remember now
      That scene of long ago —
      The Kamo Festival,
      The jostling carriages.
      No one could tell
      Who their owners were,
      But thick as dewdrops
PRIEST: The splendid ranks crowded the place.
MIYASUDOKORO: Pleasure carriages of every description,
      And one among them of special magnificence,
      The Princess Aoi's.
PRIEST: "Make way for Her Highness' carriage!"
      The servants cried, clearing the crowd,
      And in the confusion
MIYASUDOKORO: I answered, "My carriage is small,
      I have nowhere else to put it."
      I stood my ground,
PRIEST: But around the carriage
MIYASUDOKORO: Men suddenly swarmed.
            [*Her gestures suggest the actions described.*]
CHORUS: Grasping the shafts,
      They pushed my carriage back

Into the ranks of the servants.
My carriage had come for no purpose,
My pleasure was gone,
And I knew my helplessness.
I realized now
That all that happened
Was surely retribution
For the sins of former lives.
Even now I am in agony:
Like the wheels of my carriage
I return again and again —
How long must I still keep returning?
I beg you, dispel this delusion!
I beg you, dispel my suffering!
         [*She presses her palms together in supplication.*]
MIYASUDOKORO:  Remembering the vanished days
         I dance, waving at the moon
         My flowerlike sleeves,
CHORUS:  As if begging it to restore the past.
         [*She goes to the* shite-*position and begins to dance. As her dance ends, the
         text resumes.*]
MIYASUDOKORO:  Even the moon
         At the Shrine in the Fields
         Must remember the past;
CHORUS:  Its light forlornly trickles
         Through the leaves to the forest dew.
         Through the leaves to the forest dew.
MIYASUDOKORO:  This place, once my refuge,
         This garden, still lingers
CHORUS:  Unchanged from long ago,
MIYASUDOKORO:  A beauty nowhere else,
CHORUS:  Though transient, insubstantial
MIYASUDOKORO:  As this little wooden fence
CHORUS:  From which he used to brush the dew.
         [*She brushes the fence with her fan.*]
I, whom he visited,
And he, my lover too,
The whole world turned to dreams,
To aging ruins;
Whom shall I pine for now?
The voices of pine-crickets
Trill *rin, rin,*
The wind howls:
         [*She advances to stage front. She gazes at the* torii.]
How I remember
Nights at the Shrine in the Fields!
         [*Weeping, she withdraws to the area before the musicians and starts to
         dance. The text resumes when her dance has ended.*]

CHORUS: At this shrine we have always worshiped
   The divine wind that blows from Ise,
      [*She goes before the* torii.]
   The Inner and Outer Shrines.
   As I pass to and fro through this *torii*
   I seem to wander on the path of delusion:
   I waver between life and death.
      [*She passes back and forth through the* torii.]
   The gods will surely reject me!
   Again she climbs in her carriage and rides out
   The gate of the Burning House,
   The gate of the Burning House.[8]

---

[8] An image for this world, which an enlightened person should flee as eagerly as from a burning building

# William Shakespeare

# Hamlet, Prince of Denmark

*DRAMATIS PERSONAE*

CLAUDIUS, *King of Denmark*
HAMLET, *son to the former and nephew to the present King*
POLONIUS, *Lord Chamberlain*
HORATIO, *friend to Hamlet*
LAERTES, *son to Polonius*

VOLTEMAND
CORNELIUS
ROSENCRANTZ       } *courtiers*
GUILDENSTERN
OSRIC
A GENTLEMAN

A PRIEST

MARCELLUS        } *officers*
BERNARDO

FRANCISCO, *a soldier*
REYNALDO, *servant to Polonius*
PLAYERS
TWO CLOWNS, *grave-diggers*
FORTINBRAS, *Prince of Norway*
A NORWEGIAN CAPTAIN
ENGLISH AMBASSADORS
GERTRUDE, *Queen of Denmark, and mother of Hamlet*
OPHELIA, *daughter to Polonius*
GHOST *of Hamlet's father*
LORDS, LADIES, OFFICERS, SOLDIERS, SAILORS, MESSENGERS, AND ATTENDANTS

SCENE——*Denmark.*

## ACT I

SCENE I——*Elsinore. The guard-platform of the Castle.*

[FRANCISCO *at his post. Enter to him* BERNARDO.]
BERNARDO: Who's there?
FRANCISCO: Nay, answer me. Stand and unfold yourself.
BERNARDO: Long live the King!
FRANCISCO: Bernardo?

BERNARDO: He.

FRANCISCO: You come most carefully upon your hour.

BERNARDO: 'Tis now struck twelve; get thee to bed, Francisco.

FRANCISCO: For this relief much thanks. 'Tis bitter cold,
        And I am sick at heart.

BERNARDO: Have you had quiet guard?

FRANCISCO: Not a mouse stirring.

BERNARDO: Well; good night.
        If you do meet Horatio and Marcellus,
        The rivals of my watch, bid them make haste.
            [*Enter* HORATIO *and* MARCELLUS.]

FRANCISCO: I think I hear them. Stand, ho! Who is there?

HORATIO: Friends to this ground.

MARCELLUS: And liegemen to the Dane.

FRANCISCO: Give you good night.

MARCELLUS: O, farewell, honest soldier!
        Who hath reliev'd you?

FRANCISCO: Bernardo hath my place.
        Give you good night.                                   [*Exit.*]

MARCELLUS: Holla, Bernardo!

BERNARDO: Say —
        What, is Horatio there?

HORATIO: A piece of him.

BERNARDO: Welcome, Horatio; welcome, good Marcellus.

HORATIO: What, has this thing appear'd again to-night?

BERNARDO: I have seen nothing.

MARCELLUS: Horatio says 'tis but our fantasy,
        And will not let belief take hold of him
        Touching this dreaded sight, twice seen of us;
        Therefore I have entreated him along
        With us to watch the minutes of this night,
        That, if again this apparition come,
        He may approve our eyes and speak to it.

HORATIO: Tush, tush, 'twill not appear.

BERNARDO: Sit down awhile,
        And let us once again assail your ears,
        That are so fortified against our story,
        What we have two nights seen.

HORATIO: Well, sit we down,
        And let us hear Bernardo speak of this.

BERNARDO: Last night of all,
        When yond same star that's westward from the pole
        Had made his course t' illume that part of heaven
        Where now it burns, Marcellus and myself,
        The bell then beating one —
            [*Enter* GHOST.]

MARCELLUS: Peace, break thee off; look where it comes again.

BERNARDO: In the same figure, like the King that's dead.

MARCELLUS: Thou art a scholar; speak to it, Horatio.

BERNARDO: Looks 'a not like the King? Mark it, Horatio.

HORATIO: Most like. It harrows me with fear and wonder.

BERNARDO: It would be spoke to.

MARCELLUS: Question it, Horatio.

HORATIO: What art thou that usurp'st this time of night
       Together with that fair and warlike form
       In which the majesty of buried Denmark
       Did sometimes march? By heaven I charge thee, speak!

MARCELLUS: It is offended.

BERNARDO: See, it stalks away.

HORATIO: Stay! speak, speak! I charge thee, speak!
       [*Exit* GHOST.]

MARCELLUS: 'Tis gone, and will not answer.

BERNARDO: How now, Horatio! You tremble and look pale.
       Is not this something more than fantasy?
       What think you on't?

HORATIO: Before my God, I might not this believe
       Without the sensible and true avouch
       Of mine own eyes.

MARCELLUS: Is it not like the King?

HORATIO: As thou art to thyself:
       Such was the very armour he had on
       When he the ambitious Norway combated;
       So frown'd he once when, in an angry parle,
       He smote the sledded Polacks on the ice.
       'Tis strange.

MARCELLUS: Thus twice before, and jump at this dead hour,
       With martial stalk hath he gone by our watch.

HORATIO: In what particular thought to work I know not;
       But, in the gross and scope of mine opinion,
       This bodes some strange eruption to our state.

MARCELLUS: Good now, sit down, and tell me, he that knows,
       Why this same strict and most observant watch
       So nightly toils the subject of the land;
       And why such daily cast of brazen cannon,
       And foreign mart for implements of war;
       Why such impress of shipwrights, whose sore task
       Does not divide the Sunday from the week;
       What might be toward, that this sweaty haste
       Doth make the night joint-labourer with the day:
       Who is't that can inform me?

HORATIO: That can I;
       At least, the whisper goes so. Our last King,
       Whose image even but now appear'd to us,
       Was, as you know, by Fortinbras of Norway,
       Thereto prick'd on by a most emulate pride,
       Dar'd to the combat; in which our valiant Hamlet—

For so this side of our known world esteem'd him —
Did slay this Fortinbras; who, by a seal'd compact,
Well ratified by law and heraldry,
Did forfeit, with his life, all those his lands
Which he stood seiz'd of, to the conqueror;
Against the which a moiety competent
Was gaged by our King; which had return'd
To the inheritance of Fortinbras,
Had he been vanquisher; as, by the same comart
And carriage of the article design'd,
His fell to Hamlet. Now, sir, young Fortinbras,
Of unimproved mettle hot and full,
Hath in the skirts of Norway, here and there,
Shark'd up a list of lawless resolutes,
For food and diet, to some enterprise
That hath a stomach in't; which is no other,
As it doth well appear unto our state,
But to recover of us, by strong hand
And terms compulsatory, those foresaid lands
So by his father lost; and this, I take it,
Is the main motive of our preparations,
The source of this our watch, and the chief head
Of this post-haste and romage in the land.

BERNARDO: I think it be no other but e'en so.
Well may it sort, that this portentous figure
Comes armed through our watch; so like the King
That was and is the question of these wars.

HORATIO: A mote it is to trouble the mind's eye.
In the most high and palmy state of Rome,
A little ere the mightiest Julius fell,
The graves stood tenantless, and the sheeted dead
Did squeak and gibber in the Roman streets;
As, stars with trains of fire, and dews of blood,
Disasters in the sun; and the moist star
Upon whose influence Neptune's empire stands
Was sick almost to doomsday with eclipse;
And even the like precurse of fear'd events,
As harbingers preceding still the fates
And prologue to the omen coming on,
Have heaven and earth together demonstrated
Unto our climatures and countrymen.
        [*Re-enter* GHOST.]
But, soft, behold! Lo, where it comes again!
I'll cross it, though it blast me. Stay, illusion.
        [GHOST *spreads its arms.*]
If thou hast any sound or use of voice,
Speak to me.
If there be any good thing to be done,

That may to thee do ease and grace to me,
Speak to me.
If thou art privy to thy country's fate,
Which happily foreknowing may avoid,
O, speak!
Or if thou hast uphoarded in thy life
Extorted treasure in the womb of earth,
For which, they say, you spirits oft walk in death,
   [*The cock crows.*]
Speak of it. Stay, and speak. Stop it, Marcellus.
MARCELLUS: Shall I strike at it with my partisan?
HORATIO: Do, if it will not stand.
BERNARDO:                         'Tis here!
HORATIO:                                    'Tis here!
MARCELLUS: 'Tis gone!                                            [*Exit* GHOST.]
   We do it wrong, being so majestical,
   To offer it the show of violence;
   For it is, as the air, invulnerable,
   And our vain blows malicious mockery.
BERNARDO: It was about to speak, when the cock crew.
HORATIO: And then it started like a guilty thing
   Upon a fearful summons. I have heard
   The cock, that is the trumpet to the morn,
   Doth with his lofty and shrill-sounding throat
   Awake the god of day; and at his warning,
   Whether in sea or fire, in earth or air,
   Th' extravagant and erring spirit hies
   To his confine; and of the truth herein
   This present object made probation.
MARCELLUS: It faded on the crowing of the cock.
   Some say that ever 'gainst that season comes
   Wherein our Saviour's birth is celebrated,
   This bird of dawning singeth all night long;
   And then, they say, no spirit dare stir abroad,
   The nights are wholesome, then no planets strike,
   No fairy takes, nor witch hath power to charm,
   So hallowed and so gracious is that time.
HORATIO: So have I heard, and do in part believe it.
   But look, the morn, in russet mantle clad,
   Walks o'er the dew of yon high eastward hill.
   Break we our watch up; and, by my advice,
   Let us impart what we have seen to-night
   Unto young Hamlet; for, upon my life,
   This spirit, dumb to us, will speak to him.
   Do you consent we shall acquaint him with it,
   As needful in our loves, fitting our duty?
MARCELLUS: Let's do't, I pray; and I this morning know
   Where we shall find him most convenient.                     [*Exeunt.*]

SCENE II——*Elsinore. The Castle.*

[*Flourish. Enter* CLAUDIUS KING OF DENMARK, GERTRUDE THE QUEEN, *and* COUNCILLORS, *including* POLONIUS, *his son* LAERTES, VOLTEMAND, CORNELIUS, *and* HAMLET.]

KING: Though yet of Hamlet our dear brother's death
The memory be green; and that it us befitted
To bear our hearts in grief, and our whole kingdom
To be contracted in one brow of woe;
Yet so far hath discretion fought with nature
That we with wisest sorrow think on him,
Together with remembrance of ourselves.
Therefore our sometime sister, now our queen,
Th' imperial jointress to this warlike state,
Have we, as 'twere with a defeated joy,
With an auspicious and a dropping eye,
With mirth in funeral, and with dirge in marriage,
In equal scale weighing delight and dole,
Taken to wife; nor have we herein barr'd
Your better wisdoms, which have freely gone
With this affair along. For all, our thanks.
Now follows that you know: young Fortinbras,
Holding a weak supposal of our worth,
Or thinking by our late dear brother's death
Our state to be disjoint and out of frame,
Co-leagued with this dream of his advantage —
He hath not fail'd to pester us with message
Importing the surrender of those lands
Lost by his father, with all bands of law,
To our most valiant brother. So much for him.
Now for ourself, and for this time of meeting,
Thus much the business is: we have here writ
To Norway, uncle of young Fortinbras —
Who, impotent and bed-rid, scarcely hears
Of this his nephew's purpose — to suppress
His further gait herein, in that the levies,
The lists, and full proportions, are all made
Out of his subject; and we here dispatch
You, good Cornelius, and you, Voltemand,
For bearers of this greeting to old Norway;
Giving to you no further personal power
To business with the King more than the scope
Of these dilated articles allow.
Farewell; and let your haste commend your duty.

CORNELIUS:
VOLTEMAND: } In that and all things will we show our duty.

KING: We doubt it nothing; heartily farewell.

[*Exeunt* VOLTEMAND *and* CORNELIUS.]

And now, Laertes, what's the news with you?
You told us of some suit; what is't, Laertes?
You cannot speak of reason to the Dane
And lose your voice. What wouldst thou beg, Laertes,
That shall not be my offer, not thy asking?
The head is not more native to the heart,
The hand more instrumental to the mouth,
Than is the throne of Denmark to thy father.
What wouldst thou have, Laertes?

LAERTES: My dread lord,
Your leave and favour to return to France;
From whence though willingly I came to Denmark
To show my duty in your coronation,
Yet now, I must confess, that duty done,
My thoughts and wishes bend again toward France,
And bow them to your gracious leave and pardon.

KING: Have you your father's leave? What says Polonius?

POLONIUS: 'A hath, my lord, wrung from me my slow leave
By laboursome petition; and at last
Upon his will I seal'd my hard consent.
I do beseech you, give him leave to go.

KING: Take thy fair hour, Laertes; time be thine,
And thy best graces spend it at thy will!
But now, my cousin Hamlet, and my son—

HAMLET: [*Aside*] A little more than kin, and less than kind.

KING: How is it that the clouds still hang on you?

HAMLET: Not so, my lord; I am too much in the sun.

QUEEN: Good Hamlet, cast thy nighted colour off,
And let thine eye look like a friend on Denmark.
Do not for ever with thy vailed lids
Seek for thy noble father in the dust.
Thou know'st 'tis common—all that lives must die,
Passing through nature to eternity.

HAMLET: Ay, madam, it is common.

QUEEN:                                        If it be,
Why seems it so particular with thee?

HAMLET: Seems, madam! Nay, it is; I know not seems.           *depression*
'Tis not alone my inky cloak, good mother,
Nor customary suits of solemn black,
Nor windy suspiration of forc'd breath,
No, nor the fruitful river in the eye,
Nor the dejected haviour of the visage,
Together with all forms, moods, shapes of grief,
That can denote me truly. These, indeed, seem;
For they are actions that a man might play;
But I have that within which passes show—
These but the trappings and the suits of woe.

KING: 'Tis sweet and commendable in your nature, Hamlet,

To give these mourning duties to your father;
But you must know your father lost a father;
That father lost, lost his; and the survivor bound,
In filial obligation, for some term
To do obsequious sorrow. But to persever
In obstinate condolement is a course
Of impious stubbornness; 'tis unmanly grief;
It shows a will most incorrect to heaven,
A heart unfortified, a mind impatient,
An understanding simple and unschool'd;
For what we know must be, and is as common
As any the most vulgar thing to sense,
Why should we in our peevish opposition
Take it to heart? Fie! 'tis a fault to heaven,
A fault against the dead, a fault to nature,
To reason most absurd; whose common theme
Is death of fathers, and who still hath cried,
From the first corse till he that died to-day,
'This must be so.' We pray you throw to earth
This unprevailing woe, and think of us
As of a father; for let the world take note
You are the most immediate to our throne;
And with no less nobility of love
Than that which dearest father bears his son
Do I impart toward you. For your intent
In going back to school in Wittenberg,
It is most retrograde to our desire;
And we beseech you bend you to remain
Here, in the cheer and comfort of our eye,
Our chiefest courtier, cousin, and our son.

QUEEN: Let not thy mother lose her prayers, Hamlet:
I pray thee stay with us; go not to Wittenberg.

HAMLET: I shall in all my best obey you, madam.

KING: Why, 'tis a loving and a fair reply.
Be as ourself in Denmark. Madam, come;
This gentle and unforc'd accord of Hamlet
Sits smiling to my heart; in grace whereof,
No jocund health that Denmark drinks to-day
But the great cannon to the clouds shall tell,
And the King's rouse the heaven shall bruit again,
Re-speaking earthly thunder. Come away.
        [*Flourish. Exeunt all but* HAMLET.]

HAMLET: O, that this too too solid flesh would melt,
Thaw, and resolve itself into a dew!
Or that the Everlasting had not fix'd
His canon 'gainst self-slaughter! O God! God!
How weary, stale, flat, and unprofitable,
Seem to me all the uses of this world!

Fie on't! Ah, fie! 'tis an unweeded garden,
That grows to seed; things rank and gross in nature
Possess it merely. That it should come to this!
But two months dead! Nay, not so much, not two.
So excellent a king that was to this
Hyperion to a satyr; so loving to my mother,
That he might not beteem the winds of heaven
Visit her face too roughly. Heaven and earth!
Must I remember? Why, she would hang on him
As if increase of appetite had grown
By what it fed on; and yet, within a month—
Let me not think on't. Frailty, thy name is woman!—
A little month, or ere those shoes were old
With which she followed my poor father's body,
Like Niobe, all tears—why she, even she—
O God! a beast that wants discourse of reason
Would have mourn'd longer—married with my uncle,
My father's brother; but no more like my father
Than I to Hercules. Within a month,
Ere yet the salt of most unrighteous tears
Had left the flushing in her galled eyes,
She married. O, most wicked speed, to post
With such dexterity to incestuous sheets!
It is not, nor it cannot come to good.
But break, my heart, for I must hold my tongue.
            [*Enter* HORATIO, MARCELLUS, *and* BERNARDO.]
HORATIO: Hail to your lordship!
HAMLET: I am glad to see you well.
        Horatio—or I do forget myself.
HORATIO: The same, my lord, and your poor servant ever.
HAMLET: Sir, my good friend. I'll change that name with you.
        And what make you from Wittenberg, Horatio?
        Marcellus?
MARCELLUS: My good lord!
HAMLET: I am very glad to see you. [*to* BERNARDO] Good even, sir.—
        But what, in faith, make you from Wittenberg?
HORATIO: A truant disposition, good my lord.
HAMLET: I would not hear your enemy say so;
        Nor shall you do my ear that violence,
        To make it truster of your own report
        Against yourself. I know you are no truant.
        But what is your affair in Elsinore?
        We'll teach you to drink deep ere you depart.
HORATIO: My lord, I came to see your father's funeral.
HAMLET: I prithee do not mock me, fellow-student;
        I think it was to see my mother's wedding.
HORATIO: Indeed, my lord, it followed hard upon.

HAMLET: Thrift, thrift, Horatio! The funeral bak'd-meats
 Did coldly furnish forth the marriage tables.
 Would I had met my dearest foe in heaven
 Or ever I had seen that day, Horatio!
 My father — methinks I see my father.
HORATIO: Where, my lord?
HAMLET: In my mind's eye, Horatio.
HORATIO: I saw him once; 'a was a goodly king.
HAMLET: 'A was a man, take him for all in all,
 I shall not look upon his like again.
HORATIO: My lord, I think I saw him yesternight.
HAMLET: Saw who?
HORATIO: My lord, the King your father.
HAMLET: The King my father!
HORATIO: Season your admiration for a while
 With an attent ear, till I may deliver,
 Upon the witness of these gentlemen,
 This marvel to you.
HAMLET: For God's love, let me hear.
HORATIO: Two nights together had these gentlemen,
 Marcellus and Bernardo, on their watch,
 In the dead waste and middle of the night,
 Been thus encount'red. A figure like your father,
 Armed at point exactly, cap-a-pe,
 Appears before them, and with solemn march
 Goes slow and stately by them; thrice he walk'd
 By their oppress'd and fear-surprised eyes,
 Within his truncheon's length; whilst they, distill'd
 Almost to jelly with the act of fear,
 Stand dumb and speak not to him. This to me
 In dreadful secrecy impart they did;
 And I with them the third night kept the watch;
 Where, as they had delivered, both in time,
 Form of the thing, each word made true and good,
 The apparition comes. I knew your father;
 These hands are not more like.
HAMLET: But where was this?
MARCELLUS: My lord, upon the platform where we watch.
HAMLET: Did you not speak to it?
HORATIO: My lord, I did;
 But answer made it none; yet once methought
 It lifted up its head and did address
 Itself to motion, like as it would speak;
 But even then the morning cock crew loud,
 And at the sound it shrunk in haste away
 And vanish'd from our sight.
HAMLET: 'Tis very strange.

HORATIO:  As I do live, my honour'd lord, 'tis true;
          And we did think it writ down in our duty
          To let you know of it.
HAMLET:  Indeed, indeed, sirs, but this troubles me.
          Hold you the watch to-night?
ALL:  We do, my lord.
HAMLET:  Arm'd, say you?
ALL:  Arm'd, my lord.
HAMLET:  From top to toe?
ALL:  My lord, from head to foot.
HAMLET:  Then saw you not his face?
HORATIO:  O yes, my lord; he wore his beaver up.
HAMLET:  What, look'd he frowningly?
HORATIO:  A countenance more in sorrow than in anger.
HAMLET:  Pale or red?
HORATIO:  Nay, very pale.
HAMLET:  And fix'd his eyes upon you?
HORATIO:  Most constantly.
HAMLET:  I would I had been there.
HORATIO:  It would have much amaz'd you.
HAMLET:  Very like, very like. Stay'd it long?
HORATIO:  While one with moderate haste might tell a hundred.
BOTH:  Longer, longer.
HORATIO:  Not when I saw't.
HAMLET:  His beard was grizzl'd — no?
HORATIO:  It was, as I have seen it in his life,
          A sable silver'd.
HAMLET:  I will watch to-night;
          Perchance 'twill walk again.
HORATIO:  I warr'nt it will.
HAMLET:  If it assume my noble father's person.
          I'll speak to it, though hell itself should gape
          And bid me hold my peace, I pray you all,
          If you have hitherto conceal'd this sight,
          Let it be tenable in your silence still;
          And whatsoever else shall hap to-night,
          Give it an understanding, but no tongue;
          I will requite your loves. So, fare you well —
          Upon the platform, 'twixt eleven and twelve,
          I'll visit you.
ALL:  Our duty to your honour.
HAMLET:  Your loves, as mine to you; farewell.
          [*Exeunt all but* HAMLET.]
          My father's spirit in arms! All is not well.
          I doubt some foul play. Would the night were come!
          Till then sit still, my soul. Foul deeds will rise,
          Though all the earth o'erwhelm them, to men's eyes.          [*Exit.*]

SCENE III——*Elsinore. The house of* POLONIUS.

[*Enter* LAERTES *and* OPHELIA *his sister.*]

LAERTES:  My necessaries are embark'd. Farewell.
And, sister, as the winds give benefit
And convoy is assistant, do not sleep,
But let me hear from you.

OPHELIA:  Do you doubt that?

LAERTES:  For Hamlet, and the trifling of his favour,
Hold it a fashion and a toy in blood,
A violet in the youth of primy nature,
Forward not permanent, sweet not lasting,
The perfume and suppliance of a minute;
No more.

OPHELIA:  No more but so?

LAERTES:  Think it no more;
For nature crescent does not grow alone
In thews and bulk, but as this temple waxes,
The inward service of the mind and soul
Grows wide withal. Perhaps he loves you now,
And now no soil nor cautel doth besmirch
The virtue of his will; but you must fear,
His greatness weigh'd, his will is not his own;
For he himself is subject to his birth:
He may not, as unvalued persons do,
Carve for himself; for on his choice depends
The sanity and health of this whole state;
And therefore must his choice be circumscrib'd
Unto the voice and yielding of that body
Whereof he is the head. Then if he says he loves you,
It fits your wisdom so far to believe it
As he in his particular act and place
May give his saying deed; which is no further
Than the main voice of Denmark goes withal.
Then weigh what loss your honour may sustain,
If with too credent ear you list his songs,
Or lose your heart, or your chaste treasure open
To his unmast'red importunity.
Fear it, Ophelia, fear it, my dear sister;
And keep you in the rear of your affection,
Out of the shot and danger of desire.
The chariest maid is prodigal enough
If she unmask her beauty to the moon.
Virtue itself scapes not calumnious strokes;
The canker galls the infants of the spring
Too oft before their buttons be disclos'd;
And in the morn and liquid dew of youth

Contagious blastments are most imminent.
Be wary, then; best safety lies in fear:
Youth to itself rebels, though none else near.
OPHELIA: I shall the effect of this good lesson keep
     As watchman to my heart. But, good my brother,
     Do not, as some ungracious pastors do,
     Show me the steep and thorny way to heaven,
     Whiles, like a puff'd and reckless libertine,
     Himself the primrose path of dalliance treads
     And recks not his own rede.
LAERTES: O, fear me not!
          [*Enter* POLONIUS.]
     I stay too long. But here my father comes.
     A double blessing is a double grace;
     Occasion smiles upon a second leave.
POLONIUS: Yet here, Laertes! Aboard, aboard, for shame!
     The wind sits in the shoulder of your sail,
     And you are stay'd for. There — my blessing with thee!
     And these few precepts in thy memory
     Look thou character. Give thy thoughts no tongue,
     Nor any unproportion'd thought his act.
     Be thou familiar, but by no means vulgar.
     Those friends thou hast, and their adoption tried,
     Grapple them to thy soul with hoops of steel;
     But do not dull thy palm with entertainment
     Of each new-hatch'd, unfledg'd comrade. Beware
     Of entrance to a quarrel; but, being in,
     Bear't that th' opposed may beware of thee.
     Give every man thy ear, but few thy voice;
     Take each man's censure, but reserve thy judgment.
     Costly thy habit as thy purse can buy,
     But not express'd in fancy; rich, not gaudy;
     For the apparel oft proclaims the man;
     And they in France of the best rank and station
     Are of a most select and generous choice in that.
     Neither a borrower nor a lender be;
     For loan oft loses both itself and friend,
     And borrowing dulls the edge of husbandry.
     This above all — to thine own self be true,
     And it must follow, as the night the day,
     Thou canst not then be false to any man.
     Farewell; my blessing season this in thee!
LAERTES: Most humbly do I take my leave, my lord.
POLONIUS: The time invites you; go, your servants tend.
LAERTES: Farewell, Ophelia; and remember well
     What I have said to you.
OPHELIA: 'Tis in my memory lock'd,
     And you yourself shall keep the key of it.

LAERTES: Farewell.                                                              [*Exit.*]

POLONIUS: What is't, Ophelia, he hath said to you?

OPHELIA: So please you, something touching the Lord Hamlet.

POLONIUS: Marry, well bethought!
　　　'Tis told me he hath very oft of late
　　　Given private time to you; and you yourself
　　　Have of your audience been most free and bounteous.
　　　If it be so — as so 'tis put on me,
　　　And that in way of caution — I must tell you
　　　You do not understand yourself so clearly
　　　As it behoves my daughter and your honour.
　　　What is between you? Give me up the truth.

OPHELIA: He hath, my lord, of late made many tenders
　　　Of his affection to me.

POLONIUS: Affection! Pooh! You speak like a green girl,
　　　Unsifted in such perilous circumstance.
　　　Do you believe his tenders, as you call them?

OPHELIA: I do not know, my lord, what I should think.

POLONIUS: Marry, I will teach you: think yourself a baby
　　　That you have ta'en these tenders for true pay
　　　Which are not sterling. Tender yourself more dearly;
　　　Or — not to crack the wind of the poor phrase,
　　　Running it thus — you'll tender me a fool.

OPHELIA: My lord, he hath importun'd me with love
　　　In honourable fashion.

POLONIUS: Ay, fashion you may call it; go to, go to.

OPHELIA: And hath given countenance to his speech, my lord,
　　　With almost all the holy vows of heaven.

POLONIUS: Ay, springes to catch woodcocks! I do know,
　　　When the blood burns, how prodigal the soul
　　　Lends the tongue vows. These blazes, daughter,
　　　Giving more light than heat — extinct in both,
　　　Even in their promise, as it is a-making —
　　　You must not take for fire. From this time
　　　Be something scanter of your maiden presence;
　　　Set your entreatments at a higher rate
　　　Than a command to parle. For Lord Hamlet,
　　　Believe so much in him, that he is young,
　　　And with a larger tether may he walk
　　　Than may be given you. In few, Ophelia,
　　　Do not believe his vows; for they are brokers,
　　　Not of that dye which their investments show,
　　　But mere implorators of unholy suits,
　　　Breathing like sanctified and pious bonds,
　　　The better to beguile. This is for all —
　　　I would not, in plain terms, from this time forth
　　　Have you so slander any moment leisure
　　　As to give words or talk with the Lord Hamlet.

Look to't, I charge you. Come your ways.
OPHELIA: I shall obey, my lord.                              [*Exeunt.*]


SCENE IV——*Elsinore. The guard-platform of the Castle.*

[*Enter* HAMLET, HORATIO, *and* MARCELLUS.]
HAMLET: The air bites shrewdly; it is very cold.
HORATIO: It is a nipping and an eager air.
HAMLET: What hour now?
HORATIO: I think it lacks of twelve.
MARCELLUS: No, it is struck.
HORATIO: Indeed? I heard it not. It then draws near the season
    Wherein the spirit held his wont to walk.
        [*A flourish of trumpets, and two pieces go off.*]
    What does this mean, my lord?
HAMLET: The King doth wake to-night and takes his rouse,
    Keeps wassail, and the swagg'ring up-spring reels,
    And, as he drains his draughts of Rhenish down,
    The kettle-drum and trumpet thus bray out
    The triumph of his pledge.
HORATIO: Is it a custom?
HAMLET: Ay, marry, is't;
    But to my mind, though I am native here
    And to the manner born, it is a custom
    More honour'd in the breach than the observance.
    This heavy-headed revel east and west
    Makes us traduc'd and tax'd of other nations;
    They clepe us drunkards, and with swinish phrase
    Soil our addition; and, indeed, it takes
    From our achievements, though perform'd at height,
    The pith and marrow of our attribute.
    So, oft it chances in particular men
    That, for some vicious mole of nature in them,
    As in their birth, wherein they are not guilty,
    Since nature cannot choose his origin;
    By the o'ergrowth of some complexion,
    Oft breaking down the pales and forts of reason;
    Or by some habit that too much o'er-leavens
    The form of plausive manners—that these men,
    Carrying, I say, the stamp of one defect,
    Being nature's livery or fortune's star,
    His virtues else, be they as pure as grace,
    As infinite as man may undergo,
    Shall in the general censure take corruption
    From that particular fault. The dram of eale
    Doth all the noble substance of a doubt
    To his own scandal.
        [*Enter* GHOST.]

HORATIO: Look, my lord, it comes.
HAMLET: Angels and ministers of grace defend us!
    Be thou a spirit of health or goblin damn'd,
    Bring with thee airs from heaven or blasts from hell,
    Be thy intents wicked or charitable,
    Thou com'st in such a questionable shape
    That I will speak to thee. I'll call thee Hamlet,
    King, father, royal Dane. O, answer me!
    Let me not burst in ignorance, but tell
    Why thy canoniz'd bones, hearsed in death,
    Have burst their cerements; why the sepulchre
    Wherein we saw thee quietly enurn'd
    Have op'd his ponderous and marble jaws
    To cast thee up again. What may this mean
    That thou, dead corse, again in complete steel
    Revisits thus the glimpses of the moon,
    Making night hideous, and we fools of nature
    So horridly to shake our disposition
    With thoughts beyond the reaches of our souls?
    Say, why is this? wherefore? What should we do?
        [GHOST *beckons* HAMLET.]
HORATIO: It beckons you to go away with it,
    As if it some impartment did desire
    To you alone.
MARCELLUS: Look with what courteous action
    It waves you to a more removed ground.
    But do not go with it.
HORATIO: No, by no means.
HAMLET: It will not speak; then I will follow it.
HORATIO: Do not, my lord.
HAMLET: Why, what should be the fear?
    I do not set my life at a pin's fee;
    And for my soul, what can it do to that,
    Being a thing immortal as itself?
    It waves me forth again; I'll follow it.
HORATIO: What if it tempt you toward the flood, my lord,
    Or to the dreadful summit of the cliff
    That beetles o'er his base into the sea,
    And there assume some other horrible form,
    Which might deprive your sovereignty of reason
    And draw you into madness? Think of it:
    The very place puts toys of desperation,
    Without more motive, into every brain
    That looks so many fathoms to the sea
    And hears it roar beneath.
HAMLET: It waves me still.
    Go on; I'll follow thee.
MARCELLUS: You shall not go, my lord.

HAMLET: Hold off your hands.
HORATIO: Be rul'd; you shall not go.
HAMLET: My fate cries out,
 And makes each petty arture in this body
 As hardy as the Nemean lion's nerve.                    [GHOST *beckons.*]
 Still am I call'd. Unhand me, gentlemen.
 By heaven, I'll make a ghost of him that lets me.
 I say, away! Go on; I'll follow thee.
  [*Exeunt* GHOST *and* HAMLET.]
HORATIO: He waxes desperate with imagination.
MARCELLUS: Let's follow; 'tis not fit thus to obey him.
HORATIO: Have after. To what issue will this come?
MARCELLUS: Something is rotten in the state of Denmark.
HORATIO: Heaven will direct it.
MARCELLUS: Nay, let's follow him.                          [*Exeunt.*]


 SCENE V——*Elsinore. The battlements of the Castle.*

  [*Enter* GHOST *and* HAMLET.]
HAMLET: Whither wilt thou lead me? Speak. I'll go no further.
GHOST: Mark me.
HAMLET: I will.
GHOST: My hour is almost come,
 When I to sulph'rous and tormenting flames
 Must render up myself.
HAMLET: Alas, poor ghost!
GHOST: Pity me not, but lend thy serious hearing
 To what I shall unfold.
HAMLET: Speak; I am bound to hear.
GHOST: So art thou to revenge, when thou shalt hear.
HAMLET: What?
GHOST: I am thy father's spirit,
 Doom'd for a certain term to walk the night,
 And for the day confin'd to fast in fires,
 Till the foul crimes done in my days of nature
 Are burnt and purg'd away. But that I am forbid
 To tell the secrets of my prison-house,
 I could a tale unfold whose lightest word
 Would harrow up thy soul, freeze thy young blood,
 Make thy two eyes, like stars, start from their spheres,
 Thy knotted and combined locks to part,
 And each particular hair to stand an end,
 Like quills upon the fretful porpentine.
 But this eternal blazon must not be
 To ears of flesh and blood. List, list, O, list!
 If thou didst ever thy dear father love —
HAMLET: O God!
GHOST: Revenge his foul and most unnatural murder.

HAMLET: Murder!

GHOST: Murder most foul, as in the best it is;
But this most foul, strange, and unnatural.

HAMLET: Haste me to know't, that I, with wings as swift
As meditation or the thoughts of love,
May sweep to my revenge.

GHOST: I find thee apt;
And duller shouldst thou be than the fat weed
That roots itself in ease on Lethe wharf,
Wouldst thou not stir in this. Now, Hamlet, hear:
'Tis given out that, sleeping in my orchard,
A serpent stung me; so the whole ear of Denmark
Is by a forged process of my death
Rankly abus'd; but know, thou noble youth,
The serpent that did sting thy father's life
Now wears his crown.

HAMLET: O my prophetic soul!
My uncle!

GHOST: Ay, that incestuous, that adulterate beast,
With witchcraft of his wits, with traitorous gifts—
O wicked wit and gifts that have the power
So to seduce!—won to his shameful lust
The will of my most seeming virtuous queen.
O Hamlet, what a falling off was there,
From me, whose love was of that dignity
That it went hand in hand even with the vow
I made to her in marriage; and to decline
Upon a wretch whose natural gifts were poor
To those of mine!
But virtue, as it never will be moved,
Though lewdness court it in a shape of heaven,
So lust, though to a radiant angel link'd,
Will sate itself in a celestial bed
And prey on garbage.
But soft! methinks I scent the morning air.
Brief let me be. Sleeping within my orchard,
My custom always of the afternoon,
Upon my secure hour thy uncle stole,
With juice of cursed hebona in a vial,
And in the porches of my ears did pour
The leperous distilment; whose effect
Holds such an enmity with blood of man
That swift as quicksilver it courses through
The natural gates and alleys of the body;
And with a sudden vigour it doth posset
And curd, like eager droppings into milk,
The thin and wholesome blood. So did it mine;
And a most instant tetter bark'd about,

Most lazar-like, with vile and loathsome crust,
All my smooth body.
Thus was I, sleeping, by a brother's hand
Of life, of crown, of queen, at once dispatch'd;
Cut off even in the blossoms of my sin,
Unhous'led, disappointed, unanel'd;
No reck'ning made, but sent to my account
With all my imperfections on my head.
O, horrible! O, horrible! most horrible!
If thou hast nature in thee, bear it not;
Let not the royal bed of Denmark be
A couch for luxury and damned incest.
But, howsomever thou pursuest this act,
Taint not thy mind, nor let thy soul contrive
Against thy mother aught; leave her to heaven,
And to those thorns that in her bosom lodge
To prick and sting her. Fare thee well at once.
The glowworm shows the matin to be near,
And gins to pale his uneffectual fire.
Adieu, adieu, adieu! Remember me.                          [*Exit.*]
HAMLET:  O all you host of heaven! O earth! What else?
And shall I couple hell? O, fie! Hold, hold, my heart;
And you, my sinews, grow not instant old,
But bear me stiffly up. Remember thee!
Ay, thou poor ghost, whiles memory holds a seat
In this distracted globe. Remember thee!
Yea, from the table of my memory
I'll wipe away all trivial fond records,
All saws of books, all forms, all pressures past,
That youth and observation copied there,
And thy commandment all alone shall live
Within the book and volume of my brain,
Unmix'd with baser matter. Yes, by heaven!
O most pernicious woman!
O villain, villain, smiling, damned villain!
My tables — meet it is I set it down
That one may smile, and smile, and be a villain;
At least I am sure it may be so in Denmark. [*writing*]
So, uncle, there you are. Now to my word:
It is 'Adieu, adieu! Remember me.'
I have sworn't.
HORATIO:  [*within*] My lord, my lord!
           [*Enter* HORATIO *and* MARCELLUS.]
MARCELLUS:  Lord Hamlet!
HORATIO:  Heavens secure him!
HAMLET:  So be it!
MARCELLUS:  Illo, ho, ho, my lord!
HAMLET:  Hillo, ho, ho, boy! Come, bird, come.

MARCELLUS: How is't, my noble lord?

HORATIO: What news, my lord?

HAMLET: O, wonderful!

HORATIO: Good my lord, tell it.

HAMLET: No; you will reveal it.

HORATIO: Not I, my lord, by heaven!

MARCELLUS: Nor I, my lord.

HAMLET: How say you, then; would heart of man once think it?
　　But you'll be secret?

BOTH: Ay, by heaven, my lord!

HAMLET: There's never a villain dwelling in all Denmark
　　But he's an arrant knave.

HORATIO: There needs no ghost, my lord, come from the grave
　　To tell us this.

HAMLET: Why, right; you are in the right;
　　And so, without more circumstance at all,
　　I hold it fit that we shake hands and part;
　　You, as your business and desire shall point you —
　　For every man hath business and desire,
　　Such as it is; and for my own poor part,
　　Look you, I will go pray.

HORATIO: These are but wild and whirling words, my lord.

HAMLET: I am sorry they offend you, heartily;
　　Yes, faith, heartily.

HORATIO: There's no offence, my lord.

HAMLET: Yes, by Saint Patrick, but there is, Horatio,
　　And much offence too. Touching this vision here —
　　It is an honest ghost, that let me tell you.
　　For your desire to know what is between us,
　　O'ermaster't as you may. And now, good friends,
　　As you are friends, scholars, and soldiers,
　　Give me one poor request.

HORATIO: What is't, my lord? We will.

HAMLET: Never make known what you have seen to-night.

BOTH: My lord, we will not.

HAMLET: Nay, but swear't.

HORATIO: In faith,
　　My lord, not I.

MARCELLUS: Nor I, my lord, in faith.

HAMLET: Upon my sword.

MARCELLUS: We have sworn, my lord, already.

HAMLET: Indeed, upon my sword, indeed.

GHOST: [*cries under the stage*] Swear.

HAMLET: Ha, ha, boy! say'st thou so? Art thou there, true-penny?
　　Come on. You hear this fellow in the cellarage:
　　Consent to swear.

HORATIO: Propose the oath, my lord.

HAMLET: Never to speak of this that you have seen,

Swear by my sword.
GHOST: [*beneath*] Swear.
HAMLET: Hic et ubique? Then we'll shift our ground.
    Come hither, gentlemen,
    And lay your hands again upon my sword.
    Swear by my sword
    Never to speak of this that you have heard.
GHOST: [*beneath*] Swear, by his sword.
HAMLET: Well said, old mole! Canst work i' th' earth so fast?
    A worthy pioneer! Once more remove, good friends.
HORATIO: O day and night, but this is wondrous strange!
HAMLET: And therefore as a stranger give it welcome.
    There are more things in heaven and earth, Horatio,
    Than are dreamt of in your philosophy.
    But come.
    Here, as before, never, so help you mercy,
    How strange or odd some'er I bear myself—
    As I perchance hereafter shall think meet
    To put an antic disposition on—
    That you, at such times, seeing me, never shall,
    With arms encumb'red thus, or this head-shake,
    Or by pronouncing of some doubtful phrase,
    As 'Well, well, we know' or 'We could, an if we would'
    Or 'If we list to speak' or 'There be, an if they might'
    Or such ambiguous giving out, to note
    That you know aught of me—this do swear,
    So grace and mercy at your most need help you.
GHOST: [*beneath*] Swear.
HAMLET: Rest, rest, perturbèd spirit! So, gentlemen,
    With all my love I do commend me to you;
    And what so poor a man as Hamlet is
    May do t'express his love and friending to you,
    God willing, shall not lack. Let us go in together;
    And still your fingers on your lips, I pray.
    The time is out of joint. O cursed spite,
    That ever I was born to set it right!
    Nay, come, let's go together.                    [*Exeunt.*]

## ACT II

SCENE I——*Elsinore. The house of* POLONIUS.

[*Enter* POLONIUS *and* REYNALDO.]
POLONIUS: Give him this money and these notes, Reynaldo.
REYNALDO: I will, my lord.
POLONIUS: You shall do marvellous wisely, good Reynaldo,
    Before you visit him, to make inquire
    Of his behaviour.

REYNALDO: My lord, I did intend it.
POLONIUS: Marry, well said; very well said. Look you, sir,
    Enquire me first what Danskers are in Paris;
    And how, and who, what means, and where they keep,
    What company, at what expense; and finding
    By this encompassment and drift of question
    That they do know my son, come you more nearer
    Than your particular demands will touch it.
    Take you, as 'twere, some distant knowledge of him;
    As thus: 'I know his father and his friends,
    And in part him.' Do you mark this, Reynaldo?
REYNALDO: Ay, very well, my lord.
POLONIUS: 'And in part him — but' you may say 'not well;
    But if't be he I mean, he's very wild;
    Addicted so and so'; and there put on him
    What forgeries you please; marry, none so rank
    As may dishonour him; take heed of that;
    But, sir, such wanton, wild, and usual slips
    As are companions noted and most known
    To youth and liberty.
REYNALDO: As gaming, my lord.
POLONIUS: Ay, or drinking, fencing, swearing, quarrelling.
    Drabbing — you may go so far.
REYNALDO: My lord, that would dishonour him.
POLONIUS: Faith, no; as you may season it in the charge.
    You must not put another scandal on him,
    That he is open to incontinency;
    That's not my meaning. But breathe his faults so quaintly
    That they may seem the taints of liberty;
    The flash and outbreak of a fiery mind,
    A savageness in unreclaimed blood,
    Of general assault.
REYNALDO: But, my good lord —
POLONIUS: Wherefore should you do this?
REYNALDO: Ay, my lord,
    I would know that.
POLONIUS: Marry, sir, here's my drift,
    And I believe it is a fetch of warrant:
    You laying these slight sullies on my son,
    As 'twere a thing a little soil'd wi' th' working,
    Mark you,
    Your party in converse, him you would sound,
    Having ever seen in the prenominate crimes
    The youth you breathe of guilty, be assur'd
    He closes with you in this consequence —
    'Good sir' or so, or 'friend' or 'gentleman'
    According to the phrase or the addition
    Of man and country.

REYNALDO: Very good, my lord.

POLONIUS: And then, sir, does 'a this — 'a does — What was I
    about to say? By the mass, I was about to say something;
    where did I leave?

REYNALDO: At 'closes in the consequence,' at 'friend or so'
    and 'gentleman.'

POLONIUS: At 'closes in the consequence' — ay, marry,
    He closes thus: 'I know the gentleman;
    I saw him yesterday, or t'other day,
    Or then, or then; with such, or such; and, as you say,
    There was 'a gaming; there o'ertook in's rouse;
    There falling out at tennis'; or perchance
    'I saw him enter such a house of sale,'
    Videlicet, a brothel, or so forth. See you now
    Your bait of falsehood take this carp of truth;
    And thus do we of wisdom and of reach,
    With windlasses and with assays of bias,
    By indirections find directions out;
    So, by my former lecture and advice,
    Shall you my son. You have me, have you not?

REYNALDO: My lord, I have.

POLONIUS: God buy ye; fare ye well.

REYNALDO: Good my lord!

POLONIUS: Observe his inclination in yourself.

REYNALDO: I shall, my lord.

POLONIUS: And let him ply his music.

REYNALDO: Well, my lord.

POLONIUS: Farewell!                                 [*Exit* REYNALDO.]
        [*Enter* OPHELIA.]
    How now, Ophelia! What's the matter?

OPHELIA: O my lord, my lord, I have been so affrighted!

POLONIUS: With what, i' th' name of God?

OPHELIA: My lord, as I was sewing in my closet,
    Lord Hamlet, with his doublet all unbrac'd,
    No hat upon his head, his stockings fouled,
    Ungart'red and down-gyved to his ankle;
    Pale as his shirt, his knees knocking each other,
    And with a look so piteous in purport
    As if he had been loosed out of hell
    To speak of horrors — he comes before me.

POLONIUS: Mad for thy love?

OPHELIA: My lord, I do not know,
    But truly I do fear it.

POLONIUS: What said he?

OPHELIA: He took me by the wrist, and held me hard;
    Then goes he to the length of all his arm,
    And, with his other hand thus o'er his brow,
    He falls to such a perusal of my face

As 'a would draw it. Long stay'd he so.
At last, a little shaking of mine arm,
And thrice his head thus waving up and down,
He rais'd a sigh so piteous and profound
As it did seem to shatter all his bulk
And end his being. That done, he lets me go,
And, with his head over his shoulder turn'd,
He seem'd to find his way without his eyes;
For out adoors he went without their help
And to the last bended their light on me.

POLONIUS: Come, go with me. I will go seek the King.
This is the very ecstasy of love,
Whose violent property fordoes itself,
And leads the will to desperate undertakings
As oft as any passion under heaven
That does afflict our natures. I am sorry—
What, have you given him any hard words of late?

OPHELIA: No, my good lord; but, as you did command,
I did repel his letters, and denied
His access to me.

POLONIUS: That hath made him mad.
I am sorry that with better heed and judgment
I had not quoted him. I fear'd he did but trifle,
And meant to wreck thee; but beshrew my jealousy!
By heaven, it is as proper to our age
To cast beyond ourselves in our opinions
As it is common for the younger sort
To lack discretion. Come, go we to the King.
This must be known; which, being kept close, might move
More grief to hide than hate to utter love.
Come.                                                    [*Exeunt.*]


SCENE II——*Elsinore. The Castle.*

[*Flourish. Enter* KING, QUEEN, ROSENCRANTZ, GUILDENSTERN, *and attendants.*]

KING: Welcome, dear Rosencrantz and Guildenstern!
Moreover that we much did long to see you,
The need we have to use you did provoke
Our hasty sending. Something have you heard
Of Hamlet's transformation; so I call it,
Sith nor th' exterior nor the inward man
Resembles that it was. What it should be,
More than his father's death, that thus hath put him
So much from th' understanding of himself,
I cannot deem of. I entreat you both
That, being of so young days brought up with him,
And sith so neighboured to his youth and haviour,

That you vouchsafe your rest here in our court
Some little time; so by your companies
To draw him on to pleasures, and to gather,
So much as from occasion you may glean,
Whether aught to us unknown afflicts him thus
That, open'd, lies within our remedy.

QUEEN: Good gentlemen, he hath much talk'd of you;
And sure I am two men there is not living
To whom he more adheres. If it will please you
To show us so much gentry and good will
As to expend your time with us awhile
For the supply and profit of our hope,
Your visitation shall receive such thanks
As fits a king's remembrance.

ROSENCRANTZ:                         Both your Majesties
Might, by the sovereign power you have of us,
Put your dread pleasures more into command
Than to entreaty.

GUILDENSTERN: But we both obey,
And here give up ourselves, in the full bent,
To lay our service freely at your feet,
To be commanded.

KING: Thanks, Rosencrantz and gentle Guildenstern.

QUEEN: Thanks, Guildenstern and gentle Rosencrantz.
And I beseech you instantly to visit
My too much changed son. Go, some of you,
And bring these gentlemen where Hamlet is.

GUILDENSTERN: Heavens make our presence and our practices
Pleasant and helpful to him!

QUEEN: Aye amen! [*Exeunt* ROSENCRANTZ, GUILDENSTERN, *and some attendants.*]
        [*Enter* POLONIUS.]

POLONIUS: Th' ambassadors from Norway, my good lord,
Are joyfully return'd.

KING: Thou still hast been the father of good news.

POLONIUS: Have I, my lord? I assure you, my good liege,
I hold my duty, as I hold my soul,
Both to my God and to my gracious King;
And I do think — or else this brain of mine
Hunts not the trail of policy so sure
As it hath us'd to do — that I have found
The very cause of Hamlet's lunacy.

KING: O, speak of that; that do I long to hear.

POLONIUS: Give first admittance to th' ambassadors;
My news shall be the fruit to that great feast.

KING: Thyself do grace to them, and bring them in.
        [*Exit* POLONIUS.]
He tells me, my dear Gertrude, he hath found
The head and source of all your son's distemper.

QUEEN: I doubt it is no other but the main,
    His father's death and our o'erhasty marriage.
KING: Well, we shall sift him.
        [*Re-enter* POLONIUS, *with* VOLTEMAND *and* CORNELIUS.]
    Welcome, my good friends!
    Say, Voltemand, what from our brother Norway?
VOLTEMAND: Most fair return of greetings and desires.
    Upon our first, he sent out to suppress
    His nephew's levies; which to him appear'd
    To be a preparation 'gainst the Polack;
    But, better look'd into, he truly found
    It was against your Highness. Whereat griev'd,
    That so his sickness, age, and impotence,
    Was falsely borne in hand, sends out arrests
    On Fortinbras; which he, in brief, obeys;
    Receives rebuke from Norway; and, in fine,
    Makes vow before his uncle never more
    To give th' assay of arms against your Majesty.
    Whereon old Norway, overcome with joy,
    Gives him threescore thousand crowns in annual fee,
    And his commission to employ those soldiers,
    So levied as before, against the Polack;
    With an entreaty, herein further shown, [*gives a paper*]
    That it might please you to give quiet pass
    Through your dominions for this enterprise,
    On such regards of safety and allowance
    As therein are set down.
KING: It likes us well;
    And at our more considered time we'll read,
    Answer, and think upon this business.
    Meantime we thank you for your well-took labour.
    Go to your rest; at night we'll feast together.
    Most welcome home!        [*Exeunt* AMBASSADORS *and attendants.*]
POLONIUS: This business is well ended.
    My liege, and madam, to expostulate
    What majesty should be, what duty is,
    Why day is day, night night, and time is time,
    Were nothing, but to waste night, day, and time.
    Therefore, since brevity is the soul of wit,
    And tediousness the limbs and outward flourishes,
    I will be brief. Your noble son is mad.
    Mad call I it; for, to define true madness,
    What is't but to be nothing else but mad?
    But let that go.
QUEEN: More matter with less art.
POLONIUS: Madam, I swear I use no art at all.
    That he's mad, 'tis true: 'tis true 'tis pity;
    And pity 'tis 'tis true. A foolish figure!

But farewell it, for I will use no art.
Mad let us grant him, then; and now remains
That we find out the cause of this effect;
Or rather say the cause of this defect,
For this effect defective comes by cause.
Thus it remains, and the remainder thus.
Perpend.
I have a daughter — have while she is mine —
Who in her duty and obedience, mark,
Hath given me this. Now gather, and surmise. [*reads*]
'To the celestial, and my soul's idol, the most beautified Ophelia.' That's an ill
phrase, a vile phrase; 'beautified' is a vile phrase. But you shall hear. Thus:
[*reads*]
'In her excellent white bosom, these, &c.'

QUEEN: Came this from Hamlet to her?

POLONIUS: Good madam, stay awhile; I will be faithful. [*reads*]
     'Doubt thou the stars are fire;
      Doubt that the sun doth move;
     Doubt truth to be a liar;
      But never doubt I love.
'O dear Ophelia, I am ill at these numbers. I have not art to reckon my groans;
but that I love thee best, O most best, believe it. Adieu.
        'Thine evermore, most dear lady, whilst
           this machine is to him,
               HAMLET.'

This, in obedience, hath my daughter shown me;
And more above, hath his solicitings,
As they fell out by time, by means, and place,
All given to mine ear.

KING: But how hath she
Receiv'd his love?

POLONIUS: What do you think of me?

KING: As of a man faithful and honourable.

POLONIUS: I would fain prove so. But what might you think,
When I had seen this hot love on the wing,
As I perceiv'd it, I must tell you that,
Before my daughter told me — what might you,
Or my dear Majesty your Queen here, think,
If I had play'd the desk or table-book;
Or given my heart a winking, mute and dumb;
Or look'd upon this love with idle sight —
What might you think? No, I went round to work,
And my young mistress thus I did bespeak:
'Lord Hamlet is a prince out of thy star;
This must not be.' And then I prescripts gave her,
That she should lock herself from his resort,
Admit no messengers, receive no tokens.
Which done, she took the fruits of my advice;

And he repelled, a short tale to make,
Fell into a sadness, then into a fast,
Thence to a watch, thence into a weakness,
Thence to a lightness, and, by this declension,
Into the madness wherein now he raves
And all we mourn for.

KING: Do you think 'tis this?

QUEEN: It may be, very like.

POLONIUS: Hath there been such a time — I would fain know that —
That I have positively said ' 'Tis so,'
When it prov'd otherwise?

KING: Not that I know.

POLONIUS: Take this from this, if this be otherwise.
If circumstances lead me, I will find
Where truth is hid, though it were hid indeed
Within the centre.

KING: How may we try it further?

POLONIUS: You may know sometimes he walks four hours together,
Here in the lobby.

QUEEN: So he does, indeed.

POLONIUS: At such a time I'll loose my daughter to him.
Be you and I behind an arras then;
Mark the encounter: if he love her not,
And be not from his reason fall'n thereon,
Let me be no assistant for a state,
But keep a farm and carters.

KING: We will try it.
[*Enter* HAMLET, *reading on a book.*]

QUEEN: But look where sadly the poor wretch comes reading.

POLONIUS: Away, I do beseech you, both away:
I'll board him presently. O, give me leave.
[*Exeunt* KING *and* QUEEN.]
How does my good Lord Hamlet?

HAMLET: Well, God-a-mercy.

POLONIUS: Do you know me, my lord?

HAMLET: Excellent well; you are a fishmonger.

POLONIUS: Not I, my lord.

HAMLET: Then I would you were so honest a man.

POLONIUS: Honest, my lord!

HAMLET: Ay, sir; to be honest, as this world goes, is to be one man pick'd out of ten thousand.

POLONIUS: That's very true, my lord.

HAMLET: For if the sun breed maggots in a dead dog, being a good kissing carrion —
Have you a daughter?

POLONIUS: I have, my lord.

HAMLET: Let her not walk i' th' sun. Conception is a blessing. But as your daughter may conceive — friend, look to't.

POLONIUS: How say you by that? [*aside*] Still harping on my daughter. Yet he knew

me not at first; 'a said I was a fishmonger. 'A is far gone, far gone. And truly in
my youth I suff'red much extremity for love. Very near this. I'll speak to him
again. — What do you read, my lord?

HAMLET: Words, words, words.

POLONIUS: What is the matter, my lord?

HAMLET: Between who?

POLONIUS: I mean, the matter that you read, my lord.

HAMLET: Slanders, sir; for the satirical rogue says here that old men have grey beards;
that their faces are wrinkled; their eyes purging thick amber and plum-tree
gum; and that they have a plentiful lack of wit, together with most weak
hams — all which, sir, though I most powerfully and potently believe, yet I
hold it not honesty to have it thus set down; for you yourself, sir, shall grow old
as I am, if, like a crab, you could go backward.

POLONIUS: [aside] Though this be madness, yet there is method in't. — Will you
walk out of the air, my lord?

HAMLET: Into my grave?

POLONIUS: Indeed, that's out of the air. [aside] How pregnant sometimes his replies
are! a happiness that often madness hits on, which reason and sanity could not
so prosperously be delivered of. I will leave him, and suddenly contrive the
means of meeting between him and my daughter. — My lord. I will take my
leave of you.

HAMLET: You cannot, sir, take from me anything that I will more willingly part
withal — except my life, except my life, except my life.

[*Enter* ROSENCRANTZ *and* GUILDENSTERN.]

POLONIUS: Fare you well, my lord.

HAMLET: These tedious old fools!

POLONIUS: You go to seek the Lord Hamlet; there he is.

ROSENCRANTZ: [*to* POLONIUS] God save you, sir!

[*Exit* POLONIUS.]

GUILDENSTERN: My honour'd lord!

ROSENCRANTZ: My most dear lord!

HAMLET: My excellent good friends! How dost thou, Guildenstern? Ah, Rosencrantz! Good lads, how do you both?

ROSENCRANTZ: As the indifferent children of the earth.

GUILDENSTERN: Happy in that we are not over-happy;
On fortune's cap we are not the very button.

HAMLET: Nor the soles of her shoe?

ROSENCRANTZ: Neither, my lord.

HAMLET: Then you live about her waist, or in the middle of her favours?

GUILDENSTERN: Faith, her privates we.

HAMLET: In the secret parts of Fortune? O, most true; she is a strumpet. What news?

ROSENCRANTZ: None, my lord, but that the world's grown honest.

HAMLET: Then is doomsday near. But your news is not true. Let me question more
in particular. What have you, my good friends, deserved at the hands of
Fortune, that she sends you to prison hither?

GUILDENSTERN: Prison, my lord!

HAMLET: Denmark's a prison.

ROSENCRANTZ: Then is the world one.

HAMLET: A goodly one; in which there are many confines, wards, and dungeons, Denmark being one o' th' worst.

ROSENCRANTZ: We think not so, my lord.

HAMLET: Why, then, 'tis none to you; for there is nothing either good or bad, but thinking makes it so. To me it is a prison.

ROSENCRANTZ: Why, then your ambition makes it one; 'tis too narrow for your mind.

HAMLET: O God, I could be bounded in a nutshell and count myself a king of infinite space, were it not that I have bad dreams.

GUILDENSTERN: Which dreams indeed are ambition; for the very substance of the ambitious is merely the shadow of a dream.

HAMLET: A dream itself is but a shadow.

ROSENCRANTZ: Truly, and I hold ambition of so airy and light a quality that it is but a shadow's shadow.

HAMLET: Then are our beggars bodies, and our monarchs and oustretch'd heroes the beggars' shadows. Shall we to th' court? for, by my fay, I cannot reason.

BOTH: We'll wait upon you.

HAMLET: No such matter. I will not sort you with the rest of my servants; for, to speak to you like an honest man, I am most dreadfully attended. But, in the beaten way of friendship, what make you at Elsinore?

ROSENCRANTZ: To visit you, my lord; no other occasion.

HAMLET: Beggar that I am, I am even poor in thanks; but I thank you; and sure, dear friends, my thanks are too dear a half-penny. Were you not sent for? Is it your own inclining? It is a free visitation? Come, come, deal justly with me. Come, come; nay, speak.

GUILDENSTERN: What should we say, my lord?

HAMLET: Why any thing. But to th' purpose: you were sent for; and there is a kind of confession in your looks, which your modesties have not craft enough to colour; I know the good King and Queen have sent for you.

ROSENCRANTZ: To what end, my lord?

HAMLET: That you must teach me. But let me conjure you by the rights of our fellowship, by the consonancy of our youth, by the obligation of our ever-preserved love, and by what more dear a better proposer can charge you withal, be even and direct with me, whether you were sent for or no?

ROSENCRANTZ: [*aside to* GUILDENSTERN] What say you?

HAMLET: [*aside*] Nay, then, I have an eye of you. — If you love me, hold not off.

GUILDENSTERN: My lord, we were sent for.

HAMLET: I will tell you why; so shall my anticipation prevent your discovery, and your secrecy to the King and Queen moult no feather. I have of late — but wherefore I know not — lost all my mirth, forgone all custom of exercises; and indeed it goes so heavily with my disposition that this goodly frame, the earth, seems to me a sterile promontory; this most excellent canopy the air, look you, this brave o'er-hanging firmament, this majestical roof fretted with golden fire — why, it appeareth no other thing to me than a foul and pestilent congregation of vapours. What a piece of work is a man! How noble in reason! how infinite in faculties! in form and moving, how express and admirable! in action, how like an angel! in apprehension, how like a god! the beauty of the world! the paragon of animals! And yet, to me, what is this quintessence of dust? Man delights not me — no, nor woman neither, though by your smiling you seem to say so.

ROSENCRANTZ: My lord, there was no such stuff in my thoughts.

HAMLET: Why did ye laugh, then, when I said 'Man delights not me'?

ROSENCRANTZ: To think, my lord, if you delight not in man, what lenten entertainment the players shall receive from you. We coted them on the way; and hither are they coming to offer you service.

HAMLET: He that plays the king shall be welcome — his Majesty shall have tribute on me; the adventurous knight shall use his foil and target; the lover shall not sigh gratis; the humorous man shall end his part in peace; the clown shall make those laugh whose lungs are tickle o' th' sere; and the lady shall say her mind freely, or the blank verse shall halt for't. What players are they?

ROSENCRANTZ: Even those you were wont to take such delight in — the tragedians of the city.

HAMLET: How chances it they travel? Their residence, both in reputation and profit, was better both ways.

ROSENCRANTZ: I think their inhibition comes by the means of the late innovation.

HAMLET: Do they hold the same estimation they did when I was in the city? Are they so followed?

ROSENCRANTZ: No, indeed, are they not.

HAMLET: How comes it? Do they grow rusty?

ROSENCRANTZ: Nay, their endeavour keeps in the wonted pace; but there is, sir, an eyrie of children, little eyases that cry out on the top of question, and are most tyrannically clapp'd for't. These are now the fashion, and so berattle the common stages — so they call them — that many wearing rapiers are afraid of goose quills and dare scarce come thither.

HAMLET: What, are they children? Who maintains 'em? How are they escoted? Will they pursue the quality no longer than they can sing? Will they not say afterwards, if they should grow themselves to common players — as it is most like, if their means are no better — their writers do them wrong to make them exclaim against their own succession?

ROSENCRANTZ: Faith, there has been much to-do on both sides; and the nation holds it no sin to tarre them to controversy. There was for a while no money bid for argument, unless the poet and the player went to cuffs in the question.

HAMLET: Is't possible?

GUILDENSTERN: O, there has been much throwing about of brains.

HAMLET: Do the boys carry it away?

ROSENCRANTZ: Ay, that they do, my lord — Hercules and his load too.

HAMLET: It is not very strange; for my uncle is King of Denmark, and those that would make mows at him while my father lived give twenty, forty, fifty, a hundred ducats apiece for his picture in little. 'Sblood, there is something in this more than natural, if philosophy could find it out.

[A *flourish.*]

GUILDENSTERN: There are the players.

HAMLET: Gentlemen, you are welcome to Elsinore. Your hands, come then; th' appurtenance of welcome is fashion and ceremony. Let me comply with you in this garb; lest my extent to the players, which, I tell you, must show fairly outwards, should more appear like entertainments than yours. You are welcome. But my uncle-father and aunt-mother are deceived.

GUILDENSTERN: In what, my dear lord?

HAMLET: I am but mad north-north-west; when the wind is southerly I know a hawk from a handsaw.

[*Re-enter* POLONIUS.]

POLONIUS: Well be with you, gentlemen!

HAMLET: Hark you, Guildenstern, and you too — at each ear a hearer: that great baby you see there is not yet out of his swaddling clouts.

ROSENCRANTZ: Happily he is the second time come to them; for they say an old man is twice a child.

HAMLET: I will prophesy he comes to tell me of the players; mark it. You say right, sir: a Monday morning; 'twas then indeed.

POLONIUS: My lord, I have news to tell you.

HAMLET: My lord, I have news to tell you. When Roscius was an actor in Rome —

POLONIUS: The actors are come hither, my lord.

HAMLET: Buzz, buzz!

POLONIUS: Upon my honour —

HAMLET: They came each actor on his ass —

POLONIUS: The best actors in the world, either for tragedy, comedy, history, pastoral, pastoral-comical, historical-pastoral, tragical-historical, tragical-comical-historical-pastoral, scene individable, or poem unlimited. Seneca cannot be too heavy nor Plautus too light. For the law of writ and the liberty, these are the only men.

HAMLET: O Jephthah, judge of Israel, what a treasure hadst thou!

POLONIUS: What a treasure had he, my lord?

HAMLET: Why —

> 'One fair daughter, and no more,
> The which he loved passing well.'

POLONIUS: [*aside*] Still on my daughter.

HAMLET: Am I not i' th' right, old Jephthah?

POLONIUS: If you call me Jephthah, my lord, I have a daughter that I love passing well.

HAMLET: Nay, that follows not.

POLONIUS: What follows then, my lord?

HAMLET: Why —

> 'As by lot, God wot'

and then, you know,

> 'It came to pass, as most like it was.'

The first row of the pious chanson will show you more; for look where my abridgement comes.

[*Enter the* PLAYERS.]

You are welcome, masters; welcome, all. — I am glad to see thee well. — Welcome, good friends. — O, my old friend! Why thy face is valanc'd since I saw thee last; com'st thou to beard me in Denmark? — What, my young lady and mistress! By'r lady, your ladyship is nearer to heaven than when I saw you last by the altitude of a chopine. Pray God, your voice, like a piece of uncurrent gold, be not crack'd within the ring. — Masters, you are all welcome. We'll e'en to't like French falconers, fly at anything we see. We'll have a speech straight. Come, give us a taste of your quality; come, a passionate speech.

FIRST PLAYER: What speech, my good lord?

HAMLET: I heard thee speak me a speech once, but it was never acted; or, if it was, not
above once; for the play, I remember, pleas'd not the million; 'twas caviary to
the general. But it was — as I received it, and others whose judgments in such
matters cried in the top of mine — an excellent play, well digested in the
scenes, set down with as much modesty as cunning. I remember one said there
were no sallets in the lines to make the matter savoury, nor no matter in the
phrase that might indict the author of affectation; but call'd it an honest
method, as wholesome as sweet, and by very much more handsome than fine.
One speech in it I chiefly lov'd; 'twas Aeneas' tale to Dido; and thereabout of it
especially where he speaks of Priam's slaughter. If it live in your memory,
begin at this line — let me see:
'The rugged Pyrrhus, like th' Hyrcanian beast,'
'Tis not so; it begins with Pyrrhus.
'The rugged Pyrrhus, he whose sable arms,
Black as his purpose, did the night resemble
When he lay couched in the ominous horse,
Hath now this dread and black complexion smear'd
With heraldry more dismal; head to foot
Now is he total gules, horridly trick'd
With blood of fathers, mothers, daughters, sons,
Bak'd and impasted with the parching streets,
That lend a tyrannous and damned light
To their lord's murder. Roasted in wrath and fire,
And thus o'er-sized with coagulate gore,
With eyes like carbuncles, the hellish Pyrrhus
Old grandsire Priam seeks.'
So proceed you.

POLONIUS: Fore God, my lord, well spoken, with good accent and good discretion.

FIRST PLAYER: 'Anon he finds him
Striking too short at Greeks; his antique sword,
Rebellious to his arm, lies where it falls,
Repugnant to command. Unequal match'd,
Pyrrhus at Priam drives, in rage strikes wide;
But with the whiff and wind of his fell sword
Th' unnerved father falls. Then senseless Ilium,
Seeming to feel this blow, with flaming top
Stoops to his base, and with a hideous crash
Takes prisoner Pyrrhus' ear. For, lo! his sword,
Which was declining on the milky head
Of reverend Priam, seem'd i' th' air to stick.
So, as a painted tyrant, Pyrrhus stood
And, like a neutral to his will and matter,
Did nothing.
But as we often see, against some storm,
A silence in the heavens, the rack stand still,
The bold winds speechless, and the orb below

As hush as death, anon the dreadful thunder
Doth rend the region; so, after Pyrrhus' pause,
A roused vengeance sets him new a-work;
And never did the Cyclops' hammers fall
On Mars' armour, forg'd for proof eterne,
With less remorse than Pyrrhus' bleeding sword
Now falls on Priam.
Out, out, thou strumpet, Fortune! All you gods,
In general synod, take away her power;
Break all the spokes and fellies from her wheel,
And bowl the round nave down the hill of heaven,
As low as to the fiends.'

POLONIUS: This is too long.

HAMLET: It shall to the barber's, with your beard. Prithee say on. He's for a jig, or a tale of bawdry, or he sleeps. Say on; come to Hecuba.

FIRST PLAYER: 'But who, ah, who had seen the mobled queen —'

HAMLET: 'The mobled queen'?

POLONIUS: That's good; 'mobled queen' is good.

FIRST PLAYER: 'Run barefoot up and down, threat'ning the flames
With bisson rheum; a clout upon that head
Where late the diadem stood, and for a robe,
About her lank and all o'er teemed loins,
A blanket, in the alarm of fear caught up —
Who this had seen, with tongue in venom steep'd,
'Gainst Fortune's state would treason have pronounc'd.
But if the gods themselves did see her then,
When she saw Pyrrhus make malicious sport
In mincing with his sword her husband's limbs,
The instant burst of clamour that she made —
Unless things mortal move them not at all —
Would have made milch the burning eyes of heaven,
And passion in the gods.'

POLONIUS: Look whe'er he has not turn'd his colour, and has tears in 's eyes, Prithee no more.

HAMLET: 'Tis well; I'll have thee speak out the rest of this soon. — Good my lord, will you see the players well bestowed? Do you hear: let them be well used; for they are the abstract and brief chronicles of the time; after your death you were better have a bad epitaph than their ill report while you live.

POLONIUS: My lord, I will use them according to their desert.

HAMLET: God's bodykins, man, much better. Use every man after his desert, and who shall scape whipping? Use them after your own honour and dignity; the less they deserve, the more merit is in your bounty. Take them in.

POLONIUS: Come, sirs.

HAMLET: Follow him, friends. We'll hear a play to-morrow. Dost thou hear me, old friend; can you play 'The Murder of Gonzago'?

FIRST PLAYER: Ay, my lord.

HAMLET: We'll ha't to-morrow night. You could, for a need, study a speech of some dozen or sixteen lines which I would set down and insert in't, could you not?

FIRST PLAYER: Ay, my lord.

HAMLET: Very well. Follow that lord; and look you mock him not. [*Exeunt* POLONIUS
   *and* PLAYERS.] My good friends, I'll leave you till night. You are welcome to
   Elsinore.

ROSENCRANTZ: Good my lord!

      [*Exeunt* ROSENCRANTZ *and* GUILDENSTERN.]

HAMLET: Ay, so God buy to you! Now I am alone.
   O, what a rogue and peasant slave am I!
   Is it not monstrous that this player here,
   But in a fiction, in a dream of passion,
   Could force his soul so to his own conceit
   That from her working all his visage wann'd;
   Tears in his eyes, distraction in's aspect,
   A broken voice, and his whole function suiting
   With forms to his conceit? And all for nothing!
   For Hecuba!
   What's Hecuba to him or he to Hecuba,
   That he should weep for her? What would he do,
   Had he the motive and the cue for passion
   That I have? He would drown the stage with tears,
   And cleave the general ear with horrid speech;
   Make mad the guilty, and appal the free,
   Confound the ignorant, and amaze indeed
   The very faculties of eyes and ears.
   Yet I,
   A dull and muddy-mettl'd rascal, peak,
   Like John-a-dreams, unpregnant of my cause,
   And can say nothing; no, not for a king
   Upon whose property and most dear life
   A damn'd defeat was made. Am I a coward?
   Who calls me villain, breaks my pate across,
   Plucks off my beard and blows it in my face,
   Tweaks me by the nose, gives me the lie i' th' throat
   As deep as to the lungs? Who does me this?
   Ha!
   'Swounds, I should take it; for it cannot be
   But I am pigeon-liver'd and lack gall
   To make oppression bitter, or ere this
   I should 'a fatted all the region kites
   With this slave's offal. Bloody, bawdy villian!
   Remorseless, treacherous, lecherous, kindless villain!
   O, vengeance!
   Why, what an ass am I! This is most brave,
   That I, the son of a dear father murder'd,
   Prompted to my revenge by heaven and hell,
   Must, like a whore, unpack my heart with words,
   And fall a-cursing like a very drab,
   A scullion! Fie upon't! foh!

About, my brains. Hum — I have heard
That guilty creatures, sitting at a play,
Have by the very cunning of the scene
Been struck so to the soul that presently
They have proclaim'd their malefactions;
For murder, though it have no tongue, will speak
With most miraculous organ. I'll have these players
Play something like the murder of my father
Before mine uncle. I'll observe his looks;
I'll tent him to the quick. If 'a do blench,
I know my course. The spirit that I have seen
May be a devil; and the devil hath power
T'assume a pleasing shape; yea and perhaps
Out of my weakness and my melancholy,
As he is very potent with such spirits,
Abuses me to damn me. I'll have grounds
More relative than this. The play's the thing
Wherein I'll catch the conscience of the King.      *[Exit.]*

# ACT III

### SCENE I——*Elsinore. The Castle.*

[*Enter* KING, QUEEN, POLONIUS, OPHELIA, ROSENCRANTZ, *and* GUILDEN-
STERN.]

KING: And can you by no drift of conference
    Get from him why he puts on this confusion,
    Grating so harshly all his days of quiet
    With turbulent and dangerous lunacy?
ROSENCRANTZ: He does confess he feels himself distracted,
    But from what cause 'a will by no means speak.
GUILDENSTERN: Nor do we find him forward to be sounded;
    But, with a crafty madness, keeps aloof
    When we would bring him on to some confession
    Of his true state.
QUEEN: Did he receive you well?
ROSENCRANTZ: Most like a gentleman.
GUILDENSTERN: But with much forcing of his disposition.
ROSENCRANTZ: Niggard of question; but of our demands
    Most free in his reply.
QUEEN: Did you assay him
    To any pastime?
ROSENCRANTZ: Madam, it so fell out that certain players
    We o'er-raught on the way. Of these we told him;
    And there did seem in him a kind of joy
    To hear of it. They are here about the court,
    And, as I think, they have already order
    This night to play before him.

POLONIUS: 'Tis most true;
   And he beseech'd me to entreat your Majesties
   To hear and see the matter.
KING: With all my heart; and it doth much content me
   To hear him so inclin'd.
   Good gentlemen, give him a further edge,
   And drive his purpose into these delights.
ROSENCRANTZ: We shall, my lord.
     [*Exeunt* ROSENCRANTZ *and* GUILDENSTERN.]
KING: Sweet Gertrude, leave us too;
   For we have closely sent for Hamlet hither,
   That he, as 'twere by accident, may here
   Affront Ophelia.
   Her father and myself—lawful espials—
   Will so bestow ourselves that, seeing unseen,
   We may of their encounter frankly judge,
   And gather by him, as he is behav'd,
   If 't be th' affliction of his love or no
   That thus he suffers for.
QUEEN: I shall obey you;
   And for your part, Ophelia, I do wish
   That your good beauties be the happy cause
   Of Hamlet's wildness; so shall I hope your virtues
   Will bring him to his wonted way again,
   To both your honours.
OPHELIA: Madam, I wish it may.                              [*Exit* QUEEN.]
POLONIUS: Ophelia, walk you here.—Gracious, so please you,
   We will bestow ourselves.—Read on this book;
   That show of such an exercise may colour
   Your loneliness.—We are oft to blame in this:
   'Tis too much prov'd, that with devotion's visage
   And pious action we do sugar o'er
   The devil himself.
KING: [*aside*] O, 'tis too true!
   How smart a lash that speech doth give my conscience!
   The harlot's cheek, beautied with plast'ring art,
   Is not more ugly to the thing that helps it
   Than is my deed to my most painted word.
   O heavy burden!
POLONIUS: I hear him coming; let's withdraw, my lord.
    [*Exeunt* KING *and* POLONIUS.]
    [*Enter* HAMLET.]
HAMLET: To be, or not to be—that is the question;
   Whether 'tis nobler in the mind to suffer
   The slings and arrows of outrageous fortune,
   Or to take arms against a sea of troubles,
   And by opposing end them? To die, to sleep—

No more; and by a sleep to say we end
The heart-ache and the thousand natural shocks
That flesh is heir to. 'Tis a consummation
Devoutly to be wish'd. To die, to sleep;
To sleep, perchance to dream. Ay, there's the rub;
For in that sleep of death what dreams may come,
When we have shuffled off this mortal coil,
Must give us pause. There's the respect
That makes calamity of so long life;
For who would bear the whips and scorns of time,
Th' oppressor's wrong, the proud man's contumely,
The pangs of despis'd love, the law's delay,
The insolence of office, and the spurns
That patient merit of th' unworthy takes,
When he himself might his quietus make
With a bare bodkin? Who would these fardels bear,
To grunt and sweat under a weary life,
But that the dread of something after death —
The undiscover'd country, from whose bourn
No traveller returns — puzzles the will,
And makes us rather bear those ills we have
Than fly to others that we know not of?
Thus conscience does make cowards of us all;
And thus the native hue of resolution
Is sicklied o'er with the pale cast of thought,
And enterprises of great pitch and moment,
With this regard, their currents turn awry
And lose the name of action. — Soft you now!
The fair Ophelia. — Nymph, in thy orisons
Be all my sins rememb'red.

OPHELIA: Good my lord,
How does your honour for this many a day?

HAMLET: I humbly thank you; well, well, well.

OPELIA: My lord, I have remembrance of yours
That I have longed to re-deliver.
I pray you now receive them.

HAMLET: No, not I;
I never gave you aught.

OPHELIA: My honour'd lord, you know right well you did,
And with them words of so sweet breath compos'd
As made the things more rich; their perfume lost,
Take these again; for to the noble mind
Rich gifts wax poor when givers prove unkind.
There, my lord.

HAMLET: Ha, Ha! Are you honest?

OPHELIA: My lord?

HAMLET: Are you fair?

OPHELIA: What means your lordship?

HAMLET: That if you be honest and fair, your honesty should admit no discourse to your beauty.

OPHELIA: Could beauty, my lord, have better commerce than with honesty?

HAMLET: Ay, truly; for the power of beauty will sooner transform honesty from what it is to a bawd than the force of honesty can translate beauty into his likeness. This was sometime a paradox, but now the time gives it proof. I did love you once.

OPHELIA: Indeed, my lord, you made me believe so.

HAMLET: You should not have believ'd me; for virtue cannot so inoculate our old stock but we shall relish of it. I loved you not.

OPHELIA: I was the more deceived.

HAMLET: Get thee to a nunnery. Why wouldst thou be a breeder of sinners? I am myself indifferent honest, but yet I could accuse me of such things that it were better my mother had not borne me: I am very proud, revengeful, ambitious; with more offences at my beck than I have thoughts to put them in, imagination to give them shape, or time to act them in. What should such fellows as I do crawling between earth and heaven? We are arrant knaves, all; believe none of us. Go thy ways to a nunnery. Where's your father?

OPHELIA: At home, my lord.

HAMLET: Let the doors be shut upon him, that he may play the fool nowhere but in's own house. Farewell.

OPHELIA: O, help him, you sweet heavens!

HAMLET: If thou dost marry, I'll give thee this plague for thy dowry: be thou as chaste as ice, as pure as snow, thou shalt not escape calumny. Get thee to a nunnery, go, farewell. Or, if thou wilt needs marry, marry a fool; for wise men know well enough what monsters you make of them. To a nunnery go; and quickly too. Farewell.

OPHELIA: O heavenly powers, restore him!

HAMLET: I have heard of your paintings too, well enough; God hath given you one face, and you make yourselves another. You jig and amble, and you lisp, and nickname God's creatures, and make your wantonness your ignorance. Go to, I'll no more on't; it hath made me mad. I say we will have no more marriage: those that are married already, all but one, shall live; the rest shall keep as they are. To a nunnery, go.

[*Exit.*]

OPHELIA: O, what a noble mind is here o'erthrown!
The courtier's, soldier's, scholar's, eye, tongue, sword;
Th' expectancy and rose of the fair state,
The glass of fashion and the mould of form,
Th' observ'd of all observers — quite, quite down!
And I, of ladies most deject and wretched,
That suck'd the honey of his music vows,
Now see that noble and most sovereign reason,
Like sweet bells jangled, out of time and harsh;
That unmatch'd form and feature of blown youth
Blasted with ecstasy. O, woe is me
T' have seen what I have seen, see what I see!

[*Re-enter* KING *and* POLONIUS.]

KING: Love! His affections do not that way tend;
    Nor what he spake, though it lack'd form a little,
    Was not like madness. There's something in his soul
    O'er which his melancholy sits on brood;
    And I do doubt the hatch and the disclose
    Will be some danger; which to prevent
    I have in quick determination
    Thus set it down: he shall with speed to England
    For the demand of our neglected tribute.
    Haply the seas and countries different,
    With variable objects, shall expel
    This something-settled matter in his heart
    Whereon his brains still beating puts him thus
    From fashion of himself. What think you on't?
POLONIUS: It shall do well. But yet do I believe
    The origin and commencement of his grief
    Sprung from neglected love. How now, Ophelia!
    You need not tell us what Lord Hamlet said;
    We heard it all. My lord, do as you please;
    But if you hold it fit, after the play
    Let his queen mother all alone entreat him
    To show his grief. Let her be round with him;
    And I'll be placed, so please you, in the ear
    Of all their conference. If she find him not,
    To England send him; or confine him where
    Your wisdom best shall think.
KING: It shall be so:
    Madness in great ones must not unwatch'd go.         [*Exeunt.*]

<br>

SCENE II——*Elsinore. The Castle.*

[*Enter* HAMLET *and three of the* PLAYERS.]

HAMLET: Speak the speech, I pray you, as I pronounc'd it to you, trippingly on the
    tongue; but if you mouth it, as many of our players do, I had as lief the
    towncrier spoke my lines. Nor do not saw the air too much with your hand,
    thus, but use all gently; for in the very torrent, tempest, and, as I may say,
    whirlwind of your passion, you must acquire and beget a temperance that may
    give it smoothness. O, it offends me to the soul to hear a robustious periwig-
    pated fellow tear a passion to tatters, to very rags, to split the ears of the
    groundlings, who, for the most part, are capable of nothing but inexplicable
    dumb shows and noise. I would have such a fellow whipp'd for o'erdoing
    Termagant; it out-herods Herod. Pray you avoid it.
FIRST PLAYER: I warrant your honour.
HAMLET: Be not too tame neither, but let your own discretion be your tutor. Suit the
    action to the word, the word to the action; with this special observance, that
    you o'erstep not the modesty of nature; for anything so o'erdone is from the
    purpose of playing, whose end, both at the first and now, was and is to hold, as

'twere, the mirror up to nature; to show virtue her own feature, scorn her own image, and the very age and body of the time his form and pressure. Now, this overdone or come tardy off, though it makes the unskilful laugh, cannot but make the judicious grieve; the censure of the which one must, in your allowance, o'erweigh a whole theatre of others. O, there be players that I have seen play — and heard others praise, and that highly — not to speak it profanely, that, neither having th' accent of Christians, nor the gait of Christian, pagan, nor man, have so strutted and bellowed that I have thought some of Nature's journeymen had made men, and not made them well, they imitated humanity so abominably.

FIRST PLAYER: I hope we have reform'd that indifferently with us, sir.

HAMLET: O, reform it altogether. And let those that play your clowns speak no more than is set down for them; for there be of them that will themselves laugh, to set on some quantity of barren spectators to laugh too, though in the meantime some necessary question of the play be then to be considered. That's villainous, and shows a most pitiful ambition in the fool that uses it. Go, make you ready.

    [*Exeunt* PLAYERS.]

    [*Enter* POLONIUS, ROSENCRANTZ, *and* GUILDENSTERN.]

How now, my lord! Will the King hear this piece of work?

POLONIUS: And the Queen too, and that presently.

HAMLET: Bid the players make haste.                     [*Exit* POLONIUS.]

    Will you two help to hasten them?

ROSENCRANTZ: Ay, my lord.                             [*Exeunt they two.*]

HAMLET: What, ho, Horatio!

    [*Enter* HORATIO.]

HORATIO: Here, sweet lord, at your service.

HAMLET: Horatio, thou art e'en as just a man
    As e'er my conversation cop'd withal.

HORATIO: O my dear lord!

HAMLET: Nay, do not think I flatter;
    For what advancement may I hope from thee,
    That no revenue hast but thy good spirits
    To feed and clothe thee? Why should the poor be flatter'd?
    No, let the candied tongue lick absurd pomp,
    And crook the pregnant hinges of the knee
    Where thrift may follow fawning. Dost thou hear?
    Since my dear soul was mistress of her choice
    And could of men distinguish her election,
    Sh'hath seal'd thee for herself; for thou hast been
    As one, in suff'ring all, that suffers nothing;
    A man that Fortune's buffets and rewards
    Hast ta'en with equal thanks; and blest are those
    Whose blood and judgment are so well commingled
    That they are not a pipe for Fortune's finger
    To sound what stop she please. Give me that man
    That is not passion's slave, and I will wear him
    In my heart's core, ay, in my heart of heart,

As I do thee. Something too much of this.
There is a play to-night before the King;
One scene of it comes near the circumstance
Which I have told thee of my father's death.
I prithee, when thou seest that act afoot,
Even with the very comment of thy soul
Observe my uncle. If his occulted guilt
Do not itself unkennel in one speech,
It is a damned ghost that we have seen,
And my imaginations are as foul
As Vulcan's stithy. Give him heedful note;
For I mine eyes will rivet to his face;
And, after, we will both our judgments join
In censure of his seeming.

HORATIO: Well, my lord.
If 'a steal aught the whilst this play is playing,
And scape detecting, I will pay the theft.

[*Enter trumpets and kettledrums. Danish march. Sound a flourish. Enter* KING, QUEEN, POLONIUS, OPHELIA, ROSENCRANTZ, GUILDENSTERN, *and other* LORDS *attendant, with the guard carrying torches.*]

HAMLET: They are coming to the play; I must be idle.
Get you a place.

KING: How fares our cousin Hamlet?

HAMLET: Excellent, i' faith; of the chameleon's dish. I eat the air promise-cramm'd; you cannot feed capons so.

KING: I have nothing with this answer, Hamlet; these words are not mine.

HAMLET: No, nor mine now. [*to* POLONIUS] My lord, you play'd once in th' university, you say?

POLONIUS: That did I, my lord, and was accounted a good actor.

HAMLET: What did you enact?

POLONIUS: I did enact Julius Caesar; I was kill'd i' th' Capitol; Brutus kill'd me.

HAMLET: It was a brute part of him to kill so capital a calf there. Be the players ready?

ROSENCRANTZ: Ay, my lord; they stay upon your patience.

QUEEN: Come hither, my dear Hamlet, sit by me.

HAMLET: No, good mother; here's metal more attractive.

POLONIUS: [*to the* KING] O, ho! do you mark that?

HAMLET: Lady, shall I lie in your lap? [*lying down at* OPHELIA's *feet*]

OPHELIA: No, my lord.

HAMLET: I mean, my head upon your lap?

OPHELIA: Ay, my lord.

HAMLET: Do you think I meant country matters?

OPHELIA: I think nothing, my lord.

HAMLET: That's a fair thought to lie between maids' legs.

OPHELIA: What is, my lord?

HAMLET: Nothing.

OPHELIA: You are merry, my lord.

HAMLET: Who, I?

OPHELIA: Ay, my lord.

HAMLET: O God, your only jig-maker! What should a man do but be merry? For look you how cheerfully my mother looks, and my father died within's two hours.

OPHELIA: Nay, 'tis twice two months, my lord.

HAMLET: So long? Nay then, let the devil wear black, for I'll have a suit of sables. O heavens! die two months ago, and not forgotten yet? Then there's hope a great man's memory may outlive his life half a year; but, by'r lady, 'a must build churches, then; or else shall 'a suffer not thinking on, with the hobby-horse, whose epitaph is 'For O, for O, the hobby-horse is forgot!'

> *[The trumpet sounds. Hautboys play. The Dumb Show enters.]*
>
> *[Enter a* KING *and a* QUEEN, *very lovingly; the* QUEEN *embracing him and he her. She kneels, and makes a show of protestation unto him. He takes her up, and declines his head upon her neck. He lies him down upon a bank of flowers; she, seeing him asleep, leaves him. Anon comes in a* FELLOW, *takes off his crown, kisses it, pours poison in the sleeper's ears, and leaves him. The* QUEEN *returns; finds the* KING *dead, and makes passionate action. The* POISONER, *with some two or three* MUTES, *comes in again, seeming to condole with her. The dead body is carried away. The* POISONER *woos the* QUEEN *with gifts: she seems harsh awhile, but in the end accepts his love. Exeunt.]*

OPHELIA: What means this, my lord?

HAMLET: Marry, this is miching mallecho; it means mischief.

OPHELIA: Belike this show imports the argument of the play.

> *[Enter* PROLOGUE.*]*

HAMLET: We shall know by this fellow: the players cannot keep counsel; they'll tell all.

OPHELIA: Will 'a tell us what this show meant?

HAMLET: Ay, or any show that you show him. Be not you asham'd to show, he'll not shame to tell you what it means.

OPHELIA: You are naught, you are naught. I'll mark the play.

PROLOGUE: *For us, and for our tragedy,*
> *Here stooping to your clemency,*
> *We beg your hearing patiently.*
> *[Exit.]*

HAMLET: Is this a prologue, or the posy of a ring?

OPHELIA: 'Tis brief, my lord.

HAMLET: As woman's love.

> *[Enter the* PLAYER KING *and* QUEEN.*]*

PLAYER KING: *Full thirty times hath Phoebus' cart gone round*
> *Neptune's salt wash and Tellus' orbed ground,*
> *And thirty dozen moons with borrowed sheen*
> *About the world have times twelve thirties been,*
> *Since love our hearts and Hymen did our hands*
> *Unite comutual in most sacred bands.*

PLAYER QUEEN: *So many journeys may the sun and moon*
> *Make us again count o'er ere love be done!*
> *But, woe is me, you are so sick of late,*
> *So far from cheer and from your former state,*

That I distrust you. Yet, though I distrust,
Discomfort you, my lord, it nothing must;
For women fear too much even as they love,
And women's fear and love hold quantity,
In neither aught, or in extremity.
Now, what my love is, proof hath made you know;
And as my love is siz'd, my fear is so.
Where love is great, the littlest doubts are fear;
Where little fears grow great, great love grows there.

PLAYER KING: Faith, I must leave thee, love, and shortly too:
My operant powers their functions leave to do;
And thou shalt live in this fair world behind,
Honour'd, belov'd; and haply one as kind
For husband shalt thou —

PLAYER QUEEN: O, confound the rest!
Such love must needs be treason in my breast.
In second husband let me be accurst!
None wed the second but who kill'd the first.

HAMLET: That's wormwood, wormwood.

PLAYER QUEEN: The instances that second marriage move
Are base respects of thrift, but none of love.
A second time I kill my husband dead,
When second husband kisses me in bed.

PLAYER KING: I do believe you think what now you speak;
But what we do determine oft we break.
Purpose is but the slave to memory,
Of violent birth, but poor validity;
Which now, the fruit unripe, sticks on the tree;
But fall unshaken when they mellow be.
Most necessary 'tis that we forget
To pay ourselves what to ourselves is debt.
What to ourselves in passion we propose,
The passion ending, doth the purpose lose.
The violence of either grief or joy
Their own enactures with themselves destroy.
Where joy most revels grief doth most lament;
Grief joys, joy grieves, on slender accident.
This world is not for aye; nor 'tis not strange
That even our loves should with our fortunes change;
For 'tis a question left us yet to prove,
Whether love lead fortune or else fortune love.
The great man down, you mark his favourite flies;
The poor advanc'd makes friends of enemies.
And hitherto doth love on fortune tend;
For who not needs shall never lack a friend,
And who in want a hollow friend doth try,
Directly seasons him his enemy.
But, orderly to end where I begun,

*Our wills and fates do so contrary run*
*That our devices still are overthrown;*
*Our thoughts are ours, their ends none of our own.*
*So think thou wilt no second husband wed;*
*But die thy thoughts when thy first lord is dead.*

PLAYER QUEEN: *Nor earth to me give food, nor heaven light,*
*Sport and repose lock from me day and night,*
*To desperation turn my trust and hope,*
*An anchor's cheer in prison be my scope,*
*Each opposite that blanks the face of joy*
*Meet what I would have well, and it destroy,*
*Both here and hence pursue my lasting strife,*
*If, once a widow, ever I be wife!*

HAMLET: If she should break it now!

PLAYER KING: *'Tis deeply sworn. Sweet, leave me here awhile;*
*My spirits grow dull, and fain I would beguile*
*The tedious day with sleep.*                          [*Sleeps.*]

PLAYER QUEEN: *Sleep rock thy brain,*
*And never come mischance between us twain!*

HAMLET: Madam, how like you this play?

QUEEN: The lady doth protest too much, methinks.

HAMLET: O, but she'll keep her word.

KING: Have you heard the argument? Is there no offence in't?

HAMLET: No, no; they do but jest, poison in jest; no offence i' th' world.

KING: What do you call the play?

HAMLET: 'The Mouse-trap.' Marry, how? Tropically. This play is the image of a murder done in Vienna: Gonzago is the duke's name; his wife, Baptista. You shall see anon. 'Tis a knavish piece of work; but what of that? Your Majesty, and we that have free souls, it touches us not. Let the galled jade wince, our withers are unwrung.

[*Enter* LUCIANUS.]

This is one Lucianus, nephew to the King.

OPHELIA: You are as good as a chorus, my lord.

HAMLET: I could interpret between you and your love, if I could see the puppets dallying.

OPHELIA: You are keen, my lord, you are keen.

HAMLET: It would cost you a groaning to take off mine edge.

OPHELIA: Still better, and worse.

HAMLET: So you mis-take your husbands. — Begin, murderer; pox, leave thy damnable faces and begin. Come; the croaking raven doth bellow for revenge.

LUCIANUS: *Thoughts black, hands apt, drugs fit, and time agreeing;*
*Confederate season, else no creature seeing;*
*Thou mixture rank, of midnight weeds collected,*
*With Hecat's ban thrice blasted, thrice infected.*
*Thy natural magic and dire property*
*On wholesome life usurps immediately.*

[*Pours the poison in his ears.*]

HAMLET: 'A poisons him i' th' garden for his estate. His name's Gonzago. The story
    is extant, and written in very choice Italian. You shall see anon how the
    murderer gets the love of Gonzago's wife.
OPHELIA: The King rises.
HAMLET: What, frighted with false fire!
QUEEN: How fares my lord?
POLONIUS: Give o'er the play.
KING: Give me some light. Away!
POLONIUS: Lights, lights, lights!

[*Exeunt all but* HAMLET *and* HORATIO.]

HAMLET: Why, let the strucken deer go weep,
        The hart ungalled play;
    For some must watch, while some must sleep;
        Thus runs the world away.
    Would not this, sir, and a forest of feathers—if the rest of my fortunes turn
    Turk with me—with two Provincial roses on my raz'd shoes, get me a
    fellowship in a cry of players, sir?
HORATIO: Half a share.
HAMLET: A whole one, I.
    For thou dost know, O Damon dear,
        This realm dismantled was
    Of Jove himself; and now reigns here
        A very, very—peacock.
HORATIO: You might have rhym'd.
HAMLET: O good Horatio, I'll take the ghost's word for a thousand pound. Didst
    perceive?
HORATIO: Very well, my lord.
HAMLET: Upon the talk of the poisoning.
HORATIO: I did very well note him.
HAMLET: Ah, ha! Come, some music. Come, the recorders.
    For if the King like not the comedy,
    Why, then, belike he likes it not, perdy.
    Come, some music.

[*Re-enter* ROSENCRANTZ *and* GUILDENSTERN.]

GUILDENSTERN: Good my lord, vouchsafe me a word with you.
HAMLET: Sir, a whole history.
GUILDENSTERN: The King, sir—
HAMLET: Ay, sir, what of him?
GUILDENSTERN: Is, in his retirement, marvellous distemp'red.
HAMLET: With drink, sir?
GUILDENSTERN: No, my lord, rather with choler.
HAMLET: Your wisdom should show itself more richer to signify this to his doctor; for
    for me to put him to his purgation would perhaps plunge him into far more
    choler.

GUILDENSTERN: Good my lord, put your discourse into some frame, and start not so wildly from my affair.

HAMLET: I am tame, sir. Pronounce.

GUILDENSTERN: The Queen, your mother, in most great affliction of spirit, hath sent me to you.

HAMLET: You are welcome.

GUILDENSTERN: Nay, good my lord, this courtesy is not of the right breed. If it shall please you to make me a wholesome answer, I will do your mother's commandment; if not, your pardon and my return shall be the end of my business.

HAMLET: Sir, I cannot.

ROSENCRANTZ: What, my lord?

HAMLET: Make you a wholesome answer; my wit's diseas'd. But, sir, such answer as I can make, you shall command: or rather, as you say, my mother. Therefore no more, but to the matter: my mother, you say —

ROSENCRANTZ: Then thus she says: your behaviour hath struck her into amazement and admiration.

HAMLET: O wonderful son, that can so stonish a mother! But is there no sequel at the heels of this mother's admiration? Impart.

ROSENCRANTZ: She desires to speak with you in her closet ere you go to bed.

HAMLET: We shall obey, were she ten times our mother. Have you any further trade with us?

ROSENCRANTZ: My lord, you once did love me.

HAMLET: And do still, by these pickers and stealers.

ROSENCRANTZ: Good my lord, what is your cause of distemper? You do surely bar the door upon your own liberty, if you deny your griefs to your friend.

HAMLET: Sir, I lack advancement.

ROSENCRANTZ: How can that be, when you have the voice of the King himself for your succession in Denmark?

HAMLET: Ay, sir, but 'While the grass grows' — the proverb is something musty.
    [*Re-enter the* PLAYERS, *with recorders.*]
    O, the recorders! Let me see one. To withdraw with you — why do you go about to recover the wind of me, as if you would drive me into a toil?

GUILDENSTERN: O my lord, if my duty be too bold, my love is too unmannerly.

HAMLET: I do not well understand that. Will you play upon this pipe?

GUILDENSTERN: My lord, I cannot.

HAMLET: I pray you.

GUILDENSTERN: Believe me, I cannot.

HAMLET: I do beseech you.

GUILDENSTERN: I know no touch of it, my lord.

HAMLET: It is as easy as lying: govern these ventages with your fingers and thumb, give it breath with your mouth, and it will discourse most eloquent music. Look you, these are the stops.

GUILDENSTERN: But these cannot I command to any utterance of harmony; I have not the skill.

HAMLET: Why, look you now, how unworthy a thing you make of me! You would play upon me; you would seem to know my stops; you would pluck out the heart of my mystery; you would sound me from my lowest note to the top of my compass; and there is much music, excellent voice, in this little organ, yet cannot you make it speak. 'Sblood, do you think I am easier to be play'd on than a pipe? Call me what instrument you will, though you can fret me, yet you cannot play upon me.

[*Re-enter* POLONIUS.]

God bless you, sir!

POLONIUS: My lord, the Queen would speak with you, and presently.

HAMLET: Do you see yonder cloud that's almost in shape of a camel?

POLONIUS: By th' mass, and 'tis like a camel indeed.

HAMLET: Methinks it is like a weasel.

POLONIUS: It is back'd like a weasel.

HAMLET: Or like a whale?

POLONIUS: Very like a whale.

HAMLET: Then I will come to my mother by and by. [*aside*] They fool me to the top of my bent. — I will come by and by.

POLONIUS: I will say so. [*Exit* POLONIUS.]

HAMLET: 'By and by' is easily said. Leave me, friends.

[*Exeunt all but* HAMLET.]

'Tis now the very witching time of night,
When churchyards yawn, and hell itself breathes out
Contagion to this world. Now could I drink hot blood,
And do such bitter business as the day
Would quake to look on. Soft! now to my mother.
O heart, lose not thy nature; let not ever
The soul of Nero enter this firm bosom.
Let me be cruel, not unnatural:
I will speak daggers to her, but use none.
My tongue and soul in this be hypocrites —
How in my words somever she be shent,
To give them seals never, my soul, consent! [*Exit.*]

SCENE III ——— *Elsinore. The Castle.*

[*Enter* KING, ROSENCRANTZ, *and* GUILDENSTERN.]

KING: I like him not; nor stands it safe with us
To let his madness range. Therefore prepare you;
I your commission will forthwith dispatch,
And he to England shall along with you.
The terms of our estate may not endure
Hazard so near's as doth hourly grow
Out of his brows.

GUILDENSTERN: We will ourselves provide.
Most holy and religious fear it is
To keep those many many bodies safe
That live and feed upon your Majesty.

ROSENCRANTZ: The single and peculiar life is bound
With all the strength and armour of the mind
To keep itself from noyance; but much more
That spirit upon whose weal depends and rests

The lives of many. The cease of majesty
Dies not alone, but like a gulf doth draw
What's near it with it. It is a massy wheel,
Fix'd on the summit of the highest mount,
To whose huge spokes ten thousand lesser things
Are mortis'd and adjoin'd; which when it falls,
Each small annexment, petty consequence,
Attends the boist'rous ruin. Never alone
Did the king sigh, but with a general groan.

KING: Arm you, I pray you, to this speedy voyage;
For we will fetters put about this fear,
Which now goes too free-footed.

ROSENCRANTZ: We will haste us.

[*Exeunt* ROSENCRANTZ *and* GUILDENSTERN.]
[*Enter* POLONIUS.]

POLONIUS: My lord, he's going to his mother's closet.
Behind the arras I'll convey myself
To hear the process. I'll warrant she'll tax him home;
And, as you said, and wisely was it said,
'Tis meet that some more audience than a mother,
Since nature makes them partial, should o'erhear
The speech, of vantage. Fare you well, my liege.
I'll call upon you ere you go to bed,
And tell you what I know.

KING: Thanks, dear my lord.                              [*Exit* POLONIUS.]
O, my offence is rank, it smells to heaven;
It hath the primal eldest curse upon't —
A brother's murder! Pray can I not,
Though inclination be as sharp as will.
My stronger guilt defeats my strong intent,
And, like a man to double business bound,
I stand in pause where I shall first begin,
And both neglect. What if this cursed hand
Were thicker than itself with brother's blood,
Is there not rain enough in the sweet heavens
To wash it white as snow? Whereto serves mercy
But to confront the visage of offence?
And what's in prayer but this twofold force,
To be forestalled ere we come to fall,
Or pardon'd being down? Then I'll look up;
My fault is past. But, O, what form of prayer
Can serve my turn? 'Forgive me my foul murder'!
That cannot be; since I am still possess'd
Of those effects for which I did the murder —
My crown, mine own ambition, and my queen.
May one be pardon'd and retain th' offence?
In the corrupted currents of this world
Offence's gilded hand may shove by justice;

And oft 'tis seen the wicked prize itself
Buys out the law. But 'tis not so above:
There is no shuffling; there the action lies
In his true nature; and we ourselves compell'd,
Even to the teeth and forehead of our faults,
To give in evidence. What then? What rests?
Try what repentance can. What can it not?
Yet what can it when one cannot repent?
O wretched state! O bosom black as death!
O limed soul, that, struggling to be free,
Art more engag'd! Help, angels. Make assay:
Bow, stubborn knees; and, heart, with strings of steel,
Be soft as sinews of the new-born babe.
All may be well.                                    [*He kneels.*]
      [*Enter* HAMLET.]
HAMLET: Now might I do it pat, now 'a is a-praying;
   And now I'll do't — and so 'a goes to heaven,
   And so am I reveng'd. That would be scann'd:
   A villain kills my father; and for that,
   I, his sole son, do this same villain send
   To heaven.
   Why, this is hire and salary, not revenge.
   'A took my father grossly, full of bread,
   With all his crimes broad blown, as flush as May;
   And how his audit stands who knows save heaven?
   But in our circumstance and course of thought
   'Tis heavy with him; and am I then reveng'd
   To take him in the purging of his soul,
   When he is fit and season'd for his passage?
   No.
   Up, sword, and know thou a more horrid hent.
   When he is drunk asleep, or in his rage;
   Or in th' incestuous pleasure of his bed;
   At game, a-swearing, or about some act
   That has no relish of salvation in't —
   Then trip him, that his heels may kick at heaven,
   And that his soul may be as damn'd and black
   As hell, whereto it goes. My mother stays.
   This physic but prolongs thy sickly days.          [*Exit.*]
KING: [*rising*] My words fly up, my thoughts remain below.
   Words without thoughts never to heaven go.          [*Exit.*]


SCENE IV ——— *The* QUEEN'*s closet.*

[*Enter* QUEEN *and* POLONIUS.]
POLONIUS: 'A will come straight. Look you lay home to him;
   Tell him his pranks have been too broad to bear with,
   And that your Grace hath screen'd and stood between

Much heat and him. I'll silence me even here.
Pray you be round with him.
HAMLET: [*within*] Mother, mother, mother!
QUEEN: I'll warrant you. Fear me not.
Withdraw, I hear him coming.
[POLONIUS *goes behind the arras.*]
[*Enter* HAMLET.]
HAMLET: Now, mother, what's the matter?
QUEEN: Hamlet, thou hast thy father much offended.
HAMLET: Mother, you have my father much offended.
QUEEN: Come, come, you answer with an idle tongue.
HAMLET: Go, go, you question with a wicked tongue.
QUEEN: Why, how now, Hamlet!
HAMLET: What's the matter now?
QUEEN: Have you forgot me?
HAMLET: No, by the rood, not so:
You are the Queen, your husband's brother's wife;
And—would it were not so!—you are my mother.
QUEEN: Nay then, I'll set those to you that can speak.
HAMLET: Come, come, and sit you down; you shall not budge.
You go not till I set you up a glass
Where you may see the inmost part of you.
QUEEN: What wilt thou do? Thou wilt not murder me?
Help, help, ho!
POLONIUS: [*behind*] What, ho! help, help, help!
HAMLET: [*draws*] How now! a rat?
Dead, for a ducat, dead!
[*kills* POLONIUS *with a pass through the arras*]
POLONIUS: [*behind*] O, I am slain!
QUEEN: O me, what hast thou done?
HAMLET: Nay, I know not:
Is it the King?
QUEEN: O, what a rash and bloody deed is this!
HAMLET: A bloody deed!—almost as bad, good mother,
As kill a king and marry with his brother.
QUEEN: As kill a king!
HAMLET: Ay, lady, it was my word. [*parting the arras*]
Thou wretched, rash, intruding fool, farewell!
I took thee for thy better. Take thy fortune;
Thou find'st to be too busy is some danger.
Leave wringing of your hands. Peace; sit you down,
And let me wring your heart; for so I shall,
If it be made of penetrable stuff;
If damned custom have not braz'd it so
That it be proof and bulwark against sense.
QUEEN: What have I done that thou dar'st wag thy tongue
In noise so rude against me?
HAMLET: Such an act

That blurs the grace and blush of modesty;
Calls virtue hypocrite; takes off the rose
From the fair forehead of an innocent love,
And sets a blister there; makes marriage-vows
As false as dicers' oaths. O, such a deed
As from the body of contraction plucks
The very soul, and sweet religion makes
A rhapsody of words. Heaven's face does glow
O'er this solidity and compound mass
With heated visage, as against the doom —
Is thought-sick at the act.

QUEEN: Ay me, what act,
That roars so loud and thunders in the index?

HAMLET: Look here upon this picture and on this,
The counterfeit presentment of two brothers.
See what a grace was seated on this brow;
Hyperion's curls; the front of Jove himself;
An eye like Mars, to threaten and command;
A station like the herald Mercury
New lighted on a heaven-kissing hill —
A combination and a form indeed
Where every god did seem to set his seal,
To give the world assurance of a man.
This was your husband. Look you now what follows:
Here is your husband, like a mildew'd ear
Blasting his wholesome brother. Have you eyes?
Could you on this fair mountain leave to feed,
And batten on this moor? Ha! have you eyes?
You cannot call it love; for at your age
The heyday in the blood is tame, it's humble,
And waits upon the judgment; and what judgment
Would step from this to this? Sense, sure, you have,
Else could you not have motion; but sure that sense
Is apoplex'd; for madness would not err,
Nor sense to ecstasy was ne'er so thrall'd
But it reserv'd some quantity of choice
To serve in such a difference. What devil was't
That thus hath cozen'd you at hoodman-blind?
Eyes without feeling, feeling without sight,
Ears without hands or eyes, smelling sans all,
Or but a sickly part of one true sense
Could not so mope. O shame! where is thy blush?
Rebellious hell,
If thou canst mutine in a matron's bones,
To flaming youth let virtue be as wax
And melt in her own fire; proclaim no shame
When the compulsive ardour gives the charge,
Since frost itself as actively doth burn,

And reason panders will.

QUEEN: O Hamlet, speak no more!
Thou turn'st my eyes into my very soul;
And there I see such black and grained spots
As will not leave their tinct.

HAMLET: Nay, but to live
In the rank sweat of an enseamed bed,
Stew'd in corruption, honeying and making love
Over the nasty sty!

QUEEN: O, speak to me no more!
These words like daggers enter in my ears;
No more, sweet Hamlet.

HAMLET: A murderer and a villain!
A slave that is not twentieth part the tithe
Of your precedent lord; a vice of kings;
A cutpurse of the empire and the rule,
That from a shelf the precious diadem stole
And put it in his pocket!

QUEEN: No more!

       [*Enter* GHOST.]

HAMLET: A king of shreds and patches —
Save me, and hover o'er me with your wings,
You heavenly guards! What would your gracious figure?

QUEEN: Alas, he's mad!

HAMLET: Do you not come your tardy son to chide,
That, laps'd in time and passion, lets go by
Th' important acting of your dread command?
O, say!

GHOST: Do not forget; this visitation
Is but to whet thy almost blunted purpose.
But look, amazement on thy mother sits.
O, step between her and her fighting soul!
Conceit in weakest bodies strongest works.
Speak to her, Hamlet.

HAMLET: How is it with you, lady?

QUEEN: Alas, how is't with you,
That you do bend your eye on vacancy,
And with th' incorporal air do hold discourse?
Forth at your eyes and spirits wildly peep;
And, as the sleeping soldiers in th' alarm,
Your bedded hairs like life in excrements
Start up and stand an end. O gentle son,
Upon the heat and flame of thy distemper
Sprinkle cool patience! Whereon do you look?

HAMLET: On him, on him! Look you how pale he glares.
His form and cause conjoin'd, preaching to stones,
Would make them capable. — Do not look upon me,
Lest with this piteous action you convert

My stern effects; then what I have to do
Will want true colour — tears perchance for blood.
QUEEN: To whom do you speak this?
HAMLET: Do you see nothing there?
QUEEN: Nothing at all; yet all that is I see.
HAMLET: Nor did you nothing hear?
QUEEN: No, nothing but ourselves.
HAMLET: Why, look you there. Look how it steals away.
    My father, in his habit as he liv'd!
    Look where he goes even now out at the portal.
       [*Exit* GHOST.]
QUEEN: This is the very coinage of your brain.
    This bodiless creation ecstasy
    Is very cunning in.
HAMLET: Ecstasy!
    My pulse as yours doth temperately keep time.
    And makes as healthful music. It is not madness
    That I have utt'red. Bring me to the test,
    And I the matter will re-word which madness
    Would gambol from. Mother, for love of grace,
    Lay not that flattering unction to your soul,
    That not your trespass but my madness speaks:
    It will but skin and film the ulcerous place,
    Whiles rank corruption, mining all within,
    Infects unseen. Confess yourself to heaven;
    Repent what's past; avoid what is to come;
    And do not spread the compost on the weeds,
    To make them ranker. Forgive me this my virtue;
    For in the fatness of these pursy times
    Virtue itself of vice must pardon beg,
    Yea, curb and woo for leave to do him good.
QUEEN: O Hamlet, thou hast cleft my heart in twain.
HAMLET: O, throw away the worser part of it,
    And live the purer with the other half.
    Good night — but go not to my uncle's bed;
    Assume a virtue, if you have it not.
    That monster custom, who all sense doth eat,
    Of habits devil, is angel yet in this,
    That to the use of actions fair and good
    He likewise gives a frock or livery
    That aptly is put on. Refrain to-night;
    And that shall lend a kind of easiness
    To the next abstinence; the next more easy;
    For use almost can change the stamp of nature,
    And either curb the devil, or throw him out,
    With wondrous potency. Once more, good night;
    And when you are desirous to be blest,
    I'll blessing beg of you. For this same lord

I do repent; but Heaven hath pleas'd it so,
To punish me with this, and this with me,
That I must be their scourge and minister.
I will bestow him, and will answer well
The death I gave him. So, again, good night.
I must be cruel only to be kind;
Thus bad begins and worse remains behind.
One word more, good lady.

QUEEN: What shall I do?

HAMLET: Not this, by no means, that I bid you do:
Let the bloat King tempt you again to bed;
Pinch wanton on your cheek; call you his mouse;
And let him, for a pair of reechy kisses,
Or paddling in your neck with his damn'd fingers,
Make you to ravel all this matter out,
That I essentially am not in madness,
But mad in craft. 'Twere good you let him know;
For who that's but a queen, fair, sober, wise,
Would from a paddock, from a bat, a gib,
Such dear concernings hide? Who would do so?
No, in despite of sense and secrecy,
Unpeg the basket on the house's top,
Let the birds fly, and, like the famous ape,
To try conclusions, in the basket creep
And break your own neck down.

QUEEN: Be thou assur'd, if words be made of breath
And breath of life, I have no life to breathe
What thou hast said to me.

HAMLET: I must to England; you know that?

QUEEN: Alack,
I had forgot. 'Tis so concluded on.

HAMLET: There's letters seal'd; and my two school-fellows,
Whom I will trust as I will adders fang'd—
They bear the mandate; they must sweep my way
And marshal me to knavery. Let it work;
For 'tis the sport to have the engineer
Hoist with his own petar; and't shall go hard
But I will delve one yard below their mines
And blow them at the moon. O, 'tis most sweet
When in one line two crafts directly meet.
This man shall set me packing.
I'll lug the guts into the neighbour room.
Mother, good night. Indeed, this counsellor
Is now most still, most secret, and most grave,
Who was in life a foolish prating knave.
Come, sir, to draw toward an end with you.
Good night, mother.
         [*Exeunt severally*; HAMLET *tugging in* POLONIUS.]

# ACT IV

SCENE I——*Elsinore. The Castle.*

[*Enter* KING, QUEEN, ROSENCRANTZ, *and* GUILDENSTERN.]

KING: There's matter in these sighs, these profound heaves,
You must translate; 'tis fit we understand them.
Where is your son?

QUEEN: Bestow this place on us a little while.

[*Exeunt* ROSENCRANTZ *and* GUILDENSTERN.]
Ah, mine own lord, what have I seen to-night!

KING: What, Gertrude? How does Hamlet?

QUEEN: Mad as the sea and wind, when both contend
Which is the mightier. In his lawless fit,
Behind the arras hearing something stir,
Whips out his rapier, cries 'A rat, a rat!'
And in this brainish apprehension kills
The unseen good old man.

KING: O heavy deed!
It had been so with us had we been there.
His liberty is full of threats to all —
To you yourself, to us, to every one.
Alas, how shall this bloody deed be answer'd?
It will be laid to us, whose providence
Should have kept short, restrain'd, and out of haunt,
This mad young man. But so much was our love,
We would not understand what was most fit;
But, like the owner of a foul disease,
To keep it from divulging, let it feed
Even on the pith of life. Where is he gone?

QUEEN: To draw apart the body he hath kill'd;
O'er whom his very madness, like some ore
Among a mineral of metals base,
Shows itself pure: 'a weeps for what is done.

KING: O Gertrude, come away!
The sun no sooner shall the mountains touch
But we will ship him hence; and this vile deed
We must with all our majesty and skill
Both countenance and excuse. Ho Guildenstern!

[*Re-enter* ROSENCRANTZ *and* GUILDENSTERN.]
Friends, both go join you with some further aid:
Hamlet in madness hath Polonius slain,
And from his mother's closet hath he dragg'd him;
Go seek him out; speak fair, and bring the body
Into the chapel. I pray you haste in this.

[*Exeunt* ROSENCRANTZ *and* GUILDENSTERN.]
Come, Gertrude, we'll call up our wisest friends
And let them know both what we mean to do
And what's untimely done; so haply slander —

Whose whisper o'er the world's diameter,
As level as the cannon to his blank,
Transports his pois'ned shot — may miss our name,
And hit the woundless air. O, come away!
My soul is full of discord and dismay.                              *[Exeunt.]*

SCENE II ———— *Elsinore. The Castle.*

[*Enter* HAMLET.]

HAMLET: Safely stow'd.

GENTLEMEN: [*within*] Hamlet! Lord Hamlet!

HAMLET: But soft! What noise? Who calls on Hamlet? O, here they come!
        [*Enter* ROSENCRANTZ *and* GUILDENSTERN.]

ROSENCRANTZ: What have you done, my lord, with the dead body?

HAMLET: Compounded it with dust, whereto 'tis kin.

ROSENCRANTZ: Tell us where 'tis, that we may take it thence. And bear it to the
        chapel.

HAMLET: Do not believe it.

ROSENCRANTZ: Believe what?

HAMLET: That I can keep your counsel, and not mine own. Besides, to be demanded
        of a sponge — what replication should be made by the son of a king?

ROSENCRANTZ: Take you me for a sponge, my lord?

HAMLET: Ay, sir; that soaks up the King's countenance, his rewards, his authorities.
        But such officers do the King best service in the end: he keeps them, like an ape
        an apple in the corner of his jaw; first mouth'd to be last swallowed; when he
        needs what you have glean'd, it is but squeezing you and, sponge, you shall be
        dry again.

ROSENCRANTZ: I understand you not, my lord.

HAMLET: I am glad of it; a knavish speech sleeps in a foolish ear.

ROSENCRANTZ: My lord, you must tell us where the body is, and go with us to the
        King.

HAMLET: The body is with the King, but the King is not with the body. The King is a
        thing —

GUILDENSTERN: A thing, my lord!

HAMLET: Of nothing. Bring me to him. Hide fox, and all after.        *[Exeunt.]*

SCENE III ———— *Elsinore. The Castle.*

[*Enter* KING, *attended.*]

KING: I have sent to seek him, and to find the body.
      How dangerous is it that this man goes loose!
      Yet must not we put the strong law on him:
      He's lov'd of the distracted multitude,
      Who like not in their judgment but their eyes;
      And where 'tis so, th' offender's scourge is weigh'd,
      But never the offence. To bear all smooth and even,
      This sudden sending him away must seem
      Deliberate pause. Diseases desperate grown
      By desperate appliance are reliev'd,

Or not at all.

[*Enter* ROSENCRANTZ.]

How now! what hath befall'n?

ROSENCRANTZ: Where the dead body is bestow'd, my lord,
We cannot get from him.

KING: But where is he?

ROSENCRANTZ: Without, my lord; guarded, to know your pleasure.

KING: Bring him before us.

ROSENCRANTZ: Ho, Guildenstern! bring in the lord.

[*Enter* HAMLET *and* GUILDENSTERN.]

KING: Now, Hamlet, where's Polonius?

HAMLET: At supper.

KING: At supper! Where?

HAMLET: Not where he eats, but where 'a is eaten; a certain convocation of politic
worms are e'en at him. Your worm is your only emperor for diet: we fat all
creatures else to fat us, and we fat ourselves for maggots; your fat king and your
lean beggar is but variable service — two dishes, but to one table. That's the
end.

KING: Alas, alas!

HAMLET: A man may fish with the worm that hath eat of a king, and eat of the fish
that hath fed of that worm.

KING: What dost thou mean by this?

HAMLET: Nothing but to show you how a king may go a progress through the guts of
a beggar.

KING: Where is Polonius?

HAMLET: In heaven; send thither to see; if your messenger find him not there, seek
him i' th' other place yourself. But if, indeed, you find him not within this
month, you shall nose him as you go up the stairs into the lobby.

KING: [*to attendants*] Go seek him there.

HAMLET: 'A will stay till you come.                          [*Exeunt attendants.*]

KING: Hamlet, this deed, for thine especial safety —
Which we do tender, as we dearly grieve
For that which thou hast done — must send thee hence
With fiery quickness. Therefore prepare thyself;
The bark is ready, and the wind at help,
Th' associates tend, and everything is bent
For England.

HAMLET: For England!

KING: Ay, Hamlet.

HAMLET: Good!

KING: So is it, if thou knew'st our purposes.

HAMLET: I see a cherub that sees them. But, come; for England! Farewell, dear
mother.

KING: Thy loving father, Hamlet.

HAMLET: My mother: father and mother is man and wife; man and wife is one flesh;
and so, my mother. Come, for England.                              [*Exit.*]

KING: Follow him at foot; tempt him with speed aboard;
Delay it not; I'll have him hence to-night.

Away! for everything is seal'd and done
That else leans on th' affair. Pray you make haste.
        [*Exeunt all but the* KING.]
And, England, if my love thou hold'st at aught —
As my great power thereof may give thee sense,
Since yet thy cicatrice looks raw and red
After the Danish sword, and thy free awe
Pays homage to us — thou mayst not coldly set
Our sovereign process; which imports at full,
By letters congruing to that effect,
The present death of Hamlet. Do it, England:
For like the hectic in my blood he rages,
And thou must cure me. Till I know 'tis done,
Howe'er my haps, my joys were ne'er begun.                    [*Exit.*]


SCENE IV——*A plain in Denmark.*

        [*Enter* FORTINBRAS *with his army over the stage.*]
FORTINBRAS:  Go, Captain, from me greet the Danish king.
        Tell him that by his license Fortinbras
        Craves the conveyance of a promis'd march
        Over his kingdom. You know the rendezvous.
        If that his Majesty would aught with us,
        We shall express our duty in his eye;
        And let him know so.
CAPTAIN:  I will do't, my lord.
FORTINBRAS:  Go softly on.                    [*Exeunt all but the* CAPTAIN.]
        [*Enter* HAMLET, ROSENCRANTZ, GUILDENSTERN, *and others.*]
HAMLET:  Good sir, whose powers are these?
CAPTAIN:  They are of Norway, sir.
HAMLET:  How purpos'd, sir, I pray you?
CAPTAIN:  Against some part of Poland.
HAMLET:  Who commands them, sir?
CAPTAIN:  The nephew to old Norway, Fortinbras.
HAMLET:  Goes it against the main of Poland, sir,
        Or for some frontier?
CAPTAIN:  Truly to speak, and with no addition,
        We go to gain a little patch of ground
        That hath in it no profit but the name.
        To pay five ducats, five, I would not farm it;
        Nor will it yield to Norway or the Pole
        A ranker rate should it be sold in fee.
HAMLET:  Why, then the Polack never will defend it.
CAPTAIN:  Yes, it is already garrison'd.
HAMLET:  Two thousand souls and twenty thousand ducats
        Will not debate the question of this straw.
        This is th' imposthume of much wealth and peace,
        That inward breaks, and shows no cause without

Why the man dies. I humbly thank you, sir.
CAPTAIN: God buy you, sir.                                                    ]*Exit.*]
ROSENCRANTZ: Will't please you go, my lord?
HAMLET: I'll be with you straight. Go a little before.
      [*Exeunt all but* HAMLET.]
      How all occasions do inform against me,
      And spur my dull revenge! What is a man,
      If his chief good and market of his time
      Be but to sleep and feed? A beast, no more!
      Sure he that made us with such large discourse,
      Looking before and after, gave us not
      That capability and godlike reason
      To fust in us unus'd. Now, whether it be
      Bestial oblivion, or some craven scruple
      Of thinking too precisely on th' event —
      A thought which, quarter'd, hath but one part wisdom
      And ever three parts coward — I do not know
      Why yet I live to say 'This thing's to do,'
      Sith I have cause, and will, and strength, and means,
      To do't. Examples gross as earth exhort me:
      Witness this army, of such mass and charge,
      Led by a delicate and tender prince,
      Whose spirit, with divine ambition puff'd,
      Makes mouths at the invisible event,
      Exposing what is mortal and unsure
      To all that fortune, death, and danger dare,
      Even for an egg-shell. Rightly to be great
      Is not to stir without great argument,
      But greatly to find quarrel in a straw,
      When honour's at the stake. How stand I, then,
      That have a father kill'd, a mother stain'd,
      Excitements of my reason and my blood,
      And let all sleep, while to my shame I see
      The imminent death of twenty thousand men
      That, for a fantasy and trick of fame,
      Go to their graves like beds, fight for a plot
      Whereon the numbers cannot try the cause,
      Which is not tomb enough and continent
      To hide the slain? O, from this time forth,
      My thoughts be bloody, or be nothing worth!                    [*Exit.*]

SCENE V——*Elsinore. The Castle.*

      [*Enter* QUEEN, HORATIO, *and a* GENTLEMAN.]
QUEEN: I will not speak with her.
GENTLEMAN: She is importunate, indeed distract.
      Her mood will needs be pitied.

QUEEN: What would she have?

GENTLEMAN: She speaks much of her father; says she hears
There's tricks i' th' world, and hems, and beats her heart;
Spurns enviously at straws; speaks things in doubt,
That carry but half sense. Her speech is nothing,
Yet the unshaped use of it doth move
The hearers to collection; they yawn at it,
And botch the words up fit to their own thoughts;
Which, as her winks and nods and gestures yield them,
Indeed would make one think there might be thought,
Though nothing sure, yet much unhappily.

HORATIO: 'Twere good she were spoken with; for she may strew
Dangerous conjectures in ill-breeding minds.

QUEEN: Let her come in.                            [*Exit* GENTLEMAN.]
[*aside*] To my sick soul, as sin's true nature is,
Each toy seems prologue to some great amiss.
So full of artless jealousy is guilt,
It spills itself in fearing to be spilt.
      [*Enter* OPHELIA *distracted.*]

OPHELIA: Where is the beauteous Majesty of Denmark?

QUEEN: How now, Ophelia!

OPHELIA: [*sings*]
                    How should I your true love know
                       From another one?
                    By his cockle hat and staff,
                       And his sandal shoon.

QUEEN: Alas, sweet lady, what imports this song?

OPHELIA: Say you? Nay, pray you, mark.                    [*sings*]
                    He is dead and gone, lady,
                       He is dead and gone;
                    At his head a grass-green turf,
                       At his heels a stone.

      O, ho!

QUEEN: Nay, but, Ophelia —

OPHELIA: Pray you, mark.                                   [*sings*]
                    White his shroud as the mountain snow —
         [*Enter* KING.]

QUEEN: Alas, look here, my lord.

OPHELIA:                        Larded with sweet flowers;
                    Which bewept to the grave did not go
                          With true-love showers.

KING: How do you, pretty lady?

OPHELIA: Well, God dild you! They say the owl was a baker's daughter. Lord, we
know that we are, but know not what we may be. God be at your table!

KING: Conceit upon her father.

OPHELIA: Pray let's have no words of this; but when they ask you what it means, say
you this:                                                  [*sings*]

> To-morrow is Saint Valentine's day,
> All in the morning betime,
> And I a maid at your window,
> To be your Valentine.
> Then up he rose, and donn'd his clothes,
> And dupp'd the chamber-door;
> Let in the maid, that out a maid
> Never departed more.

KING: Pretty Ophelia!

OPHELIA: Indeed, la, without an oath, I'll make an end on't.       *[sings]*

> By Gis and by Saint Charity,
> Alack, and fie for shame!
> Young men will do't, if they come to't;
> By Cock, they are to blame.
> Quoth she 'Before you tumbled me,
> You promis'd me to wed.'

He answers:

> 'So would I 'a done, by yonder sun,
> An thou hadst not come to my bed.'

KING: How long hath she been thus?

OPHELIA: I hope all will be well. We must be patient; but I cannot choose but weep to think they would lay him i' th' cold ground. My brother shall know of it; and so I thank you for your good counsel. Come, my coach! Good night, ladies; good night, sweet ladies, good night, good night.

    *[Exit.]*

KING: Follow her close; give her good watch, I pray you.

    *[Exeunt* HORATIO *and* GENTLEMAN.*]*

> O, this is the poison of deep grief; it springs
> All from her father's death. And now behold—
> O Gertrude, Gertude!
> When sorrows come, they come not single spies,
> But in battalions! First, her father slain;
> Next, your son gone, and he most violent author
> Of his own just remove; the people muddied,
> Thick and unwholesome in their thoughts and whispers
> For good Polonius' death; and we have done but greenly
> In hugger-mugger to inter him; poor Ophelia
> Divided from herself and her fair judgment,
> Without the which we are pictures, or mere beasts;
> Last, and as much containing as all these,
> Her brother is in secret come from France;
> Feeds on his wonder, keeps himself in clouds,
> And wants not buzzers to infect his ear
> With pestilent speeches of his father's death;
> Wherein necessity, of matter beggar'd,
> Will nothing stick our person to arraign
> In ear and ear. O my dear Gertrude, this,

Like to a murd'ring piece, in many places
Gives me superfluous death.                                    [*A noise within.*]
QUEEN: Alack, what noise is this?
KING: Attend!
        [*Enter a* GENTLEMAN.]
Where are my Switzers? Let them guard the door.
What is the matter?
GENTLEMAN: Save yourself, my lord:
        The ocean, overpeering of his list,
        Eats not the flats with more impetuous haste
        Than young Laertes, in a riotous head,
        O'erbears your officers. The rabble call him lord;
        And, as the world were now but to begin,
        Antiquity forgot, custom not known,
        The ratifiers and props of every word,
        They cry 'Choose we; Laertes shall be king.'
        Caps, hands, and tongues, applaud it to the clouds,
        'Laertes shall be king, Laertes king.'
QUEEN: How cheerfully on the false trail they cry!
        [*Noise within.*]
        O, this is counter, you false Danish dogs!
KING: The doors are broke.
        [*Enter* LAERTES, *with others, in arms.*]
LAERTES: Where is this king? — Sirs, stand you all without.
ALL: No, let's come in.
LAERTES: I pray you give me leave.
ALL: We will, we will.
        [*Exeunt.*]
LAERTES: I thank you. Keep the door. — O thou vile king,
        Give me my father!
QUEEN: Calmly, good Laertes.
LAERTES: That drop of blood that's calm proclaims me bastard;
        Cries cuckold to my father; brands the harlot
        Even here, between the chaste unsmirched brow
        Of my true mother.
KING: What is the cause, Laertes,
        That thy rebellion looks so giant-like?
        Let him go, Gertrude; do not fear our person:
        There's such divinity doth hedge a king
        That treason can but peep to what it would,
        Acts little of his will. Tell me, Laertes,
        Why thou art thus incens'd. Let him go, Gertrude.
        Speak, man.
LAERTES: Where is my father?
KING: Dead.
QUEEN: But not by him.
KING: Let him demand his fill.

LAERTES: How came he dead? I'll not be juggled with.
　　　To hell, allegiance! Vows, to the blackest devil!
　　　Conscience and grace, to the profoundest pit!
　　　I dare damnation. To this point I stand,
　　　That both the worlds I give to negligence,
　　　Let come what comes; only I'll be reveng'd
　　　Most thoroughly for my father.
KING: Who shall stay you?
LAERTES: My will, not all the world's.
　　　And for my means, I'll husband them so well
　　　They shall go far with little.
KING: Good Laertes,
　　　If you desire to know the certainty
　　　Of your dear father, is't writ in your revenge
　　　That, swoopstake, you will draw both friend and foe,
　　　Winner and loser?
LAERTES: None but his enemies.
KING: Will you know them, then?
LAERTES: To his good friends thus wide I'll ope my arms
　　　And, like the kind life-rend'ring pelican,
　　　Repast them with my blood.
KING: Why, now you speak
　　　Like a good child and a true gentleman.
　　　That I am guiltless of your father's death,
　　　And am most sensibly in grief for it,
　　　It shall as level to your judgment 'pear
　　　As day does to your eye.

　　　　　　　　　　　　[A *noise within:* 'Let her come in.']

LAERTES: How now! What noise is that?
　　　　[*Re-enter* OPHELIA.]
　　　O, heat dry up my brains! tears seven times salt
　　　Burn out the sense and virtue of mine eye!
　　　By heaven, thy madness shall be paid with weight
　　　Till our scale turn the beam. O rose of May!
　　　Dear maid, kind sister, sweet Ophelia!
　　　O heavens! is't possible a young maid's wits
　　　Should be as mortal as an old man's life?
　　　Nature is fine in love; and where 'tis fine
　　　It sends some precious instance of itself
　　　After the thing it loves.
OPHELIA: [*sings*]
　　　　　　　　They bore him barefac'd on the bier;
　　　　　　　　Hey non nonny, nonny, hey nonny;
　　　　　　　　And in his grave rain'd many a tear—
　　　Fare you well, my dove!
LAERTES: Hadst thou thy wits, and didst persuade revenge,
　　　It could not move thus.

OPHELIA: You must sing 'A-down, a-down,' an you call him a-down-a. O, how the
wheel becomes it! It is the false steward, that stole his master's daughter.

LAERTES: This nothing's more than matter.

OPHELIA: There's rosemary, that's for remembrance; pray you, love, remember.
And there is pansies, that's for thoughts.

LAERTES: A document in madness—thoughts and remembrance fitted.

OPHELIA: There's fennel for you, and columbines. There's rue for you; and here's
some for me. We may call it herb of grace a Sundays. O, you must wear your
rue with a difference. There's a daisy. I would give you some violets, but they
wither'd all when my father died. They say 'a made a good end.

[*sings*] For bonny sweet Robin is all my joy.

LAERTES: Thought and affliction, passion, hell itself,
She turns to favour and to prettiness.

OPHELIA: [*sings*]

> And will 'a not come again?
> And will 'a not come again?
>    No, no, he is dead,
>    Go to thy death-bed,
> He never will come again.
>
>
> His beard was as white as snow,
> All flaxen was his poll;
>    He is gone, he is gone,
>    And we cast away moan:
> God-a-mercy on his soul!

And of all Christian souls, I pray God. God buy you.
[*Exit.*]

LAERTES: Do you see this, O God?

KING: Laertes, I must commune with your grief,
Or you deny me right. Go but apart,
Make choice of whom your wisest friends you will,
And they shall hear and judge 'twixt you and me.
If by direct or by collateral hand
They find us touch'd, we will our kingdom give,
Our crown, our life, and all that we call ours,
To you in satisfaction; but if not,
Be you content to lend your patience to us,
And we shall jointly labour with your soul
To give it due content.

LAERTES: Let this be so.
His means of death, his obscure funeral—
No trophy, sword, nor hatchment, o'er his bones,
No noble rite nor formal ostentation—
Cry to be heard, as 'twere from heaven to earth,
That I must call't in question.

KING: So you shall;
And where th' offence is, let the great axe fall.
I pray you go with me.                                                          [*Exeunt.*]

SCENE VI———*Elsinore. The Castle.*

[*Enter* HORATIO *with an* ATTENDANT.]

HORATIO:  What are they that would speak with me?

ATTENDANT:  Sea-faring men, sir; they say they have letters for you.

HORATIO:  Let them come in.                              [*Exit* ATTENDANT.]
          I do not know from what part of the world
          I should be greeted, if not from Lord Hamlet.
                  [*Enter sailors.*]

SAILOR:  God bless you, sir.

HORATIO:  Let Him bless thee too.

SAILOR:  'A shall, sir, an't please Him. There's a letter for you, sir; it came from th'
         ambassador that was bound for England — if your name be Horatio, as I am let
         to know it is.

HORATIO:  [*reads*] 'Horatio, when thou shalt have overlook'd this, give these fellows
          some means to the King: they have letters for him. Ere we were two days old at
          sea, a pirate of very warlike appointment gave us chase. Finding ourselves too
          slow of sail, we put on a compelled valour; and in the grapple I boarded them.
          On the instant they got clear of our ship; so I alone became their prisoner.
          They have dealt with me like thieves of mercy; but they knew what they did; I
          am to do a good turn for them. Let the King have the letters I have sent; and
          repair thou to me with as much speed as thou wouldest fly death. I have words
          to speak in thine ear will make thee dumb; yet are they much too light for the
          bore of the matter. These good fellows will bring thee where I am. Rosen-
          crantz and Guildenstern hold their course for England; of them I have much
          to tell thee. Farewell.
                                            'He that thou knowest thine, HAMLET.'
          Come, I will give you way for these your letters,
          And do't the speedier that you may direct me
          To him from whom you brought them.                          [*Exeunt.*]

SCENE VII———*Elsinore. The Castle.*

[*Enter* KING *and* LAERTES.]

KING:  Now must your conscience my acquittance seal,
       And you must put me in your heart for friend,
       Sith you have heard, and with a knowing ear,
       That he which hath your noble father slain
       Pursu'd my life.

LAERTES:  It well appears. But tell me
          Why you proceeded not against these feats,
          So crimeful and so capital in nature,
          As by your safety, wisdom, all things else,
          You mainly were stirr'd up.

KING:  O, for two special reasons,
       Which may to you, perhaps, seem much unsinew'd,
       But yet to me th' are strong. The Queen his mother
       Lives almost by his looks; and for myself,
       My virtue or my plague, be it either which —

She is so conjunctive to my life and soul
That, as the star moves not but in his sphere,
I could not but by her. The other motive,
Why to a public count I might not go,
Is the great love the general gender bear him;
Who, dipping all his faults in their affection,
Work like the spring that turneth wood to stone,
Convert his gyves to graces; so that my arrows,
Too slightly timber'd for so loud a wind,
Would have reverted to my bow again,
But not where I have aim'd them.

LAERTES: And so have I a noble father lost;
A sister driven into desp'rate terms,
Whose worth, if praises may go back again,
Stood challenger on mount of all the age
For her perfections. But my revenge will come.

KING: Break not your sleeps for that. You must not think
That we are made of stuff so flat and dull
That we can let our beard be shook with danger,
And think it pastime. You shortly shall hear more.
I lov'd your father, and we love our self;
And that, I hope, will teach you to imagine—
[*Enter a* MESSENGER *with letters.*]
How now! What news?

MESSENGER: Letters, my lord, from Hamlet:
These to your Majesty; this to the Queen.

KING: From Hamlet! Who brought them?

MESSENGER: Sailors, my lord, they say; I saw them not.
They were given me by Claudio; he receiv'd them
Of him that brought them.

KING: Laertes, you shall hear them.
Leave us.                                        [*Exit* MESSENGER.]
[*reads*] 'High and Mighty. You shall know I am set naked on your kingdom.
To-morrow shall I beg leave to see your kingly eyes; when I shall, first asking
your pardon thereunto, recount the occasion of my sudden and more strange
return.

HAMLET.'

What should this mean? Are all the rest come back?
Or is it some abuse, and no such thing?

LAERTES: Know you the hand?

KING: 'Tis Hamlet's character. 'Naked'!
And in a postscript here, he says 'alone.'
Can you devise me?

LAERTES: I am lost in it, my lord. But let him come;
It warms the very sickness in my heart
That I shall live and tell him to his teeth
'Thus didest thou.'

KING: If it be so, Laertes—

As how should it be so, how otherwise? —
Will you be rul'd by me?
LAERTES: Ay, my lord;
So you will not o'errule me to a peace.
KING: To thine own peace. If he be now return'd,
As checking at his voyage, and that he means
No more to undertake it, I will work him
To an exploit now ripe in my device,
Under the which he shall not choose but fall;
And for his death, no wind of blame shall breathe;
But even his mother shall uncharge the practice
And call it accident.
LAERTES: My lord, I will be rul'd
The rather, if you could devise it so
That I might be the organ.
KING:                                        It falls right.
You have been talk'd of since your travel much,
And that in Hamlet's hearing, for a quality
Wherein they say you shine. Your sum of parts
Did not together pluck such envy from him
As did that one; and that, in my regard,
Of the unworthiest siege.
LAERTES: What part is that, my lord?
KING: A very riband in the cap of youth,
Yet needful too; for youth no less becomes
The light and careless livery that it wears
Than settled age his sables and his weeds,
Importing health and graveness. Two months since
Here was a gentleman of Normandy —
I have seen myself, and serv'd against, the French,
And they can well on horseback; but this gallant
Had witchcraft in't; he grew into his seat,
And to such wondrous doing brought his horse,
As had he been incorps'd and demi-natur'd
With the brave beast. So far he topp'd my thought,
That I, in forgery of shapes and tricks,
Come short of what he did.
LAERTES:                              A Norman was't?
KING: A Norman.
LAERTES:          Upon my life, Lamord.
KING:                                        The very same.
LAERTES: I know him well. He is the brooch indeed
And gem of all the nation.
KING: He made confession of you;
And gave you such a masterly report
For art and exercise in your defence,
And for your rapier most especial,
That he cried out 'twould be a sight indeed

If one could match you. The scrimers of their nation
He swore had neither motion, guard, nor eye,
If you oppos'd them. Sir, this report of his
Did Hamlet so envenom with his envy
That he could nothing do but wish and beg
Your sudden coming o'er, to play with you.
Now out of this —
LAERTES: What out of this, my lord?
KING: Laertes, was your father dear to you?
Or are you like the painting of a sorrow,
A face without a heart?
LAERTES:                          Why ask you this?
KING: Not that I think you did not love your father;
But that I know love is begun by time,
And that I see, in passages of proof,
Time qualifies the spark and fire of it.
There lives within the very flame of love
A kind of wick or snuff that will abate it;
And nothing is at a like goodness still;
For goodness, growing to a pleurisy,
Dies in his own too much. That we would do,
We should do when we would; for this 'would' changes,
And hath abatements and delays as many
As there are tongues, are hands, are accidents;
And then this 'should' is like a spendthrift's sigh
That hurts by easing. But to the quick of th' ulcer:
Hamlet comes back; what would you undertake
To show yourself in deed your father's son
More than in words?
LAERTES: To cut his throat i' th' church.
KING: No place, indeed, should murder sanctuarize;
Revenge should have no bounds. But, good Laertes,
Will you do this? Keep close within your chamber.
Hamlet return'd shall know you are come home.
We'll put on those shall praise your excellence,
And set a double varnish on the fame
The Frenchman gave you; bring you, in fine, together,
And wager on your heads. He, being remiss,
Most generous, and free from all contriving,
Will not peruse the foils; so that with ease
Or with a little shuffling, you may choose
A sword unbated, and, in a pass of practice,
Requite him for your father.
LAERTES:                          I will do't;
And for that purpose I'll anoint my sword.
I bought an unction of a mountebank,
So mortal that but dip a knife in it,
Where it draws blood no cataplasm so rare,

Collected from all simples that have virtue
Under the moon, can save the thing from death
That is but scratch'd withal. I'll touch my point
With this contagion, that, if I gall him slightly,
It may be death.

KING:                              Let's further think of this;
Weigh what convenience both of time and means
May fit us to our shape. If this should fail,
And that our drift look through our bad performance,
'Twere better not assay'd, therefore this project
Should have a back or second, that might hold
If this did blast in proof. Soft! let me see.
We'll make a solemn wager on your cunnings —
I ha't.
When in your motion you are hot and dry —
As make your bouts more violent to that end —
And that he calls for drink, I'll have preferr'd him
A chalice for the nonce; whereon but sipping,
If he by chance escape your venom'd stuck,
Our purpose may hold there. Buy stay; what noise?
       [*Enter* QUEEN.]
QUEEN: One woe doth tread upon another's heel,
So fast they follow. Your sister's drown'd, Laertes.
LAERTES: Drown'd? O, where?
QUEEN: There is a willow grows aslant the brook
That shows his hoar leaves in the glassy stream;
Therewith fantastic garlands did she make
Of crowflowers, nettles, daisies, and long purples
That liberal shepherds give a grosser name,
But our cold maids do dead men's fingers call them.
There, on the pendent boughs her coronet weeds
Clamb'ring to hang, an envious sliver broke;
When down her weedy trophies and herself
Fell in the weeping brook. Her clothes spread wide
And, mermaid-like, awhile they bore her up;
Which time she chanted snatches of old lauds,
As one incapable of her own distress,
Or like a creature native and indued
Unto that element; but long it could not be
Till that her garments, heavy with their drink,
Pull'd the poor wretch from her melodious lay
To muddy death.
LAERTES:                         Alas, then she is drown'd!
QUEEN: Drown'd, drown'd.
LAERTES: Too much of water hast thou, poor Ophelia,
And therefore I forbid my tears; but yet
It is our trick; nature her custom holds,
Let shame say what it will. When these are gone,

The woman will be out. Adieu, my lord.
I have a speech o' fire that fain would blaze
But that this folly douts it.                                                    [*Exit.*]
KING: Let's follow, Gertrude.
How much I had to do to calm his rage!
Now fear I this will give it start again;
Therefore let's follow.                                                        [*Exeunt.*]


# ACT V

SCENE I———*Elsinore. A churchyard.*

[*Enter two* CLOWNS *with spades and picks.*]

FIRST CLOWN: Is she to be buried in Christian burial when she wilfully seeks her own
salvation?

SECOND CLOWN: I tell thee she is; therefore make her grave straight. The crowner
hath sat on her, and finds it Christian burial.

FIRST CLOWN: How can that be, unless she drown'd herself in her own defence?

SECOND CLOWN: Why, 'tis found so.

FIRST CLOWN: It must be 'se offendendo'; it cannot be else. For here lies the point: if
I drown myself wittingly, it argues an act; and an act hath three branches — it is
to act, to do, to perform; argal, she drown'd herself wittingly.

SECOND CLOWN: Nay, but hear you, Goodman Delver.

FIRST CLOWN: Give me leave. Here lies the water; good. Here stands the man; good.
If the man go to this water and drown himself, it is, will he, nill he, he
goes — mark you that; but if the water come to him and drown him, he drowns
not himself. Argal, he that is not guilty of his own death shortens not his own
life.

SECOND CLOWN: But is this law?

FIRST CLOWN: Ay, marry, is't; crowner's quest law.

SECOND CLOWN: Will you ha' the truth an't? If this had not been a gentlewoman, she
should have been buried out a Christian burial.

FIRST CLOWN: Why, there thou say'st; and the more pity that great folk should have
count'nance in this world to drown or hang themselves more than their even
Christen. Come, my spade. There is no ancient gentlemen but gard'ners,
ditchers, and grave-makers; they hold up Adam's profession.

SECOND CLOWN: Was he a gentleman?

FIRST CLOWN: 'A was the first that ever bore arms.

SECOND CLOWN: Why, he had none.

FIRST CLOWN: What, art a heathen? How dost thou understand the Scripture? The
Scripture says Adam digg'd. Could he dig without arms? I'll put another
question to thee. If thou answerest me not to the purpose, confess thyself —

SECOND CLOWN: Go to.

FIRST CLOWN: What is he that builds stronger than either the mason, the shipwright,
or the carpenter?

SECOND CLOWN: The gallows-maker; for that frame outlives a thousand tenants.

FIRST CLOWN: I like thy wit well; in good faith the gallows does well; but how does it
well? It does well to those that do ill. Now thou dost ill to say the gallows is built

stronger than the church; argal, the gallows may do well to thee. To't again, come.

SECOND CLOWN: Who builds stronger than a mason, a shipwright, or a carpenter?

FIRST CLOWN: Ay, tell me that, and unyoke.

SECOND CLOWN: Marry, now I can tell.

FIRST CLOWN: To 't.

SECOND CLOWN: Mass, I cannot tell.

[*Enter* HAMLET *and* HORATIO, *afar off.*]

FIRST CLOWN: Cudgel thy brains no more about it, for your dull ass will not mend his pace with beating; and when you are ask'd this question next, say 'a grave-maker': the house he makes lasts till doomsday. Go, get thee to Yaughan; fetch me a stoup of liquor. [*Exit* SECOND CLOWN.]

[*digs and sings*]

> In youth, when I did love, did love
> Methought it was very sweet,
> To contract-o-the time for-a my behove,
> O, methought there-a-was nothing-a meet.

HAMLET: Has this fellow no feeling of his business, that 'a sings in grave-making?

HORATIO: Custom hath made it in him a property of easiness.

HAMLET: 'Tis e'en so; the hand of little employment hath the daintier sense.

FIRST CLOWN: [*sings*]

> But age, with his stealing steps,
> Hath clawed me in his clutch,
> And hath shipped me intil the land,
> As if I had never been such.

[*throws up a skull*]

HAMLET: That skull had a tongue in it, and could sing once. How the knave jowls it to the ground, as if 'twere Cain's jawbone, that did the first murder! This might be the pate of a politician, which this ass now o'erreaches; one that would circumvent God, might it not?

HORATIO: It might, my lord.

HAMLET: Or of a courtier; which could say 'Good morrow, sweet lord! How dost thou, sweet lord?' This might be my Lord Such-a-one, that praised my Lord Such-a-one's horse, when 'a meant to beg it — might it not?

HORATIO: Ay, my lord.

HAMLET: Why, e'en so; and now my Lady Worm's, chapless, and knock'd about the mazard with a sexton's spade. Here's fine revolution, an we had the trick to see't. Did these bones cost no more the breeding but to play at loggats with them? Mine ache to think on't.

FIRST CLOWN: [*sings*]

> A pick-axe and a spade, a spade
> For and a shrouding sheet:
> O, a pit of clay for to be made
> For such a guest is meet.

[*throws up another skull*]

HAMLET: There's another. Why may not that be the skull of a lawyer? Where be his guiddities now, his quillets, his cases, his tenures, and his tricks? Why does he suffer this rude knave now to knock him about the sconce with a dirty shovel, and will not tell him of his action of battery? Hum! This fellow might be in's time a great buyer of land, with his statutes, his recognizances, his fines, his double vouchers, his recoveries. Is this the fine of his fines, and the recovery of his recoveries, to have his fine pate full of fine dirt? Will his vouchers vouch him no more of his purchases, and double ones too, than the length and breadth of a pair of indentures? The very conveyances of his lands will scarcely lie in this box; and must th' inheritor himself have no more, ha?

HORATIO: Not a jot more, my lord.

HAMLET: Is not parchment made of sheep-skins?

HORATIO: Ay, my lord, and of calves' skins too.

HAMLET: They are sheep and calves which seek out assurance in that. I will speak to this fellow. Whose grave's this, sirrah?

FIRST CLOWN: Mine, sir.                                                                     [*sings*]
                          O, a pit of clay for to be made
                          For such a guest is meet.

HAMLET: I think it be thine indeed, for thou liest in't.

FIRST CLOWN: You lie out on't, sir, and therefore 'tis not yours. For my part, I do not lie in't, yet it is mine.

HAMLET: Thou dost lie in't, to be in't and say it is thine; 'tis for the dead, not for the quick; therefore thou liest.

FIRST CLOWN: 'Tis a quick lie, sir; 'twill away again from me to you.

HAMLET: What man dost thou dig it for?

FIRST CLOWN: For no man, sir.

HAMLET: What woman, then?

FIRST CLOWN: For none neither.

HAMLET: Who is to be buried in't?

FIRST CLOWN: One that was a woman, sir; but, rest her soul, she's dead.

HAMLET: How absolute the knave is! We must speak by the card, or equivocation will undo us. By the Lord, Horatio, this three years I have took note of it: the age is grown so picked that the toe of the peasant comes so near the heel of the courtier, he galls his kibe. How long hast thou been a grave-maker?

FIRST CLOWN: Of all the days i' th' year, I came to't that day that our last King Hamlet overcame Fortinbras.

HAMLET: How long is that since?

FIRST CLOWN: Cannot you tell that? Every fool can tell that: it was that very day that young Hamlet was born—he that is mad, and sent into England.

HAMLET: Ay, marry, why was he sent into England?

FIRST CLOWN: Why, because 'a was mad: 'a shall recover his wits there; or, if 'a do not, 'tis no great matter there.

HAMLET: Why?

FIRST CLOWN: 'Twill not be seen in him there: there the men are as mad as he.

HAMLET: How came he mad?

FIRST CLOWN: Very strangely, they say.

HAMLET: How strangely?

FIRST CLOWN: Faith, e'en with losing his wits.

HAMLET: Upon what ground?

FIRST CLOWN: Why, here in Denmark. I have been sexton here, man and boy, thirty years.

HAMLET: How long will a man lie i' th' earth ere he rot?

FIRST CLOWN: Faith, if 'a be not rotten before 'a die — as we have many pocky corses now-a-days that will scarce hold the laying in — 'a will last you some eight year or nine year. A tanner will last you nine year.

HAMLET: Why he more than another?

FIRST CLOWN: Why, sir, his hide is so tann'd with his trade that 'a will keep out water a great while; and your water is a sore decayer of your whoreson dead body. Here's a skull now; this skull has lien you i' th' earth three and twenty years.

HAMLET: Whose was it?

FIRST CLOWN: A whoreson mad fellow's it was. Whose do you think it was?

HAMLET: Nay, I know not.

FIRST CLOWN: A pestilence on him for a mad rogue! 'A poured a flagon of Rhenish on my head once. This same skull, sir, was, sir, Yorick's skull, the King's jester.

HAMLET: This?

FIRST CLOWN: E'en that.

HAMLET: Let me see. [*takes the skull*] Alas, poor Yorick! I knew him, Horatio: a fellow of infinite jest, of most excellent fancy; he hath borne me on his back a thousand times. And now how abhorred in my imagination it is! My gorge rises at it. Here hung those lips that I have kiss'd I know not how oft. Where be your gibes now, your gambols, your songs, your flashes of merriment that were wont to set the table on a roar? Not one now to mock your own grinning — quite chap-fall'n? Now get you to my lady's chamber, and tell her, let her paint an inch thick, to this favour she must come; make her laugh at that. Prithee, Horatio, tell me one thing.

HORATIO: What's that, my lord?

HAMLET: Dost thou think Alexander look'd a this fashion i' th' earth?

HORATIO: E'en so.

HAMLET: And smelt so? Pah! [*throws down the skull*]

HORATIO: E'en so, my lord.

HAMLET: To what base uses we may return, Horatio! Why may not imagination trace the noble dust of Alexander till 'a find it stopping a bung-hole?

HORATIO: 'Twere to consider too curiously to consider so.

HAMLET: No, faith, not a jot; but to follow him thither with modesty enough, and likelihood to lead it, as thus: Alexander died, Alexander was buried, Alexander returneth to dust; the dust is earth; of earth we make loam, and why of that loam whereto he was converted might they not stop a beer-barrel?
> Imperious Caesar, dead and turn'd to clay,
> Might stop a hole to keep the wind away.
> O, that that earth which kept the world in awe
> Should patch a wall t' expel the winter's flaw!
But soft! but soft! awhile. Here comes the King.
[*Enter the* KING, QUEEN, LAERTES, *in funeral procession after the coffin, with* PRIEST *and* LORDS *attendant.*]
The Queen, the courtiers. Who is this they follow?
And with such maimed rites? This doth betoken
The corse they follow did with desperate hand
Fordo it own life. 'Twas of some estate.
Couch we awhile and mark. [*retiring with* HORATIO]

LAERTES: What ceremony else?

HAMLET: That is Laertes, a very noble youth. Mark.

LAERTES: What ceremony else?

PRIEST: Her obsequies have been so far enlarg'd
   As we have warrantise. Her death was doubtful;
   And, but that great command o'ersways the order,
   She should in ground unsanctified have lodg'd
   Till the last trumpet; for charitable prayers,
   Shards, flints, and pebbles, should be thrown on her;
   Yet here she is allow'd her virgin crants,
   Her maiden strewments, and the bringing home
   Of bell and burial.

LAERTES: Must there no more be done?

PRIEST: No more be done.
   We should profane the service of the dead
   To sing sage requiem and such rest to her
   As to peace-parted souls.

LAERTES: Lay her i' th' earth;
   And from her fair and unpolluted flesh
   May violets spring! I tell thee, churlish priest,
   A minist'ring angel shall my sister be
   When thou liest howling.

HAMLET: What, the fair Ophelia!

QUEEN: Sweets to the sweet; farewell! [*scattering flowers*]
   I hop'd thou shouldst have been my Hamlet's wife;
   I thought thy bride-bed to have deck'd, sweet maid,
   And not have strew'd thy grave.

LAERTES:        O, treble woe
   Fall ten times treble on that cursed head
   Whose wicked deed thy most ingenious sense
   Depriv'd thee of! Hold off the earth awhile,
   Till I have caught her once more in mine arms.
    [*leaps into the grave*]
   Now pile your dust upon the quick and dead,
   Till of this flat a mountain you have made
   T' o'er-top old Pelion or the skyish head
   Of blue Olympus.

HAMLET: [*advancing*] What is he whose grief
   Bears such an emphasis, whose phrase of sorrow
   Conjures the wand'ring stars, and makes them stand
   Like wonder-wounded hearers? This is I,
   Hamlet, the Dane.         [*leaps into the grave*]

LAERTES: The devil take thy soul! [*grappling with him*]

HAMLET: Thou pray'st not well.
   I prithee take thy fingers from my throat;
   For, though I am not splenitive and rash,
   Yet have I in me something dangerous,
   Which let thy wiseness fear. Hold off thy hand.

KING: Pluck them asunder.

QUEEN: Hamlet! Hamlet!

ALL: Gentlemen!

HORATIO: Good my lord, be quiet.

[*The attendants part them, and they come out of the grave.*]

HAMLET: Why, I will fight with him upon this theme
Until my eyelids will no longer wag.

QUEEN: O my son, what theme?

HAMLET: I lov'd Ophelia: forty thousand brothers
Could not, with all their quantity of love
Make up my sum. What wilt thou do for her?

KING: O, he is mad, Laertes.

QUEEN: For love of God, forbear him.

HAMLET: 'Swounds, show me what th'owt do:
Woo't weep, woo't fight, woo't fast, woo't tear thyself,
Woo't drink up eisel, eat a crocodile?
I'll do't. Dost come here to whine?
To outface me with leaping in her grave?
Be buried quick with her, and so will I;
And, if thou prate of mountains, let them throw
Millions of acres on us, till our ground,
Singeing his pate against the burning zone,
Make Ossa like a wart! Nay, an thou'lt mouth,
I'll rant as well as thou.

QUEEN: This is mere madness;
And thus awhile the fit will work on him;
Anon, as patient as the female dove
When that her golden couplets are disclos'd
His silence will sit drooping.

HAMLET: Hear you, sir:
What is the reason that you use me thus?
I lov'd you ever. But it is no matter.
Let Hercules himself do what he may,
The cat will mew, and dog will have his day.        [*Exit.*]

KING: I pray thee, good Horatio, wait upon him.

[*Exit* HORATIO.]

[*to* LAERTES] Strengthen your patience in our last night's speech;
We'll put the matter to the present push. —
Good Gertrude, set some watch over your son. —
This grave shall have a living monument.
An hour of quiet shortly shall we see;
Till then in patience our proceeding be.        [*Exeunt.*]

SCENE II———*Elsinore. The Castle.*

[*Enter* HAMLET *and* HORATIO.]

HAMLET: So much for this, sir; now shall you see the other. You do remember all
the circumstance?

HORATIO: Remember it, my lord!

HAMLET: Sir, in my heart there was a kind of fighting
          That would not let me sleep. Methought I lay
          Worse than the mutines in the bilboes. Rashly,
          And prais'd be rashness for it—let us know,
          Our indiscretion sometime serves us well,
          When our deep plots do pall; and that should learn us
          There's a divinity that shapes our ends,
          Rough-hew them how we will.
HORATIO:                              That is most certain.
HAMLET: Up from my cabin,
          My sea-gown scarf'd about me, in the dark
          Grop'd to find out them; had my desire;
          Finger'd their packet, and in fine withdrew
          To mine own room again, making so bold,
          My fears forgetting manners, to unseal
          Their grand commission; where I found, Horatio,
          Ah, royal knavery! an exact command,
          Larded with many several sorts of reasons,
          Importing Denmark's health and England's too,
          With, ho! such bugs and goblins in my life—
          That, on the supervise, no leisure bated,
          No, not to stay the grinding of the axe,
          My head should be struck off.
HORATIO:                              Is't possible?
HAMLET: Here's the commission; read it at more leisure.
          But wilt thou hear now how I did proceed?
HORATIO: I beseech you.
HAMLET: Being thus benetted round with villainies—
          Ere I could make a prologue to my brains,
          They had begun the play—I sat me down;
          Devis'd a new commission; wrote it fair.
          I once did hold it, as our statists do,
          A baseness to write fair, and labour'd much
          How to forget that learning; but sir, now
          It did me yeoman's service. Wilt thou know
          Th' effect of what I wrote?
HORATIO:                              Ay, good my lord.
HAMLET: An earnest conjuration from the King,
          As England was his faithful tributary,
          As love between them like the palm might flourish,
          As peace should still her wheaten garland wear
          And stand a comma 'tween their amities,
          And many such like as-es of great charge,
          That, on the view and knowing of these contents,
          Without debatement further more or less,
          He should those bearers put to sudden death,
          Not shriving-time allow'd.
HORATIO:                              How was this seal'd?

HAMLET: Why, even in that was heaven ordinant.
I had my father's signet in my purse,
Which was the model of that Danish seal;
Folded the writ up in the form of th' other;
Subscrib'd it, gave't th' impression, plac'd it safely,
The changeling never known. Now, the next day
Was our sea-fight; and what to this was sequent
Thou knowest already.

HORATIO: So Guildenstern and Rosencrantz go to't.

HAMLET: Why, man, they did make love to this employment;
They are not near my conscience; their defeat
Does by their own insinuation grow:
'Tis dangerous when the baser nature comes
Between the pass and fell incensed points
Of mighty opposites.

HORATIO:                            Why, what a king is this!

HAMLET: Does it not, think thee, stand me now upon —
He that hath kill'd my king and whor'd my mother;
Popp'd in between th' election and my hopes;
Thrown out his angle for my proper life,
And with such coz'nage — is't not perfect conscience
To quit him with this arm? And is't not to be damn'd
To let this canker of our nature come
In further evil?

HORATIO: It must be shortly known to him from England
What is the issue of the business there.

HAMLET: It will be short; the interim is mine.
And a man's life's no more than to say 'one.'
But I am very sorry, good Horatio,
That to Laertes I forgot myself;
For by the image of my cause I see
The portraiture of his. I'll court his favours.
But sure the bravery of his grief did put me
Into a tow'ring passion.

HORATIO:                            Peace; who comes here?

[*Enter young* OSRIC.]

OSRIC: Your lordship is right welcome back to Denmark.

HAMLET: I humbly thank you, sir. [*aside to* HORATIO] Dost know this water-fly?

HORATIO: [*aside to* HAMLET] No, my good lord.

HAMLET: [*aside to* HORATIO] Thy state is the more gracious; for 'tis a vice to know him. He hath much land, and fertile. Let a beast be lord of beasts, and his crib shall stand at the king's mess. 'Tis a chough; but, as I say, spacious in the possession of dirt.

OSRIC: Sweet lord, if your lordship were at leisure, I should impart a thing to you from his Majesty.

HAMLET: I will receive it, sir, with all diligence of spirit. Put your bonnet to his right use, 'tis for the head.

OSRIC: I thank your lordship; it is very hot.

HAMLET: No, believe me, 'tis very cold; the wind is northerly.

OSRIC: It is indifferent cold, my lord, indeed.

HAMLET: But yet methinks it is very sultry and hot for my complexion.

OSRIC: Exceedingly, my lord; it is very sultry, as 'twere — I cannot tell how. But, my lord, his Majesty bade me signify to you that 'a has laid a great wager on your head. Sir, this is the matter —

HAMLET: I beseech you, remember.

[HAMLET *moves him to put on his hat.*]

OSRIC: Nay, good my lord; for my ease, in good faith. Sir, here is newly come to court Laertes; believe me, an absolute gentleman, full of most excellent differences, of very soft society and great showing. Indeed, to speak feelingly of him, he is the card or calendar of gentry, for you shall find in him the continent of what part a gentleman would see.

HAMLET: Sir, his definement suffers no perdition in you; though, I know, to divide him inventorially would dozy th' arithmetic of memory, and yet but yaw neither in respect of his quick sail. But, in the verity of extolment, I take him to be a soul of great article, and his infusion of such dearth and rareness, as to make true diction of him, his semblable is his mirror, and who else would trace him, his umbrage, nothing more.

OSRIC: Your lordship speaks most infallibly of him.

HÁMLET: The concernancy, sir? Why do we wrap the gentleman in our more rawer breath?

OSRIC: Sir?

HORATIO: [*aside to* HAMLET] Is't not possible to understand in another tongue? You will to't, sir, really.

HAMLET: What imports the nomination of this gentleman?

OSRIC: Of Laertes?

HORATIO: [*aside*] His purse is empty already; all's golden words are spent.

HAMLET: Of him, sir.

OSRIC: I know you are not ignorant —

HAMLET: I would you did, sir; yet, in faith, if you did, it would not much approve me. Well, sir.

OSRIC: You are not ignorant of what excellence Laertes is —

HAMLET: I dare not confess that, lest I should compare with him in excellence; but to know a man well were to know himself.

OSRIC: I mean, sir, for his weapon; but in the imputation laid on him by them, in his meed he's unfellowed.

HAMLET: What's his weapon?

OSRIC: Rapier and dagger.

HAMLET: That's two of his weapons — but well.

OSRIC: The King, sir, hath wager'd with him six Barbary horses; against the which he has impon'd, as I take it, six French rapiers and poniards, with their assigns, as girdle, hangers, and so — three of the carriages, in faith, are very dear to fancy, very responsive to the hilts, most delicate carriages, and of very liberal conceit.

HAMLET: What call you the carriages?

HORATIO: [*aside to* HAMLET] I knew you must be edified by the margent ere you had done.

OSRIC: The carriages, sir, are the hangers.

HAMLET: The phrase would be more germane to the matter if we could carry a cannon by our sides. I would it might be hangers till then. But on: six Barbary horses against six French swords, their assigns, and three liberal conceited carriages; that's the French bet against the Danish. Why is this all impon'd, as you call it?

OSRIC: The King, sir, hath laid, sir, that in a dozen passes between yourself and him he shall not exceed you three hits; he hath laid on twelve for nine, and it would come to immediate trial if your lordship would vouchsafe the answer.

HAMLET: How if I answer no?

OSRIC: I mean, my lord, the opposition of your person in trial.

HAMLET: Sir, I will walk here in the hall. If it please his Majesty, it is the breathing time of day with me; let the foils be brought, the gentleman willing, and the King hold his purpose, I will win for him an I can; if not, I will gain nothing but my shame and the odd hits.

OSRIC: Shall I redeliver you e'en so?

HAMLET: To this effect, sir, after what flourish your nature will.

OSRIC: I commend my duty to your lordship.

HAMLET: Yours, yours. [*Exit* OSRIC.] He does well to commend it himself; there are no tongues else for's turn.

HORATIO: This lapwing runs away with the shell on his head.

HAMLET: 'A did comply, sir, with his dug before 'a suck'd it. Thus has he, and many more of the same bevy, that I know the drossy age dotes on, only got the tune of the time and outward habit of encounter — a kind of yesty collection, which carries them through and through the most fann'd and winnowed opinions; and do but blow them to their trial, the bubbles are out.

[*Enter a* LORD.]

LORD: My lord, his Majesty commended him to you by young Osric, who brings back to him that you attend him in the hall. He sends to know if your pleasure hold to play with Laertes, or that you will take longer time.

HAMLET: I am constant to my purposes; they follow the king's pleasure: if his fitness speaks, mine is ready now — or whensoever, provided I be so able as now.

LORD: The King and Queen and all are coming down.

HAMLET: In happy time.

LORD: The Queen desires you to use some gentle entertainment to Laertes before you fall to play.

HAMLET: She well instructs me. [*Exit* LORD.]

HORATIO: You will lose this wager, my lord.

HAMLET: I do not think so; since he went into France I have been in continual practice. I shall win at the odds. But thou wouldst not think how ill all's here about my heart; but it is no matter.

HORATIO: Nay, good my lord —

HAMLET: It is but foolery; but it is such a kind of gaingiving as would perhaps trouble a woman.

HORATIO: If your mind dislike anything, obey it. I will forestall their repair hither, and say you are not fit.

HAMLET: Not a whit, we defy augury: there is a special providence in the fall of a sparrow. If it be now, 'tis not to come; if it be not to come, it will be now; if it be not now, yet it will come — the readiness is all. Since no man owes of aught he leaves, what is't to leave betimes? Let be.

  [*A table prepared. Trumpets, drums, and officers with cushions, foils and daggers. Enter* KING, QUEEN, LAERTES, *and all the state.*]

KING:  Come, Hamlet, come, and take this hand from me.

  [*The* KING *puts* LAERTES' *hand into* HAMLET'S.]

HAMLET:  Give me your pardon, sir. I have done you wrong;
  But pardon't, as you are a gentleman.
  This presence knows,
  And you must needs have heard how I am punish'd
  With a sore distraction. What I have done
  That might your nature, honour, and exception,
  Roughly awake, I here proclaim was madness.
  Was 't Hamlet wrong'd Laertes? Never Hamlet.
  If Hamlet from himself be ta'en away,
  And when he's not himself does wrong Laertes,
  Then Hamlet does it not, Hamlet denies it.
  Who does it, then? His madness. If 't be so,
  Hamlet is of the faction that is wrong'd;
  His madness is poor Hamlet's enemy.
  Sir, in this audience,
  Let my disclaiming from a purpos'd evil
  Free me so far in your most generous thoughts
  That I have shot my arrow o'er the house
  And hurt my brother.

LAERTES:      I am satisfied in nature,
  Whose motive in this case should stir me most
  To my revenge; but in my terms of honour
  I stand aloof, and will no reconcilement
  Till by some elder masters of known honour
  I have a voice and precedent of peace
  To keep my name ungor'd — but till that time
  I do receive your offer'd love like love,
  And will not wrong it.

HAMLET:      I embrace it freely;
  And will this brother's wager frankly play.
  Give us the foils. Come on.

LAERTES:      Come, one for me.

HAMLET:  I'll be your foil, Laertes; in mine ignorance
  Your skill shall, like a star i' th' darkest night,
  Stick fiery off indeed.

LAERTES:     You mock me, sir.

HAMLET:  No, by this hand.

KING:  Give them the foils, young Osric. Cousin Hamlet,
  You know the wager?

HAMLET:     Very well, my lord;
  Your Grace has laid the odds a' th' weaker side.

KING: I do not fear it: I have seen you both;
　　　But since he's better'd, we have therefore odds.
LAERTES: This is too heavy; let me see another.
HAMLET: This likes me well. These foils have all a length?
　　　[*They prepare to play.*]
OSRIC: Ay, my good lord.
KING: Set me the stoups of wine upon that table.
　　　If Hamlet give the first or second hit,
　　　Or quit in answer of the third exchange,
　　　Let all the battlements their ordnance fire;
　　　The King shall drink to Hamlet'd better breath,
　　　And in the cup an union shall he throw,
　　　Richer than that which four successive kings
　　　In Denmark's crown have worn. Give me the cups;
　　　And let the kettle to the trumpet speak,
　　　The trumpet to the cannoneer without,
　　　The cannons to the heavens, the heaven to earth,
　　　'Now the King drinks to Hamlet.' Come, begin —
　　　And you, the judges, bear a wary eye.
HAMLET: Come on, sir.
LAERTES: 　　　　　　Come, my lord. 　　　　　　　　　　[*They play.*]
HAMLET: 　　　　　　　　　One.
LAERTES: 　　　　　　　　　　No.
HAMLET: Judgement?
OSRIC: A hit, a very palpable hit.
LAERTES: 　　　　　　　　　Well, again.
KING: Stay, give me drink. Hamlet, this pearl is thine;
　　　Here's to thy health. [*Drum, trumpets, and shot.*] Give him the cup.
HAMLET: I'll play this bout first; set it by awhile.
　　　Come. [*They play.*] Another hit; what say you?
LAERTES: A touch, a touch, I do confess't.
KING: Our son shall win.
QUEEN: 　　　　　　　　He's fat, and scant of breath.
　　　Here, Hamlet, take my napkin, rub thy brows.
　　　The Queen carouses to thy fortune, Hamlet.
HAMLET: Good madam!
KING: 　　　　　　　Gertrude, do not drink.
QUEEN: I will, my lord; I pray you pardon me.
KING: [*aside*] It is the poison'd cup; it is too late.
HAMLET: I dare not drink yet, madam; by and by.
QUEEN: Come, let me wipe thy face.
LAERTES: My lord, I'll hit him now.
KING: 　　　　　　　　　　I do not think't.
LAERTES: [*aside*] And yet it is almost against my conscience.
HAMLET: Come, for the third. Laertes, you do but dally;
　　　I pray you pass with your best violence;
　　　I am afeard you make a wanton of me.
LAERTES: Say you so? Come on. 　　　　　　　　　　　[*They play.*]

OSRIC: Nothing, neither way.

LAERTES: Have at you now!

> [LAERTES *wounds* HAMLET: *then, in scuffling, they change rapiers, and* HAMLET *wounds* LAERTES.]

KING: Part them; they are incens'd.

HAMLET: Nay, come again.                                     [*The* QUEEN *falls.*]

OSRIC:                          Look to the Queen there, ho!

HORATIO: They bleed on both sides. How is it, my lord?

OSRIC: How is't, Laertes?

LAERTES: Why, as a woodcock, to mine own springe, Osric;
> I am justly kill'd with mine own treachery.

HAMLET: How does the Queen?

KING:                                She swoons to see them bleed.

QUEEN: No, no, the drink, the drink! O my dear Hamlet!
> The drink, the drink! I am poison'd.                        [*dies*]

HAMLET: O, villainy! Ho! let the door be lock'd.
> Treachery! seek it out.                                     [LAERTES *falls.*]

LAERTES: It is here, Hamlet. Hamlet, thou art slain;
> No med'cine in the world can do thee good;
> In thee there is not half an hour's life;
> The treacherous instrument is in thy hand,
> Unbated and envenom'd. The foul practice
> Hath turn'd itself on me; lo, here I lie,
> Never to rise again. Thy mother's poison'd.
> I can no more. The King, the King's to blame.

HAMLET: The point envenom'd too!
> Then, venom, to thy work.                                   [*stabs the* KING]

ALL: Treason! treason!

KING: O, yet defend me, friends; I am but hurt.

HAMLET: Here, thou incestuous, murd'rous, damned Dane,
> Drink off this potion. Is thy union here?
> Follow my mother.                                           [KING *dies.*]

LAERTES: He is justly serv'd:
> It is a poison temper'd by himself.
> Exchange forgiveness with me, noble Hamlet.
> Mine and my father's death come not upon thee,
> Nor thine on me!                                            [*dies*]

HAMLET: Heaven make thee free of it! I follow thee.
> I am dead, Horatio. Wretched Queen, adieu!
> You that look pale and tremble at this chance,
> That are but mutes or audience to this act,
> Had I but time, as this fell sergeant Death
> Is strict in his arrest, O, I could tell you—
> But let it be. Horatio, I am dead:
> Thou livest; report me and my cause aright
> to the unsatisfied.

HORATIO:                       Never believe it.
> I am more an antique Roman than a Dane;

Here's yet some liquor left.

HAMLET:                               As th'art a man,
Give me the cup. Let go. By heaven, I'll ha't.
O good Horatio, what a wounded name,
Things standing thus unknown, shall live behind me!
If thou didst ever hold me in thy heart,
Absent thee from felicity awhile,
And in this harsh world draw thy breath in pain,
To tell my story. [*March afar off, and shot within.*] What warlike noise is this?

OSRIC: Young Fortinbras, with conquest come from Poland,
To th' ambassadors of England gives
This warlike volley.

HAMLET:                               O, I die, Horatio!
The potent poison quite o'er-crows my spirit.
I cannot live to hear the news from England,
But I do prophesy th' election lights
On Fortinbras; he has my dying voice.
So tell him, with th' occurrents, more and less,
Which have solicited — the rest is silence.                               [*dies*]

HORATIO: Now cracks a noble heart. Good night, sweet prince,
And flights of angels sing thee to thy rest!                    [*March within.*]
Why does the drum come hither?

[*Enter* FORTINBRAS *and* ENGLISH AMBASSADORS, *with drum, colours, and
attendants.*]

FORTINBRAS: Where is this sight?

HORATIO:                               What is it you would see?
If aught of woe or wonder, cease your search.

FORTINBRAS: This quarry cries on havoc. O proud death,
What feast is toward in thine eternal cell
That thou so many princes at a shot
So bloodily hast struck?

FIRST AMBASSADOR: The sight is dismal;
And our affairs from England come too late:
The ears are senseless that should give us hearing
To tell him his commandment is fulfill'd
That Rosencrantz and Guildenstern are dead.
Where should we have our thanks?

HORATIO: Not from his mouth,
Had it th' ability of life to thank you:
He never gave commandment for their death.
But since, so jump upon this bloody question,
You from the Polack wars, and you from England,
And here arrived, give order that these bodies
High on a stage be placed to the view;
And let me speak to th' yet unknowing world
How these things came about. So shall you hear
Of carnal, bloody, and unnatural acts;
Of accidental judgments, casual slaughters;

Of deaths put on by cunning and forc'd cause;
And, in this upshot, purposes mistook
Fall'n on th' inventors' heads — all this can I
Truly deliver.

FORTINBRAS:          Let us haste to hear it,
And call the noblest to the audience.
For me, with sorrow I embrace my fortune;
I have some rights to memory in this kingdom,
Which now to claim my vantage doth invite me.

HORATIO:  Of that I shall have also cause to speak,
And from his mouth whose voice will draw on more.
But let this same be presently perform'd,
Even while men's minds are wild, lest more mischance
On plots and errors happen.

FORTINBRAS:                        Let four captains
Bear Hamlet like a soldier to the stage;
For he was likely, had he been put on,
To have prov'd most royal; and for his passage
The soldier's music and the rite of war
Speak loudly for him.
Take up the bodies. Such a sight as this
Becomes the field, but here shows much amiss.
Go, bid the soldiers shoot.

          [*Exeunt marching. A peal of ordnance shot off.*]

# Molière

# Tartuffe

## Translated into English Verse by Richard Wilbur

### CHARACTERS

MME PERNELLE, *Orgon's mother*
ORGON, *Elmire's husband*
ELMIRE, *Orgon's wife*
DAMIS, *Orgon's son, Elmire's stepson*
MARIANE, *Orgon's daughter, Elmire's stepdaughter, in love with Valère*
VALÈRE, *in love with Mariane*
CLÉANTE, *Orgon's brother-in-law*
TARTUFFE, *a hypocrite*
DORINE, *Mariane's lady's-maid*
M. LOYAL, *a bailiff*
A POLICE OFFICER
FLIPOTE, *Mme Pernelle's maid*

*The scene throughout:* ORGON'S *house in Paris*

## ACT I

### SCENE I

MADAME PERNELLE: Come, come, Flipote; it's time I left this place.
ELMIRE: I can't keep up, you walk at such a pace.
MADAME PERNELLE: Don't trouble, child; no need to show me out.
    It's not your manners I'm concerned about.
ELMIRE: We merely pay you the respect we owe.
    But, Mother, why this hurry? Must you go?
MADAME PERNELLE: I must. This house appals me. No one in it
    Will pay attention for a single minute.
    Children, I take my leave much vexed in spirit.
    I offer good advice, but you won't hear it.
    You all break in and chatter on and on.
    It's like a madhouse with the keeper gone.
DORINE: If . . .
MADAME PERNELLE: Girl, you talk too much, and I'm afraid
    You're far too saucy for a lady's-maid.
    You push in everywhere and have your say.
DAMIS: But . . .
MADAME PERNELLE: You, boy, grow more foolish every day.

To think my grandson should be such a dunce!
I've said a hundred times, if I've said it once,
That if you keep the course on which you've started,
You'll leave your worthy father broken-hearted.
MARIANE: I think . . .
MADAME PERNELLE: And you, his sister, seem so pure,
So shy, so innocent, and so demure.
But you know what they say about still waters.
I pity parents with secretive daughters.
ELMIRE: Now, Mother . . .
MADAME PERNELLE: And as for you, child, let me add
That your behavior is extremely bad,
And a poor example for these children, too.
Their dear, dead mother did far better than you.
You're much too free with money, and I'm distressed
To see you so elaborately dressed.
When it's one's husband that one aims to please,
One has no need of costly fripperies.
CLÉANTE: Oh, Madam, really . . .
MADAME PERNELLE: You are her brother, Sir,
And I respect and love you; yet if I were
My son, this lady's good and pious spouse,
I wouldn't make you welcome in my house.
You're full of worldly counsels which, I fear,
Aren't suitable for decent folk to hear.
I've spoken bluntly, Sir; but it behooves us
Not to mince words when righteous fervor moves us.
DAMIS: Your man Tartuffe is full of holy speeches . . .
MADAME PERNELLE: And practices precisely what he preaches.
He's a fine man, and should be listened to.
I will not hear him mocked by fools like you.
DAMIS: Good God! Do you expect me to submit
To the tyranny of that carping hypocrite?
Must we forgo all joys and satisfactions
Because that bigot censures all our actions?
DORINE: To hear him talk — and he talks all the time —
There's nothing one can do that's not a crime.
He rails at everything, your dear Tartuffe.
MADAME PERNELLE: Whatever he reproves deserves reproof.
He's out to save your souls, and all of you
Must love him, as my son would have you do.
DAMIS: Ah no, Grandmother, I could never take
To such a rascal, even for my father's sake.
That's how I feel, and I shall not dissemble.
His every action makes me seethe and tremble
With helpless anger, and I have no doubt
That he and I will shortly have it out.
DORINE: Surely it is a shame and a disgrace

To see this man usurp the master's place —
To see this beggar who, when first he came,
Had not a shoe or shoestring to his name
So far forget himself that he behaves
As if the house were his, and we his slaves.

MADAME PERNELLE: Well, mark my words, your souls would fare far better
  If you obeyed his precepts to the letter.

DORINE: You see him as a saint. I'm far less awed;
  In fact, I see right through him. He's a fraud.

MADAME PERNELLE: Nonsense!

DORINE: His man Laurent's the same, or worse;
  I'd not trust either with a penny purse.

MADAME PERNELLE: I can't say what his servant's morals may be;
  His own great goodness I can guarantee.
  You all regard him with distaste and fear
  Because he tells you what you're loathe to hear,
  Condemns your sins, points out your moral flaws,
  And humbly strives to further Heaven's cause.

DORINE: If sin is all that bothers him, why is it
  He's so upset when folk drop in to visit?
  Is Heaven so outraged by a social call
  That he must prophesy against us all?
  I'll tell you what I think: if you ask me,
  He's jealous of my mistress' company.

MADAME PERNELLE: Rubbish! [*to* ELMIRE] He's not alone, child, in complaining
  Of all of your promiscuous entertaining.
  Why, the whole neighborhood's upset, I know,
  By all these carriages that come and go,
  With crowds of guests parading in and out
  And noisy servants loitering about.
  In all of this, I'm sure there's nothing vicious;
  But why give people cause to be suspicious?

CLÉANTE: They need no cause; they'll talk in any case.
  Madam, this world would be a joyless place
  If, fearing what malicious tongues might say,
  We locked our doors and turned our friends away.
  And even if one did so dreary a thing,
  D'you think those tongues would cease their chattering?
  One can't fight slander; it's a losing battle;
  Let us instead ignore their tittle-tattle.
  Let's strive to live by conscience' clear decrees,
  And let the gossips gossip as they please.

DORINE: If there is talk against us, I know the source:
  It's Daphne and her little husband, of course.
  Those who have greatest cause for guilt and shame
  Are quickest to besmirch a neighbor's name.
  When there's a chance for libel, they never miss it;
  When something can be made to seem illicit

They're off at once to spread the joyous news,
Adding to fact what fantasies they choose.
By talking up their neighbor's indiscretions
They seek to camouflage their own transgressions,
Hoping that others' innocent affairs
Will lend a hue of innocence to theirs,
Or that their own black guilt will come to seem
Part of a general shady color-scheme.

MADAME PERNELLE: All that is quite irrelevant. I doubt
That anyone's more virtuous and devout
Than dear Orante; and I'm informed that she
Condemns your mode of life most vehemently.

DORINE: Oh, yes, she's strict, devout, and has no taint
Of worldliness; in short, she seems a saint.
But it was time which taught her that disguise;
She's thus because she can't be otherwise.
So long as her attractions could enthrall,
She flounced and flirted and enjoyed it all,
But now that they're no longer what they were
She quits a world which fast is quitting her,
And wears a veil of virtue to conceal
Her bankrupt beauty and her lost appeal.
That's what becomes of old coquettes today:
Distressed when all their lovers fall away,
They see no recourse but to play the prude,
And so confer a style on solitude.
Thereafter, they're severe with everyone,
Condemning all our actions, pardoning none,
And claiming to be pure, austere, and zealous
When, if the truth were known, they're merely jealous,
And cannot bear to see another know
The pleasures time has forced them to forgo.

MADAME PERNELLE: [*initially to* ELMIRE] That sort of talk is what you like to hear;
Therefore you'd have us all keep still, my dear,
While Madam rattles on the livelong day.
Nevertheless, I mean to have my say.
I tell you that you're blest to have Tartuffe
Dwelling, as my son's guest, beneath this roof;
That Heaven has sent him to forestall its wrath
By leading you, once more, to the true path;
That all he reprehends is reprehensible,
And that you'd better heed him, and be sensible.
These visits, balls, and parties in which you revel
Are nothing but inventions of the Devil.
One never hears a word that's edifying:
Nothing but chaff and foolishness and lying,
As well as vicious gossip in which one's neighbor
Is cut to bits with epee, foil, and saber.

People of sense are driven half-insane
At such affairs, where noise and folly reign
And reputations perish thick and fast.
As a wise preacher said on Sunday last,
Parties are Towers of Babylon, because
The guests all babble on with never a pause;
And then he told a story which, I think . . .
[*to* CLÉANTE]: I heard that laugh, Sir, and I saw that wink!
Go find your silly friends and laugh some more!
Enough; I'm going; don't show me to the door.
I leave this household much dismayed and vexed;
I cannot say when I shall see you next.
[*slapping* FLIPOTE]: Wake up, don't stand there gaping into space!
I'll slap some sense into that stupid face.
Move, move, you slut.

SCENE II

CLÉANTE:  I think I'll stay behind;
I want no further pieces of her mind.
How that old lady . . .
DORINE:  Oh, what wouldn't she say
If she could hear you speak of her that way!
She'd thank you for the *lady*, but I'm sure
She'd find the *old* a little premature.
CLÉANTE:  My, what a scene she made, and what a din!
And how this man Tartuffe has taken her in!
DORINE:  Yes, but her son is even worse deceived;
His folly must be seen to be believed.
In the late troubles, he played an able part
And served his king with wise and loyal heart,
But he's quite lost his senses since he fell
Beneath Tartuffe's infatuating spell.
He calls him brother, and loves him as his life,
Preferring him to mother, child, or wife.
In him and him alone will he confide;
He's made him his confessor and his guide;
He pets and pampers him with love more tender
Than any pretty mistress could engender,
Gives him the place of honor when they dine,
Delights to see him gorging like a swine,
Stuffs him with dainties till his guts distend,
And when he belches, cries "God bless you, friend!"
In short, he's mad; he worships him; he dotes;
His deeds he marvels at, his words he quotes,
Thinking each act a miracle, each word
Oracular as those that Moses heard.
Tartuffe, much pleased to find so easy a victim,

Has in a hundred ways beguiled and tricked him,
Milked him of money, and with his permission
Established here a sort of Inquisition.
Even Laurent, his lackey, dares to give
Us arrogant advice on how to live;
He sermonizes us in thundering tones
And confiscates our ribbons and colognes.
Last week he tore a kerchief into pieces
Because he found it pressed in a *Life of Jesus*:
He said it was a sin to juxtapose
Unholy vanities and holy prose.

SCENE III

ELMIRE: [*to* CLÉANTE] You did well not to follow; she stood in the door
And said *verbatim* all she'd said before.
I saw my husband coming. I think I'd best
Go upstairs now, and take a little rest.
CLÉANTE: I'll wait and greet him here; then I must go.
I've really only time to say hello.
DAMIS: Sound him about my sister's wedding, please.
I think Tartuffe's against it, and that he's
Been urging Father to withdraw his blessing.
As you well know, I'd find that most distressing.
Unless my sister and Valère can marry,
My hopes to wed *his* sister will miscarry,
And I'm determined . . .
DORINE: He's coming.

SCENE IV

ORGON: Ah, Brother, good-day.
CLÉANTE: Well, welcome back. I'm sorry I can't stay.
How was the country? Blooming, I trust, and green?
ORGON: Excuse me, Brother; just one moment.
[*to* DORINE] Dorine . . .
[*to* CLÉANTE] To put my mind at rest, I always learn
The household news the moment I return.
[*to* DORINE] Has all been well, these two days I've been gone?
How are the family? What's been going on?
DORINE: Your wife, two days ago, had a bad fever,
And a fierce headache which refused to leave her.
ORGON: Ah. And Tartuffe?
DORINE: Tartuffe? Why, he's round and red,
Bursting with health, and excellently fed.
ORGON: Poor fellow!
DORINE: That night, the mistress was unable
To take a single bite at the dinner-table.
Her headache-pains, she said, were simply hellish.

ORGON: Ah. And Tartuffe?
DORINE: He ate his meal with relish,
    And zealously devoured in her presence
    A leg of mutton and a brace of pheasants.
ORGON: Poor fellow!
DORINE: Well, the pains continued strong,
    And so she tossed and tossed the whole night long,
    Now icy-cold, now burning like a flame.
    We sat beside her bed till morning came.
ORGON: Ah. And Tartuffe?
DORINE: Why, having eaten, he rose
    And sought his room, already in a doze,
    Got into his warm bed, and snored away
    In perfect peace until the break of day.
ORGON: Poor fellow!
DORINE: After much ado, we talked her
    Into dispatching someone for the doctor.
    He bled her, and the fever quickly fell.
ORGON: Ah. And Tartuffe?
DORINE: He bore it very well.
    To keep his cheerfulness at any cost,
    And make up for the blood *Madame* had lost,
    He drank, at lunch, four beakers full of port.
ORGON: Poor fellow!
DORINE: Both are doing well, in short.
    I'll go and tell *Madame* that you've expressed
    Keen sympathy and anxious interest.

SCENE V

CLÉANTE: That girl was laughing in your face, and though
    I've no wish to offend you, even so
    I'm bound to say that she had some excuse.
    How can you possibly be such a goose?
    Are you so dazed by this man's hocus-pocus
    That all the world, save him, is out of focus?
    You've given him clothing, shelter, food, and care;
    Why must you also . . .
ORGON: Brother, stop right there.
    You do not know the man of whom you speak.
CLÉANTE: I grant you that. But my judgment's not so weak
    That I can't tell, by his effect on others . . .
ORGON: Ah, when you meet him, you two will be like brothers!
    There's been no loftier soul since time began.
    He is a man who . . . a man who . . . an excellent man.
    To keep his precepts is to be reborn,
    And view this dunghill of a world with scorn.
    Yes, thanks to him I'm a changed man indeed.

Under his tutelage my soul's been freed
From earthly loves, and every human tie:
My mother, children, brother, and wife could die,
And I'd not feel a single moment's pain.
CLÉANTE: That's a fine sentiment, Brother; most humane.
ORGON: Oh, had you seen Tartuffe as I first knew him,
    Your heart, like mine, would have surrendered to him.
    He used to come into our church each day
    And humbly kneel nearby, and start to pray.
    He'd draw the eyes of everybody there
    By the deep fervor of his heartfelt prayer;
    He'd sigh and weep, and sometimes with a sound
    Of rapture he would bend and kiss the ground;
    And when I rose to go, he'd run before
    To offer me holy-water at the door.
    His serving-man, no less devout than he,
    Informed me of his master's poverty;
    I gave him gifts, but in his humbleness
    He'd beg me every time to give him less.
    "Oh, that's too much," he'd cry, "too much by twice!
    I don't deserve it. The half, Sir, would suffice."
    And when I wouldn't take it back, he'd share
    Half of it with the poor, right then and there.
    At length, Heaven prompted me to take him in
    To dwell with us, and free our souls from sin.
    He guides our lives, and to protect my honor
    Stays by my wife, and keeps an eye upon her;
    He tells me whom she sees, and all she does,
    And seems more jealous than I ever was!
    And how austere he is! Why, he can detect
    A mortal sin where you would least suspect;
    In smallest trifles, he's extremely strict.
    Last week, his conscience was severely pricked
    Because, while praying, he had caught a flea
    And killed it, so he felt, too wrathfully.
CLÉANTE: Good God, man! Have you lost your common sense—
    Or is this all some joke at my expense?
    How can you stand there and in all sobriety . . .
ORGON: Brother, your language savors of impiety.
    Too much free-thinking's made your faith unsteady,
    And as I've warned you many times already,
    'Twill get you into trouble before you're through.
CLÉANTE: So I've been told before by dupes like you:
    Being blind, you'd have all others blind as well;
    The clear-eyed man you call an infidel,
    And he who sees through humbug and pretense
    Is charged, by you, with want of reverence.
    Spare me your warnings, Brother; I have no fear

Of speaking out, for you and Heaven to hear,
Against affected zeal and pious knavery.
There's true and false in piety, as in bravery,
And just as those whose courage shines the most
In battle, are the least inclined to boast,
So those whose hearts are truly pure and lowly
Don't make a flashy show of being holy.
There's a vast difference, so it seems to me,
Between true piety and hypocrisy:
How do you fail to see it, may I ask?
Is not a face quite different from a mask?
Cannot sincerity and cunning art,
Reality and semblance, be told apart?
Are scarecrows just like men, and do you hold
That a false coin is just as good as gold?
Ah, Brother, man's a strangely fashioned creature
Who seldom is content to follow Nature,
But recklessly pursues his inclination
Beyond the narrow bounds of moderation,
And often, by transgressing Reason's laws,
Perverts a lofty aim or noble cause.
A passing observation, but it applies.

ORGON: I see, dear Brother, that you're profoundly wise;
You harbor all the insight of the age.
You are our one clear mind, our only sage,
The era's oracle, its Cato too,
And all mankind are fools compared to you.

CLÉANTE: Brother, I don't pretend to be a sage,
Nor have I all the wisdom of the age.
There's just one insight I would dare to claim:
I know that true and false are not the same;
And just as there is nothing I more revere
Than a soul whose faith is steadfast and sincere,
Nothing that I more cherish and admire
Than honest zeal and true religious fire,
So there is nothing that I find more base
Than specious piety's dishonest face—
Than these bold mountebanks, these histrios
Whose impious mummeries and hollow shows
Exploit our love of Heaven, and make a jest
Of all that men think holiest and best;
These calculating souls who offer prayers
Not to their Maker, but as public wares,
And seek to buy respect and reputation
With lifted eyes and sighs of exaltation;
These charlatans, I say, whose pilgrim souls
Proceed, by way of Heaven, toward earthly goals,
Who weep and pray and swindle and extort,

Who preach the monkish life, but haunt the court,
Who make their zeal the partner of their vice —
Such men are vengeful, sly, and cold as ice,
And when there is an enemy to defame
They cloak their spite in fair religion's name,
Their private spleen and malice being made
To seem a high and virtuous crusade,
Until, to mankind's reverent applause,
They crucify their foe in Heaven's cause.
Such knaves are all too common; yet, for the wise,
True piety isn't hard to recognize,
And happily, these present times provide us
With bright examples to instruct and guide us.
Consider Ariston and Périandre;
Look at Oronte, Alcidamas, Clitandre;
Their virtue is acknowledged; who could doubt it?
But you won't hear them beat the drum about it.
They're never ostentatious, never vain,
And their religion's moderate and humane;
It's not their way to criticize and chide:
They think censoriousness a mark of pride,
And therefore, letting others preach and rave,
They show, by deeds, how Christians should behave.
They think no evil of their fellow man,
But judge of him kindly as they can.
They don't intrigue and wangle and conspire;
To lead a good life is their one desire;
The sinner wakes no rancorous hate in them;
It is the sin alone which they condemn;
Nor do they try to show a fiercer zeal
For Heaven's cause than Heaven itself could feel.
These men I honor, these men I advocate
As models for us all to emulate.
Your man is not their sort at all, I fear:
And, while your praise of him is quite sincere,
I think that you've been dreadfully deluded.

ORGON: Now then, dear Brother, is your speech concluded?
CLÉANTE: Why, yes.
ORGON: Your servant, Sir. [*He turns to go.*]
CLÉANTE: No, Brother; wait.
    There's one more matter. You agreed of late
    That young Valère might have your daughter's hand.
ORGON: I did.
CLÉANTE: And set the date, I understand.
ORGON: Quite so.
CLÉANTE: You've now postponed it; is that true?
ORGON: No doubt.
CLÉANTE: The match no longer pleases you?

ORGON: Who knows?

CLÉANTE: D'you mean to go back on your word?

ORGON: I won't say that.

CLÉANTE: Has anything occurred
Which might entitle you to break your pledge?

ORGON: Perhaps.

CLÉANTE: Why must you hem, and haw, and hedge?
The boy asked me to sound you in this affair . . .

ORGON: It's been a pleasure.

CLÉANTE: But what shall I tell Valère?

ORGON: Whatever you like.

CLÉANTE: But what have you decided?
What are your plans?

ORGON: I plan, Sir, to be guided
By Heaven's will.

CLÉANTE: Come, Brother, don't talk rot.
You've given Valère your word; will you keep it, or not?

ORGON: Good day.

CLÉANTE: This looks like poor Valère's undoing;
I'll go and warn him that there's trouble brewing.

## ACT II

### SCENE I

ORGON: Mariane

MARIANE: Yes, Father?

ORGON: A word with you; come here.

MARIANE: What are you looking for?

ORGON: [*peering into a small closet*] Eavesdroppers, dear.
I'm making sure we shan't be overheard.
Someone in there could catch our every word.
Ah, good, we're safe. Now, Mariane, my child,
You're a sweet girl who's tractable and mild,
Whom I hold dear, and think most highly of.

MARIANE: I'm deeply grateful, Father, for your love.

ORGON: That's well said, Daughter; and you can repay me
If, in all things, you'll cheerfully obey me.

MARIANE: To please you, Sir, is what delights me best.

ORGON: Good, good. Now, what d'you think of Tartuffe, our
guest?

MARIANE: I, Sir?

ORGON: Yes. Weigh your answer; think it through.

MARIANE: Oh, dear. I'll say whatever you wish me to.

ORGON: That's wisely said, my Daughter. Say of him, then,
That he's the very worthiest of men,
And that you're fond of him, and would rejoice
In being his wife, if that should be my choice.

Well?

MARIANE: What?

ORGON: What's that?

MARIANE: I . . .

ORGON: Well?

MARIANE: Forgive me, pray.

ORGON: Did you not hear me?

MARIANE: Of *whom*, Sir, must I say
    That I am fond of him, and would rejoice
    In being his wife, if that should be your choice?

ORGON: Why, of Tartuffe.

MARIANE: But, Father, that's false, you know.
    Why would you have me say what isn't so?

ORGON: Because I am resolved it shall be true.
    That it's my wish should be enough for you.

MARIANE: You can't mean, Father . . .

ORGON: Yes, Tartuffe shall be
    Allied by marriage to this family,
    And he's to be your husband, is that clear?
    It's a father's privilege . . .

### SCENE II

ORGON: [*to* DORINE] What are you doing in here?
    Is curiosity so fierce a passion
    With you, that you must eavesdrop in this fashion?

DORINE: There's lately been a rumor going about—
    Based on some hunch or chance remark, no doubt—
    That you mean Mariane to wed Tartuffe.
    I've laughed it off, of course, as just a spoof.

ORGON: You find it so incredible?

DORINE: Yes, I do.
    I won't accept that story, even from you.

ORGON: Well, you'll believe it when the thing is done.

DORINE: Yes, yes, of course. Go on and have your fun.

ORGON: I've never been more serious in my life.

DORINE: Ha!

ORGON: Daughter, I mean it; you're to be his wife.

DORINE: No, don't believe your father; it's all a hoax.

ORGON: See here, young woman . . .

DORINE: Come, Sir, no more jokes;
    You can't fool us.

ORGON: How dare you talk that way?

DORINE: All right, then: we believe you, sad to say.
    But how a man like you, who looks so wise
    And wears a moustache of such splendid size,
    Can be so foolish as to . . .

ORGON: Silence, please!

My girl, you take too many liberties.
I'm master here, as you must not forget.
DORINE:  Do let's discuss this calmly; don't be upset.
You can't be serious, Sir, about this plan.
What should that bigot want with Mariane?
Praying and fasting ought to keep him busy.
And then, in terms of wealth and rank, what is he?
Why should a man of property like you
Pick out a beggar son-in-law?
ORGON:  That will do.
Speak of his poverty with reverence.
His is pure and saintly indigence
Which far transcends all worldly pride and pelf.
He lost his fortune, as he says himself,
Because he cared for Heaven alone, and so
Was careless of his interests here below.
I mean to get him out of his present straits
And help him to recover his estates—
Which, in his part of the world, have no small fame.
Poor though he is, he's a gentleman just the same.
DORINE:  Yes, so he tells us; and, Sir, it seems to me
Such pride goes very ill with piety.
A man whose spirit spurns this dungy earth
Ought not to brag of lands and noble birth;
Such worldly arrogance will hardly square
With meek devotion and the life of prayer.
 . . . But this approach, I see, has drawn a blank;
Let's speak, then, of his person, not his rank.
Doesn't it seem to you a trifle grim
To give a girl like her to a man like him?
When two are so ill-suited, can't you see
What the sad consequence is bound to be?
A young girl's virtue is imperilled, Sir,
When such a marriage is imposed on her;
For if one's bridegroom isn't to one's taste,
It's hardly an inducement to be chaste,
And many a man with horns upon his brow
Has made his wife the thing that she is now.
It's hard to be a faithful wife, in short,
To certain husbands of a certain sort,
And he who gives his daughter to a man she hates
Must answer for her sins at Heaven's gates.
Think, Sir, before you play so risky a role.
ORGON:  This servant-girl presumes to save my soul!
DORINE:  You would do well to ponder what I've said.
ORGON:  Daughter, we'll disregard this dunderhead.
Just trust your father's judgment. Oh, I'm aware
That I once promised you to young Valère;

But now I hear he gambles, which greatly shocks me;
What's more, I've doubts about his orthodoxy.
His visits to church, I note, are very few.
DORINE: Would you have him go at the same hours as you,
And kneel nearby, to be sure of being seen?
ORGON: I can dispense with such remarks, Dorine.
[*to* MARIANE]
Tartuffe, however, is sure of Heaven's blessing,
And that's the only treasure worth possessing.
This match will bring you joys beyond all measure;
Your cup will overflow with every pleasure;
You two will interchange your faithful loves
Like two sweet cherubs, or two turtle-doves.
No harsh word shall be heard, no frown be seen,
· And he shall make you happy as a queen.
DORINE: And she'll make him a cuckold, just wait and see.
ORGON: What language!
DORINE: Oh, he's a man of destiny;
He's *made* for horns, and what the stars demand
Your daughter's virtue surely can't withstand.
ORGON: Don't interrupt me further. Why can't you learn
That certain things are none of your concern?
DORINE: It's for your own sake that I interfere.
[*She repeatedly interrupts* ORGON *just as he is turning to speak to his daughter.*]
ORGON: Most kind of you. Now, hold your tongue, d'you hear?
DORINE: If I didn't love you . . .
ORGON: Spare me your affection.
DORINE: I'll love you, Sir, in spite of your objection.
ORGON: Blast!
DORINE: I can't bear, Sir, for your honor's sake,
To let you make this ludicrous mistake.
ORGON: You mean to go on talking?
DORINE: If I didn't protest
This sinful marriage, my conscience couldn't rest.
ORGON: If you don't hold your tongue, you little shrew . . .
DORINE: What, lost your temper? A pious man like you?
ORGON: Yes! Yes! You talk and talk. I'm maddened by it.
Once and for all, I tell you to be quiet.
DORINE: Well, I'll be quiet. But I'll be thinking hard.
ORGON: Think all you like, but you had better guard
That saucy tongue of yours, or I'll . . . [*turning back to* MARIANE] Now, child,
I've weighed this matter fully.
DORINE: [*aside*] It drives me wild
That I can't speak.
[ORGON *turns his head, and she is silent.*]
ORGON: Tartuffe is no young dandy,

But, still, his person . . .
DORINE: [*aside*] Is as sweet as candy.
ORGON: Is such that, even if you shouldn't care
  For his other merits . . .
    [*He turns and stands facing* DORINE, *arms crossed.*]
DORINE: [*aside*] They'll make a lovely pair.
  If I were she, no man would marry me
  Against my inclination, and go scot-free.
  He'd learn, before the wedding-day was over,
  How readily a wife can find a lover.
ORGON: [*to* DORINE] It seems you treat my orders as a joke.
DORINE: Why, what's the matter? 'Twas not to you I spoke.
ORGON: What *were* you doing?
DORINE: Talking to myself, that's all.
ORGON: Ah! [*aside*]: One more bit of impudence and gall,
  And I shall give her a good slap in the face.
    [*He puts himself in position to slap her;* DORINE, *whenever he glances at
    her, stands immobile and silent.*]
  Daughter, you shall accept, and with good grace,
  The husband I've selected . . . Your wedding-day . . .
  [*to* DORINE] Why don't you talk to yourself?
DORINE: I've nothing to say.
ORGON: Come, just one word.
DORINE: No thank you, Sir. I pass.
ORGON: Come, speak; I'm waiting.
DORINE: I'd not be such an ass.
ORGON: [*turning to* MARIANE] In short, dear Daughter, I mean to be obeyed,
  And you must bow to the sound choice I've made.
DORINE: [*moving away*] I'd not wed such a monster, even in jest.
    [ORGON *attempts to slap her, but misses.*]
ORGON: Daughter, that maid of yours is a thorough pest;
  She makes me sinfully annoyed and nettled.
  I can't speak further; my nerves are too unsettled.
  She's so upset me by her insolent talk,
  I'll calm myself by going for a walk.


### SCENE III

DORINE: [*returning*] Well, have you lost your tongue, girl? Must I play
  Your part, and say the lines you ought to say?
  Faced with a fate so hideous and absurd,
  Can you not utter one dissenting word?
MARIANE: What good would it do? A father's power is great.
DORINE: Resist him now, or it will be too late.
MARIANE: But . . .
DORINE: Tell him one cannot love at a father's whim;
  That you shall marry for yourself, not him;
  That since it's you who are to be the bride,

It's you, not he, who must be satisfied;
And that if his Tartuffe is so sublime,
He's free to marry him at any time.

MARIANE: I've bowed so long to Father's strict control,
I couldn't oppose him now, to save my soul.

DORINE: Come, come, Mariane. Do listen to reason, won't you?
Valère has asked your hand. Do you love him, or don't
you?

MARIANE: Oh, how unjust of you! What can you mean
By asking such a question, dear Dorine?
You know the depth of my affection for him;
I've told you a hundred times how I adore him.

DORINE: I don't believe in everything I hear;
Who knows if your professions were sincere?

MARIANE: They were, Dorine, and you do me wrong to doubt it;
Heaven knows that I've been all too frank about it.

DORINE: You love him, then?

MARIANE: Oh, more than I can express.

DORINE: And he, I take it, cares for you no less?

MARIANE: I think so.

DORINE: And you both, with equal fire,
Burn to be married?

MARIANE: That is our one desire.

DORINE: What of Tartuffe, then? What of your father's plan?

MARIANE: I'll kill myself, if I'm forced to wed that man.

DORINE: I hadn't thought of that recourse. How splendid!
Just die, and all your troubles will be ended!
A fine solution. Oh, it maddens me
To hear you talk in that self-pitying key.

MARIANE: Dorine, how harsh you are! It's most unfair.
You have no sympathy for my despair.

DORINE: I've none at all for people who talk drivel
And, faced with difficulties, whine and snivel.

MARIANE: No doubt I'm timid, but it would be wrong . . .

DORINE: True love requires a heart that's firm and strong.

MARIANE: I'm strong in my affection for Valère,
But coping with my father is his affair.

DORINE: But if your father's brain has grown so cracked
Over his dear Tartuffe that he can retract
His blessing, though your wedding-day was named,
It's surely not Valère who's to be blamed.

MARIANE: If I defied my father, as you suggest,
Would it not seem unmaidenly, at best?
Shall I defend my love at the expense
Of brazenness and disobedience?
Shall I parade my heart's desires, and flaunt . . .

DORINE: No, I ask nothing of you. Clearly you want
To be Madame Tartuffe, and I feel bound

Not to oppose a wish so very sound.
What right have I to criticize the match?
Indeed, my dear, the man's a brilliant catch.
Monsieur Tartuffe! Now, there's a man of weight!
Yes, yes, Monsieur Tartuffe, I'm bound to state,
Is quite a person; that's not to be denied;
'Twill be no little thing to be his bride.
The world already rings with his renown;
He's a great noble—in his native town;
His ears are red, he has a pink complexion,
And all in all, he'll suit you to perfection.
MARIANE: Dear God!
DORINE: Oh, how triumphant you will feel
At having caught a husband so ideal!
MARIANE: Oh, do stop teasing, and use your cleverness
To get me out of this appalling mess.
Advise me, and I'll do whatever you say.
DORINE: Ah no, a dutiful daughter must obey
Her father, even if he weds her to an ape.
You've a bright future; why struggle to escape?
Tartuffe will take you back where his family lives,
To a small town aswarm with relatives—
Uncles and cousins whom you'll be charmed to meet.
You'll be received at once by the elite,
Calling upon the bailiff's wife, no less—
Even, perhaps, upon the mayoress,
Who'll sit you down in the *best* kitchen chair.
Then, once a year, you'll dance at the village fair
To the drone of bagpipes—two of them, in fact—
And see a puppet-show, or an animal act.
Your husband . . .
MARIANE: Oh, you turn my blood to ice!
Stop torturing me, and give me your advice.
DORINE: [*threatening to go*] Your servant, Madam.
MARIANE: Dorine, I beg of you . . .
DORINE: No, you deserve it; this marriage must go through.
MARIANE: Dorine!
DORINE: No.
MARIANE: Not Tartuffe! You know I think him . . .
DORINE: Tartuffe's your cup of tea, and you shall drink him.
MARIANE: I've always told you everything, and relied . . .
DORINE: No. You deserve to be tartuffified.
MARIANE: Well, since you mock me and refuse to care,
I'll henceforth seek my solace in despair:
Despair shall be my counsellor and friend,
And help me bring my sorrows to an end.
[*She starts to leave.*]
DORINE: There now, come back; my anger has subsided.

You do deserve some pity, I've decided.
MARIANE: Dorine, if Father makes me undergo
    This dreadful martyrdom, I'll die, I know.
DORINE: Don't fret; it won't be difficult to discover
    Some plan of action . . . But here's Valère, your lover.

SCENE IV

VALÈRE: Madam, I've just received some wondrous news
    Regarding which I'd like to hear your views.
MARIANE: What news?
VALÈRE: You're marrying Tartuffe.
MARIANE: I find
    That Father does have such a match in mind.
VALÈRE: Your father, Madam . . .
MARIANE:    . . . has just this minute said
    That it's Tartuffe he wishes me to wed.
VALÈRE: Can he be serious?
MARIANE: Oh, indeed he can;
    He's clearly set his heart upon the plan.
VALÈRE: And what position do you propose to take,
    Madam?
MARIANE: Why—I don't know.
VALÈRE: For heaven's sake—
    You don't know?
MARIANE: No.
VALÈRE: Well, well!
MARIANE: Advise me, do.
VALÈRE: Marry the man. That's my advice to you.
MARIANE: That's your advice?
VALÈRE: Yes.
MARIANE: Truly?
VALÈRE: Oh, absolutely.
    You couldn't choose more wisely, more astutely.
MARIANE: Thanks for this counsel; I'll follow it, of course.
VALÈRE: Do, do; I'm sure 'twill cost you no remorse.
MARIANE: To give it didn't cause your heart to break.
VALÈRE: I gave it, Madam, only for your sake.
MARIANE: And it's for your sake that I take it, Sir.
DORINE: [*withdrawing to the rear of the stage*]
    Let's see which fool will prove the stubborner.
VALÈRE: So! I am nothing to you, and it was flat
    Deception when you . . .
MARIANE: Please, enough of that.
    You've told me plainly that I should agree
    To wed the man my father's chosen for me,
    And since you've deigned to counsel me so wisely,
    I promise, Sir, to do as you advise me.

VALÈRE: Ah, no, 'twas not by me that you were swayed.
No, your decision was already made;
Though now, to save appearances, you protest
That you're betraying me at my behest.
MARIANE: Just as you say.
VALÈRE: Quite so. And I now see
That you were never truly in love with me.
MARIANE: Alas, you're free to think so if you choose.
VALÈRE: I choose to think so, and here's a bit of news:
You've spurned my hand, but I know where to turn
For kinder treatment, as you shall quickly learn.
MARIANE: I'm sure you do. Your noble qualities
Inspire affection . . .
VALÈRE: Forget my qualities, please.
They don't inspire you overmuch, I find.
But there's another lady I have in mind
Whose sweet and generous nature will not scorn
To compensate me for the loss I've borne.
MARIANE: I'm no great loss, and I'm sure that you'll transfer
Your heart quite painlessly from me to her.
VALÈRE: I'll do my best to take it in my stride.
The pain I feel at being cast aside
Time and forgetfulness may put an end to.
Or if I can't forget, I shall pretend to.
No self-respecting person is expected
To go on loving once he's been rejected.
MARIANE: Now, that's fine, high-minded sentiment.
VALÈRE: One to which any sane man would assent.
Would you prefer it if I pined away
In hopeless passion till my dying day?
Am I to yield you to a rival's arms
And not console myself with other charms?
MARIANE: Go then: console yourself; don't hesitate.
I wish you to; indeed, I cannot wait.
VALÈRE: You wish me to?
MARIANE: Yes.
VALÈRE: That's the final straw.
Madam, farewell. Your wish shall be my law.
  [*He starts to leave, and then returns: this repeatedly.*]
MARIANE: Splendid.
VALÈRE: [*coming back again*] This breach, remember, is of your making;
It's you who've driven me to the step I'm taking.
MARIANE: Of course.
VALÈRE: [*coming back again*] Remember, too, that I am merely
Following your example.
MARIANE: I see that clearly.
VALÈRE: Enough. I'll go and do your bidding, then.
MARIANE: Good.

VALÈRE: [*coming back again*] You shall never see my face again.

MARIANE: Excellent.

VALÈRE: [*walking to the door, then turning about*] Yes?

MARIANE: What?

VALÈRE: What's that? What did you say?

MARIANE: Nothing. You're dreaming.

VALÈRE: Ah. Well, I'm on my way.
Farewell, *Madame*.
[*He moves slowly away.*]

MARIANE: Farewell.

DORINE: [*to* MARIANE] If you ask me,
Both of you are as mad as mad can be.
Do stop this nonsense, now. I've only let you
Squabble so long to see where it would get you.
Whoa there, Monsieure Valère!
[*She goes and seizes Valère by the arm; he makes a great show of resistance.*]

VALÈRE: What's this, Dorine?

DORINE: Come here.

VALÈRE: No, no, my heart's too full of spleen.
Don't hold me back; her wish must be obeyed.

DORINE: Stop!

VALÈRE: It's too late now; my decision's made.

DORINE: Oh, pooh!

MARIANE: [*aside*] He hates the sight of me, that's plain.
I'll go, and so deliver him from pain.

DORINE: [*leaving* VALÈRE, *running after* MARIANE] And now *you* run away!
Come back.

MARIANE: No, no.
Nothing you say will keep me here. Let go!

VALÈRE: [*aside*] She cannot bear my presence, I perceive.
To spare her further torment, I shall leave.

DORINE: [*leaving* MARIANE, *running after* VALÈRE] Again! You'll not escape, Sir;
don't you try it.
Come here, you two. Stop fussing, and be quiet.
[*She takes* VALÈRE *by the hand, then* MARIANE, *and draws them together.*]

VALÈRE: [*to* DORINE] What do you want of me?

MARIANE: [*to* DORINE] What is the point of this?

DORINE: We're going to have a little armistice.
[*to* VALÈRE] Now, weren't you silly to get so overheated?

VALÈRE: Didn't you see how badly I was treated?

DORINE: [*to* MARIANE] Aren't you a simpleton, to have lost your head?

MARIANE: Didn't you hear the hateful things he said?

DORINE: [*to* VALÈRE] You're both great fools. Her sole desire, Valère,
Is to be yours in marriage. To that I'll swear.
[*to* MARIANE] He loves you only, and he wants no wife
But you, Mariane. On that I'll stake my life.

MARIANE: [*to* VALÈRE] Then why you advised me so, I cannot see.

VALÈRE: [*to* MARIANE] On such a question, why ask advice of *me?*
DORINE: Oh, you're impossible. Give me your hands, you two.
    [*to* VALÈRE] Yours first.
VALÈRE: [*giving* DORINE *his hand*] But why?
DORINE: [*to* MARIANE] And now a hand from you.
MARIANE: [*also giving* DORINE *her hand*] What are you doing?
DORINE: There: a perfect fit.
    You suit each other better than you'll admit.
        [VALÈRE *and* MARIANE *hold hands for some time without looking at each
        other.*]
VALÈRE: [*turning toward* MARIANE] Ah, come, don't be so haughty. Give a man
    A look of kindness, won't you, Mariane?
        [MARIANE *turns toward* VALÈRE *and smiles.*]
DORINE: I'll tell you, lovers are completely mad!
VALÈRE: [*to* MARIANE] Now come, confess that you were very bad
    To hurt my feelings as you did just now.
    I have a just complaint, you must allow.
MARIANE: *You* must allow that you were most unpleasant . . .
DORINE: Let's table that discussion for the present;
    Your father has a plan which must be stopped.
MARIANE: Advise us, then; what means must we adopt?
DORINE: We'll use all manner of means, and all at once.
    [*to* MARIANE] Your father's addled; he's acting like a dunce.
    Therefore you'd better humor the old fossil.
    Pretend to yield to him, be sweet and docile,
    And then postpone, as often as necessary,
    The day on which you have agreed to marry.
    You'll thus gain time, and time will turn the trick.
    Sometimes, for instance, you'll be taken sick,
    And that will seem good reason for delay;
    Or some bad omen will make you change the day —
    You'll dream of muddy water, or you'll pass
    A dead man's hearse, or break a looking-glass
    If all else fails, no man can marry you
    Unless you take his ring and say "I do."
    But now, let's separate. If they should find
    Us talking here, our plot might be divined.
    [*to* VALÈRE] Go to your friends, and tell them what's occurred,
    And have them urge her father to keep his word.
    Meanwhile, we'll stir her brother into action,
    And get Elmire, as well, to join our faction.
    Good-bye.
VALÈRE: [*to* MARIANE] Though each of us will do his best,
    It's your true heart on which my hopes shall rest.
MARIANE: [*to* VALÈRE] Regardless of what Father may decide,
    None but Valère shall claim me as his bride.
VALÈRE: Oh, how those words content me! Come what will . . .
DORINE: Oh, lovers, lovers! Their tongues are never still.

Be off, now.

VALÈRE: [*turning to go, then turning back*] One last word . . .

DORINE:  No time to chat:

You leave by this door; and *you* leave by that.

> [DORINE *pushes them, by the shoulders, toward opposing doors.*]


## ACT III

### SCENE I

DAMIS:  May lightning strike me even as I speak,
        May all men call me cowardly and weak,
        If any fear or scruple holds me back
        From settling things, at once, with that great quack!

DORINE:  Now, don't give way to violent emotion.
        Your father's merely talked about this notion,
        And words and deeds are far from being one.
        Much that is talked about is left undone.

DAMIS:  No, I must stop that scoundrel's machinations;
        I'll go and tell him off; I'm out of patience.

DORINE:  Do calm down and be practical. I had rather
        My mistress dealt with him — and with your father.
        She has some influence with Tartuffe, I've noted.
        He hangs upon her words, seems most devoted,
        And may, indeed, be smitten by her charm.
        Pray Heaven it's true! 'Twould do our cause no harm.
        She sent for him, just now, to sound him out
        On this affair you're so incensed about;
        She'll find out where he stands, and tell him, too
        What dreadful strife and trouble will ensue
        If he lends countenance to your father's plan.
        I couldn't get in to see him, but his man
        Says that he's almost finished with his prayers.
        Go, now. I'll catch him when he comes downstairs.

DAMIS:  I want to hear this conference, and I will.

DORINE:  No, they must be alone.

DAMIS:  Oh, I'll keep still.

DORINE:  Not you. I know your temper. You'd start a brawl,
        And shout and stamp your foot and spoil it all.
        Go on.

DAMIS:  I won't; I have a perfect right . . .

DORINE:  Lord, you're a nuisance! He's coming; get out of sight.

> [DAMIS *conceals himself in a closet at the rear of the stage.*]


### SCENE II

TARTUFFE: [*observing* DORINE, *and calling to his manservant offstage*] Hang up
         my hair-shirt, put my scourge in place,
        And pray, Laurent, for Heaven's perpetual grace.

I'm going to the prison now, to share
My last few coins with the poor wretches there.
DORINE: [*aside*] Dear God, what affectation! What a fake!
TARTUFFE: You wished to see me?
DORINE: Yes . . .
TARTUFFE: [*taking a handkerchief from his pocket*] For mercy's sake,
Please take this handkerchief, before you speak.
DORINE: What?
TARTUFFE: Cover that bosom, girl. The flesh is weak,
And unclean thoughts are difficult to control.
Such sights as that can undermine the soul.
DORINE: Your soul, it seems, has very poor defenses,
And flesh makes quite an impact on your senses.
It's strange that you're so easily excited;
My own desires are not so soon ignited,
And if I saw you naked as a beast,
Not all your hide would tempt me in the least.
TARTUFFE: Girl, speak more modestly; unless you do,
I shall be forced to take my leave of you.
DORINE: Oh, no, it's I who must be on my way;
I've just one little message to convey.
*Madame* is coming down, and begs you, Sir,
To wait and have a word or two with her.
TARTUFFE: Gladly.
DORINE: [*aside*] *That* had a softening effect!
I think my guess about him was correct.
TARTUFFE: Will she be long?
DORINE: No: that's her step I hear.
Ah, here she is, and I shall disappear.

### SCENE III

TARTUFFE: May heaven, whose infinite goodness we adore,
Preserve your body and soul forevermore,
And bless your days, and answer thus the plea
Of one who is its humblest votary.
ELMIRE: I thank you for that pious wish. But please,
Do take a chair and let's be more at ease.
[*They sit down.*]
TARTUFFE: I trust that you are once more well and strong?
ELMIRE: Oh, yes: the fever didn't last for long.
TARTUFFE: My prayers are too unworthy, I am sure,
To have gained from Heaven this most gracious cure;
But lately, Madam, my every supplication
Has had for object your recuperation.
ELMIRE: You shouldn't have troubled so. I don't deserve it.
TARTUFFE: Your health is priceless, Madam, and to preserve it
I'd gladly give my own, in all sincerity.

ELMIRE: Sir, you outdo us all in Christian charity.
    You've been most kind. I count myself your debtor.
TARTUFFE: 'Twas nothing, Madam. I long to serve you better.
ELMIRE: There's a private matter I'm anxious to discuss.
    I'm glad there's no one here to hinder us.
TARTUFFE: I too am glad; it floods my heart with bliss
    To find myself alone with you like this.
    For just this chance I've prayed with all my power—
    But prayed in vain, until this happy hour.
ELMIRE: This won't take long, Sir, and I hope you'll be
    Entirely frank and unconstrained with me.
TARTUFFE: Indeed, there's nothing I had rather do
    Than bare my inmost heart and soul to you.
    First, let me say that what remarks I've made
    About the constant visits you are paid
    Were prompted not by any mean emotion,
    But rather by a pure and deep devotion,
    A fervent zeal . . .
ELMIRE: No need for explanation.
    Your sole concern, I'm sure, was my salvation.
TARTUFFE: [*taking* ELMIRE's *hand and pressing her fingertips*] Quite so; and such
        great fervor do I feel . . .
ELMIRE: Ooh! Please! You're pinching!
TARTUFFE: 'Twas from excess of zeal.
    I never meant to cause you pain, I swear.
    I'd rather . . . [*He places his hand on* ELMIRE's *knee.*]
ELMIRE: What can your hand be doing there?
TARTUFFE: Feeling your gown; what soft, fine-woven stuff!
ELMIRE: Please, I'm extremely ticklish. That's enough.
        [*She draws her chair away;* TARTUFFE *pulls his after her.*]
TARTUFFE: [*fondling the lace collar of her gown*] My, my, what lovely lacework
        on your dress!
    The workmanship's miraculous, no less.
    I've not seen anything to equal it.
ELMIRE: Yes, quite. But let's talk business for a bit.
    They say my husband means to break his word
    And give his daughter to you, Sir. Had you heard?
TARTUFFE: He did once mention it. But I confess
    I dream of quite a different happiness.
    It's elsewhere, Madam, that my eyes discern
    The promise of that bliss for which I yearn.
ELMIRE: I see: you care for nothing here below.
TARTUFFE: Ah, well—my heart's not made of stone, you know.
ELMIRE: All your desires mount heavenward, I'm sure,
    In scorn of all that's earthly and impure.
TARTUFFE: A love of heavenly beauty does not preclude
    A proper love for earthly pulchritude;

Our senses are quite rightly captivated
By perfect works our Maker has created.
Some glory clings to all that Heaven has made;
In you, all Heaven's marvels are displayed.
On that fair face, such beauties have been lavished,
The eyes are dazzled and the heart is ravished;
How could I look on you, O flawless creature,
And not adore the Author of all Nature,
Feeling a love both passionate and pure
For you, his triumph of self-portraiture?
At first, I trembled lest that love should be
A subtle snare that Hell had laid for me;
I vowed to flee the sight of you, eschewing
A rapture that might prove my soul's undoing;
But soon, fair being, I became aware
That my deep passion could be made to square
With rectitude, and with my bounden duty.
I thereupon surrendered to your beauty.
It is, I know, presumptuous on my part
To bring you this poor offering of my heart,
And it is not my merit, Heaven knows,
But your compassion on which my hopes repose.
You are my peace, my solace, my salvation;
On you depends my bliss — or desolation;
I bide your judgment and, as you think best,
I shall be either miserable or blest.

ELMIRE: Your declaration is most gallant, Sir,
But don't you think it's out of character?
You'd have done better to restrain your passion
And think before you spoke in such a fashion.
It ill becomes a pious man like you . . .

TARTUFFE: I may be pious, but I'm human too:
With your celestial charms before his eyes,
A man has not the power to be wise.
I know such words sound strangely, coming from me,
But I'm no angel, nor was meant to be,
And if you blame my passion, you must needs
Reproach as well the charms on which it feeds.
Your loveliness I had no sooner seen
Than you became my soul's unrivalled queen;
Before your seraph glance, divinely sweet,
My heart's defenses crumbled in defeat,
And nothing fasting, prayer, or tears might do
Could stay my spirit from adoring you.
My eyes, my sighs have told you in the past
What now my lips make bold to say at last,
And if, in your great goodness, you will deign

To look upon your slave, and ease his pain, —
If, in compassion for my soul's distress,
You'll stoop to comfort my unworthiness,
I'll raise to you, in thanks for that sweet manna,
An endless hymn, an infinite hosanna.
With me, of course, there need be no anxiety,
No fear of scandal or of notoriety.
These young court gallants, whom all the ladies fancy,
Are vain in speech, in action rash and chancy;
When they succeed in love, the world soon knows it;
No favor's granted them but they disclose it
And by the looseness of their tongues profane
The very altar where their hearts have lain.
Men of my sort, however, love discreetly,
And one may trust our reticence completely.
My keen concern for my good name insures
The absolute security of yours;
In short, I offer you, my dear Elmire,
Love without scandal, pleasure without fear.

ELMIRE: I've heard your well-turned speeches to the end,
And what you urge I clearly apprehend.
Aren't you afraid that I may take a notion
To tell my husband of your warm devotion,
And that, supposing he were duly told,
His feelings toward you might grow rather cold?

TARTUFFE: I know, dear lady, that your exceeding charity
Will lead your heart to pardon my temerity;
That you'll excuse my violent affection
As human weakness, human imperfection;
And that—O fairest!—you will bear in mind
That I'm but flesh and blood, and am not blind.

ELMIRE: Some women might do otherwise, perhaps,
But I shall be discreet about your lapse;
I'll tell my husband nothing of what's occurred
If, in return, you'll give your solemn word
To advocate as forcefully as you can
The marriage of Valère and Mariane,
Renouncing all desire to dispossess
Another of his rightful happiness,
And . . .

### SCENE IV

DAMIS: [*Emerging from the closet where he has been hiding*] No! We'll not hush
up this vile affair;
I heard it all inside that closet there,
Where Heaven, in order to confound the pride

Of this great rascal, prompted me to hide.
Ah, now I have my long-awaited chance
To punish his deceit and arrogance,
And give my father clear and shocking proof
Of the black character of his dear Tartuffe.

ELMIRE: Ah no, Damis; I'll be content if he
Will study to deserve my leniency.
I've promised silence — don't make me break my word;
To make a scandal would be too absurd.
Good wives laugh off such trifles, and forget them;
Why should they tell their husbands, and upset them?

DAMIS: You have your reasons for taking such a course,
And I have reasons, too, of equal force.
To spare him now would be insanely wrong.
I've swallowed my just wrath for far too long
And watched this insolent bigot bringing strife
And bitterness into our family life.
Too long he's meddled in my father's affairs,
Thwarting my marriage-hopes, and poor Valère's.
It's high time that my father was undeceived,
And now I've proof that can't be disbelieved —
Proof that was furnished me by Heaven above.
It's too good not to take advantage of.
This is my chance, and I deserve to lose it
If, for one moment, I hesitate to use it.

ELMIRE: Damis . . .

DAMIS: No, I must do what I think right.
Madam, my heart is bursting with delight,
And, say whatever you will, I'll not consent
To lose the sweet revenge on which I'm bent.
I'll settle matters without more ado;
And here, most opportunely, is my cue.

### SCENE V

DAMIS: Father, I'm glad you've joined us. Let us advise you
Of some fresh news which doubtless will surprise you.
You've just now been repaid with interest
For all your loving-kindness to our guest.
He's proved his warm and grateful feelings toward you;
It's with a pair of horns he would reward you.
Yes, I surprised him with your wife, and heard
His whole adulterous offer, every word.
She, with her all too gentle disposition,
Would not have told you of his proposition;
But I shall not make terms with brazen lechery,
And feel that not to tell you would be treachery.

ELMIRE:  And I hold that one's husband's peace of mind
                Should not be spoilt by tattle of this kind.
                One's honor doesn't require it: to be proficient
                In keeping men at bay is quite sufficient.
                These are my sentiments, and I wish, Damis,
                That you had heeded me and held your peace.                    [*Exit.*]


                                    SCENE VI

ORGON:  Can it be true, this dreadful thing I hear?
TARTUFFE:  Yes, Brother, I'm a wicked man, I fear:
                A wretched sinner, all depraved and twisted,
                The greatest villain that has ever existed.
                My life's one heap of crimes, which grows each minute;
                There's naught but foulness and corruption in it;
                And I perceive that Heaven, outraged by me,
                Has chosen this occasion to mortify me.
                Charge me with any deed you wish to name;
                I'll not defend myself, but take the blame.
                Believe what you are told, and drive Tartuffe
                Like some base criminal from beneath your roof;
                Yes, drive me hence, and with a parting curse:
                I shan't protest, for I deserve far worse.
ORGON:  [*to* DAMIS] Ah, you deceitful boy, how dare you try
                To stain his purity with so foul a lie?
DAMIS:  What! Are you taken in by such a bluff?
                Did you not hear  . . . ?
ORGON:  Enough, you rogue, enough!
TARTUFFE:  Ah, Brother, let him speak: you're being unjust.
                Believe his story; the boy deserves your trust.
                Why, after all, should you have faith in me?
                How can you know what I might do, or be?
                Is it on my good actions that you base
                Your favor? Do you trust my pious face?
                Ah, no, don't be deceived by hollow shows;
                I'm far, alas, from being what men suppose;
                Though the world takes me for a man of worth,
                I'm truly the most worthless man on earth.
                [*to* DAMIS] Yes, my dear son, speak out now: call me the chief
                Of sinners, a wretch, a murderer, a thief;
                Load me with all the names men most abhor;
                I'll not complain; I've earned them all, and more;
                I'll kneel here while you pour them on my head
                As a just punishment for the life I've led.
ORGON:  [*to* TARTUFFE] This is too much, dear Brother.
                [*to* DAMIS] Have you no heart?
DAMIS:  Are you so hoodwinked by this rascal's art  . . . ?
ORGON:  Be still, you monster.

[*to* TARTUFFE] Brother, I pray you, rise.
[*to* DAMIS] Villain!
DAMIS: But . . .
ORGON: Silence!
DAMIS: Can't you realize . . . ?
ORGON: Just one word more, and I'll tear you limb from limb.
TARTUFFE: In God's name, Brother, don't be harsh with him.
I'd rather far be tortured at the stake
Than see him bear one scratch for my poor sake.
ORGON: [*to* DAMIS] Ingrate!
TARTUFFE: If I must beg you, on bended knee,
To pardon him . . .
ORGON: [*falling to his knees, addressing* TARTUFFE] Such goodness cannot be!
[*to* DAMIS] Now, *there's* true charity!
DAMIS: What, you . . . ?
ORGON: Villain, be still!
I know your motives; I know you wish him ill:
Yes, all of you—wife, children, servants, all—
Conspire against him and desire his fall,
Employing every shameful trick you can
To alienate me from this saintly man.
Ah, but the more you seek to drive him away,
The more I'll do to keep him. Without delay,
I'll spite this household and confound its pride
By giving him my daughter as his bride.
DAMIS: You're going to force her to accept his hand?
ORGON: Yes, and this very night, d'you understand?
I shall defy you all, and make it clear
That I'm the one who gives the orders here.
Come, wretch, kneel down and clasp his blessed feet,
And ask his pardon for your black deceit.
DAMIS: I ask that swindler's pardon? Why, I'd rather . . .
ORGON: So! You insult him, and defy your father!
A stick! A stick! [*to* TARTUFFE] No, no—release me, do.
    [*to* DAMIS]
Out of my house this minute! Be off with you,
And never dare set foot in it again.
DAMIS: Well, I shall go, but . . .
ORGON: Well, go quickly, then.
I disinherit you; an empty purse
Is all you'll get from me—except my curse!

### SCENE VII

ORGON: How he blasphemed your goodness! What a son!
TARTUFFE: Forgive him, Lord, as I've already done.
[*to* ORGON] You can't know how it hurts when someone tries
To blacken me in my dear Brother's eyes.

ORGON: Ahh!

TARTUFFE: The mere thought of such ingratitude
 Plunges my soul into so dark a mood . . .
 Such horror grips my heart . . . I gasp for breath,
 And cannot speak, and feel myself near death.

ORGON: [*He runs, in tears, to the door through which he has just driven his son.*]
 You blackguard! Why did I spare you? Why did I not
 Break you in little pieces on the spot?
 Compose yourself, and don't be hurt, dear friend.

TARTUFFE: These scenes, these dreadful quarrels, have got to end.
 I've much upset your household, and I perceive
 That the best thing will be for me to leave.

ORGON: What are you saying!

TARTUFFE: They're all against me here;
 They'd have you think me false and insincere.

ORGON: Ah, what of that? Have I ceased believing in you?

TARTUFFE: Their adverse talk will certainly continue,
 And charges which you now repudiate
 You may find credible at a later date.

ORGON: No, Brother, never.

TARTUFFE: Brother, a wife can sway
 Her husband's mind in many a subtle way.

ORGON: No, no.

TARTUFFE: To leave at once is the solution;
 Thus only can I end their persecution.

ORGON: No, no, I'll not allow it; you shall remain.

TARTUFFE: Ah, well; 'twill mean much martyrdom and pain,
 But if you wish it . . .

ORGON: Ah!

TARTUFFE: Enough; so be it.
 But one thing must be settled, as I see it.
 For your dear honor, and for our friendship's sake,
 There's one precaution I feel bound to take.
 I shall avoid your wife, and keep away . . .

ORGON: No, you shall not, whatever they may say.
 It pleases me to vex them, and for spite
 I'd have them see you with her day and night.
 What's more, I'm going to drive them to despair
 By making you my only son and heir;
 This very day, I'll give to you alone
 Clear deed and title to everything I own.
 A dear, good friend and son-in-law-to-be
 Is more than wife, or child, or kin to me.
 Will you accept my offer, dearest son?

TARTUFFE: In all things, let the will of Heaven be done.

ORGON: Poor fellow! Come, we'll go draw up the deed.
 Then let them burst with disappointed greed!

# ACT IV

## SCENE I

CLÉANTE: Yes, all the town's discussing it, and truly,
   Their comments do not flatter you unduly.
   I'm glad we've met, Sir, and I'll give my view
   Of this sad matter in a word or two.
   As for who's guilty, that I shan't discuss;
   Let's say it was Damis who caused the fuss;
   Assuming, then, that you have been ill-used
   By young Damis, and groundlessly accused,
   Ought not a Christian to forgive, and ought
   He not to stifle every vengeful thought?
   Should you stand by and watch a father make
   His only son an exile for your sake?
   Again I tell you frankly, be advised:
   The whole town, high and low, is scandalized;
   This quarrel must be mended, and my advice is
   Not to push matters to a further crisis.
   No, sacrifice your wrath to God above,
   And help Damis regain his father's love.
TARTUFFE: Alas, for my part I should take great joy
   In doing so. I've nothing against the boy.
   I pardon all, I harbor no resentment;
   To serve him would afford me much contentment.
   But Heaven's interest will not have it so:
   If he comes back then I shall have to go.
   After his conduct—so extreme, so vicious—
   Our further intercourse would look suspicious.
   God knows what people would think! Why, they'd describe
   My goodness to him as a sort of bribe;
   They'd say that out of guilt I made pretense
   Of loving-kindness and benevolence—
   That, fearing my accuser's tongue, I strove
   To buy his silence with a show of love.
CLÉANTE: Your reasoning is badly warped and stretched,
   And these excuses, Sir, are most farfetched.
   Why put yourself in charge of Heaven's cause?
   Does Heaven need our help to enforce its laws?
   Leave vengeance to the Lord, Sir; while we live,
   Our duty's not to punish, but forgive;
   And what the Lord commands, we should obey
   Without regard to what the world may say.
   What! Shall the fear of being misunderstood
   Prevent our doing what is right and good?
   No, no; let's simply do what Heaven ordains,
   And let no other thoughts perplex our brains.

TARTUFFE: Again, Sir, let me say that I've forgiven
    Damis, and thus obeyed the laws of Heaven;
    But I am not commanded by the Bible
    To live with one who smears my name with libel.
CLÉANTE: Were you commanded, Sir, to indulge the whim
    Of poor Orgon, and to encourage him
    In suddenly transferring to your name
    A large estate to which you have no claim?
TARTUFFE: 'Twould never occur to those who know me best
    To think I acted from self-interest.
    The treasures of this world I quite despise;
    Their specious glitter does not charm my eyes;
    And if I have resigned myself to taking
    The gift which my dear Brother insists on making,
    I do so only, as he well understands,
    Lest so much wealth fall into wicked hands,
    Lest those to whom it might descend in time
    Turn it to purposes of sin and crime,
    And not, as I shall do, make use of it
    For Heaven's glory and mankind's benefit.
CLÉANTE: Forget these trumped-up fears. Your argument
    Is one the rightful heir might well resent;
    It *is* a moral burden to inherit
    Such wealth, but give Damis a chance to bear it.
    And would it not be worse to be accused
    Of swindling, than to see that wealth misused?
    I'm shocked that you allowed Orgon to broach
    This matter, and that you feel no self-reproach;
    Does true religion teach that lawful heirs
    May freely be deprived of what is theirs?
    And if the Lord has told you in your heart
    That you and young Damis must dwell apart,
    Would it not be the decent thing to beat
    A generous and honorable retreat,
    Rather than let the son of the house be sent,
    For your convenience, into banishment?
    Sir, if you wish to prove the honesty
    Of your intentions . . .
TARTUFFE: Sir, it is half-past three.
    I've certain pious duties to attend to,
    And hope my prompt departure won't offend you.
CLÉANTE: [*alone*] Damn.


SCENE II

DORINE: Stay, Sir, and help Mariane, for Heaven's sake!
    She's suffering so, I fear her heart will break.
    Her father's plan to marry her off tonight

Has put the poor child in a desperate plight.
I hear him coming. Let's stand together, now,
And see if we can't change his mind, somehow,
About this match we all deplore and fear.

SCENE III

ORGON: Hah! Glad to find you all assembled here.
[*to* MARIANE] This contract, child, contains your happiness,
And what it says I think your heart can guess.
MARIANE: [*falling to her knees*] Sir, by that Heaven which sees me here distressed,
And by whatever else can move your breast,
Do not employ a father's power, I pray you,
To crush my heart and force it to obey you,
Nor by your harsh commands oppress me so
That I'll begrudge the duty which I owe —
And do not so embitter and enslave me
That I shall hate the very life you gave me.
If my sweet hopes must perish, if you refuse
To give me to the one I've dared to choose,
Spare me at least — I beg you, I implore —
The pain of wedding one whom I abhor;
And do not, by a heartless use of force,
Drive me to contemplate some desperate course.
ORGON: [*feeling himself touched by her*] Be firm, my soul. No human weakness,
now.
MARIANE: I don't resent your love for him. Allow
Your heart free rein, Sir; give him your property,
And if that's not enough, take mine from me;
He's welcome to my money; take it, do,
But don't, I pray, include my person too.
Spare me, I beg you; and let me end the tale
Of my sad days behind a convent veil.
ORGON: A convent! Hah! When crossed in their amours,
All lovesick girls have the same thought as yours.
Get up! The more you loathe the man, and dread him,
The more ennobling it will be to wed him.
Marry Tartuffe, and mortify your flesh!
Enough; don't start that whimpering afresh.
DORINE: But why . . . ?
ORGON: Be still, there. Speak when you're spoken to.
Not one more bit of impudence out of you.
CLÉANTE: If I may offer a word of counsel here . . .
ORGON: Brother, in counseling you have no peer;
All your advice is forceful, sound, and clever;
I don't propose to follow it, however.
ELMIRE: [*to* ORGON] I am amazed, and don't know what to say;
Your blindness simply takes my breath away.

        You are indeed bewitched, to take no warning
        From our account of what occurred this morning.
ORGON: Madam, I know a few plain facts, and one
        Is that you're partial to my rascal son;
        Hence, when he sought to make Tartuffe the victim
        Of a base lie, you dared not contradict him.
        Ah, but you underplayed your part, my pet;
        You should have looked more angry, more upset.
ELMIRE: When men make overtures, must we reply
        With righteous anger and a battle-cry?
        Must we turn back their amorous advances
        With sharp reproaches and with fiery glances?
        Myself, I find such offers merely amusing,
        And make no scenes and fusses in refusing;
        My taste is for good-natured rectitude,
        And I dislike the savage sort of prude
        Who guards her virtue with her teeth and claws,
        And tears men's eyes out for the slightest cause:
        The Lord preserve me from such honor as that,
        Which bites and scratches like an alley-cat!
        I've found that a polite and cool rebuff
        Discourages a lover quite enough.
ORGON: I know the facts, and I shall not be shaken.
ELMIRE: I marvel at your power to be mistaken.
        Would it, I wonder, carry weight with you
        If I could *show* you that our tale was true?
ORGON: Show me?
ELMIRE: Yes.
ORGON: Rot.
ELMIRE: Come, what if I found a way
        To make you see the facts as plain as day?
ORGON: Nonsense.
ELMIRE: Do answer me; don't be absurd.
        I'm not now asking you to trust our word.
        Suppose that from some hiding-place in here
        You learned the whole sad truth by eye and ear—
        What would you say of your good friend, after that?
ORGON: Why, I'd say . . . nothing, by Jehoshaphat!
        It can't be true.
ELMIRE:                You've been too long deceived,
        And I'm quite tired of being disbelieved.
        Come now: let's put my statements to the test,
        And you shall see the truth made manifest.
ORGON: I'll take that challenge. Now do your uttermost.
        We'll see how you make good your empty boast.
ELMIRE: [*to* DORINE] Send him to me.
DORINE:                      He's crafty; it may be hard
        To catch the cunning scoundrel off his guard.

ELMIRE: No, amorous men are gullible. Their conceit
    So blinds them that they're never hard to cheat.
    Have him come down. [*to* CLÉANTE & MARIANE] Please leave us, for a bit.

SCENE IV

ELMIRE: Pull up this table, and get under it.
ORGON: What?
ELMIRE: It's essential that you be well-hidden.
ORGON: Why there?
ELMIRE: Oh, Heavens! Just do as you are bidden.
    I have my plans; we'll soon see how they fare.
    Under the table, now; and once you're there,
    Take care that you are neither seen nor heard.
ORGON: Well, I'll indulge you, since I gave my word
    To see you through this infantile charade.
ELMIRE: Once it is over, you'll be glad we played.
       [*to her husband, who is now under the table*]
    I'm going to act quite strangely, now, and you
    Must not be shocked at anything I do.
    Whatever I may say, you must excuse
    As part of that deceit I'm forced to use.
    I shall employ sweet speeches in the task
    Of making that imposter drop his mask;
    I'll give encouragement to his bold desires,
    And furnish fuel to his amorous fires.
    Since it's for your sake, and for his destruction,
    That I shall seem to yield to his seduction,
    I'll gladly stop whenever you decide
    That all your doubts are fully satisfied.
    I'll count on you, as soon as you have seen
    What sort of man he is, to intervene,
    And not expose me to his odious lust
    One moment longer than you feel you must.
    Remember: you're to save me from my plight
    Whenever . . . He's coming! Hush! Keep out of sight!

SCENE V

TARTUFFE: You wish to have a word with me, I'm told.
ELMIRE: Yes. I've a little secret to unfold.
    Before I speak, however, it would be wise
    To close that door, and look for spies.
       [TARTUFFE *goes to the door, closes it, and returns.*]
    The very last thing that must happen now
    Is a repetition of this morning's row.
    I've never been so badly caught off guard.
    Oh, how I feared for you! You saw how hard
    I tried to make that troublesome Damis

Control his dreadful temper, and hold his peace.
In my confusion, I didn't have the sense
Simply to contradict his evidence;
But as it happened, that was for the best,
And all has worked out in our interest.
This storm has only bettered your position;
My husband doesn't have the least suspicion,
And now, in mockery of those who do,
He bids me be continually with you.
And that is why, quite fearless of reproof,
I now can be alone with my Tartuffe,
And why my heart — perhaps too quick to yield —
Feels free to let its passion be revealed.

TARTUFFE: Madam, your words confuse me. Not long ago,
  You spoke in quite a different style, you know.

ELMIRE: Ah, Sir, if that refusal made you smart,
  It's little that you know of woman's heart,
  Or what that heart is trying to convey
  When it resists in such a feeble way!
  Always, at first, our modesty prevents
  The frank avowal of tender sentiments;
  However high the passion which inflames us,
  Still, to confess its power somehow shames us.
  Thus we reluct, at first, yet in a tone
  Which tells you that our heart is overthrown,
  That what our lips deny, our pulse confesses,
  And that, in time, all noes will turn to yesses.
  I fear my words are all too frank and free,
  And a poor proof of woman's modesty;
  But since I'm started, tell me, if you will —
  Would I have tried to make Damis be still,
  Would I have listened, calm and unoffended,
  Until your lengthy offer of love was ended,
  And be so very mild in my reaction,
  Had your sweet words not given me satisfaction?
  And when I tried to force you to undo
  The marriage-plans my husband has in view,
  What did my urgent pleading signify
  If not that I admired you, and that I
  Deplored the thought that someone else might own
  Part of a heart I wished for mine alone?

TARTUFFE: Madam, no happiness is so complete
  As when, from lips we love, come words so sweet;
  Their nectar floods my every sense, and drains
  In honeyed rivulets through all my veins.
  To please you is my joy, my only goal;
  Your love is the restorer of my soul;
  And yet I must beg leave, now, to confess

Some lingering doubts as to my happiness.
Might this not be a trick? Might not the catch
Be that you wish me to break off the match
With Mariane, and so have feigned to love me?
I shan't quite trust your fond opinion of me
Until the feelings you've expressed so sweetly
Are demonstrated somewhat more concretely,
And you have shown, by certain kind concessions,
That I may put my faith in your professions.

ELMIRE: [*She coughs, to warn her husband.*] Why be in such a hurry? Must my heart
Exhaust its bounty at the very start?
To make that sweet admission cost me dear,
But you'll not be content, it would appear,
Unless my store of favors is disbursed
To the last farthing, and at the very first.

TARTUFFE: The less we merit, the less we dare to hope,
And with our doubts, mere words can never cope.
We trust no promised bliss till we receive it;
Not till a joy is ours can we believe it.
I, who so little merit your esteem,
Can't credit this fulfillment of my dream,
And shan't believe it, Madam, until I savor
Some palpable assurance of your favor.

ELMIRE: My, how tyrannical your love can be,
And how it flusters and perplexes me!
How furiously you take one's heart in hand,
And make your every wish a fierce command!
Come, must you hound and harry me to death?
Will you not give me time to catch my breath?
Can it be right to press me with such force,
Give me no quarter, show me no remorse,
And take advantage, by your stern insistence,
Of the fond feelings which weaken my resistance?

TARTUFFE: Well, if you look with favor upon my love,
Why, then, begrudge me some clear proof thereof?

ELMIRE: But how can I consent without offense
To Heaven, toward which you feel such reverence?

TARTUFFE: If Heaven is all that holds you back, don't worry.
I can remove that hindrance in a hurry.
Nothing of that sort need obstruct our path.

ELMIRE: Must one not be afraid of Heaven's wrath?

TARTUFFE: Madam, forget such fears, and be my pupil,
And I shall teach you how to conquer scruple.
Some joys, it's true, are wrong in Heaven's eyes;
Yet Heaven is not averse to compromise;
There is a science, lately formulated,
Whereby one's conscience may be liberated,
And any wrongful act you care to mention

May be redeemed by purity of intention.
I'll teach you, Madam, the secrets of that science;
Meanwhile, just place on me your full reliance.
Assuage my keen desires, and feel no dread:
The sin, if any, shall be on my head.
     [ELMIRE *coughs, this time more loudly.*]
You've a bad cough.

ELMIRE: Yes, yes. It's bad indeed.

TARTUFFE: [*producing a little paper bag*] A bit of licorice may be what you need.

ELMIRE: No, I've a stubborn cold, it seems. I'm sure it
Will take much more than licorice to cure it.

TARTUFFE: How aggravating.

ELMIRE: Oh, more than I can say.

TARTUFFE: If you're still troubled, think of things this way:
No one shall know our joys, save us alone,
And there's no evil till the act is known;
It's scandal, Madam, which makes it an offense,
And it's no sin to sin in confidence.

ELMIRE: [*having coughed once more*] Well, clearly I must do as you require,
And yield to your importunate desire.
It is apparent, now, that nothing less
Will satisfy you, and so I acquiesce.
To go so far is much against my will;
I'm vexed that it should come to this; but still,
Since you are so determined on it, since you
Will not allow mere language to convince you,
And since you ask for concrete evidence, I
See nothing for it, now, but to comply.
If this is sinful, if I'm wrong to do it,
So much the worse for him who drove me to it.
The fault can surely not be charged to me.

TARTUFFE: Madam, the fault is mine, if fault there be,
And . . .

ELMIRE: Open the door a little, and peek out;
I wouldn't want my husband poking about.

TARTUFFE: Why worry about the man? Each day he grows
More gullible; one can lead him by the nose.
To find us here would fill him with delight,
And if he saw the worst, he'd doubt his sight.

ELMIRE: Nevertheless, do step out for a minute
Into the hall, and see that no one's in it.

### SCENE VI

ORGON: [*coming out from under the table*] That man's a perfect monster, I must admit!
I'm simply stunned. I can't get over it.

ELMIRE: What, coming out so soon? How premature!

Get back in hiding, and wait until you're sure.
Stay till the end, and be convinced completely;
We mustn't stop till things are proved concretely.
ORGON: Hell never harbored anything so vicious!
ELMIRE: Tut, don't be hasty. Try to be judicious.
Wait, and be certain that there's no mistake.
No jumping to conclusions, for Heaven's sake!
[*She places* ORGON *behind her, as* TARTUFFE *re-enters.*]

SCENE VII

TARTUFFE: [*not seeing* ORGON] Madam, all things have worked out to perfection;
I've given the neighboring rooms a full inspection;
No one's about; and now I may at last . . .
ORGON: [*intercepting him*] Hold on, my passionate fellow, not so fast!
I should advise a little more restraint.
Well, so you thought you'd fool me, my dear saint!
How soon you wearied of the saintly life —
Wedding my daughter, and coveting my wife!
I've long suspected you, and had a feeling
That soon I'd catch you at your double-dealing.
Just now, you've given me evidence galore;
It's quite enough; I have no wish for more.
ELMIRE: [*to* TARTUFFE] I'm sorry to have treated you so slyly,
But circumstances forced me to be wily.
TARTUFFE: Brother, you can't think . . .
ORGON: No more talk from you;
Just leave this household, without more ado.
TARTUFFE: What I intended . . .
ORGON: That seems fairly clear.
Spare me your falsehoods and get out of here.
TARTUFFE: No, I'm the master, and you're the one to go!
This house belongs to me, I'll have you know,
And I shall show you that you can't hurt *me*
By this contemptible conspiracy,
That those who cross me know not what they do,
And that I've means to expose and punish you,
Avenge offended Heaven, and make you grieve
That ever you dared order me to leave.

SCENE VIII

ELMIRE: What was the point of all that angry chatter?
ORGON: Dear God, I'm worried. This is no laughing matter.
ELMIRE: How so?
ORGON: I fear I understood his drift.
I'm much disturbed about that deed of gift.
ELMIRE: You gave him . . . ?
ORGON: Yes, it's all been drawn and signed.

But one thing more is weighing on my mind.
ELMIRE: What's that?
ORGON: I'll tell you; but first let's see if there's
      A certain strong-box in his room upstairs.


# ACT V

## SCENE I

CLÉANTE: Where are you going so fast?
ORGON: God knows!
CLÉANTE: Then wait;
      Let's have a conference, and deliberate
      On how this situation's to be met.
ORGON: That strong-box has me utterly upset;
      This is the worst of many, many shocks.
CLÉANTE: Is there some fearful mystery in that box?
ORGON: My poor friend Argas brought that box to me
      With his own hands, in utmost secrecy;
      'Twas on the very morning of his flight.
      It's full of papers which, if they came to light,
      Would ruin him — or such is my impression.
CLÉANTE: Then why did you let it out of your possession?
ORGON: Those papers vexed my conscience, and it seemed best
      To ask the counsel of my pious guest.
      The cunning scoundrel got me to agree
      To leave the strong-box in his custody,
      So that, in case of an investigation,
      I could employ a slight equivocation
      And swear I didn't have it, and thereby,
      At no expense to conscience, tell a lie.
CLÉANTE: It looks to me as if you're out on a limb.
      Trusting him with that box, and offering him
      That deed of gift, were actions of a kind
      Which scarcely indicate a prudent mind.
      With two such weapons, he has the upper hand,
      And since you're vulnerable, as matters stand,
      You erred once more in bringing him to bay.
      You should have acted in some subtler way.
ORGON: Just think of it: behind that fervent face,
      A heart so wicked, and a soul so base!
      I took him in, a hungry beggar, and then . . .
      Enough, by God! I'm through with pious men:
      Henceforth I'll hate the whole false brotherhood,
      And persecute them worse than Satan could.
CLÉANTE: Ah, there you go — extravagant as ever!
      Why can you not be rational? You never
      Manage to take the middle course, it seems,
      But jump, instead, between absurd extremes.

You've recognized your recent grave mistake
In falling victim to a pious fake;
Now, to correct that error, must you embrace
An even greater error in its place,
And judge our worthy neighbors as a whole
By what you've learned of one corrupted soul?
Come, just because one rascal made you swallow
A show of zeal which turned out to be hollow,
Shall you conclude that all men are deceivers,
And that, today, there are no true believers?
Let atheists make that foolish inference;
Learn to distinguish virtue from pretense,
Be cautious in bestowing admiration,
And cultivate a sober moderation.
Don't humor fraud, but also don't asperse
True piety; the latter fault is worse,
And it is best to err, if err one must,
As you have done, upon the side of trust.

### SCENE II

DAMIS: Father, I hear that scoundrel's uttered threats
    Against you; that he pridefully forgets
    How, in his need, he was befriended by you,
    And means to use your gifts to crucify you.
ORGON: It's true, my boy. I'm too distressed for tears.
DAMIS: Leave it to me, Sir; let me trim his ears.
    Faced with such insolence, we must not waver.
    I shall rejoice in doing you the favor
    Of cutting short his life, and your distress.
CLÉANTE: What a display of young hotheadedness!
    Do learn to moderate your fits of rage.
    In this just kingdom, this enlightened age,
    One does not settle things by violence.

### SCENE III

MADAME PERNELLE: [*entering with* ELMIRE *and* MARIANE]
    I hear strange tales of very strange events.
ORGON: Yes, strange events which these two eyes beheld.
    The man's ingratitude is unparalleled.
    I save a wretched pauper from starvation,
    House him, and treat him like a blood relation,
    Shower him every day with my largesse,
    Give him my daughter, and all that I possess;
    And meanwhile the unconscionable knave
    Tries to induce my wife to misbehave;
    And not content with such extreme rascality,
    Now threatens me with my own liberality,

And aims, by taking base advantage of
The gifts I gave him out of Christian love,
To drive me from my house, a ruined man,
And make me end a pauper, as he began.

DORINE: Poor fellow!

MADAME PERNELLE: No, my son, I'll never bring
Myself to think him guilty of such a thing.

ORGON: How's that?

MADAME PERNELLE: The righteous always were maligned.

ORGON: Speak clearly, Mother. Say what's on your mind.

MADAME PERNELLE: I mean that I can smell a rat, my dear.
You know how everybody hates him, here.

ORGON: That has no bearing on the case at all.

MADAME PERNELLE: I told you a hundred times, when you were small,
That virtue in this world is hated ever;
Malicious men may die, but malice never.

ORGON: No doubt that's true, but how does it apply?

MADAME PERNELLE: They've turned you against him by a clever lie.

ORGON: I've told you, I was there and saw it done.

MADAME PERNELLE: Ah, slanderers will stop at nothing, Son.

ORGON: Mother, I'll lose my temper . . . For the last time,
I tell you I was witness to the crime.

MADAME PERNELLE: The tongues of spite are busy night and noon,
And to their venom no man is immune.

ORGON: You're talking nonsense. Can't you realize
I saw it; saw it; saw it with my eyes?
Saw, do you understand me? Must I shout it
Into your ears before you'll cease to doubt it?

MADAME PERNELLE: Appearances can deceive, my son. Dear me,
We cannot always judge by what we see.

ORGON: Drat! Drat!

MADAME PERNELLE: One often interprets things awry;
Good can seem evil to a suspicious eye.

ORGON: Was I to see his pawing at Elmire
As an act of charity?

MADAME PERNELLE: Till his guilt is clear,
A man deserves the benefit of the doubt.
You should have waited, to see how things turned out.

ORGON: Great God in Heaven, what more proof did I need?
Was I to sit there, watching, until he'd . . .
You drive me to the brink of impropriety.

MADAME PERNELLE: No, no, a man of such surpassing piety
Could not do such a thing. You cannot shake me.
I don't believe it, and you shall not make me.

ORGON: You vex me so that, if you weren't my mother,
I'd say to you . . . some dreadful thing or other.

DORINE: It's your turn now, Sir, not to be listened to;
You'd not trust us, and now she won't trust you.

CLÉANTE:  My friends, we're wasting time which should be spent
    In facing up to our predicament.
    I fear that scoundrel's threats weren't made in sport.
DAMIS:  Do you think he'd have the nerve to go to court?
ELMIRE:  I'm sure he won't: they'd find it all too crude
    A case of swindling and ingratitude.
CLÉANTE:  Don't be too sure. He won't be at a loss
    To give his claims a high and righteous gloss;
    And clever rogues with far less valid cause
    Have trapped their victims in a web of laws.
    I say again that to antagonize
    A man so strongly armed was most unwise.
ORGON:  I know it; but the man's appalling cheek
    Outraged me so, I couldn't control my pique.
CLÉANTE:  I wish to Heaven that we could devise
    Some truce between you, or some compromise.
ELMIRE:  If I had known what cards he held, I'd not
    Have roused his anger by my little plot.
ORGON:  [*to* DORINE, *as* M. LOYAL *enters*] What is that fellow looking for? Who is he?
    Go talk to him — and tell him that I'm busy.


SCENE IV

MONSIEUR LOYAL:  Good day, dear sister. Kindly let me see
    Your master.
DORINE:  He's involved with company,
    And cannot be disturbed just now, I fear.
MONSIEUR LOYAL:  I hate to intrude; but what has brought me here
    Will not disturb your master, in any event.
    Indeed, my news will make him most content.
DORINE:  Your name?
MONSIEUR LOYAL:  Just say that I bring greetings from
    Monsieur Tartuffe, on whose behalf I've come.
DORINE:  [*to* ORGON] Sir, he's a very gracious man, and bears
    A message from Tartuffe, which, he declares,
    Will make you most content.
CLÉANTE:  Upon my word,
    I think this man had best be seen, and heard.
ORGON:  Perhaps he has some settlement to suggest.
    How shall I treat him? What manner would be best?
CLÉANTE:  Control your anger, and if he should mention
    Some fair adjustment, give him your full attention.
MONSIEUR LOYAL:  Good health to you, good Sir. May Heaven confound
    Your enemies, and may your joys abound.
ORGON:  [*aside, to* CLÉANTE] A gentle salutation: it confirms
    My guess that he is here to offer terms.
MONSIEUR LOYAL:  I've always held your family most dear;
    I served your father, Sir, for many a year.

ORGON: Sir, I must ask your pardon; to my shame,
   I cannot now recall your face or name.
MONSIEUR LOYAL: Loyal's my name; I come from Normandy,
   And I'm a bailiff, in all modesty.
   For forty years, praise God, it's been my boast
   To serve with honor in that vital post,
   And I am here, Sir, if you will permit
   The liberty, to serve you with this writ . . .
ORGON: To—*what?*
MONSIEUR LOYAL: Now, please, Sir, let us have no friction:
   It's nothing but an order of eviction.
   You are to move your goods and family out
   And make way for new occupants, without
   Deferment or delay, and give the keys . . .
ORGON: I? Leave this house?
MONSIEUR LOYAL: Why yes, Sir, if you please.
   This house, Sir, from the cellar to the roof,
   Belongs now to the good Monsieur Tartuffe,
   And he is lord and master of your estate
   By virtue of a deed of present date,
   Drawn in due form, with clearest legal phrasing . . .
DAMIS: Your insolence is utterly amazing!
MONSIEUR LOYAL: Young man, my business here is not with you,
   But with your wise and temperate father, who,
   Like every worthy citizen, stands in awe
   Of justice, and would never obstruct the law.
ORGON: But . . .
MONSIEUR LOYAL: Not for a million, Sir, would you rebel
   Against authority; I know that well.
   You'll not make trouble, Sir, or interfere
   With the execution of my duties here.
DAMIS: Someone may execute a smart tattoo
   On that black jacket of yours, before you're through.
MONSIEUR LOYAL: Sir, bid your son be silent. I'd much regret
   Having to mention such a nasty threat
   Of violence, in writing my report.
DORINE: [*aside*] This man Loyal's a most disloyal sort!
MONSIEUR LOYAL: I love all men of upright character,
   And when I agreed to serve these papers, Sir,
   It was your feelings that I had in mind.
   I couldn't bear to see the case assigned
   To someone else, who might esteem you less
   And so subject you to unpleasantness.
ORGON: What's more unpleasant than telling a man to leave
   His house and home?
MONSIEUR LOYAL: You'd like a short reprieve?
   If you desire it, Sir, I shall not press you,
   But wait until tomorrow to dispossess you.

Splendid. I'll come and spend the night here, then,
Most quietly, with half a score of men.
For form's sake, you might bring me, just before
You go to bed, the keys to the front door.
My men, I promise, will be on their best
Behavior, and will not disturb your rest.
But bright and early, Sir, you must be quick
And move out all your furniture, every stick:
The men I've chosen are both young and strong,
And with their help it shouldn't take you long.
In short, I'll make things pleasant and convenient,
And since I'm being so extremely lenient,
Please show me, Sir, a like consideration,
And give me your entire cooperation.
ORGON: [*aside*] I may be all but bankrupt, but I vow
    I'd give a hundred louis, here and now,
    Just for the pleasure of landing one good clout
    Right on the end of that complacent snout.
CLÉANTE: Careful; don't make things worse.
DAMIS: My bootsole itches
    To give that beggar a good kick in the breeches.
DORINE: Monsieur Loyal, I'd love to hear the whack
    Of a stout stick across your fine broad back.
MONSIEUR LOYAL: Take care: a woman too may go to jail if
    She uses threatening language to a bailiff.
CLÉANTE: Enough, enough, Sir. This must not go on.
    Give me that paper, please, and then begone.
MONSIEUR LOYAL: Well, *au revoir*. God give you all good cheer!
ORGON: May God confound you, and him who sent you here!

SCENE V

ORGON: Now, Mother, was I right or not? This writ
    Should change your notion of Tartuffe a bit.
    Do you perceive his villainy at last?
MADAME PERNELLE: I'm thunderstruck. I'm utterly aghast.
DORINE: Oh, come, be fair. You mustn't take offense
    At this new proof of his benevolence.
    He's acting out of selfless love, I know.
    Material things enslave the soul, and so
    He kindly has arranged your liberation
    From all that might endanger your salvation.
ORGON: Will you not ever hold your tongue, you dunce?
CLÉANTE: Come, you must take some action, and at once.
ELMIRE: Go tell the world of the low trick he's tried.
    The deed of gift is surely nullified
    By such behavior, and public rage will not
    Permit the wretch to carry out his plot.

### SCENE VI

VALÈRE:  Sir, though I hate to bring you more bad news,
            Such is the danger that I cannot choose.
            A friend who is extremely close to me
            And knows my interest in your family
            Has, for my sake, presumed to violate
            The secrecy that's due to things of state,
            And sends me word that you are in a plight
            From which your one salvation lies in flight.
            That scoundrel who's imposed upon you so
            Denounced you to the King an hour ago
            And, as supporting evidence, displayed
            The strong-box of a certain renegade
            Whose secret papers, so he testified,
            You had disloyally agreed to hide.
            I don't know just what charges may be pressed,
            But there's a warrant out for your arrest;
            Tartuffe has been instructed, furthermore,
            To guide the arresting officer to your door.
CLÉANTE:  He's clearly done this to facilitate
            His seizure of your house and your estate.
ORGON:  That man, I must say, is a vicious beast!
VALÈRE:  Quick, Sir; you mustn't tarry in the least.
            My carriage is outside, to take you hence;
            This thousand louis should cover all expense.
            Let's lose no time, or you shall be undone;
            The sole defense, in this case, is to run.
            I shall go with you all the way, and place you
            In a safe refuge to which they'll never trace you.
ORGON:  Alas, dear boy, I wish that I could show you
            My gratitude for everything I owe you.
            But now is not the time; I pray the Lord
            That I may live to give you your reward.
            Farewell, my dears; be careful . . .
CLÉANTE:  Brother, hurry.
            We shall take care of things; you needn't worry.

### SCENE VII

TARTUFFE:  Gently, Sir, gently; stay right where you are.
            No need for haste; your lodging isn't far.
            You're off to prison, by order of the Prince.
ORGON:  This is the crowning blow, you wretch; and since
            It means my total ruin and defeat,
            Your villainy is now at last complete.
TARTUFFE:  You needn't try to provoke me; it's no use.
            Those who serve Heaven must expect abuse.
CLÉANTE:  You are indeed most patient, sweet, and blameless.
DORINE:  How he exploits the name of Heaven! It's shameless.

TARTUFFE: Your taunts and mockeries are all for naught;
    To do my duty is my only thought.
MARIANE: Your love of duty is most meritorious,
    And what you've done is little short of glorious.
TARTUFFE: All deeds are glorious, Madam, which obey
    The sovereign prince who sent me here today.
ORGON: I rescued you when you were destitute;
    Have you forgotten that, you thankless brute?
TARTUFFE: No, no, I well remember everything;
    But my first duty is to serve my King.
    That obligation is so paramount
    That other claims, beside it, do not count;
    And for it I would sacrifice my wife,
    My family, my friend, or my own life.
ELMIRE: Hypocrite!
DORINE: All that we most revere, he uses
    To cloak his plots and camouflage his ruses.
CLÉANTE: If it is true that you are animated
    By pure and loyal zeal, as you have stated,
    Why was this zeal not roused until you'd sought
    To make Orgon a cuckold, and been caught?
    Why weren't you moved to give your evidence
    Until your outraged host had driven you hence?
    I shan't say that the gift of all his treasure
    Ought to have damped your zeal in any measure;
    But if he is a traitor, as you declare,
    How could you condescend to be his heir?
TARTUFFE: [*to the* OFFICER] Sir, spare me all this clamor; it's growing shrill.
    Please carry out your orders, if you will.
OFFICER: Yes, I've delayed too long, Sir. Thank you kindly.
    You're just the proper person to remind me.
    Come, you are off to join the other boarders
    In the King's prison, according to his orders.
TARTUFFE: Who? I, Sir?
OFFICER: Yes.
TARTUFFE: To prison? This can't be true!
OFFICER: I owe an explanation, but not to you.
    [*to* ORGON] Sir, all is well; rest easy, and be grateful.
    We serve a Prince to whom all sham is hateful,
    A Prince who sees into our inmost hearts,
    And can't be fooled by any trickster's arts.
    His royal soul, though generous and human,
    Views all things with discernment and acumen;
    His sovereign reason is not lightly swayed,
    And all his judgments are discreetly weighed.
    He honors righteous men of every kind,
    And yet his zeal for virtue is not blind,
    Nor does his love of piety numb his wits
    And make him tolerant of hypocrites.

'Twas hardly likely that this man could cozen
A King who's foiled such liars by the dozen.
With one keen glance, the King perceived the whole
Perverseness and corruption of his soul,
And thus high Heaven's justice was displayed:
Betraying you, the rogue stood self-betrayed.
The King soon recognized Tartuffe as one
Notorious by another name, who'd done
So many vicious crimes that one could fill
Ten volumes with them, and be writing still.
But to be brief: our sovereign was appalled
By this man's treachery toward you, which he called
The last, worst villainy of a vile career,
And bade me follow the impostor here
To see how gross his impudence could be,
And force him to restore your property.
Your private papers, by the King's command,
I hereby seize and give into your hand.
The King, by royal order, invalidates
The deed which gave this rascal your estates,
And pardons, furthermore, your grave offense
In harboring an exile's documents.
By these decrees, our Prince rewards you for
Your loyal deeds in the late civil war,
And shows how heartfelt is his satisfaction
In recompensing any worthy action,
How much he prizes merit, and how he makes
More of men's virtues than of their mistakes.

DORINE: Heaven be praised!

MADAME PERNELLE: I breathe again, at last.

ELMIRE: We're safe.

MARIANE: I can't believe the danger's past.

ORGON: [*to* TARTUFFE] Well, traitor, now you see . . .

CLÉANTE: Ah, Brother, please,
Let's not descend to such indignities.
Leave the poor wretch to his unhappy fate,
And don't say anything to aggravate
His present woes; but rather hope that he
Will soon embrace an honest piety,
And mend his ways, and by a true repentance
Move our just King to moderate his sentence.
Meanwhile, go kneel before your sovereign's throne
And thank him for the mercies he has shown.

ORGON: Well said: let's go at once and, gladly kneeling,
Express the gratitude which all are feeling.
Then, when that first great duty has been done,
We'll turn with pleasure to a second one,
And give Valère, whose love has proven so true,
The wedded happiness which is his due.

# Carlo Goldoni

# The Servant of Two Masters

## English Version by Edward J. Dent

CHARACTERS

PANTALONE DEI BISOGNOSI, *a Venetian merchant*
CLARICE, *his daughter*
DR. LOMBARDI
SILVIO, *his son*
BEATRICE RASPONI, *a lady of Turin, disguised as her brother* FEDERIGO RASPONI
FLORINDO ARETUSI, *of Turin, lover of* BEATRICE
BRIGHELLA, *an innkeeper*
SMERALDINA, *maidservant to* CLARICE
TRUFFALDINO, *servant first to* BEATRICE, *and afterward to* FLORINDO
FIRST WAITER
SECOND WAITER
FIRST PORTER
SECOND PORTER

*The scene is laid in Venice. The action takes place within a single day.*

ACT I

SCENE I——*A Room in the House of* PANTALONE.

SILVIO: [*offering his hand to* CLARICE] Here is my hand, and with it I give you my whole heart.
PANTALONE: [*to* CLARICE] Come, come, not so shy, give him your hand too. Then you will be betrothed, and very soon you will be married.
CLARICE: Dear Silvio, here is my hand. I promise to be your wife.
SILVIO: And I promise to be your husband.
    [*They take hands.*]
DR. LOMBARDI: Well done. Now that is settled, and there's no going back on it.
SMERALDINA: [*aside*] There's luck for you! And me just bursting to get married!
PANTALONE: [*to* BRIGHELLA *and* SMERALDINA] You two shall be witnesses of this betrothal of my daughter Clarice to Signor Silvio, the worthy son of our good Dr. Lombardi!
BRIGHELLA: [*to* PANTALONE] We will, sir, and I thank you for the honor.
PANTALONE: Look you, I was witness at your wedding, and now you are a witness to

my daughter's. I have asked no great company of friends and relations, for the doctor too is a man of my sort. We will have dinner together; we will enjoy ourselves and nobody shall disturb us.

[*To* CLARICE *and* SILVIO.]

What say you, children, does that suit you?

SILVIO: I desire nothing better than to be near my beloved bride.

SMERALDINA: [*aside*] Yes, that's the best of all foods.

DR. LOMBARDI: My son is no lover of vanities. He is an honest lad; he loves your daughter and thinks of nothing else.

PANTALONE: Truly we may say that this marriage was made in Heaven, for had it not been for the death of Federigo Rasponi, my correspondent at Turin, you know, I had promised my daughter to him.

[*To* SILVIO.]

I could not then have given her to my dear son-in-law.

SILVIO: I can call myself fortunate indeed, sir; I know not if Signora Clarice will say the same.

CLARICE: You wrong me, dear Silvio. You should know if I love you. I should have married Signor Rasponi in obedience to my father; but my heart has always been yours.

DR. LOMBARDI: 'Tis true indeed, the will of Heaven is wrought in unexpected ways.

[*To* PANTALONE.]

Pray, sir, how did Federigo Rasponi come to die?

PANTALONE: Poor wretch, I hardly know. He was killed one night on account of some affair about his sister. Someone ran a sword through him and that was the end of him.

BRIGHELLA: Did that happen at Turin, sir?

PANTALONE: At Turin.

BRIGHELLA: Alas, poor gentleman! I am indeed sorry to hear it.

PANTALONE: [*to* BRIGHELLA] Did you know Signor Federigo Rasponi?

BRIGHELLA: Indeed and I did, sir. I was three years at Turin. I knew his sister too — a fine high-spirited young woman — dressed like a man and rode a-horseback; and he loved her more than anyone in the world. Lord! Who'd ha' thought it?

PANTALONE: Well, misfortune waits for all of us. But come, let us talk no more of sad things. Do you know what I have in mind, good master Brighella? I know you love to show your skill in the kitchen. Now, I would have you make us a few dishes of your best.

BRIGHELLA: 'Tis a pleasure to serve you, sir. Though I say it that shouldn't, customers are always well contented at my house. They say there's no place where they eat as they do there. You shall taste something fine, sir.

PANTALONE: Good, good. Let's have something with plenty of gravy that we can sop the bread in.

[*A knock at the door.*]

Oh! Someone is knocking. Smeraldina, see who it is.

SMERALDINA: Yes, sir.

[*Goes to door.*]

CLARICE: [*wishing to retire*] Sir, may I beg your leave?

PANTALONE: Wait; we are all coming. Let us hear who is there.

SMERALDINA: [*coming back*] Sir, there is a gentleman's servant below who desires to give you a message. He would tell me nothing. He says he would speak to the master.

PANTALONE: Tell him to come up. We'll hear what he has to say.

SMERALDINA: I'll fetch him, sir.

    [*Exit.*]

CLARICE: May I not go, sir?

PANTALONE: Whither then, madam?

CLARICE: I know not — to my own room —

PANTALONE: No, madam, no; you stay here.

    [*Aside to* DR. LOMBARDI.]

These lovebirds can't be left alone just yet for a while.

DR. LOMBARDI: [*aside to* PANTALONE] Prudence above all things!

    SMERALDINA *brings in* TRUFFALDINO.

TRUFFALDINO: My most humble duty to the ladies and gentlemen. And a very fine company too, to be sure! Ve-ry fine, indeed!

PANTALONE: Who are you, my good friend? And what is your business?

TRUFFALDINO: [*to* PANTALONE, *pointing to* CLARICE] Who is this fair gentlewoman?

PANTALONE: That is my daughter.

TRUFFALDINO: Delighted to hear it.

SMERALDINA: [*to* TRUFFALDINO] What's more, she is going to be married.

TRUFFALDINO: I'm sorry to hear it. And who are you?

SMERALDINA: I am her maid, sir.

TRUFFALDINO: I congratulate her.

PANTALONE: Come, sir, have done with ceremony. What do you want with me? Who are you? Who sends you hither?

TRUFFALDINO: Patience, patience, my good sir, take it easy. Three questions at once is too much for a poor man.

PANTALONE: [*aside to* DR. LOMBARDI] I think the man's a fool.

DR. LOMBARDI: [*aside to* PANTALONE] I think he's playing the fool.

TRUFFALDINO: [*to* SMERALDINA] Is it you that are going to be married?

SMERALDINA: [*sighs*] No, sir.

PANTALONE: Will you tell me who you are, or will you go about your business?

TRUFFALDINO: If you only want to know who I am, I'll tell you in two words. I am the servant of my master.

    [*Turns to* SMERALDINA.]

To go back to what I was saying —

PANTALONE: But who is your master?

TRUFFALDINO: [*to* PANTALONE] He is a gentleman who desires the honor of paying his respects to you.

    [*To* SMERALDINA.]

We must have a talk about this marriage.

PANTALONE: Who is this gentleman, I say? What is his name?

TRUFFALDINO: Oh, that's a long story. Si'or Federigo Rasponi of Turin, that's my master, and he sends his compliments, and he has come to see you, and he's down below, and he sends me to say that he would like to come up and he's waiting for an answer. Anything else, or will that do?

    [*All look surprised.*]

    [*To* SMERALDINA, *as before.*]

Let's begin again.

PANTALONE: Come here and talk to me. What the devil do you mean?

TRUFFALDINO: And if you want to know who I am, I am Truffaldin' Battocchio from Bergamo.

PANTALONE: I don't care who *you* are. Tell me again, who is this master of yours? I fear I did not understand you rightly.

TRUFFALDINO: Poor old gentleman! He must be hard of hearing. My master is Si'or Federigo Rasponi of Turin.

PANTALONE: Away! You must be mad. Signor Federigo Rasponi of Turin is dead.

TRUFFALDINO: Dead?

PANTALONE: To be sure he's dead, worse luck for him.

TRUFFALDINO: [*aside*] The devil! My master dead? Why, I left him alive downstairs!
[*To* PANTALONE.]
You really mean he is dead?

PANTALONE: I tell you for an absolute certainty, he is dead.

DR. LOMBARDI: 'Tis the honest truth; he is dead; we can have no doubt about it.

TRUFFALDINO: [*aside*] Alas, my poor master! He must have met with an accident.
[*To* PANTALONE *as if retiring.*]
Your very humble servant, sir.

PANTALONE: Can I do nothing more for you?

TRUFFALDINO: If he's dead, there's nothing more to do.
[*Aside.*]
But I'm going to see if it's true or not.
[*Exit.*]

PANTALONE: What are we to make of this fellow? Is he knave or fool?

DR. LOMBARDI: I really don't know. Probably a little of both.

BRIGHELLA: I should say he was just a zany. He comes from Bergamo; I can't think he is a knave.

SMERALDINA: He's not such a fool, neither.
[*Aside.*]
I like that little dark fellow.

PANTALONE: But what is this nightmare about Signor Federigo?

CLARICE: If 'tis true indeed that he is here, it would be the worst of news for me.

PANTALONE: What nonsense! Did not you see the letters yourself?

SILVIO: If he *is* alive and here after all, he has come too late.
[*Re-enter* TRUFFALDINO.]

TRUFFALDINO: Gentlemen, I am surprised at you. Is that the way to treat a poor man? Is that the way you deceive strangers? Is that the behavior of a gentleman? I shall insist upon satisfaction.

PANTALONE: [*to* DR. LOMBARDI] We must be careful, the man's mad.
[*To* TRUFFALDINO.]
What's the matter? What have they done to you?

TRUFFALDINO: To go and tell me that Si'or Federigo Rasponi was dead!

PANTALONE: Well, what then?

TRUFFALDINO: What then? Well, he's here, safe and sound, in good health and spirits, and he desires to pay his respects to you, with your kind permission.

PANTALONE: Signor Federigo?

TRUFFALDINO: Si'or Federigo.

PANTALONE: Rasponi?

TRUFFALDINO: Rasponi.

PANTALONE: Of Turin?

TRUFFALDINO: Of Turin.

PANTALONE: Be off to Bedlam, my lad; that's the place for you.

TRUFFALDINO: The Devil take *you* there, sir! You'll make me swear like a Turk. I tell you he's here, in the house, in the next room, bad luck to you.

PANTALONE: If you say any more I'll break your head.

DR. LOMBARDI: No, no, Signor Pantalone; I tell you what to do. Tell him to bring in this person whom he thinks to be Federigo Rasponi.

PANTALONE: Well, bring in this man that is risen from the dead.

TRUFFALDINO: He may have been dead and risen from the dead, for all I know. That's no affair of mine. But he's alive now, sure enough, and you shall see him with your own eyes. I'll go and tell him to come.

[*Angrily to* PANTALONE.]

And 'tis time you learned how to behave properly to strangers, to gentlemen of my position, to honorable citizens of Bergamo.

[*To* SMERALDINA.]

Young woman, we will have some talk together when you will.

[*Exit.*]

CLARICE: Silvio, I am all of a tremble.

SILVIO: Have no fear; whatever happens, you shall be mine.

DR. LOMBARDI: Now we shall discover the truth.

PANTALONE: Some rogue, I dare say, come to tell me a string of lies.

BRIGHELLA: Sir, as I told you just now, I knew Signor Federigo; we shall see if it be he.

SMERALDINA: [*aside*] That little dark fellow doesn't look like a liar. I wonder, now, if —

[*Curtsy to* PANTALONE.]

By your good leave, sir.

[*Exit.*]

[*Enter* BEATRICE, *dressed as a man.*]

BEATRICE: Signor Pantalone, that courtesy which I have so much admired in your correspondence is but ill matched in the treatment which I have received from you in person. I send my servant to pay you my respects, and you keep me standing in the street for half an hour before you condescend to allow me to enter.

PANTALONE: [*nervously*] I ask your pardon. But, sir, who are you?

BEATRICE: Your obedient servant, sir, Federigo Rasponi of Turin.

[*All look bewildered.*]

PANTALONE: Extraordinary!

BRIGHELLA: [*aside*] What does this mean? This is not Federigo, this is his sister Beatrice.

PANTALONE: I rejoice to see you, sir, alive and in health, after the bad news which we had received.

[*Aside to* DR. LOMBARDI.]

I tell you, I am not convinced yet.

BEATRICE: I know; 'twas reported that I was killed in a duel. Heaven be praised, I was but wounded; and no sooner was I restored to health than I set out for Venice, according to our previous arrangement.

PANTALONE: I don't know what to say. You have the appearance of an honest man, sir, but I have sure and certain evidence that Signor Federigo is dead, and you will understand that if you cannot give us proof of the contrary —

BEATRICE: Your doubt is most natural; I recognize that I must give you proof of my identify. Here are four letters from correspondents of yours whom you know personally; one of them is from the manager of our bank. You will recognize the signatures and you will satisfy yourself as to who I am.

[*Gives four letters to* PANTALONE, *who reads them to himself.*]

CLARICE: Ah, Silvio, we are lost.

SILVIO: I will lose my life before I lose you.

BEATRICE: [*noticing* BRIGHELLA, *aside*] Heavens! Brighella! How the devil does he come to be here? If he betrays me —

[*Aloud to* BRIGHELLA.]

Friend, I think I know you.

BRIGHELLA: Indeed yes, sir; do you not remember Brighella Cavicchio at Turin?

BEATRICE: Ah yes, now I recognize you.

[*Goes up to him.*]

And what are you doing in Venice, my good fellow?

[*Aside to* BRIGHELLA.]

For the love of heaven do not betray me.

BRIGHELLA: [*aside to* BEATRICE] Trust me.

[*Aloud.*]

I keep an inn, sir, at your service.

BEATRICE: The very thing for me; as I have the pleasure of your acquaintance, I shall come to lodge at your inn.

BRIGHELLA: You do me honor, sir.

[*Aside.*]

Running contraband, I'll be bound.

PANTALONE: I have read the letters. Certainly they present Signor Federigo Rasponi to me, and if you present them, I am bound to believe that you are — the person named therein.

BEATRICE: If you are still in doubt, here is Master Brighella; he knows me, he can assure you as to who I am.

BRIGHELLA: Of course, sir, I am happy to assure you.

PANTALONE: Well, if that be so, and my good friend Brighella confirms the testimony of the letters, then, dear Signor Federigo, I am delighted to see you and I ask your pardon for having doubted your word.

CLARICE: Then, sir, this gentleman is indeed Signor Federigo Rasponi?

PANTALONE: But of course he is.

CLARICE: [*aside to* SILVIO] Oh misery, what will happen to us?

SILVIO: [*aside to* CLARICE] Don't be frightened; you are mine and I will protect you.

PANTALONE: [*aside to* DR. LOMBARDI] What do you say to it, Doctor? He has come just in the nick of time.

DR. LOMBARDI: *Accidit in puncto, quod non contingit in anno.*

BEATRICE: [*pointing to* CLARICE] Signor Panatlone, who is that young lady?

PANTALONE: That is my daughter Clarice.

BEATRICE: The one who was promised in marriage to me?

PANTALONE: Precisely, sir; that is she.

> [*Aside.*]
> Now I am in a pretty mess.

BEATRICE: [*to* CLARICE] Madam, permit me to have the honor.

CLARICE: [*stiffly*] Your most humble servant, sir.

BEATRICE: [*to* PANTALONE] She receives me somewhat coldly.

PANTALONE: You must forgive her, she is shy by nature.

BEATRICE: [*to* PANTALONE, *pointing at* SILVIO] And this gentleman is a relative of yours?

PANTALONE: Yes, sir; he is a nephew of mine.

SILVIO: [*to* BEATRICE] No, sir, I am not his nephew at all; I am the promised husband of Signora Clarice.

DR. LOMBARDI: [*aside to* SILVIO] Well said, my boy! Don't lose your chance! Stand up for your rights, but do nothing rash.

BEATRICE: What? You the promised husband of Signora Clarice? Was she not promised to me?

PANTALONE: There, there, I'll explain the whole matter. My dear Signor Federigo, I fully believed that the story of your accident was true, that you were dead, in fact, and so I had promised my daughter to Signor Silvio; but there is not the least harm done. You have arrived at last, just in time. Clarice is yours, if you will have her, and I am here to keep my word. Signor Silvio, I don't know what to say; you can see the position yourself. You remember what I said to you; and you will have no cause to bear me ill-will.

SILVIO: But Signor Federigo will never consent to take a bride who has given her hand to another.

BEATRICE: Oh, I am not so fastidious. I will take her in spite of that.

> [*Aside.*]
> I mean to have some fun out of this.

DR. LOMBARDI: [*sarcastically*] There's a fine fashionable husband! I like him.

BEATRICE: I hope Signora Clarice will not refuse me her hand.

SILVIO: Sir, you have arrived too late. Signora Clarice is to be *my* wife, and you need have no hope that I will yield her to you. If Signor Pantalone does me wrong, I will be avenged upon him; and whoever presumes to desire Clarice will have to fight for her against this sword.

DR. LOMBARDI: [*aside*] That's a fine boy, by the Lord!

BEATRICE: [*aside*] Thank you, but I don't mean to die just yet.

DR. LOMBARDI: Sir, I must beg to inform you that you are too late. Signora Clarice is to marry my son. The law, the law, sir, is clear on the point. *Prior in tempore, potior in jure.*

> [*Exeunt* DR. LOMBARDI *and* SILVIO.]

BEATRICE: [*to* CLARICE] And you, madam bride, do you say nothing?

CLARICE: I say — I say — I'd sooner marry the hangman.

> [*Exit.*]

PANTALONE: What, you minx! What did you say?

> [*Starts to run after her.*]

BEATRICE: Stay, Signor Pantalone; I am sorry for her. It is not the moment for severity. In course of time I hope I may deserve her favor. Meanwhile let us go into our accounts together, for, as you know, that is one of the two reasons that have brought me to Venice.

PANTALONE: Everything is in order for your inspection. You shall see the books; your money is ready for you, and we will make up the account whenever you like.

BEATRICE: I will call on you at some more convenient time. Now, if you will allow me, I will go with Brighella to settle some little business which I have to do.

PANTALONE: You shall do as you please, and if you have need of anything, I am at your service.

BEATRICE: Well, if you could give me a little money, I should be greatly obliged; I did not bring any with me, for fear of being robbed on the way.

PANTALONE: I am delighted to serve you; but the cashier is not here just now. The moment he comes I will send the money to your lodgings. Are you not staying at my friend Brighella's?

BEATRICE: Yes, I lie there. But I will send my servant; he is entirely honest. You can trust him with anything.

PANTALONE: Very well. I will carry out your wishes, and if you may be pleased to take pot luck with me, I am yours to command.

BEATRICE: For today I thank you. Another day I shall be happy to wait upon you.

PANTALONE: Then I shall expect you.

[*Enter* SMERALDINA.]

SMERALDINA: [*to* PANTALONE] Sir, you are asked for.

PANTALONE: Who is it?

SMERALDINA: I couldn't say, sir.

PANTALONE: I will come directly. Sir, I beg you to excuse me. Brighella, you are at home here; be good enough to attend Signor Federigo.

BEATRICE: Pray do not put yourself about for me, sir.

PANTALONE: I must go. Farewell, sir.

[*Aside.*]

I don't want to have trouble in my house.

[*Exit with* SMERALDINA.]

BRIGHELLA: May I ask, Signora Beatrice —?

BEATRICE: Hush, for the love of Heaven, don't betray me. My poor brother is dead. 'Twas thought Florindo Aretusi killed him in a duel. You remember, Florindo loved me, and my brother would not have it. They fought, Federigo fell, and Florindo fled from justice. I heard he was making for Venice, so I put on my brother's clothes and followed him. Thanks to the letters of credit, which are my brother's, and thanks still more to you, Signor Pantalone takes me for Federigo. We are to make up our accounts; I shall draw the money, and then I shall be able to help Florindo too, if he has need of it. Be my friend, dear Brighella, help me, please! You shall be generously rewarded.

BRIGHELLA: That's all very well, but I don't want to be responsible for Signor Pantalone paying you out money in good faith and then finding himself made a fool of.

BEATRICE: Made a fool of? If my brother is dead, am I not his heir?

BRIGHELLA: Very true. Then why not say so?

BEATRICE: If I do that, I can do nothing. Pantalone will begin by treating me as if he were my guardian; then they will all worry me and say my conduct is unbecoming and all that sort of thing. I want my liberty. Help me to it. 'Twill not last long.

BRIGHELLA: Well, well, you were always one for having your own way. Trust me, and I'll do my best for you.

BEATRICE: Thank you. And now let us go to your inn.

BRIGHELLA: Where is your servant?

BEATRICE: I told him to wait for me in the street.

BRIGHELLA: Wherever did you get hold of that idiot? He cannot even speak plain.

BEATRICE: I picked him up on the journey. He seems a fool at times; but he isn't really a fool and I can rely on his loyalty.

BRIGHELLA: Yes, loyalty's a fine thing. Well, I am at your service. To think what love will make people do!

BEATRICE: Oh, this is nothing. Love makes people do far worse things than this.

BRIGHELLA: Well, here's a good beginning. If you go on that way, Lord knows what may come of it!

[*Exeunt* BEATRICE *and* BRIGHELLA.]


SCENE II——*A Street with* BRIGHELLA's *Inn.*

TRUFFALDINO: I'm sick of waiting; I can hold out no longer. With this master of mine there's not enough to eat, and the less there is the more I want it. The town clock struck twelve half an hour ago, and my belly struck two hours ago at least. If I only knew where we were going to lodge! With my other masters the first thing they did, as soon as they came to a town, was to go to a tavern. This gentleman — Lord no! He leaves his trunks in the boat at the landing stage, goes off to pay visits, and forgets all about his poor servant. When they say we ought to serve our masters with love, they ought to tell the masters to have a little charity toward their servants.

    Here's an inn. I've half a mind to go in and see if I could find something to tickle my teeth; but what if my master comes to look for me? His own fault; he ought to know better. I'll go in — but now I come to think of it, there's another little difficulty that I hadn't remembered; I haven't a penny. Oh poor Truffaldin'! Rather than be a servant, devil take me, I'd — what indeed? By the grace of Heaven there's nothing I *can* do.

[*Enter* FLORINDO *in traveling dress with a* PORTER *carrying a trunk on his shoulder.*]

PORTER: I tell you, sir, I can go no farther; the weight's enough to kill me.

FLORINDO: Here is the sign of an inn. Can't you carry it these few steps?

PORTER: Help! The trunk is falling.

FLORINDO: I told you you could not carry it; you're too weak; you have no strength at all.

[FLORINDO *rearranges the trunk on the* PORTER's *shoulder.*]

TRUFFALDINO: Here's a chance for sixpence.

[*To* FLORINDO.]

Sir, can I do anything for you?

FLORINDO: My good man, be so good as to carry this trunk into the inn there.

TRUFFALDINO: Yes, sir, let me take it, sir. See how I do it.
> [*To the* PORTER.]

You be off!
> [TRUFFALDINO *puts his shoulder under the trunk and takes it by himself, knocking the* PORTER *down at the same time.*]

FLORINDO: Well done!

TRUFFALDINO: It weighs nothing. A mere trifle.
> [*Goes into the inn with the trunk.*]

FLORINDO: [*to* PORTER] There! You see how it's done.

PORTER: I can do no more. I work as a porter for my misfortune, but I am the son of a respectable person.

FLORINDO: What did your father do?

PORTER: My father? He skinned lambs in the town.

FLORINDO: The fellow's mad.
> [*To* PORTER.]

That will do.
> [*Going towards the inn.*]

PORTER: Please your honor —

FLORINDO: What do you want?

PORTER: The money for the porterage.

FLORINDO: How much am I to give you for ten yards? There's the landing stage!
> [*Pointing off.*]

PORTER: I didn't count them. I want my pay.
> [*Holds out his hand.*]

FLORINDO: There's twopence.
> [*Gives money.*]

PORTER: I want my pay.
> [*Still holding out his hand.*]

FLORINDO: Lord, what obstinacy! Here's twopence more.
> [*Gives money.*]

PORTER: I want my pay.

FLORINDO: [*kicks him*] Go and be hanged!

PORTER: Thank you, sir, that's enough.
> [*Exit.*]

FLORINDO: There's a humorous fellow! He was positively waiting for me to kick him. Well, let us go and see what the inn is like —
> [*Re-enter* TRUFFALDINO.]

TRUFFALDINO: Sir, everything is ready for you.

FLORINDO: What lodging is there here?

TRUFFALDINO: 'Tis a very good place, sir. Good beds, fine looking glasses, and a grand kitchen with a smell to it that is very comforting. I have talked with the waiter. You will be served like a king.

FLORINDO: What's *your* trade?

TRUFFALDINO: Servant

FLORINDO: Are you a Venetian?

TRUFFALDINO: Not from Venice, but of the State. I'm from Bergamo, at your service.

FLORINDO: Have you a master now?

TRUFFALDINO: At the moment — to tell the truth, I have not.

FLORINDO: You are without a master?

TRUFFALDINO: You see me, sir. I am without a master.
>  [*Aside.*]
>  My master is not here, so I tell no lies.

FLORINDO: Will you come and be *my* servant?

TRUFFALDINO: Why not?
>  [*Aside.*]
>  If his terms are better.

FLORINDO: At any rate, for as long as I stay in Venice.

TRUFFALDINO: Very good, sir. How much will you give me?

FLORINDO: How much do you want?

TRUFFALDINO: I'll tell you: another master I had, who is here no more, he gave me a shilling a day and all found.

FLORINDO: Good, I will give you as much.

TRUFFALDINO: You must give me a little more than that.

FLORINDO: How much more do you want?

TRUFFALDINO: A halfpenny a day for snuff.

FLORINDO: Oh, I'll give you that and welcome.

TRUFFALDINO: If that's so, I'm your man, sir.

FLORINDO: But I should like to know a little more about you.

TRUFFALDINO: If you want to know all about me, you go to Bergamo; anyone there will tell you who I am.

FLORINDO: Have you nobody in Venice who knows you?

TRUFFALDINO: I only arrived this morning, sir.

FLORINDO: Well, well, I take you for an honest man. I will give you a trial.

TRUFFALDINO: You give me a trial and you shall see.

FLORINDO: First of all, I am anxious to know if there are letters at the Post for me. Here is half a crown; go to the Turin Post and ask if there are letters for Florindo Aretusi; if there are, take them and bring them at once. I shall wait for you.

TRUFFALDINO: Meanwhile you will order dinner, sir?

FLORINDO: Yes, well said! I will order it.
>  [*Aside.*]
>  He is a wag, I like him. I'll give him a trial.
>  [FLORINDO *goes into the inn.*]

TRUFFALDINO: A halfpenny more a day, that's fifteen pence a month. 'Tis not true that the other gentleman gave me a shilling; he gives me six pennies. Maybe six pennies make a shilling, but I'm not quite sure. And this gentleman from Turin is nowhere to be seen. He's mad. He's a young fellow without a beard and without any sense neither. He may go about his business; I shall go to the Post for my new gentleman.
>  [*As he is going,* BEATRICE *enters with* BRIGHELLA *and meets him.*]

BEATRICE: That's a nice way to behave! Is that the way you wait for me?

TRUFFALDINO: Here I am, sir. I am still waiting for you.

BEATRICE: And how do you come to be waiting for me here, and not in the street where I told you? 'Tis a mere accident that I have found you.

TRUFFALDINO: I went for a bit of a walk to take away my appetite.

BEATRICE: Well, go at once to the landing stage; fetch my trunk and take it to the inn of Master Brighella.

BRIGHELLA: There's my inn, you cannot mistake it.

BEATRICE: Very well, then, make haste, and I will wait for you.

TRUFFALDINO: The devil! In *that* inn?

BEATRICE: Here, you will go at the same time to the Turin Post and ask if there are any letters for me. You may ask if there are letters for Federigo Rasponi and also for Beatrice Rasponi. That's my sister. Some friends of hers might perhaps write to her; so be sure to see if there are letters either for her or for me.

TRUFFALDINO: [*aside*] What *am* I to do? Here's a pretty kettle of fish!

BRIGHELLA: [*to* BEATRICE] Why do you expect letters in your real name if you left home secretly?

BEATRICE: I told the steward to write to me; and I don't know which name he may use. I'll tell you more later.

> [*To* TRUFFALDINO.]

Make haste, be off with you to the Post and the landing stage. Fetch the letters and have the trunk brought to the inn; I shall be there.

> [*Exit* BEATRICE *into the inn.*]

TRUFFALDINO: Are you the landlord?

BRIGHELLA: Yes, I am. You behave properly and you need have no fear, I will do you well.

> [*Exit* BRIGHELLA *into the inn.*]

TRUFFALDINO: There's luck! There are many that look in vain for a master, and I have found two. What the devil am I to do? I cannot wait upon them both. No? Why not? Wouldn't it be a fine thing to wait upon both of them, earn two men's wages and eat and drink for two? 'Twould be a fine thing indeed, if neither of them found out. And if they did? What then? No matter! If one sends me away, I stay with the other. I swear I'll try it. If it last but a day, I'll try it. Whatever happens I shall have done a fine thing. Here goes. Let's go to the Post for both of 'em.

> [*Enter* SILVIO *and meets* TRUFFALDINO.]

SILVIO: [*aside*] That is the servant of Federigo Rasponi.

> [*To* TRUFFALDINO.]

My good man.

TRUFFALDINO: Sir?

SILVIO: Where is your master?

TRUFFALDINO: My master? He's in that inn there.

SILVIO: Go at once and tell your master that I wish to speak to him; if he be a man of honor let him come down; I wait for him.

TRUFFALDINO: My dear sir —

SILVIO: [*angrily*] Go at once.

TRUFFALDINO: But I must tell you, my master —

SILVIO: Don't answer me; or, by Heaven, I'll —

TRUFFALDINO: But which do you want?

SILVIO: At once, I say, or I'll beat you.

TRUFFALDINO: [*aside*] Well, I don't know — I'll send the first I can find.

> [*Exit* TRUFFALDINO *into the inn.*]

SILVIO: No, I will never suffer the presence of a rival. Federigo may have got off once with his life, but he shall not always have the same fortune. Either he shall renounce all claims to Clarice, or he shall give me the satisfaction of a gentleman. Here are some more people coming out of the inn. I don't want to be disturbed.

[*Retires to the opposite side.*]

[*Enter* TRAFFALDINO *with* FLORINDO.]

TRUFFALDINO: [*points out* SILVIO *to* FLORINDO] There's the fire-eating gentleman, sir.

FLORINDO: I do not know him. What does he want with me?

TRUFFALDINO: I don't know. I go to fetch the letters, with your good leave, sir.

[*Aside.*]

I don't want any more trouble.

[*Exit.*]

SILVIO: [*aside*] Federigo does not come?

FLORINDO: [*aside*] I must find out what the truth is.

[*To* SILVIO.]

Sir, are you the gentleman who inquired for me?

SILVIO: I, sir? I have not even the honor of your acquaintance.

FLORINDO: But that servant who has just gone told me that with a loud and threatening voice you made bold to challenge me.

SILVIO: He misunderstood. I said I wished to speak to his master.

FLORINDO: Very well, I am his master.

SILVIO: You his master?

FLORINDO: Certainly. He is in my service.

SILVIO: Then I ask your pardon. Either your servant is exactly like another whom I saw this morning, or he waits on another person.

FLORINDO: You may set your mind at rest; he waits on me.

SILVIO: If that be so, I ask your pardon again.

FLORINDO: No harm done. Mistakes often occur.

SILVIO: Are you a stranger here, sir?

FLORINDO: From Turin, sir, at your service.

SILVIO: The man whom I would have provoked was from Turin.

FLORINDO: Then perhaps I may know him; if he has given you offence, I shall gladly assist you to obtain just satisfaction.

SILVIO: Do you know one Federigo Rasponi?

FLORINDO: Ah! I knew him only too well.

SILVIO: He makes claim, on the strength of her father's word, to the lady who this morning swore to be my wife.

FLORINDO: My good friend, Federigo Rasponi cannot take your wife away from you. He is dead.

SILVIO: Yes, we all believed that he was dead; but this morning to my disgust he arrived in Venice safe and sound.

FLORINDO: Sir, you petrify me.

SILVIO: No wonder! I was petrified myself.

FLORINDO: I assure you Federigo Rasponi is dead.

SILVIO: I assure you that Federigo Rasponi is alive.

FLORINDO: Take care you are not deceived.

SILVIO: Signor Pantalone dei Bisognosi, the young lady's father, has made all possible inquiries to assure himself and is in possession of incontestable proofs that he is here in person.

FLORINDO: [*aside*] Then he was not killed in the duel, as everybody believed!

SILVIO: Either he or I must renounce claim to the love of Clarice or to life.

FLORINDO: [*aside*] Federigo here?

SILVIO: I am surprised that you have not seen him. He was to lodge at this very inn.

FLORINDO: I have not seen him. They told me that there was no one else at all staying there.

SILVIO: He must have changed his mind. Forgive me, sir, if I have troubled you. If you see him, tell him that for his own welfare he must abandon the idea of this marriage. Silvio Lombardi is my name; I am your most obedient servant, sir.

FLORINDO: I shall be greatly pleased to have the honor of your friendship.

    [*Aside.*]

I am confounded.

SILVIO: May I beg to know your name, sir?

FLORINDO: [*aside*] I must not discover myself.

    [*To* SILVIO.]

Your servant, sir, Orazio Ardenti.

SILVIO: Signor Orazio, I am yours to command.

    [*Exit* SILVIO.]

FLORINDO: I was told he died on the spot. Yet I fled so hurriedly when accused of the crime that I had no chance of finding out the truth. Then, since he is not dead, it will be better for me to go back to Turin and console my beloved Beatrice, who is perhaps in suffering and sorrow for my absence.

    [*Enter* TRUFFALDINO, *with another* PORTER *who carries* BEATRICE'S *trunk.* TRUFFALDINO *comes forward a few steps, sees* FLORINDO *and, fearing to be seen himself, makes the* PORTER *retire.*]

TRUFFALDINO: Come along. This way — The devil! There's my other master. Go back, friend, and wait for me at that corner.

    [*Exit* PORTER.]

FLORINDO: [*continuing to himself*] Yes, without delay. I will go back to Turin.

TRUFFALDINO: Here I am, sir.

FLORINDO: Truffaldino, will you come to Turin with me?

TRUFFALDINO: When?

FLORINDO: Now; at once.

TRUFFALDINO: Before dinner?

FLORINDO: No, we will have dinner, and then we will go.

TRUFFALDINO: Very good, sir. I'll think it over at dinner.

FLORINDO: Have you been to the Post?

TRUFFALDINO: Yes, sir.

FLORINDO: Have you found my letters?

TRUFFALDINO: I have, sir.

FLORINDO: Where are they?

TRUFFALDINO: I will give you them.

    [*Takes three letters out of his pocket. Aside.*]

The devil! I have mixed up one master's letters with the other's. How shall I find out which are his? I cannot read.

FLORINDO: Come, give me my letters.

TRUFFALDINO: Directly, sir.

[*Aside.*]

Here's a muddle.

[*To* FLORINDO.]

I must tell you, sir; these three letters are not all for your honor. I met another servant, who knows me; we were in service together in Bergamo; I told him I was going to the Post, and he asked me to see whether there was anything for *his* master. I think there was one letter, but I don't know which of them it was.

FLORINDO:  Let me see; I will take mine and give you the other back.

TRUFFALDINO:  There, sir; I only wanted to do my friend a good turn.

FLORINDO:  [*aside*] What is this? A letter addressed to Beatrice Rasponi? To Beatrice Rasponi at Venice?

TRUFFALDINO:  Did you find the one that belongs to my mate?

FLORINDO:  Who is this mate of yours who asked you to do this for him?

TRUFFALDINO:  He is a servant — his name is Pasqual' —

FLORINDO:  Whom does he wait upon?

TRUFFALDINO:  I do not know, sir.

FLORINDO:  But if he told you to fetch his master's letters, he must have told you his name.

TRUFFALDINO:  Of course he did.

[*Aside.*]

The muddle's getting thicker.

FLORINDO:  Well, what name did he tell you?

TRUFFALDINO:  I don't remember.

FLORINDO:  What?

TRUFFALDINO:  He wrote it down on a bit of paper.

FLORINDO:  And where is the paper?

TRUFFALDINO:  I left it at the Post.

FLORINDO:  [*aside*] Confusion! What does this mean?

TRUFFALDINO:  [*aside*] I am learning my part as I go along.

FLORINDO:  Where does this fellow Pasquale live?

TRUFFALDINO:  Indeed, sir, I haven't the slightest idea.

FLORINDO:  How will you be able to give him the letter?

TRUFFALDINO:  He said he would meet me in the Piazza.

FLORINDO:  [*aside*] I don't know what to make of it.

TRUFFALDINO:  [*aside*] If I get through this business clean 'twill be a miracle.

[*To* FLORINDO.]

Pray give me the letter, sir, and I shall find him somewhere.

FLORINDO:  No; I mean to open this letter.

TRUFFALDINO:  Oh, sir, do not do that, sir. Besides, you know how wrong it is to open letters.

FLORINDO:  I care not; this letter interests me too much. It is addressed to a person on whom I have a certain claim. I can open it without scruple.

[*Opens letter.*]

TRUFFALDINO:  As you will, sir.

[*Aside.*]

He has opened it.

FLORINDO:  [*reads*] "Madam, your departure from this city has given rise to much talk, and all understand that you have gone to join Signor Florindo. The Court of Justice has discovered that you have fled in man's dress and intends to have you arrested. I have not sent this letter by the courier from Turin to Venice, so as not to reveal the place whither you were bound, but I have sent it to a friend at Genoa to be forwarded to Venice. If I have any more news to tell you, I will not fail to send it by the same means. Your most humble servant, Antonio."

TRUFFALDINO: That's a nice way to behave! Reading other people's letters!

FLORINDO: [*aside*] What is all this? Beatrice has left home? In man's dress? To join me? Indeed she loves me. Heaven grant I may find her in Venice.

[*To* TRUFFALDINO.]

Here, my good Truffaldino, go and do all you can to find Pasquale; find out from him who his master is, and if he be man or woman. Find out where he lodges, and if you can, bring him here to me, and both he and you shall be handsomely rewarded.

TRUFFALDINO: Give me the letter; I will try to find him.

FLORINDO: There it is. I count upon you. This matter is of infinite importance to me.

TRUFFALDINO: But am I to give him the letter open like this?

FLORINDO: Tell him it was a mistake, an accident. Don't make difficulties.

TRUFFALDINO: And are you going to Turin now?

FLORINDO: No, not for the present. Lose no time. Go and find Pasquale.

[*Aside*]

Beatrice in Venice, Federigo in Venice! If her brother finds her, unhappy woman! I will do all I can to discover her first.

[*Exit toward the town.*]

TRUFFALDINO: Upon my word, I hope he is not going away. I want to see how my two jobs will work out. I'm on my mettle. This letter, now, which I have to take to my other master — I don't like to have to give it to him opened. I must try to fold it again.

[*Tries various awkward folds.*]

And now it must be sealed. If I only knew how to do it! I have seen my grandmother sometimes seal letters with chewed bread. I'll try it.

[*Takes a piece of bread out of his pocket.*]

It's a pity to waste this little piece of bread, but still something must be done.

[*Chews a little bread to seal the letter and accidentally swallows it.*]

The devil! It has gone down. I must chew another bit.

[*Same business.*]

No good, nature rebels. I'll try once more.

[*Chews again; would like to swallow the bread, but restrains himself and with great difficulty removes the bread from his mouth.*]

Ah, here it is; I'll seal the letter.

[*Seals the letter with the bread.*]

I think that looks quite well. I'm always a great man for doing things cleanly. Lord! I had forgotten the porter.

[*Calls off.*]

Friend, come hither; take the trunk on your shoulder.

[*Re-enter* PORTER.]

PORTER: Here I am; where am I to carry it?

TRUFFALDINO: Take it into that inn; I am coming directly.

[BEATRICE *comes out of the inn.*]

BEATRICE: Is this my trunk?

TRUFFALDINO: Yes, sir.

BEATRICE: [to PORTER] Carry it into my room.

PORTER: Which is your room?

BEATRICE: Ask the waiter.

PORTER: There's one and threepence to pay.

BEATRICE: Go on, I will pay you.

PORTER: Please be quick about it.

BEATRICE: Don't bother me.

PORTER: I've half a mind to throw the trunk down in the middle of the street.
    [Goes into the inn.]

TRUFFALDINO: Great folk for politeness, these porters!

BEATRICE: Have you been to the Post?

TRUFFALDINO: Yes, sir.

BEATRICE: Any letters for me?

TRUFFALDINO: One for your sister.

BEATRICE: Good; where is it?

TRUFFALDINO: Here.
    [Gives letter.]

BEATRICE: This letter has been opened.

TRUFFALDINO: Opened? No! Impossible!

BEATRICE: Yes, opened, and then sealed with bread.

TRUFFALDINO: I can't think how that can have happened.

BEATRICE: You cannot think, eh? Rascal, who has opened this letter? I must know.

TRUFFALDINO: Sir, I'll tell you, I'll confess the truth. We are all liable to make
    mistakes. At the Post there was a letter for me; I can't read very much, and by
    mistake, instead of opening my letter, I opened yours. I ask your pardon —

BEATRICE: If that was all, there's no great harm done.

TRUFFALDINO: 'Tis true, on the word of a poor man.

BEATRICE: Have you read this letter? Do you know what is in it?

TRUFFALDINO: Not a word. I can't read the handwriting.

BEATRICE: Has anyone else seen it?

TRUFFALDINO: [with an air of great indignation] Oh!

BEATRICE: Take care now —

TRUFFALDINO: [same business] Sir!

BEATRICE: [aside] I hope he is not deceiving me.
    [Reads to herself.]

TRUFFALDINO: That's all put straight.

BEATRICE: [aside] Antonio is a faithful servant and I am obliged to him.
    [To TRUFFALDINO.]
    Listen; I have some business to do close by. You go into the inn, open the
    trunk — here are my keys — and unpack my things. When I come back, we
    will have dinner.
    [Aside.]
    I have seen nothing of Signor Pantalone, and I am anxious to have my money.
    [Exit.]

TRUFFALDINO: Come, that all went well; it couldn't have gone better. I'm a great
    fellow; I think a deal more of myself than I did before.
    [Enter PANTALONE.]

PANTALONE:  Tell me, my good man, is your master in the house?

TRUFFALDINO:  No, sir, he is not there.

PANTALONE:  Do you know where he may be?

TRUFFALDINO:  Not that neither.

PANTALONE:  Is he coming home to dinner?

TRUFFALDINO:  Yes, I should think so.

PANTALONE:  Here, as soon as he comes home give him this purse with these hundred guineas. I cannot stay, I have business. Good day to you.
> [*Exit* PANTALONE.]

TRUFFALDINO:  And a good day to you, sir! He never told me to which of my masters I was to give it.
> [*Enter* FLORINDO.]

FLORINDO:  Well, did you find Pasquale?

TRUFFALDINO:  No sir, I did not find Pasqual', but I found a gentleman who gave me a purse with a hundred guineas in it.

FLORINDO:  A hundred guineas? What for?

TRUFFALDINO:  Tell me truly, sir, were you expecting money from anyone?

FLORINDO:  Yes; I had presented a letter of credit to a merchant.

TRUFFALDINO:  Then this money will be for you.

FLORINDO:  What did he say when he gave it to you?

TRUFFALDINO:  He told me to give it to my master.

FLORINDO:  Then of course it is mine. Am I not your master? What doubt could you have?

TRUFFALDINO:  [*aside*] Yes, but what about t'other one?

FLORINDO:  And you do not know who gave you the money?

TRUFFALDINO:  No, sir; I think I have seen his face somewhere, but I don't remember exactly.

FLORINDO:  It will have been the merchant to whom I had a letter.

TRUFFALDINO:  Yes, of course, sir.

FLORINDO:  You won't forget Pasquale.

TRUFFALDINO:  I'll find him after dinner.

FLORINDO:  Then let us go and order our meal.
> [*Goes into the inn.*]

TRUFFALDINO:  We will. Lucky I made no mistake this time. I've given the purse to the right one.
> [*Goes into the inn.*]

SCENE III———*A Room in the House of* PANTALONE.

PANTALONE:  That's the long and short of it; Signor Federigo is to be your husband. I have given my word and I am not to be cozened.

CLARICE:  You have my obedience, sir; but I beseech you, this is tyranny.

PANTALONE:  When Signor Federigo first asked for your hand, I told you; you never replied that you did not wish to marry him. You should have spoken then; now it is too late.

CLARICE:  My fear of you, sir, and my respect, made me dumb.

PANTALONE:  Then your fear and respect should do the same now.

CLARICE: Indeed I cannot marry him, sir.

PANTALONE: No? And why not?

CLARICE: Nothing shall induce me to marry Federigo.

PANTALONE: You dislike him so much?

CLARICE: He is odious in my eyes.

PANTALONE: And supposing I were to show you how you might begin to like him a little?

CLARICE: What do you mean, sir?

PANTALONE: Put Signor Silvio out of your mind, and you will soon like Federigo well enough.

CLARICE: Silvio is too firmly stamped upon my heart; and your own approval, sir, has rooted him there the more securely.

PANTALONE: [*aside*] In some ways I am sorry for her.
[*To* CLARICE.]
You have got to make a virtue of necessity.

CLARICE: My heart is not capable of so great an effort.

PANTALONE: Come, come; you shall!
[*Enter* SMERALDINA.]

SMERALDINA: Sir, Signor Federigo is here and desires to speak with you.

PANTALONE: Tell him to come in; I am at his service.

CLARICE: [*weeping*] Alas! What torture!

SMERALDINA: What is it, madam? You are weeping? Truly you do wrong. Have you not noticed how handsome Signor Federigo is? If I had such luck, I would not cry; no, I would laugh with the whole of my mouth.
[*Exit* SMERALDINA.]

PANTALONE: There, there, my child; you must not be seen crying.

CLARICE: But if I feel my heart bursting!
[*Enter* BEATRICE *in man's dress.*]

BEATRICE: My respects to Signor Pantalone.

PANTALONE: Your servant, sir. Did you receive a purse with a hundred guineas in it?

BEATRICE: No.

PANTALONE: But I gave it to your servant just now. You told me he was a trustworthy man.

BEATRICE: Yes, indeed; there is no danger. I did not see him. He will give me the money when I come home again.
[*Aside to* PANTALONE.]
What ails Signora Clarice that she is weeping?

PANTALONE: [*aside to* BEATRICE] Dear Signor Federigo, you must have pity on her. The news of your death was the cause of this trouble. I hope it will pass away in time.

BEATRICE: [*to* PANTALONE] Do me a kindness, Signor Pantalone, and leave me alone with her a moment, to see if I cannot obtain a kind word from her.

PANTALONE: With pleasure, sir. I will go, and come back again.
[*To* CLARICE.]
My child, stay here, I will be back directly. You must entertain your promised husband awhile.
[*Softly to* CLARICE.]
Now, be careful.

[*Exit* PANTALONE.]

BEATRICE: Signora Clarice, I beg you —

CLARICE: Stand away, and do not dare to importune me.

BEATRICE: So severe with him who is your destined husband?

CLARICE: They may drag me by force to the altar, but you will have only my hand, never my heart.

BEATRICE: You disdain me, but I hope to appease you.

CLARICE: I shall abhor you to all eternity.

BEATRICE: But if you knew me, you would not say so.

CLARICE: I know you well enough as the destroyer of my happiness.

BEATRICE: But I can find a way to comfort you.

CLARICE: You deceive yourself; there is no one who can comfort me but Silvio.

BEATRICE: 'Tis true, I cannot give you the same comfort as your Silvio might, but I can at least contribute to your happiness.

CLARICE: I think it is quite enough, sir, that although I speak to you as harshly as I can, you should continue to torture me.

BEATRICE: [*aside*] Poor girl! I can't bear to see her suffer.

CLARICE: [*aside*] I'm so angry, I don't care how rude I am.

BEATRICE: Signora Clarice, I have a secret to tell you.

CLARICE: I make no promise to keep it; you had better not tell it me.

BEATRICE: Your severity deprives me of the means to make you happy.

CLARICE: You can never make me anything but miserable.

BEATRICE: You are wrong, and to convince you I will speak plainly. You have no desire for me, I have no use for you. You have promised your hand to another, I to another have already pledged my heart.

CLARICE: Oh! Now you begin to please me.

BEATRICE: Did I not tell you that I knew how to comfort you?

CLARICE: Ah, I feared you would deceive me.

BEATRICE: Nay, madam, I speak in all sincerity; and if you promise me that discretion which you refused me just now, I will confide to you a secret, which will ensure your peace of mind.

CLARICE: I vow I will observe the strictest silence.

BEATRICE: I am not Federigo Rasponi, but his sister Beatrice.

CLARICE: What! I am amazed. You a woman?

BEATRICE: I am indeed. Imagine my feelings when I claimed you as my bride!

CLARICE: And what news have you of your brother?

BEATRICE: He died indeed by the sword. A lover of mine was thought to have killed him, and 'tis he whom I am seeking now in these clothes. I beseech you by all the holy laws of friendship and of love not to betray me.

CLARICE: Won't you let me tell Silvio?

BEATRICE: No; on the contrary I forbid you absolutely.

CLARICE: Well, I will say nothing.

BEATRICE: Remember I count upon you.

CLARICE: You have my promise. I will be silent.

BEATRICE: Now, I hope, you will treat me more kindly.

CLARICE: I will be your friend indeed; and if I can be of service to you, dispose of me.

BEATRICE: I too swear eternal friendship to you. Give me your hand.

CLARICE: I don't quite like to —

BEATRICE: Are you afraid I am not a woman after all? I will give you proof positive.

CLARICE: It all seems just like a dream.

BEATRICE: Yes. 'Tis a strange business.

CLARICE: 'Tis indeed fantastic.

BEATRICE: Come, I must be going. Let us embrace in sign of honest friendship and loyalty.

CLARICE: There! I doubt you no longer.

[*Enter* PANTALONE.]

PANTALONE: Well done, well done; I congratulate you.

[*To* CLARICE.]

My child, you have been very quick in adapting yourself.

BEATRICE: Did I not tell you, Signor Pantalone, that I should win her round?

PANTALONE: Magnificent! You have done more in four minutes than I should have done in four years.

CLARICE: [*aside*] Now I am in a worse tangle than ever.

PANTALONE: [*to* CLARICE] Then we will have the wedding at once.

CLARICE: Pray do not be in too much haste, sir.

PANTALONE: What? Holding hands on the sly and kissing, and then in no haste about it? No, no, I don't want you to get yourself into trouble. You shall be married tomorrow.

BEATRICE: Signor Pantalone, 'twill be necessary first of all to arrange the settlement and to go into our accounts.

PANTALONE: We will do all that. These things can be done in a couple of hours.

CLARICE: Sir, I beseech you —

PANTALONE: Madam, I am going straight away to say a word to Signor Silvio.

CLARICE: For the love of Heaven do not anger him.

PANTALONE: What, what? Do you want two husbands?

CLARICE: Not exactly — but —

PANTALONE: Butt me no buts. 'Tis all settled. Your servant, sir.

[*Going.*]

BEATRICE: [*to* PANTALONE] Listen, sir —

PANTALONE: You are husband and wife.

[*Going.*]

CLARICE: Had you not better —

PANTALONE: We will talk about it this evening.

[*Exit.*]

CLARICE: Oh, Signora Beatrice, 'tis worse than it was before!

## ACT II

SCENE I——*The Courtyard of* PANTALONE'S *House.*

SILVIO: Sir, I entreat you to leave me alone.

DR. LOMBARDI: Stay, answer me.

SILVIO: I am beside myself.

DR. LOMBARDI: What are you doing in the courtyard of Signor Pantalone?

SILVIO: I intend either that he should keep his word that he has given me, or that he should render me account for this intolerable insult.

DR. LOMBARDI: But you cannot do this in Pantalone's own house. You are a fool to let yourself be so transported with anger.

SILVIO: A man who behaves so abominably deserves no consideration.

DR. LOMBARDI: True; but that is no reason why you should be so rash. Leave him to me, my dear boy, leave him to me; let me talk to him; maybe I can bring him to reason and make him see where his duty lies. Go away somewhere and wait for me; leave this courtyard; do not let us make a scene. I will wait for Signor Pantalone.

SILVIO: But sir, I —

DR. LOMBARDI: But, sir, I will have you obey me.

SILVIO: I obey you, sir. I will go. Speak to him. I wait for you at the apothecary's. But if Signor Pantalone persists, he will have to settle with me.

    [*Exit* SILVIO.]

DR. LOMBARDI: Poor dear boy, I feel truly sorry for him. Signor Pantalone ought never to have led him on so far before he was quite certain that man from Turin was dead. I must see him quietly; I must not let my temper get the better of me.

    [*Enter* PANTALONE.]

PANTALONE: [*aside*] What is the doctor doing in my house?

DR. LOMBARDI: Oh, Signor Pantalone, your servant.

PANTALONE: Your servant, Doctor. I was just going to look for you and your son.

DR. LOMBARDI: Indeed? Good! I suppose you were coming to give us your assurance that Signora Clarice is to be Silvio's wife.

PANTALONE: [*much embarrassed*] Well, the fact is, I was coming to tell you —

DR. LOMBARDI: No, no; there is no need for explanations. You have my sympathy in a very awkward situation. But we are old friends and we will let bygones be bygones.

PANTALONE: [*still hesitating*] Yes, of course, in view of the promise made to Signor Federigo —

DR. LOMBARDI: He took you by surprise, and you had no time for reflection; you did not think of the affront you were giving to our family.

PANTALONE: You can hardly talk of an affront, when a previous contract —

DR. LOMBARDI: I know what you are going to say. It seemed at first sight out of the question that your promise to the Turin gentleman could be repudiated, because it was a formal contract. But that was a contract merely between you and him; whereas ours is confirmed by the girl himself.

PANTALONE: Very true, but —

DR. LOMBARDI: And as you know, in matrimonial cases, *consensus, et non concubitus, facit virum.*

PANTALONE: I am no Latin scholar; but I must tell you —

DR. LOMBARDI: And girls must not be sacrificed.

PANTALONE: Have you anything more to say?

DR. LOMBARDI: I have nothing more to say.

PANTALONE: Have you finished?

DR. LOMBARDI: I have finished.

PANTALONE: May I speak?

DR. LOMBARDI: You may.

PANTALONE: My dear Doctor, with all your learning—

DR. LOMBARDI: As regards the dowry, we can easily arrange matters. A little more or a little less, I will make no difficulties.

PANTALONE: I must begin all over again. Will you allow me to speak?

DR. LOMBARDI: With pleasure.

PANTALONE: I must tell you; I have the greatest respect for your legal learning, but in this case it does not apply.

DR. LOMBARDI: And you mean to tell me that this other marriage is to take place?

PANTALONE: For my part I have given my word and I cannot go back upon it. My daughter is content; what impediment can there be? I was just coming to look for you or Signor Silvio, to tell you this. I am extremely sorry, but I see no help for it.

DR. LOMBARDI: I am not surprised at your daughter's behavior. But I am surprised at yours, sir, at your treating me in this disgraceful way. If you were not perfectly certain about the death of Signor Federigo, you had no business to enter into an engagement with my son; and having entered into an engagement with him, you are bound to maintain that engagement whatever it may cost you. The news of Federigo's death was quite sufficient to justify, even to Federigo, your new intention; he could have no right to reproach you, still less to demand compensation. The marriage which was contracted this morning between Signora Clarice and my son *coram testibus* cannot be dissolved by a mere word given by you to another party. If I were to listen to my son I should insist upon the annulment of the new contract and compel your daughter to marry him; but I should be ashamed to receive into my house so disreputable a daughter-in-law, the daughter of a man who breaks his word as you do. Signor Pantalone, you have done me an injury, you have done an injury to the house of Lombardi. The time will come when you will have to pay for it; yes, sir, the time will come—*omnia tempus habent.*

[*Exit* DOCTOR.]

PANTALONE: You may go to the devil for all I care. I don't care a fig, I'm not afraid of you. The Rasponis are worth a hundred of the Lombardis. An only son, and as rich as he is—you won't find that every day. It has got to be.

[*Enter* SILVIO.]

SILVIO: [*aside*] 'Tis all very fine for my father to talk. Let him keep his temper who can.

PANTALONE: [*seeing* SILVIO, *aside*] Here comes the other.

SILVIO: [*rudely*] Your servant, sir.

PANTALONE: Yours to command, sir.

　　　[*Aside.*]

He is boiling.

SILVIO: I have just heard something from my father; am I to believe that it is true?

PANTALONE: If your father said it, it must certainly be true.

SILVIO: Then the marriage is settled between Signora Clarice and Signor Federigo?

PANTALONE: Yes, sir, settled and concluded.

SILVIO: I am amazed that you should have the face to tell me so. You are a man of no reputation, you are no gentleman.

PANTALONE: What is all this? Is that the way you speak to a man of my age?

SILVIO: I don't care how old you are; I have a mind to run you straight through the body.

PANTALONE: I am not a frog, sir, to be spitted. Do you come into my own house to make all this turmoil?

SILVIO: Come outside then.

PANTALONE: I am surprised at you, sir.

SILVIO: Come on, if you are a man of honor.

PANTALONE: I am accustomed to be treated with respect.

SILVIO: You are a low fellow, a coward, and a villain.

PANTALONE: You are a most impertinent young puppy.

SILVIO: I swear to Heaven —
　　　　[*Lays his hand to his sword.*]

PANTALONE: Help! Murder!
　　　　[*Draws a pistol.*]
　　　　[*Enter* BEATRICE *with a drawn sword.*]

BEATRICE: [*to* PANTALONE] I am here to defend you.

PANTALONE: My dear son-in-law, I am much obliged to you.

SILVIO: [*to* BEATRICE] You are the very man I want to fight.

BEATRICE: [*aside*] I am in for it now.

SILVIO: [*to* BEATRICE] Come on, sir.

PANTALONE: [*frightened*] My dear son-in-law —

BEATRICE: It is not the first time that I have been in danger.
　　　　[*To* SILVIO.]
　　I am not afraid of you.
　　　　[*Presents sword.*]

PANTALONE: Help! Help!
　　　　[PANTALONE *runs toward the street.* BEATRICE *and* SILVIO *fight.* SILVIO *falls and drops his sword.* BEATRICE *holds her point to his heart.*]

CLARICE: [*to* BEATRICE] Stop, stop!

BEATRICE: Fair Clarice, at your request I grant Silvio his life, and in consideration of my mercy, I beg you to remember your oath.
　　　　[*Exit* BEATRICE.]

CLARICE: Dear Silvio, are you hurt?

SILVIO: Dear Silvio! Faithless deceiver! Dear Silvio! To a lover disdained, to a betrayed husband!

CLARICE: No, Silvio, I do not deserve your reproaches. I love you, I adore you, I am indeed faithful.

SILVIO: Oh, lying jade! Faithful to me, forsooth! You call that fidelity, to plight your troth to another?

CLARICE: I never did so, nor will I ever. I will die rather than desert you.

SILVIO: I heard just now that you have given your oath.

CLARICE: My oath does not bind me to marry him.

SILVIO: Then what did you swear?

CLARICE: Dear Silvio, have mercy on me; I cannot tell you.

SILVIO: Why not?

CLARICE: Because I am sworn to silence.

SILVIO: That proves your guilt.

CLARICE: No, I am innocent.

SILVIO: Innocent people have no secrets.

CLARICE: Indeed I should be guilty if I spoke.

SILVIO: And to whom have you sworn this silence?

CLARICE: To Federigo.

SILVIO: And you will observe it so jealously?

CLARICE: I will observe it, rather than be a perjuress.

SILVIO: And you tell me you do not love him? He's a fool that believes you. I do not believe you, cruel, deceiver! Begone from my sight!

CLARICE: If I did not love you, I should not have run hither in all haste to save your life.

SILVIO: Then I loathe my life, if I must owe it to one so ungrateful.

CLARICE: I love you with all my heart.

SILVIO: I abhor you with all my soul.

CLARICE: I will die, if you are not to be appeased.

SILVIO: I would sooner see you dead than unfaithful.

CLARICE: Then you shall have that satisfaction.

> [*Picks up his sword.*]

SILVIO: Yes, that sword should avenge my wrongs.

CLARICE: Are you so cruel to your Clarice?

SILVIO: 'Twas you that taught me cruelty.

CLARICE: Then you desire my death?

SILVIO: I know not what I desire.

CLARICE: I do.

> [*Points the sword at her breast.*]
>
> [*Enter* SMERALDINA.]

SMERALDINA: Stop, stop! What on earth are you doing?

> [*Takes the sword away from* CLARICE.]

And you, you dog, you would have let her die?

> [*To* SILVIO.]

Have you the heart of a tiger, of a hyena, of a devil? Look at you, you're a pretty little fellow, that expects ladies to disembowel themselves for you! You are much too kind to him, madam. He doesn't want you any more, I suppose? The man that doesn't want you doesn't deserve you. Let this murderer go to the devil; and you come along with me. There's no shortage of men; I'll promise to find you a dozen before evening.

> [*She throws down the sword,* SILVIO *picks it up.*]

CLARICE: [*weeping*] Ungrateful! Can it be that my death should cost you not a single sigh? But I *shall* die, and die of grief. I shall die, and you will be content. But one day you will know that I am innocent, and then, when it is too late, you will be sorry you did not believe me, you will weep for my misfortune and for your own barbarous cruelty.

> [*Exit* CLARICE.]

SMERALDINA: Here's something I really don't understand. Here's a girl on the point of killing herself, and you sit there looking on, just as if you were at a play.

SILVIO: Nonsense, woman! Do you suppose she really meant to kill herself?

SMERALDINA:  How should I know? I know that if I had not arrived in time, she would have been gone, poor thing.

SILVIO:  The point was nowhere near her heart.

SMERALDINA:  Did you ever hear such a lie? It was just ready to pierce her.

SILVIO:  You women always invent things.

SMERALDINA:  We should indeed, if we were like you. It's as the old saw says; we get the kicks and you the halfpence. They say women are unfaithful, but men are committing infidelities all day long. People talk about the women, and they never say a word about the men. We get all the blame, and you are allowed to do as you please. Do you know why? Because 'tis the men who have made the laws. If the women had made them, things would be just the other way. If I were a queen, I'd make every man who was unfaithful carry a branch of a tree in his hand, and I know all the towns would look like forests.

[*Exit* SMERALDINA.]

SILVIO:  Clarice faithless! Clarice a traitress! Her pretense at suicide was a trick to deceive me, to move my compassion. But though fate made me fall before my rival, I will never give up the thought of revenge. That wretch shall die, and my ungrateful Clarice shall see her lover wallowing in his own gore.

[*Exit* SILVIO.]


SCENE II———*A Room in* BRIGHELLA'S *Inn, with a door at each side and two doors at the back, facing the audience.*

TRUFFALDINO:  Just my luck! Two masters and neither of them comes home to dinner. 'Tis two o'clock, and not one to be seen. Sure enough they will both come at the same time, and I shall be in a mess; I shall not be able to wait on both together, and the whole thing will be found out. Hush, here comes one. All the better.

[*Enter* FLORINDO.]

FLORINDO:  Well, did you find that fellow Pasquale?

TRUFFALDINO:  Didn't we say, sir, that I was to look for him after dinner?

FLORINDO:  I am impatient to see him.

TRUFFALDINO:  You should have come back to dinner a little sooner.

FLORINDO:  [*aside*] I can find no way of making certain whether Beatrice is here.

TRUFFALDINO:  You told me to go and order dinner, and then you go out. The dinner will have been spoiled.

FLORINDO:  I don't want to eat anything.

[*Aside.*]

I shall go to the Post; I must go myself; then perhaps I shall find out something.

TRUFFALDINO:  You know, sir, at Venice you must eat; if you do not, you will fall sick.

FLORINDO:  I must go out; I have important business. If I come back to dinner, well and good; if not, I shall eat in the evening. You can get yourself some food, if you like.

TRUFFALDINO:  Very good, sir; just as you please, sir; you're the master.

FLORINDO:  This money is heavy; here, put it in my trunk. There is the key.

[*Gives* TRUFFALDINO *the purse and his keys.*]

TRUFFALDINO:  Certainly, sir; I'll bring the key back at once.

FLORINDO: No, no, you can give it me later. I can't stop. If I do not come back to dinner come to the Piazza; I can't rest till you have found Pasquale.

[*Exit* FLORINDO.]

TRUFFALDINO: Well, anyway, he said I could get myself some food; we are agreed about that. If he won't eat his dinner, he can leave it. My complexion was not made for fasting. I'll just put away this purse, and then —

[*Enter* BEATRICE.]

BEATRICE: Oh, Truffaldino!

TRUFFALDINO: [*aside*] The devil!

BEATRICE: Did Signor Pantalone dei Bisognosi give you a purse of a hundred guineas?

TRUFFALDINO: Yes, indeed he did.

BEATRICE: Then why did you not give it to me?

TRUFFALDINO: Was it meant for your honor?

BEATRICE: Was it meant for me? What did he say when he gave you the purse?

TRUFFALDINO: He told me I was to give it to my master.

BEATRICE: Well, and who is your master?

TRUFFALDINO: Your honor.

BEATRICE: Then why do you ask if the purse is mine?

TRUFFALDINO: Then it will be yours.

BEATRICE: Where is it?

TRUFFALDINO: Here, sir.

[*Gives* BEATRICE *the purse.*]

BEATRICE: Is the money all there?

TRUFFALDINO: I never touched it, sir.

BEATRICE: [*aside*] I shall count it.

TRUFFALDINO: [*aside*] I made a mistake over the purse; but that puts it straight. I wonder what the other gentleman will say? Oh well, if the money wasn't his, he'll say nothing at all.

BEATRICE: Is the landlord in?

TRUFFALDINO: Yes, sir.

BEATRICE: Tell him I shall have a friend to dinner with me, and he must get it ready as soon as he can.

TRUFFALDINO: What do you want for dinner, sir? How many dishes?

BEATRICE: Oh, Signor Pantalone dei Bisognosi is not a man who expects a great deal. Tell him to give us five or six dishes; something good.

TRUFFALDINO: You leave it all to me, sir?

BEATRICE: Yes, you order it, do the best you can. I am going to fetch the gentleman, he is not far off; see that all is ready by the time we come back.

[*Going*]

TRUFFALDINO: You shall see how they serve you here.

BEATRICE: Look! Take this paper; put it in my trunk. Be careful with it; 'tis a bill of exchange for four thousand crowns.

TRUFFALDINO: Be sure of it, sir, I'll put it away at once.

BEATRICE: See that everything is ready.

[*Aside.*]

Poor old Signor Pantalone — I gave him a terrible fright! I must cheer him up a little.

[*Exit* BEATRICE.]

TRUFFALDINO: Now's the time to do myself proud. 'Tis the first time this master of mine has told me to order him a dinner. I'll show him I am a man of good taste. I'll just put away this paper and then — no, I'll put it away afterward, I must not waste time. Ho there! Is nobody at home?

[*Calling into the inn.*]

Call Master Brighella, tell him I want to talk to him.

[*Returning.*]

Now with a really good dinner 'tis not the having such and such dishes, but the way it is served. A properly laid table is worth more than a mountain of dishes.

[*Enter* BRIGHELLA.]

BRIGHELLA: What is it, Si'or Truffaldin'? What can I do for you?

TRUFFALDINO: My master has got a gentleman to dine with him. He wants a good dinner, and that quickly. Have you got enough in the kitchen?

BRIGHELLA: I always have plenty of everything. In half an hour I can put on any sort of dinner you like.

TRUFFALDINO: Very well, then. Tell me what you can give us.

BRIGHELLA: For two persons, we will have two courses of four dishes each; will that do?

TRUFFALDINO: He said five or six dishes — better say six or eight. That will do. What will you give us?

BRIGHELLA: For the first course, I shall give you soup, fried, boiled, and a fricandeau.

TRUFFALDINO: Three of the dishes I know, but I do not know the last.

BRIGHELLA: 'Tis a French dish — a ragout — very tasty indeed.

TRUFFALDINO: Very well, that will do for the first course; now the second.

BRIGHELLA: For the second course the roast, the salad, a meat pie — and a trifle.

TRUFFALDINO: [*indignant*] What's that? A trifle? My master and his guest are gentlemen of substance; they won't be satisfied with a mere trifle. A trifle indeed!

BRIGHELLA: You don't understand. I said

[*Impressively.*]

a trifle! That's an English dish, a pudding, my very own speciality; there's not another man in Venice knows how to make it!

TRUFFALDINO: [*nonchalantly*] Oh well, I dare say it will do. But how are you going to arrange the table?

BRIGHELLA: Oh, that's easy enough. The waiter will see to that.

TRUFFALDINO: No, my good friend, laying the table is a very important matter; that's the first thing about a dinner, to have the table properly laid.

BRIGHELLA: Well, you might put the soup here, the fried there, there the boiled and here the fricandeau.

[*Makes an imaginary arrangement.*]

TRUFFALDINO: I don't like that. Don't you put something in the middle?

BRIGHELLA: Then we should want five dishes.

TRUFFALDINO: Good, then let us have five.

BRIGHELLA: We can put the gravy in the middle.

TRUFFALDINO: No, no, friend, you know nothing about laying a table; you can't put the gravy in the middle; soup always goes in the middle.

BRIGHELLA: Then the meat on one side, and the gravy on the other.

TRUFFALDINO: Lord, lord, that won't do at all. You innkeepers may know how to cook, but you have no idea of butlering. Now I'll show you.

[*Kneels down on one knee and points to the floor.*]

Suppose this is the table. Now you look how we arrange the five dishes. Like this: here in the middle the soup.

[*He tears off a piece of the bill of exchange and puts in on the floor to represent a dish.*]

Now the boiled meat.

[*Same business.*]

Here we put the fried opposite,

[*Same business.*]

here the gravy and here that — what-d'ye-call-it. There now! Won't that look fine?

BRIGHELLA: H'm, 'twill do; but you have put the gravy too far away from the meat.

TRUFFALDINO: Very well, we must see if we can't put it a little nearer.

[*Enter* BEATRICE *and* PANTALONE.]

BEATRICE: What are you doing on your knees?

TRUFFALDINO: [*stands up*] I was just planning how to have the table laid.

BEATRICE: What is that paper?

TRUFFALDINO: [*aside*] The devil! The letter that he gave me!

BEATRICE: That is my bill of exchange.

TRUFFALDINO: I am very sorry, sir; I will stick it together again.

BEATRICE: You rascal! Is that the way you look after my things? Things of such value too! You deserve a good thrashing. What say you, Signor Pantalone? Did you ever see such a piece of folly?

PANTALONE: To tell the truth, I cannot help laughing. 'Twould be a serious matter if it could not be mended, but I will write you out another and then all will be in order.

BEATRICE: But just think if the bill had been made out not here but in some place a long way off!

[*To* TRUFFALDINO.]

You ignorant fool!

TRUFFALDINO: This has all come about because Brighella doesn't know how to lay a table.

BRIGHELLA: He finds fault with everything I do.

TRUFFALDINO: I am a man that knows his business.

BEATRICE: [*to* TRUFFALDINO] Go away.

TRUFFALDINO: Things must be done properly.

BEATRICE: Be off, I tell you.

TRUFFALDINO: In the matter of pantry work I won't give way to the first butler in the land.

[*Exit* TRUFFALDINO.]

BRIGHELLA: I don't understand that fellow; sometimes he is a knave and sometimes a fool.

BEATRICE: This tomfoolery is all put on. Well, is dinner ready?

BRIGHELLA: If you will have five dishes to each course, 'twill take a little time.

PANTALONE: What's this about courses of five dishes? We'll take pot luck — a risotto, a couple of other dishes, and I shall be most obliged to you. My tastes are simple.

BEATRICE: [*to* BRIGHELLA] You hear that? That will do nicely.

BRIGHELLA: Very good, sir; but will you please to tell me if there might be anything you would particularly fancy?

PANTALONE: I should like some rissoles if you have them; my teeth are not very good nowadays.

BEATRICE: You hear? Rissoles.

BRIGHELLA: Very good, sir. If you will sit down here for a moment, gentlemen, dinner will be ready directly.

BEATRICE: Tell Truffaldino to come and wait on us.

BRIGHELLA: I'll tell him, sir.
[*Exit* BRIGHELLA.]

BEATRICE: Signor Pantalone, I fear you will indeed have to be content with pot luck.

PANTALONE: My dear sir, I am overcome with all the attention you show me; in fact you are doing for me what I ought to be doing for you. But, you see, I have that girl of mine at home, and until everything is finally settled it would not be proper for you to be together. So I accept your kind hospitality to raise my spirits a little; indeed I still feel quite upset. Had it not been for you, that young scoundrel would have done for me.

BEATRICE: I am glad that I arrived in time.
[WAITERS *enter from the kitchen and carry glasses, wine, bread, etc., into the room where* BEATRICE *and* PANTALONE *are to dine.*]

PANTALONE: They are very quick about their business here.

BEATRICE: Brighella is a smart fellow. He was servant to a great nobleman at Turin, and still wears his livery.

PANTALONE: There's a very good tavern on the other side of the Grand Canal oposite the Rialto where you can eat very well; I have often been there with various good friends of mine, very sound men, too; I often think of that place. They had some wonderful Burgundy wine there to — 'twas a wine for the gods.

BEATRICE: There's nothing one enjoys more than good wine in good company.

PANTALONE: Good company! Ah, if you had known them! That was good company! Good honest fellows, with many a good story to tell. God bless them. Seven or eight of them there were, and there wasn't the like of them in all the world.
[*The* WAITERS *come out of the room and return to the kitchen.*]

BEATRICE: You often had a merry time with these gentlemen, eh?

PANTALONE: And I hope I may live to have many more.
[*Enter* TRUFFALDINO *carrying the soup tureen.*]

TRUFFALDINO: [*to* BEATRICE] Dinner is ready for you in that room, sir.

BEATRICE: Go and put the soup on the table.

TRUFFALDINO: [*makes a bow*] After you, sir.

PANTALONE: A queer fellow, that servant of yours.
[*Goes in.*]

BEATRICE: [*to* TRUFFALDINO] I want less wit and more attention.
[*Goes in.*]

TRUFFALDINO: Call that a dinner! One dish at a time! They have money to spend, but they get nothing good for it. I wonder if this soup is worth eating; I'll try it.

[*Takes a spoon out of his pocket and tastes the soup.*]
I always carry my weapons about me. Not bad; it might be worse.
[*Goes into room with soup.*]
[*Enter* FIRST WAITER *with a dish.*]
FIRST WAITER: When is that man coming to take the dishes?
TRUFFALDINO: [*re-entering*] Here I am, friend. What have you got for me?
FIRST WAITER: Here's the boiled meat. There's another dish to follow.
[*Exit* FIRST WAITER.]
TRUFFALDINO: Mutton? Or veal? Mutton, I think. Let's taste it.
[*Tastes.*]
No, 'tis neither mutton nor veal; 'tis lamb, and very good, too.
[*Goes toward* BEATRICE'S *room.*]
[*Enter* FLORINDO.]
FLORINDO: Where are you going?
TRUFFALDINO: [*aside*] Oh dear, oh dear!
FLORINDO: What are you doing with that dish?
TRUFFALDINO: I was just putting it on the table, sir.
FLORINDO: For whom?
TRUFFALDINO: For you, sir.
FLORINDO: Why do you serve dinner before I come in?
TRUFFALDINO: I saw you from the window.
[*Aside.*]
I must find some excuse.
FLORINDO: And you begin with boiled meat instead of soup?
TRUFFALDINO: You must know, sir, at Venice soup is always taken last.
FLORINDO: I have other habits. I want my soup. Take that back to the kitchen.
TRUFFALDINO: Yes, sir, as you wish, sir.
FLORINDO: Make haste; afterward I want to have a nap.
TRUFFALDINO: Yes, sir.
[*Makes as if going to the kitchen.*]
FLORINDO: [*aside*] Shall I never find Beatrice again?
[FLORINDO *goes into the other room. As soon as he is in,* TRUFFALDINO *quickly takes the dish in to* BEATRICE. *Enter* FIRST WAITER *with another dish.* FLORINDO *calls from his room.*]
FLORINDO: Truffaldino! Truffaldino! Am I always to be kept waiting?
TRUFFALDINO: [*coming out of* BEATRICE'S *room*] Coming, sir.
[*To* FIRST WAITER.]
Quick, go and lay the table in that other room, the other gentleman has arrived; bring the soup at once.
FIRST WAITER: Directly.
[*Exit* FIRST WAITER.]
TRUFFALDINO: What may this dish be? This must be the "fricandeau."
[*Tastes it.*]
That's good, upon my word.
[*Takes it in to* BEATRICE.]
[WAITERS *enter and carry glasses, wine, bread, etc., into* FLORINDO'S *room.*]
TRUFFALDINO: [*to* WAITERS] Good lads, that's right.

[*Aside.*]
They're as lively as kittens. Well, if I can manage to wait at table on two masters at once, 'twill be a great accomplishment indeed.

[*The* WAITERS *come back out of* FLORINDO'S *room and go toward the kitchen.*]

TRUFFALDINO: Hurry up, lads, the soup!

FIRST WAITER: You look after your own table; we'll take care of this one.

[*Exeunt* WAITERS.]

TRUFFALDINO: I want to look after both, if I can.

[*Re-enter* FIRST WAITER *with* FLORINDO'S *soup.*]

TRUFFALDINO: Here, give me that; I'll take it. Go and get the stuff for the other room.

[*Takes soup from* FIRST WAITER *and carries it into* FLORINDO'S *room.*]

FIRST WAITER: That's a strange fellow. He wants to wait on everyone. Let him. They will have to give me *my* tip all the same.

[TRUFFALDINO *comes out of* FLORINDO'S *room.*]

BEATRICE: [*calling from her room*] Truffaldino!

FIRST WAITER: [*to* TRUFFALDINO] Your master's calling.

TRUFFALDINO: Coming, sir.

[*Goes into* BEATRICE'S *room.*]

[SECOND WAITER *brings the boiled meat for* FLORINDO. TRUFFALDINO *brings the dirty plates out of* BEATRICE'S *room.*]

TRUFFALDINO: Here, give it to me.

[*Exit* SECOND WAITER.]

FLORINDO: [*calls*] Truffaldino!

TRUFFALDINO: [*wishes to take the meat from* WAITER] Give it to me.

FIRST WAITER: No, I'm taking this.

TRUFFALDINO: Didn't you hear him call for me?

[*Takes meat from him and carries it in to* FLORINDO.]

FIRST WAITER: Well, that's fine! He wants to do everything.

[SECOND WAITER *brings in a dish of rissoles, gives it to the* FIRST WAITER *and exit.*]

I would take this in myself, but I don't want to have words with that fellow.

[*Re-enter* TRUFFALDINO *from* FLORINDO'S *room with dirty plates.*]

Here, master Jack-of-all-trades; take these rissoles to your master.

TRUFFALDINO: [*takes dish*] Rissoles?

FIRST WAITER: Yes, the rissoles he ordered.

[*Exit* FIRST WAITER.]

TRUFFALDINO: Oh, fine! Now which table are these to go to? I wonder which the devil of my two masters can have ordered them? If I go to the kitchen and ask, they'll begin to suspect; if I make a mistake and carry them to the one who didn't order them, then the other will ask for them and I shall be found out. I know what I'll do; I'll divide them on two plates, take half to each, and then I shall see who ordered them.

[*Takes plates and divides the rissoles.*]

That's four and that's four. There's one over. Who's to have that? We mustn't cause ill-feeling; I'll eat that one myself.

[*Eats it.*]

Now. We'll take the rissoles to this gentleman.

TRUFFALDINO *puts one plate of rissoles on the floor and takes the other in to* BEATRICE. FIRST WAITER *enters with an English pudding (trifle).*]

FIRST WAITER: Truffaldino!

TRUFFALDINO: [*comes out of* BEATRICE'S *room*] Coming!

FIRST WAITER: Take this pudding —

TRUFFALDINO: Wait a moment, I'm coming.
    [*Takes the other dish of rissoles and is going to* FLORINDO'S *room.*

FIRST WAITER: That's not right, the rissoles belong there.

TRUFFALDINO: I know they do, sir; I have carried them there; and my master sends these four as a courtesy to this gentleman.
    [*Goes into* FLORINDO'S *room.*]

FIRST WAITER: I see, they know each other — friends, you might say? They might as well have dined together.

TRUFFALDINO: [*re-entering*] What's this affair?

FIRST WAITER: That's an English pudding.

TRUFFALDINO: Who is it for?

FIRST WAITER: For your master.
    [*Exit* FIRST WAITER.]

TRUFFALDINO: What the devil is this "pudding"? It smells delicious, and looks like polenta. Oh! If it is polenta, that would be good indeed. I'll taste it.
    [*Brings a fork out of his pocket and tries the pudding.*]
It's not polenta, but it's very much like it.
    [*Eats.*]
Much better than polenta.
    [*Goes on eating.*]

BEATRICE: [*calling*] Truffaldino!

TRUFFALDINO: [*with mouth full*] Coming, sir.

FLORINDO: [*calling*] Truffaldino!

TRUFFALDINO: [*with mouth full*] Coming, sir.
    [*To himself.*]
Oh what wonderful stuff! Just another mouthful and then I'll go.
    [*Goes on eating.*]
    [BEATRICE *comes out of her room, sees* TRUFFALDINO *eating, kicks him, and says:*]

BEATRICE: You come and wait on me.
    [*She goes back to her room.*]
Truffaldino!

TRUFFALDINO: Coming!
    [TRUFFALDINO *puts the pudding on the floor and goes into* BEATRICE'S *room.* FLORINDO *comes out of his.*]

FLORINDO: [*calling*] Truffaldino! Where the devil is he?
    [TRUFFALDINO *comes out of* BEATRICE'S *room.*]

TRUFFALDINO: Here, sir.
    [*Seeing* FLORINDO.]

FLORINDO: What are you doing? Where have you been?

TRUFFALDINO: I just went to fetch the next course, sir.

FLORINDO: Is there anything more to eat?

TRUFFALDINO: I'll go and see.

FLORINDO: Make haste, I tell you, because I want to have a nap afterward.
[*Goes back into his room.*]
TRUFFALDINO: Very good, sir.
[*Calling.*]
Waiter, is there anything more to come?
[*Aside.*]
I'll put this pudding aside for myself.
[*Hides it.*]
[*Enter* FIRST WAITER *with dish.*]
FIRST WAITER: Here's the roast.
TRUFFALDINO: [*takes the roast*] Quick, the dessert!
FIRST WAITER: Lord, what a fluster! In a minute.
[*Exit* FIRST WAITER.]
TRUFFALDINO: I'll take the roast to this gentleman.
[*Takes it to* FLORINDO.]
[*Re-enter* FIRST WAITER.]
FIRST WAITER: [*with plate of fruit*] Here's the dessert; where are you?
TRUFFALDINO: [*re-entering from* FLORINDO's *room*] Here.
FIRST WAITER: [*gives him the fruit*] There. Anything more?
TRUFFALDINO: Wait.
[*Takes the dessert to* BEATRICE.]
FIRST WAITER: He jumps about here and there like the devil himself.
TRUFFALDINO: [*re-entering*] That will do. Nobody wants any more.
FIRST WAITER: I'm glad to hear it.
TRUFFALDINO: And now lay the table for *me*.
FIRST WAITER: In a moment.
[*Exit* FIRST WAITER.]
TRUFFALDINO: Now for my pudding! Hurrah! I've got through it all, they are all content, they want nothing more, they've had a very good dinner. I have waited at table on two masters at once, and neither of 'em knew anything about the other. But if I have waited for two, now I am going to eat for four.

SCENE III———*A Street with* BRIGHELLA's *Inn.*

[*Enter* SMERALDINA.]
SMERALDINA: A very proper sort of young lady my mistress is! To send me all alone with a letter to a tavern, a young girl like me! Waiting on a woman in love is a sad business. This young lady of mine does a thousand crazy things, and what I cannot understand is this — if she is so much in love with Signor Silvio as to be ready to disembowel herself for him, why does she send letters to another gentleman? One for summer and one for winter, I suppose! Well, there it is! I am not going inside that tavern. I'll call; somebody will come out. Hey there! Anyone at home?
[FIRST WAITER *comes out of the inn.*]
FIRST WAITER: Now, young woman, what do you want?
SMERALDINA: [*aside*] I feel thoroughly ashamed.
[*To* WAITER.]
Tell me — a certain Signor Federigo Rasponi lodges here, does he not?
FIRST WAITER: Yes, indeed. He has just this moment finished dinner.

SMERALDINA: I have something to say to him.

FIRST WAITER: A message? You can come inside.

SMERALDINA: And what sort of a girl do you take me for? I am the waiting maid of the lady he is to marry.

FIRST WAITER: [*more politely*] Well then, pray step this way.

SMERALDINA: Oh, but I don't like to go in there.

FIRST WAITER: Do you expect me to bring him out into the street for you? That would not be at all the right thing; more especially as he has Signor Pantalone dei Bisognosi with him.

SMERALDINA: What, my master? Worse and worse! I'll not come in.

FIRST WAITER: I can send his servant, if you like.

SMERALDINA: The little dark man?

FIRST WAITER: Exactly so.

SMERALDINA: Yes, do send him.

FIRST WAITER: [*aside*] I understand. She fancies the little dark man, and is ashamed to come inside. She is not ashamed to be seen with him in the middle of the street. [*Goes in.*]

SMERALDINA: If the master sees me, whatever shall I say? I'll tell him I came to look for *him*; that will do nicely. I'm never short of an answer.

[*Enter* TRUFFALDINO *with a bottle in his hand, a glass and a napkin.*]

TRUFFALDINO: Who sent for me?

SMERALDINA: I did, sir. I ask pardon if I have troubled you.

TRUFFALDINO: Not a bit of it. I am here to receive your commands.

SMERALDINA: I fear I must have taken you from your dinner.

TRUFFALDINO: I was having dinner, but I can go back to it.

SMERALDINA: I am truly sorry.

TRUFFALDINO: I am delighted. The fact is, I have had my bellyful, and your bright eyes are just the right thing to make me digest it.

SMERALDINA: [*aside*] Very gallant!

TRUFFALDINO: I'll just set down this bottle, and then I'm with you, my dear.

SMERALDINA: [*aside*] He called me "my dear"!

[*To* TRUFFALDINO.]

My mistress sends this letter to Signor Federigo Rasponi; I do not like to come into the tavern, so I thought I might put you to this trouble, as you are his man.

TRUFFALDINO: I'll take it with pleasure; but first, you must know that I have a message for *you*.

SMERALDINA: From whom?

TRUFFALDINO: From a very honest man. Tell me, are you acquainted with one Truffaldin' Battocchio?

SMERALDINA: I think I have heard him spoken of, but I am not sure.

[*Aside.*]

It must be himself.

TRUFFALDINO: He's a good-looking man; short, thickset, with plenty of wit to his talk. Understands butlering too —

SMERALDINA: I don't know him from Adam.

TRUFFALDINO: Yes, you do; and what's more, he's in love with you.

SMERALDINA: Oh! You are making fun of me.

TRUFFALDINO: And if he could only have just a little hope that his affections were returned, he would make himself known.

SMERALDINA: Well, sir, if I were to see him, and he took my fancy, it might possibly be that I should return his affection.

TRUFFALDINO: Shall I show him to you?

SMERALDINA: I should like to see him.

TRUFFALDINO: Just a moment.

     *[Goes into the inn.]*

SMERALDINA: Then 'tis not he.

     *[*TRUFFALDINO *comes out of the inn, makes low bows to* SMERALDINA, *passes close to her, sighs, and goes back into the inn.]*

SMERALDINA: I do not understand this play-acting.

TRUFFALDINO: *[re-entering]* Did you see him?

SMERALDINA: See whom?

TRUFFALDINO: The man who is in love with your beauty.

SMERALDINA: I saw no one but you.

TRUFFALDINO: *[sighs]* Well!

SMERALDINA: It is you, then, who profess to be in love with me?

TRUFFALDINO: It is.

     *[Sighs.]*

SMERALDINA: Why did you not say so before?

TRUFFALDINO: Because I am rather shy.

SMERALDINA: *[aside]* He would make a stone fall in love with him.

TRUFFALDINO: Well, and what do you say?

SMERALDINA: I say —

TRUFFALDINO: Come, tell me.

SMERALDINA: Oh — I am rather shy too.

TRUFFALDINO: Then if we were joined up, 'twould be a marriage of two people who are rather shy.

SMERALDINA: I must say, you are just my fancy.

TRUFFALDINO: Are you a maid?

SMERALDINA: Need you ask?

TRUFFALDINO: I suppose that means "certainly not."

SMERALDINA: On the contrary, it means "certainly I am."

TRUFFALDINO: I am a bachelor too.

SMERALDINA: I could have been married fifty times, but I never found the man I really fancied.

TRUFFALDINO: Do you think there is any hope for me?

SMERALDINA: Well — to tell the truth — really — I must say — there's a — something about you — No, I won't say another word.

TRUFFALDINO: If somebody wanted to marry you, what would he have to do?

SMERALDINA: I have neither father nor mother. He would have to speak to my master, or to my mistress.

TRUFFALDINO: And if I speak to them, what will they say?

SMERALDINA: They will say, that if I am content —

TRUFFALDINO: And what will you say?

SMERALDINA: I shall say — that if they are content too —

TRUFFALDINO: That will do. We shall all be content. Give me the letter and when I bring you back the answer, we will have a talk.

SMERALDINA: Here's the letter.

TRUFFALDINO: Do you know what is in it?

SMERALDINA: No — if you only knew how curious I am to know!

TRUFFALDINO: I hope it is not a disdainful letter, or I shall get my face spoiled.

SMERALDINA: Who knows? It can't be a love letter.

TRUFFALDINO: I don't want to get into trouble. If I don't know what is in the letter, I am not going to take it.

SMERALDINA: We could open it — but how are we to seal it again?

TRUFFALDINO: Leave it to me; sealing letters is just my job. No one will ever know anything.

SMERALDINA: Then let us open it.

TRUFFALDINO: Can you read?

SMERALDINA: A little. But you can read quite well, I'm sure.

TRUFFALDINO: Yes, I too can read just a little.

SMERALDINO: Then let us hear.

TRUFFALDINO: We must open it cleanly.
　　　[*Tears off a piece.*]

SMERALDINA: Oh! What have you done?

TRUFFALDINO: Nothing. I've a secret way to mend it. Here it is, open.

SMERALDINA: Quick, read it.

TRUFFALDINO: *You* read it. You will know your young lady's handwriting better than I do.

SMERALDINA: [*looking at the letter*] Really, I can't make out a word.

TRUFFALDINO: [*same business*] Nor I neither.

SMERALDINA: Then what was the good of opening it?

TRUFFALDINO: [*takes the letter*] Wait; let me think; I can make out some of it.

SMERALDINA: Oh I know some of the letters too.

TRUFFALDINO: Let us try one by one. Isn't that an M?

SMERALDINA: No! That's an R!

TRUFFALDINO: Between R and M there is very little difference.

SMERALDINA: *Ri, ri, o.* No, no: keep quiet; I think it *is* an M — *Mi, mi, o* — *mio!*

TRUFFALDINO: It's not *mio*, it's *mia*.

SMERALDINA: But it is, there's the hook —

TRUFFALDINO: That proves it is *mia*.
　　　[BEATRICE *comes out of the inn with* PANTALONE.]

PANTALONE: [*to* SMERALDINA] What are you doing here?

SMERALDINA: [*frightened*] Nothing sir; I came to look for *you*.

PANTALONE: [*to* SMERALDINA] What do you want with me?

SMERALDINA: The mistress wants you, sir.

BEATRICE: [*to* TRUFFALDINO] What is this paper?

TRUFFALDINO: [*frightened*] Nothing, just a bit of paper —

BEATRICE: Let me see.

TRUFFALDINO: [*gives paper, trembling*] Yes, sir.

BEATRICE: What? This is a letter addressed to me. Villain, will you open all my letters?

TRUFFALDINO: I know nothing about it, sir —

BEATRICE: Look, Signor Pantalone, here is a letter from Signora Clarice, in which she tells me of Silvio's insane jealousy — and this rascal has the impudence to open it!

PANTALONE: [*to* SMERALDINA] And you helped him to do so?

SMERALDINA: I know nothing about it, sir.

BEATRICE: Who opened this letter?

TRUFFALDINO: Not I.

SMERALDINA: Nor I.

PANTALONE: Well, who brought it?

SMERALDINA: Truffaldino brought it to his master.

TRUFFALDINO: And Smeraldina brought it to Truffaldino.

SMERALDINA: [*aside*] Sneak! I don't like you any more.

PANTALONE: You meddlesome little hussy, so you are the cause of all this trouble, are you? I've a good mind to smack your face.

SMERALDINA: I've never had my face smacked by any man; I'm surprised at you.

PANTALONE: [*coming near her*] Is that the way you answer me?

SMERALDINA: You won't catch me. You're too rheumatic, you can't run.
    [*Exit running.*]

PANTALONE: You saucy minx, I'll show you if I can run; I'll catch you.
    [*Runs after her.*]

TRUFFALDINO: [*aside*] If I only knew how to get out of this!

BEATRICE: [*looking at the letter, aside*] Poor Clarice! She is in despair over Silvio's jealousy; 'twill be best for me to discover myself and set her mind at rest.

TRUFFALDINO: [*tries to steal away quietly*] I don't think he is looking. I'll try to get away.

BEATRICE: Where are you off to?

TRUFFALDINO: Nowhere.
    [*Stops.*]

BEATRICE: Why did you open this letter?

TRUFFALDINO: It was Smeraldina; I had nothing to do with it.

BEATRICE: Smeraldina, forsooth! You did it, you rascal. One and one make two. That's the second letter of mine you have opened today. Come here.

TRUFFALDINO: [*approaching timidly*] Oh, for mercy's sake, sir —

BEATRICE: Come here, I say.

TRUFFALDINO: [*same business*] Oh, for the love of Heaven —
    [BEATRICE *takes the stick which* TRUFFALDINO *has at his flank (i.e., Harlequin's wooden sword or baton) and beats him well, she standing with her back to the inn.* FLORINDO *appears at the window and sees the beating.*]

FLORINDO: What's this? Beating my servant?
    [*Leaves window.*]

TRUFFALDINO: Stop, stop, sir, for pity's sake.

BEATRICE: Take that, rascal, and learn to open my letters.
    [*Throws stick on the ground, and exit to street.*]

TRUFFALDINO: [*after* BEATRICE *has gone*] My blood! My body! Is that the way to treat a man of my sort? Beat a man like me? If a servant is no good, you can send him away, but you don't beat him.
    [FLORINDO *comes out, unseen by* TRUFFALDINO.]

FLORINDO: What's that?

TRUFFALDINO: [*seeing* FLORINDO] Oh! I said people had no business to beat other people's servants like that. This is an insult to my master.
    [*Looking toward direction of* BEATRICE's *exit.*]

FLORINDO:  Yes, 'tis an affront put upon *me*. Who was it gave you a thrashing?

TRUFFALDINO:  I couldn't say, sir; I do not know him.

FLORINDO:  Why did he thrash you?

TRUFFALDINO:  Because I — I spat on his shoe.

FLORINDO:  And you let yourself be beaten like that? Did nothing? Made no attempt
to defend yourself? And you expose your master to insult, with perhaps serious
consequences? Ass! Poltroon!

> [*Picks up the stick.*]

Since you enjoy being thrashed, I'll give you your pleasure, I'll thrash you
myself as well.

> [*Thrashes him and exit into inn.*]

TRUFFALDINO:  Well, there's no mistake about my being the servant of two masters.
They have both paid me my wages.

> [*Exit into the inn.*]


## ACT III

SCENE I———A *Room in* BRIGHELLA'S *inn.*

TRUFFALDINO:  I don't care that for my beating! I have eaten well, I've dined well,
and this evening I shall sup still better; and as long as I can serve two masters,
there's this at least, that I draw double wages.

   And now what's to be done? Master number one is out of doors, master
number two is fast asleep; why, it's just the moment to give those clothes an
airing — take them out of the trunks and see if there's anything wants doing.
Here are the keys. This room will do nicely. I'll get the trunks out and make a
proper job of it. I must have someone to help me though.

> [*Calls.*]

Waiter!

> [*Enter* WAITERS.]

FIRST WAITER:  What do you want?

TRUFFALDINO:  I want you to lend a hand to bring some trunks out of those rooms, to
give the clothes an airing.

FIRST WAITER:  [*to* SECOND WAITER] Go and help him.

TRUFFALDINO:  [*to* SECOND WAITER] Come along, and I'll give you a good handful of
what my masters gave me.

> [TRUFFALDINO *and* SECOND WAITER *go into* BEATRICE'S *room.*]

FIRST WAITER:  He looks like a rare good servant — quick, ready, and most attentive;
but I'll warrant he has his faults somewhere. I've been a servant myself and I
know the ropes. Nobody does anything just for love. Whatever they do, either
they are robbing their masters or they are throwing dust in their eyes.

> [TRUFFALDINO *comes out of the room with the* SECOND WAITER *carrying a
> trunk.*]

TRUFFALDINO:  Gently! Let's put it down here.

> [*They put the trunk in the middle of the room.*]

Now let's fetch the other. But quietly, for my master is in there asleep.

> [TRUFFALDINO *and* SECOND WAITER *go into* FLORINDO'S *room.*]

FIRST WAITER:  Either he's a real first-rate fellow, or he's a real knave; I never saw anybody wait on two gentlemen at once like that. I shall just keep my eyes open; maybe, under the pretense of waiting on two gentlemen at once, he means to rob them both.

[TRUFFALDINO *and* SECOND WAITER *re-enter with the other trunk.*]

TRUFFALDINO: And we'll put this one here.

[*They put it down a little way off from the other.*]

[*To* SECOND WAITER.]

There! You can run along now, if you like. I don't want anything more.

FIRST WAITER: [*to* SECOND WAITER] Go on; off with you to the kitchen.

[*Exit* SECOND WAITER.]

[*To* TRUFFALDINO.]

Can I help you?

TRUFFALDINO: No, thank you; I can do my work myself.

FIRST WAITER: I must say, you are a giant for work; it's a marvel to me how you get through it all.

[*Exit* FIRST WAITER.]

TRUFFALDINO: Now I'm going to do my work properly, in peace and quiet, with no one to worry me.

[*Takes a key out of his pocket.*]

Now which key is this, I wonder? Which trunk does it fit? Let's try.

[*Opens one trunk.*]

I guessed right at once. I'm the cleverest man on earth. And this other will open t'other trunk.

[*Takes out second key and opens second trunk.*]

Now they are both open. Let's take everything out.

[*He takes all the clothes out of both trunks and puts them on the table. In each trunk there must be a black suit, books and papers, and anything else ad lib.*]

I'll just see if there is anything in the pockets. You never know, sometimes they leave biscuits or sweets in them.

[*Searches the pockets of* BEATRICE'S *suit and finds a portrait.*]

My word, what a pretty picture! There's a handsome man! Who can it be? A queer thing, I seem to know him, but yet I can't remember. He is just the least little bit like my other master; but no, *he* never wears clothes like that, nor that wig neither.

[FLORINDO *calls from his room.*]

FLORINDO: Truffaldino!

TRUFFALDINO: Oh, plague take him! He has woken up. If the devil tempts him to come out and he sees this other trunk, he'll want to know — quick, quick — I'll lock it up and say I don't know whose it is.

[*Begins putting clothes in again.*]

FLORINDO: [*calling*] Truffaldino!

TRUFFALDINO: Coming, sir!

[*Aside.*]

I must put these things away first. But I can't remember which trunk this coat came from, nor these papers neither.

FLORINDO: [*calling*] Come here, I say; or must I fetch a stick to you?

TRUFFALDINO: In a minute, sir.

[*Aside.*]

Quick, before he comes! I'll put all straight when he goes out.
> *Stuffs the things into the trunks anyhow and locks them.* FLORINDO *comes out in a dressing gown.*]

FLORINDO: What the devil are you doing?

TRUFFALDINO: Pray, sir, didn't you tell to give your clothes an airing? I was just about to do it here.

FLORINDO: And this other trunk, whose is that?

TRUFFALDINO: I couldn't say, sir; 'twill belong to some other gentleman.

FLORINDO: Give me my black coat.

TRUFFALDINO: Very good, sir.
> [*Opens* FLORINDO'S *trunk and gives him the black suit.* FLORINDO *takes off his dressing gown with* TRUFFALDINO'S *help and puts on the black coat; then puts his hand into the pockets and finds the portrait.*]

FLORINDO: [*much surprised*] What is this?

TRUFFALDINO: [*aside*] Oh Lord, I've made a mistake. I ought to have put it into the other gentleman's pocket. 'Tis the color made me go wrong.

FLORINDO: [*aside*] Heavens! There can be no mistake. This is my own portrait; the one I gave to my beloved Beatrice.
> [*To* TRUFFALDINO.]
Tell me, how ever did this portrait come to be in the pocket of my coat? It wasn't there before.

TRUFFALDINO: [*aside*] Now what's the answer to that? I don't know. Let me think —

FLORINDO: Come on, out with it, answer me. How did this portrait come to be in my pocket?

TRUFFALDINO: Sir, be kind and forgive me for taking a liberty. The portrait belongs to me, and I hid it there for safety, for fear I might lose it.

FLORINDO: How did you come by this portrait?

TRUFFALDINO: My master left it to me.

FLORINDO: Left it to you?

TRUFFALDINO: Yes, sir; I had a master who died, and he left me a few trifles which I sold, all except this portrait, sir.

FLORINDO: Great heavens! And how long is it since this master of yours died?

TRUFFALDINO: 'Twill be just about a week ago, sir.
> [*Aside.*]
I say the first thing that comes into my head.

FLORINDO: What was your master's name?

TRUFFALDINO: I do not know, sir; he lived incognito.

FLORINDO: Incognito? How long were you in his service?

TRUFFALDINO: Only a short time, sir; ten or twelve days.

FLORINDO: [*aside*] Heavens! More and more do I fear that it was Beatrice. She escaped in man's dress; she concealed her name — Oh, wretched me, if it be true!

TRUFFALDINO: [*aside*] As he believes it all, I may as well go on with the fairy tale.

FLORINDO: [*despairingly*] Tell me, was your master young?

TRUFFALDINO: Yes, sir, quite a young gentleman.

FLORINDO: Without a beard?

TRUFFALDINO: Without a beard, sir.

FLORINDO: [*aside, with a sigh*] 'Twas she, doubtless.

TRUFFALDINO: [*aside*] I hope I'm not in for another thrashing.

FLORINDO: At least, you know where your late master came from?

TRUFFALDINO: I did know, sir, but I can't now call it to mind.

FLORINDO: Was it from Turin?

TRUFFALDINO: Turin it was, sir.

FLORINDO: [*aside*] Every word he speaks is a sword thrust in my heart.
[*To* TRUFFALDINO.]
Tell me again, this young gentleman from Turin, is he really dead?

TRUFFALDINO: He is dead indeed, sir.

FLORINDO: Of what did he die?

TRUFFALDINO: He met with an accident, and that was the end of him.
[*Aside.*]
That seems to be the best way out.

FLORINDO: Where was he buried?

TRUFFALDINO: [*aside*] I wasn't ready for that one.
[*To* FLORINDO.]
He wasn't buried, sir.

FLORINDO: What!

TRUFFALDINO: No, sir, another servant from the same place got permission to have him put into a coffin and sent home, sir.

FLORINDO: And was it, by any chance, the same servant who got you to fetch his letters for him from the Post this morning?

TRUFFALDINO: Exactly so, sir; it was Pasqual'.

FLORINDO: [*aside*] Then all hope is lost. Beatrice is dead. Unhappy Beatrice! The discomforts of the journey and the tortures of her heart must have killed her. Oh! I can no longer endure the agony of my grief!
[*Exit into his room.*]

TRUFFALDINO: That portrait has touched him in the guts. He must have known the gentleman. Well, I had better take the trunks back to the rooms again, or I shall be in for more trouble of the same sort. Oh dear! Here comes my other master.
[*Enter* BEATRICE *and* PANTALONE.]

BEATRICE: I assure you, Signor Pantalone, the last consignment of mirrors and wax candles has been put down twice over.

PANTALONE: Maybe my young men have made a mistake. We will go through the books again, and then we shall find out exactly how things stand.

BEATRICE: I too have a list copied from my own books. We will compare them. Perhaps that may decide the point either in your favor or mine. Truffaldino!

TRUFFALDINO: Here, sir.

BEATRICE: Have you the key of my trunk?

TRUFFALDINO: Yes, sir; here it is.

BEATRICE: Why have you brought my trunk in here?

TRUFFALDINO: To air your clothes, sir.

BEATRICE: Have you aired them?

TRUFFALDINO: I have, sir.

BEATRICE: Open the trunk and give me — Whose is that other trunk?

TRUFFALDINO: It belongs to another gentleman who has just come.

BEATRICE: Give me the memorandum book which you will find there.

TRUFFALDINO: Yes, sir.
[*Aside.*]

The Lord help me this time!

[*Opens trunk and looks for the book.*]

PANTALONE: As I say, they may have made a mistake; of course, if there is a mistake, you will not have to pay.

BEATRICE: We may find that all is in order; we shall see.

TRUFFALDINO: Is this the book, sir?

[*Holding out a book to* BEATRICE.]

BEATRICE: I expect so.

[*Takes the book without looking carefully and opens it.*]

No, this is not it — Whose is this book?

TRUFFALDINO: [*aside*] I've done it now!

BEATRICE: [*aside*] These are two letters which I wrote to Florindo. Alas, these notes, these accounts belong to him. I tremble, I am in a cold sweat, I know not where I am.

PANTALONE: What ails you, Signor Federigo? Are you unwell?

BEATRICE: 'Tis nothing.

[*Aside to* TRUFFALDINO.]

Truffaldino, how did this book come to be in my trunk? It is not mine.

TRUFFALDINO: I hardly know, sir —

BEATRICE: Come, out with it — tell me the truth.

TRUFFALDINO: I ask your pardon for the liberty I took, sir, putting the book into your trunk. It belongs to me, and I put it there for safety.

[*Aside.*]

That was a good enough story for the other gentleman, I hope 'twill do for this one too.

BEATRICE: The book is your own, you say, and yet you gave it to me instead of mine, without noticing?

TRUFFALDINO: [*aside*] He's much too clever.

[*To* BEATRICE.]

I'll tell you, sir; I have only had the book a very short time, so I did not recognize it at once.

BEATRICE: And how came you by this book?

TRUFFALDINO: I was in service with a gentleman at Venice, and he died and left the book to me.

BEATRICE: How long ago?

TRUFFALDINO: I don't remember exactly — ten or twelve days.

BEATRICE: How can that be, when I met you at Verona?

TRUFFALDINO: I had just come away from Venice on account of my poor master's death.

BEATRICE: [*aside*] Alas for me!

[*To* TRUFFALDINO.]

Your master — was his name — Florindo?

TRUFFALDINO: Yes, sir; Florindo.

BEATRICE: And his family name Aretusi?

TRUFFALDINO: That was it, sir; Aretusi.

BEATRICE: And you are sure he is dead?

TRUFFALDINO: As sure as I stand here.

BEATRICE: Of what did he die? Where was he buried?

TRUFFALDINO:  He tumbled into the canal and was drowned and never seen again.
BEATRICE:  Oh, wretched that I am! Florindo is dead, my beloved is dead; my one and
      only hope is dead. All is lost. Love's stratagems are fruitless! I leave my home, I
      leave my relatives, I dress as a man, I confront danger, I hazard my very life, all
      for Florindo — and Florindo is dead. Unhappy Beatrice! Was the loss of my
      brother so little to me that Fate must make me lose my lover as well? Oh! Grief
      overwhelms me, I can no longer bear the light of day. My adored one, my
      beloved, I will follow you to the tomb.
            [*Exits into her room raving.*]
PANTALONE:  [*who has listened to her speech with astonishment*] Truffaldino!
TRUFFALDINO:  Si'or Pantalon'?
PANTALONE:  A woman!
TRUFFALDINO:  A female!
PANTALONE:  Most extraordinary!
TRUFFALDINO:  Who'd have thought it?
PANTALONE:  I'm struck all of a heap.
TRUFFALDINO:  You might knock me down with a feather.
PANTALONE:  I shall go straight home and tell my daughter.
            [*Exit.*]
TRUFFALDINO:  It seems I am not the servant of two masters but of a master and a
      mistress.
            [*Exit.*]


                          SCENE II ———— A *Street*.

            [*Enter* DR. LOMBARDI *meeting* PANTALONE.]
DR. LOMBARDI:  [*aside*] This doddering old villain Pantalone sticks in my gizzard.
      The more I think about him, the more I abominate him.
PANTALONE:  [*cheerfully*] Good day, my dear Doctor, your servant.
DR. LOMBARDI:  I am surprised that you have the effrontery to address me.
PANTALONE:  I have news for you. Do you know —
DR. LOMBARDI:  You are going to tell me that the marriage has already been per-
      formed? I care not a fig if it has.
PANTALONE:  The whole story is untrue. Let me speak, plague take you.
DR. LOMBARDI:  Speak on then, pox on you.
PANTALONE:  [*aside*] I should like to give him a good doctoring with my fists.
            [*To* DR. LOMBARDI.]
      My daughter shall marry your son whenever you please.
DR. LOMBARDI:  I am vastly obliged to you. Pray do not put yourself to inconvenience.
      My son is not prepared to stomach that, sir. You may give her to the Turin
      gentleman.
PANATLONE:  If you knew who the Turin gentleman is, you would say differently.
DR. LOMBARDI:  He may be who he will. Your daughter has been seen with him, *et
      hoc sufficit.*
PANTALONE:  But 'tis not true that he is —
DR. LOMBARDI:  I will not hear another word.
PANTALONE:  If you won't hear me, 'twill be the worse for you.
DR. LOMBARDI:  We shall see for whom it will be the worse.

PANTALONE: My daughter is a girl of unblemished reputation, and —

DR. LOMBARDI: The devil take you.

PANTALONE: The devil take you, sir.

DR. LOMBARDI: You disreputable old villain!

[*Exit* DR. LOMBARDI.]

PANTALONE: Damn you! He is more like a beast than a man. Why, how could I ever tell him that the man was a woman? Not a bit of it, he wouldn't let me speak. But here comes that young lout of a son of his; now I shall be in for more impertinence.

[*Enter* SILVIO.]

SILVIO: [*aside*] There is Pantalone. I should like to run a sword through his paunch.

PANTALONE: Signor Silvio, if you will give me leave, I should like to give you a piece of good news, if you will condescend to allow me to speak, and not behave like that windmill of a father of yours.

SILVIO: What have you to say to me? Pray speak, sir.

PANTALONE: You must know, sir, that the marriage of my daughter to Signor Federigo has come to nothing.

SILVIO: Indeed? Do not deceive me.

PANTALONE: 'Tis true indeed, and if you are still of your former mind, my daughter is ready to give you her hand.

SILVIO: Oh, heavens! You bring me back from death to life.

PANTALONE: [*aside*] Well, well, he is not quite such a bear as his father.

SILVIO: But heavens! How can I clasp to my bosom her who has for so long been the bride of another?

PANTALONE: To cut a long story short, Federigo Rasponi has turned into Beatrice his sister.

SILVIO: What? I do not understand you.

PANTALONE: Then you are very thickheaded. The person whom we thought to be Federigo has been discovered to be Beatrice.

SILVIO: Dressed as a man?

PANTALONE: Dressed as a man.

SILVIO: At last I understand.

PANTALONE: About time you did.

SILVIO: How did it happen? Tell me.

PANTALONE: Let us go to my house. My daughter knows nothing of it. I need only tell the story once to satisfy you both.

SILVIO: I will come, sir; and I must humbly beg your forgiveness, for having allowed myself to be transported by passion —

PANTALONE: 'Twas a mere nothing; I appreciate your feelings. I know what love is. Now, my dear boy, come along with me.

[*Going.*]

SILVIO: [*aside*] Who is happier than I am? What heart could be more contented?

[*Exit with* PANTALONE.]

SCENE III——*A Room in* BRIGHELLA's *Inn.*

BEATRICE *and* FLORINDO *come out of their rooms simultaneously; each holds a sword or dagger and is on the point of committing suicide.* BRIGHELLA *is restraining* BEATRICE *and the* FIRST WAITER *restraining* FLORINDO.

*They all come forward in such a way that* BEATRICE *and* FLORINDO *are unaware of each other's presence.*]

BRIGHELLA: [*seizing* BEATRICE's *hand*] Stop, stop!

BEATRICE: [*trying to break loose*] For pity's sake, let me go.

FIRST WAITER: [*holding* FLORINDO] This is madness.

FLORINDO: [*breaks away from* WAITER] Go to the devil.

BEATRICE: [*breaking away from* BRIGHELLA] You shall not hinder me.

[*Both come forward, determined to kill themselves, they see each other, recognize each other, and stand dazed.*]

FLORINDO: What do I see?

BEATRICE: Florindo!

FLORINDO: Beatrice!

BEATRICE: Are you alive?

FLORINDO: Are you too living?

BEATRICE: Oh, destiny!

FLORINDO: Oh, my adored one!

[*They drop their weapons and embrace.*]

BRIGHELLA: [*jokingly to the* WAITER] You had better mop up the blood; we don't want a mess here.

[*Exit* BRIGHELLA.]

FIRST WAITER: [*aside*] Anyway I'll pick up the weapons and I shall not give them back again.

[*Picks up the daggers and exits.*]

FLORINDO: What brought you to attempt such an act of madness?

BEATRICE: The false news of your death.

FLORINDO: Who told you that I was dead?

BEATRICE: My servant.

FLORINDO: And mine gave me to believe that you were dead; and I too, carried away by the same agony of grief, intended to take my life.

BEATRICE: I was this book caused me to believe the story.

FLORINDO: That book was in my trunk. How came it into your hands? Ah, now I know. By the same means, no doubt, as the portrait I found in my coat pocket. Here it is. The one I gave you in Turin.

BEATRICE: Those rascally servants of ours— Heaven only knows what they have been up to.

FLORINDO: Where are they, I wonder?

BEATRICE: Nowhere to be seen.

FLORINDO: Let us find them and confront them.

[*Calling.*]

Ho there! Is nobody there?

[*Enter* BRIGHELLA.]

BRIGHELLA: Did you call, sir?

FLORINDO: Where are our servants?

BRIGHELLA: I don't know, sir. Shall I send to look for them?

FLORINDO: Find them at once if you can and send them to us here.

BRIGHELLA: For myself I only know one of them; I will ask the waiters, they will know them both. I congratulate you, sir, and madam, on having made such a satisfactory end of yourselves; if you want to get yourselves buried, you must try some other establishment; that's more than *we* can undertake. Your servant, madam and sir.

[*Exit* BRIGHELLA.]

FLORINDO: Then you too are lodged in this inn?

BEATRICE: I arrived this morning.

FLORINDO: I too this morning. And yet we never saw each other.

BEATRICE: Fate has been pleased to torment us a little.

FLROINDO: Tell me: your brother Federigo — is he dead?

BEATRICE: Have you any doubt? He died on the spot.

FLORINDO: I was told he was alive and here in Venice.

BEATRICE: It was I who traveled in his name and in these clothes to follow —

FLORINDO: To follow me — I know, my dearest; I read it in a letter from your servant in Turin.

BEATRICE: How came it into your hands?

FLORINDO: My servant gave it me by mistake and seeing it was addressed to you, I could not help opening it.

BEATRICE: I suppose a lover's curiosity is always legitimate.

FLORINDO: But where are these servants of ours? Ah!

[*Sees* TRUFFALDINO *approaching.*]

Here is one.

BEATRICE: He looks like the worse knave of the two.

FLORINDO: I think you are not far wrong.

[*Enter* TRUFFALDINO *brought in by force by* BRIGHELLA *and the* FIRST WAITER.]

FLORINDO: Come here, come here, don't be frightened.

BEATRICE: We shall do you no harm.

TRUFFALDINO: [*aside*] H'm, I still remember the thrashing.

BRIGHELLA: We have found this one; if we can find the other, we will bring him.

FLORINDO: Yes, we *must* have them both here together.

BRIGHELLA: [*aside to* WAITER] Do you know the other?

FIRST WAITER: [*to* BRIGHELLA] Not I.

BRIGHELLA: We'll ask in the kitchen. Someone there will know him.

FIRST WAITER: If he had been there, I should have known him too.

[*Exeunt* FIRST WAITER *and* BRIGHELLA.]

FLORINDO: [*to* TRUFFALDINO] Come, now, tell us what happened about that changing of the portrait and the book, and why you and that other rascal conspired to drive us distracted.

TRUFFALDINO: [*signs to both with his finger to keep silence*] Hush!

[*To* FLORINDO.]

Pray, sir, a word with you in private.

[*To* BEATRICE *just as he turns to speak to* FLORINDO.]

I will tell you everything directly.

[*To* FLORINDO.]

You must know, sir, I am not to blame for anything that has happened; it's all Pasqual's fault, the servant of that lady there.

[*Cautiously pointing at* BEATRICE.]

It was he mixed up the things, and put into one trunk what belonged to the other, without my knowledge. The poor man begged and prayed me to take the blame, for fear his master should send him away, and as I am a kindhearted fellow that would let himself be drawn and quartered for his friends, I made up all these stories to see if I could help him. I never dreamed it was a portrait of you or that you would be so much upset at hearing of the death of the owner. Now I have told you the whole truth, sir, as an honest man and a faithful servant.

BEATRICE: [*aside*] 'Tis a very long story he is telling. I am curious to know what the mystery is about.

FLORINDO: [*aside to* TRUFFALDINO] Then the man who got you to fetch that letter from the Post was the servant of Signora Beatrice?

TRUFFALDINO: [*aside to* FLORINDO] Yes, sir, that was Pasqual'.

FLORINDO: Then why conceal from me a fact I so urgently desired to know?

TRUFFALDINO: He begged me not to tell anyone, sir.

FLORINDO: Who?

TRUFFALDINO: Pasqual'.

FLORINDO: Why didn't you obey your master?

TRUFFALDINO: For the love of Pasqual'.

FLORINDO: You and Pasquale deserve a sound thrashing together.

TRUFFALDINO: [*aside to himself*] In that case I should get both.

BEATRICE: Have you not yet finished this long cross-examination?

FLORINDO: This fellow has been telling me—

TRUFFALDINO: [*aside to* FLORINDO] For the love of Heaven, your honor, do not say it was Pasqual'. I'd rather you told the lady it was me. You can give me a beating if you like, but don't, don't let any trouble come to Pasqual'.

FLORINDO: [*aside to* TRUFFALDINO] Are you so devoted a friend to Pasquale?

TRUFFALDINO: I love him as if he were my very own self. Now I am going to the lady, and I am going to tell her that it was all my fault; she may scold me as she pleases and do what she will to me, but I *will* protect Pasqual'.

[TRUFFALDINO *moves toward* BEATRICE.]

FLORINDO: [*aside*] Well, he's certainly a very loyal and affectionate character.

TRUFFALDINO: [*to* BEATRICE] Here I am, madam.

BEATRICE: [*aside to* TRUFFALDINO] What is all this long story you've been telling Signor Florindo?

TRUFFALDINO: [*aside to* BEATRICE] You must know, madam, that that gentleman has a servant called Pasqual'; he is the most arrant noddy in the world; it was he made all that mess of things; but because the poor man was afraid his master would send him away, I made up all the story about the book and the master who was dead and drowned, and all the rest of it. And just now I've been telling Si'or Florindo that I was the cause of it all.

BEATRICE: But why accuse yourself of faults which you have never committed?

TRUFFALDINO: Madam, 'tis all for the love I bear Pasqual'.

FLORINDO: [*aside*] This seems a very long business.

TRUFFALDINO: [*to* BEATRICE *as before*] Dear madam, I beg of you, don't get him into trouble.

BEATRICE: Whom?

TRUFFALDINO: Pasqual'.

BEATRICE: Pasquale and you are a pretty pair of rascals.

TRUFFALDINO: [*aside to himself*] I fear I'm the only one.

FLORINDO: Come. That's enough. Signora Beatrice, our servants certainly deserve to be punished; but in consideration of our own great happiness, we surely may forgive what is past.

BEATRICE: True; but your servant —

TRUFFALDINO: [*aside to* BEATRICE] For the love of Heaven don't mention Pasqual'.

BEATRICE: [*to* FLORINDO] Well, I must go and call upon Signor Pantalone dei Bisognosi; will you accompany me?

FLORINDO: I would do so with pleasure, but I have to wait here and see my banker. I will come later, if you are in haste.

BEATRICE: I am, I must go at once. I shall expect you at Signor Pantalone's; and shall stay there till you come.

FLORINDO: I don't know where he lives.

TRUFFALDINO: I know, sir, I'll show you the way.

BEATRICE: Very well, and now I must go to my room and tidy myself up.

TRUFFALDINO: [*aside to* BEATRICE] Very good, madam; I am at your service directly.

BEATRICE: Dear Florindo! What torments have I not endured for love of you!

[BEATRICE *goes into her room.*]

FLORINDO: Mine have been no less.

TRUFFALDINO: Sir, Pasqual' is not here, and Si'ora Beatrice has no one to help her dress; will you give me leave to wait upon her instead of Pasqual'?

FLORINDO: Yes, by all means. Wait upon her with diligence; I am delighted.

TRUFFALDINO: [*aside*] For invention, for promptness and for intrigue I will challenge the attorney general.

[TRUFFALDINO *goes into* BEATRICE'S *room.*]

FLORINDO: What strange things have happened in the course of this one day! Tears, lamentations, and anguish, and then at last consolation and happiness. From tears to laughter is a happy step, which makes us forget our agonies, but when we pass from pleasure to pain the change is even yet more acutely perceptible.

[*Re-enter* BEATRICE *followed by* TRUFFALDINO.]

BEATRICE: Here I am, have I not been quick?

FLORINDO: When will you change these clothes?

BEATRICE: Do I not look well in them?

FLORINDO: I long to see you in a woman's dress. Your beauties ought not to be so completely disguised.

BEATRICE: Well, I shall expect you at Signor Pantalone's; make Truffaldino show you the way.

FLORINDO: I must wait for the banker; if he does not come soon another time will do.

BEATRICE: Show me your love in your anxiety to attend me.

[*About to go.*]

TRUFFALDINO: [*aside to* BEATRICE] Do you wish me to stay and wait upon this gentleman?

BEATRICE: Yes, you will show him the way to Signor Pantalone's.

TRUFFALDINO: Yes, madam, certainly, as Pasqual' is not here.

BEATRICE: Wait upon him, I shall be pleased indeed.

[*Aside to herself.*]

I love him more than my very self.

[*Exit* BEATRICE.]

TRUFFALDINO: The fellow's nowhere to be seen. His master wants to dress, and he goes out on his own and is nowhere to be found.

FLORINDO: Of whom are you speaking?

TRUFFALDINO: Of Pasqual'. I love him, he is a good friend of mine, but he's a lazy dog. Now I am a servant worth two.

FLORINDO: Come and dress my wig. The banker will be here directly.

TRUFFALDINO: Please your honor, I hear your honor has to go to Si'or Pantalon's.

FLORINDO: Yes, what then?

TRUFFALDINO: I want to ask a favor of you.

FLORINDO: Well, you deserve it after all you have done.

TRUFFALDINO: If there has been any trouble, you know, sir, 'tis all the fault of Pasqual'.

FLORINDO: But where on earth *is* this cursed Pasquale? Can't one see him?

TRUFFALDINO: He'll come, the knave. And so, sir, I want to ask you this favor.

FLORINDO: What do you want?

TRUFFALDINO: You see, sir, I'm in love too.

FLORINDO: In love?

TRUFFALDINO: Yes, sir, and my young woman is maidservant to Si'or Pantalon'; and it would be very kind if your honor —

FLORINDO: How do I come into it?

TRUFFALDINO: I won't say, sir, that you come into it; but I being your servant, you might say a word for me to Si'or Pantalon'.

FLORINDO: We must see first whether the girl wants you.

TRUFFALDINO: The girl wants me, no mistake. All I want is a word to Si'or Pantalon'; I beg you, sir, of your charity.

FLORINDO: Certainly, I will speak for you, but how can you keep a wife?

TRUFFALDINO: I shall do what I can. I shall ask for help from Pasqual'.

FLORINDO: You had better ask help from someone with more sense.

[FLORINDO *goes into his room.*]

TRUFFALDINO: Well, if I don't show sense this time, I shall never show it again.

[TRUFFALDINO *follows* FLORINDO *into his room.*]


SCENE IV——*A Room in the House of* PANTALONE.

PANTALONE: Come, Clarice, pull yourself together. You see that Signor Silvio has repented and asks your foregiveness. If he acted foolishly, it was all for love of you; I have forgiven him his extravagances, you ought to forgive him too.

SILVIO: Measure my agony by your own, Signora Clarice, and rest assured that I most truly love you, since 'twas the fear of losing you that rendered me distracted. Heaven desires our happiness; do not be ungrateful for the blessings of Providence. Do not let the idea of revenge spoil the most beautiful day of your life.

DR. LOMBARDI: I join my prayers to those of my son; Signora Clarice, my dear daughter-in-law, have pity on the poor young man; he nearly went out of his mind.

SMERALDINA: Come, dear madam, what would you? Men are all cruel to us, some more, some less. They demand the most absolute fidelity, and on the least shadow of suspicion they bully us, ill-treat us and are like to murder us. Well, you have got to marry one or another of them some day, so I say to you as one says to sick people — since you have got to take your nasty medicine, take it.

PANTALONE: There, do you hear that? Smeraldina calls matrimony medicine. You must not think it is poison.

[*Aside to* DR. LOMBARDI.]

We must try to cheer her up.

DR. LOMBARDI: Certainly, 'tis not poison, nor even nasty medicine. Matrimony is a lollipop, a jujube, a lozenge!

SILVIO: But dear Clarice, won't you say a word? I know I deserve to be punished by you, but, of your mercy, punish me with hard words rather than with silence. Behold me at your feet; have pity upon me.

CLARICE: [*to* SILVIO *with a sigh*] Cruel!

PANTALONE: [*aside to* DR. LOMBARDI] You heard that little sigh? A good sign.

DR. LOMBARDI: [*aside to* SILVIO] Strike while the iron is hot.

SMERALDINA: [*aside*] A sigh is like lightning; it promises rainfall.

SILVIO: If I could think that you desired my blood to avenge my supposed cruelty, I give it you with all my heart. But, oh God! instead of the blood of my veins, accept, I beg you, that which gushes from my eyes.

[*Weeps.*]

PANTALONE: Bravo! Bravo! Well said!

DR. LOMBARDI: Capital! Capital!

CLARICE: [*sighing as before, but more tenderly*] Cruel!

DR. LOMBARDI: [*aside to* PANTALONE] She's done to a turn.

PANTALONE: Here, come up with you.

[*He raises* SILVIO, *takes him by the hand.*]

Stand over there.

[*Takes* CLARICE'S *hand.*]

And you come here too, madam. Now, join your hands together again; and make peace. So no more tears, be happy, no more nonsense and Heaven bless you both.

DR. LOMBARDI: There; 'tis done.

SMERALDINA: 'Tis done, 'tis done.

SILVIO: [*holding* CLARICE'S *hand*] Oh, Signora Clarice, for pity's sake—

CLARICE: Ungrateful!

SILVIO: Dearest!

CLARICE: Inhuman!

SILVIO: Beloved!

CLARICE: Monster!

SILVIO: Angel!

CLARICE: [*sighs*] Ah!

PANTALONE: [*aside*] Going, going—

SILVIO: Forgive me, for the love of Heaven.

CLARICE: [*sighs*] I forgive you.

PANTALONE: [*aside*] Gone!

DR. LOMBARDI: Come, Silvio, she has forgiven you.

SMERALDINA: The patient is ready; give her her medicine.

[*Enter* BRIGHELLA.]

BRIGHELLA: By your leave, sir, may I come in?

PANTALONE: Pray come in, good friend Brighella. 'Twas you, was it not, that told me all these pretty stories, who assured me that that party was Signor Federigo— eh?

BRIGHELLA: My dear sir, who would not have been deceived? They were twin brother and sister, as like as two peas. In those clothes I would have wagered my head that it was he.

PANTALONE: Enough. That's all done with. What is the news?

BRIGHELLA: Signora Beatrice is here, and desires to pay her respects.

PANTALONE: Let her come in; she is most welcome.

CLARICE: Poor Signora Beatrice, I am happy to think that her troubles are over.

SILVIO: You are sorry for her?

CLARICE: I am indeed.

SILVIO: And for me?

CLARICE: Oh, cruel!

PANTALONE: [*aside to* DR. LOMBARDI] You hear these loving words?

DR. LOMBARDI: [*aside to* PANTALONE] Ah, my son has a way with him.

PANTALONE: My daughter, poor dear child, has a very good heart.

SMERALDINA: Yes, they will both of them do their duty by each other.
          [*Enter* BEATRICE.]

BEATRICE: Ladies and gentlemen, I come to ask your pardon and forgiveness, that you should on my account have been put to inconvenience —

CLARICE: No, no, my dear; come to me.
          [*Embraces her.*]

SILVIO: [*annoyed at the embrace*] How now?

BEATRICE: [*to* SILVIO] What! May she not even embrace a woman?

SILVIO: [*aside*] 'Tis those clothes again.

PANTALONE: Well, well, Signora Beatrice, I must say, for a young woman of your age you have a wonderful courage.

DR. LOMBARDI: [*to* BEATRICE] Too much spirit, madam.

BEATRICE: Love makes one do great things.

PANTALONE: And you have found your young gentleman at last? So I hear.

BEATRICE: Yes, Heaven has made us happy.

DR. LOMBARDI: A nice reputation you have made yourself!

BEATRICE: Sir, you have no business in my affairs.

SILVIO: [*to* DR. LOMBARDI] Sir, I beg you, let everyone do as they will; do not be so put out about it. Now that I am happy, I want all the world to be happy too. Is anyone else going to be married? Let them all get married!

SMERALDINA: [*to* SILVIO] What about me, sir?

SILVIO: Whom are you going to marry?

SMERALDINA: The first man that comes along, sir.

SILVIO: Find him then, here am I.

CLARICE: [*to* SILVIO] You? What for?

SILVIO: To give her a wedding present.

CLARICE: That is no affair of yours.

SMERALDINA: [*aside*] She's afraid everybody will eat him. She likes the taste of him, I see.
          [*Enter* TRUFFALDINO.]

TRUFFALDINO: My respects to the company.

BEATRICE: [*to* TRUFFALDINO] Where is Signor Florindo?

TRUFFALDINO: He is here and would like to come in, by your leave.

BEATRICE: Signor Pantalone, will you give Signor Florindo leave?

PANTALONE: Is that your young gentleman?

BEATRICE: He is going to marry me.

PANTALONE: I shall be pleased to meet him.

BEATRICE: [*to* TRUFFALDINO] Show him in.

TRUFFALDINO: [*aside to* SMERALDINA] Young woman, my respects to you.

SMERALDINA: [*aside to* TRUFFALDINO] Pleased to see you, my little darkie.

TRUFFALDINO: We will have to talk.

SMERALDINA: What about?

TRUFFALDINO: [*makes as though giving her a wedding ring*] Are you willing?

SMERALDINA: Why not?

TRUFFALDINO: We'll have a talk.

> [*Exit* TRUFFALDINO.]

SMERALDINA: [*to* CLARICE] Madam, with the company's leave, I want a favor of you.

CLARICE: [*going aside to listen to* SMERALDINA] What is it?

SMERALDINA: [*to* CLARICE] I too am a poor young girl that would like to settle myself; there's the servant of Signora Beatrice who wants to marry me; now if you would say a kind word to his mistress, and get her to allow him to take me to wife, I should be the happiest girl in the world.

CLARICE: Dear Smeraldina, with all the pleasure in life; as soon as I can speak freely to Beatrice, I will certainly do so.

PANTALONE: [*to* CLARICE] What is all this whispering about?

CLARICE: Nothing, sir. She had something to say to me.

SILVIO: [*to* CLARICE] May I not know?

CLARICE: How inquisitive they all are! And then they talk about us women!

> [*Enter* FLORINDO *shown in by* TRUFFALDINO.]

FLORINDO: Your most humble servant, ladies and gentlemen.

> [*All bow and curtsy.*]
> [*To* PANTALONE.]

Are you the master of the house, sir?

PANTALONE: Yours to command, sir.

FLORINDO: Allow me, sir, to have the honor of waiting upon you this evening; I present myself by command of the Signora Beatrice, whose adventures will be known to you, and mine too.

PANTALONE: I am happy to know you, sir, and to see you here; I congratulate you most heartily on your good fortune.

FLORINDO: Signora Beatrice is to be my wife, and if you will not disdain to do us the honor, I hope you will give away the bride.

PANTALONE: Whatever has to be done, let it be done at once. Give her your hand.

FLORINDO: Signora Beatrice, I am willing.

BEATRICE: Here is my hand, Signor Florindo.

SMERALDINA: [*aside*] They don't want pressing.

PANTALONE: Afterward we will settle up our accounts. You will put yours in order; then we will settle ours.

CLARICE: [*to* BEATRICE] Dear friend, I congratulate you.

BEATRICE: [*to* CLARICE] And I you, with all my heart.

SILVIO: [*to* FLORINDO] Sir, do you know me again?

FLORINDO: [*to* SILVIO] Indeed I do, sir; you would have provoked me to a duel.

SILVIO: 'Twas to my own disaster. Here is the adversary.

[*Pointing to* BEATRICE.]
who disarmed me and very nearly killed me.

BEATRICE: And gave you your life too, you might say.

SILVIO: 'Tis true.

CLARICE: At my entreaty.

SILVIO: That is very true.

PANTALONE: Everything is in order, everything is settled.

TRUFFALDINO: The best is yet to come, ladies nd gentlemen.

PANTALONE: What is yet to come?

TRUFFALDINO: [*to* FLORINDO, *taking him apart*] With your good leave, sir, one word.

FLORINDO: What do you want?

TRUFFALDINO: You remember what you promised me, sir?

FLORINDO: What did I promise? I do not recollect.

TRUFFALDINO: To ask Si'or Pantalon' for Smeraldina as my wife.

FLORINDO: Of course, now I remember; I will do so at once.

TRUFFALDINO: [*aside*] I, too, poor man, want to put myself right with the world.

FLORINDO: Signor Pantalone, although this is the first occasion on which I have had the honor of knowing you, I make bold to desire a favor of you.

PANTALONE: You may command me, sir; I will serve you the best of my powers.

FLORINDO: My manservant desires to marry your maid; have you any objection to giving your consent?

SMERALDINA: [*aside*] Wonderful! Here's another who wants to marry me! Who the devil can he be? I wish I knew him.

PANTALONE: For my part I am agreed.
[*To* SMERALDINA.]
What say you, girl?

SMERALDINA: If I thought he would make a good husband—

PANTALONE: Is he a good honest man, this servant of yours?

FLORINDO: For the short time he has been with me he has certainly proved himself trusty, and he seems to be intelligent.

CLARICE: Signor Florindo, you have anticipated me in something that *I* ought to have done. I was to propose the marriage of my maid with the manservant of Signora Beatrice. You have asked for her for *your* servant, I can say no more.

FLORINDO: No, no; since you so earnestly desire this, I withdraw altogether and leave you completely free.

CLARICE: Indeed, sir, I could never permit myself to have my own wishes preferred to yours. Besides, I must admit that I am not fully authorized. Pray continue in your proposal.

FLORINDO: You say so out of courtesy, madam. Signor Pantalone, I withdraw all that I have said. I will not say another word on behalf of my servant; on the contrary, I am absolutely opposed to his marrying her.

CLARICE: If *your* man is not to marry her, no more shall the other man. We must be fair on both sides.

TRUFFALDINO: [*aside*] Here's a state of things! They pay each other compliments, and meanwhile I am left without a wife at all.

SMERALDINA: [*aside*] It looks as if I should have neither one nor the other.

PANTALONE: Come, we *must* settle it somehow; this poor girl wants to get married, let us give her either to the one or the other.

FLORINDO: Not to *my* man. Nothing shall induce me to do Signora Clarice an injustice.

CLARICE: Nor will I ever tolerate an injustice to Signor Florindo.

TRUFFALDINO: Sir, madam, I can settle the matter myself.
　　　　　[*With his usual air of great ingenuity.*]
　　　　　Si'or Florindo, did you not ask the hand of Smeraldina for your servant?

FLORINDO: I did; did you not hear me?

TRUFFALDINO: And you, Si'ora Clarice, did you not intend Smeraldina to marry the servant of Si'ora Beatrice?

CLARICE: Most certainly I was to do so.

TRUFFALDINO: Good; then if that is so, give me your hand, Smeraldina.

PANTALONE: And pray what right have *you* to ask for her hand?

TRUFFALDINO: Because I am the servant of Si'or Florindo and of Si'ora Beatrice too.

FLORINDO: What?

BEATRICE: What do you say?

TRUFFALDINO: Pray be calm. Si'or Florindo, who asked you to ask Si'or Pantalon' for Smeraldina?

FLORINDO: You did.

TRUFFALDINO: And you, Si'ora Clarice, whom had you in mind as the intended husband of Smeraldina?

CLARICE: Yourself.

TRUFFALDINO: *Ergo*, Smeraldina is mine.

FLORINDO: Signora Beatrice, where is your servant?

BEATRICE: Why, here! Truffaldino, of course.

FLORINDO: Truffaldino? He is *my* servant!

BEATRICE: Is not yours called Pasquale?

FLORINDO: Pasquale? I thought Pasquale was *yours!*

BEATRICE: [*to* TRUFFALDINO] How do you explain this?
　　　　　[TRUFFALDINO *makes silent gentures asking for forgiveness.*]

FLORINDO: You rascal!

BEATRICE: You knave!

FLORINDO: So you waited on two masters at once?

TRUFFALDINO: Yes, sir, I did, that was the very trick. I took on the job without thinking; just to see what I could do. It did not last long, 'tis true; but at any rate I can boast that nobody would ever have found me out, if I had not given myself away for love of this girl here. I have done a hard day's work, and I dare say I had my shortcomings, but I hope that in consideration of the fun of the thing, all these ladies and gentlemen will forgive me.

# Henrik Ibsen

# The Wild Duck

## Translated by William Archer

### PERSONS OF THE PLAY

WERLE, *a merchant*
GREGERS WERLE, *his son*
OLD EKDAL
HIALMAR EKDAL, *his son, a photographer*
GINA EKDAL, *Hialmar's wife*
HEDVIG, *their daughter, a girl of fourteen*
MRS SORBY, *Werle's housekeeper*
RELLING, *a doctor*
MOLVIK, *a student of theology*
GRABERG, *Werle's bookkeeper*
PETTERSEN, *Werle's servant*
JENSEN, *a hired waiter*
A FLABBY GENTLEMAN
A THIN-HAIRED GENTLEMAN
A SHORTSIGHTED GENTLEMAN
SIX OTHER GENTLEMEN, *guests at Werle's dinner party*
SEVERAL HIRED WAITERS

*The action takes place in the home of* WERLE *and the studio of* HIALMAR EKDAL.

## ACT I

SCENE——*At* WERLE'S *house A richly and comfortably furnished study; bookcases and upholstered furniture; a writing table, with papers and documents, in the center of the room; lighted lamps with green shades, giving a subdued light. At the back open folding doors with curtains drawn back. Within is seen a large and handsome room, brilliantly lighted with lamps and branching candlesticks. In front, on the right (in the study), a small baize door leads into* WERLE'S *office. On the left, in front, a fireplace with a glowing coal fire and farther back a double door leading into the dining room.*

[WERLE'S *servant,* PETTERSEN, *in livery, and* JENSEN, *the hired waiter, in black, are putting the study in order. In the large room two or three other hired waiters are moving about arranging things and lighting more candles. From the dining room the hum of conversation and laughter of many voices are heard; a glass is tapped with a knife; silence follows, and a toast is proposed; shouts of "Bravo!" and then again a buzz of conversation.*]

298

PETTERSEN: [*lights a lamp on the chimney place and places a shade over it*] Listen to them, Jensen! Now the old man's on his legs giving a long speech about Mrs Sorby.

JENSEN: [*pushing forward an armchair*] Is it true, what folks say, that they're — very good friends, eh?

PETTERSEN: Lord knows.

JENSEN: I've heard tell as he's been a lively customer in his day.

PETTERSEN: May be.

JENSEN: And he's giving this spread in honor of his son, they say.

PETTERSEN: Yes. His son came home yesterday.

JENSEN: This is the first time I ever heard as Mr Werle had a son.

PETTERSEN: Oh yes, he has a son right enough. But he's a fixture, as you might say, up at the Höidal works. He's never once come to town all the years I've been in service here.

A WAITER: [*in the doorway of the other room*] Pettersen, here's an old fellow wanting —

PETTERSEN: [*mutters*] The devil — who's this now?

[OLD EKDAL *appears from the right, in the inner room. He is dressed in a threadbare overcoat with a high collar; he wears woolen mittens and carries in his hand a stick and a fur cap. Under his arm a brown paper parcel. Dirty red-brown wig and small gray mustache.*]

PETTERSEN: [*goes toward him*] Good lord! — what do you want here?

EKDAL: [*in the doorway*] Must get into the office, Pettersen.

PETTERSEN: The office was closed an hour ago, and —

EKDAL: So they told me at the front door. But Graberg's in there still. Let me slip in this way, Pettersen; there's a good fellow. [*points toward the baize door*] It's not the first time I've come this way.

PETTERSEN: Well, you may pass. [*opens the door*] But mind you go out again the proper way, for we've got company.

EKDAL: I know, I know — h'm! Thanks, Pettersen, good old friend! Thanks! [*mutters softly*] Ass! [*He goes into the office;* PETTERSEN *shuts the door after him.*]

JENSEN: Is he one of the office people?

PETTERSEN: No, he's only an outside hand that does odd jobs of copying. But he's been a topnotcher in his day, has old Ekdal.

JENSEN: You can see he's been through a lot.

PETTERSEN: Yes; he was an army officer, you know.

JENSEN: You don't say so?

PETTERSEN: No mistake about it. But then he went into the timber trade or something of the sort. They say he once played Mr Werle a very nasty trick. They were partners in the Höidal works at the time. Oh, I know old Ekdal well, I do. Many a nip of bitters and a bottle of ale we two have drunk at Madam Eriksen's.

JENSEN: He don't look as if he'd much to stand treat with.

PETTERSEN: Why, bless you, Jensen, it's me that stands treat. I always think there's no harm in being a bit civil to folks that have seen better days.

JENSEN: Did he go bankrupt then?

PETTERSEN: Worse than that. He went to jail.

JENSEN: To jail!

PETTERSEN: Or perhaps it was the penitentiary. [*listens*] Sh! They're leaving the table.

[*The dining-room door is thrown open from within by a couple of waiters.* MRS SORBY *comes out conversing with two gentlemen. Gradually the whole company follows, among them* WERLE. *Last come* HIALMAR EKDAL *and* GREGERS WERLE.]

MRS SORBY: [*in passing, to the servant*] Tell them to serve the coffee in the music room, Pettersen.

PETTERSEN: Very well, madam.

[*She goes with the two gentlemen into the inner room and thence out to the right.* PETTERSEN *and* JENSEN *go out the same way.*]

A FLABBY GENTLEMAN: [*to a* THIN-HAIRED GENTLEMAN] Whew! What a dinner! It was no joke to do it justice.

THE THIN-HAIRED GENTLEMAN: Oh, with a little good will one can get through a lot in three hours.

THE FLABBY GENTLEMAN: Yes, but afterward, afterward, my dear Chamberlain!

A THIRD GENTLEMAN: I hear the coffee and liqueur are to be served in the music room.

THE FLABBY GENTLEMAN: Bravo! Then perhaps Mrs Sorby will play us something.

THE THIN-HAIRED GENTLEMAN: [*in a low voice*] I hope Mrs Sorby doesn't play us a tune we don't like, one of these days!

THE FLABBY GENTLEMAN: Oh no, Bertha will never turn against her old friends.

[*They laugh and pass into the inner room.*]

WERLE: [*in a low voice, dejectedly*] I don't think anybody noticed it, Gregers.

GREGERS: [*looks at him*] Noticed what?

WERLE: Didn't you notice it either?

GREGERS: What do you mean?

WERLE: We were thirteen at table.

GREGERS: Really? Were there thirteen of us?

WERLE: [*glances toward* HIALMAR EKDAL] Our usual party is twelve. [*to the others*] This way, gentlemen!

[WERLE *and the others, all except* HIALMAR *and* GREGERS, *go out by the back, to the right.*]

HIALMAR: [*who has overheard the conversation*] You ought not to have invited me, Gregers.

GREGERS: What! Not ask my best and only friend to a party supposed to be in my honor?

HIALMAR: But I don't think your father likes it. You see, I am quite outside his circle.

GREGERS: So I hear. But I wanted to see you and have a talk with you, and I certainly shan't be staying long. Ah, we two old schoolfellows have drifted apart from each other. It must be sixteen or seventeen years since we met.

HIALMAR: Is it so long?

GREGERS: It is. Well, how goes it with you? You look well. You have put on flesh and grown almost stout.

HIALMAR: Well, "stout" is scarcely the word, but I daresay I look a little more of a man than I used to.

GREGERS: Yes, you do; your outer man is in first-rate condition.

HIALMAR: [*in a tone of gloom*] Ah, but the inner man! That is a very different matter,

I can tell you! Of course you know of the terrible catastrophe that has befallen me since last we met.

GREGERS: [*more softly*] How are things going with your father now?

HIALMAR: Don't let us talk of it, old fellow. Of course my poor unhappy father lives with me. He hasn't another soul in the world to care for him. But you can understand that this is a miserable subject for me. Tell me, rather, how you have been getting on up at the works.

GREGERS: I have had a delightfully lonely time of it — plenty of leisure to think and think about things. Come over here; we may as well make ourselves comfortable.

[*He seats himself in an armchair by the fire and draws* HIALMAR *down into another alongside of it.*]

HIALMAR: [*sentimentally*] After all, Gregers, I thank you for inviting me to your father's table; for I take it as a sign that you have got over your feeling against me.

GREGERS: [*surprised*] How could you imagine I had any feeling against you?

HIALMAR: You had at first, you know.

GREGERS: How at first?

HIALMAR: After the great misfortune. It was natural enough that you should. Your father was within an ace of being drawn into that — well, that terrible business.

GREGERS: Why should that give me any feeling against you? Who can have put that into your head?

HIALMAR: I know it did, Gregers; your father told me so himself.

GREGERS: [*starts*] My father! Oh, indeed. H'm. Was that why you never let me hear from you? — not a single word.

HIALMAR: Yes.

GREGERS: Not even when you made up your mind to become a photographer?

HIALMAR: Your father said I had better not write to you at all, about anything.

GREGERS: [*looking straight before him*] Well, well, perhaps he was right. But tell me now, Hialmar: are you pretty well satisfied with your present position?

HIALMAR: [*with a little sigh*] Oh yes, I am; I have really no cause to complain. At first, as you may guess, I felt it a little strange. It was such a totally new state of things for me. But of course my whole circumstances were totally changed. Father's utter, irretrievable ruin — the shame and disgrace of it, Gregers —

GREGERS: [*affected*] Yes, yes; I understand.

HIALMAR: I couldn't think of remaining at college; there wasn't a shilling to spare; on the contrary, there were debts — mainly to your father, I believe —

GREGERS: H'm.

HIALMAR: In short, I thought it best to break, once for all, with my old surroundings and associations. It was your father that specially urged me to it, and since he interested himself so much in me —

GREGERS: My father did?

HIALMAR: Yes, you surely knew that, didn't you? Where do you suppose I found the money to learn photography and to furnish a studio and make a start? All that costs money, I can tell you.

GREGERS: And my father provided it?

HIALMAR: Yes, my dear fellow, didn't you know? I understood him to say he had written to you about it.

GREGERS: Not a word about his part in the business. He must have forgotten it. Our correspondence has always been purely a business one. So it was my father that —

HIALMAR: Yes, certainly. He didn't wish it to be generally known, but he it was. And of course it was he, too, that put me in a position to marry. Don't you — don't you know about that either?

GREGERS: No, I haven't heard a word of it. [*shakes him by the arm*] But, my dear Hialmar, I can't tell you what pleasure all this gives me — pleasure and self-reproach. I have perhaps done my father injustice after all — in some things. This proves that he has a heart. It shows a sort of compunction —

HIALMAR: Compunction?

GREGERS: Yes, yes — whatever you like to call it. Oh, I can't tell you how glad I am to hear this of Father. So you are a married man, Hialmar! That is further than I shall ever get. Well, I hope you are happy in your married life?

HIALMAR: Yes, thoroughly happy. She is as good and capable a wife as any man could wish for. And she is by no means without culture.

GREGERS: [*rather surprised*] No, of course not.

HIALMAR: You see, life is itself an education. Her daily intercourse with me — And then we know one or two rather remarkable men who come a good deal about us. I assure you, you would hardly know Gina again.

GREGERS: Gina?

HIALMAR: Yes; had you forgotten that her name was Gina?

GREGERS: Whose name? I haven't the slightest idea —

HIALMAR: Don't you remember that she used to be in service here?

GREGERS: [*looks at him*] Is it Gina Hansen?

HIALMAR: Yes, of course it is Gina Hansen.

GREGERS: — who kept house for us during the last year of my mother's illness?

HIALMAR: Yes, exactly. But, my dear friend, I'm quite sure your father told you that I was married.

GREGERS: [*who has risen*] Oh yes, he mentioned it, but not that —[*walking about the room*] Stay — perhaps he did — now that I think of it. My father always writes such short letters. [*half seats himself on the arm of the chair*] Now tell me, Hialmar — this is interesting — how did you come to know Gina — your wife?

HIALMAR: The simplest thing in the world. You know Gina did not stay here long; everything was so much upset at that time, owing to your mother's illness and so forth, that Gina was not equal to it all; so she gave notice and left. That was the year before your mother died — or it may have been the same year.

GREGERS: It was the same year. I was up at the works then. But afterward?

HIALMAR: Well, Gina lived at home with her mother, Madam Hansen, an excellent, hard-working woman who kept a little eating house. She had a room to let too, a very nice comfortable room.

GREGERS: And I suppose you were lucky enough to secure it?

HIALMAR: Yes; in fact, it was your father that recommended it to me. So it was there, you see, that I really came to know Gina.

GREGERS: And then you got engaged?

HIALMAR: Yes. It doesn't take young people long to fall in love — h'm.

GREGERS: [*rises and moves about a little*] Tell me: was it after your engagement — was it then that my father — I mean was it then that you began to take up photography?

HIALMAR: Yes, precisely. I wanted to make a start and to set up house as soon as possible, and your father and I agreed that this photography business was the readiest way. Gina thought so too. Oh, and there was another thing in its favor, by the bye; it happened luckily, that Gina had learned to retouch.

GREGERS: That chimed in marvelously.

HIALMAR: [*pleased, rises*] Yes, didn't it? Don't you think it was a marvelous piece of luck?

GREGERS: Oh, unquestionably. My father seems to have been almost a kind of providence to you.

HIALMAR: [*with emotion*] He did not forsake his old friend's son in the hour of his need. For he has a heart, you see.

MRS SORBY: [*enters arm in arm with* WERLE] Nonsense, my dear Mr Werle; you mustn't stay there any longer staring at all the lights. It's very bad for you.

WERLE: [*lets go her arm and passes his hand over his eyes*] I daresay you are right.
[PETTERSEN *and* JENSEN *carry round refreshment trays.*]

MRS SORBY: [*to the guests in the other room*] This way, if you please, gentlemen. Whoever wants a glass of punch must be so good as to come in here.

THE FLABBY GENTLEMAN: [*comes up to* MRS SORBY] Surely it isn't possible that you have suspended our cherished right to smoke?

MRS. SORBY: Yes, No smoking here, in Mr Werle's sanctum, Chamberlain.

THE THIN-HAIRED GENTLEMAN: When did you enact these stringent amendments on the cigar law, Mrs Sorby?

MRS SORBY: After the last dinner, Chamberlain, when certain persons permitted themselves to overstep the mark.

THE THIN-HAIRED GENTLEMAN: And may one never overstep the mark a little bit, Madame Bertha? Not the least little bit?

MRS SORBY: Not in any respect whatsoever, Mr Balle.
[*Most of the guests have assembled in the study; servants hand round glasses of punch.*]

WERLE: [*to* HIALMAR, *who is studying beside a table*] What are you studying so intently, Ekdal?

HIALMAR: Only an album, Mr Werle.

THE THIN-HAIRED GENTLEMAN: [*who is wandering about*] Ah, photographs! They are quite in your line of course.

THE FLABBY GENTLEMAN: [*in an armchair*] Haven't you brought any of your own with you?

HIALMAR: No, I haven't.

THE FLABBY GENTLEMAN: You ought to have; it's very good for the digestion to sit and look at pictures.

THE THIN-HAIRED GENTLEMAN: And it contributes to the entertainment, you know.

THE SHORTSIGHTED GENTLEMAN: And all contributions are thankfully received.

MRS SORBY: The chamberlains think that when one is invited out to dinner one ought to exert oneself a little in return, Mr Ekdal.

THE FLABBY GENTLEMAN: Where one dines so well, that duty becomes a pleasure.

THE THIN-HAIRED GENTLEMAN: And when it's a case of the struggle for existence, you know —

MRS SORBY: I quite agree with you!
[*They continue the conversation with laughter and joking.*]

GREGERS: [*softly*] You must join in, Hialmar.

HIALMAR: [*writhing*] What am I to talk about?

THE FLABBY GENTLEMAN: Don't you think, Mr Werle, that Tokay may be considered one of the more wholesome sorts of wine?

WERLE: [*by the fire*] I can answer for the Tokay you had today, at any rate; it's one of the very finest seasons. Of course you would notice that.

THE FLABBY GENTLEMAN: Yes, it had a remarkably delicate flavor.

HIALMAR: [*shyly*] Is there any difference between the seasons?

THE FLABBY GENTLEMAN: [*laughs*] Come! That's good!

WERLE: [*smiles*] It really doesn't pay to set fine wine before you.

THE THIN-HAIRED GENTLEMAN: Tokay is like photographs, Mr Ekdal; they both need sunshine. Am I not right?

HIALMAR: Yes, light is important, no doubt.

MRS SORBY: And it's exactly the same with the chamberlains — they, too, depend very much on sunshine, as the saying is.

THE THIN-HAIRED GENTLEMAN: Oh, shame! That's a very threadbare joke!

THE SHORTSIGHTED GENTLEMAN: Mrs Sorby is coming out —

THE FLABBY GENTLEMAN: — and at our expense too. [*holds up his finger reprovingly*] Oh, Madame Bertha, Madame Bertha!

MRS SORBY: Yes, and there's not the least doubt that the seasons differ greatly. The old vintages are the finest.

THE SHORTSIGHTED GENTLEMAN: Do you count me among the old vintages?

MRS SORBY: Oh, far from it.

THE THIN-HAIRED GENTLEMAN: There now! But me, dear Mrs Sorby —

THE FLABBY GENTLEMAN: Yes, and me? What vintage should you say that we belong to?

MRS SORBY: Why, to the sweet vintages, gentlemen.[*She sips a glass of punch. The gentlemen laugh and flirt with her.*]

WERLE: Mrs Sorby can always find a loophole — when she wants to. Fill your glasses, gentlemen! Pettersen, will you see to it? Gregers, suppose we have a glass together. [GREGERS *does not move.*] Won't you join us, Ekdal? I found no opportunity of drinking with you at table.

[GRABERG, *the bookkeeper, looks in at the baize door.*]

GRABERG: Excuse me, sir, but I can't get out.

WERLE: Have you been locked in again?

GRABERG: Yes, and Flakstad has carried off the keys.

WERLE: Well, you can pass out this way.

GRABERG: But there's someone else —

WERLE: All right; come through, both of you. Don't be afraid.

[GRABERG *and* OLD EKDAL *come out of the office.*]

WERLE: [*involuntarily*] Ugh!

[*The laughter and talk among the guests cease.* HIALMAR *starts at the sight of his father, puts down his glass and turns toward the fireplace.*]

EKDAL: [*does not look up but makes little bows to both sides as he passes, murmuring*] Beg pardon, come the wrong way. Door locked — door locked. Beg pardon.

[*He and* GRABERG *go out by the back, to the right.*]

WERLE: [*between his teeth*] That idiot Graberg.

GREGERS: [*open-mouthed and staring, to* HIALMAR] Why, surely that wasn't —

THE FLABBY GENTLEMAN: What's the matter? Who was it?

GREGERS: Oh, nobody; only the bookkeeper and someone with him.

THE SHORTSIGHTED GENTLEMAN: [*to* HIALMAR] Did you know that man?

HIALMAR: I don't know — I didn't notice —

THE FLABBY GENTLEMAN: What the devil has come over everyone? [*He joins another group who are talking softly.*]

MRS SORBY: [*whispers to the* SERVANT] Give him something to take with him — something good, mind.

PETTERSEN: [*nods*] I'll see to it.
    [*Goes out.*]

GREGERS: [*softly and with emotion, to* HIALMAR] So that was really he!

HIALMAR: Yes.

GREGERS: And you could stand there and deny that you knew him.

HIALMAR: [*whispers vehemently*] But how could I —

GREGERS: — acknowledge your own father?

HIALMAR: [*with pain*] Oh, if you were in my place —
    [*The conversation among the guests, which has been carried on in a low tone, now swells into constrained joviality.*]

THE THIN-HAIRED GENTLEMAN: [*approaching* HIALMAR *and* GREGERS *in a friendly manner*] Ah! Reviving old college memories, eh? Don't you smoke, Mr Ekdal? May I give you a light? Oh, by the bye, we mustn't —

HIALMAR: No, thank you, I won't —

THE FLABBY GENTLEMAN: Haven't you a nice little poem you could recite to us, Mr Ekdal? You used to recite so charmingly.

HIALMAR: I am sorry, I can't remember anything.

THE FLABBY GENTLEMAN: Oh, that's a pity. Well, what shall we do, Balle?
    [*Both gentlemen move away and pass into the other room.*]

HIALMAR: [*gloomily*] Gregers — I am going! When a man has felt the crushing hand of Fate, you see — Say good-by to your father for me.

GREGERS: Yes, yes. Are you going straight home?

HIALMAR: Yes. Why?

GREGERS: Oh, because I may perhaps look in on you later.

HIALMAR: No, you mustn't do that. You must not come to my home. Mine is a melancholy abode, Gregors; especially after a splendid banquet like this. We can always arrange to meet somewhere in the town.

MRS SORBY: [*who has quietly approached*] Are you going, Ekdal?

HIALMAR: Yes.

MRS SORBY: Remember me to Gina.

HIALMAR: Thanks.

MRS SORBY: And say I am coming up to see her one of these days.

HIALMAR: Yes, thank you. [*to* GREGERS] Stay here; I will slip out unobserved.
    [*He saunters away, then into the other room and so out to the right.*]

MRS SORBY: [*softly to the* SERVANT, *who has come back*] Well, did you give the old man something?

PETTERSEN: Yes; I sent him off with a bottle of brandy.

MRS SORBY: Oh, you might have thought of something better than that.

PETTERSEN: Oh no, Mrs Sorby; brandy is what he likes best in the world.

THE FLABBY GENTLEMAN: [*in the doorway with a sheet of music in his hand*] Shall we play a duet, Mrs. Sorby?

MRS SORBY: Yes, suppose we do.

THE GUESTS: Bravo, bravo!

[*She goes with all the guests through the back room out to the right.* GREGERS *remains standing by the fire.* WERLE *is looking for something on the writing table and appears to wish that* GREGERS *would go; as* GREGERS *does not move* WERLE *goes toward the door.*]

GREGERS: Father, won't you stay a moment?

WERLE: [*stops*] What is it?

GREGERS: I must have a word with you.

WERLE: Can't it wait until we are alone?

GREGERS: No, it can't, for perhaps we shall never be alone together.

WERLE: [*drawing nearer*] What do you mean by that?

[*During what follows the pianoforte is faintly heard from the distant music room.*]

GREGERS: How has that family been allowed to go so miserably to the wall?

WERLE: You mean the Ekdals, I suppose.

GREGERS: Yes, I mean the Ekdals. Lieutenant Ekdal was once so closely associated with you.

WERLE: Much too closely; I have felt that to my cost for many a year. It is thanks to him that I — yes I — have had a kind of slur cast upon my reputation.

GREGERS: [*softly*] Are you sure that he alone was to blame?

WERLE: Who else do you suppose?

GREGERS: You and he acted together in that affair of the forests —

WERLE: But was it not Ekdal that drew the map of the tracts we had bought — that fraudulent map! It was he who felled all that timber illegally on government ground. In fact, the whole management was in his hands. I was quite in the dark as to what Lieutenant Ekdal was doing.

GREGERS: Lieutenant Ekdal himself seems to have been very much in the dark as to what he was doing.

WERLE: That may be. But the fact remains that he was found guilty and I acquitted.

GREGERS: Yes, I know that nothing was proved against you.

WERLE: Acquittal is acquittal. Why do you rake up these old miseries that turned my hair gray before its time? Is that the sort of thing you have been brooding over up there, all these years? I can assure you, Gregers, here in the town the whole story has been forgotten long ago — as far as *I* am concerned.

GREGERS: But that unhappy Ekdal family —

WERLE: What would you have me do for the people? When Ekdal came out of prison he was a broken-down being, past all help. There are people in the world who dive to the bottom the moment they get a couple of slugs in their body and never come to the surface again. You may take my word for it, Gregers, I have done all I could without positively laying myself open to all sorts of suspicion and gossip.

GREGERS: Suspicion? Oh, I see.

WERLE: I have given Ekdal copying to do for the office, and I pay him far, far more for it than his work is worth.

GREGERS: [*without looking at him*] H'm; that I don't doubt.

WERLE: You laugh? Do you think I am not telling you the truth? Well, I certainly can't refer you to my books, for I never enter payments of that sort.

GREGERS: [*smiles coldly*] No, there are certain payments it is best to keep no account of.

WERLE: [*taken aback*] What do you mean by that?

GREGERS: [*mustering up courage*] Have you entered what it cost you to have Hial-mar Ekdal taught photography?

WERLE: I? How "entered" it?

GREGERS: I have learned that it was you who paid for his training. And I have learned, too, that it was you who enabled him to set up house so comfortably.

WERLE: Well, and yet you talk as though I had done nothing for the Ekdals! I can assure you these people have cost me enough in all conscience.

GREGERS: Have you entered any of these expenses in your books?

WERLE: Why do you ask?

GREGERS: Oh, I have my reasons. Now tell me: when you interested yourself so warmly in your old friend's son — it was just before his marriage, was it not?

WERLE: Why, deuce take it — after all these years how can I —

GREGERS: You wrote me a letter about that time — a business letter, of course — and in a postscript you mentioned — quite briefly — that Hialmar Ekdal had married a Miss Hansen.

WERLE: Yes, that was quite right. That was her name.

GREGERS: But you did not mention that this Miss Hansen was Gina Hansen — our former housekeeper.

WERLE: [*with a forced laugh of derision*] No; to tell the truth, it didn't occur to me that you were so particularly interested in our former houskeeper.

GREGERS: Nor was I. But [*lowers his voice*] there were others in this house who were particularly interested in her.

WERLE: What do you mean by that? [*flaring up*] You are not alluding to me, I hope?

GREGERS: [*softly but firmly*] Yes, I am alluding to you.

WERLE: And you dare — You presume to — How can that ungrateful hound — that photographer fellow — how dare he go making such insinuations!

GREGERS: Hialmar has never breathed a word about this. I don't believe he has the faintest suspicion of such a thing.

WERLE: Then where have you got it from? Who can have put such notions in your head?

GREGERS: My poor unhappy mother told me, the very last time I saw her.

WERLE: Your mother! I might have known as much! You and she — you always stuck together. It was she who turned you against me from the first.

GREGERS: No, it was all that she had to suffer and submit to, until she broke down and came to such a pitiful end.

WERLE: Oh, she had nothing to suffer or submit to; not more than most people, at all events. But there's no getting on with morbid, overstrained creatures — that I have learned to my cost. And you could go on nursing such a suspicion — burrowing into all sorts of slanders against your own father! I must say, Gregers, I really think at your age you might find something more useful to do.

GREGERS: Yes, it is high time.

WERLE: Then perhaps your mind would be easier than it seems to be now. What can be your object in remaining up at the works year out and year in, drudging away like a common clerk and not drawing a farthing more than the ordinary monthly wage? It is downright folly.

GREGERS: Ah, if I were only sure of that.

WERLE: I understand you well enough. You want to be independent; you won't be beholden to me for anything. Well, now there happens to be an opportunity for you to become independent, your own master in everything.

GREGERS: Indeed? In what way?

WERLE: When I wrote you insisting on your coming to town at once — h'm —

GREGERS: Yes, what is it you really want of me? I have been waiting all day to know.

WERLE: I want to propose that you should enter the firm as partner.

GREGERS: I! Join your firm? As partner?

WERLE: Yes. It would not involve our being constantly together. You could take over the business here in town, and I would move up to the works.

GREGERS: You would?

WERLE: The fact is, I am not so fit for work as I once was. I am obliged to spare my eyes, Gregers; they have begun to trouble me.

GREGERS: They have always been weak.

WERLE: Not as they are now. And besides, circumstances might possibly make it desirable for me to live up there — for a time, at any rate.

GREGERS: That is certainly quite a new idea to me.

WERLE: Listen, Gregers, there are many things that stand between us; but we are father and son after all. We ought surely to be able to come to some sort of understanding with each other.

GREGERS: Outwardly, you mean, of course?

WERLE: Well, even that would be something. Think it over, Gregers. Don't you think it ought to be possible? Eh?

GREGERS: [*looking at him coldly*] There is something behind all this.

WERLE: How so?

GREGERS: You want to make use of me in some way.

WERLE: In such a close relationship as ours the one can always be useful to the other.

GREGERS: Yes, so people say.

WERLE: I want very much to have you at home with me for a time. I am a lonely man, Gregers; I have always felt lonely all my life through, but most of all now that I am getting up in years. I feel the need of someone about me —

GREGERS: You have Mrs Sorby.

WERLE: Yes, I have her, and she has become, I may say, almost indispensable to me. She is lively and even tempered; she brightens up the house; and that is a very great thing for me.

GREGERS: Well, then, you have everything as you wish it.

WERLE: Yes, but I am afraid it can't last. A woman so situated may easily find herself in a false position in the eyes of the world. For that matter, it does a man no good either.

GREGERS: Oh, when a man gives such dinners as you give he can risk a great deal.

WERLE: Yes, but how about the woman, Gregers? I fear she won't accept the situation much longer, and even if she did — even if, out of attachment to me, she were to take her chance of gossip and scandal and all that — do you think, Gregers, you with your strong sense of justice —

GREGERS: [*interrupts him*] Tell me in one word: are you thinking of marrying her?

WERLE: Suppose I were thinking of it? What then?

GREGERS: That's what I say: What then?

WERLE: Should you be inflexibly opposed to it?

GREGERS: Not at all. Not by any means.

WERLE: I was not sure whether your devotion to your mother's memory —

GREGERS: I am not overstrained.

WERLE: Well, whatever you may or not be, at all events you have lifted a great weight from my mind. I am extremely pleased that I can reckon on your concurrence in this matter.

GREGERS: [looking intently at him] Now I see the use you want to put me to.

WERLE: Use to put you to? What an expression!

GREGERS: Oh, don't let us be nice in our choice of words — not when we are alone together, at any rate. [with a short laugh] Well, well. So this is what made it absolutely essential that I should come to town in person. For the sake of Mrs Sorby we are to get up a pretense at family life in the house — a tableau of filial affection. That will be something new, indeed.

WERLE: How dare you speak in that tone!

GREGERS: Was there ever any family life here? Never since I can remember. But now, your plans demand something of the sort. No doubt it will have an excellent effect when it is reported that the son has hastened home, on the wings of filial piety, to the gray-haired father's wedding feast. What will then remain of all the rumors as to the wrongs the poor dead mother had to submit to? Not a scrap. Her son annihilates them at one stroke.

WERLE: Gregers — I believe there is no one in the world you detest as you do me.

GREGERS: [softly] I have seen you at too close quarters.

WERLE: You have seen me with your mother's eyes. [lowers his voice a little] But you should remember that her eyes were — clouded now and then.

GREGERS: [quivering] I see what you are hinting at. But who was to blame for mother's unfortunate weakness? Why, you and all those — The last of them was this woman that you palmed off upon Hialmar Ekdal when you were — Ugh!

WERLE: [shrugs his shoulders] Word for word as if it were your mother speaking!

GREGERS: [without heeding] And there he is now, with his great, confiding childlike mind, compassed about with all this treachery — living under the same roof with such a creature and never dreaming that what he calls his home is built up on a lie! [comes a step nearer] When I look back upon your past I seem to see a battlefield with shattered lives on every hand.

WERLE: I begin to think that the chasm that divides us is too wide.

GREGERS: [bowing with self-command] So I have observed, and therefore I take my hat and go.

WERLE: You are going? Out of the house?

GREGERS: Yes. For at last I see my mission in life.

WERLE: What mission?

GREGERS: You would only laugh if I told you.

WERLE: A lonely man doesn't laugh so easily, Gregers.

GREGERS: [pointing toward the background] Look, Father — the chamberlains are playing blindman's buff with Mrs Sorby. Good night and good-by.

[He goes out by the back to the right. Sound of laughter and merriment from the company, who are now visible in the outer room.]

WERLE: [muttering contemptuously after GREGERS] Ha! Poor wretch — and he says he is not overstrained!

## ACT II

SCENE———HIALMAR EKDAL's *studio, a good-sized room, evidently in the top story of the building. On the right a sloping roof of large panes of glass half covered by a blue curtain. In the right-hand corner, at the back, the entrance door; farther forward, on the same side, a door leading to the sitting room. Two doors on the opposite side and between them an iron stove. At the back a wide double sliding door. The studio is plainly but comfortably furnished. Between the door on the right, standing out a little from the wall, a sofa with a table and some chairs; on the table a lighted lamp with a shade; beside the stove an old armchair. Photographic instruments and apparatus of different kinds lying about the room. Against the back wall, to the left of the double door, stands a bookcase containing a few books, boxes and bottles of chemicals, instruments, tools and other objects. Photographs and small articles, such as camel's-hair pencils, paper and so forth, lie on the table.*

[GINA EKDAL *sits on a chair by the table, sewing.* HEDVIG *is sitting on the sofa, with her hands shading her eyes and her thumbs in her ears, reading a book.*]

GINA: [*glances once or twice at* HEDVIG, *as if with secret anxiety, then says*] Hedvig!
[HEDVIG *does not hear.*]

GINA: [*repeats more loudly*] Hedvig!

HEDVIG: [*takes away her hands and looks up*] Yes, Mother?

GINA: Hedvig dear, you mustn't sit reading any longer now.

HEDVIG: Oh Mother, mayn't I read a little more? Just a little bit?

GINA: No, no, you must put away your book now. Father doesn't like it; he never reads himself in the evening.

HEDVIG: [*shuts the book*] No, Father doesn't care much about reading.

GINA: [*puts aside her sewing and takes up a lead pencil and a little account book from the table*] Can you remember how much we paid for the butter today?

HEDVIG: It was one crown sixty-five.

GINA: That's right. [*puts it down*] It's terrible what a lot of butter we get through in this house. Then there was the smoked sausage and the cheese — let me see [*writes*] — and the ham. [*adds up*] Yes, that makes just—

HEDVIG: And then the beer.

GINA: Yes, to be sure. [*writes*] How it do mount up! But we can't manage with no less.

HEDVIG: And then you and I didn't need anything hot for dinner, as Father was out.

GINA: No, that was so much to the good. And then I took eight crowns fifty for the photographs.

HEDVIG: Really! As much as that?

GINA: Exactly eight crowns fifty.

[*Silence.* GINA *takes up her sewing again;* HEDVIG *takes paper and pencil and begins to draw, shading her eyes with her left hand.*]

HEDVIG: Isn't it jolly to think that Father is at Mr Werle's big dinner party?

GINA: You know he's not really Mr Werle's guest. It was the son invited him. [*after a pause*] We have nothing to do with that Mr Werle.

HEDVIG: I'm longing for Father to come home. He promised to ask Mrs Sorby for something nice for me.

GINA: Yes, there's plenty of good things in that house, I can tell you.

HEDVIG: [*goes on drawing*] And I believe I'm a little hungry too.

[OLD EKDAL, *with the paper parcel under his arm and another parcel in his coat pocket, comes in by the entrance door.*]

GINA: How late you are today, Grandfather!

EKDAL: They had locked the office door. Had to wait in Graberg's room. And then they let me through — h'm.

HEDVIG: Did you get some more copying to do, Grandfather?

EKDAL: This whole packet. Just look.

GINA: That's fine.

HEDVIG: And you have another parcel in your pocket.

EKDAL: Eh? Oh, never mind, that's nothing. [*puts his stick away in a corner*] This work will keep me going a long time, Gina. [*opens one of the sliding doors in the back wall a little*] Hush! [*peeps into the room for a moment, then pushes the door carefully to again*] Hee-hee! They're fast asleep, all the lot of them. And she's gone into the basket herself. Hee-hee!

HEDVIG: Are you sure she isn't cold in that basket, Grandfather?

EKDAL: Not a bit of it! Cold? With all that straw? [*goes toward the farther door on the left*] There are matches in here, I suppose.

GINA: The matches is on the drawers.

[EKDAL *goes into his room.*]

HEDVIG: It's nice that Grandfather has got all that copying.

GINA: Yes, poor old Father; it means a bit of pocket money for him.

HEDVIG: And he won't be able to sit the whole forenoon down at that horrid Madam Eriksen's.

GINA: No more he won't. [*short silence*]

HEDVIG: Do you suppose they are still at the dinner table?

GINA: Goodness knows; as like as not.

HEDVIG: Think of all the delicious things Father is having to eat! I'm certain he'll be in splendid spirits when he comes. Don't you think so, Mother?

GINA: Yes; and if only we could tell him that we'd rented the room —

HEDVIG: But we don't need that this evening.

GINA: Oh, we'd be none the worst of it, I can tell you. It's no use to us as it is.

HEDVIG: I mean we don't need it this evening, for Father will be in good humor at any rate. It is best to keep the renting of the room for another time.

GINA: [*looks across at her*] You like having some good news to tell Father when he comes home in the evening?

HEDVIG: Yes, for then things are pleasanter somehow.

GINA: [*thinking to herself*] Yes, yes, there's something in that.

[OLD EKDAL *comes in again and is going out by the foremost door to the left.*]

GINA: [*half turning in her chair*] Do you want something in the kitchen, Grandfather?

EKDAL: Yes, yes, I do. Don't you trouble. [*Goes out.*]

GINA: He's not poking away at the fire, is he? [*waits a moment*] Hedvig, go and see what he's about.

[EKDAL *comes in again with a small jug of steaming hot water.*]

HEDVIG: Have you been getting some hot water, Grandfather?

EKDAL: Yes, hot water. Want it for something. Want to write, and the ink has got as thick as porridge — h'm.

GINA: But you'd best have your supper first, Grandfather. It's laid in there.

EKDAL: Can't be bothered with supper, Gina. Very busy, I tell you. No one's to come to my room. No one—h'm.

[*He goes into his room;* GINA *and* HEDVIG *look at each other.*]

GINA: [*softly*] Can you imagine where he's got money from?

HEDVIG: From Graberg, perhaps.

GINA: Not a bit of it. Graberg always sends the money to me.

HEDVIG: Then he must have got a bottle on credit somewhere.

GINA: Poor Grandfather, who'd give him credit?

[HIALMAR EKDAL, *in an overcoat and gray felt hat, comes in from the right.*]

GINA: [*throws down her sewing and rises*] Why, Ekdal, is that you already?

HEDVIG: [*at the same time jumping up*] Fancy your coming so soon, Father!

HIALMAR: [*taking off his hat*] Yes, most of the people were coming away.

HEDVIG: So early?

HIALMAR: Yes, it was a dinner party, you know. [*Takes off his overcoat.*]

GINA: Let me help you.

HEDVIG: Me too.

[*They draw off his coat;* GINA *hangs it up on the back wall.*]

HEDVIG: Were there many people there, Father?

HIALMAR: On no, not many. We had about twelve or fourteen at table.

GINA: And you had some talk with them all?

HIALMAR: Oh yes, a little; but Gregers took me up most of the time.

GINA: Is Gregers as ugly as ever?

HIALMAR: Well, he's not very much to look at. Hasn't the old man come home?

HEDVIG: Yes, Grandfather is in his room, writing.

HIALMAR: Did he say anaything?

GINA: No, what should he say?

HIALMAR: Didn't he say anything about—I heard something about his having been with Graberg. I'll go in an see him for a moment.

GINA: No, no, better not.

HIALMAR: Why not? Did he say he didn't want me to go in?

GINA: I don't think he wants to see nobody this evening.

HEDVIG: [*making signs*] H'm—h'm!

GINA: [*not noticing*] He has been in to fetch hot water—

HIALMAR: Aha! Then he's—

GINA: Yes, I suppose so.

HIALMAR: Oh God! My poor old white-haired father! Well, well, there let him sit and get all the enjoyment he can.

[OLD EKDAL, *in an indoor coat and with a lighted pipe, comes from his room.*]

EKDAL: Got home? Thought it was you I heard talking.

HIALMAR: Yes, I have just come.

EKDAL: You didn't see me, did you?

HIALMAR: No, but they told me you had passed through—so I thought I would follow you.

EKDAL: H'm, good of you, Hialmar. Who were they, all those fellows?

HIALMAR: Oh, all sorts of people. There was Chamberlain Flor and Chamberlain Balle and Chamberlain Kaspersen and Chamberlain—this, that and the other—I don't know who all.

EKDAL: [*nodding*] Hear that, Gina! Chamberlains every one of them!

GINA: Yes, I hear as they're terrible genteel in that house nowadays.

HEDVIG: Did the chamberlains sing, Father? Or did they read aloud?

HIALMAR: No, they only talked nonsense. They wanted me to recite something for them, but I knew better than that.

EKDAL: You weren't to be persuaded, eh?

GINA: Oh, you might have done it.

HIALMAR: No; one mustn't be at everybody's beck and call. [*walks about the room*] That's not my way, at any rate.

EKDAL: No, No; Hialmar's not to be had for the asking, he isn't.

HIALMAR: I don't see why I should bother myself to entertain people on the rare occasions when I go into society. Let the others exert themselves. These fellows go from one great dinner table to the next and gorge and guzzle day out and day in. It's for them to bestir themselves and do something in return for all the good feeding they get.

GINA: But you didn't say that?

HIALMAR: [*humming*] Ho-ho-ho; I gave them a bit of my mind.

EKDAL: Not the chamberlains?

HIALMAR: Oh, why not? [*lightly*] After that we had a little discussion about Tokay.

EKDAL: Tokay! There's a fine wine for you!

HIALMAR: [*comes to a standstill*] It may be a fine wine. But of course you know the vintages differ; it all depends on how much sunshine the grapes have had.

GINA: Why, you know everything, Ekdal.

EKDAL: And did they argue that?

HIALMAR: They tried to, but they were requested to observe it was just the same with chamberlains — that with them, too, different batches were of different qualities.

GINA: What things you do think of!

EKDAL: Hee-hee! So they got that in their pipes too?

HIALMAR: Right in their teeth.

EKDAL: Do you hear that, Gina? He said it right in the very teeth of all the chamberlains.

GINA: Fancy! Right in their teeth!

HIALMAR: Yes, but I don't want it talked about. One doesn't speak of such things. The whole affair passed off quite amicably, of course. They were nice genial fellows; I didn't want to wound them — not I!

EKDAL: Right in their teeth, though!

HEDVIG: [*caressingly*] How nice it is to see you in a dress coat! It suits you so well, Father.

HIALMAR: Yes, don't you think so? And this one really fits to perfection. It fits almost as if it had been made for me — a little tight in the armholes, perhaps; help me, Hedvig. [*takes off the coat*] I think I'll put on my jacket. Where is my jacket, Gina?

GINA: Here it is. [*Brings the jacket and helps him.*]

HIALMAR: That's it! Don't forget to send the coat back to Molvik first thing tomorrow morning.

GINA: [*laying it away*] I'll be sure and see to it.

HIALMAR: [*stretching himself*] After all, there's a more homely feeling about this. A free-and-easy indoor costume suits my whole personality better. Don't you think so, Hedvig?

HEDVIG: Yes, Father.

HIALMAR: When I loosen my necktie into a pair of flowing ends — like this — eh?

HEDVIG: Yes, and that goes so well with your mustache and the sweep of your curls.

HIALMAR: I should not call them curls exactly; I should rather say locks.

HEDVIG: Yes, they are too big for curls.

HIALMAR: Locks describes them better.

HEDVIG: [*after a pause, twitching his jacket*] Father!

HIALMAR: Well, what is it?

HEDVIG: Oh, you know very well.

HIALMAR: No, really I don't.

HEDVIG: [*half laughing, half whispering*] Oh yes, Father; now don't tease me any longer!

HIALMAR: Why, what do you mean?

HEDVIG: [*shaking him*] Oh, what nonsense! Come, where are they, Father? All the good things you promised me, you know?

HIALMAR: Oh — if I haven't forgotten all about them!

HEDVIG: Now you're only teasing me, Father! Oh, it's too bad of you! Where have you put them?

HIALMAR: No, I positively forgot to get anything. But wait a little! I have something else for you, Hedvig.

[*Goes and searches in the pockets of the coat.*]

HEDVIG: [*skipping and clapping her hands*] Oh, Mother, Mother!

HIALMAR: [*with a paper*] Look, here it is.

GINA: There, you see; if you only give him time —

HEDVIG: That? Why, that's only a paper.

HIALMAR: That is the bill of fare, my dear; the whole bill of fare. Here you see "Menu" — that means bill of fare.

HEDVIG: Haven't you anything else?

HIALMAR: I forgot the other things, I tell you. But you may take my word for it, these dainties are very unsatisfying. Sit down at the table and read the bill of fare, and then I'll describe to you how the dishes taste. Here you are, Hedvig.

HEDVIG: [*gulping down her tears*] Thank you.

[*She seats herself but does not read;* GINA *makes signs to her;* HIALMAR *notices it.*]

HIALMAR: [*pacing up and down the room*] It's monstrous what absurd things the father of a family is expected to think of, and if he forgets the smallest trifle he is treated to sour faces at once. Well, well, one gets used to that too. [*stops near the stove by the old man's chair*] Have you peeped in there this evening, Father?

EKDAL: Yes, to be sure I have. She's gone into the basket.

HIALMAR: Ah, she has gone into the basket. Then she's beginning to get used to it.

EKDAL: Yes, just as I prophesied. But you know there are still a few little things —

HIALMAR: A few improvements, yes.

EKDAL: They've got to be made, you know.

HIALMAR: Yes, let us have a talk about the improvements, Father. Come, let us sit on the sofa.

EKDAL: All right. H'm — think I'll just fill my pipe first. Must clean it out too. H'm. [*He goes into his room.*]

GINA: [*smiling to* HIALMAR] His pipe!

HIALMAR: Oh yes, yes, Gina; let him alone — the poor shipwrecked old man. Yes, these improvements — we had better get them out of the way tomorrow.

GINA: You'll hardly have time tomorrow, Ekdal.

HEDVIG: [*interposing*] Oh yes, he will, Mother!

GINA: — for remember them prints that has to be retouched; they've sent for them time after time.

HIALMAR: There now! Those prints again! I shall get them finished all right. Have any new orders come in?

GINA: No, worse luck; tomorrow I have nothing to do but those two sittings, you know.

HIALMAR: Nothing else? Oh no, if people won't set about things with a will —

GINA: But what more can I do? Don't I advertise in the papers as much as we can afford?

HIALMAR: Yes, the papers; you see how much good they do. And I suppose no one has been to look at the room either?

GINA: No, not yet.

HIALMAR: That was only to be expected. If people won't keep their eyes open — Nothing can be done without a real effort, Gina!

HEDVIG: [*going toward him*] Shall I fetch you the flute, Father?

HIALMAR: No; no flute for me; *I* want no pleasures in this world. [*pacing about*] Yes indeed, I will work tomorrow; you shall see if I don't. You may be sure I shall work as long as my strength holds out.

GINA: But, my dear good Ekdal, I didn't mean it in that way.

HEDVIG: Father, mayn't I bring in a bottle of beer?

HIALMAR: No, certainly not. I require nothing, nothing. [*comes to a standstill*] Beer? Was it beer you were talking about?

HEDVIG: [*cheerfully*] Yes, Father; beautiful fresh beer.

HIALMAR: Well — since you insist upon it, you may bring in a bottle.

GINA: Yes, do; and we'll be nice and cosy.

[HEDVIG *runs toward the kitchen door.*]

HIALMAR: [*by the stove, stops her, looks at her, puts his arm round her neck and presses her to him*] Hedvig, Hedvig!

HEDVIG: [*with tears of joy*] My dear, kind father!

HIALMAR: No, don't call me that. Here have I been feasting at the rich man's table — battening at the groaning board! And I couldn't even —

GINA: [*sitting at the table*] Oh, nonsense, nonsense, Ekdal.

HIALMAR: It's not nonsense! And yet you mustn't be too hard upon me. You know that I love you for all that.

HEDVIG: [*throwing her arms round him*] And we love you, oh, so dearly, Father!

HIALMAR: And if I am unreasonable once in a while — why, then — you must remember that I am a man beset by a host of cares. There, there! [*dries his eyes*] No beer at such a moment as this. Give me the flute.

[HEDVIG *runs to the bookcase and fetches it.*]

HIALMAR: Thanks! That's right. With my flute in my hand and you two at my side — ah!

[HEDVIG *seats herself at the tabale near* GINA; HIALMAR *paces backward and forward, pipes up vigorously and plays a Bohemian peasant dance, but in a slow plaintive tempo and with sentimental expression.*]

HIALMAR: [*breaking off the melody, holds out his left hand to* GINA *and says with emotion*] Our roof may be poor and humble, Gina, but it is home. And with all my heart I say: here dwells my happiness.

[*He begins to play again; almost immediately after a knocking is heard at the entrance door.*]

GINA: [*rising*] Hush, Ekdal — I think there's someone at the door.

HIALMAR: [*laying the flute on the bookcase*] There! Again!

[GINA *goes and opens the door.*]

GREGERS: [*in the passage*] Excuse me —

GINA: [*starting back slightly*] Oh!

GREGERS: — doesn't Mr Ekdal, the photographer, live here?

GINA: Yes, he does.

HIALMAR: [*going toward the door*] Gregers! You here after all? Well, come in then.

GREGERS: [*coming in*] I told you I would come and look you up.

HIALMAR: But this evening — Have you left the party?

GREGERS: I have left both the party and my father's house. Good evening, Mrs Ekdal. I don't know whether you recognize me?

GINA: Oh yes, it's not difficult to know young Mr Werle again.

GREGERS: No, I am like my mother, and no doubt you remember her.

HIALMAR: Left your father's house, did you say?

GREGERS: Yes, I have gone to a hotel.

HIALMAR: Indeed. Well, since you're here, take off your coat and sit down.

GREGERS: Thanks. [*He takes off his overcoat. He is now dressed in a plain gray suit of a countrified cut.*]

HIALMAR: Here on the sofa. Make yourself comfortable.

GREGERS: [*looking around him*] So these are your quarters, Hialmar — this is your home.

HIALMAR: This is the studio, as you see.

GINA: But it's the largest of our rooms, so we generally sit here.

HIALMAR: We used to live in a better place, but this flat has one great advantage: there are such capital outer rooms —

GINA: And we have a room on the other side of the passage that we can rent.

GREGERS: [*to* HIALMAR] Ah — so you have lodgers too?

HIALMAR: No, not yet. They're not so easy to find, you see; you have to keep your eyes open. [*to* HEDVIG] How about that beer, eh?

[HEDVIG *nods and goes out into the kitchen.*]

GREGERS: So that is your daughter?

HIALMAR: Yes, that is Hedvig.

GREGERS: And she is your only child?

HIALMAR: Yes, the only one. She is the joy of our lives, and [*lowering his voice*] at the same time our deepest sorrow, Gregers.

GREGERS: What do you mean?

HIALMAR: She is in serious danger of losing her eyesight.

GREGERS: Becoming blind?

HIALMAR: Yes. Only the first symptoms have appeared as yet, and she may not feel it much for some time. But the doctor has warned us. It is coming inexorably.

GREGERS: What a terrible misfortune! How do you account for it?

HIALMAR: [*sighs*] Hereditary, no doubt.

GREGERS: [*starting*] Hereditary?

GINA: Ekdal's mother had weak eyes.

HIALMAR: Yes, so my father says; I can't remember her.

GREGERS: Poor child! And how does she take it?

HIALMAR: Oh, you can imagine we haven't the heart to tell her of it. She dreams of no danger. Gay and careless and chirping like a little bird, she flutters onward into a life of endless night. [*overcome*] Oh, it is cruelly hard on me, Gregers.

[HEDVIG *brings a tray with beer and glasses which she sets upon the table.*]

HIALMAR: [*stroking her hair*] Thanks, thanks, Hedvig.

[HEDVIG *puts her arm around his neck and whispers in his ear.*]

HIALMAR: No, no bread and butter just now. [*looks up*] But perhaps you would like some, Gregers?

GREGERS: [*with a gesture of refusal*] No, no thank you.

HIALMAR: [*still melancholy*] Well, you can bring in a little all the same. If you have a crust, that is all I want. And plenty of butter on it, mind.

[HEDVIG *nods gaily and goes out into the kitchen again.*]

GREGERS: [*who has been following her with his eyes*] She seems strong and healthy otherwise.

GINA: Yes. In other ways there's nothing amiss with her, thank goodness.

GREGERS: She promises to be very like you, Mrs Ekdal. How old is she now?

GINA: Hedvig is close on fourteen; her birthday is the day after tomorrow.

GREGERS: She is pretty tall for her age then.

GINA: Yes, she's shot up wonderful this last year.

GREGERS: It makes one realize one's own age to see these young people growing up. How long is it now since you were married?

GINA: We've been married—let me see—just on fifteen years.

GREGERS: Is it so long as that?

GINA: [*becomes attentive, looks at him*] Yes, it is indeed.

HIALMAR: Yes, so it is. Fifteen years, all but a few months. [*changing his tone*] They must have been long years for you up at the works, Gregers.

GREGERS: They seemed long while I was living them; now they are over, I hardly know how the time has gone.

[OLD EKDAL *comes from his room without his pipe but with his old-fashioned uniform cap on his head; his gait is somewhat unsteady.*]

EKDAL: Come now, Hialmar, let's sit down and have a good talk about this—h'm—what was it again?

HIALMAR: [*going toward him*] Father, we have a visitor here—Gregers Werle—I don't know if you remember him.

EKDAL: [*looking at* GREGERS, *who has risen*] Werle? Is that the son? What does he want with me?

HIALMAR: Nothing! It's me he has come to see.

EKDAL: Oh! Then there's nothing wrong?

HIALMAR: No, no, of course not.

EKDAL: [*with a large gesture*] Not that I'm afraid, you know; but—

GREGERS: [*goes over to him*] I bring you a greeting from your old hunting grounds, Lieutenant Ekdal.

EKDAL: Hunting grounds?

GREGERS: Yes, up in Höidal, about the works, you know.

EKDAL: Oh, up there. Yes, I knew all those places well in the old days.

GREGERS: You were a great sportsman then.

EKDAL: So I was, I don't deny it. You're looking at my uniform cap. I don't ask anybody's leave to wear it in the house. So long as I don't go out in the streets with it —

> [HEDVIG *brings a plate of bread and butter which she puts upon the table.*]

HIALMAR: Sit down, Father, and have a glass of beer. Help yourself, Gregers.

> [EKDAL *mutters and stumbles over to the sofa.* GREGERS *seats himself on the chair neareset to him,* HIALMAR *on the other side of* GREGERS. GINA *sits a little way from the table, sewing;* HEDVIG *stands beside her father.*]

GREGERS: Can you remember, Lieutenant Ekdal, how Hialmar and I used to come up and visit you in the summer and at Christmas?

EKDAL: Did you? No, no, no; I don't remember it. But, sure enough, I've been a tidy bit of sportsman in my day. I've shot bears too. I've shot nine of 'em no less.

GREGERS: [*looking sympathetically at him*] And now you never get any shooting?

EKDAL: Can't say that, sir. Get a shot now and then, perhaps. Of course not in the old way. For the woods, you see — the woods, the woods — [*drinks*] Are the woods fine up there now?

GREGERS: Not so fine as in your time. They have been thinned out a good deal.

EKDAL: Thinned? [*more softly and as if afraid*] It's dangerous work, that. Bad things come of it. The woods revenge themselves.

HIALMAR: [*filling up his glass*] Come — a little more, Father.

GREGERS: How can a man like you — such a man for the open air — live in the midst of a stuffy town, boxed within four walls?

EKDAL: [*laughs quietly and glances at* HIALMAR] Oh, it's not so bad here. Not at all so bad.

GREGERS: But don't you miss all the things that used to be a part of your very being — the cool sweeping breezes, the free life in the woods and on the uplands, among beasts and birds?

EKDAL: [*smiling*] Hialmar, shall we let him see it?

HIALMAR: [*hastily and a little embarrassed*] Oh no, no, Father; not this evening.

GREGERS: What does he want to show me?

HIALMAR: Oh, it's only something — you can it another time.

GREGERS: [*continues, to the old man*] You see, I have been thinking, Lieutenant Ekdal, that you should come up with me to the works; I am sure to be going back soon. No doubt you could get some copying there too. And here you have nothing on earth to interest you — nothing to liven you up.

EKDAL: [*stares in astonishment at him*] Have I nothing on earth to —

GREGERS: Of course you have Hialmar, but then he has his own family. And a man like you, who has always had such a passion for what is free and wild —

EKDAL: [*thumps the table*] Hialmar, he shall see it!

HIALMAR: Oh, do you think it's worth while, Father? It's all dark.

EKDAL: Nonsense; it's moonlight. [*rises*] He shall see it, I tell you. Let me pass! Come on and help me, Hialmar.

HEDVIG: Oh yes, do, Father!

HIALMAR: [*rising*] Very well then.

GREGERS: [*to* GINA] What is it?

GINA: Oh, nothing so wonderful after all.

[EKDAL *and* HIALMAR *have gone to the back wall and are each pushing back a side of the sliding door;* HEDVIG *helps the old man;* GREGERS *remains standing by the sofa;* GINA *sits still and sews. Through the open doorway a large, deep irregular garret is seen with odd nooks and corners, a couple of stovepipes running through it from rooms below. There are skylights through which clear moonbeams shine in on some parts of the great room; others lie in deep shadow.*]

EKDAL: [*to* GREGERS] You may come close up if you like.

GREGERS: [*going over to them*] Why, what is it?

EKDAL: Look for yourself, h'm.

HIALMAR: [*somewhat embarrassed*] This belongs to Father, you understand.

GREGERS: [*at the door, looks into the garret*] Why, you keep poultry, Lieutenant Ekdal.

EKDAL: Should think we did keep poultry. They've gone to roost now. But you should see our fowls by daylight, sir!

HEDVIG: And there's a —

EKDAL: Sh — sh! Don't say anything about it yet.

GREGERS: And you have pigeons too, I see.

EKDAL: Oh yes, haven't we just got pigeons! They have their nest boxes up there under the rooftree; for pigeons like to roost high, you see.

HIALMAR: They aren't all common pigeons.

EKDAL: Common! Should think not, indeed! We have tumblers and a pair of pouters too. But come here! Can you see that hutch down there by the wall?

GREGERS: Yes; what do you use it for?

EKDAL: That's where the rabbits sleep, sir.

GREGERS: Dear me, so you have rabbits too?

EKDAL: Yes, you may take my word for it, we have rabbits! He wants to know if we have rabbits, Hialmar! H'm! But now comes the thing, let me tell you! Here we have it! Move away, Hedvig. Stand here; that's right — and now look down there. Don't you see a basket with straw in it?

GREGERS: Yes. And I can see a fowl lying in the basket.

EKDAL: H'm — "a fowl" —

GREGERS: Isn't it a duck?

EKDAL: [*hurt*] Why, of course it's a duck.

HIALMAR: But what kind of a duck, do you think?

HEDVIG: It's not just a common duck.

EKDAL: Sh!

GREGERS: And it's not a Muscovy duck either.

EKDAL: No, Mr — Werle; it's not a Muscovy duck, for it's a wild duck!

GREGERS: Is it really? A wild duck?

EKDAL: Yes, that's what it is. That "fowl" — as you call it — is the wild duck. It's our wild duck, sir.

HEDVIG: My wild duck. It belongs to me.

GREGERS: And can it live up here in the garret? Does it thrive?

EKDAL: Of course it has a trough of water to splash about in, you know.

HIALMAR: Fresh water every other day.

GINA: [*turning toward* HIALMAR] But, my dear Ekdal, it's getting icy cold here.

EKDAL: H'm, we had better shut up then. It's as well not to disturb their night's rest too. Close up, Hedvig.

[HIALMAR *and* HEDVIG *push the garret doors together.*]

EKDAL: Another time you shall see her properly. [*seats himself in the armchair by the stove*] Oh, they're curious things, these wild ducks, I can tell you.

GREGERS: How did you manage to catch it, Lieutenant Ekdal?

EKDAL: *I* didn't catch it. There's a certain man in this town whom we have to thank for it.

GREGERS: [*starts slightly*] That man was not my father, was he?

EKDAL: You've hit it. Your father and no one else. H'm.

HIALMAR: Strange that you should guess that, Gregers.

GREGERS: You were telling me that you owed so many things to my father, and so I thought perhaps —

GINA: But we didn't get the duck from Mr Werle himself.

EKDAL: It's Hakon Werle we have to thank for her, all the same, Gina. [*to* GREGERS] He was shooting from a boat, you see, and he brought her down. But your father's sight is not very good now. H'm; she was only wounded.

GREGERS: Ah! She got a couple of slugs in her body, I suppose?

HIALMAR: Yes, two or three.

HEDVIG: She was hit under the wing so that she couldn't fly.

GREGERS: And I suppose she dived to the bottom, eh?

EKDAL: [*sleepily, in a thick voice*] Of course. Always do that, wild ducks do. They shoot to the bottom as deep as they can get, sir — and catch themselves in the tangle and seaweed — and all the devil's own mess that grows down there. And they never come up again.

GREGERS: But your wild duck came up again, Lieutenant Ekdal.

EKDAL: He had such an amazingly clever dog, your father had. And that dog — he dived in after the duck and fetched her up again.

GREGERS: [*who has turned to* HIALMAR] And then she was sent to you here?

HIALMAR: Not at once; at first your father took her home. But she wouldn't thrive there, so Pettersen was told to put an end to her.

EKDAL: [*half asleep*] H'm — yes — Pettersen — that ass —

HIALMAR: [*speaking more softly*] That was how we got her, you see; for Father knows Pettersen a little, and when he heard about the wild duck he got him to hand her over to us.

GREGERS: And now she thrives as well as possible in the garret there?

HIALMAR: Yes, wonderfully well. She has got fat. You see, she has lived in there so long now that she has forgotten her natural wild life, and it all depends on that.

GREGERS: You are right there, Hialmar. Be sure you never let her get a glimpse of the sky and the sea. But I mustn't stay any longer; I think your father is asleep.

HIALMAR: Oh, as for that —

GREGERS: But by the bye — you said you had a room to let — a spare room?

HIALMAR: Yes; what then? Do you know of anybody?

GREGERS: Can *I* have that room?

HIALMAR: You?

GINA: Oh no, Mr Werle, you —

GREGERS: May I have the room? If so, I'll take possession first thing tomorrow morning.

HIALMAR: Yes, with the greatest pleasure.

GINA: But, Mr Werle, I'm sure it's not at all the sort of room for you.

HIALMAR: Why, Gina! How can you say that?

GINA: Why, because the room's neither large enough nor light enough, and—

GREGERS: That really doesn't matter, Mrs Ekdal.

HIALMAR: I call it quite a nice room, and not at all badly furnished either.

GINA: But remember the pair of them underneath.

GREGERS: What pair?

GINA: Well, there's one as has been a tutor.

HIALMAR: That's Molvik—Mr Molvik, B.A.

GINA: And then there's a doctor by the name of Relling.

GREGERS: Relling? I know him a little; he practiced for a time up in Höidal.

GINA: They're a regular rackety pair, they are. As often as not they're out on the loose in the evenings, and then they come home at all hours, and they are not always just—

GREGERS: One soon gets used to that sort of thing. I daresay I shall be like the wild duck.

GINA: H'm; I think you ought to sleep upon it first, anyway.

GREGERS: You seem very unwilling to have me in the house, Mrs Ekdal.

GINA: Oh no! What makes you think that?

HIALMAR: Well, you really behave strangely about it, Gina. [*to* GREGERS] Then I suppose you intend to remain in town for the present?

GREGERS: [*putting on his overcoat*] Yes, now I intend to remain here.

HIALMAR: And yet not at your father's? What do you propose to do then?

GREGERS: Ah, if I only knew that, Hialmar, I shouldn't be so badly off! But when one has the misfortune to be called Gregers!—"Gregers"—and then "Werle" after it; did you ever hear of anything so hideous?

HIALMAR: Oh, I don't think so at all.

GREGERS: Ugh! Bah! I feel I should like to spit on the fellow that answers to such a name. But when a man is once for all doomed to be Gregers Werle—in this world—as I am—

HIALMAR: [*laughs*] Ha, ha! If you weren't Gregers Werle, what would you like to be?

GREGERS: If I should chose, I should like best to be a clever dog.

GINA: A dog!

HEDVIG: [*involuntarily*] Oh no!

GREGERS: Yes, an amazingly clever dog; one that goes to the bottom after wild ducks when they dive and catch themselves fast in tangle and seaweed down among the ooze.

HIALMAR: Upon my word now. Gregers—I don't in the least know what you are driving at.

GREGERS: Oh well, you might not be much the wiser if you did. It's understood, then, that I move in early tomorrow morning. [*to* GINA] I won't give you any trouble; I do everything for myself. [*to* HIALMAR] We will talk about the rest tomorrow. Good night, Mrs Ekdal. [*nods to* HEDVIG] Good night.

HEDVIG: Good night.

HIALMAR: [*who has lighted a candle*] Wait a moment; I must show you a light; the stairs are sure to be dark.

[GREGERS *and* HIALMAR *go out by the passage door.*]

GINA: [*looking straight before her with her sewing in her lap*] Wasn't that queer-like talk about wanting to be a dog?

HEDVIG: Do you know, Mother — I believe he meant something quite different by that.

GINA: Why, what should he mean?

HEDVIG: Oh, I don't know, but it seemed to me he meant something different from what he said — all the time.

GINA: Do you think so? Yes, it was sort of queer.

HIALMAR: [*comes back*] The lamp was still burning. [*puts out the candle and sets it down*] Ah, now one can get a mouthful of food at last. [*begins to eat the bread and butter*] Well, you see, Gina — if only you keep your eyes open —

GINA: How keep your eyes open?

HIALMAR: Why, haven't we at last had the luck to rent the room? And just think — to a person like Gregers — a good old friend.

GINA: Well, I don't know what to say about it.

HEDVIG: Oh Mother, you'll see: it'll be such fun!

HIALMAR: You're very strange. You were so bent upon getting the room rented before, and now you don't like it.

GINA: Yes, I do, Ekdal; if it had only been to someone else. But what do you suppose Mr Werle will say?

HIALMAR: Old Werle? It doesn't concern him.

GINA: But surely you can see that there's something wrong between them again, or the young man wouldn't be leaving home. You know very well those two can't get on with each other.

HIALMAR: Very likely not, but —

GINA: And now Mr Werle may think it's you that has egged him on —

HIALMAR: Let him think so, then! Mr Werle has done a great deal for me; far be it from me to deny it. But that doesn't make me everlastingly dependent upon him.

GINA: But, my dear Ekdal, maybe Grandfather'll suffer for it. He may lose the little bit of work he gets from Graberg.

HIALMAR: I could almost say: so much the better! Is it not humiliating for a man like me to see his gray-haired father treated as a pariah? But now I believe the fullness of time is at hand. [*takes a fresh piece of bread and butter*] As sure as I have a mission in life, I mean to fulfill it now!

HEDVIG: Oh yes, Father, do!

GINA: Hush! Don't wake him!

HIALMAR: [*more softly*] I will fulfill it, I say. The day shall come when — And that is why I say it's a good thing we have rented the room, for that makes me more independent. The man who has a mission in life must be independent. [*by the armchair, with emotion*] Poor old white-haired Father! Rely on your Hialmar. He has broad shoulders — strong shoulders, at any rate. You shall yet wake up some fine day and — [*to* GINA] Do you not believe it?

GINA: [*rising*] Yesa, of course I do, but in the meantime suppose we see about getting him to bed.

HIALMAR: Yes, come.

[*They take hold of the old man carefully.*]

# ACT III

SCENE——HIALMAR EKDAL's *studio. It is morning; the daylight shines through the large window in the slanting roof; the curtain is drawn back.*

[HIALMAR *is sitting at the table, busy retouching a photograph; several others lie before him. Presently* GINA, *wearing her hat and cloak, enters by the passage door; she has a covered basket on her arm.*]

HIALMAR: Back already, Gina?

GINA: Oh yes, one can't let the grass grow under one's feet. [*Sets her basket on a chair and takes off her things.*]

HIALMAR: Did you look in at Gregers' room?

GINA: Yes, I did. It's a rare sight, I can tell you; he's made a pretty mess to start off with.

HIALMAR: How so?

GINA: He was determined to do everything for himself, he said; so he sets to work to light the stove, and what must he do but screw down the damper till the whole room is full of smoke. Ugh! There was a smell fit to—

HIALMAR: Well, really!

GINA: But that's not the worse of it; for then he thinks he'll put out the fire and goes and empties his water jug into the stove and so makes the whole floor one filthy puddle.

HIALMAR: How annoying!

GINA: I've got the porter's wife to clear up after him, the pig! But the room won't be fit to live in till the afternoon.

HIALMAR: What's he doing with himself in the meantime?

GINA: He said he was going out for a little while.

HIALMAR: I looked in upon him too, for a moment—after you had gone.

GINA: So I heard. You've asked him to lunch.

HIALMAR: Just to a little bit of early lunch, you know. It's his first day—we can hardly do less. You've got something in the house, I suppose?

GINA: I shall have to find something or other.

HIALMAR: And don't cut it too fine, for I fancy Relling and Molvik are coming up too. I just happened to meet Relling on the stairs, you see; so I had to—

GINA: Oh, are we to have those two as well?

HIALMAR: Good lord—a couple more or less can't make any difference.

OLD EKDAL: [*opens his door and looks in*] I say, Hialmar—[*sees* GINA] Oh!

GINA: Do you want anything, Grandfather?

EKDAL: Oh no, it doesn't matter. H'm! [*Retires again.*]

GINA: [*takes up the basket*] Be sure you see that he doesn't go out.

HIALMAR: All right, all right. And, Gina, a little herring salad wouldn't be a bad idea. Relling and Molvik were out on the loose again last night.

GINA: If only they don't come before I'm ready for them—

HIALMAR: No, of course they won't; take your own time.

GINA: Very well, and meanwhile you can be working a bit.

HIALMAR: Well, I am working! I am working as hard as I can!

GINA: Then you'll have that job off your hands, you see. [*She goes out to the kitchen with her basket.* HIALMAR *sits for a time penciling away at the photograph in an indolent and listless manner.*]

EKDAL: [*peeps in, looks round the studio and says softly*] Are you busy?

HIALMAR: Yes, I'm toiling at these wretched pictures.

EKDAL: Well, well, never mind—since you're so busy—h'm!

    [*He goes out again; the door stands open.*]

HIALMAR: [*continues for some time in silence, then he lays down his brush and goes over to the door*] Are you busy, Father?

EKDAL: [*in a grumbling tone within*] If you're busy, I'm busy too. H'm!

HIALMAR: Oh, very well then. [*Goes to his work again.*]

EKDAL: [*presently coming to the door again*] H'm; I say Hialmar, I'm not so very busy, you know.

HIALMAR: I thought you were writing.

EKDAL: Oh, devil take it! Can't Graberg wait a day or two? After all, it's not a matter of life and death.

HIALMAR: No, and you're not his slave either.

EKDAL: And about that other business in there—

HIALMAR: Just what I was thinking of. Do you want to go in? Shall I open the door for you?

EKDAL: Well, it wouldn't be a bad notion.

HIALMAR: [*rises*] Then we'd have that off our hands.

EKDAL: Yes, exactly. It's got to be ready first thing tomorrow. It is tomorrow, isn't it? H'm?

HIALMAR: Yes, of course it's tomorrow.

    [HIALMAR *and* EKDAL *push aside each his half of the sliding door. The morning sun is shining in through the skylights; some doves are flying about; others sit cooing upon the perches; the hens are heard clucking now and then further back in the garret.*]

HIALMAR: There; now you can get to work, Father.

EKDAL: [*goes in*] Aren't you coming too?

HIALMAR: Well, really, you know—I almost think—[*sees* GINA *at the kitchen door*] I? No; I haven't time; I must work—But now for our new contrivance—
    [*He pulls a cord; a curtain slips down inside, the lower part consisting of a piece of old sailcloth, the upper part of a stretched fishing net. The floor of the garret is thus no longer visible.*]

HIALMAR: [*goes to the table*] So! Now perhaps I can sit in peace for a little while.

GINA: Is he rampaging in there again?

HIALMAR: Would you rather have him slip down to Madam Eriksen's? [*seats himself*] Do you want anything? You know you said—

GINA: I only wanted to ask if you think we can lay the table for lunch here?

HIALMAR: Yes; we have no early appointment, I suppose?

GINA: No, I expect no one today except those two sweethearts that are to be taken together.

HIALMAR: Why the devil couldn't they be taken together another day?

GINA: Don't you know, I told them to come in the afternoon, when you are having your nap.

HIALMAR: Oh, that's capital. Very well, let us have lunch here then.

GINA: All right, but there's no hurry about laying the cloth; you can have the table for a good while yet.

HIALMAR: Do you think I am not sticking to my work? I'm at it as hard as I can!

GINA: Then you'll be free later on, you know.

[*Goes out into the kitchen again. Short pause.*]

EKDAL: [*in the garret doorway, behind the net*] Hialmar!

HIALMAR: Well?

EKDAL: Afraid we shall have to move the water trough after all.

HIALMAR: What else have I been saying all along?

EKDAL: H'm — h'm — h'm.

[*Goes away from the door again.* HIALMAR *goes on working a little, glances toward the garret and half rises.* HEDVIG *comes in from the kitchen.*]

HIALMAR: [*sits down again hurriedly*] What do you want!

HEDVIG: I only wanted to come in beside you, Father.

HIALMAR: [*after a pause*] What makes you go prying around like that? Perhaps you are told to watch me?

HEDVIG: No, no.

HIALMAR: What is your mother doing out there?

HEDVIG: Oh, Mother's in the middle of making the herring salad. [*goes to the table*] Isn't there any little thing I could help you with, Father?

HIALMAR: Oh no. It is right that I should bear the whole burden — so long as my strength holds out. Set your mind at rest, Hedvig; if only your father keeps his health —

HEDVIG: Oh no, Father! You mustn't talk in that horrid way.

[*She wanders about a little, stops by the doorway and looks into the garret.*]

HIALMAR: Tell me, what is he doing?

HEDVIG: I think he's making a new path to the water trough.

HIALMAR: He can never manage that by himself! And here am I doomed to sit!

HEDVIG: [*goes to him*] Let me take the brush, Father; I can do it quite well.

HIALMAR: Oh, nonsense; you will only hurt your eyes.

HEDVIG: Not a bit. Give me the brush.

HIALMAR: [*rising*] Well, it won't take more than a minute or two.

HEDVIG: Pooh, what harm can it do then? [*takes the brush*] There! [*seats herself*] I can begin upon this one.

HIALMAR: But mind you don't hurt your eyes! Do you hear? *I* won't be answerable; you do it on your own responsibility — understand that.

HEDVIG: [*retouching*] Yes, yes, I understand.

HIALMAR: You are quite clever at it, Hedvig. Only a minute or two, you know.

[*He slips through by the edge of the curtain into the garret.* HEDVIG *sits at her work.* HIALMAR *and* EKDAL *are heard disputing inside.*]

HIALMAR: [*appears behind the net*] I say, Hedvig — give me those pliers that are lying on the shelf. And the chisel. [*turns away inside*] Now you shall see, Father. Just let me show you first what I mean!

[HEDVIG *has fetched the required tools from the shelf and hands them to him through the net.*]

HIALMAR: Ah, thanks. I didn't come a moment too soon.

[*Goes back from the curtain again; they are heard carpentering and talking inside.* HEDVIG *stands looking in at them. A moment later there is a knock at the passage door; she does not notice it.*]

GREGERS WERLE: [*bareheaded, in indoor dress, enters and stops near the door*] H'm!

HEDVIG: [*turns and goes toward him*] Good morning. Please come in.

GREGERS: Thank you. [*looking toward the garret*] You seem to have work-people in the house.

HEDVIG: No, it's only Father and Grandfather. I'll tell them you are here.

GREGERS: No, no, don't do that; I would rather wait a little. [*Seats himself on the sofa.*]

HEDVIG: It looks so untidy here — [*Begins to clear away the photographs.*]

GREGERS: Oh, don't take them away. Are those prints that have to be finished off?

HEDVIG: Yes, they are a few I was helping Father with.

GREGERS: Please don't let me disturb you.

HEDVIG: Oh no.

[*She gathers the things to her and sits down to work;* GREGERS *looks at her meanwhile in silence.*]

GREGERS: Did the wild duck sleep well last night?

HEDVIG: Yes, I think so, thanks.

GREGERS: [*turning toward the garret*] It looks quite different by day from what it did last night in the moonlight.

HEDVIG: Yes, it changes ever so much. It looks different in the morning and in the afternoon, and it's different on rainy days from what it is in fine weather.

GREGERS: Have you noticed it?

HEDVIG: Yes, how could I help it?

GREGERS: Are you too fond of being in there with the wild duck?

HEDVIG: Yes, when I can manage it.

GREGERS: But I suppose you haven't much spare time; you go to school, no doubt.

HEDVIG: No, not now; Father is afraid of my hurting my eyes.

GREGERS: Oh, then he reads with you himself?

HEDVIG: Father has promised to read with me, but he has never had time yet.

GREGERS: Then is there nobody else to give you a little help?

HEDVIG: Yes, there is Mr Molvik, but he is not always exactly — quite —

GREGERS: Sober?

HEDVIG: Yes, I suppose that's it!

GREGERS: Why, then, you must have any amount of time on your hands. And in there I suppose it is a sort of world by itself?

HEDVIG: Oh yes, quite. And there are such lots of wonderful things.

GREGERS: Indeed?

HEDVIG: Yes, there are big cupboards full of books, and a great many of the books have pictures in them.

GREGERS: Aha!

HEDVIG: And there's an old bureau with drawers and flaps and a big clock with figures that go out and in. But the clock isn't going now.

GREGERS: So time has come to a standstill in there — in the wild duck's world?

HEDVIG: Yes. And then there's an old paintbox and things of that sort, and all the books.

GREGERS: And you read the books, I suppose.

HEDVIG: Oh yes, when I get the chance. Most of them are English, though, and I don't understand English. But then I look at the pictures. There is one great book called *Harrison's History of London*. It must be a hundred years old, and there are such heaps of pictures in it. At the beginning there is Death with an hourglass and a woman. I think that is horrid. But then there are all the other pictures of churches and castles and streets and great ships sailing on the sea.

GREGERS: But tell me, where did all those wonderful things come from?

HEDVIG: Oh, an old sea captain once lived here, and he brought them home with him. They used to call him "The Flying Dutchman." That was curious, because he wasn't a Dutchman at all.

GREGERS: Was he not?

HEDVIG: No. But at last he was drowned at sea, and so he left all those things behind him.

GREGERS: Tell me now — when you are sitting in there looking at the pictures don't you wish you could travel and see the real world for yourself?

HEDVIG: Oh no! I mean always to stay at home and help Father and Mother.

GREGERS: To retouch photographs?

HEDVIG: No, not only that. I should love above everything to learn to engrave pictures like those in the English books.

GREGERS: H'm. What does your father say to that?

HEDVIG: I don't think Father likes it; Father is strange about such things. Only think, he talks of my learning basketmaking! But I don't think that would be much good.

GREGERS: Oh no, I don't think so either.

HEDVIG: But Father was right in saying that if I had learned basketmaking I could have made the new basket for the wild duck.

GREGERS: So you could; and it was you that ought to have done it, wasn't it?

HEDVIG: Yes, for it's my wild duck.

GREGERS: Of course it is.

HEDVIG: Yes, it belongs to me. But I lend it to Father and Grandfather as often as they please.

GREGERS: Indeed? What do they do with it?

HEDVIG: Oh, they look after it and build places for it and so on.

GREGERS: I see; no doubt the wild duck is by far the most distinguished inhabitant of the garret?

HEDVIG: Yes, indeed she is; for she is a real wild fowl, you know. And then she is so much to be pitied; she has no one to care for, poor thing.

GREGERS: She has no family, as the rabbits have.

HEDVIG: No. The hens too, many of them, were chickens together; but she has been taken right away from all her friends. And then there is so much that is strange about the wild duck. Nobody knows her, and nobody knows where she came from either.

GREGERS: And she has been down in the depths of the sea.

HEDVIG: [*with a quick glance at him, represses a smile and asks*] Why do you say "depths of the sea"?

GREGERS: What else should I say?

HEDVIG: You could say "the bottom of the sea."

GREGERS: Oh, can't I just as well say the depths of the sea?

HEDVIG: Yes, but it sounds so strange to me when other people speak of the depths of the sea.

GREGERS: Why? Tell my why?

HEDVIG: No, I won't; it's so stupid.

GREGERS: Oh no, I am sure it's not. Do tell my why you smiled.

HEDVIG: Well, this is the reason: whenever I come to realize suddenly — in a flash — what is in there, it always seems to me that the whole room and everything in it should be called "the depths of the sea." But that is so stupid.

GREGERS: You mustn't say that.

HEDVIG: Oh yes, for you know it is only a garret.

GREGERS: [*looks fixedly at her*] Are you so sure of that?

HEDVIG: [*astonished*] That it's a garret?

GREGERS: Are you quite certain of it?

> [HEDVIG *is silent and looks at him open-mouthed.* GINA *comes in from the kitchen with the table things.*]

GREGERS: [*rising*] I have come in upon you too early.

GINA: Oh, you must be somewhere, and we're nearly ready now anyway. Clear the table Hedvig.

> [HEDVIG *clears away her things; she and* GINA *lay the cloth during what follows.* GREGERS *seats himself in the armchair and turns over an album.*]

GREGERS: I hear you can retouch, Mrs Ekdal.

GINA: [*with a side glance*] Yes, I can.

GREGERS: That was exceedingly lucky.

GINA: How — lucky?

GREGERS: Since Ekdal took to photography, I mean.

HEDVIG: Mother can take photographs too.

GINA: Oh yes, I had to learn that.

GREGERS: So it is really you that carry on the business, I suppose?

GINA: Yes, when Ekdal hasn't time himself —

GREGERS: He is a great deal taken up with his old father, I daresay.

GINA: Yes; and then you can't expect a man like Ekdal to do nothing but take pictures of Dick, Tom and Harry.

GREGERS: I quite agree with you, but having once gone in for the thing —

GINA: You can surely understand, Mr Werle, that Ekdal's not like one of your common photographers.

GREGERS: Oh course not, but still —

> [A *shot is fired within the garret.*]

GREGERS: [*starting up*] What's that?

GINA: Ugh! Now they're firing again!

GREGERS: Have they firearms in there?

HEDVIG: They are out shooting.

GREGERS: What! [*at the door of the garret*] Are you shooting, Hialmar?

HIALMAR: [*inside the net*] Are you there? I didn't know; I was so taken up — [*to* HEDVIG] Why did you not let us know? [*Comes into the studio.*]

GREGERS: Do you go shooting in the garret?

HIALMAR: [*showing a double-barreled pistol*] Oh, only with this thing.

GINA: Yes, you and Grandfather will hurt yourselves someday with that there pigstol.

HIALMAR: [*with irritation*] I believe I have told you that this kind of firearm is called a pistol.

GINA: Oh, that doesn't make it much better that I can see.

GREGERS: So you have become a sportsman too, Hialmar?

HIALMAR: Only a little rabbit shooting now and then. Mostly to please Father, you understand.

GINA: Men are strange beings; they must always have something to pervert themselves with.

HIALMAR: [*snappishly*] Just so; we must always have something to divert ourselves with.

GINA: Yes, that's just what I say.

HIALMAR: H'm. [*to* GREGERS] You see, the garret is fortunately so situated that no one can hear us shooting. [*lays the pistol on the top shelf of the bookcase*] Don't touch the pistol, Hedvig! One of the barrels is loaded; remember that.

GREGERS: [*looking through the net*] You have a fowling piece too, I see.

HIALMAR: That is Father's old gun. It's of no use now. Something has gone wrong with the lock. But it's fun to have it all the same, for we can take it to pieces now and then and clean and grease it and screw it together again. Of course it's mostly Father that fiddles with all that sort of thing.

HEDVIG: [*beside* GREGERS] Now you can see the wild duck properly.

GREGERS: I was just looking at her. One of her wings seems to me to droop a bit.

HEDVIG: Well, no wonder; her wing was broken, you know.

GREGERS: And she trails one foot a little. Isn't that so?

HIALMAR: Perhaps a very little bit.

HEDVIG: Yes, it was by that foot the dog took hold of her.

HIALMAR: But otherwise she hasn't the least thing the matter with her, and that is simply marvelous for a creature that has a charge of shot in her body and has been between a dog's teeth —

GREGERS: [*with a glance at* HEDVIG] — and that has lain in the depths of the sea — so long.

HEDVIG: [*smiling*] Yes.

GINA: [*laying the table*] That blessed wild duck! What a lot of fuss you do make over her.

HIALMAR: H'm — will lunch soon be ready?

GINA: Yes, directly. Hedvig, you must come and help me now.

[GINA *and* HEDVIG *go out into the kitchen.*]

HIALMAR: [*in a low voice*] I think you had better not stand there looking in at Father; he doesn't like it. [GREGERS *moves away from the garret door*] Besides, I may as well shut up before the others come. [*claps his hands to drive the fowls back*] Shh — shh, in with you! [*draws up the curtain and pulls the doors together*] All the contrivances are my own convention. Its really quite amusing to have things of this sort to potter with and to put to rights when they get out of order. And its absolutely necessary too, for Gina objects to having rabbits and fowls in the studio.

GREGERS: To be sure, and I suppose the studio is your wife's special department?

HIALMAR: As a rule I leave the everyday details of business to her, for then I can take refuge in the parlor and give my mind to more important things.

GREGERS: What things are they Hialmar?

HIALMAR: I wonder you have not asked that question sooner. But perhaps you haven't heard of the invention?

GREGERS: The invention? No.

HIALMAR: Really? Haven't you? Oh no, out there in the wilds —

GREGERS: So you have invented something, have you?

HIALMAR: It is not quite completed yet, but I am working at it. You can easily imagine that when I resolved to devote myself to photography it wasn't simply with the idea of taking likenesses of all sorts of commonplace people.

GREGERS: No; your wife was saying the same thing just now.

HIALMAR: I swore that if I concentrated my powers to this handicraft I would so exalt it that it should become both an art and a science. And to that end I determined to make this great invention.

GREGERS: And what is the nature of the invention? What purpose does it serve?

HIALMAR: Oh, my dear fellow, you mustn't ask for details yet. It takes time, you see. And you must not think that my motive is vanity. It is not for my own sake that I am working. Oh no; it is my life's mission that stands before me night and day.

GREGERS: What is your life's mission?

HIALMAR: Do you forget the old man with the silver hair?

GREGERS: Your poor father? Well, but what can you do for him?

HIALMAR: I can raise up his self-respect from the dead by restoring the name of Ekdal to honor and dignity.

GREGERS: Then that is your life's mission?

HIALMAR: Yes. I will rescue the shipwrecked man. For shipwrecked he was, by the very first blast of the storm. Even while those terrible investigations were going on he was no longer himself. That pistol there — the one we used to shoot rabbits with — has played its part in the tragedy of the house of Ekdal.

GREGERS: The pistol? Indeed?

HIALMAR: When the sentence of imprisonment was passed — he had the pistol in his hand.

GREGERS: Had he?

HIALMAR: Yes, but he dared not use it. His courage failed him. So broken, so demoralized was he even then! Oh, can you understand it? He, a soldier; he, who had shot nine bears and who was descended from two lieutenant colonels — one after the other, of course. Can you understand it, Gregers?

GREGERS: Yes, I understand it well enough.

HIALMAR: I cannot. And once more the pistol played a part in the history of our house. When he had put on the gray clothes and was under lock and key — oh, that was a terrible time for me, I can tell you. I kept the blinds drawn down over both my windows. When I peeped out I saw the sun shining as if nothing had happened. I could not understand it. I saw people going along the street, laughing and talking about indifferent things. I could not understand it. It seemed to me that the whole of existence must be at a standstill — as if under an eclipse.

GREGERS: I felt that too, when my mother died.

HIALMAR: It was in such an hour that Hialmar Ekdal pointed the pistol at his own breast.

GREGERS: You, too, thought of —

HIALMAR: Yes.

GREGERS: But you did not fire?

HIALMAR: No. At the decisive moment I won the victory over myself. I remained in life. But I can assure you it takes some courage to choose life under circumstances like those.

GREGERS: Well, that depends on how you look at it.

HIALMAR: Yes indeed, it takes courage. But I am glad I was firm, for now I shall soon perfect my invention; and Doctor Relling thinks, as I do myself, that Father may be allowed to wear his uniform again. I will demand that as my sole reward.

GREGERS: So that is what he meant about his uniform?

HIALMAR: Yes, that is what he most yearns for. You can't think how my heart bleeds for him. Every time we celebrate any little family festival — Gina's and my wedding day or whatever it may be — in comes the old man in the lieutenant's uniform of happier days. But if he only hears a knock at the door — for he daren't show himself to strangers, you know — he hurries back to his room again as fast as his old legs can carry him. Oh, it's heart-rending for a son to see such things!

GREGERS: How long do you think it will take you to finish your invention?

HIALMAR: Come now, you mustn't expect me to enter into particulars like that. An invention is not a thing completely under one's own control. It depends largely on inspiration — on intuition — and it is almost impossible to predict when the inspiration may come.

GREGERS: But it's advancing?

HIALMAR: Yes, certainly it is advancing. I turn it over in my mind every day; I am full of it. Every afternoon, when I have had my dinner, I shut myself up in the parlor where I can ponder undisturbed. But I can't be goaded to it; it's not a bit of good. Relling says so too.

GREGERS: And you don't think that all that business in the garret draws you off and distracts you too much?

HIALMAR: No, no, no; quite the contrary. You mustn't say that. I cannot be everlastingly absorbed in the same laborious train of thought. I must have something alongside of it to fill up the time of waiting. The inspiration, the intuition, you see — when it comes it comes, and there's an end of it.

GREGERS: My dear Hialmar, I almost think you have something of the wild duck in you.

HIALMAR: Something of the wild duck? How do you mean?

GREGERS: You have dived down and caught yourself fast in the undergrowth.

HIALMAR: Are you alluding to the almost fatal shot that has broken my father's wing — and mine too?

GREGERS: Not exactly to that. I don't say that your wing has been broken, but you have strayed into a poisonous marsh, Hialmar; an insidious disease has taken hold of you, and you have sunk down to die in the dark.

HIALMAR: I? To die in the dark? Look here, Gregers, you must really stop talking such nonsense.

GREGERS: Don't be afraid; I shall find a way to help you up again. I, too, have a mission in life now; I found it yesterday.

HIALMAR: That's all very well, but you will please leave me out of it. I can assure you that — apart from my very natural melancholy, of course — I am as contented as anyone can wish to be.

GREGERS: Your contentment is an effect of the marsh poison.

HIALMAR: Now, my dear Gregers, pray do not go on about disease and poison; I am not used to that sort of talk. In my house nobody ever speaks to me about unpleasant things.

GREGERS: Ah, that I can easily believe.

HIALMAR: It's not good for me, you see. And there are no marsh poisons here, as you express it. The poor photographer's roof is lowly, I know — and my circumstances are narrow. But I am an inventor, and I am the breadwinner of a family. That exalts me above my mean surroundings. Ah, here comes lunch!

[GINA *and* HEDVIG *bring bottles of ale, a decanter of brandy, glasses, etc. At the same time* RELLING *and* MOLVIK *enter from the passage; they are both without hat or overcoat.* MOLVIK *is dressed in black.*]

GINA: [*placing the things upon the table*] Ah you two have come in the nick of time.

RELLING: Molvik got it into his head that he could smell herring salad, and then there was no holding him. Good morning again, Ekdal.

HIALMAR: Gregers, let me introduce you to Mr Molvik — Doctor — Oh, you know Relling, don't you?

GREGERS: Yes, slightly.

RELLING: Oh, Mr Werle junior! Yes, we two have had one or two little skirmishes up at the Höidal works. You've just moved in?

GREGERS: I moved in this morning.

RELLING: Molvik and I live right under you, so you haven't far to go for the doctor and the clergyman if you should need anything in that line.

GREGERS: Thanks; it's not quite unlikely, for yesterday we were thirteen at table.

HIALMAR: Oh, come now, don't let us get upon unpleasant subjects again!

RELLING: You may make your mind easy, Ekdal; I'll be hanged if the finger of fate points to you.

HIALMAR: I should hope not, for the sake of my family. But let us sit down now and eat and drink and be merry.

GREGERS: Shall we not wait for your father?

HIALMAR: No, his lunch will be taken in to him later. Come along!

[*The men seat themselves at table and eat and drink.* GINA *and* HEDVIG *go in and out and wait upon them.*]

RELLING: Molvik was frightfully drunk yesterday, Mrs Ekdal.

GINA: Really? Yesterday again?

RELLING: Didn't you hear him when I brought him home last night?

GINA: No, I can't say I did.

RELLING: That was a good thing, for Molvik was disgusting last night.

GINA: Is that true, Molvik?

MOLVIK: Let us draw a veil over last night's proceedings. That sort of thing is totally foreign to my better self.

RELLING: [*to* GREGERS] It comes over him like a sort of possession, and then I have to go out on the loose with him. Mr Molvik is demonic, you see.

GREGERS: Demonic?

RELLING: Molvik is demonic, yes.

GREGERS: H'm!

RELLING: And demonic natures are not made to walk straight through the world; they must meander a little now and then. Well, so you still stay up there at those horrible grimy works?

GREGERS: I have stayed there until now.

RELLING: And did you ever manage to collect that claim you went about presenting?

GREGERS: Claim? [*understands him*] Ah, I see.

HIALMAR: Have you been presenting claims, Gregers?

GREGERS: Oh, nonsense.

RELLING: Faith, but he has, though! He went round to all the cotters' cabins presenting something he called "the claim of the ideal."

GREGERS: I was young then.

RELLING: You're right; you were very young. And as for the claim of the ideal — you never got it honored while *I* was up there.

GREGERS: Nor since either.

RELLING: Ah, then you've learned to knock a little discount off, I expect.

GREGERS: Never, when I have a true man to deal with.

HIALMAR: No, I should think not, indeed. A little butter, Gina.

RELLING: And a slice of bacon for Molvik.

MOLVIK: Ugh! not bacon!

[*A knock at the garret door.*]

HIALMAR: Open the door, Hedvig; Father wants to come out.

[HEDVIG *goes over and opens the door a little way;* EKDAL *enters with a fresh rabbitskin; she closes the door after him.*]

EKDAL: Good morning, gentlemen! Good sport today. Shot a big one.

HIALMAR: And you've gone and skinned it without waiting for me!

EKDAL: Salted it too. It's good tender meat, is rabbit; it's sweet; it tastes like sugar. Good appetite to you, gentlemen! [*Goes into his room.*]

MOLVIK: [*rising*] Excuse me — I can't — I must get downstairs immediately —

RELLING: Drink some soda water, man!

MOLVIK: [*hurrying away*] Ugh — ugh. [*Goes out by the passage door.*]

RELLING: [*to* HIALMAR] Let us drain a glass to the old hunter.

HIALMAR: [*clinks glasses with him*] To the undaunted sportsman who has looked death in the face!

RELLING: To the gray-haired — [*drinks*] By the bye, is his hair gray or white?

HIALMAR: Something between the two, I fancy; for that matter, he has very few hairs left of any color.

RELLING: Well, well, one can get through the world with a wig. After all, you are a happy man, Ekdal; you have your noble mission to labor for —

HIALMAR: And I do labor, I can tell you.

RELLING: And then you have your excellent wife, shuffling quietly in and out in her felt slippers, with that seesaw walk of hers, and making everything cosy and comfortable about you.

HIALMAR: Yes, Gina [*nods to her*] you've been a good helpmate on the path of life.

GINA: Oh, don't sit there cricketizing me.

RELLING: And your Hedvig too, Ekdal!

HIALMAR: [*affected*] The child, yes! The child before everything! Hedvig, come here to me. [*strokes her hair*] What day is it tomorrow, eh?

HEDVIG: [*shaking him*] Oh no, you're not to say anything, Father.

HIALMAR: It cuts me to the heart when I think what a poor affair it will be; only a little festivity in the garret.

HEDVIG: Oh, but that's just what I like!

RELLING: Just you wait till the wonderful invention sees the light, Hedvig!

HIALMAR: Yes indeed—then you shall see! Hedvig, I have resolved to make your future secure. You shall live in comfort all your days. I will demand something or other—on your behalf. That shall be the poor inventor's sole reward.

HEDVIG: [*whispering, with her arms round his neck*] Oh, you dear, kind father!

RELLING: [*to* GREGERS] Come now, don't you find it pleasant, for once, to sit at a well-spread table in a happy family circle?

HIALMAR: Ah yes, I really prize these social hours.

GREGERS: For my part, I don't thrive in marsh vapors.

RELLING: Marsh vapors?

HIALMAR: Oh, don't begin with that stuff again!

GINA: Goodness knows there's no vapors in this house, Mr Werle; I give the place a good airing every blessed day.

GREGERS: [*leaves the table*] No airing you can give will drive out the taint I mean.

HIALMAR: Taint!

GINA: Yes, what do you say to that, Ekdal!

RELLING: Excuse me — may it not be you yourself that have brought the taint from those mines up there?

GREGERS: It is like you to call what I bring into this house a taint.

RELLING: [*goes up to him*] Look here, Mr Werle junior: I have a strong suspicion that you are still carrying about that "claim of the ideal" large as life in your coattail pocket.

GREGERS: I carry it in my breast.

RELLING: Well, wherever you carry it, I advise you not to come dunning us with it here as long as *I* am on the premises.

GREGERS: And if I do so nonetheless?

RELLING: Then you'll go headfirst down the stairs; now I've warned you.

HIALMAR: [*rising*] Oh, but, Relling—

GREGERS: Yes, you may turn me out.

GINA: [*interposing between them*] We can't have that, Relling. But I must say, Mr Werle, it ill becomes you to talk about vapors and taints after all the mess you made with your stove.

[*A knock at the passage door.*]

HEDVIG: Mother, there's somebody knocking.

HIALMAR: There now, we're going to have a whole lot of people!

GINA: I'll go. [*goes over and opens the door, starts and draws back*[ Oh—oh dear!

[WERLE, *in a fur coat, advances one step into the room*]

WERLE: Excuse me, but I think my son is staying here.

GINA: [*with a gulp*] Yes.

HIALMAR: [*approaching him*] Won't you do us the honor to—

WERLE: Thank you, I merely wish to speak to my son.

GREGERS: What is it? Here I am.

WERLE: I want a few words with you in your room.

GREGERS: In my room? Very well. [*About to go.*]

GINA: No, no, your room's not in a fit state.

WERLE: Well, then, out in the passage here; I want to have a few words with you alone.

HIALMAR: You can have them here, sir. Come into the parlor, Relling.

> [HIALMAR *and* RELLING *go off to the right;* GINA *takes* HEDVIG *with her into the kitchen.*]

GREGERS: [*after a short pause*] Well, now we are alone.

WERLE: From something you let fall last evening, and from your coming to lodge with the Ekdals, I can't help inferring that you intend to make yourself unpleasant to me in one way or another.

GREGERS: I intend to open Hialmar Ekdal's eyes. He shall see his position as it really is — that is all.

WERLE: Is that the mission in life you spoke of yesterday?

GREGERS: Yes. You have left me no other.

WERLE: Is it I, then, that have crippled your mind, Gregers?

GREGERS: You have crippled my whole life. I am not thinking of all that about Mother — but it's thanks to you that I am continually haunted and harassed by a guilty conscience.

WERLE: Indeed! It is your conscience that troubles you, is it?

GREGERS: I ought to have taken a stand against you when the trap was set for Lieutenant Ekdal. I ought to have cautioned him, for I had a misgiving as to what was in the wind.

WERLE: Yes, that was the time to have spoken.

GREGERS: I did not dare to, I was so cowed and spiritless. I was mortally afraid of you — not only then, but long afterward.

WERLE: You have got over that fear now, it appears.

GREGERS: Yes, fortunately. The wrong done to old Ekdal, both by me and by others, can never be undone; but Hialmar I can rescue from all the falsehood and deception that are bringing him to ruin.

WERLE: Do you think that will be doing him a kindness?

GREGERS: I have not the least doubt of it.

WERLE: You think our worthy photographer is the sort of man to appreciate such friendly offices?

GREGERS: Yes, I do.

WERLE: H'm — we shall see.

GREGERS: Besides, if I am to go on living, I must try to find some cure for my sick conscience.

WERLE: It will never be sound. Your conscience has been sickly from childhood. That is a legacy from your mother, Gregers — the only one she left you.

GREGERS: [*with a scornful half-smile*] Have you not yet forgiven her for the mistake you made in supposing she would bring you a fortune?

WERLE: Don't let us wander from the point. Then you hold to your purpose of setting young Ekdal upon what you imagine to be the right scent?

GREGERS: Yes, that is my fixed resolve.

WERLE: Well, in that case I might have spared myself this visit, for of course it is useless to ask whether you will return home with me?

GREGERS: Quite useless.

WERLE: And I suppose you won't enter the firm either?

GREGERS: No.

WERLE: Very good. But as I am thinking of marrying again, your share in the property will fall to you at once.

GREGERS: [*quickly*] No, I do not want that.

WERLE: You don't want it?

GREGERS: No, I dare not take it, for conscience' sake.

WERLE: [*after a pause*] Are you going up to the works again?

GREGERS: No; I consider myself released from your service.

WERLE: But what are you going to do?

GREGERS: Only fulfill my mission, nothing more.

WERLE: Well, but afterward? What are you going to live upon?

GREGERS: I have laid by a little out of my salary.

WERLE: How long will that last?

GREGERS: I think it will last my time.

WERLE: What do you mean?

GREGERS: I shall answer no more questions.

WERLE: Good-by, then, Gregers.

GREGERS: Good-by.

　　　　[WERLE *goes.*]

HIALMAR: [*peeping in*] He's gone, isn't he?

GREGERS: Yes.

　　　　[HIALMAR *and* RELLING *enter; also* GINA *and* HEDVIG *from the kitchen.*]

RELLING: That luncheon party was a failure.

GREGERS: Put on your coat, Hialmar; I want you to come for a long walk with me.

HIALMAR: With pleasure. What was it your father wanted? Had it anything to do with me?

GREGERS: Come along. We must have a talk. I'll go and put on my overcoat.

　　　　[*Goes out by the passage door.*]

GINA: You shouldn't go out with him, Ekdal.

RELLING: No, don't you do it. Stay where you are.

HIALMAR: [*gets his hat and overcoat*] Oh nonsense! When a friend of my youth feels impelled to open his mind to me in private —

RELLING: But devil take it — don't you see that the fellow's mad, cracked, demented!

GINA: There, what did I tell you! His mother before him had crazy fits like that sometimes.

HIALMAR: The more need for a friend's watchful eye. [*to* GINA] Be sure you have dinner ready in good time. Good-by for the present. [*Goes out by the passage door.*]

RELLING: It's a thousand pities the fellow didn't go to hell through one of the Höidal mines.

GINA: Good lord! What makes you say that?

RELLING: [*muttering*] Oh, I have my own reasons.

GINA: Do you think young Werle is really mad?

RELLING: No, worse luck; he's no madder than most other people. But one disease he has certainly got in his system.

GINA: What is it that's the matter with him?

RELLING: Well, I'll tell you, Mrs Ekdal. He is suffering from an acute attack of integrity.

GINA: Integrity?

HEDVIG: Is that a kind of disease?

RELLING: Yes, it's a national disease. But it only appears sporadically. [*nods to* GINA] Thanks for your hospitality. [*He goes out by the passage door.*]

GINA: [*moving restlessly to and fro*] Ugh, that Gregers Werle — he was always a wretched creature.

HEDVIG: [*standing by the table and looking searchingly at her*] I think all this is very strange.


## ACT IV

SCENE——HIALMAR EKDAL's *studio. A photograph has just been taken; a camera with the cloth over it, a pedestal, two chairs, a folding table, etc., are standing out in the room. Afternoon light; the sun is going down; a little later it begins to grow dusk.*

> [*Gina stands in the passage doorway with a little box and a wet glass plate in her hand and is speaking to somebody outside.*]

GINA: Yes, certainly. When I make a promise I keep it. The first dozen will be ready on Monday. Good afternoon.

> [*Someone is heard going downstairs.* GINA *shuts the door, slips the plate into the box and puts it into the covered camera.*]

HEDVIG: [*comes in from the kitchen*] Are they gone?

GINA: [*tidying up*] Yes, thank goodness. I've got rid of them at last.

HEDVIG: But can you imagine why Father hasn't come home yet?

GINA: Are you sure he's not down in Relling's room?

HEDVIG: No, he's not; I ran down the kitchen stair just now and asked.

GINA: And his dinner standing and getting cold too.

HEDVIG: Yes, I can't understand it. Father's always so careful to be home for dinner!

GINA: Oh, he'll be here directly, you'll see.

HEDVIG: I wish he would come; everything seems so queer today.

GINA: [*calls out*] There he is!

> [HIALMAR EKDAL *comes in at the passage door.*]

HEDVIG: [*going to him*] Father! Oh, what a time we've been waiting for you!

GINA: [*glancing sidelong at him*] You've been out a long time, Ekdal.

HIALMAR: [*without looking at her*] Rather long, yes.

> [*He takes off his overcoat;* GINA *and* HEDVIG *go to help him; he motions them away.*]

GINA: Perhaps you've had dinner with Werle?

HIALMAR: [*hanging up his coat*] No.

GINA: [*going toward the kitchen door*] Then I'll bring some in for you.

HIALMAR: No; let the dinner alone. I want nothing to eat.

HEDVIG: [*going nearer to him*] Are you not well, Father?

HIALMAR: Well? Oh yes, well enough. We have had a tiring walk, Gregers and I.

GINA: You didn't ought to have gone so far, Ekdal; you're not used to it.

HIALMAR: H'm; there's many a thing a man must get used to in this world. [*wanders about the room*] Has anyone been here whilst I was out?

GINA: Nobody but the two sweethearts.

HIALMAR: No new orders?

GINA: No, not today.

HEDVIG: There will be some tomorrow, Father, you'll see.

HIALMAR: I hope there will, for tomorrow I am going to set to work in real earnest.

HEDVIG: Tomorrow! Don't you remember what day it is tomorrow?

HIALMAR: Oh yes, by the bye — Well, the day after, then. Henceforth I mean to do everything myself; I shall take all the work into my own hands.

GINA: Why, what can be the good of that, Ekdal? It'll only make your life a burden to you. I can manage the photography all right, and you can go on working at your invention.

HEDVIG: And think of the wild duck, Father, and all the hens and rabbits and —

HIALMAR: Don't talk to me of all that trash! From tomorrow I will never set foot in the garret again.

HEDVIG: Oh, but, Father, you promised that we should have a little party.

HIALMAR: H'm, true. Well, then, from the day after tomorrow. I should almost like to wring that cursed wild duck's neck!

HEDVIG: [*shrieks*] The wild duck!

GINA: Well, I never!

HEDVIG: [*shaking him*] Oh no, Father; you know it's my wild duck!

HIALMAR: That is why I don't do it. I haven't the heart to — for your sake, Hedvig. But in my inmost soul I feel that I ought to do it. I ought not to tolerate under my roof a creature that has been through those hands.

GINA: Why, good gracious, even if Grandfather did get it from that poor creature Pettersen —

HEDVIG: [*going after him*] But think of the wild duck — the poor wild duck!

HIALMAR: [*stops*] I tell you I will spare it — for your sake. Not a hair of its head shall be — I mean, it shall be spared. There are greater problems than that to be dealt with. But you should go out a little now, Hedvig, as usual; it is getting dusk enough for you now.

HEDVIG: No, I don't care about going out now.

HIALMAR: Yes, do; it seems to me your eyes are blinking a great deal; all these vapors in here are bad for you. The air is heavy under this roof.

HEDVIG: Very well then, I'll run down the kitchen stair and go for a little walk. My cloak and hat? Oh, they're in my own room. Father — be sure you don't do the wild duck any harm while I'm out.

HIALMAR: Not a feather of its head shall be touched. [*draws her to him*] You and I, Hedvig — we two — Well, go along.

[HEDVIG *nods to her parents and goes out through the kitchen.*]

HIALMAR: [*walks about without looking up*] Gina.

GINA: Yes?

HIALMAR: From tomorrow — or say from the day after tomorrow — I should like to keep the household account book myself.

GINA: Do you want to keep the accounts too now?

HIALMAR: Yes; or to check the receipts at any rate.

GINA: Lord help us; that's soon done.

HIALMAR: One would hardly think so; at any rate you seem to make the money go a very long way. [*stops and looks at her*] How do you manage it?

GINA: It's because me and Hedvig, we need so little.

HIALMAR: Is it the case that Father is very liberally paid for the copying he does for Mr Werle?

GINA: I don't know as he gets anything out of the way. I don't know the rates for that sort of work.

HIALMAR: Well, what does he get, about? Let me hear!

GINA: Oh, it varies; I daresay it'll come to about as much as he costs us, with a little pocket money over.

HIALMAR: As much as he costs us! And you have never told me this before.

GINA: No, how could I tell you? It pleased you so much to think he got everything from you.

HIALMAR: And he gets it from Mr Werle.

GINA: Oh well, he has plenty and to spare, he has.

HIALMAR: Light the lamp for me, please!

GINA: [*lighting the lamp*] And of course we don't know as it's Mr Werle himself; it may be Graberg.

HIALMAR: Why attempt such an evasion?

GINA: I don't know; I only thought —

HIALMAR: H'm!

GINA: It wasn't me that got Grandfather that copying. It was Bertha, when she used to come about us.

HIALMAR: It seems to me your voice is trembling.

GINA: [*putting the lamp shade on*] Is it?

HIALMAR: And your hands are shaking, are they not?

GINA: [*firmly*] Come right out with it, Ekdal. What has he been saying about me?

HIALMAR: Is it true — can it be true that — that there was an — an understanding between you and Mr Werle while you were in service there?

GINA: That's not true. Not at that time. Mr Werle did come after me, that's a fact. And his wife thought there was something in it, and then she made such a hocus-pocus and hurly-burly, and she hustled me and bustled me about so that I left her service.

HIALMAR: But afterward, then?

GINA: Well, then I went home. And Mother — well, she wasn't the woman you took her for, Ekdal; she kept on worrying and worrying at me about one thing and another — for Mr Werle was a widower by that time.

HIALMAR: Well, and then?

GINA: I suppose you've got to know it. He gave me no peace until he'd had his way.

HIALMAR: [*striking his hands together*] And this is the mother of my child! How could you hide this from me?

GINA: Yes, it was wrong of me; I ought certainly to have told you long ago.

HIALMAR: You should have told me at the very first — then I should have known the sort of woman you were.

GINA: But would you have married me all the same?

HIALMAR: How can you dream that I would?

GINA: That's just why I didn't dare tell you anything then. For I'd come to care for you so much, you see, and I couldn't go and make myself utterly miserable.

HIALMAR: [*walks about*] And this is my Hedvig's mother! And to know that all I see before me [*kicks at chair*] — all that I call my home — I owe to a favored predecessor! Oh, that scoundrel Werle!

GINA: Do you repent of the fourteen — the fifteen years we've lived together?

HIALMAR: [*placing himself in front of her*] Have you not every day, every hour,

repented of the spider's web of deceit you have spun around me? Answer me
that! How could you help writhing with penitence and remorse?

GINA: Oh, my dear Ekdal, I've had all I could do to look after the house and get
through the day's work.

HIALMAR: Then you never think of reviewing your past?

GINA: No; heaven knows I'd almost forgotten those old stories.

HIALMAR: Oh, this dull, callous contentment! To me there is something revolting
about it. Think of it — never so much as a twinge of remorse!

GINA: But tell me, Ekdal — what would have become of you if you hadn't had a wife
like me?

HIALMAR: Like you!

GINA: Yes; for you know I've always been a bit more practical and wide awake than
you. Of course I'm a year or two older.

HIALMAR: What would have become of me!

GINA: You'd got into all sorts of bad ways when first you met me; that you can't deny.

HIALMAR: "Bad ways," do you call them? Little do you know what a man goes
through when he is in grief and despair — especially a man of my fiery
temperament.

GINA: Well, well, that may be so. And I've no reason to crow over you neither, for
you turned a fine husband, that you did, as soon as ever you had a house and
home of your own. And now we'd got everything so nice and cosy about us,
and me and Hedvig was just thinking we'd soon be able to let ourselves go a bit
in the way of both food and clothes.

HIALMAR: In the swamp of deceit, yes.

GINA: I wish to goodness that detestable thing had never set his foot inside our doors!

HIALMAR: And I, too, thought my home such a pleasant one. That was a delusion.
Where shall I now find the elasticity of spirit to bring my invention into the
world of reality? Perhaps it will die with me, and then it will be your past, Gina,
that will have killed it.

GINA: [*nearly crying*] You mustn't say such things, Ekdal. Me, that has only wanted
to do the best I could for you all my days!

HIALMAR: I ask you, what becomes of the breadwinner's dream? When I used to lie
in there on the sofa and brood over my invention I had a clear enough
presentiment that it would sap my vitality to the last drop. I felt even then that
the day when I held the patent in my hand — that day — would bring my —
release. And then it was my dream that you should live on after me, the dead
inventor's well-to-do widow.

GINA: [*drying her tears*] No, you mustn't talk like that, Ekdal. May the Lord never let
me see the day I am left a widow!

HIALMAR: Oh, the whole dream has vanished. It is all over now. All over!

[GREGERS WERLE *opens the passage door cautiously and looks in.*]

GREGERS: May I come in?

HIALMAR: Yes, come in.

GREGERS: [*comes forward, his face beaming with satisfaction, and holds out both his
hands to them*] Well, dear friends! [*looks from one to the other and whispers to*
HIALMAR] Have you not done it yet?

HIALMAR: [*aloud*] It is done.

GREGERS: It is?

HIALMAR: I have passed through the bitterest moments of my life.

GREGERS: But also, I trust, the most ennobling.

HIALMAR: Well, at any rate, we have got through it for the present.

GINA: God forgive you, Mr Werle.

GREGERS: [*in great surpirse*] But I don't understand this.

HIALMAR: What don't you understand?

GREGERS: After so great a crisis — a crisis that is to be the starting point of an entirely new life — of a communion founded on truth and free from all taint of deception —

HIALMAR: Yes, yes, I know; I know that quite well.

GREGERS: I confidently expected, when I entered the room, to find the light of transfiguration shining upon me from both husband and wife. And now I see nothing but dullness, oppression, gloom —

GINA: Oh, is that it? [*Takes off the lamp shade.*]

GREGERS: You will not understand me, Mrs Ekdal. Ah well, you, I suppose, need time to — But you, Hialmar? Surely you feel a new consecration after the great crisis?

HIALMAR: Yes, of course I do. That is — in a sort of way.

GREGERS: For surely nothing in the world can compare with the joy of forgiving one who has sinned and raising her up to oneself in love.

HIALMAR: Do you think a man can so easily throw off the bitter cup I have drained?

GREGERS: No, not a common man, perhaps. But a man like you —

HIALMAR: Good God! I know that well enough. But you must keep me up to it, Gregers. It takes time, you know.

GREGERS: You have much of the wild duck in you, Hialmar.

[RELLING *has come in at the passage door.*]

RELLING: Oho! Is the wild duck to the fore again?

HIALMAR: Yes; Mr Werle's wing-broken victim.

RELLING: Mr Werle? So it's him you are talking about?

HIALMAR: Him and — ourselves.

RELLING: [*in an undertone to* GREGERS] May the devil take you!

HIALMAR: What is that you are saying?

RELLING: Only uttering a heartfelt wish that this quack would take himself off. If he stays here he is quite equal to making an utter mess of life for both of you.

GREGERS: These two will not make a mess of life, Mr Relling. Of course I won't speak for Hialmar — him we know. But she too, in her innermost heart, has certainly something loyal and sincere —

GINA: [*almost crying*] You might have let me alone for what I was then.

RELLING: [*to* GREGERS] Is it rude to ask what you really want in this house?

GREGERS: To lay the foundations of a true marriage.

RELLING: So you don't think Ekdal's marriage is good enough as it is?

GREGERS: No doubt it is as good a marriage as most others, worse luck. But a true marriage it has yet to become.

HIALMAR: You have never had eyes for the claims of the ideal, Relling.

RELLING: Rubbish, my boy! But excuse me, Mr Werle; how many — in round numbers — how many true marriages have you seen in the course of your life?

GREGERS: Scarcely a single one.

RELLING: Nor I either.

GREGERS: But I have seen innumerable marriages of the opposite kind. And it has been my fate to see at close quarters what ruin such a marriage can work in two human souls.

HIALMAR: A man's whole moral basis may give away beneath his feet; that is the terrible part of it.

RELLING: Well, I can't say I've ever been exactly married, so I don't pretend to speak with authority. But this I know, that the child enters into the marriage problem. And you must leave the child in peace.

HIALMAR: Oh — Hedvig! My poor Hedvig!

RELLING: Yes, you must be good enough to keep Hedvig outside of all this. You two are grown-up people; you are free, in God's name, to make what mess you please of your life. But you must deal cautiously with Hedvig, I tell you; otherwise you may do her a great injury.

HIALMAR: An injury!

RELLING: Yes, or she may do herself an injury — and perhaps others too.

GINA: How can you know that, Relling?

HIALMAR: Her sight is in no immediate danger, is it?

RELLING: I am not talking about her sight. Hedvig is at a critical age. She may be getting all sorts of mischief into her head.

GINA: That's true — I've noticed it already! She's taken to carrying on with the fire out in the kitchen. She calls it playing at house on fire. I'm often scared for fear she really sets fire to the house.

RELLING: You see, I thought as much.

GREGERS: [*to* RELLING] But how do you account for that?

RELLING: [*sullenly*] Her constitution's changing, sir.

HIALMAR: So long as the child has me — so long as I am above ground —
[*A knock at the door.*]

GINA: Hush, Ekdal, there's someone in the passage. [*calls out*] Come in!
[MRS SORBY, *in walking dress, comes in.*]

MRS SORBY: Good evening.

GINA: [*going toward her*] Is it really you, Bertha?

MRS SORBY: Yes, of course it is. But I'm disturbing you, I'm afraid.

HIALMAR: No, not at all; an emissary from that house —

MRS SORBY: [*to* GINA] To tell the truth, I hoped your menfolk would be out at this time. I just ran up to have a little chat with you and to say good-by.

GINA: Good-by? Are you going away then?

MRS SORBY: Yes, tomorrow morning — up to Höidal. Mr Werle started this afternoon. [*lightly to* GREGERS] He asked me to say good-by for him.

GINA: Only fancy!

HIALMAR: I say: beware!

GREGERS: I must explain the situation. My father and Mrs Sorby are going to be married.

HIALMAR: Going to be married!

GINA: Oh, Bertha! So it's come to that at last!

RELLING: [*his voice quivering a little*] This is surely not true?

MRS SORBY: Yes, my dear Relling, it's true enough.

RELLING: You are going to marry again?

MRS SORBY: Yes, it looks like it. Werle has got a special license, and we are going to be married quietly up at the works.

GREGERS: Then I must wish you all happiness, like a dutiful stepson.

MRS SORBY: Thank you very much — if you mean what you say. I certainly hope it will lead to happiness, both for Werle and for me.

RELLING: You have every reason to hope that. Mr Werle never gets drunk — so far as I know; and I don't suppose he's in the habit of thrashing his wives, like the late lamented horse doctor.

MRS SORBY: Come now, let Sorby rest in peace. He had his good points too.

RELLING: Mr Werle has better ones, I have no doubt.

MRS SORBY: He hasn't frittered away all that was good in him, at any rate. The man who does that must take the consequences.

RELLING: I shall go out with Molvik this evening.

MRS SORBY: You mustn't do that, Relling. Don't do it — for my sake.

RELLING: There's nothing else for it. [*to* HIALMAR] If you're going with us, come along.

GINA: No, thank you. Ekdal doesn't go in for that sort of dissertation.

HIALMAR: [*half aloud, in vexation*] Oh, do hold your tongue!

RELLING: Good-by, Mrs — Werle. [*Goes out through the passage door.*]

GREGERS: [*to* MRS SORBY] You seem to know Doctor Relling pretty intimately.

MRS SORBY: Yes, we have known each other for many years. At one time it seemed as if things might have gone further between us.

GREGERS: It was surely lucky for you that they did not.

MRS SORBY: You may well say that. But I have always been wary of acting on impulse. A woman can't afford absolutely to throw herself away.

GREGERS: Are you not in the least afraid that I may let my father know about this old friendship?

MRS SORBY: Why, of course I have told him all about it myself.

GREGERS: Indeed?

MRS SORBY: Your father knows every single thing that can, with any truth, be said about me. I have told him all; it was the first thing I did when I saw what was in his mind.

GREGERS: Then you have been franker than most people, I think.

MRS SORBY: I have always been frank. We women find that the best policy.

HIALMAR: What do you say to that, Gina?

GINA: Oh, we're not all alike, us women aren't. Some are made one way, some another.

MRS SORBY: Well, for my part, Gina, I believe it's wisest to do as I've done. And Werle has no secrets either, on his side. That's really the great bond between us, you see. Now he can talk to me as openly as a child. He has never had the chance to do that before. Fancy a man like him, full of health and vigor, passing his whole youth and the best years of his life in listening to nothing but penitential sermons! And very often the sermons had for their text the most imaginary offenses — at least so I understand.

GINA: That's true enough.

GREGERS: If you ladies are going to follow up this topic, I had better withdraw.

MRS SORBY: You can stay as far as that's concerned. I shan't say a word more. But I wanted you to know that I had done nothing secretly or in an underhand way. I may seem to have come in for a great piece of luck, and so I have, in a sense. But after all, I don't think I am getting any more than I am giving. I shall stand by him always, and I can tend and care for him as no one else can, now that he is getting helpless.

HIALMAR: Getting helpless?

GREGERS: [*to* MRS SORBY] Hush, don't speak of that here.

MRS SORBY: There is no disguising it any longer, however much he would like to. He is going blind.

HIALMAR: [*starts*] Going blind? That's strange. He, too, going blind!

GINA: Lots of people do.

MRS SORBY: And you can imagine what that means to a businessman. Well, I shall try as well as I can to make my eyes take the place of his. But I mustn't stay any longer; I have heaps of things to do. Oh, by the bye, Ekdal, I was to tell you that if there is anything Werle can do for you, you must just apply to Graberg.

GREGERS: That offer I am sure Hialmar Ekdal will decline with thanks.

MRS SORBY: Indeed? I don't think he used to be so —

GINA: No, Bertha, Ekdal doesn't need anything from Mr Werle now.

HIALMAR: [*slowly and with emphasis*] Will you present my compliments to your future husband and say that I intend very shortly to call upon Mr Graberg —

GREGERS: What! You don't really mean that?

HIALMAR: To call upon Mr Graberg, I say, and obtain an account of the sum I owe his principal. I will pay that debt of honor — ha, ha, ha! a debt of honor, let us call it! In any case I will pay the whole with five per cent interest.

GINA: But, my dear Ekdal, God knows we haven't got the money to do it.

HIALMAR: Be good enough to tell your future husband that I am working assiduously at my invention. Please tell him that what sustains me in this laborious task is the wish to free myself from a torturing burden of debt. That is my reason for proceeding with the invention. The entire profits shall be devoted to releasing me from my pecuniary obligations to your future husband.

MRS SORBY: Something has happened here.

HIALMAR: Yes, you are right.

MRS SORBY: Well, good-by. I had something else to speak to you about, Gina, but it must keep till another time. Good-by.

[HIALMAR *and* GREGERS *bow silently.* GINA *follows* MRS SORBY *to the door.*]

HIALMAR: Not beyond the threshold, Gina!

[MRS SORBY *goes;* GINA *shuts the door after her.*]

HIALMAR: There now, Gregers, I have got that burden of debt off my mind.

GREGERS: You soon will, at all events.

HIALMAR: I think my attitude may be called correct.

GREGERS: You are the man I have always taken you for.

HIALMAR: In certain cases it is impossible to disregard the claim of the ideal. Yet, as the breadwinner of a family, I cannot but writhe and groan under it. I can tell you it is no joke for a man without capital to attempt the repayment of a long-standing obligation over which, so to speak, the dust of oblivion has gathered. But it cannot be helped; the man in me demands his rights.

GREGERS: [*laying his hand on* HIALMAR'*s shoulder*] My dear Hialmar — was it not a good thing I came?

HIALMAR: Yes.

GREGERS: Are you not glad to have had your true position made clear to you?

HIALMAR: [*somewhat impatiently*] Yes, of course I am. But there is one thing that is revolting to my sense of justice.

GREGERS: And what is that?

HIALMAR: It is that— But I don't know whether I ought to express myself so unreservedly about your father.

GREGERS: Say what you please so far as I am concerned.

HIALMAR: Well, then, is it not exasperating to think that it is not I, but he, who will realize the true marriage?

GREGERS: How can you say such a thing?

HIALMAR: Because it is clearly the case. Isn't the marriage between your father and Mrs Sorby founded upon complete confidence, upon entire and unreserved candor on both sides? They hide nothing from each other, they keep no secrets in the background; their relation is based, if I may put it so, on mutual confession and absolution.

GREGERS: Well, what then?

HIALMAR: Well, is not that the whole thing? Did you not yourself say that this was precisely the difficulty that had to be overcome in order to found a true marriage?

GREGERS: But this is a totally different matter, Hialmar. You surely don't compare either yourself or your wife with those two— Oh, you understood me well enough.

HIALMAR: Say what you like, there is something in all this that hurts and offends my sense of justice. It really looks as if there were no just Providence to rule the world.

GINA: Oh no, Ekdal; for God's sake don't say such things.

GREGERS: H'm; don't let us get upon those questions.

HIALMAR: And yet, after all, I cannot but recognize the guiding finger of Fate. He is going blind.

GINA: Oh, you can't be sure of that.

HIALMAR: There is no doubt about it. At all events there ought not to be, for in that very fact lies the righteous retribution. He has hoodwinked a confiding fellow creature in days gone by —

GREGERS: I fear he has hoodwinked many.

HIALMAR: And now comes inexorable, mysterious Fate and demands Werle's own eyes.

GINA: Oh, how dare you say such dreadful things! You make me quite scared.

HIALMAR: It is profitable, now and then, to plunge deep into the night side of existence.

[HEDVIG, *in her hat and cloak, comes in by the passage door. She is pleasurably excited and out of breath.*]

GINA: Are you back already?

HEDVIG: Yes, I didn't care to go any farther. It was a good thing, too, for I've just met someone at the door.

HIALMAR: It must have been that Mrs Sorby.

HEDVIG: Yes.

HIALMAR: [*walks up and down*] I hope you have seen her for the last time.

[*Silence.* HEDVIG, *discouraged, looks first at one and then at the other, trying to divine their frame of mind.*]

HEDVIG: [*approaching, coaxingly*] Father.

HIALMAR: Well—what is it, Hedvig?

HEDVIG: Mrs Sorby had something with her for me.

HIALMAR: [*stops*] For you?

HEDVIG: Yes. Something for tomorrow.

GINA: Bertha has always given you some little thing on your birthday.

HIALMAR: What is it?

HEDVIG: Oh, you mustn't see it now. Mother is to give it to me tomorrow morning before I'm up.

HIALMAR: What is all this hocus-pocus that I am to be in the dark about?

HEDVIG: [*quickly*] Oh no, you may see it if you like. It's a big letter. [*Takes the letter out of her cloak pocket.*]

HIALMAR: A letter too?

HEDVIG: Hes, it is only a letter. The rest will come afterward, I suppose. But fancy—a letter! I've never had a letter before. And there's "Miss" written upon it. [*reads*] "Miss Hedvig Ekdal." Only think—that's me!

HIALMAR: Let me see that letter.

HEDVIG: [*hands it to him*] There it is.

HIALMAR: That is Mr Werle's hand.

GINA: Are you sure of that, Ekdal?

HIALMAR: Look for yourself.

GINA: Oh, what do I know about suchlike things?

HIALMAR: Hedvig, may I open the letter—and read it?

HEDVIG: Yes, of course you may, if you want to.

GINA: No, not tonight, Ekdal; it's to be kept till tomorrow.

HEDVIG: [*softly*] Oh, can't you let him read it! It's sure to be something good, and then Father will be glad and everything will be nice again.

HIALMAR: I may open it then?

HEDVIG: Yes, do, Father. I'm so anxious to know what it is.

HIALMAR: Well and good. [*opens the letter, takes out a paper, reads it through and appears bewildered.*] What is this?

GINA: What does it say?

HEDVIG: Oh yes, Father—tell us!

HIALMAR: Be quiet. [*reads it through again; he has turned pale but says with self-control*] It is a deed of gift, Hedvig.

HEDVIG: Is it? What sort of gift am I to have?

HIALMAR: Read for yourself.

[HEDVIG *goes over and reads for a time by the lamp.*]

HIALMAR: [*half aloud, clenching his hands*] The eyes! The eyes—and then that letter!

HEDVIG: [*leaves off reading*] Yes, but it seems to me that it's Grandfather that's to have it.

HIALMAR: [*takes letter from her*] Gina—can you understand this?

GINA: I know nothing whatever about it; tell me what's the matter.

HIALMAR: Mr Werle writes to Hedvig that her old grandfather need not trouble himself any longer with the copying but that he can henceforth draw on the office for a hundred crowns a month—

GREGERS: Aha!

HEDVIG: A hundred crowns, Mother! I read that.

GINA: What a good thing for Grandfather!

HIALMAR: —a hundred crowns a month so long as he needs it—that means, of course, so long as he lives.

GINA: Well, so he's provided for, poor dear.

HIALMAR: But there is more to come. You didn't read that, Hedvig. Afterward this gift is to pass on to you.

HEDVIG: To me! The whole of it?

HIALMAR: He says that the same amount is assured to you for the whole of your life. Do you hear that, Gina?

GINA: Yes, I hear.

HEDVIG: Fancy—all that money for me! [*shakes him*] Father, Father, aren't you glad?

HIALMAR: [*eluding her*] Glad! [*walks about*] Oh, what vistas—what perspectives open up before me! It is Hedvig, Hedvig that he showers these benefactions upon!

GINA: Yes, because it's Hedvig's birthday.

HEDVIG: And you'll get it all the same, Father! You know quite well I shall give all the money to you and Mother.

HIALMAR: To Mother, yes! There we have it.

GREGERS: Hialmar, this is a trap he is setting for you.

HIALMAR: Do you think it's another trap?

GREGERS: When he was here this morning he said: Hialmar Ekdal is not the man you imagine him to be.

HIALMAR: Not the man—

GREGERS: That you shall see, he said.

HIALMAR: He meant you should see that I would let myself be bought off!

HEDVIG: Oh, Mother, what does all this mean?

GINA: Go and take off your things.

[HEDVIG *goes out by the kitchen door, half crying.*]

GREGERS: Yes, Hialmar—now is the time to show who was right, he or I.

HIALMAR: [*slowly tears the paper across, lays both pieces on the table and says*] Here is my answer.

GREGERS: Just what I expected.

HIALMAR: [*goes over to* GINA, *who stands by the stove and says in a low voice*] Now please make a clean breast of it. If the connection between you and him was quite over when you—came to care for me, as you call it—why did he place us in a position to marry?

GINA: I suppose he thought as he could come and go in our house.

HIALMAR: Only that? Was he not afraid of a possible contingency?

GINA: I don't know what you mean.

HIALMAR: I want to know whether—your child has the right to live under my roof.

GINA: [*draws herself up; her eyes flash*] You ask that!

HIALMAR: You shall answer me this one question: Does Hedvig belong to me—or —? Well?

GINA: [*looking at him with cold defiance*] I don't know.

HIALMAR: [*quivering a little*] You don't know!

GINA: How should *I* know. A creature like me—

HIALMAR: [*quietly turning away from her*] Then I have nothing more to do in this house.

GREGERS: Take care, Hialmar! Think what you are doing!

HIALMAR: [*puts on his overcoat*] In this case there is nothing for a man like me to think twice about.

GREGERS: Yes indeed, there are endless things to be considered. You three must be together if you are to attain the true frame of mind for self-sacrifice and forgiveness.

HIALMAR: I don't want to attain it. Never, never! My hat! [*takes his hat*] My home has fallen into ruins about me. [*bursts into tears*] Gregers, I have no child!

HEDVIG: [*who has opened the kitchen door*] What is that you're saying? [*coming to him*] Father, Father!

GINA: There, you see!

HIALMAR: Don't come near me, Hedvig! Keep far away. I cannot bear to see you. Oh! those eyes! Good-by.
          [*Makes for the door.*]

HEDVIG: [*clinging close to him and screaming loudly*] No! No! Don't leave me!

GINA: [*cries out*] Look at the child, Ekdal! Look at the child!

HIALMAR: I will not! I cannot! I must get out — away from all this! [*He tears himself away from* HEDVIG *and goes out by the passage door.*]

HEDVIG: [*with despairing eyes*] He is going away from us, Mother! He is going away from us! He will never come back again!

GINA: Don't cry, Hedvig. Father's sure to come back again.

HEDVIG: [*throws herself sobbing on the sofa*] No, no, he'll never come home to us any more.

GREGERS: Do you believe I meant all for the best, Mrs Ekdal?

GINA: Yes, I daresay you did, but God forgive you all the same.

HEDVIG: [*lying on the sofa*] Oh, this will kill me! What have I done to him? Mother, you must fetch him home again!

GINA: Yes, yes, yes; only be quiet, and I'll go out and look for him. [*puts on her outdoor things*] Perhaps he's gone into Relling's. But you mustn't lie there and cry. Promise me!

HEDVIG: [*weeping convulsively*] Yes, I'll stop, I'll stop; if only Father comes back!

GREGERS: [*to* GINA, *who is going*] After all, had you not better leave him to fight out his bitter fight to the end?

GINA: Oh, he can do that afterward. First of all we must get the child quieted.
          [*Goes out by the passage door.*]

HEDVIG: [*sits up and dries her tears*] Now you must tell me what all this means. Why doesn't Father want me any more?

GREGERS: You mustn't ask that till you are a big girl — quite grown up.

HEDVIG: [*sobs*] But I can't go on being as miserable as this till I'm grown up. I think I know what it is. Perhaps I'm not really Father's child.

GREGERS: [*uneasily*] How could that be?

HEDVIG: Mother might have found me. And perhaps Father has just found out; I've read of such things.

GREGERS: Well, but if it were so —

HEDVIG: I think he might be just as fond of me for all that. Yes, fonder almost. We got the wild duck as a present, you know, and I love it so dearly all the same.

GREGERS: [*turning the conversation*] Ah, the wild duck, by the bye! Let us talk about the wild duck a little, Hedvig.

HEDVIG: The poor wild duck! He doesn't want to see it any more either. Only think, he wanted to wring its neck!

GREGERS: Oh, he won't do that.

HEDVIG: No, but he said he would like to. And I think it was horrid of Father to say it, for I pray for the wild duck every night and ask that it may be preserved from death and all that is evil.

GREGERS: [*looking at her*] Do you say your prayers every night?

HEDVIG: Yes.

GREGERS: Who taught you to do that?

HEDVIG: I myself — one time when Father was very ill and said that death was staring him in the face.

GREGERS: Well?

HEDVIG: Then I prayed for him as I lay in bed, and since then I have always kept it up.

GREGERS: And now you pray for the wild duck too?

HEDVIG: I thought it best to bring in the wild duck, for she was so weak at first.

GREGERS: Do you pray in the morning too?

HEDVIG: No, of course not.

GREGERS: Why not in the morning as well?

HEDVIG: In the morning it's light, you know, and there's nothing in particular to be afraid of.

GREGERS: And your father was going to wring the neck of the wild duck that you love so dearly?

HEDVIG: No; he said he ought to wring its neck but he would spare it for my sake, and that was kind of Father.

GREGERS: [*coming a little nearer*] But suppose you were to sacrifice the wild duck of your own free will for his sake?

HEDVIG: [*rising*] The wild duck!

GREGERS: Suppose you were to make a free-will offering, for his sake, of the dearest treasure you have in the world?

HEDVIG: Do you think that would do any good?

GREGERS: Try it, Hedvig.

HEDVIG: [*softly, with flashing eyes*] Yes, I will try it.

GREGERS: Have you really the courage for it, do you think?

HEDVIG: I'll ask Grandfather to shoot the wild duck for me.

GREGERS: Yes, do. But not a word to your mother about it.

HEDVIG: Why not?

GREGERS: She doesn't understand us.

HEDVIG: The wild duck! I'll try it tomorrow morning.

     [GINA *comes in by the passage door.*]

HEDVIG: [*going toward her*] Did you find him, Mother?

GINA: No, but I heard as he had called and taken Relling with him.

GREGERS: Are you sure of that?

GINA: Yes, the porter's wife said so. Molvik went with them too, she said.

GREGERS: This evening, when his mind so sorely needs to wrestle in solitude!

GINA: [*takes off her things*] Yes, men are strange creatures, so they are. The Lord only knows where Relling has dragged him to! I ran over to Madam Eriksen's, but they weren't there.

HEDVIG: [*struggling to keep back her tears*] Oh, if he should never come home any more!

GREGERS: He will come home again. I shall have news to give him tomorrow, and then you shall see how he comes home. You may rely upon that, Hedvig, and sleep in peace. Good night. [*He goes out by the passage door.*]

HEDVIG: (*throws herself sobbing on* GINA's *neck*) Mother, Mother!

GINA: [*pats her shoulder and sighs*] Ah yes, Relling was right, he was. That's what comes of it when crazy creatures go about presenting the claim of the — what-you-may-call-it.

## ACT V

SCENE———HIALMAR EKDAL's *studio. Cold gray morning light. Wet snow lies upon the large panes of the sloping roof window.*

> [GINA *comes from the kitchen with an apron and bib on and carrying a dusting brush and a duster; she goes toward the sitting-room door. At the same moment* HEDVIG *comes hurriedly in from the passage.*]

GINA: [*stops*] Well?

HEDVIG: Oh, Mother, I almost think he's down at Relling's —

GINA: There, you see!

HEDVIG: — because the porter's wife says she could hear that Relling had two people with him when he came home last night.

GINA: That's just what I thought.

HEDVIG: But it's no use his being there if he won't come up to us.

GINA: I'll go down and speak to him at all events.

> [OLD EKDAL, *in dressing gown and slippers and with a lighted pipe, appears at the door of his room.*]

EKDAL: Hialmar — isn't Hialmar at home?

GINA: No, he's gone out.

EKDAL: So early? And in such a tearing snowstorm? Well, well, just as he pleases; I can take my morning walk alone.

> [*He slides the garret door aside;* HEDVIG *helps him; he goes in; she closes it after him.*]

HEDVIG: [*in an undertone*] Only think Mother, when poor Grandfather hears that Father is going to leave us.

GINA: Oh, nonsense; Grandfather mustn't hear anything about it. It was a heaven's mercy he wasn't at home yesterday in all that hurly-burly.

HEDVIG: Yes, but —

> [GREGERS *comes in by the passage door.*]

GREGERS: Well, have you any news of him?

GINA: They say he's down at Relling's.

GREGERS: At Relling's! Has he really been out with those creatures?

GINA: Yes, like enough.

GREGERS: When he ought to have been yearning for solitude, to collect and clear his thoughts —

GINA: Yes you may well say so.

[RELLING *enters from the passage.*]

HEDVIG: [*going to him*] Is Father in your room?

GINA: [*at the same time*] Is he there?

RELLING: Yes, to be sure he is.

HEDVIG: And you never let us know!

RELLING: Yes, I'm a brute. But in the first place I had to look after the other brute; I mean our demonic friend, of course; and then I fell so dead asleep that—

GINA: What does Ekdal say today?

RELLING: He says nothing whatever.

HEDVIG: Doesn't he speak?

RELLING: Not a blessed word.

GREGERS: No, no; I can understand that very well.

GINA: But what's he doing then?

RELLING: He's lying on the sofa, snoring.

GINA: Oh, is he? Ekdal's a rare one to snore.

HEDVIG: Asleep? Can he sleep?

RELLING: Well, it certainly looks like it.

GREGERS: No wonder, after the spiritual conflict that has torn him—

GINA: And then he's never been used to gadding about out of doors at night.

HEDVIG: Perhaps it's a good thing that he's getting sleep, Mother.

GINA: Of course it is, and we must take care we don't wake him up too early. Thank you, Relling. I must get the house cleaned up a bit now, and then— Come and help me, Hedvig.

[GINA *and* HEDVIG *go into the sitting room.*]

GREGERS: [*turning to* RELLING] What is your explanation of the spiritual tumult that is now going on in Hialmar Ekdal?

RELLING: A lot of spiritual tumult I've noticed in him.

GREGERS: What! Not at such a crisis, when his whole life has been placed on a new foundation? How can you think that such an individuality as Hialmar's—

RELLING: Oh, individuality—he! If he ever had any tendency to the abnormal developments you call individuality, I can assure you it was rooted out of him while he was still in his teens.

GREGERS: That would be strange indeed—considering the loving care with which he was brought up.

RELLING: By those two high-flown, hysterical maiden aunts, you mean?

GREGERS: Let me tell you that they were women who never forgot the claim of the ideal—but of course you will only jeer at me again.

RELLING: No, I'm in no humor for that. I know all about those ladies, for he has ladled out no end of rhetoric on the subject of his "two soul mothers." But I don't think he has much to thank them for. Ekdal's misfortune is that in his own circle he has always been looked upon as a shining light.

GREGERS: Not without reason, surely. Look at the depth of his mind!

RELLING: I have never discovered it. That his father believed in it I don't so much wonder; the old lieutenant has been an ass all his days.

GREGERS: He has had a childlike mind all his days; that is what you cannot understand.

RELLING: Well, so be it. But then when our dear sweet Hialmar went to college he at once passed for the great light of the future amongst his comrades too! He was handsome, the rascal — red and white — a shopgirl's dream of manly beauty; and with his superficially emotional temperament and his sympathetic voice and his talent for declaiming other people's verses and other people's thoughts —

GREGERS: [*indignantly*] Is it Hialmar Ekdal you are talking about in this strain?

RELLING: Yes, with your permission; I am simply giving you an inside view of the idol you are groveling before.

GREGERS: I should hardly have thought I was quite stone-blind.

RELLING: Yes, you are — or not far from it. You are a sick man too, you see.

GREGERS: You are right there.

RELLING: Yes. Yours is a complicated case. First of all there is that plaguy integrity fever, and then — what's worse — you are always in a delirium of hero worship; you must always have something to adore, outside yourself.

GREGERS: Yes, I must certainly seek it outside myself.

RELLING: But you make such shocking mistakes about every new phoenix you think you have discovered. Here again you have come to a cotter's cabin with your claim of the ideal, and the people of the house are insolvent.

GREGERS: If you don't think better than that of Hialmar Ekdal, what pleasure can you find in being everlastingly with him?

RELLING: Well, you see, I'm supposed to be a sort of a doctor — God help me! I have to give a hand to the poor sick folk who live under the same roof with me.

GREGERS: Oh, indeed! Hialmar Ekdal is sick too, is he?

RELLING: Most people are, worse luck.

GREGERS: And what remedy are you applying in Hialmar's case?

RELLING: My usual one. I am cultivating the life illusion in him.

GREGERS: Life — illusion? I didn't catch what you said.

RELLING: Yes, I said illusion. For illusion, you know, is the stimulating principle.

GREGERS: May I ask with what illusion Hialmar is inoculated?

RELLING: No, thank you; I don't betray professional secrets to quacks. You would probably go and muddle his case still more than you have already. But my method is infallible. I have applied it to Molvik as well. I have made him "demonic." That's the treatment for him.

GREGERS: Is he not really demonic then?

RELLING: What the devil do you mean by demonic? It's only a piece of gibberish I've invented to keep up a spark of life in him. But for that, the poor harmless creature would have succumbed to self-contempt and despair many a long year ago. And then the old lieutenant! But he has hit upon his own cure, you see.

GREGERS: Lieutenant Ekdal? What of him?

RELLING: Just think of the old bear hunter shutting himself up in that dark garret to shoot rabbits! I tell you there is not a happier sportsman in the world than that old man pottering about in there among all that rubbish. The four or five withered Christmas trees he has saved up are the same to him as the whole great fresh Höidal forest; the cock and the hens are big game birds in the fir tops, and the rabbits that flop about the garret floor are the bears he has to battle with — the mighty hunter of the mountains!

GREGERS: Poor unfortunate old man! Yes, he has indeed had to narrow the ideals of his youth.

RELLING: While I think of it, Mr Werle junior — don't use that foreign word: ideals. We have the excellent native word: lies.

GREGERS: Do you think the two things are related?

RELLING: Yes, just about as closely as typhus and putrid fever.

GREGERS: Doctor Relling, I shall not give up the struggle until I have rescued Hialmar from your clutches!

RELLING: So much the worse for him. Rob the average man of his life illusion and you rob him of his happiness at the same stroke. [*to* HEDVIG, *who comes in from the sitting room*] Well, little wild-duck mother. I'm just going down to see whether Papa is still lying meditating upon that wonderful invention of his. [*Goes by passage door.*]

GREGERS: [*approaches* HEDVIG] I can see by your face that you have not yet done it.

HEDVIG: What? Oh, that about the wild duck! No.

GREGERS: I suppose your courage failed when the time came?

HEDVIG: No, that wasn't it. But when I awoke this morning and remembered what we had been talking about it seemed so strange.

GREGERS: Strange?

HEDVIG: Yes, I don't know — Yesterday evening, at the moment, I thought there was something so delightful about it; but since I have slept and thought of it again, it somehow doesn't seem worth while.

GREGERS: Ah, I thought you could not have grown up quite unharmed in this house.

HEDVIG: I don't care about that, if only Father would come up —

GREGERS: Oh, if only your eyes had been opened to that which gives life its value — if you possessed the true, joyous, fearless spirit of sacrifice you would soon see how he would come up to you. But I believe in you still, Hedvig.

[*He goes out by the passage door.* HEDVIG *wanders about the room for a time; she is on the point of going into the kitchen when a knock is heard at the garret door.* HEDVIG *goes over and opens it a little;* OLD EKDAL *comes out; she pushes the door to again.*]

EKDAL: H'm, it's not much fun to take a morning walk alone.

HEDVIG: Wouldn't you like to go shooting, Grandfather?

EKDAL: It's not the weather for it today. It's so dark there you can scarcely see where you're going.

HEDVIG: Do you never want to shoot anything besides the rabbits?

EKDAL: Do you think the rabbits aren't good enough?

HEDVIG: Yes, but what about the wild duck?

EKDAL: Ho-ho! Are you afraid I shall shoot your wild duck? Never in the world. Never!

HEDVIG: No, I suppose you couldn't; they say it's very difficult to shoot wild ducks.

EKDAL: Couldn't! Should rather think I could.

HEDVIG: How would you set about it, Grandfather? I don't mean with my wild duck, but with others.

EKDAL: I should take care to shoot them in the breast, you know; that's the surest place. And then you must shoot against the feathers, you see — not the way of the feathers.

HEDVIG: Do they die then, Grandfather?

EKDAL: Yes they die right enough — when you shoot properly. Well, I must go and brush up a bit. H'm — understand — h'm. [*Goes into his room.*]

[HEDVIG *waits a little, glances toward the sitting-room door, goes over to the bookcase, stands on tiptoe, takes the double-barreled pistol down from the shelf and looks at it.* GINA, *with brush and duster, comes from the sitting room.* HEDVIG *hastily lays down the pistol unobserved.*]

GINA: Don't stand raking amongst Father's things. Hedvig.

HEDVIG: [*goes away from the bookcase*] I was only going to tidy up a little.

GINA: You'd better go into the kitchen and see if the coffee's still hot; I'll take his breakfast on a tray when I go down to him.

[HEDVIG *goes out.* GINA *begins to sweep and clean up the studio. Presently the passage door is opened with hesitation and* HIALMAR EKDAL *looks in. He has on his overcoat but not his hat; he is unwashed, and his hair is disheveled and unkempt. His eyes are dull and heavy.*]

GINA: [*standing with the brush in her hand and looking at him.*] Oh, there now, Ekdal — so you've come after all?

HIALMAR: [*comes in and answers in a toneless voice*] I come — only to depart immediately.

GINA: Yes, yes, I suppose so. But Lord help us! what a sight you are!

HIALMAR: A sight?

GINA: And your nice winter coat too! Well, that's done for.

HEDVIG: [*at the kitchen door*] Mother, hadn't I better — [*Sees* HIALMAR, *gives a loud scream of joy and runs to him*] Oh, Father, Father!

HIALMAR: [*turns away and makes a gesture of repulsion*] Away, away, away! [*to* GINA] Keep her away from me, I say!

GINA: [*in a low tone*] Go into the sitting room, Hedvig.
          [HEDVIG *does so without a word.*]

HIALMAR: [*fussily pulls out the table drawer*] I must have my books with me. Where are my books?

GINA: Which books?

HIALMAR: My scientific books, of course; the technical magazines I require for my invention.

GINA: [*searches in the bookcase*] Is it these here papercovered ones?

HIALMAR: Yes, of course.

GINA: [*lays a heap of magazines on the table*] Shan't I get Hedvig to cut them for you?

HIALMAR: I don't require to have them cut for me.
          [*Short silence.*]

GINA: Then you're still set on leaving us, Ekdal?

HIALMAR: [*rummaging amongst the books*] Yes, that is a matter of course, I should think.

GINA: Well, well.

HIALMAR: [*vehemently*] How can I live here, to be stabbed to the heart every hour of the day?

GINA: God forgive you for thinking such vile things of me.

HIALMAR: Prove —

GINA: I think it's you as has got to prove.

HIALMAR: After a past like yours? There are certain claims — I may almost call them claims of the ideal —

GINA: But what about Grandfather? What's to become of him, poor dear?

HIALMAR: I know my duty; my helpless father will come with me. I am going out into the town to make arrangements — H'm [*hesitatingly*] — has anyone found my hat on the stairs?

GINA: No. Have you lost your hat?

HIALMAR: Of course I had it on when I came in last night — there's no doubt about that — but I couldn't find it this morning.

GINA: Lord help us! Where have you been to with those two ne'er-do-wells?

HIALMAR: Oh, don't bother me about trifles. Do you suppose I am in the mood to remember details?

GINA: If only you haven't caught cold, Ekdal — [*Goes out into the kitchen.*]

HIALMAR: [*talks to himself in a low tone of irritation while he empties the table drawer*] You're a scoundrel, Relling! You're a low fellow! Ah, you shameless tempter! I wish I could get someone to stick a knife into you! [*He lays some old letters on one side, finds the torn document of yesterday, takes it up and looks at the pieces, puts it down hurriedly as* GINA *enters.*]

GINA: [*sets a tray with coffee, etc., on the table*] Here's a drop of something hot, if you'd fancy it. And there's some bread and butter and a snack of meat.

HIALMAR: [*glancing at the tray*] Meat? Never under this roof! It's true I have not had a mouthful of solid food for nearly twenty-four hours, but no matter. My memoranda! The commencement of my autobiography! What has become of my diary and all my important papers? [*opens the sitting-room door but draws back*] She is there too!

GINA: Good lord! the child must be somewhere!

HIALMAR: Come out.

[*He makes room;* HEDVIG *comes, scared, into the studio.*]

HIALMAR: [*with his hand on the door handle, says to* GINA] In these, the last moments I spend in my former home, I wish to be spared from interlopers.

[*Goes into the room.*]

HEDVIG: [*with a bound toward her mother, asks softly, trembling*] Does that mean me?

GINA: Stay out in the kitchen, Hedvig; or, no — you'd best go into your own room. [*speaks to* HIALMAR *as she goes in to him*] Wait a bit, Ekdal; don't rummage so in the drawers. I know where everything is.

HEDVIG: [*stands a moment immovable, in terror and perplexity, biting her lips to keep the tears; then she clenches her hands convulsively and says softly*] The wild duck! [*She steals over and takes the pistol from the shelf, opens the garret door a little way, creeps in and draws the door to after her.* HIALMAR *and* GINA *can be heard disputing in the sitting room.*]

HIALMAR: [*comes in with some manuscript books and old loose papers which he lays upon the table*] That portmanteau is of no use! There are a thousand and one things I must drag with me.

GINA: [*following with the portmanteau*] Why not leave all the rest for the present and only take a shirt and a pair of woolen drawers with you?

HIALMAR: Whew! All these exhausting preparations! [*Pulls off his overcoat and throws it upon the sofa.*]

GINA: And there's the coffee getting cold.

HIALMAR: H'm [*Drinks a mouthful without thinking of it and then another.*]

GINA: [*dusting the backs of the chairs*] A nice job you'll have to find such another big garret for the rabbits.

HIALMAR: What! Am I to drag all those rabbits with me too?

GINA: You don't suppose Grandfather can get on without his rabbits.

HIALMAR: He must just get used to doing without them. Have not *I* to sacrifice very much greater things than rabbits!

GINA: [*dusting the bookcase*] Shall I put the flute in the portmanteau for you?

HIALMAR: No. No flute for me. But give me the pistol!

GINA: Do you want to take the pistol with you?

HIALMAR: Yes. My loaded pistol.

GINA: [*searching for it*] It's gone. He must have taken it in with him.

HIALMAR: Is he in the garret?

GINA: Yes, of course he's in the garret.

HIALMAR: H'm — poor lonely old man. [*He takes a piece of bread and butter, eats it and finishes his cup of coffee.*]

GINA: And if we hadn't have let that room, you could have moved in there.

HIALMAR: And continued to live under the same roof with — Never — never!

GINA: But couldn't you put up with the sitting room for a day or two? You could have it all to yourself.

HIALMAR: Never within these walls!

GINA: Well, then, down with Relling and Molvik.

HIALMAR: Don't mention those wretches' names to me! The very thought of them almost takes away my appetite. Oh no, I must go out into the storm and the snowdrift — go from house to house and seek shelter for my father and myself.

GINA: But you've got no hat, Ekdal! You've gone and lost your hat, you know.

HIALMAR: Oh, those two brutes, those slaves of all the vices! A hat must be found. [*takes another piece of bread and butter*] Some arrangements must be made. For I have no mind to throw away my life either. [*Looks for something on the tray.*]

GINA: What are you looking for?

HIALMAR: Butter.

GINA: I'll get some at once. [*Goes out into the kitchen.*]

HIALMAR: [*calls after her*] Oh, it doesn't matter; dry bread is good enough for me.

GINA: [*brings a dish of butter*] Look here; this is fresh churned.

[*She pours out another cup of coffee for him; he seats himself on the sofa, spreads more butter on the already buttered bread and eats and drinks a while in silence.*]

HIALMAR: Could I, without being subject to intrusion — intrusion of any sort — could I live in the sitting room there for a day or two?

GINA: Yes, to be sure you could, if you only would.

HIALMAR: For I see no possibility of getting all Father's things out in such a hurry.

GINA: And, besides, you've surely got to tell him first as you don't mean to live with us others nor more.

HIALMAR: [*pushes away his coffee cup*] Yes, there is that too; I shall have to lay bare the whole tangled story to him — I must turn matters over; I must have breathing time. I cannot take all these burdens on my shoulders in a single day.

GINA: No, especially in such horrible weather as it is outside.

HIALMAR: [*touching* WERLE's *letter*] I see that paper still lying about here.

GINA: Yes, I haven't touched it.

HIALMAR: So far as I am concerned it is mere wastepaper—

GINA: Well, *I* have certainly no notion of making any use of it.

HIALMAR: —but we had better not let it get lost all the same, in all the upset when I move it might easily—

GINA: I'll take good care of it, Ekdal.

HIALMAR: The donation is in the first instance made to Father, and it rests with him to accept or decline it.

GINA: [*sighs*] Yes, poor old Father—

HIALMAR: To make quite safe— Where shall I find some glue?

GINA: [*goes to the bookcase*] Here's the glue pot.

HIALMAR: And a brush?

GINA: The brush is here too. [*Brings him the things.*]

HIALMAR: [*takes a pair of scissors*] Just a strip of paper at the back— [*clips and glues*] Far be it from me to lay hands upon what is not my own — and least of all upon what belongs to a destitute old man — and to— the other as well. There now! Let it lie there for a time, and when it is dry take it away. I wish never to see that document again. Never!

[GREGERS WERLE *enters from the passage.*]

GREGERS: [*somewhat surprised*] What— are you sitting here, Hialmar?

HIALMAR: [*rises hurriedly*] I had sunk down from fatigue.

GREGERS: You have been having breakfast, I see.

HIALMAR: The body sometimes makes its claims felt too.

GREGERS: What have you decided to do?

HIALMAR: For a man like me there is only one course possible. I am just putting my most important things together. But it takes time, you know.

GINA: [*with a touch of impatience*] Am I to get the room ready for you or am I to pack your suitcase?

HIALMAR: [*after a glance of annoyance at* GREGERS] Pack— and get the room ready!

GINA: [*takes the portmanteau*] Very well; then I'll put in the shirt and the other things. [*Goes into the sitting room and draws the door to after her.*]

GREGERS: [*after a short silence*] I never dreamed that this would be the end of it. Do you really feel it a necessity to leave house and home?

HIALMAR: [*wanders about restlessly*] What would you have me do? I am not fitted to bear unhappiness, Gregers. I must feel secure and at peace in my surroundings.

GREGERS: But can you not feel that here? Just try it. I should have thought you had firm ground to build upon now— if only you start afresh. And, remember, you have your invention to live for.

HIALMAR: Oh, don't talk about my invention. It's perhaps still in the dim distance.

GREGERS: Indeed!

HIALMAR: Why, great heavens, what would you have one invent? Other people have invented almost everything already. It becomes more and more difficult every day—

GREGERS: And you have devoted so much labor to it.

HIALMAR: It was that blackguard Relling that urged me to it.

GREGERS: Relling?

HIALMAR: Yes, it was he that first made me realize my aptitude for making some notable discovery in photography.

GREGERS: Aha — it was Relling!

HIALMAR: Oh, I have been so truly happy over it! Not so much for the sake of the invention itself as because Hedvig believed in it — believed in it with a child's whole eagerness of faith. At least I have been fool enough to imagine that she believed in it.

GREGERS: Can you really think Hedvig has been false toward you?

HIALMAR: I can think anything now. It is Hedvig that stands in my way. She will blot out the sunlight from my whole life.

GREGERS: Hedvig! Is it Hedvig you are talking of? How should she blot out your sunlight?

HIALMAR: [*without answering*] How unutterably I have loved that child! How unutterably happy I have felt every time I came home to my humble room and she flew to meet me with her sweet little blinking eyes. Oh, confiding fool that I have been! I loved her unutterably — and I yielded myself up to the dream, the delusion, that she loved me unutterably in return.

GREGERS: Do you call that a delusion?

HIALMAR: How should I know? I can get nothing out of Gina; and besides, she is totally blind to the ideal side of these complications. But to you I feel impelled to open my mind, Gregers. I cannot shake off this frightful doubt — perhaps Hedvig has never really and honsestly loved me.

GREGERS: What would you say if she were to give you a proof of her love? [*listens*] What's that? I thought I heard the wild duck —

HIALMAR: It's the wild duck quacking. Father's in the garret.

GREGERS: Is he? [*his face lights up with joy*] I say you may yet have proof that your poor misunderstood Hedvig loves you!

HIALMAR: Oh, what proof can she give me? I dare not believe in any assurance from that quarter.

GREGERS: Hedvig does not know what deceit means.

HIALMAR: Oh, Gregers, that is just what I cannot be sure of. Who knows what Gina and that Mrs Sorby may many a time have sat here whispering and tattling about? And Hedvig usually has her ears open, I can tell you. Perhaps the deed of gift was not such a surprise to her after all. In fact, I'm not sure but that I noticed something of the sort.

GREGERS: What spirit is this that has taken possession of you?

HIALMAR: I have had my eyes opened. Just you notice — you'll see, the deed of gift is only a beginning. Mrs Sorby has always been a good deal taken up with Hedvig, and now she has the power to do whatever she likes for the child. They can take her from me whenever they please.

GREGERS: Hedvig will never, never leave you.

HIALMAR: Don't be so sure of that. If only they beckon to her and throw out a golden bait — And oh! I have loved her so unspeakably! I would have counted it my highest happiness to take her tenderly by the hand and lead her, as one leads a timid child through a great dark empty room! I am cruelly certain now that the poor photographer in his humble attic has never really and truly been anything to her. She has only cunningly contrived to keep on a good footing with him until the time came.

GREGERS: You don't believe that yourself, Hialmar.

HIALMAR: That is just the terrible part of it — I don't know what to believe — I never can know it. But can you really doubt that it must be as I say? Ho-ho, you have far to much faith in the claim of the ideal, my good Gregers! If those others came, with the glamour of wealth about them, and called to the child: "Leave him; come to us; here life awaits you —"

GREGERS: [*quickly*] Well, what then?

HIALMAR: If I then asked her: "Hedvig, are you willing to renounce that life for me?" [*laughs scornfully*] No, thank you! You would soon hear what answer I should get.

[*A pistol shot is heard from within the garret.*]

GREGERS: [*loudly and joyfully*] Hialmar!

HIALMAR: There now; he must needs go shooting too.

GINA: [*comes in*] Oh, Ekdal, I can hear Grandfather blazing away in the garret by himself.

HIALMAR: I'll look in —

GREGERS: [*eagerly, with emotion*] Wait a moment! Do you know what that was?

HIALMAR: Yes, of course I know.

GREGERS: No, you don't know. But *I* do. That was the proof!

HIALMAR: What proof?

GREGERS: It was a child's free-will offering. She has got your father to shoot the wild duck.

HIALMAR: To shoot the wild duck!

GINA: Oh, think of that!

HIALMAR: What was that for?

GREGERS: She wanted to sacrifice to you her most cherished possession, for then she thought you would surely come to love her again.

HIALMAR: [*tenderly, with emotion*] Oh, poor child!

GINA: What things she does think of!

GREGERS: She only wanted your love again, Hialmar. She could not live without it.

GINA: [*struggling with her tears*] There, you can see for yourself, Ekdal.

HIALMAR: Gina, where is she?

GINA: [*sniffs*] Poor dear, she's sitting out in the kitchen, I daresay.

HIALMAR: [*goes over, tears open the kitchen door and says*] Hedvig, come, come in to me! [*looks around*] No, she's not here.

GINA: Then she must be in her own little room.

HIALMAR: [*without*] No, she's not here either. [*comes in*] She must have gone out.

GINA: Yes, you wouldn't have her anywheres in the house.

HIALMAR: Oh, if she would only come home quickly, so that I can tell her — Everything will come right now, Gregers; now I believe we can begin life afresh.

GREGERS: [*quietly*] I knew it; I new the child would make amends.

[OLD EKDAL *appears at the door of his room; he is in full uniform and is busy buckling on his sword.*]

HIALMAR: [*astonished*] Father! Are you there?

GINA: Have you been firing in your room?

EKDAL: [*resentfully, approaching*] So you go shooting alone, do you, Hialmar?

HIALMAR: [*excited and confused*] Then it wasn't you that fired that shot in the garret?

EKDAL: Me that fired? H'm.

GREGERS: [*calls out to* HIALMAR] She has shot the wild duck herself!

HIALMAR: What can it mean? [*hastens to the garret door, tears it aside, looks in and calls loudly*] Hedvig!

GINA: [*runs to the door*] Good God! what's that?

HIALMAR: [*goes in*] She's lying on the floor!

GREGERS: Hedvig! Lying on the floor! [*Goes in to* HIALMAR.]

GINA: [*at the same time*] Hedvig! [*inside the garret*] No, no, no!

EKDAL: Ho-ho! Does she go shooting too now?

[HIALMAR, GINA *and* GREGERS *carry* HEDVIG *into the studio; in her dangling right hand she holds the pistol clasped in her fingers.*]

HIALMAR: [*distracted*] The pistol has gone off. She has wounded herself. Call for help! Help!

GINA: [*runs into the passage and calls down*] Relling! Relling! Doctor Relling, come up as quick as you can!

[HIALMAR *and* GREGERS *lay* HEDVIG *down on the sofa.*]

EKDAL: [*quietly*] The woods avenge themselves.

HIALMAR: [*on his knees beside* HEDVIG] She'll soon come to now. She's coming to; yes, yes, yes.

GINA: [*who has come in again*] Where has she hurt herself? I can't see anything.

[RELLING *comes hurriedly, and immediately after him* MOLVIK; *the latter without his waistcoat and necktie and with his coat open.*]

RELLING: What's the matter here?

GINA: They say Hedvig shot herself.

HIALMAR: Come and help us!

RELLING: Shot herself! [*He pushes the table aside and begins to examine her.*]

HIALMAR: [*kneeling and looking anxiously up at him*] It can't be dangerous? Speak, Relling! She is scarcely bleeding at all. It can't be dangerous?

RELLING: How did it happen?

HIALMAR: Oh, we don't know —

GINA: She wanted to shoot the wild duck.

RELLING: The wild duck?

HIALMAR: The pistol must have gone off.

RELLING: H'm. Indeed.

EKDAL: The woods avenge themselves. But I'm not afraid all the same. [*Goes into the garret and closes the door after him.*]

HIALMAR: Well, Relling, why don't you say something?

RELLING: The ball has entered the breast.

HIALMAR: Yes, but she's coming to!

RELLING: Surely you can see that Hedvig is dead.

GINA: [*bursts into tears*] Oh, my child, my child —

GREGERS: [*huskily*] In the depths of the sea —

HIALMAR: [*jumps up*] No, no, she must live! Oh, for God's sake, Relling — only a moment — only just till I can tell her how unspeakably I loved her all the time.

RELLING: The bullet has gone through her heart. Internal hemorrhage. Death must have been instantaneous.

HIALMAR: And I! I hunted her from me like an animal! And she crept terrified into the garret and died for love of me! [*sobbing*] I can never atone to her! I can never tell her — [*clenches his hands and cries upward*] Oh, Thou above — if Thou be indeed! Why hast Thou done this thing to me?

GINA: Hush, hush, you mustn't go on that awful way. We had no right to keep her, I suppose.

MOLVIK: The child is not dead but sleepeth.

RELLING: Bosh!

HIALMAR: [*becomes calm, goes over the the sofa, folds his arms and looks at* HEDVIG] There she lies so stiff and still.

RELLING: [*tries to loosen the pistol*] She's holding it so tight, so tight.

GINA: No, no, Relling; don't break her fingers; let the pistol be.

HIALMAR: She shall take it with her.

GINA: Yes, let her. But the child mustn't lie here for a show. She shall go to her own room, so she shall. Help me, Ekdal.

[HIALMAR *and* GINA *take* HEDVIG *between them.*]

HIALMAR: [*as they are carrying her*] Oh Gina, Gina, can you survive this?

GINA: We must help each other to bear it. For now, at least, she belongs to both of us.

MOLVIK: [*stretches out his arms and mumbles*] Blessed be the Lord; to earth thou shalt return; to earth thou shalt return —

RELLING: [*whispers*] Hold your tongue, you fool; you're drunk.

[HIALMAR *and* GINA *carry the body out through the kitchen door.* RELLING *shuts it after them.* MOLVIK *slinks out into the passage.*]

RELLING: [*goes over to* GREGERS *and says*] No one shall ever convince me that the pistol went off by accident.

GREGERS: [*who has stood terrified, with convulsive twitchings*] Who can say how the dreadful thing happened?

RELLING: The powder has burned the body of her dress. She must have pressed the pistol right against her breast and fired.

GREGERS: Hedvig has not died in vain. Did you not see how sorrow set free what is noble in him?

RELLING: Most people are ennobled by the actual presence of death. But how long do you suppose this nobility will last in him?

GREGERS: Why should it not endure and increase throughout his life?

RELLING: Before a year is over, little Hedvig will be nothing to him but a pretty theme for declamation.

GREGERS: How dare you say that of Hialmar Ekdal?

RELLING: We will talk of this again, when the grass has first withered on her grave. Then you'll hear him spouting about "the child too early torn from her father's heart"; then you'll see him steep himself in a syrup of sentiment and self-admiration and self-pity. Just you wait!

GREGERS: If you are right and I am wrong, then life is not worth living.

RELLING: Oh, life would be quite tolerable, after all, if only we could be rid of the confounded fools that keep on pestering us, in our poverty, with the claim of the ideal.

GREGERS: [*looking straight before him*] In that case I am glad that my destiny is what it is.

RELLING: May I inquire — what is your destiny?

GREGERS: [*going*] To be the thirteenth at table.

RELLING: The devil it is.

# Eugene O'Neill

# "The Hairy Ape"

## CHARACTERS

ROBERT SMITH, "YANK"
PADDY
LONG
MILDRED DOUGLAS
HER AUNT
SECOND ENGINEER
A GUARD
A SECRETARY OF AN ORGANIZATION
STOKERS, LADIES, GENTLEMEN, ETC.

## SCENES

SCENE I: The firemen's forecastle of an ocean liner — an hour after sailing from New York.
SCENE II: Section of promenade deck, two days out — morning.
SCENE III: The stokehole. A few minutes later.
SCENE IV: Same as Scene I. Half an hour later.
SCENE V: Fifth Avenue, New York. Three weeks later.
SCENE VI: An island near the city. The next night.
SCENE VII: In the city. About a month later.
SCENE VIII: In the city. Twilight of the next day.

## SCENE I

*The firemen's forecastle of a transatlantic liner an hour after sailing from New York for the voyage across. Tiers of narrow, steel bunks, three deep, on all sides. An entrance in rear. Benches on the floor before the bunks. The room is crowded with men, shouting, cursing, laughing, singing — a confused, inchoate uproar swelling into a sort of unity, a meaning — the bewildered, furious, baffled defiance of a beast in a cage. Nearly all the men are drunk. Many bottles are passed from hand to hand. All are dressed in dungaree pants, heavy ugly shoes. Some wear singlets, but the majority are stripped to the waist.*

*The treatment of this scene, or of any other scene in the play, should by no means be naturalistic. The effect sought after is a cramped space in the bowels of a ship, imprisoned by white steel. The lines of bunks, the uprights supporting them, cross each other like the steel framework of a cage. The ceiling crushes down upon the men's heads. They cannot stand upright. This accentuates the natural stooping posture which shoveling coal and the resultant over-development of back and shoulder muscles have given them. The men themselves should resemble those pictures in which the appearance of Neanderthal Man is guessed at. All are hairy-*

362

*chested, with long arms of tremendous power, and low, receding brows above their small, fierce, resentful eyes. All the civilized white races are represented, but except for the slight differentiation in color of hair, skin, eyes, all these men are alike.*

*The curtain rises on a tumult of sound.* YANK *is seated in the foreground. He seems broader, fiercer, more truculent, more powerful, more sure of himself than the rest. They respect his superior strength — the grudging respect of fear. Then, too, he represents to them a self-expression, the very last word in what they are, their most highly developed individual.*

VOICES:  Gif me trink dere, you!
'Ave a wet!
Salute!
Gesundheit!
Skoal!
Drunk as a lord, God stiffen you!
Here's how!
Luck!
Pass back that bottle, damn you!
Pourin' it down his neck!
Ho, Froggy! Where the devil have you been?
*La Touraine.*
I hit him smash in yaw, py Gott!
Jenkins — the First — he's a rotten swine —
And the coppers nabbed him — and I run —
I like peer better. It don't pig head gif you.
A slut, I'm sayin'! She robbed me aslape —
To hell with 'em all!
Your're a bloody liar!
Say dot again!
        [*Commotion. Two men about to fight are pulled apart.*]
No scrappin' now!
Tonight —
See who's the best man!
Bloody Dutchman!
Tonight on the for'ard square.
I'll bet on Dutchy.
He packa da wallop, I tella you!
Shut up, Wop!
No fightin', maties. We're all chums, ain't we?
        [*A voice starts bawling a song.*]
                Beer, beer, glorious beer!
                Fill yourselves right up to here.
YANK:  [*for the first time seeming to take notice of the uproar about him, turns around threateningly — in a tone of contemptuous authority*] Choke off dat noise! Where d'yuh get dat beer stuff? Beer, hell! Beer's for goils — and Dutchmen. Me for somep'n wit a kick to it! Gimme a drink, one of youse guys. [*Several bottles are eagerly offered. He takes a tremendous gulp at one of them; then, keeping the bottle in his hand, glares belligerently at the owner, who hastens to*

*acquiesce in this robbery by saying*] All righto, Yank. Keep it and have another. [YANK *contemptuously turns his back on the crowd again. For a second there is an embarrassed silence. Then* — ]

VOICES:  We must be passing the Hook.

She's beginning to roll to it.

Six days in hell — and then Southampton.

Py Yesus, I vish somepody take my first vatch for me!

Gittin seasick, Square-head?

Drink up and forget it!

What's in your bottle?

Gin.

Dot's nigger trink.

Absinthe? It's doped. You'll go off your chump, Froggy!

Cochon!

Whisky, that's the ticket!

Where's Paddy?

Going asleep.

Sing us that whisky song, Paddy.

> [*They all turn to an old, wizened Irishman who is dozing, very drunk, on the benches forward. His face is extremely monkey-like with all the sad, patient pathos of that animal in his small eyes.*]

Singa da song, Caruso Pat!

He's gettin' old. The drink is too much for him.

He's too drunk.

PADDY:  [*blinking about him, starts to his feet resentfully, swaying, holding on to the edge of a bunk*] I'm never too drunk to sing. 'Tis only when I'm dead to the world I'd be wishful to sing at all. [*with a sort of sad contempt*] "Whisky Johnny," ye want? A chanty, ye want? Now that's a queer wish from the ugly like of you, God help you. But no matther. [*He starts to sing in a thin, nasal, doleful tone.*]

> Oh, whisky is the life of man!
>> Whisky! O Johnny! [*They all join in on this.*]
> Oh, whisky is the life of man!
>> Whisky for my Johnny! [*Again chorus.*]
> Oh, whisky drove my old man mad!
>> Whisky! O Johnny!
> Oh, whisky drove my old man mad!
>> Whisky for my Johnny!

YANK:  [*again turning around scornfully*] Aw hell! Nix on dat old sailing ship stuff! All dat bull's dead, see? And you're dead, too, yuh damned old Harp, on'y yuh don't know it. Take it easy, see. Give us a rest. Nix on de loud noise. [*with a cynical grin*] Can't youse see I'm tryin to t'ink?

ALL:  [*repeating the word after him as one with the same cynical amused mockery*] Think! [*The chorused word has a brazen metallic quality as if their throats were phonograph horns. It is followed by a general uproar of hard, barking laughter.*]

VOICES:  Don't be cracking your head wit ut, Yank.

You gat headache, py yingo!

One thing about it — it rhymes with drink!
Ha, ha, ha!
Drink, don't think!
Drink, don't think!
Drink, don't think!

> [A whole chorus of voices has taken up this refrain, stamping on the floor, pounding on the benches with fists.]

YANK: [taking a gulp from his bottle — good-naturedly] Aw right. Can de noise. I got yuh de foist time. [The uproar subsides. A very drunken sentimental tenor begins to sing.]

> Far away in Canada,
> Far across the sea,
> There's a lass who fondly waits
> Making a home for me —

YANK: [fiercely contemptuous] Shut up, yuh lousy boob! Where d'yuh get dat tripe? Home? Home, hell! I'll make a home for yuh! I'll knock yuh dead. Home! T'hell wit home! Where d'yuh get dat tripe? Dis is home, see? What d'yuh want wit home? [proudly] I runned away from mine when I was a kid. On'y too glad to beat it, dat was me. Home was lickings for me, dat's all. But yuh can bet your shoit no one ain't never licked me since! Wanter try it, any of youse? Huh! I guess not. [in a more placated but still contemptuous tone] Goils waitin' for yuh, huh? Aw, hell! Dat's all tripe. Dey don't wait for no one. Dey'd double-cross yuh for a nickel. Dey're all tarts, get me? Treat 'em rough, dat's me. To hell wit'em. Tarts, dat's what, de whole bunch of 'em.

LONG: [very drunk, jumps on a bench excitedly, gesticulating with a bottle in his hand] Listen 'ere, Comrades! Yank 'ere is right. 'E says this 'ere stinkin' ship is our 'ome. And 'e says as 'ome is 'ell. And 'e's right! This is 'ell. We lives in 'ell, Comrades — and right enough we'll die in it. [raging] And who's ter blame, I arsks yer? We ain't. We wasn't born this rotten way. All men is born free and ekal. That's in the bleedin' Bible, maties. But what d'they care for the Bible — them lazy, bloated swine what travels first cabin? Them's the ones. They dragged us down 'til we're on'y wage slaves in the bowels of a bloody ship, sweatin', burnin' up, eatin' coal dust! Hit's them's ter blame — the damned Capitalist clarss!

> [There had been a gradual murmur of contemptuous resentment rising among the men until now he is interrupted by a storm of catcalls, hisses, boos, hard laughter.]

VOICES: Turn it off!
Shut up!
Sit down!
Closa da face!
Tamn fool! [Etc.]

YANK: [standing up and glaring at LONG] Sit down before I knock yuh down! [LONG makes haste to efface himself. YANK goes on contemptuously.] De Bible, huh? De Cap'tlist class, huh? Aw nix on dat Salvation Army-Socialist bull. Git a soapbox! Hire a hall! Come and be saved, huh? Jerk us to Jesus, huh? Aw g'wan! I've listened to lots of guys like you, see. Yuh're all wrong. Wanter know what I t'ink? Yuh ain't no good for no one. Yuh're de bunk. Yuh ain't got no noive, get me? Yuh're yellow, dat's what. Yellow, dat's you. Say! What's dem slobs in de foist cabin got to do wit us? We're better men dan dey are, ain't we? Sure! One of us guys could clean up de whole mob wit one mit. Put one of 'em down here for one watch in de stokehole, what'd happen? Dey'd carry him off on a stretcher. Dem boids don't amount to nothin'. Dey're just baggage. Who makes dis old tub run? Ain't it us guys? Well den, we belong, don't we? We belong and dey don't. Dat's all. [A *loud chorus of approval.* YANK *goes on.*] As for dis bein' hell — aw, nuts! Yuh lost your noive, dat's what. Dis is a man's job, get me? It belongs. It runs dis tub. No stiffs need apply. But yuh're a stiff, see? Yuh're yellow, dat's you.

VOICES: [*with a great hard pride in them*]
Righto!
A man's job!
Talk is cheap, Long.
He never could hold up his end.
Divil take him!
Yank's right. We make it go.
Py Gott, Yank say right ting!
We don't need no one cryin' over us.
Makin' speeches.
Throw him out!
Yellow!
Chuck him overboard!
I'll break his jaw for him!
    [*They crowd around* LONG *threateningly.*]

YANK: [*half good-natured again — contemptuously*] Aw, take it easy. Leave him alone. He ain't woith a punch. Drink up. Here's how, whoever owns dis. [*He takes a long swallow from his bottle. All drink with him. In a flash all is hilarious amiability again, back-slapping, loud talk, etc.*]

PADDY: [*who has been sitting in a blinking, melancholy daze — suddenly cries out in a voice full of old sorrow*] We belong to this, you're saying? We make the ship to go, you're saying? Yerra then, that Almighty God have pity on us! [*His voice runs into the wail of a keen, he rocks back and forth on his bench. The men stare at him, startled and impressed in spite of themselves.*] Oh, to be back in the fine days of my youth, ochone! Oh, there was fine beautiful ships them days — clippers wid tall masts touching the sky — fine strong men in them — men that was sons of the sea as if 'twas the mother that bore them. Oh, the clean skins of them, and the clear eyes, the straight backs and full chests of them! Brave men they was, and bold men surely! We'd be sailing out, bound down round the Horn maybe. We'd be making sail in the dawn, with a fair breeze, singing a chanty song wid no care to it. And astern the land would be sinking low and dying out, but we'd give it no heed but a laugh, and never a look behind. For the day that was, was enough, for we was free men — and I'm thinking 'tis only slaves do be giving heed to the day that's gone or the day to come — until they're old like me. [*with a sort of religious exaltation*] Oh, to be scudding south again wid the power of the Trade Wind driving her on steady through the nights and the days! Full sail on her! Nights and days! Nights when the foam of the wake would be flaming wid fire, when the sky'd be blazing and winking wid stars. Or the full of the moon maybe. Then you'd see her driving through the gray night, her sails stretching aloft all silver and white, not a sound on the deck, the lot of us dreaming dreams, till you'd believe 'twas no real ship at all you was on but a ghost ship like the *Flying Dutchman* they say does be roaming the seas forevermore widout touching a port. And there was the days, too. A warm sun on the clean decks. Sun warming the blood of you, and wind over the miles of shiny green ocean like strong drink to your lungs. Work — aye, hard work — but who'd mind that at all? Sure, you worked under the sky and 'twas work wid skill and daring to it. And wid the day done, in the dog watch, smoking me pipe at ease, the lookout would be raising land maybe, and we'd see the mountains of South Americy wid the red fire of the setting sun painting their white tops and the clouds floating by them! [*His tone of exaltation ceases. He goes on mournfully.*] Yerra, what's the use of talking? 'Tis a dead man's whisper. [*to* YANK *resentfully*] 'Twas them days men belonged to ships, not now. 'Twas them days a ship was part of the sea, and a man was part of a ship, and the sea joined all together and made it one. [*scornfully*] Is it one wid this you'd be, Yank — black smoke from the funnels smudging the sea, smudging the decks — the bloody engines pounding and throbbing and shaking — wid divil a sight of sun or a breath of clean air — choking our lungs wid coal dust — breaking our backs and hearts in the hell of the stokehole — feeding the bloody furnace — feeding our lives along wid the coal, I'm thinking — caged in by steel from a sight of the sky like bloody apes in the Zoo! [*with a harsh laugh*] Ho-ho, divil mend you! Is it to belong to that you're wishing? Is it a flesh and blood wheel of the engines you'd be?

YANK: [*who has been listening with a contemptuous sneer, barks out the answer*] Sure ting! Dat's me. What about it?

PADDY: [*as if to himself — with great sorrow*] Me time is past due. That a great wave wid sun in the heart of it may sweep me over the side sometime I'd be dreaming of the days that's gone!

YANK: Aw, yuh crazy Mick! [*He springs to his feet and advances on* PADDY *threateningly — then stops, fighting some queer struggle within himself — lets his hands fall to his sides — contemptuously.*] Aw, take it easy. Yuh're aw right, at dat. Yuh're bugs, dat's all — nutty as a cuckoo. All dat tripe yuh been pullin' — Aw, dat's all right. On'y it's dead, get me? Yuh don't belong no more, see. Yuh don't got de stuff. Yuh're too old. [*disgustedly*] But aw say, come up for air onct in a while, can't yuh? See what's happened since yuh croaked. [*He suddenly bursts forth vehemently, growing more and more excited.*] Say! Sure! Sure I meant it! What de hell — Say, lemme talk! Hey! Hey, you old Harp! Hey, youse guys! Say, listen to me — wait a moment — I gotter talk, see. I belong and he don't. He's dead but I'm livin'. Listen to me! Sure I'm part of de engines! Why de hell not! Dey move, don't dey? Dey're speed, ain't dey? Dey smash trou, don't dey! Twenty-five knots a hour! Dat's goin' some! Dat's new stuff! Dat belongs! But him, he's too old. He gets dizzy. Say, listen. All dat crazy tripe about nights and days; all dat crazy tripe about stars and moons; all dat crazy tripe about suns and winds, fresh air and de rest of it — Aw hell, dat's all a dope dream! Hittin' de pipe of de past, dat's what he's doin'. He's old and don't belong no more. But me, I'm young! I'm in de pink! I move wit it! It, get me! I mean de ting dat's de guts of all dis. It ploughs trou all de tripe he's been sayin'. It blows dat up! It knocks dat dead! It slams dat offen de face of de oith! It, get me! De engines and de coal and de smoke and all de rest of it! He can't breathe and swallow coal dust, but I kin, see? Dat's fresh air for me! Dat's food for me! I'm new, get me? Hell in de stokehole? Sure! It takes a man to work in hell. Hell, sure, dat's my fav'rite climate. I eat it up! I git fat on it! It's me makes it hot! It's me makes it roar! It's me makes it move! Sure, on'y for me everything stops. It all goes dead, get me? De noise and smoke and all de engines movin' de woild, dey stop. Dere ain't nothin' no more! Dat's what I'm sayin'. Everyting else dat makes de woild move, somep'n makes it move. It can't move witout somep'n else, see? Den yuh get down to me. I'm at de bottom, get me! Dere ain't nothin' foither. I'm de end! I'm de start! I start somep'n and de woild moves! It — dat's me! — de new dat's moiderin' de old! I'm de ting in coal dat makes it boin; I'm steam and oil for de engines; I'm de ting in noise dat makes yuh hear it; I'm smoke and express trains and steamers and factory whistles; I'm de ting in gold dat makes it money! And I'm what makes iron into steel! Steel, dat stands for de whole ting! And I'm steel — steel — steel! I'm de muscles in steel, de punch behind it! [*As he says this he pounds with his fist against the steel bunks. All the men, roused to a pitch of frenzied self-glorification by his speech, do likewise. There is a deafening metallic roar, through which* YANK's *voice can be heard bellowing.*] Slaves, hell! We run de whole woiks. All de rich guys dat tink dey're somep'n, dey ain't nothin'! Dey don't belong. But us guys, we're in de move, we're at de bottom, de whole ting is us! [PADDY *from the start of* YANK's *speech has been taking one gulp after another from his bottle, at first frightenedly, as if he were afraid to listen, then desperately, as if to drown his senses, but finally has achieved complete indifferent, even amused, drunkenness.* YANK *sees his lips moving. He quells the uproar with a shout.*] Hey, youse guys, take it easy! Wait a moment! De nutty Harp is sayin' somep'n.

PADDY: [*is heard now — throws his head back a mocking burst of laughter*] Ho-ho-ho-ho-ho —

YANK: [*drawing back his fist, with a snarl*] Aw! Look out who yuh're givin' the bark!

PADDY: [*begins to sing the "Miller of Dee" with enormous good nature*]
                I care for nobody, no, not I,
                And nobody cares for me.

YANK: [*good-natured himself in a flash, interrupts* PADDY *with a slap on the bare back like a report*] Dat's de stuff! Now yuh're gettin' wise to somep'n. Care for nobody, dat's de dope! To hell wit 'em all! And nix on nobody else carin'. I kin care for myself, get me! [*Eight bells sound, muffled, vibrating through the steel walls as if some enormous brazen gong were imbedded in the heart of the ship. All the men jump up mechanically, file through the door silently close upon each other's heels in what is very like a prisoners' lockstep.* YANK *slaps* PADDY *on the back.*] Our watch, yuh old Harp! [*mockingly*] Come on down in hell. Eat up de coal dust. Drink in de heat. It's it, see! Act like yuh liked it, yuh better — or croak yuhself.

PADDY: [*with jovial defiance*] To the divil wid it! I'll not report this watch. Let thim log me and be damned. I'm no slave the like of you. I'll be sittin' here at me ease, and drinking, and thinking, and dreaming dreams.

YANK: [*contemptuously*] Tinkin' and dreamin', what'll that get yuh? What's tinkin'

got to do wit it? We move, don't we? Speed, ain't it? Fog, dat's all you stand
for. But we drive trou dat, don't we? We split dat up and smash trou —
twenty-five knots a hour! [*turns his back on* PADDY *scornfully*] Aw, yuh make
me sick! Yuh don't belong! [*He strides out the door in rear.* PADDY *hums to
himself, blinking drowsily.*]

CURTAIN

SCENE II

*Two days out. A section of the promenade deck.* MILDRED DOUGLAS *and her aunt are
discovered reclining in deck chairs. The former is a girl of twenty, slender, delicate,
with a pale, pretty face marred by a self-conscious expression of disdainful superiority. She looks fretful, nervous and discontented, bored by her own anemia. Her aunt
is a pompous and proud — and fat — old lady. She is a type even to the point of a
double chin and lorgnettes. She is dressed pretentiously, as if afraid her face alone
would never indicate her position in life.* MILDRED *is dressed all in white.*

 *The impression to be conveyed by this scene is one of the beautiful, vivid life
of the sea all about — sunshine on the deck in a great flood, the fresh sea wind
blowing across it. In the midst of this, these two incongruous, artificial figures, inert
and disharmonious, the elder like a gray lump of dough touched up with rouge, the
younger looking as if the vitality of her stock had been sapped before she was
conceived, so that she is the expression not of its life energy but merely of the
artificialities that energy had won for itself in the spending.*

MILDRED: [*looking up with affected dreaminess*] How the black smoke swirls back
 against the sky! Is it not beautiful?
AUNT: [*without looking up*] I dislike smoke of any kind.
MILDRED: My great-grandmother smoked a pipe — a clay pipe.
AUNT: [*ruffling*] Vulgar!
MILDRED: She was too distant a relative to be vulgar. Time mellows pipes.
AUNT: [*pretending boredom but irritated*] Did the sociology you took up at college
 teach you that — to play the ghoul on every possible occasion, excavating old
 bones? Why not let your great-grandmother rest in her grave?
MILDRED: [*dreamily*] With her pipe beside her — puffing in Paradise.
AUNT: [*with spite*] Yes, you are a natural born ghoul. You are even getting to look
 like one, my dear.
MILDRED: [*in a passionless tone*] I detest you, Aunt. [*looking at her critically*] Do you
 know what you remind me of? Of a cold pork pudding against a background of
 linoleum tablecloth in the kitchen of a — but the possibilities are wearisome.
 [*She closes her eyes.*]
AUNT: [*with a bitter laugh*] Merci for your candor. But since I am and must be your
 chaperon — in appearance, at least — let us patch up some sort of armed truce.
 For my part you are quite free to indulge any pose of eccentricity that beguiles
 you — as long as you observe the amenities —
MILDRED: [*drawling*] The inanities?
AUNT: [*going on as if she hadn't heard*] After exhausting the morbid thrills of social
 service work on New York's East Side — how they must have hated you, by
 the way, the poor that you made so much poorer in their own eyes! — you are

now bent on making your slumming international. Well, I hope Whitechapel
will provide the needed nerve tonic. Do not ask me to chaperon you there,
however. I told your father I would not. I loathe deformity. We will hire an
army of detectives and you may investigate everything — they allow you to
see.

MILDRED: [*protesting with a trace of genuine earnestness*] Please do not mock at my
attempts to discover how the other half lives. Give me credit for some sort of
groping sincerity in that at least. I would like to help them. I would like to be
some use in the world. Is it my fault I don't know how? I would like to be
sincere, to touch life somewhere. [*with weary bitterness*] But I'm afraid I have
neither the vitality nor integrity. All that was burnt out in our stock before I was
born. Grandfather's blast furnaces, flaming to the sky, melting steel, making
millions — then father keeping those home fires burning, making more
millions — and little me at the tail-end of it all. I'm a waste product in the
Bessemer process — like the millions. Or rather, I inherit the acquired trait of
the by-product, wealth, but none of the energy, none of the strength of the
steel that made it. I am sired by gold and damned by it, as they say at the race
track — damned in more ways than one. [*She laughs mirthlessly.*]

AUNT: [*unimpressed — superciliously*] You seem to be going in for sincerity today. It
isn't becoming to you, really — except as an obvious pose. Be as artificial as you
are, I advise. There's a sort of sincerity in that, you know. And, after all, you
must confess you like that better.

MILDRED: [*again affected and bored*] Yes, I suppose I do. Pardon me for my outburst. When a leopard complains of its spots, it must sound rather grotesque.
[*in a mocking tone*] Purr, little leopard. Purr, scratch, tear, kill, gorge yourself
and be happy — only stay in the jungle where your spots are camouflage. In a
cage they make you conspicuous.

AUNT: I don't know what you are talking about.

MILDRED: It would be rude to talk about anything to you. Let's just talk. [*She looks at
her wrist watch.*] Well, thank goodness, it's about time for them to come for
me. That ought to give me a new thrill, Aunt.

AUNT: [*affectedly troubled*] You don't mean to say you're really going? The dirt —
the heat must be frightful —

MILDRED: Grandfather started as a puddler. I should have inherited an immunity to
heat that would make a salamander shiver. It will be fun to put it to the test.

AUNT: But don't you have to have the captain's — or someone's — permission to
visit the stokehole?

MILDRED: [*with a triumphant smile*] I have it — both his and the chief engineer's.
Oh, they didn't want to at first, in spite of my social service credentials. They
didn't seem a bit anxious that I should investigate how the other half lives and
works on a ship. So I had to tell them that my father, the president of Nazareth
Steel, chairman of the board of directors of this line, had told me it would be all
right.

AUNT: He didn't.

MILDRED: How naïve age makes one! But I said he did, Aunt. I even said he had
given me a letter to them — which I had lost. And they were afraid to take the
chance that I might be lying. [*excitedly*] So it's ho! for the stokehole. The
second engineer is to escort me. [*looking at her watch again*] It's time. And
here he comes, I think.

[*The* SECOND ENGINEER *enters. He is a husky, fine-looking man of thirty-five or so. He stops before the two and tips his cap, visibly embarrassed and ill-at-ease.*]

SECOND ENGINEER: Miss Douglas?

MILDRED: Yes. [*throwing off her rugs and getting to her feet*] Are we all ready to start?

SECOND ENGINEER: In just a second, ma'am. I'm waiting for the Fourth. He's coming along.

MILDRED: [*with a scornful smile*] You don't care to shoulder this responsibility alone, is that it?

SECOND ENGINEER: [*forcing a smile*] Two are better than one. [*disturbed by her eyes, glances out to sea—blurts out*] A fine day we're having.

MILDRED: Is it?

SECOND ENGINEER: A nice warm breeze—

MILDRED: It feels cold to me.

SECOND ENGINEER: But it's hot enough in the sun—

MILDRED: Not hot enough for me. I don't like Nature. I was never athletic.

SECOND ENGINEER: [*forcing a smile*] Well, you'll find it hot enough where you're going.

MILDRED: Do you mean hell?

SECOND ENGINEER: [*flabbergasted, decides to laugh*] Ho-ho! No, I mean the stoke-hole.

MILDRED: My grandfather was a puddler. He played with boiling steel.

SECOND ENGINEER: [*all at sea—uneasily*] Is that so? Hum, you'll excuse me, ma'am, but are you intending to wear that dress?

MILDRED: Why not?

SECOND ENGINEER: You'll likely rub against oil and dirt. It can't be helped.

MILDRED: It doesn't matter. I have lots of white dresses.

SECOND ENGINEER: I have an old coat you might throw over—

MILDRED: I have fifty dresses like this. I will throw this one into the sea when I come back. That ought to wash it clean, don't you think?

SECOND ENGINEER: [*doggedly*] There's ladders to climb down that are none too clean—and dark alleyways—

MILDRED: I will wear this very dress and none other.

SECOND ENGINEER: No offense meant. It's none of my business. I was only warning you—

MILDRED: Warning? That sounds thrilling.

SECOND ENGINEER: [*looking down the deck—with a sigh of relief*] There's the Fourth now. He's waiting for us. If you'll come—

MILDRED: Go on. I'll follow you. [*He goes.* MILDRED *turns a mocking smile on her aunt.*] An oaf—but a handsome, virile oaf.

AUNT: [*scornfully*] Poser!

MILDRED: Take care. He said there were dark alleyways—

AUNT: [*in the same tone*] Poser!

MILDRED: [*biting her lips angrily*] You are right. But would that my millions were not so anemically chaste!

AUNT: Yes, for a fresh pose I have no doubt you would drag the name of Douglas in the gutter!

MILDRED: From which it sprang. Good-by, Aunt. Don't pray too hard that I may fall into the fiery furnace.

AUNT:  Poser!

MILDRED:  [*viciously*] Old hag! [*She slaps her aunt insultingly across the face and walks off, laughing gaily.*]

AUNT:  [*screams after her*] I said poser!

CURTAIN

## SCENE III

*The stokehole. In the rear, the dimly-outlined bulks of the furnaces and boilers. High overhead one hanging electric bulb sheds just enough light through the murky air laden with coal dust to pile up masses of shadows everywhere. A line of men, stripped to the waist, is before the furnace doors. They bend over, looking neither to right nor left, handling their shovels as if they were part of their bodies, with a strange, awkward, swinging rhythm. They use the shovels to throw open the furnace doors. Then from these fiery round holes in the black a flood of terrific light and heat pours full upon the men who are outlined in silhouette in the crouching, inhuman attitudes of chained gorillas. The men shovel with a rhythmic motion, swinging as on a pivot from the coal which lies in heaps on the floor behind to hurl it into the flaming mouths before them. There is a tumult of noise — the brazen clang of the furnace doors as they are flung open or slammed shut, the grating, teeth-gritting grind of steel against steel, of crunching coal. This clash of sounds stuns one's ears with its rending dissonance. But there is order in it, rhythm, a mechanical regulated recurrence, a tempo. And rising above all, making the air hum with the quiver of liberated energy, the roar of leaping flames in the furnaces, the monotonous throbbing beat of the engines.*

*As the curtain rises, the furnace doors are shut. The men are taking a breathing spell. One or two are arranging the coal behind them, pulling it into more accessible heaps. The others can be dimly made out leaning on their shovels in relaxed attitudes of exhaustion.*

PADDY:  [*from somewhere in the line — plaintively*] Yerra, will this divil's own watch nivir end? Me back is broke. I'm destroyed entirely.

YANK:  [*from the center of the line — with exuberant scorn*] Aw, yuh make me sick! Lie down and croak, why don't yuh? Always beefin', dat's you! Say, dis is a cinch! Dis was made for me! It's my meat, get me! [*A whistle is blown — a thin, shrill note from somewhere overhead in the darkness.* YANK *curses without resentment.*] Dere's de damn engineer crackin' de whip. He tinks we're loafin'.

PADDY:  [*vindictively*] God stiffen him!

YANK:  [*in an exultant tone of command*] Come on, youse guys! Git into de game! She's gittin' hungry! Pile some grub in her. Trow it into her belly! Come on now, all of youse! Open her up!

[*At this last all the men, who have followed his movements of getting into position, throw open their furnace doors with a deafening clang. The fiery light floods over their shoulders as they bend round for the coal. Rivulets of sooty sweat have traced maps on their backs. The enlarged muscles form bunches of high light and shadow.*]

YANK:  [*chanting a count as he shovels without seeming effort*] One — two — tree —

[*his voice rising exultantly in the joy of battle*] Dat's de stuff! Let her have it! All togedder now! Sling it into her! Let her ride! Shoot de piece now! Call de toin on her! Drive her into it! Feel her move! Watch her smoke! Speed, dat's her middle name! Give her coal, youse guys! Coal, dat's her booze! Drink it up, baby! Let's see yuh sprint! Dig in and gain a lap! Dere she go-o-es.

[*This last in the chanting formula of the gallery gods at the six-day bike race. He slams his furnace door shut. The others do likewise with as much unison as their wearied bodies will permit. The effect is of one fiery eye after another, being blotted out with a series of accompanying bangs.*]

PADDY: [*groaning*] Me back is broke. I'm bate out — bate —

[*There is a pause. Then the inexorable whistle sounds again from the dim regions above the electric light. There is a growl of cursing rage from all sides.*]

YANK: [*shaking his fist upward — contemptuously*] Take it easy dere, you! Who d'yuh tink's runnin' dis game, me or you? When I git ready, we move. Not before! When I git ready, get me!

VOICES: [*approvingly*]

> That's the stuff!
> Yank tal him, py golly!
> Yank ain't affeerd.
> Goot poy, Yank!
> Give 'im hell!
> Tell 'im 'e's a bloody swine!
> Bloody slave-driver!

YANK: [*contemptuously*] He ain't got no noive. He's yellow, get me? All de engineers is yellow. Dey got streaks a mile wide. Aw, to hell wit him! Let's move, youse guys. We had a rest. Come on, she needs it! Give her pep! It ain't for him. Him and his whistle, dey don't belong. But we belong, see! We gotter feed de baby! Come on!

[*He turns and flings his furnace door open. They all follow his lead. At this instant the* SECOND *and* FOURTH ENGINEERS *enter from the darkness on the left with* MILDRED *between them. She starts, turns paler, her pose is crumbling, she shivers with fright in spite of the blazing heat, but forces herself to leave the* ENGINEERS *and take a few steps nearer the men. She is right behind* YANK. *All this happens quickly while the men have their backs turned.*]

YANK: Come on, youse guys! [*He is turning to get coal when the whistle sounds again in a peremptory, irritating note. This drives* YANK *into a sudden fury. While the other men have turned full around and stopped dumbfounded by the spectacle of* MILDRED *standing there in her white dress,* YANK *does not turn far enough to see her. Besides, his head is thrown back, he blinks upward through the murk trying to find the owner of the whistle, he brandishes his shovel murderously over his head in one hand, pounding on his chest, gorilla-like, with the other, shouting.*] Toin off dat whistle! Come down outa dere, yuh yellow, brass-buttoned, Belfast bum, yuh! Come down and I'll knock yer brains out! Yuh lousy, stinkin', yellow mut of a Catholic-moiderin' bastard! Come down and I'll moider yuh! Pullin' dat whistle on me, huh? I'll show yuh! I'll crash yer skull in! I'll drive yer teet' down yer troat! I'll slam yer nose trou de back of yer head! I'll cut yer guts out for a nickel, yuh lousy boob, yuh dirty, crummy, muck-eatin' son of a — [*Suddenly he becomes conscious of all the other men staring at something directly behind his back. He whirls defensively with a snarling, murderous growl, crouching to spring, his lips drawn back over his teeth, his small eyes gleaming ferociously. He sees* MILDRED, *like a white apparition in the full light from the open furnace doors. He glares into her eyes, turned to stone. As for her, during his speech she has listened, paralyzed with horror, terror, her whole personality crushed, beaten in, collapsed, by the terrific impact of this unknown, abysmal brutality, naked and shameless. As she looks at his gorilla face, as his eyes bore into hers, she utters a low, choking cry and shrinks away from him, putting both hands up before her eyes to shut out the sight of his face, to protect her own. This startles* YANK *to a reaction. His mouth falls open, his eyes grow bewildered.*]

MILDRED: [*about to faint — to the* ENGINEERS, *who now have her one by each arm — whimperingly*] Take me away! Oh, the filthy beast!

[*She faints. They carry her quickly back, disappearing in the darkness at the left, rear. An iron door clangs shut. Rage and bewildered fury rush back on* YANK. *He feels himself insulted in some unknown fashion in the very heart of his pride. He roars.*]

YANK:  God damn yuh! [*and hurls his shovel after them at the door which has just closed. It hits the steel bulkhead with a clang and falls clattering on the steel floor. From overhead the whistle sounds again in a long, angry, insistent command.*]

CURTAIN

## SCENE IV

*The firemen's forecastle.* YANK'S *watch has just come off duty and had dinner. Their faces and bodies shine from a soap and water scrubbing but around their eyes, where a hasty dousing does not touch, the coal dust sticks like black make-up, giving them a queer, sinister expression.* YANK *has not washed either face or body. He stands out in contrast to them, a blackened, brooding figure. He is seated forward on a bench in the exact attitude of Rodin's "The Thinker." The others, most of them smoking pipes, are staring at* YANK *half-apprehensively, as if fearing an outburst; half-amusedly as if they saw a joke somewhere that tickled them.*

VOICES:  He ain't ate nothin'.
Py golly, a fallar gat to gat grub in him.
Divil a lie.
Yank feeda da fire, no feeda da face.
Ha-ha.
He ain't even washed hisself.
He's forgot.
Hey, Yank you forgot to wash.
YANK: [*sullenly*] Forgot nothin'! To hell wit washin'.
VOICES:  It'll stick to you.
It'll get under your skin.
Give yer the bleedin' itch, that's wot.

It makes spots on you — like a leopard.

Like a piebald nigger, you mean.

Better wash up, Yank.

You sleep better.

Wash up, Yank.

Wash up! Wash up!

YANK: [*resentfully*] Aw say, youse guys. Lemme alone. Can't youse see I'm tryin' to tink?

ALL: [*repeating the word after him as one with cynical mockery*] Think! [*The word has a brazen, metallic quality as if their throats were phonograph horns. It is followed by a chorus of hard, barking laughter.*]

YANK: [*springing to his feet and glaring at them belligerently*] Yes, tink! Tink, dat's what I said! What about it?

[*They are silent, puzzled by his sudden resentment at what used to be one of his jokes.* YANK *sits down again in the same attitude of "The Thinker."*]

VOICES: Leave him alone.

He's got a grouch on.

Why wouldn't he?

PADDY: [*with a wink at the others*] Sure I know what's the matther. 'Tis aisy to see. He's fallen in love, I'm telling you.

ALL: [*repeating the word after him as one with cynical mockery*] Love! [*The word has a brazen, metallic quality as if their throats were phonograph horns. It is followed by a chorus of hard, barking laughter.*]

YANK: [*with a contemptuous snort*] Love, hell! Hate, dat's what. I've fallen in hate, get me?

PADDY: [*philosophically*] 'Twould take a wise man to tell one from the other. [*with a bitter, ironical scorn, increasing as he goes on*] But I'm telling you it's love that's in it. Sure what else but love for us poor bastes in the stokehole would be bringing a fine lady, dressed like a white quane, down a mile of ladders and steps to be havin' a look at us? [*A growl of anger goes up from all sides.*]

LONG: [*jumping on a bench — hectically*] Hinsultin' us! Hinsultin' us, the bloody cow! And them bloody engineers! What right' as they got to be exhibitin' us's if we was bleedin' monkeys in a menagerie? Did we sign for hinsults to our dignity as 'onest workers? Is that in the ship's articles? You kin bloody well bet it ain't! But I knows why they done it. I arsked a deck steward 'o she was and 'e told me. 'Er old man's a bleedin' millionaire, a bloody Capitalist! 'E's got enuf bloody gold to sink this bleedin' ship! 'E makes arf the bloody steel in the world! 'E owns this bloody boat! And you and me, Comrades, we're 'is slaves! And the skipper and mates and engineers, they're 'is slaves! And she's 'is bloody daughter and we're all 'er slaves, too! And she gives 'er orders as 'ow she wants to see the bloody animals below decks and down they takes 'er!

[*There is a roar of rage from all sides.*]

YANK: [*blinking at him bewilderedly*] Say! Wait a moment! Is all dat straight goods?

LONG: Straight as string! The bleedin' steward as waits on 'em, 'e told me about 'er. And what're we goin 'ter do, I arsks yer? 'Ave we got ter swaller 'er hinsults like dogs? It ain't in the ship's articles. I tell yer we got a case. We kin go to law —

YANK: [*with abysmal contempt*] Hell! Law!

ALL: [*repeating the word after him as one with cynical mockery*] Law! [*The word has *a brazen metallic quality as if their throats were phonograph horns. It is followed by a chorus of hard, barking laughter.*]

LONG: [*feeling the ground slipping from under his feet — desperately*] As voters and citizens we kin force the bloody governments —

YANK: [*with abysmal contempt*] Hell! Governments!

ALL: [*repeating the word after him as one with cynical mockery*] Governments! [*The word has a brazen metallic quality as if their throats were phonograph horns. It is followed by a chorus of hard, barking laughter.*]

LONG: [*hysterically*] We're free and equal in the sight of God —

YANK: [*with abysmal contempt*] Hell! God!

ALL: [*repeating the word after him as one with cynical mockery*] God! [*The word has a brazen metallic quality as if their throats were phonograph horns. It is followed by a chorus of hard, barking laughter.*]

YANK: [*witheringly*] Aw, join de Salvation Army!

ALL: Sit down! Shut up! Damn fool! Sea-lawyer!
      [LONG *slinks back out of sight.*]

PADDY: [*continuing the trend of his thoughts as if he had never been interrupted — bitterly*] And there she was standing behind us, and the Second pointing at us like a man you'd hear in a circus would be saying: In this cage is a queerer kind of baboon than ever you'd find in darkest Africy. We roast them in their own sweat — and be damned if you won't hear some of thim saying they like it! [*He glances scornfully at* YANK.]

YANK: [*with a bewildered uncertain growl*] Aw!

PADDY: And there was Yank roarin' curses and turning round wid his shovel to brain her — and she looked at him, and him at her —

YANK: [*slowly*] She was all white. I tought she was a ghost. Sure.

PADDY: [*with heavy, biting sarcasm*] 'Twas love at first sight, divil a doubt of it! If you'd seen the endearin' look on her pale mug when she shriveled away with her hands over her eyes to shut out the sight of him! Sure, 'twas as if she'd seen a great hairy ape escaped from the Zoo!

YANK: [*stung — with a growl of rage*] Aw!

PADDY: And the loving way Yank heaved his shovel at the skull of her, only she was out the door! [*a grin breaking over his face*] 'Twas touching, I'm telling you! It put the touch of home, swate home in the stokehole. [*There is a roar of laughter from all.*]

YANK: [*glaring at* PADDY *menacingly*] Aw, choke dat off, see!

PADDY: [*not heeding him — to the others*] And her grabbin' at the Second's arm for protection. [*with a grotesque imitation of a woman's voice*] Kiss me, Engineer dear, for it's dark down here and me old man's in Wall Street making money! Hug me tight, darlin', for I'm afeerd in the dark and me mother's on deck makin eyes at the skipper! [*Another roar of laughter.*]

YANK: [*threateningly*] Say! What yuh tryin' to do, kid me, yuh old Harp?

PADDY: Divil a bit! Ain't I wishin' myself you'd brained her?

YANK: [*fiercely*] I'll brain her! I'll brain her yet, wait'n'see! [*coming over to* PADDY — *slowly*] Say, is dat what she called me — a hairy ape?

PADDY: She looked it at you if she didn't say the word itself.

YANK: [*grinning horribly*] Hairy ape, huh? Sure! Dat's de way she looked at me, aw right. Hairy ape! So dat's me, huh? [*bursting into rage — as if she were still in front of him*] Yuh skinny tart! Yuh white-faced bum, yuh! I'll show yuh who's a ape! [*turning to the others, bewilderment seizing him again*] Say, youse guys. I was bawlin' him out for pullin' de whistle on us. You heard me. And den I seen youse lookin' at somep'n and I tought he'd sneaked down to come up in back of me, and I hopped round to knock him dead wit de shovel. And dere she was wit de light on her! Christ, yuh coulda pushed me over with a finger! I was scared, get me? Sure! I tought she was a ghost, see? She was all in white like dey wrap around stiffs. You seen her. Kin yuh blame me? She didn't belong, dat's what. And den when I come to and seen it was a real skoit and seen de way she was lookin' at me — like Paddy said — Christ, I was sore, get me? I don't stand for dat stuff from nobody. And I flung de shovel — on'y she'd beat it. [*furiously*] I wished it'd banged her! I wished it'd knocked her block off!

LONG: And be 'anged for murder or 'lectrocuted? She ain't bleedin' well worth it.

YANK: I don't give a damn what! I'd be square wit her, wouldn't I? Tink I wanter let her put somep'n over on me? Tink I'm goin' to let her git away wit dat stuff? Yuh don't know me! No one ain't never put nothin' over on me and got away wit it, see! — not dat kind of stuff — no guy and no skoit neither! I'll fix her! Maybee she'll come down again —

VOICE: No chance, Yank. You scared her out of a year's growth.

YANK: I scared her? Why de hell should I scare her? Who de hell is she? Ain't she de same as me? Hairy ape, huh? [*with his old confident bravado*] I'll show her I'm better'n her, if she on'y knew it. I belong and she don't, see! I move and she's dead! Twenty five knots a hour, dat's me! Dat carries her but I make dat. She's on'y baggage. Sure! [*again bewilderedly*] But, Christ, she was funny lookin'! Did yuh pipe her hands? White and skinny. Yuh could see de bones through 'em. And her mush, dat was dead white, too. And her eyes, dey was like dey'd seen a ghost. Me, dat was! Sure! Hairy ape! Ghost, huh? Look at dat arm! [*He extends his right arm, swelling out the great muscles.*] I coulda took her wit dat, wit just my little finger even, and broke her in two. [*again bewilderedly*] Say, who is dat skoit, huh? What is she? What's she come from? Who made her? Who give her de noive to look at me like dat? Dis ting's got my goat right. I don't get her. She's new to me. What does a skoit like her mean, huh? She don't belong, get me! I can't see her. [*with growing anger*] But one ting I'm wise to, aw right, aw right! Youse all kin bet your skoits I'll git even wit her. I'll show her if she tinks she — She grinds de organ and I'm on de string, huh? I'll fix her! Let her come down again and I'll fling her in de furnace! She'll move den! She won't shiver at nothin', den! Speed, dat'll be her! She'll belong den! [*He grins horribly.*]

PADDY: She'll never come. She's had her belly-full, I'm telling you. She'll be in bed now, I'm thinking, wid ten doctors and nurses feedin' her salts to clean the fear out of her.

YANK: [*enraged*] Yuh tink I made her sick, too, do yuh? Just lookin' at me, huh? Hairy ape, huh? [*in a frenzy of rage*] I'll fix her! I'll tell her where to git off! She'll git down on her knees and take it back or I'll bust de face offen her! [*shaking one fist upward and beating on his chest with the other*] I'll find yuh! I'm comin', d'yuh hear? I'll fix yuh, God damn yuh! [*He makes a rush for the door.*]

VOICES: Stop him!

He'll get shot!
He'll murder her!
Trip him up!
Hold him!
He's gone crazy!
Gott, he's strong!
Hold him down!
Look out for a kick!
Pin his arms!
     [*They have all piled on him and, after a fierce struggle, by sheer weight of numbers have borne him to the floor just inside the door.*]

PADDY: [*who has remained detached*] Kape him down till he's cooled off. [*scornfully*] Yerra, Yank, you're a great fool. Is it payin' attention at all you are to the like of that skinny sow widout one drop of rale blood in her?

YANK: [*frenziedly, from the bottom of the heap*] She done me doit! She done me doit, didn't she? I'll get square wit her! I'll get her some way! Git offen me, youse guys! Lemme up! I'll show her who's a ape!

CURTAIN

SCENE V

*Three weeks later. A corner of Fifth Avenue in the Fifties on a fine Sunday morning. A general atmosphere of clean, well-tidied, wide street; a flood of mellow, tempered sunshine; gentle, genteel breezes. In the rear, the show windows of two shops, a jewelry establishment on the corner, a furrier's next to it. Here the adornments of extreme wealth are tantalizingly displayed. The jeweler's window is gaudy with glittering diamonds, emeralds, rubies, pearls, etc., fashioned in ornate tiaras, crowns, necklaces, collars, etc. From each piece hangs an enormous tag from which a dollar sign and numerals in intermittent electric lights wink out the incredible prices. The same in the furrier's. Rich furs of all varieties hang there bathed in a downpour of artificial light. The general effect is of a background of magnificence cheapened and made grotesque by commercialism, a background in tawdry disharmony with the clear light and sunshine on the street itself.*

*Up the side street* YANK *and* LONG *come swaggering.* LONG *is dressed in shore clothes, wears a black Windsor tie, cloth cap.* YANK *is in his dirty dungarees. A fireman's cap with black peak is cocked defiantly on the side of his head. He has not shaved for days and around his fierce, resentful eyes — as around those of* LONG *to a lesser degree — the black smudge of coal dust still sticks like makeup. They hesitate and stand together at the corner, swaggering, looking about them with a forced, defiant contempt.*

LONG: [*indicating it all with an oratorical gesture*] Well, 'ere we are. Fif' Avenoo. This 'ere's their bleedin private lane, as yer might say. [*bitterly*] We're trespassers 'ere. Proletarians keep orf the grass!

YANK: [*dully*] I don't see no grass, yuh boob. [*staring at the sidewalk*] Clean, ain't it? Yuh could eat a fried egg offen it. The white wings got some job sweepin' dis up. [*looking up and down the avenue — surlily*] Where's all de white-collar stiffs yuh said was here — and de skoits — *her* kind?

LONG: In church, blarst 'em! Arskin' Jesus to give 'em more money.

YANK: Choich, huh? I useter go to choich onct — sure — when I was a kid. Me old man and woman, dey made me. Dey never went demselves, dough. Always got too big a head on Sunday mornin', dat was dem. [with a grin] Dey was scrappers for fair, bot' of dem. On Satiday nights when dey bot' got a skinful dey could put up a bout oughter been staged at de Garden. When dey got trough dere wasn't a chair or table wit a leg under it. Or else dey bot' jumped on me for somep'n. Dat was where I loined to take punishment. [with a grin and a swagger] I'm a chip offen de old block, get me?

LONG: Did yer old man follow the sea?

YANK: Naw. Worked along shore. I runned away when me old lady croaked wit de tremens. I helped at truckin' and in de market. Den I shipped in de stokehole. Sure. Dat belongs. De rest was nothin'. [looking around him] I ain't never seen dis before. De Brooklyn waterfront, dat was where I was dragged up. [taking a deep breath] Dis ain't so bad at dat, huh?

LONG: Not bad? Well, we pays for it wiv our bloody sweat, if yer wants to know!

YANK: [with sudden angry disgust] Aw, hell! I don't see no one, see — like her. All dis gives me a pain. It don't belong. Say, ain't dere a back room around dis dump? Let's go shoot a ball. All dis is too clean and quiet and dolled-up, get me! It gives me a pain.

LONG: Wait and yer'll bloody well see —

YANK: I don't wait for no one. I keep on de move. Say, what yuh drag me up here for, anyway? Tryin' to kid me, yuh simp, yuh?

LONG: Yer wants to get back at 'er, don't yer? That's what yer been sayin' every bloomin' hour since she hinsulted yer.

YANK: [vehemently] Sure ting I do! Didn't I try to get even wit her in Southampton? Didn't I sneak on de dock and wait for her by de gangplank? I was goin' to spit in her pale mug, see! Sure, right in her pop-eyes! Dat woulda made me even, see? But no chanct. Dere was a whole army of plainclothes bulls around. Dey spotted me and gimme de bum's rush. I never seen her. But I'll git square wit her yet, you watch! [furiously] De lousy tart! She tinks she kin get away wit moider — but not wit me! I'll fix her! I'll tink of a way!

LONG: [as disgusted as he dares to be] Ain't that why I brought yer up 'ere — to show yer? Yer been lookin' at this 'ere 'ole affair wrong. Yer been actin' an' talkin' 's if it was all a bleedin' personal matter between yer and that bloody cow. I wants to convince yer she was on'y a representative of 'er clarss. I wants to awaken yer bloody clarss consciousness. Then yer'll see it's 'er clarss yer've got to fight, not 'er alone. There's a 'ole mob of 'em like 'er, Gawd blind 'em!

YANK: [spitting on his hands — belligerently] De more de merrier when I gits started. Bring on de gang!

LONG: Yer'll see 'em in arf a mo', when that church lets out. [He turns and sees the window display in the two stores for the first time.] Blimey! Look at that, will yer? [They both walk back and stand looking in the jeweler's. LONG flies into a fury.] Just look at this 'ere bloomin' mess! Just look at it! Look at the bleedin' prices on 'em — more'n our 'ole bloody stokehole makes in ten voyages sweatin' in 'ell! And they — 'er and 'er bloody clarss — buys 'em for toys to dangle on 'em! One of these 'ere would buy scoff for a starvin' family for a year!

YANK: Aw, cut de sob stuff! T'hell wit de starvin' family. Yuh'll be passin' de hat to me next. [*with naïve admiration*] Say, dem tings is pretty, huh? Bet yuh dey'd hock for a piece of change aw right. [*then turning away, bored*] But, aw hell, what good are dey? Let her have 'em. Dey don't belong no more'n she does. [*with a gesture of sweeping the jewelers into oblivion*] All dat don't count, get me?

LONG: [*who has moved to the furrier's — indignantly*] And I s'pose this 'ere don't neither — skins of poor, 'armless animals slaughtered so as 'er and 'ers can keep their bleedin' noses warm!

YANK: [*who has been staring at something inside — with queer excitement*] Take a slant at dat! Give it de once-over! Monkey fur — two t'ousand bucks! [*bewilderedly*] Is dat straight goods — monkey fur? What de hell — ?

LONG: [*bitterly*] It's straight enuf. [*with grim humor*] They wouldn't bloody well pay that for a 'airy ape's skin — no, nor for the 'ole livin' ape with all 'is 'ead, and body, and soul thrown in!

YANK: [*clenching his fists, his face growing pale with rage as if the skin in the window were a personal insult*] Trowin' it up in my face! Christ! I'll fix her!

LONG: [*excitedly*] Church is out. 'Ere they come, the bleedin' swine. [*after a glance at* YANK's *lowering face — uneasily*] Easy goes, Comrade. Keep yer bloomin' temper. Remember force defeats itself. It ain't our weapon. We must impress our demands through peaceful means — the votes of the onmarching proletarians of the bloody world!

YANK: [*with abysmal contempt*] Votes, hell! Votes is a joke, see. Votes for women! Let dem do it!

LONG: [*still more uneasily*] Calm, now. Treat 'em wiv the proper contempt. Observe the bleedin' parasites but 'old yer 'orses.

YANK: [*angrily*] Git away from me! Yuh're yellow, dat's what. Force, dat's me! De punch, dat's me every time, see!

> [*The crowd from church enter from the right, sauntering slowly and affectedly, their heads held stiffly up, looking neither to right nor left, talking in toneless, simpering voices. The women are rouged, calcimined, dyed, overdressed to the nth degree. The men are in Prince Alberts, high hats, spats, canes, etc. A procession of gaudy marionettes, yet with something of the relentless horror of Frankensteins in their detached, mechanical unawareness.*]

VOICES: Dear Doctor Caiaphas! He is so sincere!
What was the sermon? I dozed off.
About the radicals, my dear — and the false doctrines that are being preached.
We must organize a hundred percent American bazaar.
And let everyone contribute one one-hundredth percent of their income tax.
What an original idea!
We can devote the proceeds to rehabilitating the veil of the temple.
But that has been done so many times.

YANK: [*glaring from one to the other of them — with an insulting snort of scorn*] Huh! Huh! [*Without seeming to see him, they make wide detours to avoid the spot where he stands in the middle of the sidewalk.*]

LONG: [*frightenedly*] Keep yer bloomin' mouth shut, I tells yer.

YANK: [*viciously*] G'wan! Tell it to Sweeney! [*He swaggers away and deliberately lurches into a top-hatted gentleman, then glares at him pugnaciously.]* Say, who d'yuh tink yuh're bumpin'? Tink yuh own de oith?

GENTLEMAN: [*coldly and affectedly*] I beg your pardon. [*He has not looked at* YANK *and passes on without a glance, leaving him bewildered.*]

LONG: [*rushing up and grabbing* YANK'S *arm*] 'Ere! Come away! This wasn't what I meant. Yer'll 'ave the bloody coppers down on us.

YANK: [*savagely — giving him a push that sends him sprawling*] G'wan!

LONG: [*picks himself up — hysterically*] I'll pop orf then. This ain't what I meant. And whatever 'appens, yer can't blame me. [*He slinks off left.*]

YANK: T' hell wit youse! [*He approaches a lady — with a vicious grin and a smirking wink.*] Hello, Kiddo. How's every little ting? Got anyting on for tonight? I know an old boiler down to de docks we hin crawl into. [*The lady stalks by without a look, without a change of pace.* YANK *turns to others — insultingly.*] Holy smokes, what a mug! Go hide yuhself before de horses shy at yuh. Gee, pipe de heine on dat one! Say, youse, yuh look like de stoin of a ferryboat. Paint and powder! All dolled up to kill! Yuh look like stiffs laid out for de boneyard! Aw, g'wan, de lot of youse! Yuh give me de eye-ache. Yuh don't belong, get me! Look at me, why don't youse dare? I belong, dat's me! [*pointing to a skyscraper across the street which is in process of construction — with bravado*] See dat building goin' up dere? See de steel work? Steel, dat's me! Youse guys live on it and tink yuh'are somep'n. But I'm *in* it, see! I'm de hoistin' engine dat makes it go up! I'm it — de inside and bottom of it! Sure! I'm steel and steam and smoke and de rest of it! It moves — speed — twenty-five stories up — and me at de top and bottom — movin'! Youse simps don't move. Yuh're on'y dolls I winds up to see 'm spin. Yuh're de garbage, get me — de leavins — de ashes we dump over de side! Now, what 'a' yuh gotta say? [*But as they seem neither to see nor hear him, he flies into a fury.*] Bums! Pigs! Tarts! Bitches! [*He turns in a rage on the men, bumping viciously into them but not jarring them the least bit. Rather it is he who recoils after each collision. He keeps growling.*] Git off de oith! G'wan, yuh bum! Look where yuh're goin', can't yuh? Git outa here! Fight, why don't yuh? Put up yer mits! Don't be a dog! Fight or I'll knock yuh dead!

[*But, without seeming to see him, they all answer with mechanical affected politeness*]:

I beg your pardon. [*Then at a cry from one of the women, they all scurry to the furrier's window.*]

THE WOMAN: [*ecstatically, with a gasp of delight*] Monkey fur! [*The whole crowd of men and women chorus after her in the same tone of affected delight.*] Monkey fur!

YANK: [*with a jerk of his head back on his shoulders, as if he had received a punch full in the face — raging*] I see yuh, all in white! I see yuh, yuh white-faced tart, yuh! Hairy ape, huh? I'll hairy ape yuh!

[*He bends down and grips at the street curbing as if to pluck it out and hurl it. Foiled in this, snarling with passion, he leaps to the lamppost on the corner and tries to pull it up for a club. Just at that moment a bus is heard rumbling up. A fat, high-hatted, spatted gentleman runs out from the side street. He calls out plaintively:*] Bus! Bus! Stop there! [*and runs full tilt into the bending, straining* YANK, *who is bowled off his balance.*]

YANK: [*seeing a fight — with a roar of joy as he springs to his feet*] At last! Bus, huh? I'll bust yuh! [*He lets drive a terrific swing, his fist landing full on the fat gentleman's face. But the gentleman stands unmoved as if nothing had happened.*]

GENTLEMAN: I beg your pardon. [*then irritably*] You have made me lose my bus. [*He slaps his hands and begins to scream:*] Officer! Officer!

[*Many police whistles shrill out on the instant and a whole platoon of policemen rush in on* YANK *from all sides. He tries to fight but is clubbed to the pavement and fallen upon. The crowd at the window have not moved or noticed this disturbance. The clanging gong of the patrol wagon approaches with a clamoring din.*]

CURTAIN

## SCENE VI

*Night of the following day. A row of cells in the prison on Blackwells Island. The cells extend back diagonally from right front to left rear. They do not stop, but disappear in the dark background as if they ran on, numberless, into infinity. One electric bulb from the low ceiling of the narrow corridor sheds its light through the heavy steel bars of the cell at the extreme front and reveals part of the interior.* YANK *can be seen within, crouched on the edge of his cot in the attitude of Rodin's "The Thinker." His face is spotted with black and blue bruises. A blood-stained bandage is wrapped around his head.*

YANK: [*suddenly starting as if awakening from a dream, reaches out and shakes the bars — aloud to himself, wonderingly*] Steel. Dis is de Zoo, huh? [*A burst of hard, barking laughter comes from the unseen occupants of the cells, runs back down the tier, and abruptly ceases.*]

VOICES: [*mockingly*] The Zoo? That's a new name for this coop — a damn good name!

Steel, eh? You said a mouthful. This is the old iron house.

Who is that boob talkin'?

He's the bloke they brung in out of his head. The bulls had beat him up fierce.

YANK: [*dully*] I musta been dreamin'. I tought I was in a cage at de Zoo — but de apes don't talk, do dey?

VOICES: [*with mocking laughter*] You're in a cage aw right.

A coop!

A pen!

A sty!

A kennel! [*Hard laughter — a pause.*]

Say, guy! Who are you? No, never mind lying. What are you?

Yes, tell us your sad story. What's your game?

What did they jug yuh for?

YANK: [*dully*] I was a fireman — stokin' on de liners. [*then with sudden rage, rattling his cell bars*] I'm a hairy ape, get me? And I'll bust youse all in de jaw if yuh don't lay off kiddin' me.

VOICES: Huh! You're a hard boiled duck, ain't you!

When you spit, it bounces! [*Laughter.*]

Aw, can it. He's a regular guy. Ain't you?

What did he say he was—a ape?

YANK: [*defiantly*] Sure ting! Ain't dat what youse all are—apes?

    [A *silence. Then a furious rattling of bars from down the corridor.*]

A VOICE: [*thick with rage*] I'll show yuh who's a ape, yuh bum!

VOICES: Ssshh! Nix!

Can de noise!

Piano!

You'll have the guard down on us!

YANK: [*scornfully*] De guard? Yuh mean de keeper, don't yuh?

    [*Angry exclamations from all the cells.*]

VOICE: [*placatingly*] Aw, don't pay no attention to him. He's off his nut from the beatin'-up he got. Say, you guy! We're waitin' to hear what they landed you for—or ain't yuh tellin'?

YANK: Sure, I'll tell youse. Sure! Why de hell not? On'y—youse won't get me. Nobody gets me but me, see? I started to tell de Judge and all he says was: "Toity days to tink it over." Tink it over! Christ, dat's all I been doin' for weeks! [*after a pause*] I was tryin' to git even wit someone, see?—someone dat done me doit.

VOICES: [*cynically*] De old stuff, I bet. Your goil, huh?

Give yuh the double-cross, huh?

That's them every time!

Did yuh beat up de odder guy?

YANK: [*disgustedly*] Aw, yuh're all wrong! Sure dere was a skoit in it—but not what youse mean, not dat old tripe. Dis was a new kind of skoit. She was dolled up all in white—in de stokehole. I tought she was a ghost. Sure. [*A pause.*]

VOICES: [*whispering*] Gee, he's still nutty.

Let him rave. It's fun listenin'.

YANK: [*unheeding—groping in his thoughts*] Her hands—dey was skinny and white like dey wasn't real but painted on somep'n. Dere was a million miles from me to her—twenty-five knots a hour. She was like some dead ting de cat brung in. Sure, dat's what. She didn't belong. She belonged in de window of a toy store, or on de top of a garbage can, see! Sure! [*He breaks out angrily.*] But would yuh believe it, she had de noive to do me doit. She lamped me like she was seein' somep'n broke loose from de menagerie. Christ, yuh'd oughter seen her eyes! [*He rattles the bars of his cell furiously.*] But I'll get back at her yet, you watch! And if I can't find her I'll take it out on de gang she runs wit. I'm wise to where dey hangs out now. I'll show her who belongs! I'll show her who's in de move and who ain't. You watch my smoke!

VOICES: [*serious and joking*] Dat's de talkin'!

Take her for all she's got!

What was this dame, anyway? Who was she, eh?

YANK: I dunno. First cabin stiff. Her old man's a millionaire, dey says—name of Douglas.

VOICES: Douglas? That's the president of the Steel Trust, I bet.

Sure. I seen his mug in de papers.

He's filthy with dough.

VOICE: Hey, feller, take a tip from me. If you want to get back at that dame, you better join the Wobblies. You'll get some action then.

YANK: Wobblies? What de hell's dat?

VOICE: A gang of blokes — a tough gang. I been readin' about 'em today in the paper. The guard give me the *Sunday Times*. There's a long spiel about 'em. It's from a speech made in the Senate by a guy named Senator Queen. [*He is in the cell next to* YANK'S. *There is a rustling of paper.*] Wait'll I see if I got light enough and I'll read you. Listen. [*He reads.*] "There is a menace existing in this country today which threatens the vitals of our fair Republic — as foul a menace against the very life-blood of the American Eagle as was the foul conspiracy of Catiline against the eagles of ancient Rome!"

VOICE: [*disgustedly*] Aw, hell! Tell him to salt de tail of dat eagle!

VOICE: [*reading*] "I refer to that devil's brew of rascals, jailbirds, murderers and cutthroats who libel all honest working men by calling themselves the Industrial Workers of the World; but in the light of their nefarious plots, I call them the Industrious *Wreckers* of the World!"

YANK: [*with vengeful satisfaction*] Wreckers, dat's de right dope! Dat belongs! Me for dem!

VOICE: Ssshh! [*reading*] "This fiendish organization is a foul ulcer on the fair body of our Democracy —"

VOICE: Democracy, hell! Give him the boid, fellers — the raspberry! [*They do.*]

VOICE: Ssshh! [*reading*] "Like Cato I say to this Senate, the I. W. W. must be destroyed! For they represent an ever-present dagger pointed at the heart of the greatest nation the world has ever known, where all men are born free and equal, with equal opportunities to all, where the Founding Fathers have guaranteed to each one happiness, where Truth, Honor, Liberty, Justice, and the Brotherhood of Man are a religion absorbed with one's mother's milk, taught at our father's knee, sealed, signed, and stamped upon the glorious Constitution of these United States!" [*A perfect storm of hisses, catcalls, boos, and hard laughter.*]

VOICES: [*scornfully*] Hurrah for de Fort' of July!
Pass de hat!
Liberty!
Justice!
Honor!
Opportunity!
Brotherhood!

ALL: [*with abysmal scorn*] Aw, hell!

VOICE: Give that Queen Senator guy the bark! All togedder now — one — two — tree — [*A terrific chorus of barking and yapping.*]

GUARD: [*from a distance*] Quiet there, youse — or I'll git the hose.
[*The noise subsides.*]

YANK: [*with growling rage*] I'd like to catch dat senator guy alone for a second. I'd loin him some trute!

VOICE: Ssshh! Here's where he gits down to cases on the Wobblies. [*reads*] "They plot with fire in one hand and dynamite in the other. They stop not before murder to gain their ends, nor at the outraging of defenseless womanhood. They would tear down society, put the lowest scum in the seats of the mighty, turn Almighty God's revealed plan for the world topsy-turvy, and make of our sweet and lovely civilization a shambles, a desolation where man, God's masterpiece, would soon degenerate back to the ape!"

VOICE: [*to* YANK] Hey, you guy. There's your ape stuff again.

YANK: [*with a growl of fury*] I got him. So dey blow up tings, do dey? Dey turn tings round, do dey? Hey, lend me dat paper, will yuh?

VOICE: Sure. Give it to him. On'y keep it to yourself, see. We don't wanter listen to no more of that slop.

VOICE: Here you are. Hide it under your mattress.

YANK: [*reaching out*] Tanks. I can't read much but I kin manage. [*He sits, the paper in the hand at his side, in the attitude of Rodin's "The Thinker." A pause. Several snores from down the corridor. Suddenly* YANK *jumps to his feet with a furious groan as if some appalling thought had crashed on him — bewilderedly.*] Sure — her old man — president of de Steel Trust — makes half de steel in de world — steel — where I tought I belonged — drivin' trou — movin' — in dat — to make *her* — and cage me in for her to spit on! Christ! [*He shakes the bars of his cell door till the whole tier trembles. Irritated, protesting exclamations from those awakened or trying to get to sleep.*] He made dis — dis cage! Steel! *It* don't belong, dat's what! Cages, cells, locks, bolts, bars — dat's what it means! — holdin' me down wit him at de top! But I'll drive trou! Fire, dat melts it! I'll be fire — under de heap — fire dat never goes out — hot as hell — breakin' out in de night — [*While he has been saying this last he has shaken his cell door to a clanging accompaniment. As he comes to the "break-in' out" he seizes one bar with both hands and, putting his two feet up against the others so that his position is parallel to the floor like a monkey's, he gives a great wrench backwards. The bar bends like a licorice stick under his tremendous strength. Just at this moment the* PRISON GUARD *rushes in, dragging a hose behind him.*]

GUARD: [*angrily*] I'll loin youse bums to wake me up! [*sees* YANK] Hello, it's you, huh? Got the D. Ts., hey? Well, I'll cure 'em. I'll drown your snakes for yuh! [*noticing the bar*] Hell, look at dat bar bended! On'y a bug is strong enough for dat!

YANK: [*glaring at him*] Or a hairy ape, yuh big yellow bum! Look out! Here I come! [*He grabs another bar.*]

GUARD: [*scared now — yelling off left*] Toin de hose on, Ben! — full pressure! And call de others — and a straitjacket!

[*The curtain is falling. As it hides* YANK *from view, there is a splattering smash as the stream of water hits the steel of* YANK's *cell.*]

CURTAIN

## SCENE VII

*Nearly a month later. An I. W. W. local near the waterfront, showing the interior of a front room on the ground floor, and the street outside. Moonlight on the narrow street, buildings massed in black shadow. The interior of the room, which is general assembly room, office, and reading room, resembles some dingy settlement boys' club. A desk and high stool are in one corner. A table with papers, stacks of pamphlets, chairs about it, is at center. The whole is decidedly cheap, banal, commonplace and unmysterious as a room could well be. The secretary is perched on the stool making entries in a large ledger. An eye shade casts his face into shadows. Eight or ten men, longshoremen, iron workers, and the like, are grouped about the table. Two are playing checkers. One is writing a letter. Most of them are smoking pipes. A big signboard is on the wall at the rear, "Industrial Workers of the World — Local No. 57."*

> [YANK *comes down the street outside. He is dressed as in Scene Five. He moves cautiously, mysteriously. He comes to a point opposite the door; tiptoes softly up to it, listens, is impressed by the silence within, knocks carefully, as if he were guessing at the password to some secret rite. Listens. No answer. Knocks again a bit louder. No answer. Knocks impatiently, much louder.*]

SECRETARY: [*turning around on his stool*] What the hell is that — someone knocking? [*shouts*] Come in, why don't you?

> [*All the men in the room look up.* YANK *opens the door slowly, gingerly, as if afraid of an ambush. He looks around for secret doors, mystery, is taken aback by the commonplaceness of the room and the men in it, thinks he may have gotten in the wrong place, then sees the signboard on the wall and is reassured.*]

YANK: [*blurts out*] Hello.

MEN: [*reservedly*] Hello.

YANK: [*more easily*] I tought I'd bumped into de wrong dump.

SECRETARY: [*scrutinizing him carefully*] Maybe you have. Are you a member?

YANK: Naw, not yet. Dat's what I come for — to join.

SECRETARY: That's easy. What's your job — longshore?

YANK: Naw. Fireman — stoker on de liners.

SECRETARY: [*with satisfaction*] Welcome to our city. Glad to know you people are waking up at last. We haven't got many members in your line.

YANK: Naw. Dey're all dead to de woild.

SECRETARY: Well, you can help to wake 'em. What's your name? I'll make out your card.

YANK: [*confused*] Name? Lemme tink.

SECRETARY: [*sharply*] Don't you know your own name?

YANK: Sure; but I been just Yank for so long — Bob, dat's it — Bob Smith.

SECRETARY: [*writing*] Robert Smith. [*fills out the rest of card*] Here you are. Cost you half a dollar.

YANK: Is dat all — four bits? Dat's easy. [*gives the Secretary the money*]

SECRETARY: [*throwing it in drawer*] Thanks. Well, make yourself at home. No introductions needed. There's literature on the table. Take some of those pamphlets with you to distribute aboard ship. They may bring results. Sow the seed, only go about it right. Don't get caught and fired. We got plenty out of work. What we need is men who can hold their jobs — and work for us at the same time.

YANK: Sure. [*But he still stands, embarrassed and uneasy.*]

SECRETARY: [*looking at him — curiously*] What did you knock for? Think we had a coon in uniform to open doors?

YANK: Naw. I tought it was locked — and dat yuh'd wanter give me the once-over trou a peep-hole or somep'n to see if I was right.

SECRETARY: [*alert and suspicious but with an easy laugh*] Think we were running a crap game? That door is never locked. What put that in your nut?

YANK: [*with a knowing grin, convinced that this is all camouflage, a part of the secrecy*] Dis burg is full of bulls, ain't it?

SECRETARY: [*sharply*] What have the cops got to do with us? We're breaking no laws.

YANK: [*with a knowing wink*] Sure. Youse wouldn't for woilds. Sure. I'm wise to dat.

SECRETARY: You seem to be wise to a lot of stuff none of us knows about.

YANK: [*with another wink*] Aw, dat's aw right, see. [*then made a bit resentful by the suspicious glances from all sides*] Aw, can it! Youse needn't put me trou de toid degree. Can't youse see I belong? Sure! I'm reg'lar. I'll stick, get me? I'll shoot de woiks for youse. Dat's why I wanted to join in.

SECRETARY: [*breezily, feeling him out*] That's the right spirit. Only are you sure you understand what you've joined? It's all plain and above board; still, some guys get a wrong slant on us. [*sharply*] What's your notion of the purpose of the I. W. W.?

YANK: Aw, I know all about it.

SECRETARY: [*sarcastically*] Well, give us some of your valuable information.

YANK: [*cunningly*] I know enough not to speak outa my toin. [*then resentfully again*] Aw, say! I'm reg'lar. I'm wise to de game. I know yuh got to watch your step wit a stranger. For all youse know, I might be a plain-clothes dick, or somep'n, dat's what yuh're tinkin', huh? Aw, forget it! I belong, see? Ask any guy down to de docks if I don't.

SECRETARY: Who said you didn't?

YANK: After I'm 'nitiated, I'll show yuh.

SECRETARY: [*astounded*] Initiated? There's no initiation.

YANK: [*disappointed*] Ain't there no password — no grip nor nothin'?

SECRETARY: What'd you think this is — the Elks — or the Black Hand?

YANK: De Elks, hell! De Black Hand, dey're a lot of yellow back-stickin' Ginees. Naw. Dis is a man's gang, ain't it?

SECRETARY: You said it! That's why we stand on our two feet in the open. We got no secrets.

YANK: [*surprised but admiringly*] Yuh mean to say yuh always run wide open — like dis?

SECRETARY: Exactly.

YANK: Den yuh sure got your noive wit youse!

SECRETARY: [*sharply*] Just what was it made you want to join us? Come out with that straight.

YANK: Yuh call me? Well, I got noive, too! Here's my hand. Yuh wanter blow tings up, don't yuh? Well, dat's me! I belong!

SECRETARY: [*with pretended carelessness*] You mean change the unequal conditions of society by legitimate direct action — or with dynamite?

YANK: Dynamite! Blow if offen de oith — steel — all de cages — all de factories, steamers, buildings, jails — de Steel Trust and all dat makes it go.

SECRETARY: So — that's your idea, eh? And did you have any special job in that line you wanted to propose to us? [*He makes a sign to the men, who get up cautiously one by one and group behind* YANK.]

YANK: [*boldly*] Sure, I'll come out wit it. I'll show youse I'm one of de gang. Dere's dat millionaire guy, Douglas —

SECRETARY: President of the Steel Trust, you mean? Do you want to assassinate him?

YANK: Naw, dat don't get yuh nothin'. I mean blow up de factory, de woiks, where he makes de steel. Dat's what I'm after — to blow up de steel, knock all de steel in de woild up to de moon. Dat'll fix tings! [*eagerly, with a touch of bravado*] I'll do it by me lonesome! I'll show yuh! Tell me where his woiks is, how to get there, all de dope. Gimme de stuff, de old butter — and watch me do de rest! Watch de smoke and see it move! I don't give a damn if dey nab me — long as it's done! I'll soive life for it — and give 'em de laugh! [*half to himself*] And I'll write her a letter and tell her de hairy ape done it. Dat'll square tings.

SECRETARY: [*stepping away from* YANK] Very interesting. [*He gives a signal. The men, huskies all, throw themselves on* YANK *and before he knows it they have his legs and arms pinioned. But he is too flabbergasted to make a struggle, anyway. They feel him over for weapons.*]

MAN: No gat, no knife. Shall we give him what's what and put the boots to him?

SECRETARY: No. He isn't worth the trouble we'd get into. He's too stupid. [*He comes closer and laughs mockingly in* YANK'S *face.*] Ho-ho! By God, this is the biggest joke they've put up on us yet. Hey, you Joke! Who sent you — Burns or Pinkerton? No, by God, you're such a bonehead I'll bet you're in the Secret Service! Well, you dirty spy, you rotten agent provocator, you can go back and tell whatever skunk is paying you blood-money for betraying your brothers that he's wasting his coin. You couldn't catch a cold. And tell him that all he'll ever get on us, or ever has got, is just his own sneaking plots that he's framed up to put us in jail. We are what our manifesto says we are, neither more nor less — and we'll give him a copy of that any time he calls. And as for you — [*He glares scornfully at* YANK, *who is sunk in an oblivious stupor.*] Oh, hell, what's the use of talking? You're a brainless ape.

YANK: [*aroused by the word to fierce but futile struggles*] What's dat, yuh Sheeny bum, yuh!

SECRETARY: Throw him out, boys.

[*In spite of his struggles, this is done with gusto and éclat. Propelled by several parting kicks,* YANK *lands sprawling in the middle of the narrow cobbled street. With a growl he starts to get up and storm the closed door, but stops bewildered by the confusions in his brain, pathetically impotent. He sits there brooding, in as near to the attitude of Rodin's "Thinker" as he can get in his position.*]

YANK: [*bitterly*] So dem boids don't tink I belong, neider. Aw, to hell wit 'em! Dey're in de wrong pew — de same old bull — soap-boxes and Salvation Army — no guts! Cut out an hour offen de job a day and make me happy! Gimme a dollar more a day and make me happy! Tree square a day, and cauliflowers in de front yard — ekal rights — a woman and kids — a lousy vote — and I'm all fixed for Jesus, huh? Aw, hell! What does dat get yuh! Dis ting's in your inside, but it ain't your belly. Feedin' your face — sinkers and coffee — dat don't touch it. It's way down — at de bottom. Yuh can't grab it, and yuh can't stop it. It moves, and everything moves. It stops and de whole woild stops. Dat's me now — I don't tick, see? — I'm a busted Ingersoll, dat's what. Steel was me, and I owned de woild. Now I ain't steel, and de woild owns me. Aw, hell! I can't see — it's all dark, get me? It's all wrong! [*He turns a bitter mocking face up like an ape gibbering at the moon.*] Say, youse up dere, Man in de Moon, yuh look so wise, gimme de answer, huh? Slip me de inside dope, de information right from de stable — where do I get off at, huh?

A POLICEMAN: [*who has come up the street in time to hear this last — with grim humor*] You'll get off at the station, you boob, if you don't get up out of that and keep movin'.

YANK: [*looking up at him — with a hard, bitter laugh*] Sure! Lock me up! Put me in a cage! Dat's de on'y answer yuh know. G'wan, lock me up!

POLICEMAN: What you been doin'?

YANK: Enuf to gimme life for! I was born, see? Sure, dat's de charge. Write it in de blotter. I was born, get me!

POLICEMAN: [*jocosely*] God pity your old woman! [*then matter-of-fact*] But I've no time for kidding. You're soused. I'd run you in but it's too long a walk to the station. Come on now, get up, or I'll fan your ears with this club! Beat it now! [*He hauls* YANK *to his feet*]

YANK: [*in a vague mocking tone*] Say, where do I go from here?

POLICEMAN: [*giving him a push — with a grin, indifferently*] Go to hell.

CURTAIN

SCENE VIII

*Twilight of the next day. The monkey house at the Zoo. One spot of clear gray light falls on the front of one cage so that the interior can be seen. The other cages are vague, shrouded in shadow from which chatterings pitched in a conversational tone can be heard. On the one cage a sign from which the word "gorilla" stands out. The gigantic animal himself is seen squatting on his haunches on a bench in much the same attitude as Rodin's "Thinker."* YANK *enters from the left. Immediately a chorus of angry chattering and screeching breaks out. The gorilla turns his eyes but makes no sound or move.*

YANK: [*with a hard, bitter laugh*] Welcome to your city, huh? Hail, hail, de gang's all here! [*At the sound of his voice the chattering dies away into an attentive silence.* YANK *walks up to the gorilla's cage and, leaning over the railing, stares in at its occupant, who stares back at him, silent and motionless. There is a pause of dead stillness. Then* YANK *begins to talk in a friendly confidential tone, half-mockingly, but with a deep undercurrent of sympathy.*] Say, yuh're some hard-lookin' guy, ain't yuh? I seen lots of tough nuts dat de gang called gorillas, but yuh're de foist real one I ever seen. Some chest yuh got, and shoulders, and dem arms and mits! I bet yuh got a punch in eider fist dat'd knock 'em silly! [*This with geniune admiration. The gorilla, as if he understood, stands upright, swelling out his chest and pounding on it with his fist.* YANK *grins sympathetically.*] Sure, I get yuh. Yuh challenge de whole woild, huh? Yuh got what I was sayin' even if yuh muffed de woids. [*then bitterness creeping in*] And why wouldn't yuh get me? Ain't we both members of de same club — de Hairy Apes? [*They stare at each other — a pause — then* YANK *goes on slowly and bitterly.*] So yuh're what she seen when she looked at me, de white-faced

tart! I was you to her, get me? On'y outa de cage — broke out — free to moider
her, see? Sure! Dat's what she tought. She wasn't wise dat I was in a cage,
too — worser'n yours — sure — a damn sight — 'cause you got some chanct to
bust loose — but me — [*He grows confused.*] Aw, hell! It's all wrong, ain't it?
[*A pause.*] I s'pose yuh wanter know what I'm doin' here, huh? I been warmin'
a bench down to de Battery — ever since last night. Sure. I seen de sun come
up. Dat was pretty, too — all red and pink and green. I was lookin' at de
skyscrapers — steel — and all de ships comin' in, sailin' out, all over de oith —
and dey was steel, too. De sun was warm, dey wasn't no clouds, and dere was a
breeze blowin'. Sure, it was great stuff. I got it aw right — what Paddy said
about dat bein' de right dope — on'y I couldn't get *in* it, see? I couldn't belong
in dat. It was over my head. And I kept tinkin' — and den I beat it up here to see
what youse was like. And I waited till dey was all gone to git yuh alone. Say,
how d'yuh feel sittin' in dat pen all de time, havin' to stand for 'em comin' and
starin' at yuh — de white-faced, skinny tarts and de boobs what marry 'em —
makin' fun of yuh, laughin' at yuh, gittin' scared of you — damn 'em! [*He
pounds on the rail with his fist. The gorilla rattles the bars of his cage and
snarls. All the other monkeys set up an angry chattering in the darkness.* YANK
*goes on excitedly.*] Sure! Dat's de way it hits me, too. On'y yuh're lucky, see?
Yuh don't belong wit 'em and yuh know it. But me, I belong wit 'em — but I
don't, see? Dey don't belong wit me, dat's what. Get me? Tinkin' is hard —
[*He passes one hand across his forehead with a painful gesture. The gorilla
growls impatiently.* YANK *goes on gropingly.*] It's dis way, what I'm drivin' at.
Youse can sit and dope dream in de past, green woods, de jungle and de rest of
it. Den yuh belong and dey don't. Den yuh kin laugh at 'em, see? Yuh're de
champ of de woild. But me — I ain't got no past to tink in, nor nothin' dat's
comin', on'y what's now — and dat don't belong. Sure, you're de best off! Yuh
can't tink, can yuh? Yuh can't talk neider. But I kin make a bluff at talkin' and
tinkin' — a'most git away wit it — a'most! — and dat's where de joker comes in.
[*He laughs.*] I ain't on oith and I ain't in heaven, get me? I'm in de middle
tryin' to separate 'em, takin' all de woise punches from bot' of 'em. Maybe dat's
what dey call hell, huh? But you, yuh're at de bottom. You belong! Sure!
Yuh're de on'y one in de woild dat does, yuh lucky stiff! [*The gorilla growls
proudly.*] And dat's why dey gotter put yuh in a cage, see? [*The gorilla roars
angrily.*] Sure! Yuh get me. It beats it when you try to tink it or talk it — it's way
down — deep — behind — you 'n' me we feel it. Sure! Bot' members of dis
club! [*He laughs — then in a savage tone*] What de hell! T' hell wit it! A little
action, dat's our meat! Dat belongs! Knock 'em down and keep bustin' 'em till
dey croak yuh wit a gat — wit steel! Sure! Are yuh game? Dey've looked at
youse, ain't dey — in a cage? Wanter git even? Wanter wind up like a sport
'stead of croakin' slow in dere? [*The gorilla roars an emphatic affirmative.*
YANK *goes on with a sort of furious exaltation.*] Sure! Yuh're reg'lar! You'll
stick to de finish! Me 'n' you, huh? — bot' members of this club! We'll put up
one last star bout dat'll knock 'em offen deir seats! Dey'll have to make de cages
stronger after we're trou! [*The gorilla is straining at his bars, growling, hop-
ping from one foot to the other.* YANK *takes a jimmy from under his coat and
forces the lock on the cage door. He throws this open.*] Pardon from de
governor! Step out and shake hands. I'll take yuh for a walk down Fif' Avenoo.

We'll knock 'em offen de oith and croak wit de band playin'. Come on, Brother. [*The gorilla scrambles gingerly out of his cage. Goes to* YANK *and stands looking at him.* YANK *keeps his mocking tone — holds out his hand.*] Shake — de secret grip of our order. [*Something, the tone of mockery, perhaps, suddenly enrages the animal. With a spring he wraps his huge arms around* YANK *in a murderous hug. There is a crackling snap of crushed ribs — a gasping cry, still mocking, from* YANK.] Hey, I didn't say kiss me! [*The gorilla lets the crushed body slip to the floor; stands over it uncertainly, considering; then picks it up, throws it in the cage, shuts the door, and shuffles off menacingly into the darkness at left. A great uproar of frightened chattering and whimpering comes from the other cages. Then* YANK *moves, groaning, opening his eyes, and there is silence. He mutters painfully*] Say — dey oughter match him — wit Zybszko. He got me, aw right. I'm trou. Even him didn't tink I belonged. [*then, with sudden passionate despair*] Christ, where do I get off at? Where do I fit in? [*checking himself as suddenly*] Aw, what de hell! No squawkin', see! No quittin', get me! Croak wit your boots on! [*He grabs hold of the bars of the cage and hauls himself painfully to his feet — looks around him bewilderedly — forces a mocking laugh.*] In de cage, huh? [*in the strident tones of a circus barker*] Ladies and gents, step forward and take a slant at de one and only — [*his voice weakening*] — one and original — Hairy Ape from de wilds of —

[*He slips in a heap on the floor and dies. The monkeys set up a chattering, whimpering wail. And, perhaps, the Hairy Ape at last belongs.*]

CURTAIN

# Bertolt Brecht

# The Good Woman of Setzuan

## Revised English Version by Eric Bentley

CHARACTERS

WONG, *a water seller*
THREE GODS
SHEN TE, *a prostitute, later a shopkeeper*
MRS. SHIN, *former owner of Shen Te's shop*
A FAMILY OF EIGHT (*husband, wife, brother, sister-in-law, grandfather, nephew, niece, boy*)
AN UNEMPLOYED MAN
A CARPENTER
MRS. MI TZU, *Shen Te's landlady*
YANG SUN, *an unemployed pilot, later a factory manager*
AN OLD WHORE
A POLICEMAN
AN OLD MAN
AN OLD WOMAN, *his wife*
MR. SHU FU, *a barber*
MRS. YANG, *mother of Yang Sun*
GENTLEMEN, VOICES, CHILDREN (*three*), etc.


PROLOGUE

*At the gates of the half-Westernized city of Setzuan. Evening.*

[WONG *the water seller introduces himself to the audience.*]
WONG: I sell water here in the city of Setzuan. It isn't easy. When water is scarce, I have long distances to go in search of it, and when it is plentiful, I have no income. But in our part of the world there is nothing unusual about poverty. Many people think only the gods can save the situation. And I hear from a cattle merchant—who travels a lot—that some of the highest gods are on their way at this very moment. Informed sources have it that heaven is quite disturbed at all the complaining. I've been coming out here to the city gates for three days now to bid these gods welcome. I want to be the first to greet them. What about those fellows over there? No, no, they *work*. And that one there has ink on his fingers, he's no god, he must be a clerk from the cement factory.

*Those* two are another story. They look as though they'd like to beat you. But gods don't need to beat you, do they?

[THREE GODS *appear.*]

What about those three? Old-fashioned clothes — dust on their feet — they *must be gods!* [*he throws himself at their feet*] Do with me what you will, illustrious ones!

FIRST GOD: [*with an ear trumpet*] Ah! [*he is pleased*] So we are expected?

WONG: [*giving them water*] Oh, yes. And I *knew* you'd come.

FIRST GOD: We need somewhere to stay the night. You know of a place?

WONG: The whole town is at your service, illustrious ones! What sort of a place would you like?

[*The* GODS *eye each other.*]

FIRST GOD: Just try the first house you come to, my son.

WONG: That would be Mr. Fo's place.

FIRST GOD: Mr. Fo.

WONG: One moment! [*He knocks at the first house.*]

VOICE FROM MR. FO'S: No!

[WONG *returns a little nervously.*]

WONG: It's too bad. Mr. Fo isn't in. And his servants don't dare do a thing without his consent. He'll have a fit when he finds out who they turned away, won't he?

FIRST GOD: [*smiling*] He will, won't he?

WONG: One moment! The next house is Mr. Cheng's. Won't he be thrilled!

FIRST GOD: Mr. Cheng.

[WONG *knocks.*]

VOICE FROM MR. CHENG'S: Keep your gods. We have our own troubles!

WONG: [*back with the* GODS] Mr. Cheng is very sorry, but he has a houseful of relations. I think some of them are a bad lot, and naturally, he wouldn't like you to see them.

THIRD GOD: Are we so terrible?

WONG: Well, only with bad people, of course. Everyone knows the province of Kwan is always having floods.

SECOND GOD: Really? How's that?

WONG: Why, because they're so irreligious.

SECOND GOD: Rubbish. It's because they neglected the dam.

FIRST GOD: [*to* SECOND] Sh! [*to* WONG] You're still in hopes, aren't you, my son?

WONG: Certainly. All Setzuan is competing for the honor! What happened up to now is pure coincidence. I'll be back. [*He walks away, but then stands undecided.*]

SECOND GOD: What did I tell you?

THIRD GOD: It *could* be pure coincidence.

SECOND GOD: The same coincidence in Shun, Kwan, and Setzuan? People just aren't religious any more, let's face the fact. Our mission has failed!

FIRST GOD: Oh come, we might run into a good person any minute.

THIRD GOD: How did the resolution read? [*unrolling a scroll and reading from it*] "The world can stay as it is if enough people are found [*at the word "found" he unrolls it a little more*] living lives worthy of human beings." Good people, that is. Well, what about this water seller himself? *He's* good, or I'm very much mistaken.

SECOND GOD: You're very much mistaken. When he gave us a drink, I had the impression there was something odd about the cup. Well, look! [*He shows the cup to the* FIRST GOD.]

FIRST GOD: A false bottom!

SECOND GOD: The man is a swindler.

FIRST GOD: Very well, count *him* out. That's one man among millions. And as a matter of fact, we only need one on *our* side. These atheists are saying, "The world must be changed because no one can *be* good and *stay* good." No one, eh? I say: let us find one — just one — and we have those fellows where we want them!

THIRD GOD: [*to* WONG] Water seller, is it so hard to find a place to stay?

WONG: Nothing could be easier. It's just me. I don't go about it right.

THIRD GOD: Really?

    [*He returns to the others. A* GENTLEMAN *passes by.*]

WONG: Oh dear, they're catching on. [*He accosts the* GENTLEMAN.] Excuse the intrusion, dear sir, but three gods have just turned up. Three of the very highest. They need a place for the night. Seize this rare opportunity — to have real gods as your guests!

GENTLEMEN: [*laughing*] A new way of finding free rooms for a gang of crooks.

    [*Exit* GENTLEMAN.]

WONG: [*shouting at him*] Godless rascal! Have you no religion, gentleman of Setzuan? [*pause*] Patience, illustrious ones! [*pause*] There's only one person left. Shen Te, the prostitute. She *can't* say no. [*Calls up to a window*] Shen Te!

    [SHEN TE *opens the shutters and looks out.*]

WONG: Shen Te, it's Wong. *They're* here, and nobody wants them. Will you take them?

SHEN TE: Oh, no, Wong, I'm expecting a gentleman.

WONG: Can't you forget about him for tonight?

SHEN TE: The rent has to be paid by tomorrow or I'll be out on the street.

WONG: This is no time for calculation, Shen Te.

SHEN TE: Stomachs rumble even on the Emperor's birthday, Wong.

WONG: Setzuan is one big dung hill!

SHEN TE: Oh, very well! I'll hide till my gentleman has come and gone. Then I'll take them. [*She disappears.*]

WONG: They mustn't see her gentleman or they'll know what she is.

FIRST GOD: [*who hasn't heard any of this*] I think it's hopeless.

    [*They approach* WONG.]

WONG: [*jumping, as he finds them behind him*] A room has been found, illustrious ones! [*He wipes sweat off his brow.*]

SECOND GOD: Oh, good.

THIRD GOD: Let's see it.

WONG: [*nervously*] Just a minute. It has to be tidied up a bit.

THIRD GOD: Then we'll sit down here and wait.

WONG: [*still more nervous*] No, no! [*holding himself back*] Too much traffic, you know.

THIRD GOD: [*with a smile*] Of course, if you *want* us to move.

    [*They retire a little. They sit on a doorstep.* WONG *sits on the ground.*]

WONG: [*after a deep breath*] You'll be staying with a single girl — the finest human being in Setzuan!

THIRD GOD: That's nice.

WONG: [*to the audience*] They gave me such a look when I picked up my cup just now.

THIRD GOD: You're worn out, Wong.

WONG: A little, maybe.

FIRST GOD: Do people here have a hard time of it?

WONG: The good ones do.

FIRST GOD: What about yourself?

WONG: You mean I'm not good. That's true. And I don't have an easy time either!

[*During this dialogue, a* GENTLEMAN *has turned up in front of Shen Te's house, and has whistled several times. Each time* WONG *has given a start.*]

THIRD GOD: [*to* WONG, *softly*] Psst! I think he's gone now.

WONG: [*confused and surprised*] Ye-e-es.

[*The* GENTLEMAN *has left now, and* SHEN TE *has come down to the street.*]

SHEN TE: [*softly*] Wong!

[*Getting no answer, she goes off down the street.* WONG *arrives just too late, forgetting his carrying pole.*]

WONG: [*softly*] Shen Te! Shen Te! [*to himself*] So she's gone off to earn the rent. Oh dear, I can't go to the gods *again* with no room to offer them. Having failed in the service of the gods, I shall run to my den in the sewer pipe down by the river and hide from their sight!

[*He rushes off.* SHEN TE *returns, looking for him, but finding the* GODS. *She stops in confusion.*]

SHEN TE: You are the illustrious ones? My name is Shen Te. It would please me very much if my simple room could be of use to you.

THIRD GOD: Where is the water seller, Miss . . . Shen Te?

SHEN TE: I missed him, somehow.

FIRST GOD: Oh, he probably thought you weren't coming, and was afraid of telling us.

THIRD GOD: [*picking up the carrying pole*] We'll leave this with you. He'll be needing it.

[*Led by* SHEN TE, *they go into the house. It grows dark, then light. Dawn. Again escorted by* SHEN TE, *who leads them through the halfflight with a little lamp, the* GODS *take their leave.*]

FIRST GOD: Thank you, thank you, dear Shen Te, for your elegant hospitality! We shall not forget! And give our thanks to the water seller — he showed us a good human being.

SHEN TE: Oh, *I'm* not good. Let me tell you something: when Wong asked me to put you up, I hesitated.

FIRST GOD: It's all right to hesitate if you then go ahead! And in giving us that room you did much more than you knew. You proved that good people still exist, a point that has been disputed of late — even in heaven. Farewell!

SECOND GOD: Farewell!

THIRD GOD: Farewell!

SHEN TE: Stop, illustrious ones! I'm not sure you're right. I'd like to be good, it's true, but there's the rent to pay. And that's not all: I sell myself for a living. Even so I can't make ends meet, there's too much competition. I'd like to honor my father and mother and speak nothing but the truth and not covet my neighbor's house. I should love to stay with one man. But how? How is it done? Even breaking a few of your commandments, I can hardly manage.

FIRST GOD: [*clearing his throat*] These thoughts are but, um, the misgivings of an unusually good woman!

THIRD GOD: Good-bye, Shen Te! Give our regards to the water seller!

SECOND GOD: And above all: be good! Farewell!

FIRST GOD: Farewell!

THIRD GOD: Farewell!

[*They start to wave good-bye.*]

SHEN TE: But everything is so expensive. I don't feel sure I can do it!

SECOND GOD: That's not in our sphere. We never meddle with economics.

THIRD GOD: One moment. [*They stop.*] Isn't it true she might do better if she had more money?

SECOND GOD: Come, come! How could we ever account for it Up Above?

FIRST GOD: Oh, there are ways. [*They put their heads together and confer in dumb show. To* SHEN TE, *with embarrassment:*] As you say you can't pay your rent, well, um, we're not paupers, so of course we *insist* on paying for our room. [*Awkwardly thrusting money into her hand.*] There! [*quickly*] But don't tell anyone! The incident is open to misinterpretation.

SECOND GOD: It certainly is!

FIRST GOD: [*defensively*] But there's no law against it! It was never decreed that a god mustn't pay hotel bills!

[*The* GODS *leave.*]


SCENE I——*A small tobacco shop. The shop is not as yet completely furnished and hasn't started doing business.*

SHEN TE: [*to the audience*] It's three days now since the gods left. When they wanted to pay for the room, I looked down at my hand, and there was more than a thousand silver dollars! I bought a tobacco shop with the money, and moved in yesterday. I don't own the building, of course, but I can pay the rent, and I hope to do a lot of good here. Beginning with Mrs. Shin, who's just coming across the square with her pot. She had the shop before me, and yesterday she dropped in to ask for rice for her children. [*Enter* MRS. SHIN. *Both women bow.*] How do you do, Mrs. Shin.

MRS. SHIN: How do you do, Miss Shen Te. You like your new home?

SHEN TE: Indeed, yes. Did your children have a good night?

MRS. SHIN: In that hovel? The youngest is coughing already.

SHEN TE: Oh, dear!

MRS. SHIN: You're going to learn a thing or two in these slums.

SHEN TE: Slums? That's not what you said when you sold me the shop!

MRS. SHIN: Now don't start nagging! Robbing me and my innocent children of their home and then calling it a slum! That's the limit! [*She weeps.*]

SHEN TE: [*tactfully*] I'll get your rice.

MRS. SHIN: And a little cash while you're at it.

SHEN TE: I'm afraid I haven't sold anything yet.

MRS. SHIN: [*screeching*] I've got to have it. Strip the clothes from my back and then cut my throat, will you? I know what I'll do: I'll dump my children on your doorstep! [*She snatches the pot out of* SHEN TE'S *hands.*]

SHEN TE: Please don't be angry. You'll spill the rice.

[*Enter an elderly* HUSBAND *and* WIFE *with their shabbily dressed* NEPHEW.]

WIFE: Shen Te, dear! You've come into money, they tell me. And we haven't a roof over our heads! A tobacco shop. We had one too. But it's gone. Could we spend the night here, do you think?

NEPHEW: [*appraising the shop*] Not bad!

WIFE: He's our nephew. We're inseparable!

MRS. SHIN: And who are these . . . ladies and gentlemen?

SHEN TE: They put me up when I first came in from the country. [*to the audience*] Of course, when my small purse was empty, they put me out on the street, and they may be afraid I'll do the same to them. [*to the newcomers, kindly*] Come in, and welcome, though I've only one little room for you — it's behind the shop.

HUSBAND: That'll do. Don't worry.

WIFE: [*bringing* SHEN TE *some tea*] We'll stay over here, so we won't be in your way. Did you make it a tobacco shop in memory of your first real home? We can certainly give you a hint or two! That's one reason we came.

MRS. SHIN: [*to* SHEN TE] Very nice! As long as you have a few customers too!

HUSBAND: Sh! A customer!

[*Enter an* UNEMPLOYED MAN, *in rags.*]

UNEMPLOYED MAN: Excuse me. I'm unemployed.

[MRS. SHIN *laughs.*]

SHEN TE: Can I help you?

UNEMPLOYED MAN: Have you any damaged cigarettes? I thought there might be some damage when you're unpacking.

WIFE: What nerve, begging for tobacco! [*rhetorically*] Why don't they ask for bread?

UNEMPLOYED MAN: Bread is expensive. One cigarette butt and I'll be a new man.

SHEN TE: [*giving him cigarettes*] That's very important — to be a new man. You'll be my first customer and bring me luck.

[*The* UNEMPLOYED MAN *quickly lights a cigarette, inhales, and goes off, coughing.*]

WIFE: Was that right, Shen Te, dear?

MRS. SHIN: If this is the opening of a shop, you can hold the closing at the end of the week.

HUSBAND: I bet he had money on him.

SHEN TE: Oh, no, he said he hadn't!

NEPHEW: How d'you know he wasn't lying?

SHEN TE: [*angrily*] How do you know he was?

WIFE: [*wagging her head*] You're too good, Shen Te, dear. If you're going to keep this shop, you'll have to learn to say no.

HUSBAND: Tell them the place isn't yours to dispose of. Belongs to . . . some relative who insists on all accounts being strictly in order . . .

MRS. SHIN: That's right! What do you think you are — a philanthropist?

SHEN TE: [*laughing*] Very well, suppose I ask you for my rice back, Mrs. Shin?

WIFE: [*combatively, at* MRS. SHIN] So that's *her* rice?
        [*Enter the* CARPENTER, *a small man*.]
MRS. SHIN: [*who, at the sight of him, starts to hurry away*] See you tomorrow, Miss
        Shen Te! [*Exit* MRS. SHIN.]
CARPENTER: Mrs. Shin, it's you I want!
WIFE: [*to* SHEN TE] Has she some claim on you?
SHEN TE: She's hungry. That's a claim.
CARPENTER: Are you the new tenant? And filling up the shelves already? Well,
        they're not yours till they're paid for, ma'am. I'm the carpenter, so I should
        know.
SHEN TE: I took the shop "furnishings included."
CARPENTER: You're in league with that Mrs. Shin, of course. All right. I demand my
        hundred silver dollars.
SHEN TE: I'm afraid I haven't got a hundred silver dollars.
CARPENTER: Then you'll find it. Or I'll have you arrested
WIFE: [*whispering to* SHEN TE] That relative: make it a cousin.
SHEN TE: Can't it wait till next month?
CARPENTER: No!
SHEN TE: Be a little patient, Mr. Carpenter, I can't settle all claims at once.
CARPENTER: Who's patient with me? [*He grabs a shelf from the wall*.] Pay up — or I
        take the shelves back!
WIFE: Shen Te! Dear! Why don't you let your . . . cousin settle this affair? [*to*
        CARPENTER] Put your claim in writing. Shen Te's cousin will see you get paid.
CARPENTER: [*derisively*] Cousin, eh?
HUSBAND: Cousin, yes.
CARPENTER: I know these cousins!
NEPHEW: Don't be silly. He's a personal friend of mine.
HUSBAND: What a man! Sharp as a razor!
CARPENTER: All right. I'll put my claim in writing. [*Puts shelf on floor, sits on it,
        writes out bill*.]
WIFE: [*to* SHEN TE] He'd tear the dress off your back to get his shelves. Never
        recognize a claim. That's my motto.
SHEN TE: He's done a job, and wants something in return. It's shameful that I can't
        give it to him. What will the gods say?
HUSBAND: You did your bit when you took *us* in.
        [*Enter the* BROTHER, *limping, and the* SISTER-IN-LAW, *pregnant*.]
BROTHER: [*to* HUSBAND *and* WIFE ] So this is where you're hiding out! There's family
        feeling for you! Leaving us on the corner!
WIFE: [*embarrassed, to* SHEN TE] It's my brother and his wife. [*to them*] Now stop
        grumbling, and sit quietly in that corner. [*to* SHEN TE] It can't be helped. She's
        in her fifth month.
SHEN TE: Oh yes. Welcome!
WIFE: [*to the couple*] Say thank you. [*They mutter something*.] The cups are there.
        [*to* SHEN TE] Lucky you bought this shop when you did!
SHEN TE: [*laughing and bringing tea*] Lucky indeed!
        [*Enter* MRS. MI TZU, *the landlady*.]
MRS. MI TZU: Miss Shen Te? I am Mrs. Mi Tzu, your landlady. I hope our relation-
        ship will be a happy one. I like to think I give my tenants modern, personalized
        service. Here is your lease. [*to the others, as* SHEN TE *reads the lease*] There's

nothing like the opening of a little shop, is there? A moment of true beauty! [*she is looking around*] Not very much on the shelves, of course. But everything in the gods' good time! Where are your references, Miss Shen Te?

SHEN TE: Do I *have* to have references?

MRS. MI TZU: After all, I haven't a notion who you are!

HUSBAND: Oh, *we'd* be glad to vouch for Miss Shen Te! We'd go through fire for her!

MRS. MI TZU: And who may *you* be?

HUSBAND: [*stammering*] Ma Fu, tobacco dealer.

MRS. MI TZU: Where is your shop, Mr. . . . Ma Fu?

HUSBAND: Well, um, I haven't got a shop—I've just sold it.

MRS. MI TZU: I see. [*to* SHEN TE] Is there no one else that knows you?

WIFE: [*whispering to* SHEN TE] Your cousin! Your cousin!

MRS. MI TZU: This is a respectable house, Miss Shen Te. I never sign a lease without certain assurances.

SHEN TE: [*slowly, her eyes downcast*] I have . . . a cousin.

MRS. MI TZU: On the square? Let's go over and see him. What does he do?

SHEN TE: [*as before*] He lives . . . in another city.

WIFE: [*prompting*] Didn't you say he was in Shung?

SHEN TE: That's right. Shung.

HUSBAND: [*prompting*] I had his name on the tip of my tongue. Mr. . . .

SHEN TE: [*with an effort*] Mr. . . . Shui . . . Ta.

HUSBAND: That's it! Tall, skinny fellow!

SHEN TE: Shui Ta!

NEPHEW: [*to* CARPENTER] *You* were in touch with him, weren't you? About the shelves?

CARPENTER: [*surlily*] Give him this bill. [*He hands it over.*] I'll be back in the morning. [*Exit* CARPENTER.]

NEPHEW: [*calling after him, but with his eyes on* MRS. MI TZU] Don't worry! Mr. Shui Ta pays on the nail!

MRS. MI TZU: [*looking closely at* SHEN TE] I'll be happy to make his acquaintance, Miss Shen Te. [*Exit* MRS. MI TZU.]
 [*Pause.*]

WIFE: By tomorrow morning she'll know more about you than you do yourself.

SISTER-IN-LAW: [*to* NEPHEW] This thing isn't built to last.
 [*Enter* GRANDFATHER.]

WIFE: It's Grandfather! [*to* SHEN TE] Such a good old soul!
 [*The* BOY *enters.*]

BOY: [*over his shoulder*] Here they are!

WIFE: And the boy, how he's grown! But he always could eat enough for ten.
 [*Enter the* NIECE.]

WIFE: [*to* SHEN TE] Our little niece from the country. There are more of us now than in your time. The less we had, the more there were of us; the more there were of us, the less we had. Give me the key. We must protect ourselves from unwanted guests. [*She takes the key and locks the door.*] Just make yourself at home. I'll light the little lamp.

NEPHEW: [*a big joke*] I hope her cousin doesn't drop in tonight! The strict Mr. Shui Ta!
 [SISTER-IN-LAW *laughs.*]

BROTHER: [*reaching for a cigarette*] One cigarette more or less . . .
HUSBAND: One cigarette more or less.
    [*They pile into the cigarettes. The* BROTHER *hands a jug of wine round.*]
NEPHEW: Mr. Shui Ta'll pay for it!
GRANDFATHER: [*gravely, to* SHEN TE] How do you do?
    [SHEN TE, *a little taken aback by the belatedness of the greeting, bows. She
    has the carpenter's bill in one hand, the landlady's lease in the other.*]
WIFE: How about a bit of a song? To keep Shen Te's spirits up?
NEPHEW: Good idea. Grandfather: you start!

SONG OF THE SMOKE

GRANDFATHER:

I used to think (before old age beset me)
    That brains could fill the pantry of the poor.
But where did all my cerebration get me?
    I'm just as hungry as I was before.
        So what's the use?
            See the smoke float free
        Into ever colder coldness!
            It's the same with me.

HUSBAND:

The straight and narrow path leads to disaster
    And so the crooked path I tried to tread.
That got me to disaster even faster.
    (They say we shall be happy when we're dead.)
        So what's the use?
            See the smoke float free
        Into ever colder coldness!
            It's the same with me.

NIECE:

You older people, full of expectation,
    At any moment now you'll walk the plank!
The future's for the younger generation!
    Yes, even if that future is a blank.
        So what's the use?
            See the smoke float free
        Into ever colder coldness!
            It's the same with me.

NEPHEW: [*to the* BROTHER] Where'd you get that wine?
SISTER-IN-LAW: [*answering for the* BROTHER] He pawned the sack of tobacco.
HUSBAND: [*stepping in*] What? That tobacco was all we had to fall back on! You pig!
BROTHER: You'd call a man a pig because your wife was frigid! Did you refuse to
    drink it?
    [*They fight. The shelves fall over.*]
SHEN TE: [*imploringly*] Oh don't! Don't break everything! Take it, take it, take it all,
    but don't destroy a gift from the gods!
WIFE: [*disparagingly*] This shop isn't big enough. I should never have mentioned it
    to Uncle and the others. When *they* arrive, it's going to be disgustingly
    overcrowded.

SISTER-IN-LAW: And did you hear our gracious hostess? She cools off quick!
[*Voices outside. Knocking at the door.*]

UNCLE'S VOICE: Open the door!

WIFE: Uncle! Is that you, Uncle?

UNCLE'S VOICE: Certainly, it's me. Auntie says to tell you she'll have the children here in ten minutes.

WIFE: [*to* SHEN TE] I'll have to let him in.

SHEN TE: [*who scarcely hears her*]
The little lifeboat is swiftly sent down
Too many men too greedily
Hold on to it as they drown.

SCENE Ia——WONG's *den in a sewer pipe.*

WONG: [*crouching there*] All quiet! It's four days now since I left the city. The gods passed this way on the second day. I heard their steps on the bridge over there. They must be a long way off by this time, so I'm safe. [*Breathing a sigh of relief, he curls up and goes to sleep. In his dream the pipe becomes transparent, and the* GODS *appear. Raising an arm, as if in selfdefense:*] I know, I know, illustrious ones! I found no one to give you a room—not in all Setzuan! There, it's out. Please continue on your way!

FIRST GOD: [*mildly*] But you did find someone. Someone who took us in for the night, watched over us in our sleep, and in the early morning lighted us down to the street with a lamp.

WONG: It was . . . Shen Te that took you in?

THIRD GOD: Who else?

WONG: And I ran away! "She isn't coming," I thought, "she just can't afford it."

GODS: [*singing*]
O you feeble, well-intentioned, and yet feeble chap
Where there's need the fellow thinks there is no goodness!
When there's danger he thinks courage starts to ebb away!
Some people only see the seamy side!
What hasty judgment! What premature desperation!

WONG: I'm *very* ashamed, illustrious ones.

FIRST GOD: Do us a favor, water seller. Go back to Setzuan. Find Shen Te, and give us a report on her. We hear that she's come into a little money. Show interest in her goodness—for no one can be good for long if goodness is not in demand. Meanwhile we shall continue the search, and find other good people. After which, the idle chatter about the impossibility of goodness will stop!
[*The* GODS *vanish.*]

SCENE II

[*A knocking.*]

WIFE: Shen Te! Someone at the door. Where is she anyway?

NEPHEW: She must be getting the breakfast. Mr. Shui Ta will pay for it.
[*The* WIFE *laughs and shuffles to the door. Enter* MR. SHUI TA *and the* CARPENTER.]

WIFE: Who is it?

SHUI TA: I am Miss Shen Te's cousin.

WIFE: What?

SHUI TA: My name is Shui Ta.

WIFE: Her cousin?

NEPHEW: Her cousin?

NIECE: But that was a joke. She hasn't got a cousin.

HUSBAND: So early in the morning?

BROTHER: What's all the noise?

SISTER-IN-LAW: This fellow says he's her cousin.

BROTHER: Tell him to prove it.

NEPHEW: Right. If you're Shen Te's cousin, prove it by getting the breakfast.

SHUI TA: [*whose regime begins as he puts out the lamp to save oil; loudly, to all present, asleep or awake*] Would you all please get dressed! Customers will be coming! I wish to open my shop!

HUSBAND: *Your* shop? Doesn't it belong to our good friend Shen Te?

> [SHUI TA *shakes his head.*]

SISTER-IN-LAW: So we've been cheated. Where *is* the little liar?

SHUI TA: Miss Shen Te has been delayed. She wishes me to tell you there will be nothing she can do — now I am here.

WIFE: [*bowled over*] I thought she was good!

NEPHEW: Do you have to believe *him?*

HUSBAND: I don't.

NEPHEW: Then do something.

HUSBAND: Certainly! I'll send out a search party at once. You, you, you, and you, go out and look for Shen Te. [*as the* GRANDFATHER *rises and makes for the door*] Not you, Grandfather, you and I will hold the fort.

SHUI TA: You won't find Miss Shen Te. She has suspended her hospitable activity for an unlimited period. There are too many of you. She asked me to say: this is a tobacco shop, not a gold mine.

HUSBAND: Shen Te never said a thing like that. Boy, food! There's a bakery on the corner. Stuff your shirt full when they're not looking!

SISTER-IN-LAW: Don't overlook the raspberry tarts.

HUSBAND: And don't let the policeman see you.

> [*The* BOY *leaves.*]

SHUI TA: Don't you depend on this shop now? Then why give it a bad name by stealing from the bakery?

NEPHEW: Don't listen to him. Let's find Shen Te. She'll give him a piece of her mind.

SISTER-IN-LAW: Don't forget to leave us some breakfast.

> [BROTHER, SISTER-IN-LAW, *and* NEPHEW *leave.*]

SHUI TA: [*to the* CARPENTER] You see, Mr. Carpenter, nothing has changed since the poet, eleven hundred years ago, penned these lines:

A governor was asked what was needed
To save the freezing people in the city.
He replied:
"A blanket ten thousand feet long
to cover the city and all its suburbs."

> [*He starts to tidy up the shop.*]

CARPENTER: Your cousin owes me money. I've got witnesses. For the shelves.

SHUI TA: Yes, I have your bill. [*he takes it out of his pocket*] Isn't a hundred silver dollars rather a lot?

CARPENTER: No deductions! I have a wife and children.

SHUI TA: How many children?

CARPENTER: Three.

SHUI TA: I'll make you an offer. Twenty silver dollars.
   [*The* HUSBAND *laughs.*]

CARPENTER: You're crazy. Those shelves are real walnut.

SHUI TA: Very well, Take them away.

CARPENTER: What?

SHUI TA: They cost too much. Please take them away.

WIFE: Not bad! [*And she, too, is laughing.*]

CARPENTER: [*a little bewildered*] Call Shen Te, someone! [*to* SHUI TA] She's *good!*

SHUI TA: Certainly. She's ruined.

CARPENTER: [*provoked into taking some of the shelves*] All right, you can keep your tobacco on the floor.

SHUI TA: [*to the* HUSBAND] Help him with the shelves.

HUSBAND: [*grins and carries one shelf over to the door where the* CARPENTER *now is*] Good-bye, shelves!

CARPENTER: [*to the* HUSBAND] You dog! You want my family to starve?

SHUI TA: I repeat my offer. I have no desire to keep my tobacco on the floor. Twenty silver dollars.

CARPENTER: [*with desperate aggressiveness*] One hundred!
   [SHUI TA *shows indifference, looks through the window. The* HUSBAND *picks up several shelves.*]

CARPENTER: [*to* HUSBAND] You needn't smash them against the doorposts, you idiot! [*to* SHUI TA] These shelves were made to measure. They're no use anywhere else!

SHUI TA: Precisely.
   [*The* WIFE *squeals with pleasure.*]

CARPENTER: [*giving up, sullenly*] Take the shelves. Pay what you want to pay.

SHUI TA: [*smoothly*] Twenty silver dollars.
   [*He places two large coins on the table. The* CARPENTER *picks them up.*]

HUSBAND: [*brings the shelves in*] And quite enough too!

CARPENTER: [*slinking off*] Quite enough to get drunk on.

HUSBAND: [*happily*] Well, we got rid of him!

WIFE: [*weeping with fun, gives a rendition of the dialogue just spoken*] "Real walnut," says he. "Very well, take them away," says his lordship. "I have three children," says he. "Twenty silver dollars," says his lordship. "They're no use anywhere else," says he. "Pre-cisely," said his lordship! [*She dissolves into shrieks of merriment.*]

SHUI TA: And now: go!

HUSBAND: What's that?

SHUI TA: You're thieves, parasites. I'm giving you this chance. Go!

HUSBAND: [*summoning all his ancestral dignity*] That sort deserves no answer. Besides, one should never shout on an empty stomach.

WIFE: Where's that boy?

SHUI TA: Exactly. The boy. I want no stolen goods in this shop. [*very loudly*] I strongly advise you to leave! [*But they remain seated, noses in the air. Quietly.*] As you wish. [SHUI TA *goes to the door.* A POLICEMAN *appears.* SHUI TA *bows.*] I am addressing the officer in charge of this precinct?

POLICEMAN: That's right, Mr., um, what was the name, sir?

SHUI TA: Mr. Shui Ta.

POLICEMAN: Yes, of course, sir.
          [*They exchange a smile.*]

SHUI TA: Nice weather we're having.

POLICEMAN: A little on the warm side, sir.

SHUI TA: Oh, a little on the warm side.

HUSBAND: [*whispering to the* WIFE] If he keeps it up till the boy's back, we're done for. [*Tries to signal* SHUI TA.]

SHUI TA: [*ignoring the signal*] Weather, of course, is one thing indoors, another out on the dusty street!

POLICEMAN: Oh, quite another, sir!

WIFE: [*to the* HUSBAND] It's all right as long as he's standing in the doorway — the boy will see him.

SHUI TA: Step inside for a moment! It's quite cool indoors. My cousin and I have just opened the place. And we attach the greatest importance to being on good terms with the, um, authorities.

POLICEMAN: [*entering*] Thank you, Mr. Shui Ta. It *is* cool.

HUSBAND: [*whispering to the* WIFE] And now the boy *won't* see him.

SHUI TA: [*showing* HUSBAND *and* WIFE *to the* POLICEMAN] Visitors, I think my cousin knows them. They were just leaving.

HUSBAND: [*defeated*] Ye-e-es, we were . . . just leaving.

SHUI TA: I'll tell my cousin you couldn't wait.
          [*Noise from the street. Shouts of* "Stop, Thief!"]

POLICEMAN: What's that?
          [*The* BOY *is in the doorway with cakes and buns and rolls spilling out of his shirt. The* WIFE *signals desperately to him to leave. He gets the idea.*]

POLICEMAN: No, you don't! [*he grabs the* BOY *by the collar*] Where's all this from?

BOY: [*vaguely pointing*] Down the street.

POLICEMAN: [*grimly*] So that's it. [*Prepares to arrest the* BOY.]

WIFE: [*stepping in*] And *we* knew nothing about it. [*to the* BOY] Nasty little thief!

POLICEMAN: [*dryly*] Can you clarify the situation, Mr. Shui Ta?
          [SHUI TA *is silent.*]

POLICEMAN: [*who understands silence*] Aha. You're all coming with me — to the station.

SHUI TA: I can hardly say how sorry I am that my establishment . . .

WIFE: Oh, he saw the boy leave not ten minutes ago!

SHUI TA: And to conceal the theft asked a policeman in?

POLICEMAN: Don't listen to her, Mr. Shui Ta, I'll be happy to relieve you of their presence one and all! [*to all three*] Out! [*He drives them before him.*]

GRANDFATHER: [*leaving last, gravely*] Good morning!

POLICEMAN: Good morning!
          [SHUI TA, *left alone, continues to tidy up.* MRS. MI TZU *breezes in.*]

MRS. MI TZU: You're her cousin, are you? Then have the goodness to explain what all this means — police dragging people from a respectable house! By what right does your Miss Shen Te turn my property into a house of assignation? Well, as you see, I know all!

SHUI TA: Yes. My cousin has the worst possible reputation: that of being poor.

MRS. MI TZU: No sentimental rubbish, Mr. Shui Ta. Your cousin was a common . . .

SHUI TA: Pauper. Let's use the uglier word.

MRS. MI TZU: I'm speaking of her conduct, not her earnings. But there must have *been* earnings, or how did she buy all this? Several elderly gentlemen took care of it, I suppose. I repeat: this is a respectable house! I have tenants who prefer not to live under the same roof with such a person.

SHUI TA: [*quietly*] How much do you want?

MRS. MI TZU: [*he is ahead of her now*] I beg your pardon.

SHUI TA: To reassure yourself. To reassure your tenants. How much will it cost?

MRS. MI TZU: You're a cool customer.

SHUI TA: [*picking up the lease*] The rent is high. [*He reads on.*] I assume it's payable by the month?

MRS. MI TZU: Not in her case.

SHUI TA: [*looking up*] What?

MRS. MI TZU: Six months' rent payable in advance. Two hundred silver dollars.

SHUI TA: Six . . . ! Sheer usury! And where am I to find it?

MRS. MI TZU: You should have thought of that before.

SHUI TA: Have you no heart, Mrs. Mi Tzu? It's true Shen Te acted foolishly, being kind to all those people, but she'll improve with time. I'll see to it she does. She'll work her fingers to the bone to pay her rent, and all the time be as quiet as a mouse, as humble as a fly.

MRS. MI TZU: Her social background . . .

SHUI TA: Out of the depths! She came out of the depths! And before she'll go back there, she'll work, sacrifice, shrink from nothing. . . . Such a tenant is worth her weight in gold, Mrs. Mi Tzu.

MRS. MI TZU: It's silver dollars we were talking about, Mr. Shui Ta. Two hundred silver dollars or . . .

[*Enter the* POLICEMAN.]

POLICEMAN: Am I intruding, Mr. Shui Ta?

MRS. MI TZU: This tobacco shop is well known to the police, I see.

POLICEMAN: Mr. Shui Ta has done us a service, Mrs. Mi Tzu. I am here to present our official felicitations!

MRS. MI TZU: That means less than nothing to me, sir. Mr. Shui Ta, all I can say is: I hope your cousin will find my terms acceptable. Good day, gentlemen. [*Exit.*]

SHUI TA: Good day, ma'am.

[*Pause.*]

POLICEMAN: Mrs. Mi Tzu a bit of a stumbling block, sir?

SHUI TA: She wants six months' rent in advance.

POLICEMAN: And you haven't got it, eh? [SHUI TA *is silent.*] But surely you can get it, sir? A man like you?

SHUI TA: What about a woman like Shen Te?

POLICEMAN: You're not staying, sir?

SHUI TA: No, and I won't be back. Do you smoke?

POLICEMAN: [*taking two cigars, and placing them both in his pocket*] Thank you, sir — I see your point. Miss Te — let's mince no words — Miss Shen Te lived by selling herself. "What else could she have done?" you ask. "How else was she to pay the rent?" True. But the fact remains, Mr. Shui Ta, it is not respectable. Why not? A very deep question. But, in the first place, love — love isn't bought and sold like cigars, Mr. Shui Ta. In the second place, it isn't respectable to go waltzing off with someone that's paying his way, so to speak — it must be for love! Thirdly and lastly, as the proverb has it: not for a handful of rice but for love! [*Pause. He is thinking hard.*] "Well," you may say, "and what good is all this wisdom if the milk's already spilt?" Miss Shen Te is what she is. Is *where* she is. We have to face the fact that if she doesn't get hold of six months' rent pronto, she'll be back on the streets. The question then as I see it — everything in this world is a matter of opinion — the question as I see it is: *how* is she to get hold of this rent? How? Mr. Shui Ta: I don't know. [*Pause.*] I take that back, sir. It's just come to me. A husband. We must find her a husband!

    [*Enter a little* OLD WOMAN.]

OLD WOMAN: A good cheap cigar for my husband, we'll have been married forty years tomorrow and we're having a little celebration.

SHUI TA: Forty years? And you still want to celebrate?

OLD WOMAN: As much as we can afford to. We have the carpet shop across the square. We'll be good neighbors, I hope?

SHUI TA: I hope so too.

POLICEMAN: [*who keeps making discoveries*] Mr. Shui Ta, you know what we need? We need capital. And how do we acquire capital? We get married.

SHUI TA: [*to* OLD WOMAN] I'm afraid I've been pestering this gentleman with my personal worries.

POLICEMAN: [*lyrically*] We can't pay six months' rent, so what do we do? We marry money.

SHUI TA: That might not be easy.

POLICEMAN: Oh, I don't know. She's a good match. Has a nice, growing business. [*to the* OLD WOMAN] What do you think?

OLD WOMAN: [*undecided*] Well —

POLICEMAN: Should she put an ad in the paper?

OLD WOMAN: [*not eager to commit herself*] Well, if *she* agrees —

POLICEMAN: I'll write it for her. *You* lend us a hand, and *we* write an ad for you! [*He chuckles away to himself, takes out his notebook, wets the stump of a pencil between his lips, and writes away.*]

SHUI TA: [*slowly*] Not a bad idea.

POLICEMAN: "What . . . *respectable* . . . man . . . with small capital . . . widower . . . not excluded . . . desires . . . marriage . . . into flourishing . . . tobacco shop?" And now let's add: "Am . . . pretty . . . " No! . . . "Prepossessing appearance."

SHUI TA: If you don't think that's an exaggeration?

OLD WOMAN: Oh, not a bit. I've seen her.

    [*The* POLICEMAN *tears the page out of his notebook, and hands it over to* SHUI TA.]

SHUI TA: [*with horror in his voice*] How much luck we need to keep our heads above water! How many ideas! How many friends! [*to the* POLICEMAN] Thank you, sir, I think I see my way clear.

SCENE III———*Evening in the municipal park. Noise of a plane overhead.*

[YANG SUN, *a young man in rags, is following the plane with his eyes: one can tell that the machine is describing a curve above the park.* YANG SUN *then takes a rope out of his pocket, looking anxiously about him as he does so. He moves toward a large willow. Enter two prostitutes, one the* OLD WHORE, *the other the* NIECE *whom we have already met.*]

NIECE: Hello. Coming with me?

YANG SUN: [*taken aback*] If you'd like to buy me a dinner.

OLD WHORE: Buy you a dinner! [*to the* NIECE] Oh, we know him—it's the unemployed pilot. Waste no time on him!

NIECE: But he's the only man left in the park. And it's going to rain.

OLD WHORE: Oh, how do you know?

[*And they pass by.* YANG SUN *again looks about him, again takes his rope, and this time throws it round a branch of the willow tree. Again he is interrupted. It is the two prostitutes returning—and in such a hurry they don't notice him.*]

NIECE: It's going to pour!

[*Enter* SHEN TE.]

OLD WHORE: There's that *gorgon* Shen Te! That *drove* your family out into the cold!

NIECE: It wasn't her. It was that cousin of hers. She offered to pay for the cakes. I've nothing against her.

OLD WHORE: I have, though. [*so that* SHEN TE *can hear*] Now where would the little lady be off to? She may be rich now but that won't stop her snatching our young men, will it?

SHEN TE: I'm going to the tearoom by the pond.

NIECE: Is it true what they say? You're marrying a widower—with three children?

SHEN TE: Yes. I'm just going to see him.

YANG SUN: [*his patience at breaking point*] Move on there! This is a park, not a whorehouse!

OLD WHORE: Shut your mouth!

[*But the two prostitutes leave.*]

YANG SUN: Even in the farthest corner of the park, even when it's raining, you can't get rid of them! [*He spits.*]

SHEN TE: [*overhearing this*] And what right have you to scold them? [*But at this point she sees the rope.*] Oh!

YANG SUN: Well, what are you staring at?

SHEN TE: That rope. What is it for?

YANG SUN: Think! Think! I haven't a penny. Even if I had, I wouldn't spend it on you. I'd buy a drink of water. [*The rain starts.*]

SHEN TE: [*still looking at the rope*] What is the rope for? You mustn't!

YANG SUN: What's it to you? Clear out!

SHEN TE: [*irrelevantly*] It's raining.

YANG SUN: Well, don't try to come under this tree.

SHEN TE: Oh, no. [*She stays in the rain.*]

YANG SUN: Now go away. [*pause*] For one thing, I don't like your looks, you're bowlegged.

SHEN TE: [*indignantly*] That's not true!

YANG SUN: Well, don't show 'em to me. Look, it's raining. You better come under this tree.

[*Slowly, she takes shelter under the tree.*]

SHEN TE: Why did you want to do it?

YANG SUN: You really want to know? [*pause*] To get rid of you! [*pause*] You know what a flyer is?

SHEN TE: Oh yes, I've met a lot of pilots. At the tearoom.

YANG SUN: You call *them* flyers? Think they know what a machine is? Just 'cause they have leather helmets? They gave the airfield director a bribe, that's the way *those* fellows got up in the air! Try one of them out sometime. "Go up to two thousand feet," tell them, "then let it fall, then pick it up again with a flick of the wrist at the last moment." Know what he'll say to that? "It's not in my contract." Then again, there's the landing problem. It's like landing on your own backside. It's no different, planes are human. Those fools don't understand. [*pause*] And I'm the biggest fool for reading the book on flying in the Peking school and skipping the page where it says: "We've got enough flyers and we don't need you." I'm a mail pilot with no mail. You understand that?

SHEN TE: [*shyly*] Yes. I do.

YANG SUN: No, you don't. You'd never understand that.

SHEN TE: When we were little we had a crane with a broken wing. He made friends with us and was very good-natured about our jokes. He would strut along behind us and call out to stop us going too fast for him. But every spring and autumn when the cranes flew over the villages in great swarms, he got quite restless. [*pause*] I understand that. [*She bursts out crying.*]

YANG SUN: Don't!

SHEN TE: [*quieting down*] No.

YANG SUN: It's bad for the complexion.

SHEN TE: [*sniffing*] I've stopped.

[*She dries her tears on her big sleeve. Leaning against the tree, but not looking at her, he reaches for her face.*]

YANG SUN: You can't even wipe your own face. [*He is wiping it for her with his handkerchief. Pause.*]

SHEN TE: [*still sobbing*] I don't know *anything*!

YANG SUN: You interrupted me! What for?

SHEN TE: It's such a rainy day. You only wanted to do . . . *that* because it's such a rainy day. [*To the audience:*]

In our country
The evenings should never be somber
High bridges over rivers
The gray hour between night and morning
And the long, long winter:
Such things are dangerous
For, with all the misery,
A very little is enough
And men throw away an unbearable life.

[*Pause.*]

YANG SUN: Talk about yourself for a change.

SHEN TE: What about me? I have a shop.

YANG SUN: [*incredulous*] You have a shop, have you? Never thought of walking the streets?

SHEN TE: I did walk the streets. Now I have a shop.

YANG SUN: [*ironically*] A gift of the gods, I suppose!

SHEN TE: How did you know?

YANG SUN: [*even more ironical*] One fine evening the gods turned up saying: here's some money!

SHEN TE: [*quickly*] One fine morning.

YANG SUN: [*fed up*] This isn't much of an entertainment.
[*Pause.*]

SHEN TE: I can play the zither a little. [*pause*] And I can mimic men. [*pause*] I got the shop, so the first thing I did was to give my zither away. So I can be as stupid as a fish now, I said to myself, and it won't matter.
I'm rich now, I said
I walk alone, I sleep alone
For a whole year, I said
I'll have nothing to do with a man.

YANG SUN: And now you're marrying one! The one at the tearoom by the pond?
[SHEN TE *is silent.*]

YANG SUN: What do you know about love?

SHEN TE: Everything

YANG SUN: Nothing. [*pause*] Or d'you just mean you enjoyed it?

SHEN TE: No.

YANG SUN: [*again without turning to look at her, he strokes her cheek with his hand*] You like that?

SHEN TE: Yes.

YANG SUN: [*breaking off*] You're easily satisfied, I must say. [*pause*] What a town!

SHEN TE: You have no friends?

YANG SUN: [*defensively*] Yes, I have! [*change of tone*] But they don't want to hear I'm still unemployed. "What?" they ask. "Is there still water in the sea?" You have friends?

SHEN TE: [*hesitating*] Just a . . . cousin.

YANG SUN: Watch him carefully.

SHEN TE: He only came once. Then he went away. He won't be back. [YANG SUN *is looking away.*] But to be without hope, they say, is to be without goodness!
[*Pause.*]

YANG SUN: Go on talking. A voice is a voice.

SHEN TE: Once, when I was a little girl, I fell, with a load of brushwood. An old man picked me up. He gave me a penny too. Isn't it funny how people who don't have very much like to give some of it away? They must like to show what they can do, and how could they show it better than by being kind? Being wicked is just like being clumsy. When we sing a song, or build a machine, or plant some rice, we're being kind. You're kind.

YANG SUN: You make it sound easy.

SHEN TE: Oh, no. [*little pause*] Oh! A drop of rain!

YANG SUN: Where'd you feel it?

SHEN TE: Right between the eyes.

YANG SUN: Near the right eye? Or the left?

SHEN TE: Near the left eye.

YANG SUN: Oh, good. [*he is getting sleepy*] So you're through with men, eh?

SHEN TE: [*with a smile*] But I'm not bowlegged.

YANG SUN: Perhaps not.

SHEN TE: Definitely not.

> [*Pause.*]

YANG SUN: [*leaning wearily against the willow*] I haven't had a drop to drink all day, I haven't eaten anything for *two* days. I couldn't love you if I tried.

> [*Pause.*]

SHEN TE: I like it in the rain.

> [*Enter* WONG *the water seller, singing.*]

THE SONG OF THE WATER SELLER IN THE RAIN

"Buy my water," I am yelling
And my fury restraining
For no water I'm selling
'Cause it's raining, 'cause it's raining!
    I keep yelling: "Buy my water!"
    But no one's buying
    Athirst and dying
    And drinking and paying!
    Buy water!
    Buy water, you dogs!

Nice to dream of lovely weather!
Think of all the consternation
Were there no precipitation
Half a dozen years together!
    Can't you hear them shrieking: "Water!"
    Pretending they adore me?
    They all would go down on their knees
        before me!
    Down on your knees!
    Go down on your knees, you dogs!"

What are lawns and hedges thinking?
What are fields and forests saying?
"At the cloud's breast we are drinking!
And we've no idea who's paying!"
    I keep yelling: "Buy my water!"
    But no one's buying
    Athirst and dying
    And drinking and paying!
    Buy water
    Buy water, you dogs!

> [*The rain has stopped now,* SHEN TE *sees* WONG *and runs toward him.*]

SHEN TE: Wong! You're back! Your carrying pole's at the shop.

WONG: Oh, thank you, Shen Te. And how is life treating *you*?

SHEN TE: I've just met a brave and clever man. And I want to buy him a cup of your water.

WONG: [*bitterly*] Throw back your head and open your mouth and you'll have all the water you need—

SHEN TE: [*tenderly*]

> I want *your* water, Wong
> That water that has tired you so
> The water that you carried all this way
> The water that is hard to sell because
>     it's been raining.
> I need it for the young man over there—he's a flyer!
> A flyer is a bold man:
> Braving the storms
> In company with the clouds
> He crosses the heavens
> And brings to friends in faraway lands
> The friendly mail!

[*She pays* WONG, *and runs over to* YANG SUN *with the cup. But* YANG SUN *is fast asleep.*]

SHEN TE: [*calling to* WONG, *with a laugh*] He's fallen asleep! Despair and rain and I have worn him out!

SCENE IIIa———WONG's *den*.

[*The sewer pipe is transparent, and the* GODS *again appear to* WONG *in a dream.*]

WONG: [*radiant*] I've seen her, illustrious ones! And she hasn't changed!

FIRST GOD: That's good to hear.

WONG: She loves someone.

FIRST GOD: Let's hope the experience gives her the strength to stay good!

WONG: It does. She's doing good deeds all the time.

FIRST GOD: Ah? What sort? What sort of good deeds, Wong?

WONG: Well, she has a kind word for everybody.

FIRST GOD: [*eagerly*] And then?

WONG: Hardly anyone leaves her shop without tobacco in his pocket—even if he can't pay for it.

FIRST GOD: Not bad at all. Next?

WONG: She's putting up a family of eight.

FIRST GOD: [*gleefully, to the* SECOND GOD] Eight! [*to* WONG] And that's not all, of course!

WONG: She bought a cup of water from me even though it was raining.

FIRST GOD: Yes, yes, yes, all these smaller good deeds!

WONG: Even they run into money. A little tobacco shop doesn't make so much.

FIRST GOD: [*sententiously*] A prudent gardener works miracles on the smallest plot.

WONG: She hands out rice every morning. That eats up half her earnings.

FIRST GOD: [*a little disappointed*] Well, as a beginning . . .

WONG: They call her the Angel of the Slums—whatever the carpenter may say!

FIRST GOD: What's this? A carpenter speaks ill of her?

WONG: Oh, he only says her shelves weren't paid for in full.

SECOND GOD: [*who has a bad cold and can't pronounce his n's and m's*] What's this? Not paying a carpenter? Why was that?

WONG: I suppose she didn't have the money.

SECOND GOD: [*severely*] One pays what one owes, that's in our book of rules! First the letter of the law, then the spirit.

WONG: But it wasn't Shen Te, illustrious ones, it was her cousin. She called *him* in to help.

SECOND GOD: Then her cousin must never darken her threshold again!

WONG: Very well, illustrious ones! But in fairness to Shen Te, let me say that her cousin is a businessman.

FIRST GOD: Perhaps we should inquire what is customary? I find business quite unintelligible. But everybody's doing it. Business! Did the Seven Good Kings do business? Did King the Just sell fish?

SECOND GOD: In any case, such a thing must not occur again!

[*The* GODS *start to leave.*]

THIRD GOD: Forgive us for taking this tone with you, Wong, we haven't been getting enough sleep. The rich recommended us to the poor, and the poor tell us they haven't enough room.

SECOND GOD: Feeble, feeble, the best of them!

FIRST GOD: No great deeds! No heroic daring!

THIRD GOD: On such a *small* scale!

SECOND GOD: Sincere, yes, but what is actually *achieved*?

[*One can no longer hear them.*]

WONG: [*calling after them*] I've thought of something, illustrious ones: Perhaps you shouldn't ask — too — much — all — at — once!

SCENE IV———*The square in front of* SHEN TE's *tobacco shop. Besides Shen Te's place, two other shops are seen: the carpet shop and a barber's. Morning.*

[*Outside Shen Te's the* GRANDFATHER, *the* SISTER-IN-LAW, *the* UNEMPLOYED MAN, *and* MRS. SHIN *stand waiting.*]

SISTER-IN-LAW: She's been out all night again.

MRS. SHIN: No sooner did we get rid of that crazy cousin of hers than Shen Te herself starts carrying on! Maybe she does give us an ounce of rice now and then, but can you depend on her? Can you depend on her?

[*Loud voices from the barber's.*]

VOICE OF SHU FU: What are you doing in my shop? Get out — at once!

VOICE OF WONG: But sir. They all let me sell . . .

[WONG *comes staggering out of the barber's shop pursued by* MR. SHU FU, *the barber, a fat man carrying a heavy curling iron.*]

SHU FU: Get out, I said! Pestering my customers with your slimy old water! Get out! Take your cup!

[*He holds out the cup.* WONG *reaches out for it.* MR. SHU FU *strikes his hand with the curling iron, which is hot.* WONG *howls.*]

SHU FU: You had it coming, my man!

[*Puffing, he returns to his shop. The* UNEMPLOYED MAN *picks up the cup and gives it to* WONG.]

UNEMPLOYED MAN: You can report that to the police.

WONG: My hand! It's smashed up!

UNEMPLOYED MAN: Any bones broken?

WONG: I can't move my fingers.

UNEMPLOYED MAN: Sit down. I'll put some water on it.

[WONG *sits.*]

MRS. SHIN: The water won't cost you anything.

SISTER-IN-LAW: You might have got a bandage from Miss Shen Te till she took to staying out all night. It's a scandal.

MRS. SHIN: [*despondently*] If you ask me, she's forgotten we ever existed!

[*Enter* SHEN TE *down the street, with a dish of rice.*]

SHEN TE: [*to the audience*] How wonderful to see Setzuan in the early morning! I always used to stay in bed with my dirty blanket over my head afraid to wake up. This morning I saw the newspapers being delivered by little boys, the streets being washed by strong men, and fresh vegetables coming in from the country on ox carts. It's a long walk from where Yang Sun lives, but I feel lighter at every step. They say you walk on air when you're in love, but it's even better walking on the rough earth, on the hard cement. In the early morning, the old city looks like a great heap of rubbish! Nice, though, with all its little lights. And the sky, so pink, so transparent, before the dust comes and muddies it! What a lot you miss if you never see your city rising from its slumbers like an honest old craftsman pumping his lungs full of air and reaching for his tools as the poet says! [*cheerfully, to her waiting guests*] Good morning, everyone, here's your rice! [*Distributing the rice, she comes upon* WONG.] Good morning, Wong, I'm quite lightheaded today. On my way over, I looked at myself in all the shop windows. I'd love to be beautiful.

[*She slips into the carpet shop.* MR. SHU FU *has just emerged from his shop.*]

SHU FU: [*to the audience*] It surprises me how beautiful Miss Shen Te is looking today! I never gave her a passing thought before. But now I've been gazing upon her comely form for exactly three minutes! I begin to suspect I am in love with her. She is overpoweringly attractive! [*crossly, to* WONG] Be off with you, rascal!

[*He returns to his shop.* SHEN TE *comes back out of the carpet shop with the* OLD MAN, *its proprietor, and his wife — whom we have already met — the* OLD WOMAN. SHEN TE *is wearing a shawl. The* OLD MAN *is holding up a looking glass for her.*]

OLD WOMAN: Isn't it lovely? We'll give you a reduction because there's a little hole in it.

SHEN TE: [*looking at another shawl on the* OLD WOMAN'S *arm*] The other one's nice too.

OLD WOMAN: [*smiling*] Too bad there's no hole in that!

SHEN TE: That's right. My shop doesn't make very much.

OLD WOMAN: And your good deeds eat it all up! Be more careful, my dear. . . .

SHEN TE: [*trying on the shawl with the hole*] Just now, I'm lightheaded! Does the color suit me?

OLD WOMAN: You'd better ask a man.

SHEN TE: [*to the* OLD MAN] Does the color suit me?

OLD MAN: You'd better ask your young friend.

SHEN TE: I'd like to have your opinion.

OLD MAN: It suits you very well. But wear it this way: the dull side out.

[SHEN TE *pays up.*]

OLD WOMAN: If you decide you don't like it, you can exchange it. [*She pulls* SHEN TE *to one side.*] Has he got money?

SHEN TE: [*with a laugh*] Yang Sun? Oh, no.

OLD WOMAN: Then how're you going to pay your rent?

SHEN TE: I'd forgotten about that.

OLD WOMAN: And next Monday is the first of the month! Miss Shen Te, I've got something to say to you. After we [*indicating her husband*] got to know you, we had our doubts about that marriage ad. We thought it would be better if you'd let *us* help you. Out of our savings. We reckon we could lend you two hundred silver dollars. We don't need anything in writing — you could pledge us your tobacco stock.

SHEN TE: You're prepared to lend money to a person like me?

OLD WOMAN: It's folks like you that need it. We'd think twice about lending anything to your cousin.

OLD MAN: [*coming up*] All settled, my dear?

SHEN TE: I wish the gods could have heard what your wife was just saying, Mr. Ma. They're looking for good people who're happy — and helping me makes you happy because you know it was love that got me into difficulties!

[*The* OLD COUPLE *smile knowingly at each other.*]

OLD MAN: And here's the money, Miss Shen Te.

[*He hands her an envelope.* SHEN TE *takes it. She bows. They bow back. They return to their shop.*]

SHEN TE: [*holding up her envelope*] Look, Wong, here's six months' rent! Don't you believe in miracles now? And how do you like my new shawl?

WONG: For the young fellow I saw you with in the park?

[SHEN TE *nods.*]

MRS. SHIN: Never mind all that. It's time you took a look at his hand!

SHEN TE: Have you hurt your hand?

MRS. SHIN: That barber smashed it with his hot curling iron. Right in front of our eyes.

SHEN TE: [*shocked at herself*] And I never noticed! We must get you to a doctor this minute or who knows what will happen?

UNEMPLOYED MAN: It's not a doctor he should see, it's a judge. He can ask for compensation. The barber's filthy rich.

WONG: You think I have a chance?

MRS. SHIN: [*with relish*] If it's really good and smashed. But is it?

WONG: I think so. It's very swollen. Could I get a pension?

MRS. SHIN: You'd need a witness.

WONG: Well, you all saw it. You could all testify.

[*He looks around. The* UNEMPLOYED MAN, *the* GRANDFATHER, *and the* SISTER-IN-LAW *are all sitting against the wall of the shop eating rice. Their concentration on eating is complete.*]

SHEN TE: [*to* MRS. SHIN] You saw it yourself.

MRS. SHIN: I want nothing to do with the police. It's against my principles.

SHEN TE: [*to* SISTER-IN-LAW] What about you?

SISTER-IN-LAW: Me? I wasn't looking.

SHEN TE: [*to the* GRANDFATHER, *coaxingly*] Grandfather, *you'll* testify, won't you?

SISTER-IN-LAW: And a lot of good that will do. He's simple-minded.

SHEN TE: [*to the* UNEMPLOYED MAN] You seem to be the only witness left.

UNEMPLOYED MAN: My testimony would only hurt him. I've been picked up twice for begging.

SHEN TE: Your brother is assaulted, and you shut your eyes?
He is hit, cries out in pain, and you are silent?
The beast prowls, chooses and seizes his victim, and you say:
"Because we showed no displeasure, he has spared us."
If no one present will be a witness, I will. I'll say
I saw it.

MRS. SHIN: [*solemnly*] The name for that is perjury.

WONG: I don't know if I can accept that. Though maybe I'll have to. [*looking at his hand*] Is it swollen enough, do you think? The swelling's not going down?

UNEMPLOYED MAN: No, no. The swelling's holding up well.

WONG: Yes. It's *more* swollen if anything. Maybe my wrist is broken after all. I'd better see a judge at once.
[*Holding his hand very carefully, and fixing his eyes on it, he runs off.* MRS. SHIN *goes quickly into the barber's shop.*]

UNEMPLOYED MAN: [*seeing her*] She is getting on the right side of Mr. Shu Fu.

SISTER-IN-LAW: You and I can't change the world, Shen Te.

SHEN TE: Go away! Go away all of you!
[*The* UNEMPLOYED MAN, *the* SISTER-IN-LAW, *and the* GRANDFATHER *stalk off, eating and sulking.*]
[*To the audience.*]
They've stopped answering
They stay put
They do as they're told
They don't care
Nothing can make them look up
But the smell of food.
[*Enter* MRS. YANG, *Yang Sun's mother, out of breath.*]

MRS. YANG: Miss Shen Te. My son has told me everything. I am Mrs. Yang, Sun's mother. Just think. He's got an offer. Of a job as a pilot. A letter has just come. From the director of the airfield in Peking!

SHEN TE: So he can fly again? Isn't that wonderful!

MRS. YANG: [*less breathlessly all the time*] They won't give him the job for nothing. They want five hundred silver dollars.

SHEN TE: We can't let money stand in his way, Mrs. Yang!

MRS. YANG: If only you could help him out!

SHEN TE: I have the shop. I can try! [*She embraces* MRS. YANG.] I happen to have two hundred with me now. Take it. [*She gives her the old couple's money*.] It was a loan but they said I could repay it with my tobacco stock.

MRS. YANG: And they were calling Sun the Dead Pilot of Setzuan! A friend in need!

SHEN TE: We must find another three hundred.

MRS. YANG:  How?

SHEN TE:  Let me think. [*slowly*] I know someone who can help. I didn't want to call
on his services again, he's hard and cunning. But a flyer must fly. And I'll make
this the last time.

  [*Distant sound of a plane.*]

MRS. YANG:  If the man you mentioned can do it  . . .  Oh, look, there's the morning
mail plane, heading for Peking!

SHEN TE:  The pilot can see us, let's wave!

  [*They wave. The noise of the engine is louder.*]

MRS. YANG:  You know that pilot up there?

SHEN TE:  Wave, Mrs. Yang! I know the pilot who will be up there. He gave up hope.
But he'll do it now. One man to raise himself above the misery, above us all.
[*To the audience:*]
Yang Sun, my lover:
Braving the storms
In company with the clouds
Crossing the heavens
And bringing to friends in faraway lands
The friendly mail!


SCENE IVa———*In front of the inner curtain.*

[*Enter* SHEN TE, *carrying Shui Ta's mask. She sings:*]

THE SONG OF DEFENSELESSNESS

In our country
A useful man needs luck
Only if he finds strong backers
Can he prove himself useful.
The good can't defend themselves and
Even the gods are defenseless.

Oh, why don't the gods have their own ammunition
And launch against badness their own expedition
Enthroning the good and preventing sedition
And bringing the world to a peaceful condition?

Oh, why don't the gods do the buying and selling
Injustice forbidding, starvation dispelling
Give bread to each city and joy to each dwelling?
Oh, why don't the gods do the buying and selling?
  [*She puts on* SHUI TA's *mask and sings in his voice.*]
You can only help one of your luckless brothers
By trampling down a dozen others.

Why is it the gods do not feel indignation
And come down in fury to end exploitation

Defeat all defeat and forbid desperation
Refusing to tolerate such toleration?

Why is it?

SCENE V——— SHEN TE's *tobacco shop.*

[*Behind the counter,* MR. SHUI TA, *reading the paper.* MRS. SHIN *is cleaning up. She talks and he takes no notice.*]

MRS. SHIN: And when certain rumors get about, what *happens* to a little place like this? It goes to pot. *I* know. So, if you want my advice, Mr. Shui Ta, find out just what has been going on between Miss Shen Te and that Yang Sun from Yellow Street. And remember: a certain interest in Miss Shen Te has been expressed by the barber next door, a man with twelve houses and only one wife, who, for that matter, is likely to drop off at any time. A certain interest has been expressed. He was even inquiring about her means and, if *that* doesn't prove a man is getting serious, what would? [*Still getting no response, she leaves with her bucket.*]

YANG SUN'S VOICE: Is that Miss Shen Te's tobacco shop?

MRS. SHIN'S VOICE: Yes, it is, but it's Mr. Shui Ta who's here today.

[SHUI TA *runs to the mirror with the short, light steps of* SHEN TE, *and is just about to start primping, when he realizes his mistake, and turns away, with a short laugh. Enter* YANG SUN. MRS. SHIN *enters behind him and slips into the back room to eavesdrop.*]

YANG SUN: I am Yang Sun. [SHUI TA *bows*] Is Shen Te in?

SHUI TA: No.

YANG SUN: I guess you know our relationship? [*He is inspecting the stock.*] Quite a place! And I thought she was just talking big. I'll be flying again, all right. [*He takes a cigar, solicits and receives a light from* SHUI TA.] You think we can squeeze the other three hundred out of the tobacco stock?

SHUI TA: May I ask if it is your intention to sell at once?

YANG SUN: It was decent of her to come out with the two hundred but they aren't much use with the other three hundred still missing.

SHUI TA: Shen Te was overhasty promising so much. She might have to sell the shop itself to raise it. Haste, they say, is the wind that blows the house down.

YANG SUN: Oh, she isn't a girl to keep a man waiting. For one thing or the other, if you take my meaning.

SHUI TA: I take your meaning.

YANG SUN: [*leering*] Uh, huh.

SHUI TA: Would you explain what the five hundred silver dollars are for?

YANG SUN: Want to sound me out? Very well. The director of the Peking airfield is a friend of mine from flying school. I give him five hundred: he gets me the job.

SHUI TA: The price is high.

YANG SUN: Not as these things go. He'll have to fire one of the present pilots — for negligence. Only the man he has in mind isn't negligent. Not easy, you understand. You needn't mention that part of it to Shen Te.

SHUI TA: [*looking intently at* YANG SUN] Mr. Yang Sun, you are asking my cousin to give up her possessions, leave her friends, and place her entire fate in your hands. I presume you intend to marry her?

YANG SUN: I'd be prepared to.

       [*Slight pause.*]

SHUI TA: Those two hundred silver dollars would pay the rent here for six months. If you were Shen Te wouldn't you be tempted to continue in business?

YANG SUN: What? Can you imagine Yang Sun the flyer behind a counter? [*in an oily voice*] "A strong cigar or a mild one, worthy sir?" Not in this century!

SHUI TA: My cousin wishes to follow the promptings of her heart, and, from her own point of view, she may even have what is called the right to love. Accordingly, she has commissioned me to help you to this post. There is nothing here that I am not empowered to turn immediately into cash. Mrs. Mi Tzu, the landlady, will advise me about the sale.

       [*Enter* MRS. MI TZU.]

MRS. MI TZU: Good morning, Mr. Shui Ta, you wish to see me about the rent? As you know it falls due the day after tomorrow.

SHUI TA: Circumstances have changed, Mrs. Mi Tzu: my cousin is getting married. Her future husband here, Mr. Yang Sun, will be taking her to Peking. I am interested in selling the tobacco stock.

MRS. MI TZU: How much are you asking, Mr. Shui Ta?

YANG SUN: Three hundred sil—

SHUI TA: Five hundred silver dollars.

MRS. MI TZU: How much did she pay for it, Mr. Shui Ta?

SHUI TA: A thousand. And very little has been sold.

MRS. MI TZU: She was robbed. But I'll make you a special offer if you'll promise to be out by the day after tomorrow. Three hundred silver dollars.

YANG SUN: [*shrugging*] Take it, man, take it.

SHUI TA: It is not enough.

YANG SUN: Why not? Why not? Certainly, it's enough.

SHUI TA: Five hundred silver dollars.

YANG SUN: But why? We only need three!

SHUI TA: [*to* MRS. MI TZU] Excuse me. [*takes* YANG SUN *on one side*] The tobacco stock is pledged to the old couple who gave my cousin the two hundred.

YANG SUN: Is it in writing?

SHUI TA: No.

YANG SUN: [*to* MRS. MI TZU] Three hundred will do.

MRS. MI TZU: Of course, I need an assurance that Miss Shen Te is not in debt.

YANG SUN: Mr. Shui Ta?

SHUI TA: She is not in debt.

YANG SUN: When can you let us have the money?

MRS. MI TZU: The day after tomorrow. And remember: I'm doing this because I have a soft spot in my heart for young lovers! [*Exit.*]

YANG SUN: [*calling after her*] Boxes, jars and sacks—three hundred for the lot and the pain's over! [*to* SHUI TA] Where else can we raise money by the day after tomorrow?

SHUI TA: Nowhere. Haven't you enough for the trip and the first few weeks?

YANG SUN: Oh, certainly.

SHUI TA: How much, exactly.

YANG SUN: Oh, I'll dig it up, even if I have to steal it.

SHUI TA: I see.

YANG SUN: Well, don't fall off the roof. I'll get to Peking somehow.

SHUI TA: Two people can't travel for nothing.

YANG SUN: [*not giving* SHUI TA *a chance to answer*] I'm leaving *her* behind. No millstones round *my* neck!

SHUI TA: Oh.

YANG SUN: Don't look at me like that!

SHUI TA: How precisely is my cousin to live?

YANG SUN: Oh, you'll think of something.

SHUI TA: A small request, Mr. Yang Sun. Leave the two hundred silver dollars here until you can show me two tickets for Peking.

YANG SUN: You learn to mind your own business, Mr. Shui Ta.

SHUI TA: I'm afraid Miss Shen Te may not wish to sell the shop when she discovers that . . .

YANG SUN: You don't know women. She'll want to. Even then.

SHUI TA: [*a slight outburst*] She is a human being, sir! And not devoid of common sense!

YANG SUN: Shen Te is a woman: she *is* devoid of common sense. I only have to lay my hand on her shoulder, and church bells ring.

SHUI TA: [*with difficulty*] Mr. Yang Sun!

YANG SUN: Mr. Shui Whatever-it-is!

SHUI TA: My cousin is devoted to you . . . because . . .

YANG SUN: Because I have my hands on her breasts. Give me a cigar. [*He takes one for himself, stuffs a few more in his pocket, then changes his mind and takes the whole box.*] Tell her I'll marry her, then bring me the three hundred. Or let her bring it. One or the other. [*Exit.*]

MRS. SHIN: [*sticking her head out of the back room*] Well, he has your cousin under his thumb, and doesn't care if all Yellow Street knows it!

SHUI TA: [*crying out*] I've lost my shop! And he doesn't love me! [*He runs berserk through the room, repeating these lines incoherently. Then stops suddenly, and addresses* MRS. SHIN.] Mrs. Shin, you grew up in the gutter, like me. Are we lacking in hardness? I doubt it. If you steal a penny from me, I'll take you by the throat till you spit it out! You'd do the same to me. The times are bad, this city is hell, but we're like ants, we keep coming, up and up the walls, however smooth! Till bad luck comes. Being in love, for instance. One weakness is enough, and love is the deadliest.

MRS. SHIN: [*emerging from the back room*] You should have a little talk with Mr. Shu Fu, the barber. He's a real gentleman and just the thing for your cousin. [*She runs off.*]

SHUI TA: A caress becomes a stranglehold
A sigh of love turns to a cry of fear
Why are there vultures circling in the air?
A girl is going to meet her lover.
    [SHUI TA *sits down and* MR. SHU FU *enters with* MRS. SHIN.]

SHUI TA: Mr. Shu Fu?

SHU FU: Mr. Shui Ta.
    [*They both bow.*]

SHUI TA: I am told that you have expressed a certain interest in my cousin Shen Te. Let me set aside all propriety and confess: she is at this moment in grave danger.

SHU FU: Oh, dear!

SHUI TA: She has lost her shop, Mr. Shu Fu.

SHU FU: The charm of Miss Shen Te, Mr. Shui Ta, derives from the goodness, not of her shop, but of her heart. Men call her the Angel of the Slums.

SHUI TA: Yet her goodness has cost her two hundred silver dollars in a single day: we must put a stop to it.

SHU FU: Permit me to differ, Mr. Shui Ta. Let us, rather, open wide the gates to such goodness! Every morning, with pleasure tinged by affection, I watch her charitable ministrations. For they are hungry, and she giveth them to eat! Four of them, to be precise. Why only four? I ask. Why not four hundred? I hear she has been seeking shelter for the homeless. What about my humble cabins behind the cattle run? They are at her disposal. And so forth. And so on. Mr. Shui Ta, do you think Miss Shen Te could be persuaded to listen to certain ideas of mine? Ideas like these?

SHUI TA: Mr. Shu Fu, she would be honored.

> [*Enter* WONG *and the* POLICEMAN. MR. SHU FU *turns abruptly away and studies the shelves.*]

WONG: Is Miss Shen Te here?

SHUI TA: No.

WONG: I am Wong the water seller. You are Mr. Shui Ta?

SHUI TA: I am.

WONG: I am a friend of Shen Te's.

SHUI TA: An intimate friend, I hear.

WONG: [*to the* POLICEMAN] You see? [*to* SHUI TA] It's because of my hand.

POLICEMAN: He hurt his hand, sir that's a fact.

SHUI TA: [*quickly*] You need a sling, I see. [*He takes a shawl from the back room, and throws it to* WONG.]

WONG: But that's her new shawl!

SHUI TA: She has no more use for it.

WONG: But she bought it to please someone!

SHUI TA: It happens to be no longer necessary.

WONG: [*making the sling*] She is my only witness.

POLICEMAN: Mr. Shui Ta, your cousin is supposed to have seen the barber hit the water seller with a curling iron.

SHUI TA: I'm afraid my cousin was not present at the time.

WONG: But she was, sir! Just ask her! Isn't she in?

SHUI TA: [*gravely*] Mr. Wong, my cousin has her own troubles. You wouldn't wish her to add to them by committing perjury?

WONG: But it was she that told me to go to the judge!

SHUI TA: Was the judge supposed to heal your hand?

> [MR. SHU FU *turns quickly around.* SHUI TA *bows to* SHU FU, *and vice versa.*]

WONG: [*taking the sling off, and putting it back*] I see how it is.

POLICEMAN: Well, I'll be on my way. [*to* WONG] And you be careful. If Mr. Shu Fu wasn't a man who tempers justice with mercy, as the saying is, you'd be in jail for libel. Be off with you!

[*Exit* WONG, *followed by* POLICEMAN.]

SHUI TA: Profound apologies, Mr. Shu Fu.

SHU FU: Not at all, Mr. Shui Ta. [*pointing to the shawl*] The episode is over?

SHUI TA: It may take her time to recover. There are some fresh wounds.

SHU FU: We shall be discreet. Delicate. A short vacation could be arranged. . . .

SHUI TA: First of course, you and she would have to talk things over.

SHU FU: At a small supper in a small, but high-class, restaurant.

SHUI TA: I'll go and find her. [*Exit into back room.*]

MRS. SHIN: [*sticking her head in again*] Time for congratulations, Mr. Shu Fu?

SHU FU: Ah, Mrs. Shin! Please inform Miss Shen Te's guests they may take shelter in the cabins behind the cattle run!

    [MRS. SHIN *nods, grinning.*]

SHU FU: [*to the audience*] Well? What do you think of me, ladies and gentlemen? What could a man do more? Could he be less selfish? More farsighted? A small supper in a small but . . . Does that bring rather vulgar and clumsy thoughts into your mind? Ts, ts, ts. Nothing of the sort will occur. She won't even be touched. Not even accidentally while passing the salt. An exchange of ideas only. Over the flowers on the table — white chrysanthemums, by the way [*he writes down a note of this*] — yes, over the white chrysanthemums, two young souls will . . . shall I say "find each other"? We shall NOT exploit the misfortune of others. Understanding? Yes. An offer of assistance? Certainly. But quietly. Almost inaudibly. Perhaps with a single glance. A glance that could also — also mean more.

MRS. SHIN: [*coming forward*] Everything under control, Mr. Shu Fu?

SHU FU: Oh, Mrs. Shin, what do you know about this worthless rascal Yang Sun?

MRS. SHIN: Why, he's the most worthless rascal . . .

SHU FU: Is he really? You're sure? [*as she opens her mouth*] From now on, he doesn't exist! Can't be found anywhere!

    [*Enter* YANG SUN.]

YANG SUN: What's been going on here?

MRS. SHIN: Shall I call Mr. Shui Ta, Mr. Shu Fu? He wouldn't want strangers in here!

SHU FU: Mr. Shui Ta is in conference with Miss Shen Te. Not to be disturbed.

YANG SUN: Shen Te here? I didn't see her come in. What kind of conference?

SHU FU: [*not letting him enter the back room*] Patience, dear sir! And if by chance I have an inkling who you are, pray take note that Miss Shen Te and I are about to announce our engagement.

YANG SUN: What?

MRS. SHIN: You didn't expect that, did you?

    [YANG SUN *is trying to push past the barber into the back room when* SHEN TE *comes out.*]

SHU FU: My dear Shen Te, ten thousand apologies! Perhaps you . . .

YANG SUN: What is it, Shen Te? Have you gone crazy?

SHEN TE: [*breathless*] My cousin and Mr. Shu Fu have come to an understanding. They wish me to hear Mr. Shu Fu's plans for helping the poor.

YANG SUN: Your cousin wants to part us.

SHEN TE: Yes.

YANG SUN: And you've agreed to it?

SHEN TE: Yes.

YANG SUN:  They told you I was bad. [SHEN TE *is silent.*] And suppose I am. Does that make me need you less? I'm low, Shen Te, I have no money, I don't do the right thing but at least I put up a fight! [*He is near her now, and speaks in an undertone.*] Have you no eyes? Look at him. Have you forgotten already?

SHEN TE:  No.

YANG SUN:  How it was raining?

SHEN TE:  No.

YANG SUN:  How you cut me down from the willow tree? Bought me water? Promised me money to fly with?

SHEN TE:  [*shakily*] Yang Sun, what do you want?

YANG SUN:  I want you to come with me.

SHEN TE:  [*in a small voice*] Forgive me, Mr. Shu Fu, I want to go with Mr. Yang Sun.

YANG SUN:  We're lovers you know. Give me the key to the shop. [SHEN TE *takes the key from around her neck.* YANG SUN *puts it on the counter. To* MRS. SHIN:] Leave it under the mat when you're through. Let's go, Shen Te.

SHU FU:  But this is rape! Mr. Shui Ta!!

YANG SUN:  [*to* SHEN TE] Tell him not to shout.

SHEN TE:  Please don't shout for my cousin, Mr. Shu Fu. He doesn't agree with me, I know, but he's wrong. [*To the audience.*]

I want to go with the man I love
I don't want to count the cost
I don't want to consider if it's wise
I don't want to know if he loves me
I want to go with the man I love.

YANG SUN:  That's the spirit.

[*And the couple leave.*]

SCENE va————*In front of the inner curtain.*

[SHEN TE *in her wedding clothes, on the way to her wedding.*]

SHEN TE:  Something terrible has happened. As I left the shop with Yang Sun, I found the old carpet dealer's wife waiting on the street, trembling all over. She told me her husband had taken to his bed sick with all the worry and excitement over the two hundred silver dollars they lent me. She said it would be best if I gave it back now. Of course, I had to say I would. She said she couldn't quite trust my cousin Shui Ta or even my fiancé Yang Sun. There were tears in her eyes. With my emotions in an uproar, I threw myself into Yang Sun's arms, I couldn't resist him. The things he'd said to Shui Ta had taught Shen Te nothing. Sinking into his arms, I said to myself:

To let no one perish, not even oneself
To fill everyone with happiness, even oneself
Is so good

How could I have forgotten those two old people? Yang Sun swept me away like a small hurricane. But he's not a bad man, and he loves me. He'd rather work in the cement factory than owe his flying to a crime. Though, of course, flying *is* a great passion with Sun. Now, on the way to my wedding, I waver between fear and joy.

SCENE VI——— *The "private dining room" on the upper floor of a cheap restaurant in a poor section of town.*

[*With* SHEN TE: *the* GRANDFATHER, *the* SISTER-IN-LAW, *the* NIECE, MRS. SHIN, *the* UNEMPLOYED MAN. *In a corner, alone, a* PRIEST. A WAITER *pouring wine. Downstage,* YANG SUN *talking to his* MOTHER. *He wears a dinner jacket.*]

YANG SUN: Bad news, Mamma. She came right out and told me she can't sell the shop for me. Some idiot is bringing a claim because he lent her the two hundred she gave you.

MRS. YANG: What did you say? Of course, you can't marry her now.

YANG SUN: It's no use saying anything to *her.* I've sent for her cousin, Mr. Shui Ta. He said there was nothing in writing.

MRS. YANG: Good idea. I'll go and look for him. Keep an eye on things.

[*Exit* MRS. YANG. SHEN TE *has been pouring wine.*]

SHEN TE: [*to the audience, pitcher in hand*] I wasn't mistaken in him. He's bearing up well. Though it must have been an awful blow — giving up flying. I do love him so. [*calling across the room to him*] Sun, you haven't drunk a toast with the bride!

YANG SUN: What do we drink to?

SHEN TE: Why, to the future!

YANG SUN: When the bridegroom's dinner jacket won't be a hired one!

SHEN TE: But when the bride's dress will still get rained on sometimes!

YANG SUN: To everything we ever wished for!

SHEN TE: May all our dreams come true!

[*They drink.*]

YANG SUN: [*with loud conviviality*] And now, friends, before the wedding gets under way, I have to ask the bride a few questions. I've no idea what kind of wife she'll make, and it worries me. [*wheeling on* SHEN TE] For example. Can you make five cups of tea with three tea leaves?

SHEN TE: No.

YANG SUN: So I won't be getting very much tea. Can you sleep on a straw mattress the size of that book? [*He points to the large volume the* PRIEST *is reading.*]

SHEN TE: The two of us?

YANG SUN: The one of you.

SHEN TE: In that case, no.

YANG SUN: What a wife! I'm shocked!

[*While the audience is laughing, his* MOTHER *returns. With a shrug of her shoulders, she tells* YANG SUN *the expected guest hasn't arrived. The* PRIEST *shuts the book with a bang, and makes for the door.*]

MRS. YANG: Where are *you* off to? It's only a matter of minutes.

PRIEST: [*watch in hand*] Time goes on, Mrs. Yang, and I've another wedding to attend to. Also a funeral.

MRS. YANG: [*irately*] D'you think we planned it this way? I was hoping to manage with one pitcher of wine, and we've run through two already. [*points to empty pitcher. Loudly*] My dear Shen Te, I don't know where your cousin can be keeping himself!

SHEN TE: My cousin?!

MRS. YANG: Certainly. I'm old-fashioned enough to think such a close relative should attend the wedding.

SHEN TE: Oh, Sun, is it the three hundred silver dollars?

YANG SUN: [*not looking her in the eye*] Are you deaf? Mother says she's old-fashioned. And I say I'm considerate. We'll wait another fifteen minutes.

HUSBAND: Another fifteen minutes.

MRS. YANG: [*addressing the company*] Now you all know, don't you, that my son is getting a job as a mail pilot?

SISTER-IN-LAW: In Peking, too, isn't it?

MRS. YANG: In Peking, too! The two of us are moving to Peking!

SHEN TE: Sun, tell your mother Peking is out of the question now.

YANG SUN: Your cousin'll tell her. If he agrees. I don't agree.

SHEN TE: [*amazed, and dismayed*] Sun!

YANG SUN: I hate this godforsaken Setzuan. What people! Know what they look like when I half close my eyes? Horses! Whinnying, fretting, stamping, screwing their necks up! [*loudly*] And what is it the thunder says? They are su-per-flu-ous! [*he hammers out the syllables*] They've run their last race! They can go trample themselves to death! [*pause*] I've got to get out of here.

SHEN TE: But I've promised the money to the old couple.

YANG SUN: And since you always do the wrong thing, it's lucky your cousin's coming. Have another drink.

SHEN TE: [*quietly*] My cousin can't be coming.

YANG SUN: How d'you mean?

SHEN TE: My cousin can't be where I am.

YANG SUN: Quite a conundrum!

SHEN TE: [*desperately*] Sun, I'm the one that loves you. Not my cousin. He was thinking of the job in Peking when he promised you the old couple's money —

YANG SUN: Right. And that's why he's bringing the three hundred silver dollars. Here — to my wedding.

SHEN TE: He is not bringing the three hundred silver dollars.

YANG SUN: Huh? What makes you think that?

SHEN TE: [*looking into his eyes*] He says you only bought one ticket to Peking. [*Short pause.*]

YANG SUN: That was yesterday. [*He pulls two tickets part way out of his inside pocket, making her look under his coat.*] Two tickets. I don't want Mother to know. She'll get left behind. I sold her furniture to buy these tickets, so you see . . .

SHEN TE: But what's to become of the old couple?

YANG SUN: What's to become of me? Have another drink. Or do you believe in moderation? If I drink, I fly again. If you drink, you may learn to understand me.

SHEN TE: You want to fly. But I can't help you.

YANG SUN: "Here's a plane, my darling — but it's only got one wing!"
          [*The* WAITER *enters.*]

WAITER: Mrs. Yang!

MRS. YANG: Yes?

WAITER: Another pitcher of wine, ma'am?

MRS. YANG: We have enough, thanks. Drinking makes me sweat.

WAITER: Would you mind paying, ma'am?

MRS. YANG: [*to everyone*] Just be patient a few moments longer, everyone, Mr. Shui Ta is on his way over! [*to the* WAITER] Don't be a spoilsport.

WAITER: I can't let you leave till you've paid your bill ma'am.

MRS. YANG: But they know me here!

WAITER: That's just it.

PRIEST: [*ponderously getting up*] I humbly take my leave. [*And he does.*]

MRS. YANG: [*to the others, desperately*] Stay where you are, everybody! The priest says he'll be back in two minutes!

YANG SUN: It's no good, Mamma. Ladies and gentlemen, Mr. Shui Ta still hasn't arrived and the priest has gone home. We won't detain you any longer.
[*They are leaving now.*]

GRANDFATHER: [*in the doorway, having forgotten to put his glass down*] To the bride! [*He drinks, puts down the glass, and follows the others.*]
[*Pause*]

SHEN TE: Shall I go too?

YANG SUN: You? Aren't you the bride? Isn't this your wedding? [*he drags her across the room, tearing her wedding dress*] If we can wait, you can wait. Mother calls me her falcon. She wants to see me in the clouds. But I think it may be St. Nevercome's Day before she'll go to the door and see my plane thunder by. [*Pause. He pretends the guests are still present.*] Why such a lull in the conversation, ladies and gentlemen? Don't you like it here? The ceremony is only slightly postponed—because an important guest is expected at any moment. Also because the bride doesn't know what love is. While we're waiting, the bridegroom will sing a little song. [*He does so:*]

THE SONG OF ST. NEVERCOME'S DAY

On a certain day, as is generally known,
    One and all will be shouting: Hooray, hooray!
For the beggar maid's son has a solid-gold throne
    And the day is St. Nevercome's Day
On St. Nevercome's, Nevercome's, Nevercome's Day
    He'll sit on his solid-gold throne

Oh, hooray, hooray! That day goodness will pay!
    That day badness will cost you your head!
And merit and money will smile and be funny
    While exchanging salt and bread
On St. Nevercome's, Nevercome's, Nevercome's Day
    While exchanging salt and bread

And the grass, oh, the grass will look down at the sky
    And the pebbles will roll up the stream
And all men will be good without batting an eye
    They will make of our earth a dream

On St. Nevercome's, Nevercome's, Nevercome's Day
They will make of our earth a dream

And as for me, that's the day I shall be
A flyer and one of the best
Unemployed man, you will have work to do
Washerwoman, you'll get your rest
On St. Nevercome's, Nevercome's, Nevercome's Day
Washerwoman, you'll get your rest

MRS. YANG: It looks like he's not coming.
[*The three of them sit looking at the door.*]

SCENE VIa——WONG's *den.*

[*The sewer pipe is again transparent and again the* GODS *appear to* WONG
*in a dream.*]

WONG: I'm so glad you've come, illustrious ones. It's Shen Te. She's in great trouble
from following the rule about loving thy neighbor. Perhaps she's *too* good for
this world!

FIRST GOD: Nonsense! You are eaten up by lice and doubts!

WONG: Forgive me, illustrious one, I only meant you might deign to intervene.

FIRST GOD: Out of the question! My colleague here intervened in some squabble or
other only yesterday. [*He points to the* THIRD GOD *who has a black eye.*] The
results are before us!

WONG: She had to call on her cousin again. But not even he could help. I'm afraid
the shop is done for.

THIRD GOD: [*a little concerned*] Perhaps we should help after all?

FIRST GOD: The gods help those that help themselves.

WONG: What if we *can't* help ourselves, illustrious ones?
[*Slight pause.*]

SECOND GOD: Try, anyway! Suffering ennobles!

FIRST GOD: Our faith in Shen Te is unshaken!

THIRD GOD: We certainly haven't found any *other* good people. You can see where
we spend our nights from the straw on our clothes.

WONG: You might help her find her way by—

FIRST GOD: The good man finds his own way here below!

SECOND GOD: The good woman too.

FIRST GOD: The heavier the burden, the greater her strength!

THIRD GOD: We're only onlookers, you know.

FIRST GOD: And everything will be all right in the end, O ye of little faith!
[*They are gradually disappearing through these last lines.*]

SCENE VII——*The yard behind* SHEN TE's *shop. A few articles of furniture on a cart.*

[SHEN TE *and* MRS. SHIN *are taking the washing off the line.*]

MRS. SHIN: If you ask me, you should fight tooth and nail to keep the shop.

SHEN TE: How can I? I have to sell the tobacco to pay back the two hundred silver
dollars today.

MRS. SHIN: No husband, no tobacco, no house and home! What are you going to live on?

SHEN TE: I can work. I can sort tobacco.

MRS. SHIN: Hey, look, Mr. Shui Ta's trousers! He must have left here stark naked!

SHEN TE: Oh, he may have another pair, Mrs. Shin.

MRS. SHIN: But if he's gone for good as you say, why has he left his pants behind?

SHEN TE: Maybe he's thrown them away.

MRS. SHIN: Can I take them?

SHEN TE: Oh, no.

[*Enter* MR. SHU FU, *running.*]

SHU FU: Not a word! Total silence! I know all. You have sacrificed your own love and happiness so as not to hurt a dear old couple who had put their trust in you! Not in vain does this district — for all its malevolent tongues — call you the Angel of the Slums! That young man couldn't rise to your level, so you left him. And now, when I see you closing up the little shop, that veritable heaven of rest for the multitude, well, I cannot, I cannot let it pass. Morning after morning I have stood watching in the doorway not unmoved — while you graciously handed out rice to the wretched. Is that never to happen again? Is the good woman of Setzuan to disappear? If only you would allow *me* to assist you! Now don't say anything! No assurances, no exclamations of gratitude! [*He has taken out his checkbook.*] Here! A blank check. [*He places it on the cart.*] Just my signature. Fill it out as you wish. Any sum in the world. I herewith retire from the scene, quietly, unobtrusively, making no claims, on tiptoe, full of veneration, absolutely selflessly . . . [*He has gone.*]

MRS. SHIN: Well! You're saved. There's always some idiot of a man. . . . Now hurry! Put down a thousand silver dollars and let me fly to the bank before he comes to his senses.

SHEN TE: I can pay you for the washing without any check.

MRS. SHIN: What? You're not going to cash it just because you might have to marry him? Are you crazy? Men like him *want* to be led by the nose! Are you still thinking of that flyer? All Yellow Street knows how he treated you!

SHEN TE: When I heard his cunning laugh, I was afraid
   But when I saw the holes in his shoes, I loved him dearly.

MRS. SHIN: Defending that good-for-nothing after all that's happened!

SHEN TE: [*staggering as she holds some of the washing*] Oh!

MRS. SHIN: [*taking the washing from her, dryly*] So you feel dizzy when you stretch and bend? There couldn't be a little visitor on the way? If that's it, you can forget Mr. Shu Fu's blank check: it wasn't meant for a christening present!
   [*She goes to the back with a basket.* SHEN TE's *eyes follow* MRS. SHIN *for a moment. Then she looks down at her own body, feels her stomach, and a great joy comes into her eyes.*]

SHEN TE: O joy! A new human being is on the way. The world awaits him. In the cities the people say: he's got to be reckoned with, this new human being! [*She imagines a little boy to be present, and introduces him to the audience.*] This is my son, the well-known flyer!
   Say: Welcome
   To the conqueror of unknown mountains and unreachable regions
   Who brings us our mail across the impassable deserts!
   [*She leads him up and down by the hand.*]

Take a look at the world, my son. That's a tree. Tree, yes. Say: "Hello, tree!"
And bow. Like this. [*She bows.*] Now you know each other. And, look, here
comes the water seller. He's a friend, give him your hand. A cup of fresh water
for my little son, please. Yes, it *is* a warm day. [*handing the cup*] Oh dear, a
policeman, we'll have to make a circle round *him*. Perhaps we can pick a few
cherries over there in the rich Mr. Pung's garden. But we mustn't be seen. You
want cherries? Just like children with fathers. No, no, you can't go straight at
them like that. Don't pull. We must learn to be reasonable. Well, have it your
own way. [*She has let him make for the cherries.*] Can you reach? Where to put
them? Your mouth is the best place. [*She tries one herself.*] Mmm, they're
good. But the policeman, we must run! [*They run.*] Yes, back to the street.
Calm now, so no one will notice us. [*Walking the street with her child, she
sings.*]

> Once a plum — 'twas in Japan —
> Made a conquest of a man
> But the man's turn soon did come
> For he gobbled up the plum

[*Enter* WONG, *with a* CHILD *by the hand. He coughs.*]

SHEN TE: Wong!

WONG: It's about the carpenter, Shen Te. He's lost his shop, and he's been drinking.
His children are on the streets. This is one. Can you help?

SHEN TE: [*to the* CHILD] Come here, little man. [*Takes him down to the footlights. To
the audience:*]

> You there! A man is asking you for shelter!
> A man of tomorrow says: what about today?
> His friend the conqueror, whom you know,
> Is his advocate!

[*to* WONG] He can live in Mr. Shu Fu's cabins. I may have to go there
myself. I'm going to have a baby. That's a secret — don't tell Yang
Sun — we'd only be in his way. Can you find the carpenter for me?

WONG: I knew you'd think of something. [*to the* CHILD] Good-bye, son, I'm going for
your father.

SHEN TE: What about your hand, Wong? I wanted to help, but my cousin . . .

WONG: Oh, I can get along with one hand, don't worry. [*He shows how he can
handle his pole with his left hand alone.*]

SHEN TE: But your right hand! Look, take this cart, sell everything that's on it, and go
to the doctor with the money . . .

WONG: She's still good. But first I'll bring the carpenter. I'll pick up the cart when I
get back. [*Exit* WONG.]

SHEN TE: [*to the* CHILD] Sit down over here, son, till your father comes. [*The* CHILD
*sits cross-legged on the ground. Enter the* HUSBAND *and* WIFE, *each dragging a
large, full sack.*]

WIFE: [*furtively*] You're alone, Shen Te, dear?

[SHEN TE *nods. The* WIFE *beckons to the* NEPHEW *offstage. He comes on
with another sack.*]

WIFE: Your cousin's away? [SHEN TE *nods*] He's not coming back?

SHEN TE: No. I'm giving up the shop.

WIFE: That's why we're here. We want to know if we can leave these things in your
new home. Will you do us this favor?

SHEN TE: Why, yes, I'd be glad to.

HUSBAND: [*cryptically*] And if anyone asks about them, say they're yours.

SHEN TE: Would anyone ask?

WIFE: [*with a glance back at her husband*] Oh, someone might. The police, for instance. They don't seem to like us. Where can we put it?

SHEN TE: Well, I'd rather not get in any more trouble . . .

WIFE: Listen to her. The good woman of Setzuan!

[SHEN TE *is silent.*]

HUSBAND: There's enough tobacco in those sacks to give us a new start in life. We could have our own tobacco factory!

SHEN TE: [*slowly*] You'll have to put them in the back room.

[*The sacks are taken offstage, while the* CHILD *is alone. Shyly glancing about him, he goes to the garbage can, starts playing with the contents, and eating some of the scraps. The others return.*]

WIFE: We're counting on you, Shen Te!

SHEN TE: Yes. [*She sees the* CHILD *and is shocked.*]

HUSBAND: We'll see you in Mr. Shu Fu's cabins.

NEPHEW: The day after tomorrow.

SHEN TE: Yes. Now, go. Go! I'm not feeling well.

[*Exeunt all three, virtually pushed off.*]

He is eating the refuse in the garbage can!
Only look at his little gray mouth!

[*Pause. Music*]

As this is the world *my* son will enter
I will study to defend him.
To be good to you, my son,
I shall be a tigress to all others
If I have to.
And I shall have to.

[*She starts to go.*]

One more time, then. I hope really the last.

[*Exit* SHEN TE, *taking* SHUI TA'S *trousers.* MRS. SHIN *enters and watches her with marked interest. Enter the* SISTER-IN-LAW *and the* GRANDFATHER.]

SISTER-IN-LAW: So it's true, the shop has closed down. And the furniture's in the back yard. It's the end of the road!

MRS. SHIN: [*pompously*] The fruit of high living, selfishness, and sensuality! Down the primrose path to Mr. Shu Fu's cabins — with you!

SISTER-IN-LAW: Cabins? Rat holes! He gave them to us because his soap supplies only went moldy there!

[*Enter the* UNEMPLOYED MAN.]

UNEMPLOYED MAN: Shen Te is moving?

SISTER-IN-LAW: Yes. She was sneaking away.

MRS. SHIN: She's ashamed of herself, and no wonder!

UNEMPLOYED MAN: Tell her to call Mr. Shui Ta or she's done for this time!

SISTER-IN-LAW: Tell her to call Mr. Shui Ta or *we're* done for this time.

[*Enter* WONG *and* CARPENTER, *the latter with a* CHILD *on each hand.*]

CARPENTER: So we'll have a roof over our heads for a change!

MRS. SHIN: Roof? Whose roof?

CARPENTER: Mr. Shu Fu's cabins. And we have little Feng to thank for it. [FENG, *we find, is the name of the* CHILD *already there; his* FATHER *now takes him. To the other two]* Bow to your little brother, you two!

[*The* CARPENTER *and the two new arrivals bow to* FENG. *Enter* SHUI TA.]

UNEMPLOYED MAN: Sst! Mr. Shui Ta!

[*Pause.*]

SHUI TA: And what is this crowd here for, may I ask?

WONG: How do you do, Mr. Shui Ta? This is the carpenter. Miss Shen Te promised him space in Mr. Shu Fu's cabins.

SHUI TA: That will not be possible.

CARPENTER: We can't go there after all?

SHUI TA: All the space is needed for other purposes.

SISTER-IN-LAW: You mean we have to get out? But we've got nowhere to go.

SHUI TA: Miss Shen Te finds it possible to provide employment. If the proposition interests you, you may stay in the cabins.

SISTER-IN-LAW: [*with distaste*] You mean *work*? Work for Miss Shen Te?

SHUI TA: Making tobacco, yes. There are three bales here already. Would you like to get them?

SISTER-IN-LAW: [*trying to bluster*] We have our own tobacco! We were in the tobacco business before you were born!

SHUI TA: [*to the* CARPENTER *and the* UNEMPLOYED MAN] You *don't* have your own tobacco. What about you?

[*The* CARPENTER *and the* UNEMPLOYED MAN *get the point, and go for the sacks. Enter* MRS. MI TZU.]

MRS. MI TZU: Mr. Shui Ta? I've brought you your three hundred silver dollars.

SHUI TA: I'll sign your lease instead. I've decided not to sell.

MRS. MI TZU: What? You don't need the money for that flyer?

SHUI TA: No.

MRS. MI TZU: And you can pay six months' rent?

SHUI TA: [*takes the barber's blank check from the cart and fills it out*] Here is a check for ten thousand silver dollars. On Mr. Shu Fu's account. Look! [*He shows her the signature on the check.*] Your six months' rent will be in your hands by seven this evening. And now, if you'll excuse me.

MRS. MI TZU: So it's Mr. Shu Fu now. The flyer has been given his walking papers. These modern girls! In my day they'd have said she was flighty. That poor, deserted Mr. Yang Sun!

[*Exit* MRS. MI TZU. *The* CARPENTER *and the* UNEMPLOYED MAN *drag the three sacks back on the stage.*]

CARPENTER: [*to* SHUI TA] I don't know why I'm doing this for you.

SHUI TA: Perhaps your children want to eat, Mr. Carpenter.

SISTER-IN-LAW: [*catching sight of the sacks*] Was my brother-in-law here?

MRS. SHIN: Yes, he was.

SISTER-IN-LAW: I thought as much. I know those sacks! That's our tobacco!

SHUI TA: Really? I thought it came from my back room! Shall we consult the police on the point?

SISTER-IN-LAW: [*defeated*] No.

SHUI TA: Perhaps you will show me the way to Mr. Shu Fu's cabins?

[*Taking* FENG *by the hand,* SHUI TA *goes off, followed by the* CARPENTER *and his two older children, the* SISTER-IN-LAW, *the* GRANDFATHER, *and the*

UNEMPLOYED MAN. *Each of the last three drags a sack. Enter* OLD MAN *and* OLD WOMAN.]

MRS. SHIN: A pair of pants — missing from the clothesline one minute — and next minute on the honorable backside of Mr. Shui Ta.

OLD WOMAN: We thought Miss Shen Te was here.

MRS. SHIN: [*preoccupied*] Well, she's not.

OLD MAN: There was something she was going to give us.

WONG: She was going to help me too. [*looking at his hand*] It'll be too late soon. But she'll be back. This cousin has never stayed long.

MRS. SHIN: [*approaching a conclusion*] No, he hasn't, has he?

SCENE VIIa————*The Sewer Pipe*

[WONG *asleep. In his dream, he tells the* GODS *his fears. The* GODS *seem tired from all their travels. They stop for a moment and look over their shoulders at the water seller.*]

WONG: Illustrious ones. I've been having a bad dream. Our beloved Shen Te was in great distress in the rushes down by the river — the spot where the bodies of suicides are washed up. She kept staggering and holding her head down as if she was carrying something and it was dragging her down into the mud. When I called out to her, she said she had to take your Book of Rules to the other side, and not get it wet, or the ink would all come off. You had talked to her about the virtues, you know, the time she gave you shelter in Setzuan.

THIRD GOD: Well, but what do you suggest, my dear Wong?

WONG: Maybe a little relaxation of the rules, Benevolent One, in view of the bad times.

THIRD GOD: As for instance?

WONG: Well, um, good will, for instance, might do instead of love?

THIRD GOD: I'm afraid that would create new problems.

WONG: Or instead of justice, good sportsmanship?

THIRD GOD: That would only mean more work.

WONG: Instead of honor, outward propriety?

THIRD GOD: Still more work! No, no! The rules will have to stand, my dear Wong!

[*Wearily shaking their heads, all three journey on.*]

SCENE VIII————*Shui Ta's tobacco factory in Shu Fu's cabins.*

[*Huddled together behind bars, several families, mostly women and children. Among these people the* SISTER-IN-LAW, *the* GRANDFATHER, *the* CARPENTER, *and his* THREE CHILDREN. *Enter* MRS. YANG *followed by* YANG SUN.]

MRS. YANG: [*to the audience*] There's something I just *have* to tell you: strength and wisdom are wonderful things. The strong and wise Mr. Shui Ta has transformed my son from a dissipated good-for-nothing into a model citizen. As you may have heard, Mr. Shui Ta opened a small tobacco factory near the cattle runs. It flourished. Three months ago — I shall never forget it — I asked for an appointment, and Mr. Shui Ta agreed to see us — me and my son. I can see him now as he came through the door to meet us. . . .

[*Enter* SHUI TA *from a door.*]

SHUI TA: What can I do for you, Mrs. Yang?

MRS. YANG: This morning the police came to the house. We find you've brought an
action for breach of promise of marriage. In the name of Shen Te. You also
claim that Sun came by two hundred silver dollars by improper means.

SHUI TA: That is correct.

MRS. YANG: Mr. Shui Ta, the money's all gone. When the Peking job didn't materi-
alize, he ran through it all in three days. I know he's a good-for-nothing. He
sold my furniture. He was moving to Peking without me. Miss Shen Te
thought highly of him at one time.

SHUI TA: What do *you* say, Mr. Yang Sun?

YANG SUN: The money's gone.

SHUI TA: [*to* MRS. YANG] Mrs. Yang, in consideration of my cousin's incomprehensi-
ble weakness for your son, I am prepared to give him another chance. He can
have a job — here. The two hundred silver dollars will be taken out of his
wages.

YANG SUN: So it's the factory or jail?

SHUI TA: Take your choice.

YANG SUN: May I speak with Shen Te?

SHUI TA: You may not.
     [*Pause.*]

YANG SUN: [*sullenly*] Show me where to go.

MRS. YANG: Mr. Shui Ta, you are kindness itself: the gods will reward you! [*to* YANG
SUN] And honest work will make a man of you, my boy. [YANG SUN *follows* SHUI
TA *into the factory.* MRS. YANG *comes down again to the footlights.*] Actually,
honest work didn't agree with him — at first. And he got no opportunity to
distinguish himself till — in the third week — when the wages were being
paid . . .
     [SHUI TA *has a bag of money. Standing next to his foreman — the former*
     UNEMPLOYED MAN — he counts out the wages. It is YANG SUN's *turn.*]

UNEMPLOYED MAN: [*reading*] Carpenter, six silver dollars. Yang Sun, six silver dollars.

YANG SUN: [*quietly*] Excuse me, sir. I don't think it can be more than five. May I see?
[*He takes the foreman's list.*] It says six working days. But that's a mistake, sir. I
took a day off for court business. And I won't take what I haven't earned,
however miserable the pay is!

UNEMPLOYED MAN: Yang Sun. Five silver dollars. [*to* SHUI TA] A rare case, Mr. Shui
Ta!

SHUI TA: How is it the book says six when it should say five?

UNEMPLOYED MAN: I must've made a mistake, Mr. Shui Ta. [*with a look at* YANG SUN]
It won't happen again.

SHUI TA: [*taking* YANG SUN *aside*] You don't hold back, do you? You give your all to
the firm. You're even honest. Do the foreman's mistakes always favor the
workers?

YANG SUN: He does have . . . friends.

SHUI TA: Thank you. May I offer you any little recompense?

YANG SUN: Give me a trial period of one week, and I'll prove my intelligence is worth
more to you than my strength.

MRS. YANG: [*still down at the footlights*] Fighting words, fighting words! That eve-

ning, I said to Sun: "If you're a flyer, then fly, my falcon! Rise in the world!"
And he got to be foreman. Yes, in Mr. Shui Ta's tobacco factory, he worked
real miracles.

[*We see* YANG SUN *with his legs apart standing behind the workers who are
handing along a basket of raw tobacco above their heads.*]

YANG SUN: Faster! Faster! You, there, d'you think you can just stand around, now
you're not foreman any more? It'll be your job to lead us in song. Sing!

[UNEMPLOYED MAN *starts singing. The others join in the refrain.*]

SONG OF THE EIGHTH ELEPHANT

Chang had seven elephants — all much the same —
   But then there was Little Brother
The seven, they were wild, Little Brother, he was tame
   And to guard them Chang chose Little Brother
      Run faster!
      Mr. Chang has a forest park
      Which must be cleared before tonight
      And already it's growing dark!

When the seven elephants cleared that forest park
   Mr. Chang rode high on Little Brother
While the seven toiled and moiled till dark
   On his big behind sat Little Brother
      Dig faster!
      Mr. Chang has a forest park
      Which must be cleared before tonight
      And already it's growing dark!

And the seven elephants worked many an hour
   Till none of them could work another
Old Chang, he looked sour, on the seven he did glower
   But gave a pound of rice to Little Brother
      What was that?
      Mr. Chang has a forest park
      Which must be cleared before tonight
      And already it's growing dark!

And the seven elephants hadn't any tusks
   The one that had the tusks was Little Brother
Seven are no match for one, if the one has a gun!
   How old Chang did laugh at Little Brother!
      Keep on digging!
      Mr. Chang has a forest park
      Which must be cleared before tonight
      And already it's growing dark!

[*Smoking a cigar,* SHUI TA *strolls by.* YANG SUN, *laughing, has joined in the
refrain of the third stanza and speeded up the tempo of the last stanza by
clapping his hands.*]

MRS. YANG: And that's why I say: strength and wisdom are wonderful things. It took the strong and wise Mr. Shui Ta to bring out the best in Yang Sun. A real superior man is like a bell. If you ring it, it rings, and if you don't, it don't, as the saying is.

SCENE IX——*Shen Te's shop, now an office with club chairs and fine carpets. It is raining.*

[SHUI TA, *now fat, is just dismissing the* OLD MAN *and* OLD WOMAN. MRS. SHIN, *in obviously new clothes, looks on, smirking.*]

SHUI TA: No! I can NOT tell you when we expect her back.

OLD WOMAN: The two hundred silver dollars came today. In an envelope. There was no letter, but it must be from Shen Te. We want to write and thank her. May we have her address?

SHUI TA: I'm afraid I haven't got it.

OLD MAN: [*pulling* OLD WOMAN's *sleeve*] Let's be going.

OLD WOMAN: She's got to come back some time!

[*They move off, uncertainly, worried.* SHUI TA *bows.*]

MRS. SHIN: They lost the carpet shop because they couldn't pay their taxes. The money arrived too late.

SHUI TA: They could have come to me.

MRS. SHIN: People don't like coming to you.

SHUI TA: [*sits suddenly, one hand to his head*] I'm dizzy.

MRS. SHIN: After all, you *are* in your seventh month. But old Mrs. Shin will be there in your hour of trial! [*She cackles feebly.*]

SHUI TA: [*in a stifled voice*] Can I count on that?

MRS. SHIN: We all have our price, and mine won't be too high for the great Mr. Shui Ta! [*She opens* SHUI TA's *collar.*]

SHUI TA: It's for the child's sake. All of this.

MRS. SHIN: "All for the child," of course.

SHUI TA: I'm so fat. People must notice.

MRS. SHIN: Oh no, they think it's 'cause you're rich.

SHUI TA: [*more feelingly*] What will happen to the child?

MRS. SHIN: You ask that nine times a day. Why, it'll have the best that money can buy!

SHUI TA: He must never see Shui Ta.

MRS. SHIN: Oh, no. Always Shen Te.

SHUI TA: What about the neighbors? There are rumors, aren't there?

MRS. SHIN: As long as Mr. Shu Fu doesn't find out, there's nothing to worry about. Drink this.

[*Enter* YANG SUN *in a smart business suit, and carrying a businessman's briefcase.* SHUI TA *is more or less in* MRS. SHIN's *arms.*]

YANG SUN: [*surprised*] I guess I'm in the way.

SHUI TA: [*ignoring this, rises with an effort*] Till tomorrow, Mrs. Shin.

[MRS. SHIN *leaves with a smile, putting her new gloves on.*]

YANG SUN: Gloves now! She couldn't be fleecing you? And since when did *you* have a private life? [*taking a paper from the briefcase*] You haven't been at your desk lately, and things are getting out of hand. The police want to close us down.

They say that at the most they can only permit twice the lawful number of workers.

SHUI TA: [*evasively*] The cabins are quite good enough.

YANG SUN: For the workers maybe, not for the tobacco. They're too damp. We must take over some of Mrs. Mi Tzu's buildings.

SHUI TA: Her price is double what I can pay.

YANG SUN: Not unconditionally. If she has me to stroke her knees she'll come down.

SHUI TA: I'll never agree to that.

YANG SUN: What's wrong? Is it the rain? You get so irritable whenever it rains.

SHUI TA: Never! I will never . . .

YANG SUN: Mrs. Mi Tzu'll be here in five minutes. *You* fix it. And Shu Fu will be with her. . . . What's all that noise?

[*During the above dialogue,* WONG *is heard offstage, calling:* "The good Shen Te, where is she? Which of you has seen Shen Te, good people? Where is Shen Te?" *A knock. Enter* WONG.]

WONG: Mr. Shui Ta, I've come to ask when Miss Shen Te will be back, it's six months now. . . . There are rumors. People say something's happened to her.

SHUI TA: I'm busy. Come back next week.

WONG: [*excited*] In the morning there was always rice on her doorstep — for the needy. It's been there again lately!

SHUI TA: And what do people conclude from this?

WONG: That Shen Te is still in Setzuan! She's been . . . [*He breaks off.*]

SHUI TA: She's been what? Mr. Wong, if you're Shen Te's friend, talk a little less about her, that's my advice to you.

WONG: I don't want your advice! Before she disappeared, Miss Shen Te told me something very important — she's pregnant!

YANG SUN: What? What was that?

SHUI TA: [*quickly*] The man is lying.

WONG: A good woman isn't so easily forgotten, Mr. Shui Ta.

[*He leaves.* SHUI TA *goes quickly into the back room.*]

YANG SUN: [*to the audience*] Shen Te pregnant? So that's why. Her cousin sent her away, so I wouldn't get wind of it. I have a son, a Yang appears on the scene, and what happens? Mother and child vanish into thin air! That scroundrel, that unspeakable . . . [*The sound of sobbing is heard from the back room.*] What was that? Someone sobbing? Who was it? Mr. Shui Ta the Tobacco King doesn't weep his heart out. And where does the rice come from that's on the doorstep in the morning? [SHUI TA *returns. He goes to the door and looks out into the rain.*] Where is she?

SHUI TA: Sh! It's nine o'clock. But the rain's so heavy, you can't hear a thing.

YANG SUN: What do you want to hear?

SHUI TA: The mail plane.

YANG SUN: What?!

SHUI TA: I've been told *you* wanted to fly at one time. Is that all forgotten?

YANG SUN: Flying mail is night work. I prefer the daytime. And the firm is very dear to me — after all it belongs to my ex-fiancée, even if she's not around. And she's not, is she?

SHUI TA: What do you mean by that?

YANG SUN: Oh, well, let's say I haven't altogether — lost interest.

SHUI TA: My cousin might like to know that.

YANG SUN: I might not be indifferent — if I found she was being kept under lock and key.

SHUI TA: By whom?

YANG SUN: By you.

SHUI TA: What could you do about it?

YANG SUN: I could submit for discussion — my position in the firm.

SHUI TA: You are now my manager. In return for a more . . . appropriate position, you might agree to drop the inquiry into your ex-fiancée's whereabouts?

YANG SUN: I might.

SHUI TA: What position *would* be more appropriate?

YANG SUN: The one at the top.

SHUI TA: My own? [*silence*] And if I preferred to throw you out on your neck?

YANG SUN: I'd come back on my feet. With suitable escort.

SHUI TA: The police?

YANG SUN: The police.

SHUI TA: And when the police found no one?

YANG SUN: I might ask them not to overlook the back room. [*ending the pretense*] In short, Mr. Shui Ta, my interest in this young woman has not been officially terminated. I should like to see more of her. [*into* SHUI TA's *face*] Besides, she's pregnant and needs a friend. [*He moves to the door.*] I shall talk about it with the water seller.

> [*Exit.* SHUI TA *is rigid for a moment, then he quickly goes into the back room. He returns with Shen Te's belongings: underwear, etc. He takes a long look at the shawl of the previous scene. He then wraps the things in a bundle, which, upon hearing a noise, he hides under the table. Enter* MRS. MI TZU *and* MR. SHU FU. *They put away their umbrellas and galoshes.*]

MRS. MI TZU: I thought your manager was here, Mr. Shui Ta. He combines charm with business in a way that can only be to the advantage of all of us.

SHU FU: You sent for us, Mr. Shui Ta?

SHUI TA: The factory is in trouble.

SHU FU: It always is.

SHUI TA: The police are threatening to close us down unless I can show that the extension of our facilities is imminent.

SHU FU: Shui Ta, I'm sick and tired of your constantly expanding projects. I place cabins at your cousin's disposal; you make a factory of them. I hand your cousin a check; you present it. Your cousin disappears; you find the cabins too small and start talking of yet more —

SHUI TA: Mr. Shu Fu, I'm authorized to inform you that Miss Shen Te's return is now imminent.

SHU FU: Imminent? It's becoming his favorite word.

MRS. MI TZU: Yes, what does it mean?

SHUI TA: Mrs. Mi Tzu, I can pay you exactly half what you asked for your buildings. Are you ready to inform the police that I am taking them over?

MRS. MI TZU: Certainly, if I can take over your manager.

SHU FU: What?

MRS. MI TZU: He's so efficient.

SHUI TA: I'm afraid I need Mr. Yang Sun.

MRS. MI TZU: So do I.

SHUI TA: He will call on you tomorrow.

SHU FU: So much the better. With Shen Te likely to turn up at any moment, the presence of that young man is hardly in good taste.

SHUI TA: So we have reached a settlement. In what was once the good Shen Te's little shop we are laying the foundations for the great Mr. Shui Ta's twelve magnificent super tobacco markets. You will bear in mind that though they call me the Tobacco King of Setzuan, it is my cousin's interests that have been served . . .

VOICES: [off] The police, the police! Going to the tobacco shop! Something must have happened!

[Enter YANG SUN, WONG and the POLICEMAN.]

POLICEMAN: Quiet there, quiet, quiet! [They quiet down.] I'm sorry, Mr. Shui Ta, but there's a report that you've been depriving Miss Shen Te of her freedom. Not that I believe all I hear, but the whole city's in an uproar.

SHUI TA: That's a lie.

POLICEMAN: Mr. Yang Sun has testified that he heard someone sobbing in the back room.

SHU FU: Mrs. Mi Tzu and myself will testify that no one here has been sobbing.

MRS. MI TZU: We have been quietly smoking our cigars.

POLICEMAN: Mr. Shui Ta, I'm afraid I shall have to take a look at that room. [He does so. The room is empty.] No one there, of course, sir.

YANG SUN: But I heard sobbing. What's that? [He finds the clothes.]

WONG: Those are Shen Te's things. [to crowd] Shen Te's clothes are here!

VOICES: [off, in sequence]
— Shen Te's clothes!
— They've been found under the table!
— Body of murdered girl still missing!
— Tobacco King suspected!

POLICEMAN: Mr. Shui Ta, unless you can tell us where the girl is, I'll have to ask you to come along.

SHUI TA: I do not know.

POLICEMAN: I can't say how sorry I am, Mr. Shui Ta. [He shows him the door.]

SHUI TA: Everything will be cleared up in no time. There are still judges in Setzuan.

YANG SUN: I heard sobbing!


SCENE IXa——WONG's den.

[For the last time, the GODS appear to the water seller in his dream. They have changed and show signs of a long journey, extreme fatigue, and plenty of mishaps. The FIRST no longer has a hat; the THIRD has lost a leg; all three are barefoot.]

WONG: Illustrious ones, at last you're here. Shen Te's been gone for months and today her cousin's been arrested. They think he murdered her to get the shop. But I had a dream and in this dream Shen Te said her cousin was keeping her prisoner. You must find her for us, illustrious ones!

FIRST GOD: We've found very few good people anywhere, and even they didn't keep it up. Shen Te is still the only one that stayed good.

SECOND GOD: If she *has* stayed good.

WONG: Certainly she has. But she's vanished.

FIRST GOD: That's the last straw. All is lost!

SECOND GOD: A little moderation, dear colleague!

FIRST GOD: [*plaintively*] What's the good of moderation now? If she can't be found, we'll have to resign! The world is a terrible place! Nothing but misery, vulgarity, and waste! Even the countryside isn't what it used to be. The trees are getting their heads chopped off by telephone wires, and there's such a noise from all the gunfire, and I can't stand those heavy clouds of smoke, and—

THIRD GOD: The place is absolutely unlivable! Good intentions bring people to the brink of the abyss, and good deeds push them over the edge. I'm afraid our book of rules is destined for the scrap heap—

SECOND GOD: It's people! They're a worthless lot!

THIRD GOD: The world is too cold!

SECOND GOD: It's people! They're too weak!

FIRST GOD: Dignity, dear colleagues, dignity! Never despair! As for this world, didn't we agree that we only have to find one human being who can stand the place? Well, we found her. True, we lost her again. We must find her again, that's all. And at once!

[*They disappear.*]


SCENE X ———— *Courtroom.*

[*Groups:* SHU FU *and* MRS. MI TZU; YANG SUN *and* MRS. YANG; WONG, *the* CARPENTER, *the* GRANDFATHER, *the* NIECE, *the* OLD MAN, *the* OLD WOMAN; MRS. SHIN, *the* POLICEMAN; *the* UNEMPLOYED MAN, *the* SISTER-IN-LAW.]

OLD MAN: So much power isn't good for one man.

UNEMPLOYED MAN: And he's going to open twelve super tobacco markets!

WIFE: One of the judges is a friend of Mr. Shu Fu's.

SISTER-IN-LAW: Another one accepted a present from Mr. Shui Ta only last night. A great fat goose.

OLD WOMAN: [*to* WONG] And Shen Te is nowhere to be found

WONG: Only the gods will ever know the truth.

POLICEMAN: Order in the court! My lords the judges!

[*Enter the* THREE GODS *in judges' robes. We overhear their conversation as they pass along the footlights to their bench.*]

THIRD GOD: We'll never get away with it, our certificates were so badly forged.

SECOND GOD: My predecessor's "sudden indigestion" will certainly cause comment.

FIRST GOD: But he *had* just eaten a whole goose.

UNEMPLOYED MAN: Look at that! *New* judges.

WONG: New judges. And what good ones!

[*The* THIRD GOD *hears this, and turns to smile at* WONG. *The* GODS *sit. The* FIRST GOD *beats on the bench with his gavel. The* POLICEMAN *brings in* SHUI TA *who walks with lordly steps. He is whistled at.*]

POLICEMAN: [*to* SHUI TA] Be prepared for a surprise. The judges have been changed.

[SHUI TA *turns quickly round, looks at them, and staggers.*]

NIECE: What's the matter now?

WIFE: The great Tobacco King nearly fainted.

HUSBAND: Yes, as soon as he saw the new judges.

WONG: Does he know who they are?

[SHUI TA *picks himself up, and the proceedings open.*]

FIRST GOD: Defendant Shui Ta, you are accused of doing away with your cousin Shen Te in order to take possession of her business. Do you plead guilty or not guilty?

SHUI TA: Not guilty, my lord.

FIRST GOD: [*thumbing through the documents of the case*] The first witness is the policeman. I shall ask him to tell us something of the respective reputations of Miss Shen Te and Mr. Shui Ta.

POLICEMAN: Miss Shen Te was a young lady who aimed to please, my lord. She liked to live and let live, as the saying goes. Mr. Shui Ta, on the other hand, is a man of principle. Though the generosity of Miss Shen Te forced him at times to abandon half measures, unlike the girl he was always on the side of the law, my lord. One time, he even unmasked a gang of thieves to whom his too trustful cousin had given shelter. The evidence, in short, my lord, proves that Mr. Shui Ta was *incapable* of the crime of which he stands accused!

FIRST GOD: I see. And are there others who could testify along, shall we say, the same lines?

[SHU FU *rises.*]

POLICEMAN: [*whispering to* GODS] Mr. Shu Fu —a very important person.

FIRST GOD: [*inviting him to speak*] Mr. Shu Fu!

SHU FU: Mr. Shui Ta is a businessman, my lord. Need I say more?

FIRST GOD: Yes.

SHU FU: Very well, I will. He is Vice President of the Council of Commerce and is about to be elected a Justice of the Peace. [*He returns to his seat.*]

[MRS. MI TZU *rises.*]

WONG: Elected! *He* gave him the job!

[*With a gesture the* FIRST GOD *asks who* MRS. MI TZU *is.*]

POLICEMAN: Another very important person. Mrs. Mi Tzu.

MRS. MI TZU: My lord, as Chairman of the Committee on Social Work, I wish to call attention to just a couple of eloquent facts: Mr. Shui Ta not only has erected a model factory with model housing in our city, he is a regular contributor to our home for the disabled. [*She returns to her seat.*]

POLICEMAN: [*whispering*] And she's a great friend of the judge that ate the goose!

FIRST GOD: [*to the* POLICEMAN] Oh, thank you. What next? [*to the Court, genially*] Oh, yes. We should find out if any of the evidence is less favorable to the defendant.

[WONG, *the* CARPENTER, *the* OLD MAN, *the* OLD WOMAN, *the* UNEMPLOYED MAN, *the* SISTER-IN-LAW, *and the* NIECE *come forward.*]

POLICEMAN: [*whispering*] Just the riffraff, my lord.

FIRST GOD: [*addressing the "riffraff"*] Well, um, riffraff— do you know anything of the defendant, Mr. Shui Ta?

WONG: Too much, my lord.

UNEMPLOYED MAN: What don't we know, my lord.

CARPENTER: He ruined us.

SISTER-IN-LAW: He's a cheat.

NIECE: Liar.

WIFE: Thief.

BOY: Blackmailer.

BROTHER: Murderer.

FIRST GOD: Thank you. We should now let the defendant state his point of view.

SHUI TA: I only came on the scene when Shen Te was in danger of losing what I had understood was a gift from the gods. Because I did the filthy jobs which someone had to do, they hate me. My activities were restricted to the minimum, my lord.

SISTER-IN-LAW: He had us arrested!

SHUI TA: Certainly. You stole from the bakery!

SISTER-IN-LAW: Such concern for the bakery! You didn't want the shop for yourself, I suppose!

SHUI TA: I didn't want the shop overrun with parasites.

SISTER-IN-LAW: We had nowhere else to go.

SHUI TA: There were too many of you.

WONG: What about this old couple: Were *they* parasites?

OLD MAN: We lost our shop because of you!

OLD WOMAN: And we gave your cousin money!

SHUI TA: My cousin's fiancé was a flyer. The money had to go to *him*.

WONG: Did you care whether he flew or not? Did you care whether she married him or not? You wanted her to marry someone else! [*He points at* SHU FU.]

SHUI TA: The flyer unexpectedly turned out to be a scoundrel.

YANG SUN: [*jumping up*] Which was the reason you made him your manager?

SHUI TA: Later on he improved.

WONG: And when he improved, you sold him to her? [*he points out* MRS. MI TZU]

SHUI TA: She wouldn't let me have her premises unless she had him to stroke her knees!

MRS. MI TZU: What? The man's a pathological liar. [*to him*] Don't mention my property to me as long as you live! Murderer! [*She rustles off, in high dudgeon.*]

YANG SUN: [*pushing in*] My lord, I wish to speak for the defendant.

SISTER-IN-LAW: Naturally. He's your employer.

UNEMPLOYED MAN: And the worst slave driver in the country.

MRS. YANG: That's a lie! My lord, Mr. Shui Ta is a great man. He . . .

YANG SUN: He's this and he's that, but he is not a murderer, my lord. Just fifteen minutes before his arrest I heard Shen Te's voice in his own back room.

FIRST GOD: Oh? Tell us more!

YANG SUN: I heard sobbing, my lord!

FIRST GOD: But lots of women sob, we've been finding.

YANG SUN: Could I fail to recognize her voice?

SHU FU: No, you made her sob so often yourself, young man!

YANG SUN: Yes. But I also made her happy. Till he [*pointing at* SHUI TA] decided to sell her to you!

SHUI TA: Because you didn't love her.

WONG: Oh, no: it was for the money, my lord!

SHUI TA: And what was the money for, my lord? For the poor! And for Shen Te so she could go on being good!

WONG: For the poor? That he sent to his sweatshops? And why didn't you let Shen Te be good when you signed the big check?

SHUI TA: For the child's sake, my lord.

CARPENTER: What about *my* children? What did he do about them?

[SHUI TA *is silent.*]

WONG: The shop was to be a fountain of goodness. That was the gods' idea. You came and spoiled it!

SHUI TA: If I hadn't, it would have run dry!

MRS. SHIN: There's a lot in that, my lord.

WONG: What have you done with the good ShenTe, bad man? She *was* good, my lords, she was, I swear it! [*He raises his hand in an oath.*]

THIRD GOD: What's happened to your hand, water seller?

WONG: [*pointing to* SHUI TA] It's all his fault, my lord, *she* was going to send me to a doctor — [*to* SHUI TA] You were her worst enemy!

SHUI TA: I was her only friend!

WONG: Where is she then? Tell us where your good friend is!

[*The excitement of this exchange has run through the whole crowd.*]

ALL: Yes, where is she? Where is Shen Te? [*etc.*]

SHUI TA: Shen Te . . . had to go.

WONG: Where? Where to?

SHUI TA: I cannot tell you! I cannot tell you!

ALL: Why? Why did she have to go away? [*etc.*]

WONG: [*into the din with the first words, but talking on beyond the others*] Why not, why not? Why did she have to go away?

SHUI TA: [*shouting*] Because you'd all have torn her to shreds, that's why! My lords, I have a request. Clear the court! When only the judges remain, I will make a confession.

ALL: [*except* WONG, *who is silent, struck by the new turn of events*] So he's guilty? He's confessing! [*etc.*]

FIRST GOD: [*using the gavel*] Clear the court!

POLICEMAN: Clear the court!

WONG: Mr. Shui Ta has met his match this time.

MRS. SHIN: [*with a gesture toward the judges*] You're in for a little surprise.

[*The court is cleared. Silence.*]

SHUI TA: Illustrious ones!

[*The* GODS *look at each other, not quite believing their ears.*]

SHUI TA: Yes, I recognize you!

SECOND GOD: [*taking matters in hand, sternly*] What have you done with our good woman of Setzuan?

SHUI TA: I have a terrible confession to make: I am she! [*He takes off his mask, and tears away his clothes.* SHEN TE *stands there.*]

SECOND GOD: Shen Te!

SHEN TE: Shen Te, yes. Shui Ta *and* Shen Te. Both.

Your injunction

To be good and yet to live

Was a thunderbolt:
It has torn me in two
I can't tell how it was
But to be good to others
And myself at the same time
I could not do it
Your world is not an easy one, illustrious ones!
When we extend our hand to a begger, he tears it off for us
When we help the lost, we are lost ourselves
And so
Since not to eat is to die
Who can long refuse to be bad?
As I lay prostrate beneath the weight of good intentions
Ruin stared me in the face
It was when I was unjust that I ate good meat
And hobnobbed with the mighty
Why?
Why are bad deeds rewarded?
Good ones punished?
I enjoyed giving
I truly wished to be the Angel of the Slums
But washed by a foster mother in the water of the gutter
I developed a sharp eye
The time came when pity was a thorn in my side
And, later, when kind words turned to ashes in my mouth
And anger took over
I became a wolf
Find me guilty, then, illustrious ones,
But know:
All that I have done I did
To help my neighbor
To love my lover
And to keep my little one from want
For your great, godly deeds, I was too poor, too small.
    [*Pause.*]

FIRST GOD: [*shocked*] Don't go on making yourself miserable, Shen Te! We're overjoyed to have found you!

SHEN TE: I'm telling you I'm the bad man who committed all those crimes!

FIRST GOD: [*using — or failing to use — his ear trumpet*] The good woman who did all those good deeds?

SHEN TE: Yes, but the bad man too!

FIRST GOD: [*as if something had dawned*] Unfortunate coincidences! Heartless neighbors!

THIRD GOD: [*shouting in his ear*] But how is she to continue.

FIRST GOD: Continue? Well, she's a strong, healthy girl . . .

SECOND GOD: You didn't hear what she said!

FIRST GOD: I heard every word! She is confused, that's all! [*He begins to bluster.*] And what about this book of rules — we can't renounce our rules, can we?

[*more quietly*] Should the world be changed? How? By whom? The world should *not* be changed! [*At a sign from him, the lights turn pink, and music plays.*][1]
And now the hour of parting is at hand.
Dost thou behold, Shen Te, yon fleecy cloud?
It is our chariot. At a sign from me
'Twill come and take us back from whence we came
Above the azure vault and silver stars. . . .

SHEN TE: No! Don't go, illustrious ones!

FIRST GOD: Our cloud has landed now in yonder field
From which it will transport us back to heaven.
Farewell, Shen Te, let not thy courage fail thee. . . .
[*Exeunt* GODS.]

SHEN TE: What about the old couple? They've lost their shop! What about the water seller and his hand? And I've got to defend myself against the barber, because I don't love him! And against Sun, because I do love him! How? How?
[SHEN TE's *eyes follow the* GODS *as they are imagined to step into a cloud which rises and moves forward over the orchestra and up beyond the balcony.*]

FIRST GOD: [*from on high*] We have faith in you, Shen Te!

SHEN TE: There'll be a child. And he'll have to be fed. I can't stay here. Where shall I go?

FIRST GOD: Continue to be good, good woman of Setzuan!

SHEN TE: I need my bad cousin!

FIRST GOD: But not very often!

SHEN TE: Once a week at least!

FIRST GOD: Once a month will be quite enough!

SHEN TE: [*shrieking*] No, no! Help!
[*But the cloud continues to recede as the* GODS *sing.*]

VALEDICTORY HYMN

What a rapture, oh, it is to know
A good thing when you see it
And having seen a good thing, oh,
What rapture 'tis to flee it

Be good, sweet maid of Setzuan
Let Shui Ta be clever
Departing, we forget the man
Remember your endeavor

Because through all the length of days
Her goodness faileth never
Sing hallelujah! Make Shen Te's
Good name live on forever!

---

[1] The rest of this scene has been adapted for the many American theatres that do not have "fly-space" to lower things from ropes

SHEN TE: Help!

## EPILOGUE

You're thinking, aren't you, that this is no right
Conclusion to the play you've seen tonight?[2]
After a tale, exotic, fabulous,
A nasty ending was slipped up on us.
We feel deflated too. We too are nettled
To see the curtain down and nothing settled.
How could a better ending be arranged?
Could one change people? Can the world be changed?
Would new gods do the trick? Will atheism?
Moral rearmament? Materialism?
It is for you to find a way, my friends,
To help good men arrive at happy ends.
*You* write the happy ending to the play!
There must, there must, there's got to be a way![3]

---

[2] At *afternoon performances:*
We quite agree, our play this afternoon
Collapsed upon us like a pricked balloon

[3] When I first received the German manuscript of *Good Woman* from Brecht in 1945 it had no Epilogue.
He wrote it a little later, influenced by misunderstandings of the ending in the press on the occasion of the
Viennese première of the play. I believe that the Epilogue has sometimes been spoken by the actress
playing Shen Te, but the actor playing Wong might be a shrewder choice, since the audience has already
accepted him as a kind of chorus. On the other hand, it is not *Wong* who should deliver the Epilogue:
whichever actor delivers it should drop the character he has been playing — E. B.

# Arthur Miller

# Death of a Salesman

*CHARACTERS*

WILLY LOMAN
LINDA, *his wife*
BIFF ⎱
HAPPY ⎰ *his sons*
UNCLE BEN
CHARLEY
BERNARD
THE WOMAN
HOWARD WAGNER
JENNY
STANLEY
MISS FORSYTHE
LETTA

*The action takes place in* WILLY LOMAN'S *house and yard and in various places he visits in the New York and Boston of today.*

## ACT I

*A melody is heard, played upon a flute. It is small and fine, telling of grass and trees and the horizon. The curtain rises.*

*Before us is the Salesman's house. We are aware of towering, angular shapes behind it, surrounding it on all sides. Only the blue light of the sky falls upon the house and forestage; the surrounding area shows an angry glow of orange. As more light appears, we see a solid vault of apartment houses around the small, fragile-seeming home. An air of the dream clings to the place, a dream rising out of reality. The kitchen at center seems actual enough, for there is a kitchen table with three chairs, and a refrigerator. But no other fixtures are seen. At the back of the kitchen there is a draped entrance, which leads to the living-room. To the right of the kitchen, on a level raised two feet, is a bedroom furnished only with a brass bedstead and a straight chair. On a shelf over the bed a silver athletic trophy stands. A window opens onto the apartment house at the side.*

*Behind the kitchen, on a level raised six and a half feet, is the boys' bedroom, at present barely visible. Two beds are dimly seen, and at the back of the room a dormer window. (This bedroom is above the unseen living-room.) At the left a stairway curves up to it from the kitchen.*

*The entire setting is wholly or, in some places, partially transparent. The roof-line of the house is one-dimensional; under and over it we see the apartment buildings. Before the house lies an apron, curving beyond the forestage into the orchestra. This forward area serves as the back yard as well as the locale of all Willy's imaginings and of his city scenes. Whenever the action is in the present the actors observe the imaginary wall-lines, entering the house only through its door at the left. But in the scenes of the past these boundaries are broken, and characters enter or leave a room by stepping "through" a wall onto the forestage.*

[From the right, WILLY LOMAN, *the Salesman, enters, carrying two large sample cases. The flute plays on. He hears but is not aware of it. He is past sixty years of age, dressed quietly. Even as he crosses the stage to the doorway of the house, his exhaustion is apparent. He unlocks the door, comes into the kitchen, and thankfully lets his burden down, feeling the soreness of his palms. A word-sigh escapes his lips — it might be "Oh, boy, oh, boy." He closes the door, then carries his cases out into the living-room, through the draped kitchen doorway.*]

LINDA, *his wife, has stirred in her bed at the right. She gets out and puts on a robe, listening. Most often jovial, she has developed an iron repression of her exceptions to Willy's behavior — she more than loves him, she admires him, as though his mercurial nature, his temper, his massive dreams and little cruelties, served her only as sharp reminders of the turbulent longings within him, longings which she shares but lacks the temperament to utter and follow to their end.*]

LINDA: [*hearing* WILLY *outside the bedroom, calls with some trepidation*] Willy!

WILLY: It's all right. I came back.

LINDA: Why? What happened? [*slight pause*] Did something happen, Willy?

WILLY: No, nothing happened.

LINDA: You didn't smash the car, did you?

WILLY: [*with casual irritation*] I said nothing happened. Didn't you hear me?

LINDA: Don't you feel well?

WILLY: I'm tired to the death. [*The flute has faded away. He sits on the bed beside her, a little numb.*] I couldn't make it. I just couldn't make it, Linda.

LINDA: [*very carefully, delicately*] Where were you all day? You look terrible.

WILLY: I got as far as a little above Yonkers. I stopped for a cup of coffee. Maybe it was the coffee.

LINDA: What?

WILLY: [*after a pause*] I suddenly couldn't drive any more. The car kept going off onto the shoulder, y'know?

LINDA: [*helpfully*] Oh. Maybe it was the steering again. I don't think Angelo knows the Studebaker.

WILLY: No, it's me, it's me. Suddenly I realize I'm going' sixty miles an hour and I don't remember the last five minutes. I'm — I can't seem to — keep my mind to it.

LINDA: Maybe it's your glasses. You never went for your new glasses.

WILLY: No, I see everything. I came back ten miles an hour. It took me nearly four hours from Yonkers.

LINDA: [*resigned*]Well, you'll just have to take a rest, Willy, you can't continue this way.

WILLY: I just got back from Florida.

LINDA: But you didn't rest your mind. Your mind is overactive, and the mind is what counts, dear.

WILLY: I'll start out in the morning. Maybe I'll feel better in the morning. [*She is taking off his shoes.*] These goddam arch supports are killing me.

LINDA: Take an aspirin. Should I get you an aspirin? It'll soothe you.

WILLY: [*with wonder*] I was driving along, you understand? And I was fine. I was even observing the scenery. You can imagine, me looking at scenery, on the road every week of my life. But it's so beautiful up there, Linda, the trees are so thick, and the sun is warm. I opened the windshield and just let the warm air bathe over me. And then all of a sudden I'm goin' off the road! I'm tellin' ya, I absolutely forgot I was driving. If I'd've gone the other way over the white line I might've killed somebody. So I went on again — and five minutes later I'm dreamin' again, and I nearly — [*He presses two fingers against his eyes.*] I have such thoughts, I have such strange thoughts.

LINDA: Willy, dear. Talk to them again. There's no reason why you can't work in New York.

WILLY: They don't need me in New York. I'm the New England man. I'm vital in New England.

LINDA: But you're sixty years old. They can't expect you to keep traveling every week.

WILLY: I'll have to send a wire to Portland. I'm supposed to see Brown and Morrison tomorrow morning at ten o'clock to show the line. Goddammit, I could sell them! [*He starts putting on his jacket.*]

LINDA: [*taking the jacket from him*] Why don't you go down to the place tomorrow and tell Howard you've simply got to work in New York? You're too accommodating, dear.

WILLY: If old man Wagner was alive I'd a been in charge of New York now! That man was a prince, he was a masterful man. But that boy of his, that Howard, he don't appreciate. When I went north the first time, the Wagner Company didn't know where New England was!

LINDA: Why don't you tell those things to Howard, dear?

WILLY: [*encouraged*] I will, I definitely will. Is there any cheese?

LINDA: I'll make you a sandwich.

WILLY: No, go to sleep. I'll take some milk. I'll be up right away. The boys in?

LINDA: They're sleeping. Happy took Biff on a date tonight.

WILLY: [*interested*] That so?

LINDA: It was so nice to see them shaving together, one behind the other, in the bathroom. And going out together. You notice? The whole house smells of shaving lotion.

WILLY: Figure it out. Work a lifetime to pay off a house. You finally own it, and there's nobody to live in it.

LINDA: Well, dear, life is a casting off. It's always that way.

WILLY: No, no, some people — some people accomplish something. Did Biff say anything after I went this morning?

LINDA: You shouldn't have criticized him, Willy, especially after he just got off the train. You mustn't lose your temper with him.

WILLY: When the hell did I lose my temper? I simply asked him if he was making any money. Is that a criticism?

LINDA: But, dear, how could he make any money?

WILLY: [*worried and angered*] There's such an undercurrent in him. He became a moody man. Did he apologize when I left this morning?

LINDA: He was crestfallen, Willy. You know how he admires you. I think if he finds himself, then you'll both be happier and not fight any more.

WILLY: How can he find himself on a farm? Is that a life? A farmhand? In the beginning, when he was young, I thought, well, a young man, it's good for him to tramp around, take a lot of different jobs. But it's more than ten years now and he has yet to make thirty-five dollars a week!

LINDA: He's finding himself, Willy.

WILLY: Not finding yourself at the age of thirty-four is a disgrace!

LINDA: Shh!

WILLY: The trouble is he's lazy, goddammit!

LINDA: Willy, please!

WILLY: Biff is a lazy bum!

LINDA: They're sleeping. Get something to eat. Go on down.

WILLY: Why did he come home? I would like to know what brought him home.

LINDA: I don't know. I think he's still lost, Willy, I think he's very lost.

WILLY: Biff Loman is lost. In the greatest country in the world a young man with such — personal attractiveness, gets lost. And such a hard worker. There's one thing about Biff — he's not lazy.

LINDA: Never.

WILLY: [*with pity and resolve*] I'll see him in the morning. I'll have a nice talk with him. I'll get him a job selling. He could be big in no time. My God! Remember how they used to follow him around in high school? When he smiled at one of them their faces lit up. When he walked down the street . . . [*He loses himself in reminiscences.*]

LINDA: [*trying to bring him out of it*] Willy, dear, I got a new kind of Americantype cheese today. It's whipped.

WILLY: Why do you get American when I like Swiss?

LINDA: I just thought you'd like a change —

WILLY: I don't want a change! I want Swiss cheese. Why am I always being contradicted?

LINDA: [*with a covering laugh*] I thought it would be a surprise.

WILLY: Why don't you open a window in here, for God's sake?

LINDA: [*with infinite patience*] They're all open, dear.

WILLY: The way they boxed us in here. Bricks and windows, windows and bricks.

LINDA: We should've bought the land next door.

WILLY: The street is lined with cars. There's not a breath of fresh air in the neighborhood. The grass don't grow any more, you can't raise a carrot in the back yard. They should've had a law against apartment houses. Remember those two beautiful elm trees out there? When I and Biff hung the swing between them?

LINDA: Yeah, like being a million miles from the city.

WILLY: They should've arrested the builder for cutting those down. They massacred the neighborhood. [*lost*] More and more I think of those days, Linda. This time of year it was lilac and wisteria. And then the peonies would come out, and the daffodils. What fragrance in this room!

LINDA: Well, after all, people had to move somewhere.

WILLY: No, there's more people now.

LINDA: I don't think there's more people. I think—

WILLY: There's more people! That's what's ruining this country! Population is getting out of control. The competition is maddening! Smell the stink from that apartment house! And another one on the other side . . . How can they whip cheese?

> [*On Willy's last line,* BIFF *and* HAPPY *raise themselves up in their beds, listening.*]

LINDA: Go down, try it. And be quiet.

WILLY: [*turning to* LINDA, *guiltily*] You're not worried about me, are you, sweetheart?

BIFF: Whats the matter?

HAPPY: Listen!

LINDA: You've got too much on the ball to worry about.

WILLY: You're my foundation and my support, Linda.

LINDA: Just try to relax, dear. You make mountains out of molehills.

WILLY: I won't fight with him any more. If he wants to go back to Texas, let him go.

LINDA: He'll find his way.

WILLY: Sure. Certain men just don't get started till later in life. Like Thomas Edison, I think. Or B. F. Goodrich. One of them was deaf. [*He starts for the bedroom doorway.*] I'll put my money on Biff.

LINDA: And Willy—if it's warm Sunday we'll drive in the country. And we'll open the windshield, and take lunch.

WILLY: No, the windshields don't open on the new cars.

LINDA: But you opened it today.

WILLY: Me? I didn't. [*He stops.*] Now isn't that peculiar! Isn't that a remarkable—[*He breaks off in amazement and fright as the flute is heard distantly.*]

LINDA: What, darling?

WILLY: That is the most remarkable thing.

LINDA: What, dear?

WILLY: I was thinking of the Chevvy. [*slight pause*] Nineteen twenty-eight . . . when I had that red Chevvy— [*breaks off*] That funny? I coulda sworn I was driving that Chevvy today.

LINDA: Well, that's nothing. Something must've reminded you.

WILLY: Remarkable. Ts. Remember those days? The way Biff used to simonize that car? The dealer refused to believe there was eighty thousand miles on it. [*He shakes his head.*] Heh! [*to* LINDA] Close your eyes, I'll be right up. [*He walks out of the bedroom.*]

HAPPY: [*to* BIFF] Jesus, maybe he smashed up the car again!

LINDA: [*calling after* WILLY] Be careful on the stairs, dear! The cheese is on the middle shelf! [*She turns, goes over to the bed, takes his jacket, and goes out of the bedroom.*]

> [*Light has risen on the boys' room. Unseen,* WILLY *is heard talking to himself, "Eighty thousand miles," and a little laugh.* BIFF *gets out of bed, comes downstage a bit, and stands attentively.* BIFF *is two years older than his brother* HAPPY, *well built, but in these days bears a worn air and seems less self-assured. He has succeeded less, and his dreams are stronger and less acceptable than Happy's.* HAPPY *is tall, powerfully made. Sexuality is like a visible color on him, or a scent that many women have discovered.*]

*He, like his brother, is lost, but in a different way, for he has never allowed himself to turn his face toward defeat and is thus more confused and hard-skinned, although seemingly more content.*]

HAPPY: [*getting out of bed*] He's going to get his license taken away if he keeps that up. I'm getting nervous about him, y'know, Biff?

BIFF: His eyes are going.

HAPPY: No, I've driven with him. He sees all right. He just doesn't keep his mind on it. I drove into the city with him last week. He stops at a green light and then it turns red and he goes. [*He laughs.*]

BIFF: Maybe he's color-blind.

HAPPY: Pop? Why he's got the finest eye for color in the business. You know that.

BIFF: [*sitting down on his bed*] I'm going to sleep.

HAPPY: You're not still sour on Dad, are you, Biff?

BIFF: He's all right, I guess.

WILLY: [*underneath them, in the living-room*] Yes, sir, eighty thousand miles — eighty-two thousand!

BIFF: You smoking?

HAPPY: [*holding out a pack of cigarettes*] Want one?

BIFF: [*taking a cigarette*] I can never sleep when I smell it.

WILLY: What a simonizing job, heh!

HAPPY: [*with deep sentiment*] Funny, Biff, y'know? Us sleeping in here again? The old beds. [*He pats his bed affectionately.*] All the talk that went across those two beds, huh? Our whole lives.

BIFF: Yeah. Lotta dreams and plans.

HAPPY: [*with a deep and masculine laugh*] About five hundred women would like to know what was said in this room.
        [*They share a soft laugh.*]

BIFF: Remember that big Betsy something — what the hell was her name — over on Bushwick Avenue?

HAPPY: [*combing his hair*] With the collie dog!

BIFF: That's the one. I got you in there, remember?

HAPPY: Yeah, that was my first time — I think. Boy, there was a pig! [*They laugh, almost crudely.*] You taught me everything I know about women. Don't forget that.

BIFF: I bet you forgot how bashful you used to be. Especially with girls.

HAPPY: Oh, I still am, Biff.

BIFF: Oh, go on.

HAPPY: I just control it, that's all. I think I got less bashful and you got more so. What happened, Biff? Where's the old humor, the old confidence? [*He shakes Biff's knee.* BIFF *gets up and moves restlessly about the room.*] What's the matter?

BIFF: Why does Dad mock me all the time?

HAPPY: He's not mocking you, he —

BIFF: Everything I say there's a twist of mockery on his face. I can't get near him.

HAPPY: He just wants you to make good, that's all. I wanted to talk to you about Dad for a long time, Biff. Something's — happening to him. He — talks to himself.

BIFF: I noticed that this morning. But he always mumbled.

HAPPY: But not so noticeable. It got so embarrassing I sent him to Florida. And you know something? Most of the time he's talking to you.

BIFF: What's he say about me?

HAPPY: I can't make it out.

BIFF: What's he say about me?

HAPPY: I think the fact that you're not settled, that you're still kind of up in the air . . .

BIFF: There's one or two other things depressing him, Happy.

HAPPY: What do you mean?

BIFF: Never mind. Just don't lay it all to me.

HAPPY: But I think if you just got started — I mean — is there any future for you out there?

BIFF: I tell ya, Hap, I don't know what the future is. I don't know — what I'm supposed to want.

HAPPY: What do you mean?

BIFF: Well, I spent six or seven years after high school trying to work myself up. Shipping clerk, salesman, business of one kind or another. And it's a measly manner of existence. To get on that subway on the hot mornings in summer. To devote your whole life to keeping stock, or making phone calls, or selling or buying. To suffer fifty weeks of the year for the sake of a two-week vacation, when all you really desire is to be outdoors, with your shirt off. And always to have to get ahead of the next fella. And still — that's how you build a future.

HAPPY: Well, you really enjoy it on a farm? Are you content out there?

BIFF: [*with rising agitation*] Hap, I've had twenty or thirty different kinds of jobs since I left home before the war, and it always turns out the same. I just realized it lately. In Nebraska when I herded cattle, and the Dakotas, and Arizona, and now in Texas. It's why I came home now, I guess, because I realized it. This farm I work on, it's spring there now, see? And they've got about fifteen new colts. There's nothng more inspiring or — beautiful than the sight of a mare and a new colt. And it's cool there now, see? Texas is cool now, and it's spring. And whenever spring comes to where I am, I suddenly get the feeling, my God, I'm not gettin' anywhere! What the hell am I doing, playing around with horses, twenty-eight dollars a week! I'm thirty-four years old, I oughta be makin' my future. That's when I come running home. And now, I get here, and I don't know what to do with myself. [*after a pause*] I've always made a point of not wasting my life, and everytime I come back here I know that all I've done is to waste my life.

HAPPY: You're a poet, you know that, Biff? You're a — you're an idealist!

BIFF: No, I'm mixed up very bad. Maybe I oughta get married. Maybe I oughta get stuck into something. Maybe that's my trouble. I'm like a boy. I'm not married, I'm not in business, I just — I'm like a boy. Are you content, Hap? You're a success, aren't you? Are you content?

HAPPY: Hell, no!

BIFF: Why? You're making money, aren't you?

HAPPY: [*moving about with energy, expressiveness*] All I can do now is wait for the merchandise manager to die. And suppose I get to be merchandise manager? He's a good friend of mine, and he just built a terrific estate on Long Island. And he lived there about two months and sold it, and now he's building another one. He can't enjoy it once it's finished. And I know that's just what I would do. I don't know what the hell I'm workin' for. Sometimes I sit in my apartment — all alone. And I think of the rent I'm paying. And it's crazy. But then, it's what I always wanted. My own apartment, a car, and plenty of women. And still, goddammit, I'm lonely.

BIFF: [*with enthusiasm*] Listen, why don't you come out West with me?

HAPPY: You and I, heh?

BIFF: Sure, maybe we could buy a ranch. Raise cattle, use our muscles. Men built like we are should be working out in the open.

HAPPY: [*avidly*] The Loman Brothers, heh?

BIFF: [*with vast affection*] Sure, we'd be known all over the counties!

HAPPY: [*enthralled*] That's what I dream about, Biff. Sometimes I want to just rip my clothes off in the middle of the store and outbox that goddam merchandise manager. I mean I can outbox, outrun, and outlift anybody in that store, and I have to take orders from those common, petty sons-of-bitches till I can't stand it any more.

BIFF: I'm tellin' you, kid, if you were with me I'd be happy out there.

HAPPY: [*enthused*] See, Biff, everybody around me is so false that I'm constantly lowering my ideals . . .

BIFF: Baby, together we'd stand up for one another, we'd have someone to trust.

HAPPY: If I were around you —

BIFF: Hap, the trouble is we weren't brought up to grub for money. I don't know how to do it.

HAPPY: Neither can I!

BIFF: Then let's go!

HAPPY: The only thing is — what can you make out there?

BIFF: But look at your friend. Builds an estate and then hasn't the peace of mind to live in it.

HAPPY: Yeah, but when he walks into the store the waves part in front of him. That's fifty-two thousand dollars a year coming through the revolving door, and I got more in my pinky finger than he's got in his head.

BIFF: Yeah, but you just said —

HAPPY: I gotta show some of those pompous, self-important executives over there that Hap Loman can make the grade. I want to walk into the store the way he walks in. Then I'll go with you, Biff. We'll be together yet, I swear. But take those two we had tonight. Now weren't they gorgeous creatures?

BIFF: Yeah, yeah, most gorgeous I've had in years.

HAPPY: I get that any time I want, Biff. Whenever I feel disgusted. The only trouble is, it gets like bowling or something. I just keep knockin' them over and it doesn't mean anything. You still run around a lot?

BIFF: Naa. I'd like to find a girl — steady, somebody with substance.

HAPPY: That's what I long for.

BIFF: Go on! You'd never come home.

HAPPY: I would! Somebody with character, with resistance! Like Mom, y'know? You're gonna call me a bastard when I tell you this. That girl Charlotte I was with tonight is engaged to be married in five weeks. [*He tries on his new hat.*]

BIFF: No kiddin'!

HAPPY: Sure, the guy's in line for the vice-presidency of the store. I don't know what gets into me, maybe I just have an overdeveloped sense of competition or something, but I went and ruined her, and furthermore I can't get rid of her.

And he's the third executive I've done that to. Isn't that a crummy characteristic? And to top it all, I go to their weddings! [*indignantly, but laughing*] Like I'm not supposed to take bribes. Manufacturers offer me a hundred-dollar bill now and then to throw an order their way. You know how honest I am, but it's like this girl, see. I hate myself for it. Because I don't want the girl, and, still, I take it and—I love it!

BIFF: Let's go to sleep.

HAPPY: I guess we didn't settle anything, heh?

BIFF: I just got one idea that I think I'm going to try.

HAPPY: What's that?

BIFF: Remember Bill Oliver?

HAPPY: Sure, Oliver is very big now. You want to work for him again?

BIFF: No, but when I quit he said something to me. He put his arm on my shoulder, and he said, "Biff, if you ever need anything, come to me."

HAPPY: I remember that. That sounds good.

BIFF: I think I'll go to see him. If I could get ten thousand or even seven or eight thousand dollars I could buy a beautiful ranch.

HAPPY: I bet he'd back you. 'Cause he thought highly of you, Biff. I mean, they all do. You're well liked, Biff. That's why I say to come back here, and we both have the apartment. And I'm tellin' you, Biff, any babe you want . . .

BIFF: No, with a ranch I could do the work I like and still be something. I just wonder though. I wonder if Oliver still thinks I stole that carton of basketballs.

HAPPY: Oh, he probably forgot that long ago. It's almost ten years. You're too sensitive. Anyway, he didn't really fire you.

BIFF: Well, I think he was going to. I think that's why I quit. I was never sure whether he knew or not. I know he thought the world of me, though. I was the only one he'd let lock up the place.

WILLY: [*below*] You gonna wash the engine, Biff?

HAPPY: Shh!

> [BIFF *looks at* HAPPY, *who is gazing down, listening.* WILLY *is mumbling in the parlor.*]

HAPPY: You hear that?

> [*They listen.* WILLY *laughs warmly.*]

BIFF: [*growing angry*] Doesn't he know Mom can hear that?

WILLY: Don't get your sweater dirty, Biff!

> [A *look of pain crosses* BIFF'*s face.*]

HAPPY: Isn't that terrible? Don't leave again, will you? You'll find a job here. You gotta stick around. I don't know what to do about him, it's getting embarrassing.

WILLY: What a simonizing job!

BIFF: Mom's hearing that!

WILLY: No kiddin', Biff, you got a date? Wonderful!

HAPPY: Go on to sleep. But talk to him in the morning, will you?

BIFF: [*reluctantly getting into bed*] With her in the house. Brother!

HAPPY: [*getting into bed*] I wish you'd have a good talk with him.

> [*The light on their room begins to fade.*]

BIFF: [*to himself in bed*] That selfish, stupid . . .

HAPPY: Sh . . . Sleep, Biff.

[*Their light is out. Well before they have finished speaking,* WILLY's *form is dimly seen below in the darkened kitchen. He opens the refrigerator, searches in there, and takes out a bottle of milk. The apartment houses are fading out, and the entire house and surrounding become covered with leaves. Music insinuates itself as the leaves appear.*]

WILLY: Just wanna be careful with those girls, Biff, that's all. Don't make any promises. No promises of any kind. Because a girl, y'know, they always believe what you tell 'em, and you're very young, Biff, you're too young to be talking seriously to girls.

[*Light rises on the kitchen.* WILLY, *talking, shuts the refrigerator door and comes downstage to the kitchen table. He pours milk into a glass. He is totally immersed in himself, smiling faintly.*]

WILLY: Too young entirely, Biff. You want to watch your schooling first. Then when you're all set, there'll be plenty of girls for a boy like you. [*He smiles broadly at a kitchen chair.*] That so? The girls pay for you? [*He laughs.*] Boy, you must really be makin' a hit.

[WILLY *is gradually addressing — physically — a point offstage, speaking through the wall of the kitchen, and his voice has been rising in volume to that of a normal conversation.*]

WILLY: I been wondering why you polish the car so careful. Ha! Don't leave the hubcaps, boys. Get the chamois to the hubcaps. Happy, use newspaper on the windows, it's the easiest thing. Show him how to do it, Biff! You see, Happy? Pad it up, use it like a pad. That's it, that's it, good work. You're doin' all right, Hap. [*He pauses, then nods in approbation for a few seconds, then looks upward.*] Biff, first thing we gotta do when we get time is clip that big branch over the house. Afraid it's gonna fall in a storm and hit the roof. Tell you what. We get a rope and sling her around, and then we climb up there with a couple of saws and take her down. Soon as you finish the car, boys, I wanna see ya. I got a surprise for you, boys.

BIFF: [*offstage*] Whatta ya got, Dad?

WILLY: No, you finish first. Never leave a job till you're finished — remember that. [*looking toward the "big trees"*] Biff, up in Albany I saw a beautiful hammock. I think I'll buy it next trip, and we'll hang it right between those two elms. Wouldn't that be something? Just swingin' there under those branches. Boy, that would be . . .

[YOUNG BIFF *and* YOUNG HAPPY *appear from the direction* WILLY *was addressing.* HAPPY *carries rags and a pail of water.* BIFF, *wearing a sweater with a block "S", carries a football.*]

BIFF: [*pointing in the direction of the car offstage*] How's that, Pop, professional?

WILLY: Terrific. Terrific job, boys. Good work, Biff.

HAPPY: Where's the surprise, Pop?

WILLY: In the back seat of the car.

HAPPY: Boy! [*He runs off.*]

BIFF: What is it, Dad? Tell me, what'd you buy?

WILLY: [*laughing, cuffs him*] Never mind, something I want you to have.

BIFF: [*turns and starts off*] What is it, Hap?

HAPPY: [*offstage*] It's a punching bag!

BIFF: Oh, Pop!

WILLY: It's got Gene Tunney's signature on it!

    [HAPPY *runs onstage with a punching bag.*]

BIFF: Gee, how'd you know we wanted a punching bag?

WILLY: Well, it's the finest thing for the timing.

HAPPY: [*lies down on his back and pedals with his feet*] I'm losing weight, you notice, Pop?

WILLY: [*to* HAPPY] Jumping rope is good too.

BIFF: Did you see the new football I got?

WILLY: [*examining the ball*] Where'd you get a new ball?

BIFF: The coach told me to practice my passing.

WILLY: That so? And he gave you the ball, heh?

BIFF: Well, I borrowed it from the locker room. [*He laughs confidentially.*]

WILLY: [*laughing with him at the theft*] I want you to return that.

HAPPY: I told you he wouldn't like it!

BIFF: [*angrily*] Well, I'm bringing it back!

WILLY: [*stopping the incipient argument, to* HAPPY] Sure, he's gotta practice with a regulation ball, doesn't he? [*to* BIFF] Coach'll probably congratulate you on your initiative!

BIFF: Oh, he keeps congratulating my initiative all the time, Pop.

WILLY: That's because he likes you. If somebody else took that ball there'd be an uproar. So what's the report, boys, what's the report?

BIFF: Where'd you go this time, Dad? Gee we were lonesome for you.

WILLY: [*pleased, puts an arm around each boy and they come down to the apron*] Lonesome, heh?

BIFF: Missed you every minute.

WILLY: Don't say? Tell you a secret boys. Don't breathe it to a soul. Someday I'll have my own business, and I'll never have to leave home any more.

HAPPY: Like Uncle Charley, heh?

WILLY: Bigger than Uncle Charley! Because Charley is not — liked. He's liked, but he's not — well liked.

BIFF: Where'd you go this time, Dad?

WILLY: Well, I got on the road, and I went north to Providence. Met the Mayor.

BIFF: The Mayor of Providence!

WILLY: He was sitting in the hotel lobby.

BIFF: What'd he say?

WILLY: He said, "Morning!" And I said, "You got a fine city here, Mayor." And then he had coffee with me. And than I went to Waterbury. Waterbury is a fine city. Big clock city, the famous Waterbury clock. Sold a nice bill there. And then Boston — Boston is the cradle of the Revolution. A fine city. And a couple of other towns in Mass., and on to Portland and Bangor and straight home!

BIFF: Gee, I'd love to go with you sometime, Dad.

WILLY: Soon as summer comes.

HAPPY: Promise?

WILLY: You and Hap and I, and I'll show you all the towns. America is full of beautiful towns and fine, upstanding people. And they know me, boys, they know me up and down New England. The finest people. And when I bring you fellas up , there'll be open sesame for all of us, 'cause one thing, boys: I have friends. I can park my car in any street in New England, and the cops protect it like their own. This summer, heh?

BIFF AND HAPPY: [*together*] Yeah, You bet!

WILLY: We'll take our bathing suits.

HAPPY: We'll carry your bags, Pop!

WILLY: Oh, won't that be something! Me comin' into the Boston stores with you boys carryin' my bags. What a sensation!

[BIFF *is prancing around, practicing passing the ball.*]

WILLY: You nervous, Biff, about the game?

BIFF: Not if your're gonna be there.

WILLY: What do they say about you in school, now that they made you captain?

HAPPY: There's a crowd of girls behind him everytime the classes change.

BIFF: [*taking* WILLY's hand] This Saturday, Pop, this Saturday—just for you, I'm going to break through for a touchdown.

HAPPY: You're supposed to pass.

BIFF: I'm takin' one play for Pop. You watch me, Pop, and when I take off my helmet, that means I'm breakin' out. Then you watch me crash through that line!

WILLY: [*kisses* BIFF] Oh, wait'll I tell this in Boston!

[BERNARD *enters in knickers. He is younger than* BIFF, *earnest and loyal, a worried boy.*]

BERNARD: Biff, where are you? You're supposed to study with me today.

WILLY: Hey, looka Bernard. What're you lookin' so anemic about, Bernard?

BERNARD: He's gotta study, Uncle Willy. He's got Regents next week.

HAPPY: [*tauntingly, spinning* BERNARD *around*] Let's box, Bernard!

BERNARD: Biff! [*He gets away from* HAPPY.] Listen, Biff, I heard Mr. Birnbaum say that if you don't start studyin' math he's gonna flunk you, and you won't graduate. I heard him!

WILLY: You better study with him, Biff. Go ahead now.

BERNARD: I heard him!

BIFF: Oh, Pop, you didn't see my sneakers! [*He holds up a foot for* WILLY *to look at.*]

WILLY: Hey, that's a beautiful job of printing!

BERNARD: [*Wiping his glasses*] Just because he printed University of Virginia on his sneakers doesn't mean they've got to graduate him, Uncle Willy!

WILLY: [*angrily*] What're you talking about? With scholarships to three universities they're gonna flunk him?

BERNARD: But I heard Mr. Birnbaum say—

WILLY: Don't be a pest, Bernard! [*to his boys*] What an anemic!

BERNARD: Okay, I'm waiting for you in my house, Biff.

[BERNARD *goes off. The* LOMANS *laugh.*]

WILLY: Bernard is not well liked, is he?

BIFF: He's liked, but he's not well liked.

HAPPY: That's right, Pop.

WILLY: That's just what I mean. Bernard can get the best marks in school, y'understand, but when he gets out in the business world, y'understand, you are going to be five times ahead of him. That's why I thank Almighty God you're both built like Adonises. Because the man who makes an appearance in the business world, the man who creates personal interest, is the man who gets ahead. Be

liked and you will never want. You take me, for instance. I never have to wait
in line to see a buyer. "Willy Loman is here!" That's all they have to know, and
I go right through.

BIFF: Did you knock them dead, Pop?

WILLY: Knocked 'em cold in Providence, slaughtered 'em in Boston.

HAPPY: [*on his back, pedaling again*] I'm losing weight, you notice, Pop?
    [LINDA *enters, as of old, a ribbon in her hair, carrying a basket of washing.*]

LINDA: [*with youthful energy*] Hello, dear!

WILLY: Sweetheart!

LINDA: How'd the Chevvy run?

WILLY: Chevrolet, Linda, is the greatest car ever built. [*to the boys*] Since when do
you let your mother carry wash up the stairs?

BIFF: Grab hold there, boy!

HAPPY: Where to Mom?

LINDA: Hang them up on the line. And you better go down to your friends, Biff. The
cellar is full of boys. They don't know what to do with themselves.

BIFF: Ah, when Pop comes home they can wait!

WILLY: [*laughs appreciatively*] You better go down and tell them what to do, Biff.

BIFF: I think I'll have them sweep out the furnace room.

WILLY: Good work, Biff.

BIFF: [*goes through wall-line of kitchen to doorway at back and calls down*] Fellas!
Everybody sweep out the furnace room! I'll be right down!

VOICES: All right! Okay, Biff.

BIFF: George and Sam and Frank, come out back! We're hangin' up the wash!
Come on, Hap, on the double! [*He and* HAPPY *carry out the basket.*]

LINDA: The way they obey him!

WILLY: Well, that's training, the training. I'm tellin' you. I was sellin' thousands and
thousands, but I had to come home.

LINDA: Oh, the whole block'll be at that game. Did you sell anything?

WILLY: I did five hundred gross in Providence and seven hundred gross in Boston.

LINDA: No! Wait a minute, I've got a pencil. [*She pulls pencil and paper out of her
apron pocket.*] That makes your commission . . . Two hundred — my God!
Two hundred and twelve dollars!

WILLY: Well, I didn't figure it yet, but . . .

LINDA: How much did you do?

WILLY: Well, I — I did — about a hundred and eighty gross in Providence. Well,
no — it came to — roughly two hundred gross on the whole trip.

LINDA: [*without hesitation*] Two hundred gross. That's . . . [*She figures.*]

WILLY: The trouble was that three of the stores were half closed for inventory in
Boston. Otherwise I woulda broke records.

LINDA: Well, it makes seventy dollars and some pennies. That's very good.

WILLY: What do we owe?

LINDA: Well, on the first there's sixteen dollars on the refrigerator —

WILLY: Why sixteen?

LINDA: Well, the fan belt broke, so it was a dollar eighty.

WILLY: But it's brand new.

LINDA: Well, the man said that's the way it is. Till they work themselves in, y'know.
    [*They move through the wall-line into the kitchen.*]

WILLY: I hope we didn't get stuck on that machine.

LINDA: They got the biggest ads of any of them!

WILLY: I know, it's a fine machine. What else?

LINDA: Well, there's nine-sixty for the washing machine. And for the vacuum cleaner there's three and a half due on the fifteenth. Then the roof, you got twenty-one dollars remaining.

WILLY: It don't leak, does it?

LINDA: No, they did a wonderful job. Then you owe Frank for the carburetor.

WILLY: I'm not going to pay that man! That goddam Chevrolet, they ought to prohibit the manufacture of that car!

LINDA: Well, you owe him three and a half. And odds and ends, comes to around a hundred and twenty dollars by the fifteenth.

WILLY: A hundred and twenty dollars! My God, if business don't pick up I don't know what I'm gonna do!

LINDA: Well, next week you'll do better.

WILLY: Oh, I'll knock 'em dead next week. I'll go to Hartford. I'm very well liked in Hartford. You know, the trouble is, Linda, people don't seem to take to me.
    [*They move onto the forestage.*]

LINDA: Oh, don't be foolish.

WILLY: I know it when I walk in. They seem to laugh at me.

LINDA: Why? Why would they laugh at you? Don't talk that way, Willy.
    [WILLY *moves to the edge of the stage.* LINDA *goes into the kitchen and starts to darn stockings.*]

WILLY: I don't know the reason for it, but they just pass me by. I'm not noticed.

LINDA: But you're doing wonderful, dear. You're making seventy to a hundred dollars a week.

WILLY: But I gotta be at it ten, twelve hours a day. Other men — I don't know — they do it easier. I don't know why — I can't stop myself — I talk too much. A man oughta come in with a few words. One thing about Charley. He's a man of few words, and they respect him.

LINDA: You don't talk too much, you're just lively.

WILLY: [*smiling*] Well, I figure, what the hell, life is short, a couple of jokes. [*to himself*] I joke too much! [*The smile goes.*]

LINDA: Why? You're —

WILLY: I'm fat. I'm very — foolish to look at, Linda. I didn't tell you, but Christmas time I happened to be calling on F. H. Stewarts, and a salesman I know, as I was going in to see the buyer I heard him say something about — walrus. And I — I cracked him right across the face. I won't take that. I simply will not take that. But they do laugh at me. I know that.

LINDA: Darling . . .

WILLY: I gotta overcome it. I know I gotta overcome it. I'm not dressing to advantage, maybe.

LINDA: Willy, darling, you're the handsomest man in the world —

WILLY: Oh, no, Linda.

LINDA: To me you are. [*slight pause*] The handsomest.
    [*From the darkness is heard the laughter of a woman.* WILLY *doesn't turn to it, but it continues through* LINDA's *lines.*]

LINDA: And the boys, Willy. Few men are idolized by their children the way you are.

[*Music is heard as behind a scrim, to the left of the house,* THE WOMAN, *dimly seen, is dressing.*]

WILLY: [*with great feeling*] You're the best there is, Linda, you're a pal, you know that? On the road — on the road I want to grab you sometimes and just kiss the life outa you.

[*The laughter is loud now, and he moves into a brightening area at the left, where* THE WOMAN *has come from behind the scrim and is standing, putting on her hat, looking into a "mirror" and laughing.*]

WILLY: 'Cause I get so lonely — especially when business is bad and there's nobody to talk to. I get the feeling that I'll never sell anything again, that I won't make a living for you, or a business, a business for the boys. [*He talks through* THE WOMAN's *subsiding laughter;* THE WOMAN *primps at the "mirror."*] There's so much I want to make for—

THE WOMAN: Me? You didn't make me, Willy. I picked you.

WILLY: [*pleased*] You picked me?

THE WOMAN: [*who is quite proper-looking, Willy's age*] I did. I've been sitting at that desk watching all the salesmen go by, day in, day out. But you've got such a sense of humor, and we do have such a good time together, don't we?

WILLY: Sure, sure. [*He takes her in his arms.*] Why do you have to go now?

THE WOMAN: It's two o'clock . . .

WILLY: No, come on in! [*He pulls her.*]

THE WOMAN: . . . my sisters'll be scandalized. When'll you be back?

WILLY: Oh, two weeks about. Will you come up again?

THE WOMAN: Sure thing. You do make me laugh. It's good for me. [*She squeezes his arm, kissing him.*] And I think you're a wonderful man.

WILLY: You picked me, heh?

THE WOMAN: Sure. Because you're so sweet. And such a kidder.

WILLY: Well, I'll see you next time I'm in Boston.

THE WOMAN: I'll put you right through to the buyers.

WILLY: [*slapping her bottom*] Right. Well, bottoms up!

THE WOMAN: [*slaps him gently and laughs*] You just kill me, Willy. [*He suddenly grabs her and kisses her roughly.*] You kill me. And thanks for the stockings. I love a lot of stockings. Well, good night.

WILLY: Good night. And keep your pores open!

THE WOMAN: Oh, Willy!

[THE WOMAN *bursts out laughing, and* LINDA's *laughter blends in.* THE WOMAN *disappears into the dark. Now the area at the kitchen table brightens.* LINDA *is sitting where she was at the kitchen table, but now is mending a pair of her silk stockings.*]

LINDA: You are, Willy. The handsomest man. You've got no reason to feel that—

WILLY: [*coming out of* THE WOMAN's *dimming area and going over to* LINDA] I'll make it all up to you, Linda, I'll—

LINDA: There's nothing to make up, dear. You're doing fine, better than—

WILLY: [*noticing her mending*] What's that?

LINDA: Just mending my stockings. They're so expensive—

WILLY: [*angrily, taking them from her*] I won't have you mending stockings in this house! Now throw them out!

[LINDA *puts the stockings in her pocket.*]

BERNARD: [*entering on the run*] Where is he? If he doesn't study!

WILLY: [*moving to the forestage, with great agitation*] You'll give him the answers!

BERNARD: I do, but I can't on a Regents! That's a state exam! They're liable to arrest me!

WILLY: Where is he? I'll whip him, I'll whip him!

LINDA: And he'd better give back that football, Willy, it's not nice.

WILLY: Biff! Where is he? Why is he taking everything?

LINDA: He's too rough with the girls, Willy. All the mothers are afraid of him!

WILLY: I'll whip him!

BERNARD: He's driving the car without a license!

[THE WOMAN'S *laugh is heard.*]

WILLY: Shut up!

LINDA: All the mothers —

WILLY: Shut up!

BERNARD: [*backing quietly away and out*] Mr. Birnbaum says he's stuck up.

WILLY: Get outa here!

BERNARD: If he doesn't buckle down he'll flunk math! [*He goes off.*]

LINDA: He's right, Willy, you've gotta —

WILLY: [*exploding at her*] There's nothing the matter with him! You want him to be a worm like Bernard? He's got spirit, personality . . .

[*As he speaks,* LINDA, *almost in tears, exits into the living-room.* WILLY *is alone in the kitchen, wilting and staring. The leaves are gone. It is night again, and the apartment houses look down from behind.*]

WILLY: Loaded with it. Loaded! What is he stealing? He's giving it back, isn't he? Why is he stealing? What did I tell him? I never in my life told him anything but decent things.

[HAPPY *in pajamas has come down the stairs;* WILLY *suddenly becomes aware of* HAPPY'S *presence.*]

HAPPY: Let's go now, come on.

WILLY: [*sitting down at the kitchen table*] Huh! Why did she have to wax the floors herself? Everytime she waxes the floors she keels over. She knows that!

HAPPY: Shh! Take it easy. What brought you back tonight?

WILLY: I got an awful scare. Nearly hit a kid in Yonkers. God! Why didn't I go to Alaska with my brother Ben that time! Ben! That man was a genius, that man was success incarnate! What a mistake! He begged me to go.

HAPPY: Well, there's no use in —

WILLY: You guys! There was a man started with the clothes on his back and ended up with diamond mines!

HAPPY: Boy, someday I'd like to know how he did it.

WILLY: What's the mystery? The man knew what he wanted and went out and got it! Walked into a jungle, and comes out, the age of twenty-one, and he's rich! The world is an oyster, but you don't crack it open on a mattress!

HAPPY: Pop, I told you I'm gonna retire you for life.

WILLY: You'll retire me for life on seventy goddam dollars a week? And your women and your car and your apartment, and you'll retire me for life! Christ's sake, I couldn't get past Yonkers' today! Where are you guys, where are you? The woods are burning! I can't drive a car!

[CHARLEY *has appeared in the doorway. He is a large man, slow of speech,* laconic, immovable. In all he says, despite what he says, there is pity, and, now, trepidation. He has a robe over pajamas, slippers on his feet. He enters the kitchen.]

CHARLEY: Everything all right?

HAPPY: Yeah, Charley, everything's . . .

WILLY: What's the matter?

CHARLEY: I heard some noise. I thought something happened. Can't we do some-thing about the walls? You sneeze in here, and in my house hats blow off.

HAPPY: Let's go to bed, Dad. Come on.

[CHARLEY *signals to* HAPPY *to go.*]

WILLY: You go ahead, I'm not tired at the moment.

HAPPY: [*to* WILLY] Take it easy, huh? [*He exits.*]

WILLY: What're you doin' up?

CHARLEY: [*sitting down at the kitchen table opposite* WILLY] Couldn't sleep good. I had a heartburn.

WILLY: Well, you don't know how to eat.

CHARLEY: I eat with my mouth.

WILLY: No, you're ignorant. You gotta know about vitamins and things like that.

CHARLEY: Come on, let's shoot. Tire you out a little.

WILLY: [*hesitantly* All right. You got cards?

CHARLEY: [*taking a deck from his pocket*] Yeah, I got them. Someplace. What is it with those vitamins?

WILLY: [*dealing*] They build up your bones. Chemistry.

CHARLEY: Yeah, but there's no bones in a heartburn.

WILLY: What are you talkin' about? Do you know the first thing about it?

CHARLEY: Don't get insulted.

WILLY: Don't talk about something you don't know anything about.

[*They are playing. Pause.*]

CHARLEY: What're you doin' home?

WILLY: A little trouble with the car.

CHARLEY: Oh. [*pause*] I'd like to take a trip to California.

WILLY: Don't say.

CHARLEY: You want a job?

WILLY: I got a job. I told you that. [*after a slight pause*] What the hell are you offering me a job for?

CHARLEY: Don't get insulted.

WILLY: Don't insult me.

CHARLEY: I don't see no sense in it. You don't have to go on this way.

WILLY: I got a good job. [*slight pause*] What do you keep comin' in here for?

CHARLEY: You want me to go?

WILLY: [*after a pause, withering*] I can't understand it. He's going back to Texas again. What the hell is that?

CHARLEY: Let him go.

WILLY: I got nothin' to give him, Charley, I'm clean, I'm clean.

CHARLEY: He won't starve. None a them starve. Forget about him.

WILLY: Then what have I got to remember?

CHARLEY: You take it too hard. To hell with it. When a deposit bottle is broken you don't get your nickel back.

WILLY: That's easy enough for you to say.

CHARLEY: That ain't easy for me to say.

WILLY: Did you see the ceiling I put up in the living-room?

CHARLEY: Yeah, that's a piece of work. To put up a ceiling is a mystery to me. How do you do it?

WILLY: What's the difference?

CHARLEY: Well, talk about it.

WILLY: You gonna put up a ceiling?

CHARLEY: How could I put up a ceiling?

WILLY: Then what the hell are you bothering me for?

CHARLEY: You're insulted again.

WILLY: A man who can't handle tools is not a man. You're disgusting.

CHARLEY: Don't call me disgusting, Willy.

[UNCLE BEN, *carrying a valise and an umbrella, enters the forestage from around the right corner of the house. He is a stolid man, in his sixties, with a mustache and an authoritative air. He is utterly certain of his destiny, and there is an aura of far places about him. He enters exactly as* WILLY *speaks.*]

WILLY: I'm getting awfully tired, Ben.

[*Ben's music is heard.* BEN *looks around at everything.*]

CHARLEY: Good, keep playing; you'll sleep better. Did you call me Ben?

[BEN *looks at his watch.*]

WILLY: That's funny. For a second there you reminded me of my brother Ben.

BEN: I only have a few minutes. [*He strolls, inspecting the place.* WILLY *and* CHARLEY *continue playing.*]

CHARLEY: You never heard from him again, heh? Since that time?

WILLY: Didn't Linda tell you? Couple of weeks ago we got a letter from his wife in Africa. He died.

CHARLEY: That so.

BEN: [*chuckling*] So this is Brooklyn, eh?

CHARLEY: Maybe you're in for some of his money.

WILLY: Naa, he had seven sons. There's just one opportunity I had with that man . . .

BEN: I must make a train, William. There are several properties I'm looking at in Alaska.

WILLY: Sure, sure! If I'd gone with him to Alaska that time, everything would've been totally different.

CHARLEY: Go on, you'd froze to death up there.

WILLY: What're you talking about?

BEN: Opportunity is tremendous in Alaska, William. Surprised you're not up there.

WILLY: Sure, tremendous.

CHARLEY: Heh?

WILLY: There was the only man I ever met who knew the answers.

CHARLEY: Who?

BEN: How are you all?

WILLY: [*taking a pot, smiling*] Fine, fine.

CHARLEY: Pretty sharp tonight.

BEN: Is Mother living with you?

WILLY: No, she died a long time ago.

CHARLEY: Who?

BEN: That's too bad. Fine specimen of a lady, Mother.

WILLY: [*to* CHARLEY] Heh?

BEN: I'd hope to see the old girl.

CHARLEY: Who died?

BEN: Heard anything from Father, have you?

WILLY: [*unnerved*] What do you mean, who died?

CHARLEY: [*taking a pot*] What're you talkin' about?

BEN: [*looking at his watch*] William, it's half-past eight!

WILLY: [*as though to dispel his confusion he angrily stops* CHARLEY's *hand*] That's my build!

CHARLEY: I put the ace —

WILLY: If you don't know how to play the game I'm not gonna throw my money away on you!

CHARLEY: [*rising*] It was my ace, for God's sake!

WILLY: I'm through, I'm through!

BEN: When did Mother die?

WILLY: Long ago. Since the beginning you never knew how to play cards.

CHARLEY: [*picks up the cards and goes to the door*] All right! Next time I'll bring a deck with five aces.

WILLY: I don't play that kind of game!

CHARLEY: [*turning to him*] You ought to be ashamed of yourself!

WILLY: Yeah?

CHARLEY: Yeah! [*He goes out.*]

WILLY: [*slamming the door after him*] Ignoramus!

BEN: [*as* WILLY *comes toward him through the wall-line of the kitchen*] So you're William.

WILLY: [*shaking* BEN's *hand*] Ben! I've been waiting for you so long! What's the answer? How did you do it?

BEN: Oh, there's a story in that.

[LINDA *enters the forestage, as of old, carrying the wash basket.*]

LINDA: Is this Ben?

BEN: [*gallantly*] How do you do, my dear.

LINDA: Where've you been all these years? Willy's always wondered why you —

WILLY: [*pulling* BEN *away from her impatiently*] Where is Dad? Didn't you follow him? How did you get started?

BEN: Well, I don't know how much you remember.

WILLY: Well, I was just a baby, of course, only three or four years old —

BEN: Three years and eleven months.

WILLY: What a memory, Ben!

BEN: I have many enterprises, William, and I have never kept books.

WILLY: I remember I was sitting under the wagon in — was it Nebraska?

BEN: It was South Dakota, and I gave you a bunch of wild flowers.

WILLY: I remember you walking away down some open road.

BEN: [*laughing*] I was going to find Father in Alaska.

WILLY: Where is he?

BEN: At that age I had a very faulty view of geography, William. I discovered after a few days that I was heading due south, so instead of Alaska, I ended up in Africa.

LINDA: Africa!

WILLY: The Gold Coast!

BEN: Principally diamond mines!

LINDA: Diamond mines.

BEN: Yes, my dear. But I've only a few minutes —

WILLY: No! Boys! Boys! [YOUNG BIFF and HAPPY appear.] Listen to this. This is your Uncle Ben, a great man! Tell my boys, Ben!

BEN: Why, boys, when I was seventeen I walked into the jungle, and when I was twenty-one I walked out. [He laughs.] And by God I was rich.

WILLY: [to the boys] You see what I been talking about? The greatest things can happen!

BEN: [glancing at his watch] I have an appointment in Ketchikan Tuesday week.

WILLY: No, Ben! Please tell about Dad. I want my boys to hear. I want them to know the kind of stock they spring from. All I remember is a man with a big beard, and I was in Mamma's lap, sitting around a fire, and some kind of high music.

BEN: His flute. He played the flute.

WILLY: Sure, the flute, that's right!

[New music is heard, a high, rollicking tune.]

BEN: Father was a very great and a very wild-hearted man. We would start in Boston, and he'd toss the whole family into the wagon, and then he'd drive the team right across the country; through Ohio, and Indiana, Michigan, Illinois, and all the Western states. And we'd stop in the towns and sell the flutes that he'd made on the way. Great inventor, Father. With one gadget he made more in a week than a man like you could make in a lifetime.

WILLY: That's just the way I'm bringing them up, Ben — rugged, well liked, all-around.

BEN: Yeah? [to BIFF] Hit that, boy — hard as you can. [He pounds his stomach.]

BIFF: Oh, no, sir!

BEN: [taking boxing stance] Come on, get to me! [He laughs.]

BIFF: Okay! [He cocks his fists and starts in.]

LINDA: [to WILLY] Why must he fight, dear?

BEN: [sparring with BIFF] Good boy! Good boy!

WILLY: How's that, Ben, heh?

HAPPY: Give him the left, Biff!

LINDA: Why are you fighting?

BEN: Good boy! [Suddenly comes in, trips BIFF, and stands over him, the point of his umbrella poised over BIFF's eye.]

LINDA: Look out, Biff!

BIFF: Gee!

BEN: [patting BIFF's knee] Never fight fair with a stranger, boy. You'll never get out of the jungle that way. [taking LINDA's hand and bowing] It was an honor and a pleasure to meet you, Linda.

LINDA: [withdrawing her hand coldly, frightened] Have a nice — trip.

BEN: [to WILLY] And good luck with your — what do you do?

WILLY: Selling.

BEN: Yes. Well . . . [He raises his hand in farewell to all.]

WILLY: No, Ben, I don't want you to think . . . [*He takes* BEN's *arm to show him.*] It's Brooklyn, I know, but we hunt too.

BEN: Really, now.

WILLY: Oh, sure, there's snakes and rabbits and — that's why I moved out here. Why, Biff can fell any one of these trees in no time! Boys! Go right over to where they're building the apartment house and get some sand. We're gonna rebuild the entire front stoop right now! Watch this, Ben!

BIFF: Yes, sir! On the double, Hap!

HAPPY: [*as he and* BIFF *run off*] I lost weight, Pop, you notice?

[CHARLEY *enters in knickers, even before the boys are gone.*]

CHARLEY: Listen, if they steal any more from that building, the watchman'll put the cops on them!

LINDA: [*to* WILLY] Don't let Biff . . .

[BEN *laughs lustily.*]

WILLY: You shoulda seen the lumber they brought home last week. At least a dozen six-by-tens worth all kinds of money.

CHARLEY: Listen, if that watchman —

WILLY: I gave them hell, understand. But I got a couple of fearless characters there.

CHARLEY: Willy, the jails are full of fearless characters.

BEN: [*clapping* WILLY *on the back, with a laugh at* CHARLEY] And the stock exchange, friend!

WILLY: [*joining in* BEN's *laughter*] Where are the rest of your pants?

CHARLEY: My wife bought them.

WILLY: Now all you need is a golf club and you can go upstairs and go to sleep. [*to* BEN] Great athlete! Between him and his son Bernard they can't hammer a nail!

BERNARD: [*rushing in*] The watchman's chasing Biff!

WILLY: [*angrily*] Shut up! He's not stealing anything!

LINDA: [*alarmed, hurrying off left*] Where is he? Biff, dear! [*She exits.*]

WILLY: [*moving toward the left, away from* BEN] There's nothing wrong. What's the matter with you?

BEN: Nervy boy. Good!

WILLY: [*laughing*] Oh, nerves of iron, that Biff!

CHARLEY: Don't know what it is. My New England man comes back and he's bleedin', they murdered him up there.

WILLY: It's contacts, Charley, I got important contacts!

CHARLEY: [*sarcastically*] Glad to hear it, Willy. Come in later, we'll shoot a little casino. I'll take some of your Portland money. [*He laughs at* WILLY *and exits.*]

WILLY: [*turning to* BEN] Business is bad, it's murderous. But not for me, of course.

BEN: I'll stop by on my way back to Africa.

WILLY: [*longingly*] Can't you stay a few days? You're just what I need, Ben, because I — I have a fine position here, but I — well, Dad left when I was such a baby and I never had a chance to talk to him and I still feel — kind of temporary about myself.

BEN: I'll be late for my train.

[*They are at opposite ends of the stage.*]

WILLY: Ben, my boys — can't we talk? They'd go into the jaws of hell for me, see, but I —

BEN: William, you're being first-rate with your boys. Outstanding, manly chaps!

WILLY: [*hanging on to his words*] Oh, Ben, that's good to hear! Because sometimes I'm afraid that I'm not teaching them the right kind of — Ben, how should I teach them?

BEN: [*giving great weight to each word, and with a certain vicious audacity*] William, when I walked into the jungle, I was seventeen. When I walked out I was twenty-one. And, by God, I was rich. [*He goes off into darkness around the right corner of the house.*]

WILLY: . . . was rich! That's just the spirit I want to imbue them with! To walk into a jungle! I was right! I was right! I was right!

> [BEN *is gone, but* WILLY *is still speaking to him as* LINDA, *in nightgown and robe, enters the kitchen, glances around for* WILLY, *then goes to the door of the house, looks out and sees him. Comes down to his left. He looks at her.*]

LINDA: Willy, dear? Willy?

WILLY: I was right!

LINDA: Did you have some cheese? [*He can't answer.*] It's very late, darling. Come to bed, heh?

WILLY: [*looking straight up*] Gotta break your neck to see a star in this yard.

LINDA: You coming in?

WILLY: Whatever happened to that diamond watch fob? Remember? When Ben came from Africa that time? Didn't he give me a watch fob with a diamond in it?

LINDA: You pawned it, dear. Twelve, thirteen years ago. For Biff's radio correspondence course.

WILLY: Gee, that was a beautiful thing. I'll take a walk.

LINDA: But you're in your slippers.

WILLY: [*starting to go around the house at the left*] I was right! I was! [*half to* LINDA, *as he goes, shaking his head*] What a man! There was a man worth talking to. I was right!

LINDA: [*calling after* WILLY] But in your slippers, Willy!

> [WILLY *is almost gone when* BIFF, *in his pajamas, comes down the stairs and enters the kitchen.*]

BIFF: What is he doing out there?

LINDA: Sh!

BIFF: God Almighty, Mom, how long has he been doing this?

LINDA: Don't, he'll hear you.

BIFF: What the hell is the matter with him?

LINDA: It'll pass by morning.

BIFF: Shouldn't we do anything?

LINDA: Oh, my dear, you should do a lot of things, but there's nothing to do, so go to sleep.

> [HAPPY *comes down the stairs and sits on the steps.*]

HAPPY: I never heard him so loud, Mom.

LINDA: Well, come around more often; you'll hear him. [*She sits down at the table and mends the lining of* WILLY'S *jacket.*]

BIFF: Why didn't you ever write me about this, Mom?

LINDA: How would I write to you? For over three months you had no address.

BIFF: I was on the move. But you know I thought of you all the time. You know that, don't you, pal?

LINDA: I know, dear, I know. But he likes to have a letter. Just to know that there's still a possibility for better things.

BIFF: He's not like this all the time, is he?

LINDA: It's when you come home he's always the worst.

BIFF: When I come home?

LINDA: When you write you're coming, he's all smiles, and talks about the future, and — he's just wonderful. And then the closer you seem to come, the more shaky he gets, and then, by the time you get here, he's arguing, and he seems angry at you. I think it's just that maybe he can't bring himself to — to open up to you. Why are you so hateful to each other? Why is that?

BIFF: [*evasively*] I'm not hateful, Mom.

LINDA: But you no sooner come in the door than you're fighting!

BIFF: I don't know why. I mean to change. I'm tryin', Mom, you understand?

LINDA: Are you home to stay now?

BIFF: I don't know. I want to look around see what's doin'.

LINDA: Biff, you can't look around all your life, can you?

BIFF: I just can't take hold, Mom. I can't take hold of some kind of a life.

LINDA: Biff, a man is not a bird, to come and go with the springtime.

BIFF: Your hair . . . [*He touches her hair.*] Your hair got so gray.

LINDA: Oh, it's been gray since you were in high school. I just stopped dyeing it, that's all.

BIFF: Dye it again, will ya? I don't want my pal looking old. [*He smiles.*]

LINDA: You're such a boy! You think you can go away for a year and . . . You've got to get it into your head now that one day you'll knock on this door and there'll be strange people here —

BIFF: What are you talking about? You're not even sixty, Mom.

LINDA: But what about your father?

BIFF: [*lamely*] Well, I meant him too.

HAPPY: He admires Pop.

LINDA: Biff, dear, if you don't have any feeling for him, then you can't have any feeling for me.

BIFF: Sure I can, Mom.

LINDA: No. You can't just come to see me, because I love him. [*with a threat, but only a threat, of tears*] He's the dearest man in the world to me, and I won't have anyone making him feel unwanted and low and blue. You've got to make up your mind now, darling, there's no leeway any more. Either he's your father and you pay him that respect, or else you're not to come here. I know he's not easy to get along with — nobody knows that better than me — but . . .

WILLY: [*from the left, with a laugh*] Hey, hey, Biffo!

BIFF: [*starting to go out after* WILLY] What the hell is the matter with him? [HAPPY *stops him.*]

LINDA: Don't — don't go near him!

BIFF: Stop making excuses for him! He always, always wiped the floor with you. Never had an ounce of respect for you.

HAPPY: He's always had respect for —

BIFF: What the hell do you know about it?

HAPPY: [*surlily*] Just don't call him crazy!

BIFF: He's got no character — Charley wouldn't do this. Not in his own house — spewing out that vomit from his mind.

HAPPY: Charley never had to cope with what he's got to.

BIFF: People are worse off than Willy Loman. Believe me, I've seen them!

LINDA: Then make Charley your father, Biff. You can't do that, can you? I don't say he's a great man. Willy Loman never made a lot of money. His name was never in the paper. He's not the finest character that ever lived. But he's a human being, and a terrible thing is happening to him. So attention must be paid. He's not to be allowed to fall into his grave like an old dog. Attention, attention must be finally paid to such a person. You called him crazy —

BIFF: I didn't mean —

LINDA: No, a lot of people think he's lost his — balance. But you don't have to be very smart to know what his trouble is. The man is exhausted.

HAPPY: Sure!

LINDA: A small man can be just as exhausted as a great man. He works for a company thirty-six years this March, opens up unheard-of territories to their trademark, and now in his old age they take his salary away.

HAPPY: [*indignantly*] I didn't know that, Mom.

LINDA: You never asked, my dear! Now that you get your spending money some-place else you don't trouble your mind with him.

HAPPY: But I gave you money last —

LINDA: Christmas time, fifty dollars! To fix the hot water it cost ninety-seven fifty! For five weeks he's been on straight commission, like a beginner, an unknown!

BIFF: Those ungrateful bastards!

LINDA: Are they any worse than his sons? When he brought them business, when he was young, they were glad to see him. But now his old friends, the old buyers that loved him so and always found some order to hand him in a pinch — they're all dead, retired. He used to be able to make six, seven calls a day in Boston. Now he takes his valises out of the car and puts them back and takes them out again and he's exhausted. Instead of walking he talks now. He drives seven hundred miles, and when he gets there no one knows him any more, no one welcomes him. And what goes through a man's mind, driving seven hundred miles home without having earned a cent? Why shouldn't he talk to himself? Why? When he has to go to Charley and borrow fifty dollars a week and pretend to me that it's his pay? How long can that go on? How long? You see what I'm sitting here and waiting for? And you tell me he has no character? The man who never worked a day but for your benefit? When does he get the medal for that? Is this his reward — to turn around at the age of sixty-three and find his sons, who he loved better than his life, one a philandering bum —

HAPPY: Mom!

LINDA: That's all you are, my baby! [*to* BIFF] And you! What happened to the love you had for him? You were such pals! How you used to talk to him on the phone every night! How lonely he was till he could come home to you!

BIFF: All right, Mom. I'll live here in my room, and I'll get a job. I'll keep away from him, that's all.

LINDA: No, Biff. You can't stay here and fight all the time.

BIFF: He threw me out of this house, remember that.

LINDA: Why did he do that? I never knew why.

BIFF: Because I know he's a fake and he doesn't like anybody around who knows!

LINDA: Why a fake? In what way? What do you mean?

BIFF: Just don't lay it all at my feet. It's between me and him — that's all I have to say. I'll chip in from now on. He'll settle for half my pay check. He'll be all right. I'm going to bed. [*He starts for the stairs.*]

LINDA: He won't be all right.

BIFF: [*turning on the stairs, furiously*] I hate this city and I'll stay here. Now what do you want?

LINDA: He's dying, Biff.

[HAPPY *turns quickly to her, shocked.*]

BIFF: [*after a pause*] Why is he dying?

LINDA: He's been trying to kill himself.

BIFF: [*with great horror*] How?

LINDA: I live from day to day.

BIFF: What're you talking about?

LINDA: Remember I wrote you that he smashed up the car again? In February?

BIFF: Well?

LINDA: The insurance inspector came. He said that they have evidence. That all these accidents in the last year — weren't — weren't — accidents.

HAPPY: How can they tell that? That's a lie.

LINDA: It seems there's a woman . . . [*she takes a breath as*]

⎡BIFF: [*sharply but contained*] What woman?
⎣LINDA: [*simultaneously*] . . . and this woman . . .

LINDA: What?

BIFF: Nothing. Go ahead.

LINDA: What did you say?

BIFF: Nothing. I just said what woman?

HAPPY: What about her?

LINDA: Well, it seems she was walking down the road and saw his car. She says that he wasn't driving fast at all, and that he didn't skid. She says he came to that little bridge, and then deliberately smashed into the railing, and it was only the shallowness of the water that saved him.

BIFF: Oh, no, he probably just fell asleep again.

LINDA: I don't think he fell asleep.

BIFF: Why not?

LINDA: Last month . . . [*with great difficulty*] Oh, boys, it's so hard to say a thing like this! He's just a big stupid man to you, but I tell you there's more good in him than in many other people. [*She chokes, wipes her eyes.*] I was looking for a fuse. The lights blew out, and I went down the cellar. And behind the fuse box — it happened to fall out — was a length of rubber pipe — just short.

HAPPY: No kidding?

LINDA: There's a little attachment on the end of it. I knew right away. And sure enough, on the bottom of the water heater there's a new little nipple on the gas pipe.

HAPPY: [*angrily*] That — jerk.

BIFF: Did you have it taken off?

LINDA: I'm — I'm ashamed to. How can I mention it to him? Every day I go down and take away that little rubber pipe. But, when he comes home, I put it back where it was. How can I insult him that way? I don't know what to do. I live from day to day, boys. I tell you, I know every thought in his mind. It sounds so old-fashioned and silly, but I tell you he put his whole life into you and you've turned your backs on him. [*She is bent over in the chair, weeping, her face in her hands.*] Biff, I swear to God! Biff, his life is in your hands!

HAPPY: [*to* BIFF] How do you like that damned fool!

BIFF: [*kissing her*] All right, pal, all right. It's settled now. I've been remiss. I know that, Mom. But now I'll stay, and I swear to you, I'll apply myself. [*kneeling in front of her, in a fever of self-reproach*] It's just — you see, Mom, I don't fit in business. Not that I won't try. I'll try, and I'll make good.

HAPPY: Sure you will. The trouble with you in business was you never tried to please people.

BIFF: I know, I —

HAPPY: Like when you worked for Harrison's. Bob Harrison said you were tops, and then you go and do some damn fool thing like whistling whole songs in the elevator like a comedian.

BIFF: [*against* HAPPY] So what? I like to whistle sometimes.

HAPPY: You don't raise a guy to a responsible job who whistles in the elevator!

LINDA: Well, don't argue about it now.

HAPPY: Like when you'd go off and swim in the middle of the day instead of taking the line around.

BIFF: [*his resentment rising*] Well, don't you run off? You take off sometimes, don't you? On a nice summer day?

HAPPY: Yeah, but I cover myself!

LINDA: Boys!

HAPPY: If I'm going to take a fade the boss can call any number where I'm supposed to be and they'll swear to him that I just left. I'll tell you something that I hate to say, Biff, but in the business world some of them think you're crazy.

BIFF: [*angered*] Screw the business world!

HAPPY: All right, screw it! Great, but cover yourself!

LINDA: Hap, Hap!

BIFF: I don't care what they think! They've laughed at Dad for years, and you know why? Because we don't belong in this nuthouse of a city! We should be mixing cement on some open plain, or — or carpenters. A carpenter is allowed to whistle!

[WILLY *walks in from the entrance of the house, at left.*]

WILLY: Even your grandfather was better than a carpenter. [*Pause. They watch him.*] You never grow up. Bernard does not whistle in the elevator, I assure you.

BIFF: [*as though to laugh* WILLY *out of it*] Yeah, but you do, Pop.

WILLY: I never in my life whistled in an elevator! And who in the business world thinks I'm crazy?

BIFF: I didn't mean it like that, Pop. Now don't make a whole thing out of it, will ya?

WILLY: Go back to the West! Be a carpenter, a cowboy, enjoy yourself!

LINDA: Willy, he was just saying —

WILLY: I heard what he said!

HAPPY: [*trying to quiet* WILLY] Hey, Pop, come on now . . .

WILLY: [*continuing over* HAPPY'*s line*] They laugh at me, heh? Go to Filene's, go to the Hub, go to Slattery's, Boston. Call out the name Willy Loman and see what happens! Big shot!

BIFF: All right, Pop.

WILLY: Big!

BIFF: All right!

WILLY: Why do you always insult me?

BIFF: I didn't say a word. [*to* LINDA] Did I say a word?

LINDA: He didn't say anything, Willy.

WILLY: [*going to the doorway of the living-room*] All right, good night, good night.

LINDA: Willy, dear, he just decided . . .

WILLY: [*to* BIFF] If you get tired hanging around tomorrow, paint the ceiling I put up in the living-room

BIFF: I'm leaving early tomorrow.

HAPPY: He's going to see Bill Oliver, Pop.

WILLY: [*interestedly*] Oliver? For what?

BIFF: [*with reserve, but trying, trying*] He always said he'd stake me. I'd like to go into business, so maybe I can take him up on it.

LINDA: Isn't that wonderful?

WILLY: Don't interrupt. What's wonderful about it? There's fifty men in the City of New York who'd stake him. [*to* BIFF] Sporting goods?

BIFF: I guess so. I know something about it and—

WILLY: He knows something about it! You know sporting goods better than Spalding, for God's sake! How much is he giving you?

BIFF: I don't know, I didn't even see him yet, but—

WILLY: Then what're you talkin' about?

BIFF: [*getting angry*] Well, all I said was I'm gonna see him, that's all!

WILLY: [*turning away*] Ah, you're counting your chickens again.

BIFF: [*starting left for the stairs*] Oh, Jesus, I'm going to sleep!

WILLY: [*calling after him*] Don't curse in this house!

BIFF: [*turning*] Since when did you get so clean?

HAPPY: [*trying to stop them*] Wait a . . .

WILLY: Don't use that language to me! I won't have it!

HAPPY: [*grabbing* BIFF, *shouts*] Wait a minute! I got an idea. I got a feasible idea. Come here, Biff, let's talk this over now, let's talk some sense here. When I was down in Florida last time, I thought of a great idea to sell sporting goods. It just came back to me. You and I, Biff—we have a line, the Loman Line. We train a couple of weeks, and put on a couple of exhibitions, see?

WILLY: That's an idea!

HAPPY: Wait! We form two basketball teams, see? Two waterpolo teams. We play each other. It's a million dollars' worth of publicity. Two brothers, see? The Loman Brothers. Displays in the Royal Palms—all the hotels. And banners over the ring and the basketball court: "Loman Brothers." Baby, we could sell sporting goods!

WILLY: That is a one-million-dollar idea!

LINDA: Marvelous!

BIFF: I'm in great shape as far as that's concerned.

HAPPY: And the beauty of it is, Biff, it wouldn't be like a business. We'd be out playin' ball again . . .

BIFF: [*enthused*] Yeah, that's . . .

WILLY: Million-dollar . . .

HAPPY: And you wouldn't get fed up with it, Biff. It'd be the family again. There'd be the old honor, and comradeship, and if you wanted to go off for a swim or something' — well, you'd do it! Without some smart cooky gettin' up ahead of you!

WILLY: Lick the world! You guys together could absolutely lick the civilized world.

BIFF: I'll see Oliver tomorrow. Hap, if we could work that out . . .

LINDA: Maybe things are beginning to —

WILLY: [*wildly enthused, to* LINDA] Stop interrupting! [*to* BIFF] But don't wear sport jacket and slacks when you see Oliver.

BIFF: No, I'll —

WILLY: A business suit, and talk as little as possible, and don't crack any jokes.

BIFF: He did like me. Always liked me.

LINDA: He loved you!

WILLY: [*to* LINDA] Will you stop! [*to* BIFF] Walk in very serious. You are not applying for a boy's job. Money is to pass. Be quiet, fine, and serious. Everybody likes a kidder, but nobody lends him money.

HAPPY: I'll try to get some myself, Biff. I'm sure I can.

WILLY: I see great things for you kids, I think your troubles are over. But remember, start big and you'll end big. Ask for fifteen. How much you gonna ask for?

BIFF: Gee, I don't know —

WILLY: And don't say "Gee." "Gee" is a boy's word. A man walking in for fifteen thousand dollars does not say "Gee!"

BIFF: Ten, I think, would be top though.

WILLY: Don't be so modest. You always started too low. Walk in with a big laugh. Don't look worried. Start off with a couple of your good stories to lighten things up. It's not what you say, it's how you say it — because personality always wins the day.

LINDA: Oliver always thought the highest of him —

WILLY: Will you let me talk?

BIFF: Don't yell at her, Pop, will ya?

WILLY: [*angrily*] I was talking, wasn't I?

BIFF: I don't like you yelling at her all the time, and I'm tellin' you, that's all.

WILLY: What're you, takin' over this house?

LINDA: Willy —

WILLY: [*turning on her*] Don't take his side all the time, goddammit!

BIFF: [*furiously*] Stop yelling at her!

WILLY: [*suddenly pulling on his cheek, beaten down, guilt ridden*] Give my best to Bill Oliver — he may remember me.

[*He exits through the living-room doorway.*]

LINDA: [*her voice subdued*] What'd you have to start that for? [BIFF *turns away.*] You see how sweet he was as soon as you talked hopefully? [*She goes over to* BIFF.] Come up and say good night to him. Don't let him go to bed that way.

HAPPY: Come on, Biff, let's buck him up.

LINDA: Please, dear. Just say good night to him. It takes so little to make him happy. Come.

[*She goes through the living-room doorway, calling upstairs from within the living-room:*] Your pajamas are hanging in the bathroom, Willy!

HAPPY: [*looking toward where* LINDA *went out*] What a woman! They broke the mold when they made her. You know that, Biff?

BIFF: He's off salary. My God, working on commission!

HAPPY: Well, let's face it: he's no hot-shot selling man. Except that sometimes, you have to admit, he's a sweet personality.

BIFF: [*deciding*] Lend me ten bucks, will ya? I want to buy some new ties.

HAPPY: I'll take you to a place I know. Beautiful stuff. Wear one of my striped shirts tomorrow.

BIFF: She got gray. Mom got awful old. Gee, I'm gonna go in to Oliver tomorrow and knock him for a —

HAPPY: Come on up. Tell that to Dad. Let's give him a whirl. Come on.

BIFF: [*steamed up*] You know, with ten thousand bucks, boy!

HAPPY: [*as they go into the living-room*] That's the talk, Biff, that's the first time I've heard the old confidence out of you! [*from within the living-room, fading off*] You're gonna live with me, kid, and any babe you want just say the word . . . [*The last lines are hardly heard. They are mounting the stairs to their parents' bedroom.*]

LINDA: [*entering her bedroom and addressing* WILLY, *who is in the bathroom. She is straightening the bed for him*] Can you do anything about the shower? It drips.

WILLY: [*from the bathroom*] All of a sudden everything falls to pieces! Goddam plumbing, oughta be sued, those people. I hardly finished putting it in and the thing . . . [*his words rumble off.*]

LINDA: I'm just wondering if Oliver will remember him. You think he might?

WILLY: [*coming out of the bathroom in his pajamas*] Remember him? What's the matter with you, you crazy? If he'd've stayed with Oliver he'd be on top by now! Wait'll Oliver gets a look at him. You don't know the average caliber any more. The average young man today — [*he is getting into bed*] — is got a caliber of zero. Greatest thing in the world for him was to bum around.

[BIFF *and* HAPPY *enter the bedroom. Slight pause.*]

WILLY: [*stops short, looking at* BIFF] Glad to hear it, boy.

HAPPY: He wanted to say good night to you, sport.

WILLY: [*to* BIFF] Yeah. Knock him dead, boy. What'd you want to tell me?

BIFF: Just take it easy, Pop. Good night. [*He turns to go.*]

WILLY: [*unable to resist*] And if anything falls off the desk while you're talking to him — like a package or something — don't you pick it up. They have office boys for that.

LINDA: I'll make a big breakfast —

WILLY: Will you let me finish? [*to* BIFF] Tell him you were in the business in the West. Not farm work.

BIFF: All right, Dad.

LINDA: I think everything —

WILLY: [*going right through her speech*] And don't undersell yourself. No less than fifteen thousand dollars.

BIFF: [*unable to bear him*] Okay. Good night, Mom. [*He starts moving.*]

WILLY: Because you got a greatness in you, Biff, remember that. You got all kinds a greatness . . . [*He lies back, exhausted.*]

[BIFF *walks out.*]

LINDA: [*calling after* BIFF] Sleep well, darling!

HAPPY: I'm gonna get married, Mom. I wanted to tell you.

LINDA: Go to sleep, dear.

HAPPY: [*going*] I just wanted to tell you.

WILLY: Keep up the good work. [HAPPY *exits.*] God . . . remember that Ebbets Field game? The championship of the city?

LINDA: Just rest. Should I sing to you?

WILLY: Yeah. Sing to me. [LINDA *hums a soft lullaby.*] When that team came out — he was the tallest, remember?

LINDA: Oh, yes. And in gold.

[BIFF *enters the darkened kitchen, takes a cigarette, and leaves the house. He comes downstage into a golden pool of light. He smokes, staring at the night.*]

WILLY: Like a young god. Hercules — something like that. And the sun, the sun all around him. Remember how he waved to me? Right up from the field, with the representatives of three colleges standing by? And the buyers I brought, and the cheers when he came out — Loman, Loman, Loman! God Almighty, he'll be great yet. A star like that, magnificent, can never really fade away!

[*The light on* WILLY *is fading. The gas heater begins to glow through the kitchen wall, near the stairs, a blue flame beneath red coils.*]

LINDA: [*timidly*] Willy dear, what has he got against you?

WILLY: I'm so tired. Don't talk any more.

[BIFF *slowly returns to the kitchen. He stops, stares toward the heater.*]

LINDA: Will you ask Howard to let you work in New York?

WILLY: First thing in the morning. Everything'll be all right.

[BIFF *reaches behind the heater and draws out a length of rubber tubing. He is horrified and turns his head toward Willy's room, still dimly lit, from which the strains of* LINDA's *desperate but monotonous humming rise.*]

WILLY: [*staring through the window into the moonlight*] Gee, look at the moon moving between the buildings!

[BIFF *wraps the tubing around his hand and quickly goes up the stairs.*]


## ACT II

[*Music is heard, gay and bright. The curtain rises as the music fades away.* WILLY, *in shirt sleeves, is sitting at the kitchen table, sipping coffee, his hat in his lap.* LINDA *is filling his cup when she can.*]

WILLY: Wonderful coffee. Meal in itself.

LINDA: Can I make you some eggs?

WILLY: No. Take a breath.

LINDA: You look so rested, dear.

WILLY: I slept like a dead one. First time in months. Imagine, sleeping till ten on a Tuesday morning. Boys left nice and early, heh?

LINDA: They went out of here by eight o'clock.

WILLY: Good work!

LINDA: It was so thrilling to see them leaving together. I can't get over the shaving lotion in this house!

WILLY: [*smiling*] Mmm —

LINDA: Biff was very changed this morning. His whole attitude seemed to be hopeful. He couldn't wait to get downtown to see Oliver.

WILLY: He's heading for a change. There's no question, there simply are certain men that take longer to get — solidified. How did he dress?

LINDA: His blue suit. He's so handsome in that suit. He could be a — anything in that suit!

[WILLY *gets up from the table.* LINDA *holds his jacket for him.*]

WILLY: There's no question, no question at all. Gee, on the way home tonight I'd like to buy some seeds.

LINDA: [*laughing*] That'd be wonderful. But not enough sun gets back there. Nothing'll grow any more.

WILLY: You wait, kid, before it's all over we're gonna get a little place out in the country, and I'll raise some vegetables, a couple of chickens . . .

LINDA: You'll do it yet, dear.

[WILLY *walks out of his jacket.* LINDA *follows him*]

WILLY: And they'll get married, and come for a weekend. I'd built a little guest house. 'Cause I got so many fine tools, all I'd need would be a little lumber and some peace of mind.

LINDA: [*joyfully*] I sewed the lining . . .

WILLY: I could build two guest houses, so they'd both come. Did he decide how much he's going to ask Oliver for?

LINDA: [*getting him into the jacket*] He didn't mention it, but I imagine ten or fifteen thousand. You going to talk to Howard today?

WILLY: Yeah. I'll put it to him straight and simple. He'll just have to take me off the road.

LINDA: And Willy, don't forget to ask for a little advance, because we've got the insurance premium. It's the grace period now.

WILLY: That's a hundred . . . ?

LINDA: A hundred and eight, sixty-eight. Because we're a little short again.

WILLY: Why are we short?

LINDA: Well, you had the motor job on the car . . .

WILLY: That goddam Studebaker!

LINDA: And you got one more payment on the refrigerator . . .

WILLY: But it just broke again!

LINDA: Well, it's old, dear.

WILLY: I told you we should've bought a well-advertised machine. Charley bought a General Electric and it's twenty years old and it's still good, that son-of-a-bitch.

LINDA: But, Willy —

WILLY: Whoever heard of a Hastings refrigerator? Once in my life I would like to own something outright before it's broken! I'm always in a race with the junkyard! I just finished paying for the car and it's on its last legs. The refrigerator consumes belts like a goddam maniac. They time those things. They time them so when you finally paid for them, they're used up.

LINDA: [*buttoning up his jacket as he unbuttons it*] All told, about two hundred dollars would carry us, dear. But that includes the last payment on the mortgage. After this payment, Willy, the house belongs to us.

WILLY: It's twenty-five years!

LINDA: Biff was nine years old when we bought it.

WILLY: Well, that's a great thing. To weather a twenty-five year mortgage is —

LINDA: It's an accomplishment.

WILLY: All the cement, the lumber, the reconstruction I put in this house! There ain't a crack to be found in it any more.

LINDA: Well, it served its purpose.

WILLY: What purpose? Some stranger'll come along, move it, and that's that. If only Biff would take this house, and raise a family . . . [*He starts to go.*] Good-by, I'm late.

LINDA: [*suddenly remembering*] Oh, I forgot! You're supposed to meet them for dinner.

WILLY: Me?

LINDA: At Frank's Chop House on Forty-eighth near Sixth Avenue.

WILLY: Is that so! How about you?

LINDA: No, just the three of you. They're gonna blow you to a big meal!

WILLY: Don't say! Who thought of that?

LINDA: Biff came to me this morning, Willy, and he said, "Tell Dad. we want to blow him to a big meal." Be there six o'clock. You and your two boys are going to have dinner.

WILLY: Gee whiz! That's really somethin'. I'm gonna knock Howard for a loop, kid. I'll get an advance, and I'll come home with a New York job. Goddammit, now I'm gonna do it!

LINDA: Oh, That's the spirit, Willy!

WILLY: I will never get behind a wheel the rest of my life!

LINDA: It's changing, Willy, I can feel it changing!

WILLY: Beyond a question. G'by, I'm, late. [*He starts to go again.*]

LINDA: [*calling after him as she runs to the kitchen table for a handkerchief*] You got your glasses?

WILLY: [*feels for them, then comes back in*] Yeah, yeah, got my glasses.

LINDA: [*giving him the handkerchief*] And a handkerchief.

WILLY: Yeah, handkerchief.

LINDA: And your saccharine?

WILLY: Yeah, my saccharine.

LINDA: Be careful on the subway stairs.

[*She kisses him, and a silk stocking is seen hanging from her hand.* WILLY *notices it.*]

WILLY: Will you stop mending stockings? At least while I'm in the house. It gets me nervous. I can't tell you. Please.

[LINDA *hides the stocking in her hand as she follows* WILLY *across the forestage in front of the house.*]

LINDA: Remember, Frank's Chop House.

WILLY: [*passing the apron*] Maybe beets would grow out there.

LINDA: [*laughing*] But you tried so many times.

WILLY: Yeah. Well, don't work hard today. [*He disappears around the right corner of the house.*]

LINDA: Be careful!

[*As* WILLY *vanishes,* LINDA *waves to him. Suddenly the phone rings. She runs across the stage and into the kitchen and lifts it.*]

LINDA: Hello? Oh, Biff! I'm so glad you called, I just . . . Yes, sure, I just told him.

Yes, he'll be there for dinner at six o'clock, I didn't forget. Listen, I was just dying to tell you. You know that little rubber pipe I told you about? That he connected to the gas heater? I finally decided to go down the cellar this morning and take it away and destroy it. But it's gone! Imagine? He took it away himself, it isn't there! [*She listens.*] When? Oh, then you took it. Oh — nothing, it's just that I'd hoped he'd taken it away himself. Oh, I'm not worried, darling, because this morning he left in such high spirits, it was like the old days! I'm not afraid any more. Did Mr. Oliver see you? . . . Well, you wait there then. And make a nice impression on him, darling. Just don't perspire too much before you see him. And have a nice time with Dad. He may have big news too! . . . That's right, a New York job. And be sweet to him tonight, dear. Be loving to him. Because he's only a little boat looking for a harbor. [*She is trembling with sorrow and joy.*] Oh, that's wonderful, Biff, you'll save his life. Thanks, darling. Just put your arm around him when he comes into the restaurant. Give him a smile. That's the boy . . . Good-by, dear. . . . You got your comb? . . . That's fine. Good-by, Biff dear.

> [*In the middle of her speech,* HOWARD WAGNER, *thirty-six, wheels on a small typewriter table on which is a wire-recording machine and proceeds to plug it in. This is on the left forestage. Light slowly fades on* LINDA *as it rises on* HOWARD. HOWARD *is intent on threading the machine and only glances over his shoulder as* WILLY *appears.*]

WILLY: Pst! Pst!

HOWARD: Hello, Willy, come in.

WILLY: Like to have a little talk with you, Howard.

HOWARD: Sorry to keep you waiting. I'll be with you in a minute.

WILLY: What's that Howard?

HOWARD: Didn't you ever see one of these? Wire recorder.

WILLY: Oh. Can we talk a minute?

HOWARD: Records things. Just got delivery yesterday. Been driving me crazy, the most terrific machine I ever saw in my life. I was up all night with it.

WILLY: What do you do with it?

HOWARD: I bought if for dictation, but you can do anything with it. Listen to this. I had it home last night. Listen to what I picked up. The first one is my daughter. Get this. [*He flicks the switch and "Roll out the Barrell" is heard being whistled.*] Listen to that kid whistle.

WILLY: That is lifelike, isn't it?

HOWARD: Seven years old. Get that tone.

WILLY: Ts, ts. Like to ask a little favor if you . . .

> [*The whistling breaks off, and the voice of* HOWARD'S DAUGHTER *is heard.*]

HIS DAUGHTER: "Now you, Daddy."

HOWARD: She's crazy for me! [*Again the same song is whistled.*] That's me! Ha! [*He winks.*]

WILLY: You're very good!

> [*The whistling breaks off again. The machine runs silent for a moment.*]

HOWARD: Sh! Get this now, this is my son.

HIS SON: "The capital of Alabama is Montgomery; the capital of Arizona is Phoenix; the capital of Arkansas is Little Rock; the capital of California is Sacramento . . ." [*and on, and on*]

HOWARD: [*holding up five fingers*] Five years old, Willy!

WILLY: He'll make an announcer some day!

HIS SON: [continuing] "The capital . . ."

HOWARD: Get that—alphabetical order! [The machine breaks off suddenly.] Wait a minute. The maid kicked the plug out.

WILLY: It certainly is a—

HOWARD: Sh, for God's sake!

HIS SON: "It's nine o'clock, Bulova watch time. So I have to go to sleep."

WILLY: That really is—

HOWARD: Wait a minute! The next is my wife.

     [They wait.]

HOWARD'S VOICE: "Go on, say something." [pause] "Well, you gonna talk?"

HIS WIFE: "I can't think of anything."

HOWARD'S VOICE: "Well, talk—it's turning."

HIS WIFE: [shyly, beaten] "Hello." [silence] "Oh, Howard, I can't talk into this . . ."

HOWARD: [snapping the machine off] That was my wife.

WILLY: That is a wonderful machine. Can we—

HOWARD: I tell you, Willy, I'm gonna take my camera, and my bandsaw, and all my hobbies, and out they go. This is the most fascinating relaxation I ever found.

WILLY: I think I'll get one myself.

HOWARD: Sure, they're only a hundred and a half. You can't do without it. Supposing you wanna hear Jack Benny, see? But you can't be at home at that hour. So you tell the maid to turn the radio on when Jack Benny comes on, and this automatically goes on with the radio . . .

WILLY: And when you come home you . . .

HOWARD: You can come home twelve o'clock, one o'clock, any time you like, and you get yourself a Coke and sit yourself down, throw the switch, and there's Jack Benny's program in the middle of the night!

WILLY: I'm definitely going to get one. Because lots of time I'm on the road, and I think to myself, what I must be missing on the radio!

HOWARD: Don't you have a radio in the car?

WILLY: Yeah, but who ever thinks of turning it on?

HOWARD: Say, aren't you supposed to be in Boston?

WILLY: That's what I want to talk to you about, Howard. You got a minute?

     [He draws a chair in from the wing.]

HOWARD: What happened? What're you doing here?

WILLY: Well . . .

HOWARD: You didn't crack up again, did you?

WILLY: Oh, no. No . . .

HOWARD: Geez, you had me worried there for a minute. What's the trouble?

WILLY: Well, tell you the truth, Howard. I've come to the conclusion that I'd rather not travel any more.

HOWARD: Not travel! Well, what'll you do?

WILLY: Remember, Christmas time, when you had the party here? You said you'd try to think of some spot for me here in town.

HOWARD: With us?

WILLY: Well sure.

HOWARD: Oh, yeah, yeah. I remember. Well, I couldn't think of anything for you, Willy.

WILLY: I tell ya, Howard. The kids are all grown up, y'know. I don't need much any more. If I could take home — well, sixty-five dollars a week, I could swing it.

HOWARD: Yeah, but Willy, see I —

WILLY: I tell ya why, Howard. Speaking frankly and between the two of us, y'know — I'm just a little tired.

HOWARD: Oh, I could understand that, Willy. But you're a road man, Willy, and we do a road business. We've only got a half-dozen salesmen on the floor here.

WILLY: God knows, Howard, I never asked a favor of any man. But I was with the firm when your father used to carry you up here in his arms.

HOWARD: I know that, Willy, but —

WILLY: Your father came to me the day you were born and asked me what I thought of the name of Howard, may he rest in peace.

HOWARD: I appreciate that, Willy, but there just is no spot here for you. If I had a spot I'd slam you right in, but I just don't have a single solitary spot.

[*He looks for his lighter.* WILLY *has picked it up and gives it to him. Pause.*]

WILLY: [*with increasing anger*] Howard, all I need to set my table is fifty dollars a week.

HOWARD: But where am I going to put you, kid?

WILLY: Look, it isn't a question of whether I can sell merchandise, is it?

HOWARD: No, but it's a business, kid, and everybody's gotta pull his own weight.

WILLY: [*desperately*] Just let me tell you a story, Howard —

HOWARD: 'Cause you gotta admit, business is business.

WILLY: [*angrily*] Business is definitely business, but just listen for a minute. You don't understand this. When I was a boy — eighteen, nineteen — I was already on the road. And there was a question in my mind as to whether selling had a future for me. Because in those days I had a yearning to go to Alaska. See, there were three gold strikes in one month in Alaska, and I felt like going out. Just for the ride, you might say.

HOWARD: [*barely interested*] Don't say.

WILLY: Oh, yeah, my father lived many years in Alaska. He was an adventurous man. We've got quite a little streak of self-reliance in our family. I thought I'd go out with my older brother and try to locate him, and maybe settle in the North with the old man. And I was almost decided to go, when I met a salesman in the Parker House. His name was Dave Singleman. And he was eighty-four years old, and he'd drummed merchandise in thirty-one states. And old Dave, he'd go up to his room, y'understand, put on his green velvet slippers — I'll never forget — and pick up his phone and call the buyers, and without ever leaving his room, at the age of eighty-four, he made his living. And when I saw that, I realized that selling was the greatest career a man could want. 'Cause what could be more satisfying than to be able to go, at the age of eighty-four, into twenty or thirty different cities, and pick up a phone, and be remembered and loved and helped by so many different people? Do you know? when he died — and by the way he died the death of a salesman, in his green velvet slippers in the smoker of the New York, New Haven and Hartford, going into Boston — when he died, hundreds of salesmen and buyers were at his funeral. Things were sad on a lotta trains for months after that. [*He stands up.* HOWARD *has not looked at him.*] In those days there was personality in it, Howard. There was respect, and comradeship, and gratitude in it. Today, it's all cut and dried, and there's no chance for bringing friendship to bear — or personality. You see what I mean? They don't know me any more.

HOWARD: [*moving away, to the right*] That's just the thing, Willy.

WILLY: If I had forty dollars a week — that's all I'd need. Forty dollars, Howard.

HOWARD: Kid, I can't take blood from a stone, I —

WILLY: [*desperation is on him now*] Howard, the year Al Smith was nominated, your father came to me and —

HOWARD: [*starting to go off*] I've got to see some people, kid.

WILLY: [*stopping him*] I'm talking about your father! There were promises made across this desk! You mustn't tell me you've got people to see — I put thirty-four years into this firm, Howard, and now I can't pay my insurance! You can't eat the orange and throw the peel away — a man is not a piece of fruit! [*after a pause*] Now pay attention. Your father — in 1928 I had a big year. I averaged a hundred and seventy dollars a week in commissions.

HOWARD: [*impatiently*] Now, Willy, you never averaged —

WILLY: [*banging his hand on the desk*] I averaged a hundred and seventy dollars a week in the year of 1928! And your father came to me — or rather, I was in the office here — it was right over this desk — and he put his hand on my shoulder —

HOWARD: [*getting up*] You'll have to excuse me, Willy, I gotta see some people. Pull yourself together. [*going out*] I'll be back in a little while.

> [*On* HOWARD's *exit, the light on his chair grows very bright and strange.*]

WILLY: Pull myself together! What the hell did I say to him? My God, I was yelling at him! How could I! [WILLY *breaks off, staring at the light, which occupies the chair, animating it.*] Frank, Frank, don't you remember what you told me that time? How you put your hand on my shoulder, and Frank . . . [*He leans on the desk and as he speaks the dead man's name he accidentally switches on the recorder, and instantly*]

HOWARD'S SON: ". . . of New York is Albany. The capital of Ohio is Cincinnati, the capital of Rhode Island is . . ." [*The recitation continues.*]

WILLY: [*leaping way with fright, shouting*] Ha! Howard! Howard! Howard!

HOWARD: [*rushing in*] What happened?

WILLY: [*pointing at the machine, which continues nasally, childishly, with the capital cities*] Shut it off! Shut it off!

HOWARD: [*pulling the plug out*] Look, Willy . . .

WILLY: [*pressing his hands to his eyes*] I gotta get myself some coffee. I'll get some coffee . . .

> [WILLY *starts to walk out.* HOWARD *stops him.*]

HOWARD: [*rolling up the cord*] Willy, look . . .

WILLY: I'll go to Boston.

HOWARD: Willy, you can't go to Boston for us.

WILLY: Why can't I go?

HOWARD: I don't want you to represent us. I've been meaning to tell you for a long time now.

WILLY: Howard, are you firing me?

HOWARD: I think you need a good long rest, Willy.

WILLY: Howard —

HOWARD: And when you feel better, come back, and we'll see if we can work something out.

WILLY: But I gotta earn money, Howard. I'm in no position to—

HOWARD: Where are your sons? Why don't your sons give you a hand?

WILLY: They're working on a very big deal.

HOWARD: This is no time for false pride, Willy. You go to your sons and you tell them that you're tired. You've got two great boys, haven't you?

WILLY: Oh, no question, no question, but in the meantime . . .

HOWARD: Then that's that, heh?

WILLY: All right, I'll go to Boston tomorrow.

HOWARD: No, no.

WILLY: I can't throw myself on my sons. I'm not a cripple!

HOWARD: Look, kid, I'm busy this morning.

WILLY: [*grasping* HOWARD's *arm*] Howard, you've got to let me go to Boston!

HOWARD: [*hard, keeping himself under control*] I've got a line of people to see this morning. Sit down, take five minutes, and pull yourself together, and then go home, will ya? I need the office, Willy. [*He starts to go, turns, remembering the recorder, starts to push off the table holding the recorder.*] Oh, yeah. Whenever you can this week, stop by and drop off the samples. You'll feel better, Willy, and then come back and we'll talk. Pull yourself together, kid, there's people outside.

    [HOWARD *exits, pushing the table off left,* WILLY *stares into space, exhausted. Now the music is heard* — BEN's *music* — *first distantly, then closer. As* WILLY *speaks,* BEN *enters from the right. He carries valise and umbrella.*]

WILLY: Oh, Ben, how did you do it? What is the answer? Did you wind up the Alaska deal already?

BEN: Doesn't take much time if you know what you're doing. Just a short business trip. Boarding ship in an hour. Wanted to say good-by.

WILLY: Ben, I've got to talk to you.

BEN: [*glancing at his watch*] Haven't much time, William.

WILLY: [*crossing the apron to* BEN] Ben, nothing's working out. I don't know what to do.

BEN: Now, look here, William. I've bought timberland in Alaska and I need a man to look after things for me.

WILLY: God, timberland! Me and my boys in those grand outdoors!

BEN: You've a new continent at your doorstep, William. Get out of these cities, they're full of talk and time payments and courts of law. Screw on your fists and you can fight for a fortune up there.

WILLY: Yes, yes! Linda, Linda!

    [LINDA *enters as of old, with the wash.*]

LINDA: Oh, you're back?

BEN: I haven't much time.

WILLY: No, wait! Linda, he's got a proposition for me in Alaska.

LINDA: But you've got— [*to* BEN] He's got a beautiful job here.

WILLY: But in Alaska, kid, I could—

LINDA: You're doing well enough, Willy!

BEN: [*to* LINDA] Enough for what, my dear?

LINDA: [*frightened of* BEN *and angry at him*] Don't say those things to him! Enough to be happy right here, right now. [*to* WILLY, *while* BEN *laughs*] Why must everybody conquer the world? You're well liked, and the boys love you, and

someday — [*to* BEN] — why old man Wagner told him just the other day that if
he keeps it up he'll be a member of the firm, didn't he, Willy?

WILLY: Sure, sure. I am building something with this firm, Ben, and if a man is
building something he must be on the right track, mustn't he?

BEN: What are you building? Lay your hand on it. Where is it?

WILLY: [*hesitantly*] That's true, Linda, there's nothing.

LINDA: Why? [*to* BEN] There's a man eighty-four years old —

WILLY: That's right, Ben, that's right. When I look at that man I say, what is there to
worry about?

BEN: Bah!

WILLY: It's true, Ben. All he has to do is go into any city, pick up the phone, and he's
making his living and you know why?

BEN: [*picking up his valise*] I've got to go.

WILLY: [*holding* BEN *back*] Look at this boy!

[BIFF, *in his high school sweater, enters carrying suitcase.* HAPPY *carries*
BIFF's *shoulder guards, gold helmet, and football pants.*]

WILLY: Without a penny to his name, three great universities are begging for him,
and from there the sky's the limit, because it's not what you do, Ben. It's who
you know and the smile on your face! It's contacts, Ben, contacts! The whole
wealth of Alaska passes over the lunch table at the Commodore Hotel, and
that's the wonder, the wonder of this country, that a man can end with
diamonds here on the basis of being liked! [*he turns to* BIFF] And that's why
when you get out on that field today it's important. Because thousands of
people will be rooting for you and loving you. [*to* BEN, *who has again begun to
leave*] And Ben! when he walks into a business office his name will sound out
like a bell and all the doors will open to him! I've seen it, Ben, I've seen it a
thousand times! You can't feel it with your hand like timber, but it's there!

BEN: Good-by, William.

WILLY: Ben, am I right? Don't you think I'm right? I value your advice.

BEN: There's a new continent at your doorstep, William. You could walk out rich.
Rich! [*He is gone.*]

WILLY: We'll do it here, Ben! You hear me? We're gonna do it here!

[YOUNG BERNARD *rushes in. The gay music of the Boys is heard.*]

BERNARD: Oh, gee, I was afraid you left already!

WILLY: Why? What time is it?

BERNARD: It's half-past one!

WILLY: Well, come on, everybody! Ebbets Field next stop! Where's the pennants?
[*He rushes through the wall-line of the kitchen and out into the living-room.*]

LINDA: [*to* BIFF] Did you pack fresh underwear?

BIFF: [*who has been limbering up*] I want to go!

BERNARD: Biff, I'm carrying your helmet, ain't I?

HAPPY: No, I'm carrying the helmet.

BERNARD: Oh, Biff, you promised me.

HAPPY: I'm carrying the helmet.

BERNARD: How am I going to get in the locker room?

LINDA: Let him carry the shoulder guards. [*She puts her coat and hat on in the
kitchen.*]

BERNARD: Can I, Biff? 'Cause I told everybody I'm going to be in the locker room.

HAPPY: In Ebbets Field it's the clubhouse.

BERNARD: I meant the clubhouse. Biff!

HAPPY: Biff!

BIFF: [*grandly, after a slight pause*] Let him carry the shoulder guards.

HAPPY: [*as he gives* BERNARD *the shoulder guards*] Stay close to us now.
　　　[WILLY *rushes in with the pennants.*]

WILLY: [*handing them out*] Everybody wave when Biff comes out on the field.
　　　[HAPPY *and* BERNARD *run off.*] You set now, boy?
　　　[*The music has died away.*]

BIFF: Ready to go, Pop. Every muscle is ready.

WILLY: [*at the edge of the apron*] You realize what this means?

BIFF: That's right, Pop.

WILLY: [*feeling* BIFF's *muscles*] You're comin' home this afternoon captain of the
　　　All-Scholastic Championship Team of the City of New York.

BIFF: I got it, Pop. And remember, pal, when I take off my helmet, that touchdown is
　　　for you.

WILLY: Let's go! [*He is starting out, with his arm around* BIFF, *when* CHARLEY *enters,
　　　as of old, in knickers.*] I got no room for you, Charley.

CHARLEY: Room? For what?

WILLY: In the car.

CHARLEY: You goin' for a ride? I wanted to shoot some casino.

WILLY: [*furiously*] Casino! [*incredulously*] Don't you realize what today is?

LINDA: Oh, he knows, Willy. He's just kidding you.

WILLY: That's nothing to kid about!

CHARLEY: No, Linda, what's goin' on?

LINDA: He's playing in Ebbets Field.

CHARLEY: Baseball in this weather?

WILLY: Don't talk to him. Come on, come on! [*He is pushing them out.*]

CHARLEY: Wait a minute, didn't you hear the news?

WILLY: What?

CHARLEY: Don't you listen to the radio? Ebbets Field just blew up.

WILLY: You go to hell! [CHARLEY *laughs. Pushing them out.*] Come on, come on!
　　　We're late.

CHARLEY: [*as they go*] Knock a homer, Biff, knock a homer!

WILLY: [*the last to leave, turning to* CHARLEY] I don't think that was funny, Charley.
　　　This is the greatest day of his life.

CHARLEY: Willy, when are you going to grow up?

WILLY: Yeah, heh? When this game is over, Charley, you'll be laughing out the
　　　other side of your face. They'll be calling him another Red Grange. Twenty-
　　　five thousand a year.

CHARLEY: [*kidding*] Is that so?

WILLY: Yeah, that's so.

CHARLEY: Well, then, I'm sorry, Willy. But tell me something.

WILLY: What?

CHARLEY: Who is Red Grange?

WILLY: Put up your hands. Goddam you, put up your hands!

[CHARLEY, *chuckling, shakes his head and walks away, around the left corner of the stage.* WILLY *follows him. The music rises to a mocking frenzy.*]

WILLY: Who the hell do you think you are, better than everybody else? You don't know everything, you big, ignorant, stupid . . . Put up your hands!

[*Light rises, on the right side of the forestage, on a small table in the reception room of* CHARLEY's *office. Traffic sounds are heard.* BERNARD, *now mature, sits whistling to himself. A pair of tennis rackets and an overnight bag on the floor beside him.*]

WILLY: [*offstage*] What are you walking away for? Don't walk away! If you're going to say something say it to my face! I know you laugh at me behind my back. You'll laugh out of the other side of your goddam face after this game. Touchdown! Touchdown! Eighty thousand people! Touchdown! Right between the goal posts.

[BERNARD *is a quiet, earnest, but self-assured young man.* WILLY's *voice is coming from right upstage now.* BERNARD *lowers his feet off the table and listens.* JENNY, *his father's secretary, enters.*]

JENNY: [*distressed*] Say, Bernard, will you go out in the hall?

BERNARD: What is that noise? Who is it?

JENNY: Mr. Loman. He just got off the elevator.

BERNARD: [*getting up*] Who's he arguing with?

JENNY: Nobody. There's nobody with him. I can't deal with him any more, and your father gets all upset everytime he comes. I've got a lot of typing to do, and your father's waiting to sign it. Will you see him?

WILLY: [*entering*] Touchdown! Touch — [*He sees* JENNY.] Jenny, Jenny, good to see you. How're ya? Workin'? Or still honest?

JENNY: Fine. How've you been feeling?

WILLY: Not much any more, Jenny. Ha, ha! [*He is surprised to see the rackets.*]

BERNARD: Hello, Uncle Willy.

WILLY: [*almost shocked*] Bernard! Well, look who's here! [*He comes quickly, guiltily, to* BERNARD *and warmly shakes his hand.*]

BERNARD: How are you? Good to see you.

WILLY: What are you doing here?

BERNARD: Oh, just stopped off to see Pop. Get off my feet till my train leaves. I'm going to Washington in a few minutes.

WILLY: Is he in?

BERNARD: Yes, he's in his office with the accountants. Sit down.

WILLY: [*sitting down*] What're you going to do in Washington?

BERNARD: Oh, just a case I've got there, Willy.

WILLY: That so? [*indicating the rackets*] You going to play tennis there?

BERNARD: I'm staying with a friend who's got a court.

WILLY: Don't say. His own tennis court. Must be fine people, I bet.

BERNARD: They are, very nice. Dad tells me Biff's in town.

WILLY: [*with a big smile*] Yeah, Biff's in. Working on a very big deal, Bernard.

BERNARD: What's Biff doing?

WILLY: Well, he's been doing very big things in the West. But he decided to establish himself here. Very big. We're having dinner. Did I hear your wife had a boy?

BERNARD: That's right. Our second.

WILLY: Two boys! What do you know!

BERNARD: What kind of a deal has Biff got?

WILLY: Well, Bill Oliver — very big sporting-goods man — he wants Biff very badly. Called him in from the West. Long distance, carte blanche, special deliveries. Your friends have they own private tennis court?

BERNARD: You still with the old firm, Willy?

WILLY: [*after a pause*] I'm — I'm overjoyed to see how you made the grade, Bernard, overjoyed. It's an encouraging thing to see a young man really — really — Looks very good for Biff — very — [*He breaks off, then:*] Bernard — [*He is so full of emotion, he breaks off again.*]

BERNARD: What is it, Willy?

WILLY: [*small and alone*] What — what's the secret?

BERNARD: What secret?

WILLY: How — how did you? Why didn't he ever catch on?

BERNARD: I wouldn't know that, Willy.

WILLY: [*confidentially, desperately*] You were his friend, his boyhood friend. There's something I don't understand about it. His life ended after that Ebbets Field game. From the age of seventeen nothing good ever happened to him.

BERNARD: He never trained himself for anything.

WILLY: But he did, he did. After high school he took so many correspondence courses. Radio mechanics; television; God knows what, and never made the slightest mark.

BERNARD: [*taking off his glasses*] Willy, do you want to talk candidly?

WILLY: [*rising, faces* BERNARD] I regard you as a very brilliant man, Bernard. I value your advice.

BERNARD: Oh, the hell with the advice, Willy. I couldn't advise you. There's just one thing I've always wanted to ask you. When he was supposed to graduate, and the math teacher flunked him —

WILLY: Oh, that son-of-a-bitch ruined his life.

BERNARD: Yeah, but, Willy, all he had to do was to go to summer school and make up that subject.

WILLY: That's right, that's right.

BERNARD: Did you tell him not to go to summer school?

WILLY: Me? I begged him to go. I ordered him to go!

BERNARD: Then why wouldn't he go?

WILLY: Why? Why! Bernard, that question has been trailing me like a ghost for the last fifteen years. He flunked the subject, and laid down and died like a hammer hit him!

BERNARD: Take is easy, kid.

WILLY: Let me talk to you — I got noboby to talk to. Bernard, Bernard, was it my fault? Y'see? It keeps going around in my mind, maybe I did something to him. I got nothing to give him.

BERNARD: Don't take it so hard.

WILLY: Why did he lay down? What is the story there? You were his friend!

BERNARD: Willy, I remember, it was June, and our grades came out. And he'd flunked math.

WILLY: That son-of-a-bitch!

BERNARD: No, it wasn't right then. Biff just got very angry, I remember, and he was ready to enroll in summer school.

WILLY: [*surprised*] He was?

BERNARD: He wasn't beaten by it at all. But then, Willy, he disappeared from the block for almost a month. And I got the idea that he'd gone up to New England to see you. Did he have a talk with you then?

[WILLY *stares in silence.*]

BERNARD: Willy?

WILLY: [*with a strong edge of resentment in his voice*] Yeah, he came to Boston. What about it?

BERNARD: Well, just that when he came back — I'll never forget this, it always mystified me. Because I'd thought so well of Biff, even though he'd always taken advantage of me. I loved him, Willy, y'know? And he came back after that month and took his sneakers — remember the sneakers with "University of Virginia" printed on them? He was so proud of those, wore them every day. And he took them down in the cellar, and burned them up in the furnace. We had a fist fight. It lasted as least half an hour. Just the two of us, punching each other down the cellar, and crying right through it. I've often thought of how strange it was that I knew he'd given up his life. What happened in Boston, Willy?

[WILLY *looks at him as at an intruder.*]

BERNARD: I just bring it up because you asked me.

WILLY: [*angrily*] Nothing. What do you mean, "What happened?" What's that got to do with anything?

BERNARD: Well don't get sore.

WILLY: What are you trying to do, blame it on me? If a boy lays down is that my fault?

BERNARD: Now, Willy, don't get —

WILLY: Well, don't — don't talk to me that way! What does that mean, "What happened?"

[CHARLEY *enters. He is in his vest, and he carries a bottle of bourbon.*]

CHARLEY: Hey, you're going to miss that train. [*He waves the bottle.*]

BERNARD: Yeah, I'm going. [*He takes the bottle.*] Thanks, Pop. [*He picks up his racket and bag.*] Good-by, Willy, and don't worry about it. You know, "If at first you don't succeed . . ."

WILLY: Yes, I believe in that.

BERNARD: But sometimes, Willy, it's better for a man just to walk away.

WILLY: Walk away?

BERNARD: That's right.

WILLY: But if you can't walk away?

BERNARD: [*after a slight pause*] I guess that's when it's tough. [*Extending his hand.*] Good-by, Willy.

WILLY: [*shaking* BERNARD's *hand*] Good-by, boy.

CHARLEY: [*an arm on* BERNARD's *shoulder*] How do you like this kid? Gonna argue a case in front of the Supreme Court.

BERNARD: [*protesting*] Pop!

WILLY: [*genuinely shocked, pained, and happy*] No! The Supreme Court!

BERNARD: I gotta run. 'By, Dad!

CHARLEY: Knock 'em dead, Bernard!

[BERNARD *goes off.*]

WILLY: [*as* CHARLEY *takes out his wallet*] The Supreme Court! And he didn't even mention it!

CHARLEY: [*counting out money on the desk*] He don't have to — he's gonna do it.

WILLY: And you never told him what to do, did you? You never took any interest in him.

CHARLEY: My salvation is that I never took any interest in anything. There's some money — fifty dollars. I got an accountant inside.

WILLY: Charley, look . . . [*with difficulty*] I got my insurance to pay. If you can manage it — I need a hundred and ten dollars.

[CHARLEY *doesn't reply for a moment; merely stops moving.*]

WILLY: I'd draw it from my bank but Linda would know, and I . . .

CHARLEY: Sit down, Willy.

WILLY: [*moving toward the chair*] I'm keeping an account of everything, remember, I'll pay every penny back. [*He sits.*]

CHARLEY: Now listen to me, Willy.

WILLY: I want you to know I appreciate . . .

CHARLEY: [*sitting down on the table*] Willy, what're you doin'? What the hell is goin' on in your head?

WILLY: Why? I'm simply . . .

CHARLEY: I offered you a job. You can make fifty dollars a week. And I won't send you on the road.

WILLY: I've got a job.

CHARLEY: Without pay? What kind of job is a job without pay? [*He rises.*] Now, look, kid, enough is enough. I'm no genius but I know when I'm being insulted.

WILLY: Insulted!

CHARLEY: Why don't you want to work for me?

WILLY: What's the matter with you? I've got a job.

CHARLEY: Then what're you walkin' in here every week for?

WILLY: [*getting up*] Well, if you don't want me to walk in here —

CHARLEY: I'm offering you a job.

WILLY: I don't want your goddam job!

CHARLEY: When the hell are you going to grow up?

WILLY: [*furiously*] You big ignoramus, if you say that to me again I'll rap you one! I don't care how big you are! [*He's ready to fight.*]

[*Pause.*]

CHARLEY: [*kindly, going to him*] How much do you need, Willy?

WILLY: Charley, I'm strapped. I'm strapped. I don't know what to do. I was just fired.

CHARLEY: Howard fired you?

WILLY: That snotnose. Imagine that? I named him. I named him Howard.

CHARLEY: Willy, when're you gonna realize that them things don't mean anything? You named him Howard, but you can't sell that. The only thing you got in this world is what you can sell. And the funny thing is that you're a salesman, and you don't know that.

WILLY: I've tried to think otherwise, I guess. I always felt that if a man was impressive, and well liked, that nothing —

CHARLEY: Why must everybody like you? Who liked J. P. Morgan? Was he impressive? In a Turkish bath he'd look like a butcher. But with his pockets on he was very well liked. Now listen, Willy, I know you don't like me, and nobody can say I'm in love with you, but I'll give you a job because — just for the hell of it, put it that way. Now what do you say?

WILLY: I — I just can't work for you, Charley.

CHARLEY: What're you, jealous of me?

WILLY: I can't work for you, that's all, don't ask me why.

CHARLEY: [*angered, takes out more bills*] You been jealous of me all your life, you damned fool! Here, pay your insurance. [*He puts the money in* WILLY's *hand.*]

WILLY: I'm keeping strict accounts.

CHARLEY: I've got some work to do. Take care of yourself, and pay your insurance.

WILLY: [*moving to the right*] Funny, y'know? After all the highways, and the trains, and the appointments, and the years, you end up worth more dead than alive.

CHARLEY: Willy, nobody's worth nothin' dead. [*after a slight pause*] Did you hear what I said?

       [WILLY *stands still, dreaming.*]

CHARLEY: Willy!

WILLY: Apologize to Bernard for me when you see him. I didn't mean to argue with him. He's a fine boy. They're all fine boys, and they'll end up big — all of them. Someday they'll all play tennis together. Wish me luck, Charley. He saw Bill Oliver today.

CHARLEY: Good luck.

WILLY: [*on the verge of tears*] Charley, you're the only friend I got. Isn't that a remarkable thing? [*He goes out.*]

CHARLEY: Jesus!

       [CHARLEY *stares after him a moment and follows. All light blacks out. Suddenly raucous music is heard, and a red glow rises behind the screen at right.* STANLEY, *a young waiter, appears, carrying a table, followed by* HAPPY, *who is carrying two chairs.*]

STANLEY: [*putting the table down*] That's all right, Mr. Loman, I can handle it myself. [*He turns and takes the chairs from* HAPPY *and places them at the table.*]

HAPPY: [*glancing around*] Oh, this is better.

STANLEY: Sure, in the front there you're in the middle of all kinds of noise. Whenever you got a party, Mr. Loman, you just tell me and I'll put you back here. Y'know, there's a lotta people they don't like it private, because when they go out they like to see a lotta action around them because they're sick and tired to stay in the house by theirself. But I know you, you ain't from Hackensack. You know what I mean?

HAPPY: [*sitting down*] So how's it coming, Stanley?

STANLEY: Ah, it's a dog's life. I only wish during the war they'd a took me in the Army. I coulda been dead by now.

HAPPY: My brother's back, Stanley.

STANLEY: Oh, he come back, heh? From the Far West.

HAPPY: Yeah, big cattle man, my brother, so treat him right. And my father's coming too.

STANLEY: Oh, your father too!

HAPPY: You got a couple of nice lobsters?

STANLEY: Hundred per cent, big.

HAPPY: I want them with claws.

STANLEY: Don't worry, I don't give you no mice. [HAPPY *laughs.*] How about some wine? It'll put a head on the meal.

HAPPY: No. You remember, Stanley, that recipe I brought you from overseas? With the champagne in it?

STANLEY: Oh, yeah, sure. I still got it tacked up yet in the kitchen. But that'll have to cost a buck apiece anyways.

HAPPY: That's all right.

STANLEY: What'd you, hit a number or somethin'?

HAPPY: No, it's a little celebration. My brother is — I think he pulled off a big deal today. I think we're going into business together.

STANLEY: Great! That's the best for you. Because a family business, you know what I mean? — that's the best.

HAPPY: That's what I think.

STANLEY: 'Cause what's the difference? Somebody steals? It's in the family. Know what I mean? [*sotto voce*] Like this bartender here. The boss is goin' crazy what kinda leak he's got in the cash register. You put it in but it don't come out.

HAPPY: [*raising his head*] Sh!

STANLEY: What?

HAPPY: You notice I wasn't lookin' right or left, was I?

STANLEY: No.

HAPPY: And my eyes are closed.

STANLEY: So what's the — ?

HAPPY: Strudel's comin'.

STANLEY: [*catching on, looks around*] Ah, no, there's no —
[*He breaks off as a furred, lavishly dressed* GIRL *enters and sits at the next table. Both follow her with their eyes.*]

STANLEY: Geez, how'd ya know?

HAPPY: I got radar or something. [*staring directly at her profile*] Oooooooo . . . Stanley.

STANLEY: I think that's for you, Mr. Loman.

HAPPY: Look at that mouth. Oh God. And the binoculars.

STANLEY: Geez, you got a life, Mr. Loman.

HAPPY: Wait on her.

STANLEY: [*going to the* GIRL's *table*] Would you like a menu, ma'am?

GIRL: I'm expecting someone, but I'd like a —

HAPPY: Why don't you bring her — excuse me, miss, do you mind? I sell champagne, and I'd like you to try my brand. Bring her a champagne, Stanley.

GIRL: That's awful nice of you.

HAPPY: Don't mention it. It's all company money. [*He laughs.*]

GIRL: That's a charming product to be selling, isn't it?

HAPPY: Oh, gets to be like everything else. Selling is selling, y'know.

GIRL: I suppose.

HAPPY: You don't happen to sell, do you?

GIRL: No, I don't sell.

HAPPY: Would you object to a compliment from a stranger? You ought to be on a magazine cover.

GIRL: [*looking at him a little archly*] I have been.
[STANLEY *comes in with a glass of champagne.*]

HAPPY: What'd I say before, Stanley? You see? She's a cover girl.

STANLEY: Oh, I could see, I could see.

HAPPY: [to the GIRL] What magazine?

GIRL: Oh, a lot of them. [She takes the drink.] Thank you.

HAPPY: You know what they say in France, don't you? "Champagne is the drink of the complexion" — Hya, Biff!

[BIFF has entered and sits with HAPPY.]

BIFF: Hello, kid. Sorry I'm late.

HAPPY: I just got here. Uh, Miss — ?

GIRL: Forsythe.

HAPPY: Miss Forsythe, this is my brother.

BIFF: Is Dad here?

HAPPY: His name is Biff. You might've heard of him. Great football player.

GIRL: Really? What team?

HAPPY: Are you familiar with football?

GIRL: No, I'm afraid I'm not.

HAPPY: Biff is quarterback with the New York Giants.

GIRL: Well, that is nice, isn't it. [She drinks.]

HAPPY: Good health.

GIRL: I'm happy to meet you.

HAPPY: That's my name. Hap. It's really Harold, but at West Point they called me Happy.

GIRL: [now really impressed] Oh, I see. How do you do? [She turns her profile.]

BIFF: Isn't Dad coming?

HAPPY: You want her?

BIFF: Oh, I could never make that.

HAPPY: I remember the time that idea would never come into your head. Where's the old confidence, Biff?

BIFF: I just saw Oliver —

HAPPY: Wait a minute. I've got to see that old confidence again. Do you want her? She's on call.

BIFF: Oh, no. [He turns to look at the GIRL.]

HAPPY: I'm telling you. Watch this. [turning to the GIRL] Honey? [She turns to him.] Are you busy?

GIRL: Well, I am . . . but I could make a phone call.

HAPPY: Do that, will you, honey? And see if you can get a friend. We'll be here for a while. Biff is one of the greatest football players in the country.

GIRL: [standing up] Well, I'm certainly happy to meet you.

HAPPY: Come back soon.

GIRL: I'll try.

HAPPY: Don't try, honey, try hard.

[The GIRL exits. STANLEY follows , shaking his head in bewildered admiration.]

HAPPY: Isn't that a shame now? A beautiful girl like that? That's why I can't get married. There's not a good woman in a thousand. New York is loaded with them, kid!

BIFF: Hap, look —

HAPPY: I told you she was on call!

BIFF: [strangely unnerved] Cut it out, will ya! I want to say something to you.

HAPPY: Did you see Oliver?

BIFF: I saw him all right. Now look, I want to tell Dad a couple of things and I want you to help me.

HAPPY: What? Is he going to back you?

BIFF: Are you crazy? You're out of your goddam head, you know that?

HAPPY: Why? What happened?

BIFF: [*breathlessly*] I did a terrible thing today, Hap. It's been the strangest day I ever went through. I'm all numb, I swear.

HAPPY: You mean he wouldn't see you?

BIFF: Well, I waited six hours for him, see? All day. Kept sending my name in. Even tried to date his secretary so she'd get me to him, but no soap.

HAPPY: Because you're not showin' the old confidence, Biff. He remembered you, didn't he?

BIFF: [*stopping* HAPPY *with a gesture*] Finally, about five o'clock, he comes out. Didn't remember who I was or anything. I felt like such an idiot, Hap.

HAPPY: Did you tell him my Florida idea?

BIFF: He walked away. I saw him for one minute. I got so mad I could've torn the walls down! How the hell did I ever get the idea I was a salesman there? I even believed myself that I'd been a salesman for him! And then he gave me one look and — I realized what a ridiculous lie my whole life has been! We've been talking in a dream for fifteen years. I was a shipping clerk.

HAPPY: What'd you do?

BIFF: [*with great tension and wonder*] Well, he left, see. And the secretary went out. I was all alone in the waiting-room. I don't know what came over me, Hap. The next thing I know I'm in his office — paneled walls, everything. I can't explain it. I — Hap, I took his fountain pen.

HAPPY: Geez, did he catch you?

BIFF: I ran out. I ran down all eleven flights. I ran and ran and ran.

HAPPY: That was an awful dumb — what'd you do that for?

BIFF: [*agonized*] I don't know, I just — wanted to take something, I don't know. You gotta help me, Hap, I'm gonna tell Pop.

HAPPY: You crazy? What for?

BIFF: Hap, he's got to understand that I'm not the man somebody lends that kind of money to. He thinks I've been spiting him all these years and it's eating him up.

HAPPY: That's just it. You tell him something nice.

BIFF: I can't.

HAPPY: Say you got a lunch date with Oliver tomorrow.

BIFF: So what do I do tomorrow?

HAPPY: You leave the house tomorrow and come back at night and say Oliver is thinking it over. And he thinks it over for a couple of weeks, and gradually it fades away and nobody's the worse.

BIFF: But it'll go on forever!

HAPPY: Dad is never so happy as when he's looking forward to something!

[WILLY *enters.*]

HAPPY: Hello, scout!

WILLY: Gee, I haven't been here in years!

[STANLEY *has followed* WILLY *in and sets a chair for him.* STANLEY *starts off but* HAPPY *stops him.*]

HAPPY: Stanley!

[STANLEY *stands by, waiting for an order.*]

BIFF: [*going to* WILLY *with guilt, as to an invalid*] Sit down, Pop. You want a drink?

WILLY: Sure, I don't mind.

BIFF: Let's get a load on.

WILLY: You look worried.

BIFF: N-no. [*to* STANLEY] Scotch all around. Make it doubles.

STANLEY: Doubles, right. [*He goes.*]

WILLY: You had a couple already, didn't you?

BIFF: Just a couple, yeah.

WILLY: Well, what happened, boy? [*nodding affirmatively, with a smile*] Everything go all right?

BIFF: [*takes a breath, then reaches out and grasps* WILLY's *hand*] Pal . . .
[*He is smiling bravely, and* WILLY *is smiling too,*] I had an experience today.

HAPPY: Terrific, Pop.

WILLY: That so? What happened?

BIFF: [*high, slightly alcoholic, above the earth*] I'm going to tell you everything from first to last. It's been a strange day. [*Silence. He looks around, composes himself as best he can, but his breath keeps breaking the rhythm of his voice.*] I had to wait quite a while for him, and —

WILLY: Oliver?

BIFF: Yeah, Oliver. All day, as a matter of cold fact. And a lot of — instances — facts, Pop, facts about my life came back to me. Who was it, Pop? Who ever said I was a salesman with Oliver?

WILLY: Well, you were.

BIFF: No, Dad, I was a shipping clerk.

WILLY: But you were practically —

BIFF: [*with determination*] Dad, I don't know who said it first, but I was never a salesman for Bill Oliver.

WILLY: What're you talking about?

BIFF: Let's hold on to the facts tonight, Pop. We're not going to get anywhere bullin' around. I was a shipping clerk.

WILLY: [*angrily*] All right, now listen to me —

BIFF: Why don't you let me finish?

WILLY: I'm not interested in stories about the past or any crap of that kind because the woods are burning, boys, you understand? There's a big blaze going on all around. I was fired today.

BIFF: [*shocked*] How could you be?

WILLY: I was fired, and I'm looking for a little good news to tell your mother, because the woman has waited and the woman has suffered. The gist of it is that I haven't got a story left in my head, Biff. So don't give me a lecture about facts and aspects. I am not interested. Now what've you got to say to me?
[STANLEY *enters with three drinks. They wait until he leaves.*]

WILLY: Did you see Oliver?

BIFF: Jesus, Dad!

WILLY: You mean you didn't go up there?

HAPPY: Sure he went up there.

BIFF: I did. — I saw him. How could they fire you?

WILLY: [*on the edge of this chair*] What kind of a welcome did he give you?

BIFF: He won't even let you work on commission?

WILLY: I'm out! [*driving*] So tell me, he gave you a warm welcome?

HAPPY: Sure, Pop, sure!

BIFF: [*driven*] Well, it was kind of—

WILLY: I was wondering if he'd remember you. [*to* HAPPY] Imagine, man doesn't see him for ten, twelve years and gives him that kind of a welcome!

HAPPY: Damn right!

BIFF: [*trying to return to the offensive*] Pop, look—

WILLY: You know why he remembered you, don't you? Because you impressed him in those days.

BIFF: Let's talk quietly and get this down to the facts, huh?

WILLY: [*as though Biff had been interrupting*] Well, what happened? It's great news, Biff. Did he take you into his office or'd you talk in the waiting room?

BIFF: Well, he came in, see, and—

WILLY: [*with a big smile*] What'd he say? Betcha he threw his arm around you.

BIFF: Well, he kinda—

WILLY: He's a fine man. [*to* HAPPY] Very hard man to see, y'know.

HAPPY: [*agreeing*] Oh, I know.

WILLY: [*to* BIFF] Is that where you had the drinks?

BIFF: Yeah, he gave me a couple of—no, no!

HAPPY: [*cutting in*] He told him my Florida idea.

WILLY: Don't interrupt. [*to* BIFF] How'd he react to the Floirda idea?

BIFF: Dad, will you give me a minute to explain?

WILLY: I've been waiting for you to explain since I sat down here! What happened? He took you into his office and what?

BIFF: Well—I talked. And—and he listened, see.

WILLY: Famous for the way he listens, y'know. What was his answer?

BIFF: His answer was— [*he breaks off, suddenly angry*] Dad, you're not letting me tell you what I want to tell you!

WILLY: [*accusing, angered*] You didn't see him, did you?

BIFF: I did see him!

WILLY: What'd you insult him or something? You insulted him, didn't you?

BIFF: Listen, will you let me out of it, will you just let me out of it!

HAPPY: What the hell!

WILLY: Tell me what happened!

BIFF: [*to* HAPPY] I can't talk to him!

[*A single trumpet note jars the ear. The light of green leaves stains the house, which holds the air of night and a dream.* YOUNG BERNARD *enters and knocks on the door of the house.*]

YOUNG BERNARD: [*frantically*] Mrs. Loman, Mrs. Loman!

HAPPY: Tell him what happened!

BIFF: [*to* HAPPY] Shut up and leave me alone!

WILLY: No, no! You had to go and flunk math!

BIFF: What math? What're you talking about?

YOUNG BERNARD: Mrs. Loman, Mrs. Loman!

[LINDA *appears in the house, as of old.*]

WILLY: [*wildly*] Math, math, math!

BIFF: Take it easy, Pop!

YOUNG BERNARD: Mrs. Loman!

WILLY: [*furiously*] If you hadn't flunked you'd've been set by now!

BIFF: Now, look, I'm gonna tell you what happened, and you're going to listen to me.

YOUNG BERNARD: Mrs. Loman!

BIFF: I waited six hours —

HAPPY: What the hell are you saying?

BIFF: I kept sending in my name but he didn't see me. So finally he . . .

    [*He continues unheard as light fades low on the restaurant.*]

YOUNG BERNARD: Biff flunked math!

LINDA: No!

YOUNG BERNARD: Birnbaum flunked him! They won't graduate him!

LINDA: But they have to. He's gotta go to the university. Where is he? Biff! Biff!

YOUNG BERNARD: No, he left. He went to Grand Central.

LINDA: Grand — You mean he went to Boston!

YOUNG BERNARD: Is Uncle Willy in Boston?

LINDA: Oh, maybe Willy can talk to the teacher. Oh, the poor, poor boy!

    [*Light on house area snaps out.*]

BIFF: [*at the table, now audible, holding up a gold fountain pen*] . . . so I'm washed up with Oliver, you understand? Are you listening to me?

WILLY: [*at a loss*] Yeah, sure. If you hadn't flunked —

BIFF: Flunked what? What're you talking about?

WILLY: Don't blame everything on me! I didn't flunk math — you did! What pen?

HAPPY: That was awful dumb, Biff, a pen like that is worth —

WILLY: [*seeing the pen for the first time*] You took Oliver's pen?

BIFF: [*weakening*] Dad, I just explained it to you.

WILLY: You stole Bill Oliver's fountain pen!

BIFF: I didn't exactly steal it! That's just what I've been explaining to you!

HAPPY: He had it in his hand and just then Oliver walked in, so he got nervous and stuck it in his pocket!

WILLY: My God, Biff!

BIFF: I never intended to do it, Dad!

OPERATOR'S VOICE: Standish Arms, good evening!

WILLY: [*shouting*] I'm not in my room!

BIFF: [*frightened*] Dad, what's the matter? [*He and* HAPPY *stand up.*]

OPERATOR: Ringing Mr. Loman for you!

WILLY: I'm not there, stop it!

BIFF: [*horrified, gets down on one knee before* WILLY] Dad, I'll make good, I'll make good. [WILLY *tries to get to his feet.* BIFF *holds him down.*] Sit down now.

WILLY: No, you're no good, you're no good for anything.

BIFF: I am, Dad, I'll find something else, you unerstand? Now don't worry about anything. [*He holds up* WILLY's *face.*] Talk to me, Dad.

OPERATOR: Mr. Loman does not answer. Shall I page him?

WILLY: [*attempting to stand, as though to rush and silence the* OPERATOR] No, no, no!

HAPPY: He'll strike something, Pop.

WILLY: No, no . . .

BIFF: [*desperately, standing over* WILLY] Pop, listen! Listen to me! I'm telling you something good. Oliver talked to his partner about the Florida idea. You listening? He — he talked to his partner, and he came to me . . . I'm going to be all right, you hear? Dad, listen to me, he said it was just a question of the amount!

WILLY: Then you . . . got it?

HAPPY: He's gonna be terrific, Pop!

WILLY: [*trying to stand*] Then you got it, haven't you? You got it! You got it!

BIFF: [*agonized, holds* WILLY *down*] No, no. Look, Pop. I'm supposed to have lunch with them tomorrow. I'm just telling you this so you'll know that I can still make an impression, Pop. And I'll make good somewhere, but I can't go tomorrow, see?

WILLY: Why not? You simply —

BIFF: But the pen, Pop!

WILLY: You give it to him and tell him it was an oversight!

HAPPY: Sure, have lunch tomorrow!

BIFF: I can't say that —

WILLY: You were doing a crossword puzzle and accidentally used his pen!

BIFF: Listen, kid, I took those balls years ago, now I walk in with his fountain pen? That clinches it, don't you see? I can't face him like that! I'll try elsewhere.

PAGE'S VOICE: Paging Mr. Loman!

WILLY: Don't you want to be anything?

BIFF: Pop, how can I go back?

WILLY: You don't want to be anything, is that what's behind it?

BIFF: [*now angry at* WILLY *for not crediting his sympathy*] Don't take it that way! You think it was easy walking into that office after what I'd done to him? A team of horses couldn't have dragged me back to Bill Oliver!

WILLY: Then why'd you go?

BIFF: Why did I go? Why did I go! Look at you! Look at what's become of you!
[*Off left,* THE WOMAN *laughs.*]

WILLY: Biff, you're going to go to that lunch tomorrow, or —

BIFF: I can't go. I've got no appointment!

HAPPY: Biff, for . . . !

WILLY: Are you spiting me?

BIFF: Don't take it that way! Goddammit!

WILLY: [*strikes* BIFF *and falters away from the table*] You rotten little louse! Are you spiting me?

THE WOMAN: Someone's at the door, Willy!

BIFF: I'm no good, can't you see what I am?

HAPPY: [*separating them*] Hey, you're in a restaurant! Now cut it out, both of you!
[*The girls enter.*] Hello, girls, sit down.
[THE WOMAN *laughs, off left.*]

MISS FORSYTHE: I guess we might as well. This is Letta.

THE WOMAN: Willy, are you going to wake up?

BIFF: [*ignoring* WILLY] How're ya, miss, sit down. What do you drink?

MISS FORSYTHE: Letta might not be able to stay long.

LETTA: I gotta get up early tomorrow. I got jury duty. I'm so excited! Were you fellows ever on a jury?

BIFF: No, but I been in front of them! [*The girls laugh.*] This is my father.

LETTA: Isn't he cute? Sit down with us, Pop.

HAPPY: Sit him down, Biff!

BIFF: [*going to him*] Come on, slugger, drink us under the table. To hell with it! Come on, sit down, pal.

> [*On* BIFF's *last insistence,* WILLY *is about to sit.*]

THE WOMAN: [*now urgently*] Willy, are you going to answer the door?

> [THE WOMAN's *call pulls* WILLY *back. He starts right, befuddled.*]

BIFF: Hey, where are you going?

WILLY: Open the door.

BIFF: The door?

WILLY: The washroom . . . the door . . . where's the door?

BIFF: [*leading* WILLY *to the left*] Just go straight down.

> [WILLY *moves left.*]

THE WOMAN: Willy, Willy, are you going to get up, get up, get up, get up?

> [WILLY *exits left.*]

LETTA: I think it's sweet you bring you daddy along.

MISS FORSYTHE: Oh, he isn't really your father!

BIFF: [*at left, turning to her resentfully*] Miss Forsythe, you've just seen a prince walk by. A fine, troubled prince. A hard-working, unappreciated prince. A pal, you understand? A good companion. Always for his boys.

LETTA: That's so sweet.

HAPPY: Well, girls, what's the program? We're wasting time. Come on, Biff. Gather round. Where would you like to go?

BIFF: Why don't you do something for him?

HAPPY: Me!

BIFF: Don't you give a damm for him, Hap?

HAPPY: What're you talking about? I'm the one who—

BIFF: I sense it, you don't give a good goddam about him. [*He takes the rolled-up hose from his pocket and puts it on the table in front of* HAPPY.] Look what I found in the cellar, for Christ's sake. How can you bear to let it go on?

HAPPY: Me? Who goes away? Who runs off and—

BIFF: Yeah, but he doesn't mean anything to you. You could help him—I can't! Don't you understand what I'm talking about? He's going to kill himself, don't you know that?

HAPPY: Don't I know it! Me!

BIFF: Hap, help him! Jesus . . . help . . . Help me, help me, I can't bear to look at his face! [*Ready to weep, he hurries out, up right.*]

HAPPY: [*starting after him*] Where are you going?

MISS FORSYTHE: What's he so mad about?

HAPPY: Come on, girls, we'll catch up with him.

MISS FORSYTHE: [*as* HAPPY *pushes her out*] Say, I don't like that temper of his!

HAPPY: He's just a little overstrung, he'll be all right!

WILLY: [*off left, as* THE WOMAN *laughs*] Don't answer! Don't answer!

LETTA: Don't you want to tell your father—

HAPPY: No, that's not my father. He's just a guy. Come on, we'll catch Biff, and, honey, we're going to paint this town! Stanley, where's the check! Hey, Stanley!

[*They exit.* STANLEY *looks toward left.*]

STANLEY: [*calling to* HAPPY *indignantly*] Mr. Loman! Mr. Loman!

[STANLEY *picks up a chair and follows them off. Knocking is heard off left.* THE WOMAN *enters, laughing.* WILLY *follows her. She is in a black slip; he is buttoning his shirt. Raw, sensuous music accompanies their speech.*]

WILLLY: Will you stop laughing? Will you stop?

THE WOMAN: Aren't you going to answer the door? He'll wake the whole hotel.

WILLY: I'm not expecting anybody.

THE WOMAN: Whyn't you have another drink, honey, and stop being so damn self-centered?

WILLY: I'm so lonely.

THE WOMAN: You know you ruined me, Willy? From now on, whenever you come to the office, I'll see that you go right through to the buyers. No waiting at my desk any more, Willy. You ruined me.

WILLY: That's nice of you to say that.

THE WOMAN: Gee, you are self-centered! Why so sad? You are the saddest, self-centerdest soul I ever did see-saw. [*She laughs.*] [*He kisses her.*] Come on inside, drummer boy. It's silly to be dressing in the middle of the night. [*as knocking is heard*] Aren't you going to answer the door?

WILLY: They're knocking on the wrong door.

THE WOMAN: But I felt the knocking. And he heard us talking in here. Maybe the hotel's on fire!

WILLY: [*his terror rising*] It's a mistake.

THE WOMAN: Then tell him to go away!

WILLY: There's nobody there.

THE WOMAN: It's getting on my nerves, Willy. There's somebody standing out there and it's getting on my nerves!

WILLY: [*pushing her away from him*] All right, stay in the bathroom here, and don't come out. I think there's a law in Massachusetts about it, so don't come out. It may be that new room clerk. He looked very mean. So don't come out. It's a mistake, there's no fire.

[*The knocking is heard again. He takes a few steps away from her, and she vanishes into the wing. The light follows him, and now he is facing* YOUNG BIFF, *who carries a suitcase.* BIFF *steps toward him. The music is gone.*]

BIFF: Why didn't you answer?

WILLY: Biff! What are you doing in Boston?

BIFF: Why didn't you answer? I've been knocking for five minutes, I called you on the phone—

WILLY: I just heard you. I was in the bathroom and had the door shut. Did anything happen home?

BIFF: Dad—I let you down.

WILLY: What do you mean?

BIFF: Dad . . .

WILLY: Biffo, what's this about? [*putting his arm around* BIFF] Come on, let's go downstairs and get you a malted.

BIFF: Dad, I flunked math.

WILLY: Not for the term?

BIFF: The term. I haven't got enough credits to graduate.

WILLY: You mean to say Bernard wouldn't give you the answers?

BIFF: He did, he tried, but I only got a sixty-one.

WILLY: And they wouldn't give you four points?

BIFF: Birnbaum refused absolutely. I begged him, Pop, but he won't give me those points. You gotta talk to him before they close the school. Because if he saw the kind of man you are, and you just talked to him in your way, I'm sure he'd come through for me. The class came right before practice, see, and I didn't go enough. Would you talk to him? He'd like you, Pop. You know the way you could talk.

WILLY: You're on. We'll drive right back.

BIFF: Oh, Dad, good work! I'm sure he'll change it for you!

WILLY: Go downstairs and tell the clerk I'm checkin' out. Go right down.

BIFF: Yes, sir! See, the reason he hates me, Pop — one day he was late for class so I got up at the blackboard and imitated him. I crossed my eyes and talked with a lithp.

WILLY: [*laughing*] You did? The kids like it?

BIFF: They nearly died laughing!

WILLY: Yeah? What'd you do?

BIFF: The thquare root of thixthy twee is . . . [WILLY *bursts out laughing;* BIFF *joins him.*] And in the middle of it he walked in!

　　[WILLY *laughs and* THE WOMAN *joins in offstage.*]

WILLY: [*without hesitation*] Hurry downstairs and —

BIFF: Somebody in there?

WILLY: No, that was next door.

BIFF: Somebody got in your bathroom!

　　[THE WOMAN *laughs offstage.*]

WILLY: No, it's the next room, there's a party —

THE WOMAN: [*enters, laughing. She lisps this*] Can I come in? There's something in the bathtub, Willy, and it's moving!

　　[WILLY *looks at* BIFF, *who is staring open-mouthed and horrified at* THE WOMAN.]

WILLY: Ah — you better go back to your room. They must be finished painting by now. They're painting her room so I let her take a shower here. Go back, go back . . . [*He pushes her.*]

THE WOMAN: [*resisting*] But I've got to get dressed, Willy, I can't —

WILLY: Get out of here! Go back, go back . . . [*suddenly striving for the ordinary*] This is Miss Francis, Biff, she's a buyer. They're painting her room. Go back, Miss Francis, go back . . .

THE WOMAN: But my clothes, I can't go out naked in the hall!

WILLY: [*pushing her offstage*] Get outa here! Go back, go back!

　　[BIFF *slowly sits down on his suitcase as the argument continues offstage.*]

THE WOMAN: Where's my stockings? You promised me stockings, Willy!

WILLY: I have no stockings here!

THE WOMAN: You had two boxes of size nine sheers for me, and I want them!

WILLY: Here, for God's sake, will you get outa here!

THE WOMAN: [*enters holding a box of stockings*] I just hope there's nobody in the hall. That's all I hope. [*to* BIFF] Are you football or baseball?

BIFF: Football.

THE WOMAN: [*angry, humiliated*] That's me too. G'night. [*She snatches her clothes from* WILLY, *and walks out.*]

WILLY: [*after a pause*] Well, better get going. I want to get to the school first thing in the morning. Get my suits out of the closet. I'll get my valise. [BIFF *doesn't move.*] What's the matter? [BIFF *remains motionless, tears falling.*] She's a buyer. Buys for J. H. Simmons. She lives down the hall—they're painting. You don't imagine—[*He breaks off. After a pause:*] Now listen, pal, she's just a buyer. She sees merchandise in her room and they have to keep it looking just so . . . [*Pause. Assuming command:*] All right, get my suits. [BIFF *doesn't move.*] Now stop crying and do as I say. I gave you an order. Biff, I gave you an order! Is that what you do when I give you an order? How dare you cry! [*putting his arm around* BIFF] Now look, Biff, when you grow up you'll understand about these things. You mustn't—you mustn't overemphasize a thing like this. I'll see Birnbaum first thing in the morning.

BIFF: Never mind.

WILLY: [*getting down beside* BIFF] Never mind! He's going to give you those points. I'll see to it.

BIFF: He wouldn't listen to you.

WILLY: He certainly will listen to me. You need those points for the U. of Virginia

BIFF: I'm not going there.

WILLY: Heh? If I can't get him to change that mark you'll make it up in summer school. You've got all summer to—

BIFF: [*his weeping breaking from him*] Dad . . .

WILLY: [*infected by it*] Oh, my boy . . .

BIFF: Dad . . .

WILLY: She's nothing to me, Biff. I was lonely, I was terribly lonely.

BIFF: You—you gave her Mama's stockings! [*His tears break through and he rises to go.*]

WILLY: [*grabbing for* BIFF] I gave you an order!

BIFF: Don't touch me, you—liar!

WILLY: Apologize for that!

BIFF: You fake! You phony little fake! You fake! [*Overcome, he turns quickly and weeping fully goes out with his suitcase.* WILLY *is left on the floor on his knees.*]

WILLY: I gave you an order! Biff, come back here or I'll beat you! Come back here! I'll whip you!

[STANLEY *comes quickly in from the right and stands in front of* WILLY.]

WILLY: [*shouts at* STANLEY] I gave you an order . . .

STANLEY: Hey, let's pick it up, pick it up, Mr. Loman. [*He helps* WILLY *to his feet*] Your boys left with the chippies. They said they'll see you home.

[A SECOND WAITER *watches some distance away.*]

WILLY: But we were supposed to have dinner together.

[*Music is heard,* WILLY's *theme.*]

STANLEY: Can you make it?

WILLY: I'll—sure, I can make it. [*suddenly concerned about his clothes*] Do I—I look all right?

STANLEY: Sure, you look all right. [*He flicks a speck off* WILLY's *lapel.*]

WILLY: Here—here's a dollar.

STANLEY: Oh, your son paid me. It's all right.

WILLY: [*putting it in* STANLEY's *hand*] No, take it. You're a good boy.

STANLEY: Oh, no, you don't have to . . .

WILLY: Here—here's some more, I don't need it any more. [*after a slight pause*] Tell me—is there a seed store in the neighborhood?

STANLEY: Seeds? you mean like to plant?

[*As* WILLY *turns,* STANLEY *slips the money back into his jacket pocket.*]

WILLY: Yes. Carrots, peas . . .

STANLEY: Well, there's hardware stores on Sixth Avenue, but it may be too late now.

WILLY: [*anxiously*] Oh, I'd better hurry. I've got to get some seeds. [*He starts off to the right.*] I've got to get some seeds, right away. Nothing's planted. I don't have a thing in the ground.

[WILLY *hurries out as the light goes down.* STANLEY *moves over to the right after him, watches him off. The other waiter has been staring at* WILLY.]

STANLEY: [*to the* WAITER] Well, whatta you looking at?

[*The* WAITER *picks up the chairs and moves off right.* STANLEY *takes the table and follows him. The light fades on this area. There is a long pause, the sound of the flute coming over. The light gradually rises on the kitchen, which is empty.* HAPPY *appears at the door of the house, followed by* BIFF. HAPPY *is carrying a large bunch of long-stemmed roses. He enters the kitchen, looks around for* LINDA. *Not seeing her, he turns to* BIFF, *who is just outside the house door, and makes a gesture with his hands, indicating "Not here, I guess." He looks into the living room and freezes. Inside,* LINDA, *unseen, is seated,* WILLY's *coat on her lap. She rises ominously and quietly and moves toward* HAPPY, *who backs up into the kitchen, afraid.*]

HAPPY: Hey, what're you doing up? [LINDA *says nothing but moves toward him implacably*] Where's Pop? [*He keeps backing to the right, and now* LINDA *is in full view in the doorway to the living room.*] Is he sleeping?

LINDA: Where were you?

HAPPY: [*trying to laugh it off*] We met two girls, Mom, very fine types. Here, we brought you some flowers. [*offering them to her*] Put them in your room, Ma.

[*She knocks them to the floor at* BIFF's *feet. He has now come inside and closed the door behind him. She stares at* BIFF, *silent.*]

HAPPY: Now what'd you do that for, Mom? I want you to have some flowers—

LINDA: [*cutting* HAPPY *off, violently to* BIFF] Don't you care whether he lives or dies?

HAPPY: [*going to the stairs*] Come upstairs, Biff.

BIFF: [*with a flare of disgust, to* HAPPY] Go away from me! [*to* LINDA] What do you mean, lives or dies? Nobody's dying around here, pal.

LINDA: Get out of my sight! Get out of here!

BIFF: I wanna see the boss.

LINDA: You're not going near him!

BIFF: Where is he? [*He moves into the living room and* LINDA *follows.*]

LINDA: [*shouting after* BIFF] You invite him for dinner. He looks forward to it all day—[BIFF *appears in his parents' bedroom, looks around, and exits*]—and then you desert him there. There's no stranger you'd do that to!

HAPPY: Why? He had a swell time with us. Listen, when I—[LINDA *comes back into the kitchen*]—desert him I hope I don't outlive the day!

LINDA: Get out of here!

HAPPY: Now look, Mom . . .

LINDA: Did you have to go to women tonight? You and your lousy rotten whores!
      [BIFF *reenters the kitchen.*]
HAPPY: Mom, all we did was follow Biff around trying to cheer him up! [*to* BIFF] Boy, what a night you gave me!
LINDA: Get out of here, both of you, and don't come back! I don't want you tormenting him any more. Go on now, get your things together! [*to* BIFF] You can sleep in his apartment. [*She starts to pick up the flowers and stops herself*] Pick up this stuff, I'm not your maid any more. Pick it up, you bum, you!
      [HAPPY *turns his back to her in refusal.* BIFF *slowly moves over and gets down on his knees, picking up the flowers.*]
LINDA: You're a pair of animals! Not one, not another living soul would have had the cruelty to walk out on that man in a restaurant!
BIFF: [*not looking at her* ] Is that what he said?
LINDA: He didn't have to say anything. He was so humiliated he nearly limped when he came in.
HAPPY: But, Mom, he had a great time with us —
BIFF: [*cutting him off violently*] Shut up!
      [*Without another word,* HAPPY *goes upstairs.*]
LINDA: You! You didn't even go in to see if he was all right!
BIFF: [*still on the floor in front of* LINDA. *the flowers in his hand; with self-loathing*] No. Didn't. Didn't do a damned thing. How do you like that, heh? Left him babbling in a toilet.
LINDA: You louse. You . . .
BIFF: Now you hit it on the nose! [*He gets up, throws the flowers in the wastebasket.*] The scum of the earth, and you're looking at him!
LINDA: Get out of here!
BIFF: I gotta talk to the boss, Mom. Where is he?
LINDA: You're not going near him. Get out of this house!
BIFF: [*with absolute assurance, determination*] No. We're gonna have an abrupt conversation, him and me.
LINDA: You're not talking to him!
      [*Hammering is heard from outside the house, off right.* BIFF *turns toward the noise.*]
LINDA: [*suddenly pleading*] Will you please leave him alone?
BIFF: What's he doing out there?
LINDA: He's planting the garden!
BIFF: [*quietly*] Now? Oh, my God!
      [BIFF *moves outside,* LINDA *following. The light dies down on them and comes up on the center of the apron as* WILLY *walks into it. He is carrying a flashlight, a hoe, and a handful of seed packets. He raps the top of the hoe sharply to fix it firmly, and then moves to the left, measuring off the distance with his foot. He holds the flashlight to look at the seed packets, reading off the instructions. He is in the blue of night.*]
WILLY: Carrots . . . quarter-inch apart. Rows . . . one-foot rows. [*He measures it off.*] One foot. [*He puts down a package and measures off.*] Beets. [*He puts down another package and measures again.*] Lettuce. [*He reads the package, puts it down.*] One foot — [*He breaks off as* BEN *appears at the right and moves slowly down to him.*] What a proposition, ts, ts. Terrific, terrific. 'Cause she's

suffered, Ben, the woman has suffered. You understand me? A man can't go out the way he came in, Ben, a man has got to add up to something. You can't, you can't — [BEN *moves toward him as though to interrupt.*] You gotta consider, now. Don't answer so quick. Remember, it's a guaranteed twenty-thousand-dollar proposition. Now look, Ben, I want you to go through the ins and outs of this thing with me. I've got nobody to talk to, Ben, and the woman has suffered, you hear me?

BEN: [*standing still, considering*] What's the proposition?

WILLY: It's twenty thousand dollars on the barrelhead. Guaranteed, gilt-edged, you understand?

BEN: You don't want to make a fool of yourself. They might not honor the policy.

WILLY: How can they dare refuse? Didn't I work like a coolie to meet every premium on the nose? And now they don't pay off? Impossible!

BEN: It's called a cowardly thing, William.

WILLY: Why? Does it take more guts to stand here the rest of my life ringing up a zero?

BEN: [*yielding*] That's a point, William. [*He moves, thinking, turns.*] And twenty thousand — that *is* something one can feel with the hand, it is there.

WILLY: [*now assured, with rising power*] Oh, Ben, that's the whole beauty of it! I see it like a diamond, shining in the dark, hard and rough, that I can pick up and touch in my hand. Not like — like an appointment! This would not be another damned-fool appointment, Ben, and it changes all the aspects. Because he thinks I'm nothing, see, and so he spites me. But the funeral — [*straightening up*] Ben, that funeral will be massive! They'll come from Maine, Massachusetts, Vermont, New Hampshire! All the old-timers with the strange license plates — that boy will be thunder-struck, Ben, because he never realized — I am known! Rhode Island, New York, New Jersey — I am known, Ben, and he'll see it with his eyes once and for all. He'll see what I am, Ben! He's in for a shock, that boy!

BEN: [*coming down to the edge of the garden*] He'll call you a coward.

WILLY: [*suddenly fearful*] No, that would be terrible.

BEN: Yes. And a damned fool.

WILLY: No, no, he mustn't, I won't have that! [*He is broken and desperate.*]

BEN: He'll hate you, William.

[*The gay music of the Boys is heard.*]

WILLY: Oh, Ben, how do we get back to all the great times? Used to be so full of light, and comradeship, the sleigh-riding in winter, and the ruddiness on his cheeks. And always some kind of good news coming up, always something nice coming up ahead. And never even let me carry the valises in the house, and simonizing, simonizing that little red car! Why, why can't I give him something and not have him hate me?

BEN: Let me think about it. [*He glances at his watch.*] I still have a little time. Remarkable proposition, but you've got to be sure you're not making a fool of yourself.

[BEN *drifts off upstage and goes out of sight.* BIFF *comes down from the left.*]

WILLY: [*suddenly conscious of* BIFF, *turns and looks up at him, then begins picking up the packages of seeds in confusion*] Where the hell is that seed? [*Indignantly:*]

You can't see nothing out here! They boxed in the whole goddam neighborhood!

BIFF: There are people all around here. Don't you realize that!

WILLY: I'm busy. Don't bother me.

BIFF: [*taking the hoe from* WILLY] I'm saying good-by to you, Pop. [WILLY *looks at him, silent, unable to move.*] I'm not coming back any more.

WILLY: You're not going to see Oliver tomorrow?

BIFF: I've got no appointment, Dad.

WILLY: He put his arm around you, and you've got no appointment?

BIFF: Pop, get this now, will you? Everytime I've left it's been a fight that sent me out of here. Today I realized something about myself and I tried to explain it to you and I — I think I'm just not smart enough to make any sense out of it for you. To hell with whose fault it is or anything like that. [*He takes* WILLY's *arm.*] Let's just wrap it up, heh? Come on in, we'll tell Mom. [*He gently tries to pull* WILLY *to left.*]

WILLY: [*frozen, immobile, with guilt in his voice*] No, I don't want to see her.

BIFF: Come on! [*He pulls again, and* WILLY *tries to pull away.*]

WILLY: [*highly nervous*] No, no, I don't want to see her.

BIFF: [*tries to look into* WILLY's *face, as if to find the answer there*] Why don't you want to see her?

WILLY: [*more harshly now*] Don't bother me, will you?

BIFF: What do you mean, you don't want to see her? You don't want them calling you yellow, do you? This isn't your fault; it's me, I'm a bum. Now come inside! [WILLY *strains to get away.*] Did you hear what I said to you?

[WILLY *pulls away and quickly goes by himself into the house.* BIFF *follows.*]

LINDA: [*to* WILLY] Did you plant, dear?

BIFF: [*at the door, to* LINDA] All right, we had it out. I'm going and I'm not writing any more.

LINDA: [*going to* WILLY *in the kitchen*] I think that's the best way, dear. 'Cause there's no use drawing it out, you'll just never get along.

[WILLY *doesn't respond.*]

BIFF: People ask where I am and what I'm doing, you don't know, and you don't care. That way it'll be off your mind and you can start brightening up again. All right? That clears it, doesn't it? [WILLY *is silent, and* BIFF *goes to him.*] You gonna wish me luck, scout? [*He extends his hand.*] What do you say?

LINDA: Shake his hand, Willy.

WILLY: [*turning to her, seething with hurt*] There's no necessity to mention the pen at all, y'know.

BIFF: [*gently*] I've got no appointment, Dad.

WILLY: [*erupting fiercely*] He put his arm around . . . ?

BIFF: Dad, you're never going to see what I am, so what's the use of arguing? If I strike oil I'll send you a check. Meantime forget I'm alive.

WILLY: [*to* LINDA] Spite, see?

BIFF: Shake hands, Dad.

WILLY: Not my hand.

BIFF: I was hoping not to go this way.

WILLY: Well, this is the way you're going. Good-by.

[BIFF *looks at him a moment, then turns sharply and goes to the stairs.*]

WILLY: [*stops him with*] May you rot in hell if you leave this house!

BIFF: [*turning*] Exactly what is it that you want from me?

WILLY: I want you to know, on the train, in the mountains, in the valleys, wherever you go, that you cut down your life for spite!

BIFF: No, no.

WILLY: Spite, spite, is the word of your undoing! And when you're down and out, remember what did it. When you're rotting somewhere beside the railroad tracks, remember, and don't you dare blame it on me!

BIFF: I'm not blaming it on you!

WILLY: I won't take the rap for this, you hear?

[HAPPY *comes down the stairs and stands on the bottom step, watching.*]

BIFF: That's just what I'm telling you!

WILLY: [*sinking into a chair at the table, with full accusation*] You're trying to put a knife in me — don't think I don't know what you're doing!

BIFF: All right, phony! Then let's lay it on the line. [*He whips the rubber tube out of his pocket and puts it on the table.*]

HAPPY: You crazy —

LINDA: Biff! [*She moves to grab the hose, but* BIFF *holds it down with his hand.*]

BIFF: Leave it there! Don't move it!

WILLY: [*not looking at it*] What is that?

BIFF: You know goddam well what that is.

WILLY: [*caged, wanting to escape*] I never saw that.

BIFF: You saw it. The mice didn't bring it into the cellar! What is this supposed to do, make a hero out of you? This supposed to make me sorry for you?

WILLY: Never heard of it.

BIFF: There'll be no pity for you, you hear it? No pity!

WILLY: [*to* LINDA] You hear the spite!

BIFF: No, you're going to hear the truth — what you are and what I am!

LINDA: Stop it!

WILLY: Spite!

HAPPY: [*coming down toward* BIFF] You cut it now!

BIFF: [*to* HAPPY] The man don't know who we are! The man is gonna know! [*to* WILLY] We never told the truth for ten minutes in this house!

HAPPY: We always told the truth!

BIFF: [*turning on him*] You big blow, are you the assistant buyer? You're one of the two assistants to the assistant, aren't you?

HAPPY: Well, I'm practically —

BIFF: You're practically full of it! We all are! And I'm through with it. [*to* WILLY] Now hear this, Willy, this is me.

WILLY: I know you!

BIFF: You know why I had no address for three months? I stole a suit in Kansas City and I was in jail. [*to* LINDA, *who is sobbing*] Stop crying. I'm through with it.

[LINDA *turns away from them, her hands covering her face.*]

WILLY: I suppose that's my fault!

BIFF: I stole myself out of every good job since high school!

WILLY: And whose fault is that?

BIFF: And I never got anywhere because you blew me so full of hot air I could never stand taking orders from anybody! That's whose fault it is!

WILLY: I hear that!

LINDA: Don't, Biff!

BIFF: It's goddam time you heard that! I had to be boss big shot in two weeks, and I'm through with it!

WILLY: Then hang yourself! For spite, hang yourself!

BIFF: No! Nobody's hanging himself, Willy! I ran down eleven flights with a pen in my hand today. And suddenly I stopped, you hear me? And in the middle of that office building, do you hear this? I stopped in the middle of that building and I saw — the sky. I saw the things that I love in this world. The work and the food and time to sit and smoke. And I looked at the pen and said to myself, what the hell am I grabbing this for? Why am I trying to become what I don't want to be? What am I doing in an office, making a contemptuous, begging fool of myself, when all I want is out there, waiting for me the minute I say I know who I am! Why can't I say that, Willy?

   [*He tries to make* WILLY *face him, but* WILLY *pulls away and moves to the left.*]

WILLY: [*with hatred, threateningly*] The door of your life is wide open!

BIFF: Pop! I'm a dime a dozen, and so are you!

WILLY: [*turning on him now in an uncontrolled outburst*] I am not a dime a dozen! I am Willy Loman, and you are Biff Loman!

   [BIFF *starts for* WILLY, *but is blocked by* HAPPY. *In his fury,* BIFF *seems on the verge of attacking his father.*]

BIFF: I am not a leader of men, Willy, and neither are you. You were never anything but a hard-working drummer who landed in the ash can like all the rest of them! I'm one dollar an hour, Willy! I tried seven states and couldn't raise it. A buck an hour! Do you gather my meaning? I'm not bringing home any prizes any more, and you're going to stop waiting for me to bring them home!

WILLY: [*directly to* BIFF] You vengeful, spiteful mut!

   [BIFF *breaks from* HAPPY. WILLY, *in fright, starts up the stairs.* BIFF *grabs him.*]

BIFF: [*at the peak of his fury*] Pop, I'm nothing! I'm nothing, Pop. Can't you understand that? There's no spite in it any more. I'm just what I am, that's all.

   [BIFF'*s fury has spent itself, and he breaks down, sobbing, holding on to* WILLY, *who dumbly fumbles for* BIFF'*s face.*]

WILLY: [*astonished*] What're you doing? What're you doing? [*to* LINDA] Why is he crying?

BIFF: [*crying, broken*] Will you let me go, for Christ's sake? Will you take that phony dream and burn it before something happens? [*struggling to contain himself, he pulls away and moves to the stairs*] I'll go in the morning. Put him — put him to bed. [*Exhausted,* BIFF *moves up the stairs to his room.*]

WILLY: [*after a long pause, astonished, elevated*] Isn't that — isn't that remarkable? Biff — he likes me!

LINDA: He loves you, Willy!

HAPPY: [*deeply moved*] Always did, Pop.

WILLY: Oh, Biff! [*staring wildly*] He cried! Cried to me. [*He is choking with his love, and now cries out his promise:*] That boy — that boy is going to be magnificent!

[BEN *appears in the light just outside the kitchen.*]

BEN: Yes, outstanding, with twenty thousand behind him.

LINDA: [*sensing the racing of his mind, fearfully, carefully*] Now come to bed, Willy. It's all settled now.

WILLY: [*finding is difficult not to rush out of the house*] Yes, we'll sleep. Come on. Go to sleep, Hap.

BEN: And it does take a great kind of a man to crack the jungle.

[*In accents of dread,* BEN's *idyllic music starts up.*]

HAPPY: [*his arm around* LINDA] I'm getting married, Pop, don't forget it. I'm changing everything. I'm gonna run that department before the year is up. You'll see, Mom. [*He kisses her.*]

BEN: The jungle is dark but full of diamonds, Willy.

[WILLY *turns, moves, listening to* BEN.]

LINDA: Be good. You're both good boys, just act that way, that's all.

HAPPY: 'Night, Pop. [*He goes upstairs.*]

LINDA: [*to* WILLY] Come, dear.

BEN: [*with greater force*] One must go in to fetch a diamond out.

WILLY: [*to* LINDA, *as he moves slowly along the edge of the kitchen, toward the door*] I just want to get settled down, Linda. Let me sit alone for a little.

LINDA: [*almost uttering her fear*] I want you upstairs.

WILLY: [*taking her in his arms*] In a few minutes, Linda. I couldn't sleep right now. Go on, you look awful tired. [*He kisses her.*]

BEN: Not like an appointment at all. A diamond is rough and hard to the touch.

WILLY: Go on now. I'll be right up.

LINDA: I think this is the only way, Willy.

WILLY: Sure, it's the best thing.

BEN: Best thing!

WILLY: The only way. Everything is gonna be — go on, kid, get to bed. You look so tired.

LINDA: Come right up.

WILLY: Two minutes.

[LINDA *goes into the living-room, then reappears in her bedroom.* WILLY *moves just outside the kitchen door.*]

WILLY: Loves me. [*wonderingly*] Always loved me. Isn't that a remarkable thing? Ben, he'll worship me for it!

BEN: [*with promise*] It's dark there, but full of diamonds.

WILLY: Can you imagine that magnificence with twenty thousand dollars in his pocket?

LINDA: [*calling from her room*] Willy! Come up!

WILLY: [*calling into the kitchen* Yes! Yes. Coming! It's very smart, you realize that, don't you, sweetheart? Even Ben sees it. I gotta go, baby, 'By! 'By! [*going over to* BEN, *almost dancing*] Imagine? When the mail comes he'll be ahead of Bernard again!

BEN: A perfect proposition all around.

WILLY: Did you see how he cried to me? Oh, if I could kiss him. Ben!

BEN: Time, William, time!

WILLY: Oh, Ben, I always knew one way or another we were gonna make it, Biff and I!

BEN: [*looking at his watch*] The boat. We'll be late. [*He moves slowly off into the darkness.*]

WILLY: [*elegiacally, turning to the house*] Now when you kick off, boy, I want a seventy-yard boot, and get right down the field under the ball, and when you hit, hit low and hit hard, because it's important, boy. [*He swings around and faces the audience.*] There's all kinds of important people in the stands, and the first thing you know . . . [*suddenly realizing he is alone*] Ben! Ben, where do I . . . ? [*he makes a sudden movement of search*] Ben, how do I . . . ?

LINDA: [*calling*] Willy, you coming up?

WILLY: [*uttering a gasp of fear, whirling about as if to quiet her*] Sh! [*He turns around as if to find his way; sounds, faces, voices, seem to be swarming in upon him and he flicks at them, crying*] Sh! Sh! [*Suddenly music, faint and high, stops him. It rises in intensity, almost to an unbearable scream. He goes up and down on his toes, and rushes off around the house.*] Shhh!

LINDA: Willy?

[*There is no answer.* LINDA *waits.* BIFF *gets up off his bed. He is still in his clothes.* HAPPY *sits up.* BIFF *stands listening.*]

LINDA: [*with real fear*] Willy, answer me! Willy!

[*There is the sound of a car starting and moving away at full speed.*]

LINDA: No!

BIFF: [*rushing down the stairs*] Pop!

[*As the car speeds off, the music crashes down in a frenzy of sound, which becomes the soft pulsation of a single cello string.* BIFF *slowly returns to his bedroom. He and* HAPPY *gravely don their jackets.* LINDA *slowly walks out of her room. The music has developed into a dead march. The leaves of day are appearing over everything.* CHARLEY *and* BERNARD, *somberly dressed, appear and knock on the kitchen door.* BIFF *and* HAPPY *slowly descend the stairs to the kitchen as* CHARLEY *and* BERNARD *enter. All stop a moment when* LINDA, *in clothes of mourning, bearing a little bunch of roses, comes through the draped doorway into the kitchen. She goes to* CHARLEY *and takes his arm. Now all move toward the audience, through the wall-line of the kitchen. At the limit of the apron,* LINDA *lays down the flowers, kneels, and sits back on her heels. All stare down at the grave.*]

## REQUIEM

CHARLEY: It's getting dark, Linda.

[LINDA *doesn't react. She stares at the grave.*]

BIFF: How about it, Mom? Better get some rest, heh? They'll be closing the gate soon.

[LINDA *makes no move. Pause.*]

HAPPY: [*deeply angered*] He had no right to do that. There was no necessity for it. We would've helped him.

CHARLEY: [*grunting*] Hmmm.

BIFF: Come along, Mom.

LINDA: Why didn't anybody come?

CHARLEY: It was a very nice funeral.

LINDA: But where are all the people he knew? Maybe they blame him.

CHARLEY: Naa. It's a rough world, Linda. They couldn't blame him.

LINDA: I can't understand it. At this time especially. First time in thirty-five years we were just about free and clear. He only needed a little salary. He was even finished with the dentist.

CHARLEY: No man only needs a little salary.

LINDA: I can't understand it.

BIFF: There were a lot of nice days. When he'd come home from a trip; or on Sundays, making the stoop; finishing the cellar; putting on the new porch; when he built the extra bathroom; and put up the garage. You know something, Charley, there's more of him in that front stoop than in all the sales he ever made.

CHARLEY: Yeah. He was a happy man with a batch of cement.

LINDA: He was so wonderful with his hands.

BIFF: He had all the wrong dreams. All, all, wrong.

HAPPY: [*almost ready to fight* BIFF] Don't say that!

BIFF: He never knew who he was.

CHARLEY: [*stopping* HAPPY's *movement and reply. To* BIFF:] Nobody dast blame this man. You don't understand. Willy was a salesman. And for a salesman, there is no rock bottom to the life. He don't put a bolt to a nut, he don't tell you the law or give you medicine. He's a man way out there in the blue, riding on a smile and a shoeshine. And when they start not smiling back — that's an earthquake. And then you get yourself a couple of spots on your hat, and you're finished. Nobody dast blame this man. A salesman is got to dream, boy. It comes with the territory.

BIFF: Charley, the man didn't know who he was.

HAPPY: [*infuriated*] Don't say that!

BIFF: Why don't you come with me, Happy?

HAPPY: I'm not licked that easily. I'm staying right in this city, and I'm gonna beat this racket! [*He looks at* BIFF, *his chin set.*] The Loman Brothers!

BIFF: I know who I am, kid.

HAPPY: All right, boy. I'm gonna show you and everybody else that Willy Loman did not die in vain. He had a good dream. It's the only dream you can have — to come out number-one man. He fought it out here, and this is where I'm gonna win it for him.

BIFF: [*with a hopeless glance at* HAPPY, *bends toward his mother*] Let's go, Mom.

LINDA: I'll be with you in a minute. Go on, Charley. [*he hesitates*] I want to, just for a minute. I never had a chance to say good-by.

> [CHARLEY *moves away, followed by* HAPPY. BIFF *remains a slight distance up and left of* LINDA. *She sits there, summoning herself. The flute begins, not far away, playing behind her speech.*]

LINDA: Forgive me, dear. I can't cry. I don't know what it is, but I can't cry. I don't understand it. Why did you ever do that? Help me, Willy, I can't cry. It seems to me that you're just on another trip. I keep expecting you. Willy, dear, I can't cry. Why did you do it? I search and search and I search, and I can't understand it, Willy. I made the last payment on the house today. Today, dear. And there'll be nobody home. [*A sob rises in her throat.*] We're free and clear.

[*sobbing more fully released*] We're free. [BIFF *comes slowly toward her.*] We're free . . . We're free . . .

[BIFF *lifts her to her feet and moves out up right with her in his arms.* LINDA *sobs quietly.* BERNARD *and* CHARLEY *come together and follow them, followed by* HAPPY. *Only the music of the flute is left on the darkening stage as over the house the hard towers of the apartment buildings rise into sharp focus, and*]

THE CURTAIN FALLS

# Samuel Beckett

# Happy Days

CHARACTERS

WINNIE, *a woman about fifty*
WILLIE, *a man about sixty*

ACT I

*Expanse of scorched grass rising centre to low mound. Gentle slopes down to front and either side of stage. Back an abrupter fall to stage level. Maximum of simplicity and symmetry.*

*Blazing light.*

*Very pompier trompe-l'oeil backcloth to represent unbroken plain and sky receding to meet in far distance.*

*Imbedded up to above her waist in exact centre of mound,* WINNIE. *About fifty, well preserved, blond for preference, plump, arms and shoulders bare, low bodice, big bosom, pearl necklet. She is discovered sleeping, her arms on the ground before her, her head on her arms. Beside her on ground to her left a capacious black bag, shopping variety, and to her right a collapsible collapsed parasol, beak of handle emerging from sheath.*

*To her right and rear, lying asleep on ground, hidden by mound,* WILLIE.

*Long pause. A bell rings piercingly, say ten seconds, stops. She does not move. Pause. Bell more piercingly, say five seconds. She wakes. Bell stops. She raises her head, gazes front. Long pause. She straightens up, lays her hands flat on ground, throws back her head and gazes at zenith. Long pause.*

WINNIE: [*gazing at zenith*] Another heavenly day. [*Pause. Head back level, eyes front, pause. She clasps hands to breast, closes eyes. Lips move in inaudible prayer, say ten seconds. Lips still. Hands remain clasped. Low.*] For Jesus Christ sake Amen. [*Eyes open, hands unclasp, return to mound. Pause. She clasps hands to breast again, closes eyes, lips move again in inaudible addendum, say five seconds. Low.*] World without end Amen. [*Eyes open, hands unclasp, return to mound. Pause.*] Begin, Winnie. [*Pause.*] Begin your day, Winnie. [*Pause. She turns to bag, rummages in it without moving it from its place, brings out toothbrush, rummages again, brings out flat tube of toothpaste, turns back front, unscrews cap of tube, lays cap on ground, squeezes with difficulty small blob of paste on brush, holds tube in one hand and brushes teeth with other. She turns modestly aside and back to her right to spit out behind mound. In this position her eyes rest on* WILLIE. *She spits out. She cranes a little further back and down. Loud.*] Hoo-oo! [*Pause. Louder.*] Hoo-oo! [*Pause. Tender smile as she turns back front, lays down brush.*] Poor Willie — [*examines tube, smile off*] — running out — [*looks for cap*] — ah well — [*finds cap*] — can't be helped — [*screws on cap*] — just one of those old things — [*lays down tube*] — another of those old things — [*turns towards*

510

*bag*] — just can't be cured — [*rummages in bag*] — cannot be cured — [*brings out small mirror, turns back front*] — ah yes — [*inspects teeth in mirror*] — poor dear Willie — [*testing upper front teeth with thumb, indistinctly*] — good Lord! — [*pulling back upper lip to inspect gums, do.*] — good God! — [*pulling back corner of mouth, mouth open, do.*] — ah well — [*other corner, do.*] — no worse — [*abandons inspection, normal speech*] — no better, no worse — [*lays down mirror*] — no change — [*wipes fingers on grass*] — no pain — [*looks for toothbrush*] — hardly any — [*takes up toothbrush*] — great thing that — [*examines handle of brush*] — nothing like it — [*examines handle, reads*] — pure . . . what? — [*Pause.*] — what? — [*lays down brush*] — ah yes — [*turns towards bag*] — poor Willie — [*rummages in bag*] — no zest — [*rummages*] — for anything — [*brings out spectacles in case*] — no interest — [*turns back front*] — in life — [*takes spectacles from case*] — poor dear Willie — [*lays down case*] — sleep for ever — [*opens spectacles*] — marvellous gift — [*puts on spectacles*] — nothing to touch it — [*looks for toothbrush*] — in my opinion — [*takes up toothbrush*] — always said so — [*examines handle of brush*] — wish I had it — [*examines handle, reads*] — genuine . . . pure . . . what? — [*lays down brush*] — blind next — [*takes off spectacles*] — ah well — [*lays down spectacles*] — seen enough — [*feels in bodice for handkerchief*] — I suppose — [*takes out folded handkerchief*] — by now — [*shakes out handkerchief*] — what are those wonderful lines — [*wipes one eye*] — woe woe is me — [*wipes the other*] — to see what I see — [*looks for spectacles*] — ah yes — [*takes up spectacles*] — wouldn't miss it — [*starts polishing spectacles, breathing on lenses*] — or would I? — [*polishes*] — holy light — [*polishes*] — bob up out of dark — [*polishes*] — blaze of hellish light. [*Stops polishing, raises face to sky, pause, head back level, resumes polishing, stops polishing, cranes back to her right and down.*] Hoo-oo! [*Pause. Tender smile as she turns back front and resumes polishing. Smile off.*] Marvellous gift — [*stops polishing, lays down spectacles*] — wish I had it — [*folds handkerchief*] — ah well — [*puts handkerchief back in bodice*] — can't complain — [*looks for spectacles*] — no no — [*takes up spectacles*] — mustn't complain — [*holds up spectacles, looks through lens*] — so much to be thankful for — [*looks through other lens*] — no pain — [*puts on spectacles*] — hardly any — [*looks for toothbrush*] — wonderful thing that — [*takes up toothbrush*] — nothing like it — [*examines handle of brush*] — slight headache sometimes — [*examines handle, reads*] — guaranteed . . . genuine . . . pure . . . what? — [*looks closer*] — genuine pure . . . — [*takes handkerchief from bodice*] — ah yes — [*shakes out handkerchief*] — occasional mild migraine — [*starts wiping handle of brush*] — it comes — [*wipes*] — then goes — [*wiping mechanically*] — ah yes — [*wiping*] — many mercies — [*wiping*] — great mercies — [*stops wiping, fixed lost gaze, brokenly*] — prayers perhaps not for naught — [*Pause, do.*] — first thing — [*Pause, do.*] — last thing — [*head down, resumes wiping, stops wiping, head up, calmed, wipes eyes, folds handkerchief, puts it back in bodice, examines handle of brush, reads*] — fully guaranteed . . . genuine pure . . . — [*looks closer*] — genuine pure . . . [*Takes off spectacles, lays them and brush down, gazes before her.*] Old things. [*Pause.*] Old eyes. [*Long pause.*] On, Winnie. [*She casts about her, sees parasol, considers it at length, takes it up and develops from sheath a handle of* surprising length. Holding butt of parasol in right hand she cranes back and down to her right to hand over WILLIE.] Hoo-oo! [Pause.] Willie! [Pause.] Wonderful gift. [She strikes down at him with beak of parasol.] Wish I had it. [She strikes again. The parasol slips from her grasp and falls behind mound. It is immediately restored to her by WILLIE's invisible hand.] Thank you, dear. [She transfers parasol to left hand, turns back front and examines right palm.] Damp. [Returns parasol to right hand, examines left palm.] Ah well, no worse. [Head up, cheerfully.] No better, no worse, no change. [Pause. Do.] No pain. [Cranes back to look down at WILLIE, holding parasol by butt as before.] Don't go off on me again now dear will you please, I may need you. [Pause.] No hurry, no hurry, just don't curl up on me again. [Turns back front, lays down parasol, examines palms together, wipes them on grass.] Perhaps a shade off colour just the same. [Turns to bag, rummages in it, brings out revolver, holds it up, kisses it rapidly, puts it back, rummages, brings out almost empty bottle of red medicine, turns back front, looks for spectacles, puts them on, reads label.] Loss of spirits . . . lack of keenness . . . want of appetite . . . infants . . . children . . . adults . . . six level . . . tablespoonfuls daily —[head up, smile]—the old style!—[smile off, head down, reads]— daily . . . before and after . . . meals . . . instantaneous . . . [looks closer] improvement. [Takes off spectacles, lays them down, holds up bottle at arm's length to see level, unscrews cap, swigs it off head well back, tosses cap and bottle away in WILLIE's direction. Sound of breaking glass.] Ah that's better! [Turns to bag, rummages in it, brings out lipstick, turns back front, examines lipstick.] Running out. [Looks for spectacles.] Ah well. [Puts on spectacles, looks for mirror.] Musn't complain. [Takes up mirror, starts doing lips.] What is that wonderful line? [Lips.] Oh fleeting joys—[lips]—oh something lasting woe. [Lips. She is interrupted by disturbance from WILLIE. He is sitting up. She lowers lipstick and mirror and cranes back and down to look at him. Pause. Top back of WILLIE's bald head, trickling blood, rises to view above slope, comes to rest. WINNIE pushes up her spectacles. Pause. His hand appears with handkerchief, spreads it on skull, disappears. Pause. The hand appears with boater, club ribbon, settles it on head, rakish angle, disappears. Pause. WINNIE cranes a little further back and down.] Slip on your drawers, dear, before you get singed. [Pause.] No? [Pause.] Oh I see, you still have some of that stuff left. [Pause.] Work it well in, dear. [Pause.] Now the other. [Pause. She turns back front, gazes before her. Happy expression.] Oh this is going to be another happy day! [Pause. Happy expression off. She pulls down spectacles and resumes lips. WILLIE opens newspaper, hands invisible. Tops of yellow sheets appear on either side of his head. WINNIE finishes lips, inspects them in mirror held a little further away.] Ensign crimson. [WILLIE turns page. WINNIE lays down lipstick and mirror, turns towards bag.] Pale flag.

       [WILLIE turns page. WINNIE rummages in bag, brings out small ornate brimless hat with crumpled feather, turns back front, straightens hat, smooths feather, raises it towards head, arrests gesture as WILLIE reads.]

WILLIE:  His Grace and Most Reverend Father in God Dr Carolus Hunter dead in tub.

       [Pause.]

WINNIE:  [gazing front, hat in hand, tone of fervent reminiscence] Charlie Hunter!

[*Pause.*] I close my eyes — [*she takes off spectacles and does so, hat in one hand, spectacles in other,* WILLIE *turns page*] — and am sitting on his knees again, in the back garden at Borough Green, under the horse-beech. [*Pause. She opens eyes, puts on spectacles, fiddles with hat.*] Oh the happy memories!

[*Pause. She raises hat towards head, arrests gesture as* WILLIE *reads.*]

WILLIE: Opening for smart youth.

[*Pause. She raises hat towards head, arrests gesture, takes off spectacles, gazes front, hat in one hand, spectacles in other.*]

WINNIE: My first ball! [*Long pause.*] My second ball! [*Long pause. Closes eyes.*] My first kiss! [*Pause.* WILLIE *turns page.* WINNIE *opens eyes.*] A Mr Johnson, or Johnston, or perhaps I should say Johnstone. Very bushy moustache, very tawny. [*Reverently.*] Almost ginger! [*Pause.*] Within a toolshed, though whose I cannot conceive. We had no toolshed and he most certainly had no toolshed. [*Closes eyes.*] I see the piles of pots. [*Pause.*] The tangles of bast. [*Pause.*] The shadows deepening among the rafters.

[*Pause. She opens eyes, puts on spectacles, raises hat towards head, arrests gesture as* WILLIE *reads.*]

WILLIE: Wanted bright boy.

[*Pause.* WINNIE *puts on hat hurriedly, looks for mirror.* WILLIE *turns page.* WINNIE *takes up mirror, inspects hat, lays down mirror, turns towards bag. Paper disappears.* WINNIE *rummages in bag, brings out magnifying-glass, turns back front, looks for toothbrush. Paper reappears, folded, and begins to fan* WILLIE's *face, hand invisible.* WINNIE *takes up toothbrush and examines handle through glass.*]

WINNIE: Fully guaranteed . . . [WILLIE *stops fanning*] . . . genuine pure . . . [*Pause.* WILLIE *resumes fanning.* WINNIE *looks closer, reads.*] Fully guaranteed . . . [WILLIE *stops fanning*] . . . genuine pure . . . [*Pause.* WILLIE *resumes fanning.* WINNIE *lays down glass and brush, takes handkerchief from bodice, takes off and polishes spectacles, puts on spectacles, looks for glass, takes up and polishes glass, lays down glass, looks for brush, takes up brush and wipes handle, lays down brush, puts handkerchief back in bodice, looks for glass, takes up glass, looks for brush, takes up brush and examines handle through glass.*] Fully guaranteed . . . [WILLIE *stops fanning*] . . . genuine pure . . . [*pause,* WILLIE *resumes fanning*] . . . hog's [WILLIE *stops fanning, pause*] . . . setae. [*Pause.* WINNIE *lays down glass and brush, paper disappears,* WINNIE *takes off spectacles, lays them down, gazes front.*] Hog's setae. [*Pause.*] That is what I find so wonderful, that not a day goes by — [*smile*] — to speak in the old style — [*smile off*] — hardly a day, without some addition to one's knowledge however trifling, the addition I mean, provided one takes the pains. [WILLIE's *hand reappears with a postcard which he examines close to eyes.*] And if for some strange reason no further pains are possible, why then just close the eyes — [*she does so*] — and wait for the day to come — [*opens eyes*] — the happy day to come when flesh melts at so many degrees and the night of the moon has so many hundred hours. [*Pause.*] That is what I find so comforting when I lose heart and envy the brute beast. [*Turning towards* WILLIE.] I hope you are taking in — [*She sees postcard, bends lower.*] What is that you have there, Willie, may I see? [*She reaches down with hand and* WILLIE *hands her card. The hairy forearm appears above slope, raised in gesture of giving, the hand open to take back, and remains in this position till card is returned.* WINNIE *turns back front and examines card.*] Heavens what are they up to! [*She looks for spectacles, puts them on and examines card.*] No *but this is just* genuine pure filth! [*Examines card.*] Make any nice-minded person want to vomit! [*Impatience of* WILLIE's *fingers. She looks for glass, takes it up and examines card through glass. Long pause.*] What does the creature in the background think he's doing? [*Looks closer.*] Oh no really! [*Impatience of fingers. Last long look. She lays down glass, takes edge of card between right forefinger and thumb, averts head, takes nose between left forefinger and thumb.*] Pah! [*Drops card.*] Take it away! [WILLIE's *arm disappears. His hand reappears immediately, holding card.* WINNIE *takes off spectacles, lays them down, gazes before her. During what follows* WILLIE *continues to relish card, varying angles and distance from his eyes.*] Hog's setae. [*Puzzled expression.*] What exactly is a hog? [*Pause. Do.*] A sow of course I know, but a hog . . . [*Puzzled expression off.*] Oh well what does it matter, that is what I always say, it will come back, that is what I find so wonderful, all comes back. [*Pause.*] All? [*Pause.*] No, not all. [*Smile.*] No no. [*Smile off.*] Not quite. [*Pause.*] A part. [*Pause.*] Floats up, one fine day, out of the blue. [*Pause.*] That is what I find so wonderful. [*Pause. She turns towards bag. Hand and card disappear. She makes to rummage in bag, arrests gesture.*] No. [*She turns back front. Smile.*] No no. [*Smile off.*] Gently Winnie. [*She gazes front.* WILLIE's *hand reappears, takes off hat, disappears with hat.*] What then? [*Hand reappears, takes handkerchief from skull, disappears with handkerchief. Sharply, as to one not paying attention.*] Winnie! [WILLIE *bows head out of sight.*] What is the alternative? [*Pause.*] What *is* the al — [WILLIE *blows nose loud and long, head and hands invisible. She turns to look at him. Pause. Head reappears. Pause. Hand reappears with handkerchief, spreads it on skull, disappears. Pause. Hand reappears with boater, settles it on head, rakish angle, disappears. Pause.*] Would I had let you sleep on. [*She turns back front. Intermittent plucking at grass, head up and down, to animate following.*] Ah yes, if only I could bear to be alone, I mean prattle away with not a soul to hear. [*Pause.*] Not that I flatter myself you hear much, no Willie, God forbid. [*Pause.*] Days perhaps when you hear nothing. [*Pause.*] But days too when you answer. [*Pause.*] So that I may say at all times, even when you do not answer and perhaps hear nothing, something of this is being heard, I am not merely talking to myself, that is in the wilderness, a thing I could never bear to do — for any length of time. [*Pause.*] That is what enables me to go on, go on talking that is. [*Pause.*] Whereas if you were to die — [*smile*] — to speak in the old style — [*smile off*] — or go away and leave me, then what would I do, what *could* I do, all day long, I mean between the bell for waking and the bell for sleep? [*Pause.*] Simply gaze before me with compressed lips. [*Long pause while she does so. No more plucking.*] Not another word as long as I drew breath, nothing to break the silence of this place. [*Pause.*] Save possibly, now and then, every now and then, a sigh into my looking-glass. [*Pause.*] Or a brief . . . gale of laughter, should I happen to see the old joke again. [*Pause. Smile appears, broadens and seems about to culminate in laugh when suddenly replaced by expression of anxiety.*] My hair! [*Pause.*] Did I brush and comb my hair? [*Pause.*] I may have done. [*Pause.*] Normally I do. [*Pause.*] There is so little one *can* do. [*Pause.*] One does it all. [*Pause.*] All one can. [*Pause.*] Tis only human. [*Pause.*] Human nature. [*She begins to inspect mound, looks up.*] Human weakness. [*She resumes inspection of mound, looks up.*] Natural weakness. [*She resumes inspection of mound.*] I see no comb. [*Inspects.*] Nor any hairbrush. [*Looks up. Puzzled expression. She turns to bag, rummages in it.*] The comb is here. [*Back front. Puzzled expression.*] Perhaps I put them back, after use. [*Pause. Do.*] But normally I do not put things back, after use, no, I leave them lying about and put them back all together, at the end of the day. [*Smile.*] To speak in the old style. [*Pause.*] The sweet old style. [*Smile off.*] And yet . . . I seem . . . to remember . . . [*Suddenly careless.*] Oh well, what does it matter, that is what I always say, I shall simply brush and comb them later on, purely and simply, I have the whole — [*Pause. Puzzled.*] Them? [*Pause.*] Or it? [*Pause.*] Brush and comb it? [*Pause.*] Sounds improper somehow. [*Pause. Turning a little towards* WILLIE.] What would you say, Willie? [*Pause. Turning a little further.*] What would you say, Willie, speaking of your hair, them or it? [*Pause.*] The hair on your head, I mean. [*Pause. Turning a little further.*] The hair on your head, Willie, what would you say speaking of the hair on your head, them or it?

    [*Long pause.*]

WILLIE: It.

WINNIE: [*turning back front, joyfully*] Oh you are going to talk to me today, this is going to be a happy day! [*Pause. Joy off.*] Another happy day. [*Pause.*] Ah well, where was I, my hair, yes, later on, I shall be thankful for it later on. [*Pause.*] I have my — [*raises hand to hat*] — yes, on, my hat on — [*lowers hands*] — I cannot take it off now. [*Pause.*] To think there are times one cannot take off one's hat, not if one's life were at stake. Times one cannot put it on, times one cannot take it off. [*Pause.*] How often I have said, Put on your hat now, Winnie, there is nothing else for it, take off your hat now, Winnie, like a good girl, it will do you good, and did not. [*Pause.*] Could not. [*Pause. She raises hand, frees a strand of hair from under hat, draws it towards eye, squints at it, lets it go, hand down.*] Golden you called it, that day, when the last guest was gone — [*hand up in gesture of raising a glass*] — to your golden . . . may it never . . . [*voice breaks*] . . . may it never . . . [*Hand down. Head down. Pause. Low.*] That day. [*Pause. Do.*] What day? [*Pause. Head up. Normal voice.*] What now? [*Pause.*] Words fail, there are times when even they fail. [*Turning a little towards* WILLIE.] Is that not so, Willie? [*Pause. Turning a little further.*] Is not that so, Willie, that even words fail, at times? [*Pause. Back front.*] What is one to do then, until they come again? Brush and comb the hair, if it has not been done, or if there is some doubt, trim the nails if they are in need of trimming, these things tide one over. [*Pause.*] That is what I mean. [*Pause.*] That is all I mean. [*Pause.*] That is what I find so wonderful, that not a day goes by — [*smile*] — to speak in the old style — [*smile off*] — without some blessing — [WILLIE *collapses behind slope, his head disappears,* WINNIE *turns towards event*] — in disguise. [*She cranes back and down.*] Go back into your hole now, Willie, you've exposed yourself enough. [*Pause.*] Do as I say, Willie, don't lie sprawling there in this hellish sun, go back into your hole. [*Pause.*] Go on now, Willie. [WILLIE *invisible starts crawling left towards hole.*] That's the man. [*She follows his progress with her eyes.*] Not head first, stupid, how are you going to turn? [*Pause.*] That's it . . . right round . . . now . . . back in. [*Pause.*] Oh I know it is not easy, dear, crawling backwards, but it is rewarding in the end. [*Pause.*] You have left your vaseline behind. [*She watches as he crawls back for vaseline.*] The lid! [*She watches as he crawls back towards hole. Irritated.*] Not head first, I tell you! [*Pause.*] More to the right. [*Pause.*] The *right*, I said. [*Pause. Irritated.*] Keep your tail down, can't you! [*Pause.*] Now. [*Pause.*] There! [*All these directions loud. Now in her normal voice, still turned towards him.*] Can you hear me? [*Pause.*] I beseech you, Willie, just yes or no, can you hear me, just yes or nothing.

      [*Pause.*]

WILLIE: Yes.

WINNIE: [*turning front, same voice*] And now?

WILLIE: [*irritated*] Yes.

WINNIE: [*less loud*] And now?

WILLIE: [*more irritated*] Yes.

WINNIE: [*still less loud*] And now? [*A little louder.*] And now?

WILLIE: [*violently*] Yes!

WINNIE: [*same voice*] Fear no more the heat o' the sun. [*Pause.*] Did you hear that?

WILLIE: [*irritated*] Yes.

WINNIE: [*same voice*] What? [*Pause.*] What?

WILLIE: [*more irritated*] Fear no more.

      [*Pause.*]

WINNIE: [*same voice*] No more what? [*Pause.*] Fear no more what?

WILLIE: [*violently*] Fear no more!

WINNIE: [*normal voice, gabbled*] Bless you Willie I do appreciate your goodness I know what an effort it costs you, now you may relax I shall not trouble you again unless I am obliged to, by that I mean unless I come to the end of my own resources which is most unlikely, just to know that in theory you can hear me even though in fact you don't is all I need, just to feel you there within earshot and conceivably on the qui vive is all I ask, not to say anything I would not wish you to hear or liable to cause you pain, not to be just babbling away on trust as it is were not knowing and something gnawing at me. [*Pause for breath.*] Doubt. [*Places index and second finger on heart area, moves them about, brings them to rest.*] Here. [*Moves them slightly.*] Abouts. [*Hand away.*] Oh no doubt the time will come when before I can utter a word I must make sure you heard the one that went before and then no doubt another come another time when I must learn to talk to myself a thing I could never bear to do such wilderness. [*Pause.*] Or gaze before me with compressed lips. [*She does so.*] All day long. [*Gaze and lips again.*] No. [*Smile.*] No no. [*Smile off.*] There is of course the bag. [*Turns towards it.*] There will always be the bag. [*Back front.*] Yes, I suppose so. [*Pause.*] Even when you are gone, Willie. [*She turns a little towards him.*] You *are* going, Willie, aren't you? [*Pause. Louder.*] You *will* be going soon, Willie, won't you? [*Pause. Louder.*] Willie! [*Pause. She cranes back and down to look at him.*] So you have taken off your straw, that is wise. [*Pause.*] You do look snug, I must say, with your chin on your hands and the old blue eyes like saucers in the shadows. [*Pause.*] Can you see me from there I wonder, I still wonder. [*Pause.*] No? [*Back front.*] Oh I know it does not follow when two are gathered together — [*faltering*] — in this way — [*normal*] — that because one sees the other the other sees the one, life has taught me that . . . too. [*Pause.*] Yes, life I suppose, there is no other word. [*She turns a little towards him.*] Could you see me, Willie, do you think, from where you are, if you were to raise your eyes in my direction? [*Turns a little further.*] Lift up your eyes to me, Willie, and tell me can you see me, do that for me, I'll lean back as far as I can. [*Does so. Pause.*] No? [*Pause.*] Well never mind. [*Turns back painfully front.*] The earth is very tight today, can it be I have put on flesh, I trust not. [*Pause. Absently, eyes lowered.*] The great heat possibly. [*Starts to pat and stroke ground.*] All things expanding, some more than others. [*Pause. Patting and stroking.*] Some less. [*Pause. Do.*] Oh I can well imagine what is passing through your mind, it is not enough to have to listen to the woman, now I must look at her as well. [*Pause. Do.*] Well it is very understandable. [*Pause. Do.*] One does not appear to be asking a great deal, indeed at times it would seem hardly possible — [*voice breaks, falls to a murmur*] — to ask less — of a fellow-creature — to put it mildly — whereas actually — when you think about it — look into your heart — see the other — what he needs — peace — to be left in peace — then perhaps the moon — all this time — asking for the moon. [*Pause. Stroking hand suddenly still. Lively.*] Oh I say, what have we here? [*Bending head to ground, incredulous.*] Looks like life of some kind! [*Looks for spectacles, puts them on, bends closer. Pause.*] An emmet! [*Recoils. Shrill.*] Willie, an emmet, a live emmit! [*Seizes magnifying-glass, bends to ground again, inspects through glass.*] Where's it gone? [*Inspects.*] Ah! [*Follows its progress through grass.*] Has like a little white ball in its arms. [*Follows progress. Hand still. Pause.*] It's gone in. [*Continues a moment to gaze at spot through glass, then slowly straightens up, lays down glass, takes off spectacles and gazes before her, spectacles in hand. Finally.*] Like a little white ball.

   [*Long pause. Gesture to lay down spectacles.*]
WILLIE: Eggs.
WINNIE: [*arresting gesture*] What?
      [*Pause.*]
WILLIE: Eggs. [*Pause. Gesture to lay down glasses.*] Formication.
WINNIE: [*arresting gesture*] What!
      [*Pause.*]
WILLIE: Formication.
      [*Pause. She lay down spectacles, gazes before her. Finally.*]
WINNIE: [*murmur*] God. [*Pause.* WILLIE *laughs quietly. After a moment she joins in. They laugh quietly together.* WILLIE *stops. She laughs on a moment alone.* WILLIE *joins in. They laugh together. She stops.* WILLIE *laughs on a moment alone. He stops. Pause. Normal voice.*] Ah well what a joy in any case to hear you laugh again, Willie, I was convinced I never would, you never would. [*Pause.*] I suppose some people might think us a trifle irreverent, but I doubt it. [*Pause.*] How can one better magnify the Almighty than by sniggering with him at his little jokes, particularly the poorer ones? [*Pause.*] I think you would back me up there, Willie. [*Pause.*] Or were we perhaps diverted by two quite different things? [*Pause.*] Oh well, what does it matter, that is what I always say, so long as one . . . you know . . . what is that wonderful line . . .

laughing wild . . . something something laughing wild amid severest woe. [*Pause.*] And now? [*Long pause.*] Was I lovable once, Willie? [*Pause.*] Was I ever lovable? [*Pause.*] Do not misunderstand my question, I am not asking you if you loved me, we know all about that, I am asking you if you found me lovable — at one stage. [*Pause.*] No? [*Pause.*] You can't? [*Pause.*] Well I admit it is a teaser. And you have done more than your bit already, for the time being, just lie back now and relax, I shall not trouble you again unless I am compelled to, just to know you are there within hearing and conceivably on the semi-alert is . . . er . . . paradise enow. [*Pause.*] The day is now well advanced. [*Smile.*] To speak in the old style. [*Smile off.*] And yet it is perhaps a little soon for my song. [*Pause.*] To sing too soon is a great mistake, I find. [*Turning towards bag.*] There is of course the bag. [*Looking at bag.*] The bag. [*Back front.*] Could I enumerate its contents? [*Pause.*] No. [*Pause.*] Could I, if some kind person were to come along and ask, What all have you got in that big black bag, Winnie? give an exhaustive answer? [*Pause.*] No. [*Pause.*] The depths in particular, who knows what treasures. [*Pause.*] What comforts. [*Turns to look at bag.*] Yes, there is the bag. [*Back front.*] But something tells me, Do not overdo the bag, Winnie, make use of it of course, let it help you . . . along, when stuck, by all means, but cast your mind forward, something tells me, cast your mind forward, Winnie, to the time when words must fail — [*she closes eyes, pause, opens eyes*] — and do not overdo the bag. [*Pause. She turns to look at bag.*] Perhaps just one quick dip. [*She turns back front, closes eyes, throws out left arm, plunges hand in bag and brings out revolver. Disgusted.*] You again! [*She opens eyes, brings revolver front and contemplates it. She weighs it in her palm.*] You'd think the weight of this thing would bring it down among the . . . last rounds. But no. It doesn't. Ever uppermost, like Browning. [*Pause.*] Brownie . . . [*Turning a little toward* WILLIE] Remember Brownie, Willie? [*Pause.*] Remember how you used to keep on at me to take it away from you? Take it away, Winnie, take it away, before I put myself out of my misery. [*Back front. Derisive.*] Your misery! [*To revolver.*] Oh I suppose it's a comfort to know you're there, but I'm tired of you. [*Pause.*] I'll leave you out, that's what I'll do. [*She lays revolver on ground to her right.*] There, that's your home from this day out. [*Smile.*] The old style! [*Smile off.*] And now? [*Long pause.*] Is gravity what it was, Willie, I fancy not. [*Pause.*] Yes, the feeling more and more that if I were not held — [*gesture*] — in this way, I would simply float up into the blue. [*Pause.*] And that perhaps some day the earth will yield and let me go, the pull is so great, yes, crack all round me and let me out. [*Pause.*] Don't you ever have that feeling, Willie, of being sucked up? [*Pause.*] Don't you have to cling on sometimes, Willie? [*Pause. She turns a little towards him.*] Willie.

     [*Pause.*]

WILLIE: *Sucked* up?

WINNIE: Yes love, up into the blue, like gossamer. [*Pause.*] No? [*Pause.*] You don't? [*Pause.*] Ah well, natural laws, natural laws, I suppose it's like everything else, it all depends on the creature you happen to be. All I can say for my part is that for me they are not what they were when I was young and . . . foolish and . . . [*faltering, head down*] . . . beautiful . . . possibly . . . lovely . . . in a way . . . to look at. [*Pause. Head up.*] Forgive me, Willie, sorrow keeps breaking in. [*Normal voice.*] Ah well what a joy in any case to know you are there, as usual, and perhaps awake, and perhaps taking all this in, some of all this, what a happy day for me . . . it will have been. [*Pause.*] So far. [*Pause.*] What a blessing nothing grows, imagine if all this stuff were to start growing. [*Pause.*] Imagine. [*Pause.*] Ah yes, great mercies. [*Long pause.*] I can say no more. [*Pause.*] For the moment. [*Pause. Turns to look at bag. Back front. Smile.*] No no. [*Smile off. Looks at parasol.*] I suppose I might — [*takes up parasol*] — yes, I suppose I might . . . hoist this thing now. [*Begins to unfurl it. Following punctuated by mechanical difficulties overcome.*] One keeps putting off — putting up — for fear of putting up — too soon — and the day goes by — quite by — without one's having put up — at all. [*Parasol now fully open. Turned to her right she twirls it idly this way and that.*] Ah yes, so little to say, so little to do, and the fear so great, certain days, of finding one-self . . . left, with hours still to run, before the bell for sleep, and nothing more to say, nothing more to do, that the days go by, certain days go by, quite by, the bell goes, and little or nothing said, little or nothing done. [*Raising parasol.*] That is the danger. [*Turning front.*] To be guarded against. [*She gazes front, holding up parasol with right hand. Maximum pause.*] I used to perspire freely. [*Pause.*] Now hardly at all. [*Pause.*] The heat is much greater. [*Pause.*] The perspiration much less. [*Pause.*] That is what I find so wonderful. [*Pause.*] The way man adapts himself. [*Pause.*] To changing conditions. [*She transfers parasol to left hand. Long pause.*] Holding up wearies the arm. [*Pause.*] Not if one is going along. [*Pause.*] Only if one is at rest. [*Pause.*] That is a curious observation. [*Pause.*] I hope you heard that, Willie, I should be grieved to think you had not heard that. [*She takes parasol in both hands. Long pause.*] I am weary, holding it up, and I cannot put it down. [*Pause.*] I am worse off with it up than with it down, and I cannot put it down. [*Pause.*] Reason says, Put it down, Winnie, it is not helping you, put the thing down and get on with something else. [*Pause.*] I cannot. [*Pause.*] I cannot move. [*Pause.*] No, something must happen, in the world, take place, some change, I cannot, if I am to move again. [*Pause.*] Willie. [*Mildly.*] Help. [*Pause.*] No? [*Pause.*] Bid me put this thing down, Willie, I would obey you instantly, as I have always done, honoured and obeyed. [*Pause.*] Please, Willie. [*Mildly.*] For pity's sake. [*Pause.*] No? [*Pause.*] You can't? [*Pause.*] Well I don't blame you, no, it would ill become me, who cannot move, to blame my Willie because he cannot speak. [*Pause.*] Fortunately I am in tongue again. [*Pause.*] That is what I find so wonderful, my two lamps, when one goes out the other burns brighter. [*Pause.*] Oh yes, great mercies. [*Maximum pause. The parasol goes on fire. Smoke, flames if feasible. She sniffs, looks up, throws parasol to her right behind mound, cranes back to watch it burning. Pause.*] Ah earth you old extinguisher. [*Back front.*] I presume this has occurred before, though I cannot recall it. [*Pause.*] Can you, Willie? [*Turns a little towards him.*] Can you recall this having occurred before? [*Pause. Cranes back to look at him.*] Do you know what has occurred, Willie? [*Pause.*] Have you gone off on me again? [*Pause.*] I do not ask if you are alive to all that is going on, I merely ask if you have not gone off on me again. [*Pause.*] Your eyes appear to be closed, but that has no particular significance we know. [*Pause.*] Raise a finger, dear, will you please, if you are not quite senseless. [*Pause.*] Do that for me, Willie, please, just the little finger, if you are still conscious. [*Pause. Joyful.*] Oh all five, you are a darling today, now I may continue with an easy mind. [*Back front.*] Yes, what ever occurred that did not occur before and yet . . . I wonder, yes, I confess I wonder. [*Pause.*] With the sun blazing so much fiercer down, and hourly fiercer, is it not natural things should go on fire never known to do so, in this way I mean, spontaneous like. [*Pause.*] Shall I myself not melt perhaps in the end, or burn, oh I do not mean necessarily burst into flames, no, just little by little be charred to a black cinder, all this — [*ample gesture of arms*] — visible flesh. [*Pause.*] On the other hand, did I ever know a temperate time? [*Pause.*] No. [*Pause.*] I speak of temperate times and torrid times, they are empty words. [*Pause.*] I speak of when I was not yet caught — in this way — and had my legs and had the use of my legs, and could seek out a shady place, like you, when I was tired of the sun, or a sunny place when I was tired of the shade, like you, and they are all empty words. [*Pause.*] It is no hotter today than yesterday, it will be no hotter tomorrow than today, how could it, and so on back into the far past, forward into the far future. [*Pause.*] And should one day the earth cover my breasts, then I shall never have seen my breasts, no one ever seen my breasts. [*Pause.*] I hope you caught something of that, Willie, I should be sorry to think you had caught nothing of all that, it is not every day I rise to such heights. [*Pause.*] Yes, something seems to have occurred, something has seemed to occur, and nothing has occurred, nothing at all, you are quite right, Willie. [*Pause.*] The sunshade will be there again tomorrow, beside me on this mound, to help me through the day. [*Pause. She takes up mirror.*] I take up this little glass, I shiver it on a stone — [*does so*] — I throw it away — [*does so far behind her*] — it will be in the bag again tomorrow, without a scratch, to help me through the day. [*Pause.*] No, one can do nothing. [*Pause.*] That is what I find so wonderful, the way things . . . [*voice breaks, head down*] . . . things . . . so wonderful. [*Long pause, head down. Finally turns, still bowed, to bag, brings out unidentifiable odds and ends, stuffs them back, fumbles deeper, brings out finally musical-box, winds it up, turns it on, listens for a moment holding it in both hands, huddled over it, turns back front, straightens up and listens to tune, holding box to breast with both hands. It plays the Waltz Duet "I love you so" from* The Merry Widow. *Gradually happy expression. She sways to the rhythm. Music stops. Pause. Brief burst of hoarse song without words — musical-box tune — from* WILLIE. *Increase of happy expression. She lays down box.*] Oh this will have been a happy day! [*She claps hands.*] Again, Willie, again! [*Claps.*] Encore, Willie, please! [*Pause. Happy expression off.*] No? You won't do that for me? [*Pause.*] Well it is very understandable, very understandable. One cannot sing just to please someone, however much one loves them, no, song must come from the heart, that is what I always say, pour out from the inmost, like a thrush. [*Pause.*] How often I have said, in evil hours, Sing now, Winnie, sing your song, there is nothing else for it, and did not. [*Pause.*] Could not. [*Pause.*] No, like the thrush, or the bird of dawning, with no thought of benefit, to oneself or anyone else. [*Pause.*] And now? [*Long pause. Low.*] Strange feeling. [*Pause. Do.*] Strange feeling that someone is looking at me. I am clear, then dim, then gone, then dim again, then clear again, and so on, back and forth, in and out of someone's eye. [*Pause. Do.*] Strange? [*Pause. Do.*] No, here all is strange.

[*Pause. Normal voice.*] Something says, Stop talking now, Winnie, for a minute, don't squander all your words for the day, stop talking and do something for a change, will you? [*She raises hands and holds them open before her eyes. Apostrophic.*] Do something! [*She closes hands.*] What claws! [*She turns to bag, rummages in it, brings out finally a nailfile, turns back front and begins to file nails. Files for a time in silence, then the following punctuated by filing.*] There floats up — into my thoughts — a Mr Shower — a Mr and perhaps a Mrs Shower — no — they are holding hands — his fiancée then more likely — or just some — loved one. [*Looks closer at nails.*] Very brittle today. [*Resumes filing.*] Shower — Shower — does the name mean anything — to you, Willie — evoke any reality, I mean — for you, Willie, — don't answer if you don't — feel up to it — you have done more — than your bit — already — Shower — Shower. [*Inspects filed nails.*] Bit more like it. [*Raises head, gazes front.*] Keep yourself nice, Winnie, that's what I always say, come what may, keep yourself nice. [*Pause. Resumes filing.*] Yes — Shower — Shower — [*stops filing, raises head, gazes front, pause*] — or Cooker, perhaps I should say Cooker. [*Turning a little towards* WILLIE.] Cooker, Willie, does Cooker strike a chord? [*Pause. Turns a little further. Louder.*] Cooker, Willie, does Cooker ring a bell, the name Cooker? [*Pause. She cranes back to look at him. Pause.*] Oh really! [*Pause.*] Have you no handkerchief, darling? [*Pause.*] Have you no delicacy? [*Pause.*] Oh, Willie, you're not eating it! Spit it out, dear, spit it out! [*Pause. Back front.*] Ah well, I suppose it's only natural. [*Break in voice.*] Human. [*Pause. Do.*] What *is* one to do? [*Head down. Do.*] All day long. [*Pause. Do.*] Day after day. [*Pause. Head up. Smile. Calm.*] The old style! [*Smile off. Resumes nails.*] No, done him. [*Passes on to next.*] Should have put on my glasses. [*Pause.*] Too late now. [*Finishes left hand, inspects it.*] Bit more human. [*Starts right hand. Following punctuated as before.*] Well anyway — this man Shower — or Cooker — no matter — and the woman — hand in hand — in the other hands bags — kind of big brown grips — standing there gaping at me — and at last this man Shower — or Cooker — ends in er anyway — stake my life on that — What's she doing? he says — What's the idea? he says — stuck up to her diddies in the bleeding ground — coarse fellow — What does it mean? he says — What's it meant to mean — and so on — lot more stuff like that — usual drivel — Do you hear me? he says — I do, she says, God help me — What do you mean, he says, God help you? [*Stops filing, raises head, gazes front.*] And you, she says, what's the idea of you, she says, what are you meant to mean? It is because you're still on your two flat feet, with your old ditty full of tinned muck and changes of underwear, dragging me up and down this fornicating wilderness, coarse creature, fit mate — [*with sudden violence*] — let go of my hand and drop for God's sake, she says, drop! [*Pause. Resumes filing.*] Why doesn't he dig her out? he says — referring to you, my dear — What good is she to him like that? — What good is he to her like that? — and so one — usual tosh — Good! she says, have a heart for God's sake — Dig her out, he says, dig her out, no sense in her like that — Dig her out with what? she says — I'd dig her out with my bare hands, he says — must have been man and — wife. [*Files in silence.*] Next thing they're away — hand in hand — and the bags — dim — then gone — last human kind — to stray this way. [*Finishes right hand, inspects it, lays down *file, gazes front.*] Strange thing, time like this, drift up into the mind. [*Pause.*] Strange? [*Pause.*] No, here all is strange. [*Pause.*] Thankful for it in any case. [*Voice breaks.*] Most thankful. [*Head down. Pause. Head up. Calm.*] Bow and raise the head, bow and raise, always that. [*Pause.*] And now? [*Long pause. Starts putting things back in bag, toothbrush last. This operation, interrupted by pauses as indicated, punctuates following.*] It is perhaps a little soon — to make ready — for the night — [*stops tidying, head up, smile*] — the old style! — [*smile off, resumes tidying*] — and yet I do — make ready for the night — feeling it at hand — the bell for sleep — saying to myself — Winnie — it will not be long now, Winnie — until the bell for sleep. [*Stops tidying, head up.*] Sometimes I am wrong. [*Smile.*] But not often. [*Smile off.*] Sometimes all is over, for the day, all done, all said, all ready for the night, and the day not over, far from over, the night not ready, far, far from ready. [*Smile.*] But not often. [*Smile off.*] Yes, the bell for sleep, when I feel it at hand, and so make ready for the night — [*gesture*] — in this way, sometimes I am wrong — [*smile*] — but not often. [*Smile off. Resumes tidying.*] I used to think — I say I used to think — that all these things — put back into the bag — if too soon — put back too soon — could be taken out again — if necessary — if needed — and so on — indefinitely — back into the bag — back out of the bag — until the bell — went. [*Stops tidying, head up, smile.*] But no. [*Smile broader.*] No no. [*Smile off. Resumes tidying.*] I suppose this — might seem strange — this — what shall I say — this what I have said — yes — [*she takes up revolver*] — strange — [*she turns to put revolver in bag*] — were it not — [*about to put revolver in bag she arrests gesture and turns back front*] — were it not — [*she lays down revolver to her right, stops tidying, head up*] — that all seems strange. [*Pause.*] Most strange. [*Pause.*] Never any change. [*Pause.*] And more and more strange. [*Pause. She bends to mound again, takes up last object, i.e. toothbrush, and turns to put it in bag when her attention is drawn to disturbance from* WILLIE. *She cranes back and to her right to see. Pause.*] Weary of your hole, dear? [*Pause.*] Well I can understand that. [*Pause.*] Don't forget your straw. [*Pause.*] Not the crawler you were, poor darling. [*Pause.*] No, not the crawler I gave my heart to. [*Pause.*] The hands and knees, love, try the hands and knees. [*Pause.*] The knees! The knees! [*Pause.*] What a curse, mobility! [*She follows with eyes his progress towards her behind mound, i.e. towards place he occupied at beginning of act.*] Another foot, Willie, and you're home. [*Pause as he observes last foot.*] Ah! [*Turns back front laboriously, rubs neck.*] Crick in my neck admiring you. [*Rubs neck.*] But it's worth it, well worth it. [*Turns slightly towards him.*] Do you know what I dream sometimes? [*Pause.*] What I dream sometimes, Willie. [*Pause.*] That you'll come round and live this side where I could see you. [*Pause. Back front.*] I'd be a different woman. [*Pause.*] Unrecognizable. [*Turning slightly toward him.*] Or just now and then, come round this side just every now and then and let me feast on you. [*Back front.*] But you can't, I know. [*Head down.*] I know. [*Pause. Head up.*] Well anyway — [*looks at toothbrush in her hand*] — can't be long now — [*looks at brush*] — until the bell. [*Top back of* WILLIE's *head appears above slope.* WINNIE *looks closer at brush.*] Fully guaranteed. . . . [*head up*] . . . what's this it was? [WILLIE's *hand appears with handkerchief, spreads it on skull, disappears.*] Genuine pure . . . fully guaranteed . . .

[WILLIE's *hand appears with boater, settles it on head, rakish angle, disap-pears*] . . . genuine pure . . . ah! hog's setae. [*Pause.*] What is a hog ex-actly? [*Pause. Turns slightly towards* WILLIE.] What exactly is a hog, Willie, do you know, I can't remember. [*Pause. Turning a little further, pleading.*] What is a hog, Willie, please!

    [*Pause.*]

WILLIE:  Castrated male swine. [*Happy expression appears on* WINNIE's *face.*] Reared for slaughter.

    [*Happy expression increases.* WILLIE *opens newspaper, hands invisible. Tops of yellow sheets appear on either side of his head.* WINNIE *gazes before her with happy expression.*]

WINNIE:  Oh this *is* a happy day! This will have been another happy day! [*Pause.*] After all. [*Pause.*] So far.

    [*Pause. Happy expression off.* WILLIE *turns page. Pause. He turns another page. Pause.*]

WILLIE:  Opening for smart youth.

    [*Pause.* WINNIE *takes off hat, turns to put it in bag, arrests gesture, turns back front. Smile.*]

WINNIE:  No. [*Smile broader.*] No no. [*Smile off. Puts on hat again, gazes front, pause.*] And now? [*Pause.*] Sing. [*Pause.*] Sing your song, Winnie. [*Pause.*] No? [*Pause.*] Then pray. [*Pause.*] Pray your prayer, Winnie.

    [*Pause.* WILLIE *turns page.*]

WILLIE:  Wanted bright boy.

    [*Pause.* WINNIE *gazes before her.* WILLIE *turns page. Pause. Newspaper disappears. Long pause.*]

WINNIE:  Pray your old prayer, Winnie.

    [*Long pause.*]

CURTAIN

ACT II

*Scene* as before.

    WINNIE *embedded up to neck, hat on head, eyes closed. Her head, which she can no longer turn, nor bow, nor raise, faces front motionless throughout act. Movements of eyes as indicated.*

    *Bag and parasol as before. Revolver conspicuous to her right on mound.*

    *Long pause.*

    *Bell rings loudly. She opens eyes at once. Bell stops. She gazes front. Long pause.*

WINNIE:  Hail, holy light. [*Long pause. She closes her eyes. Bell rings loudly. She opens eyes at once. Bell stops. She gazes front. Long smile. Smile off. Long pause.*] Someone is looking at me still. [*Pause.*] Caring for me still. [*Pause.*] That is what I find so wonderful. [*Pause.*] Eyes on my eyes. [*Pause.*] What is that unforgettable line? [*Pause. Eyes right.*] Willie. [*Pause. Louder.*] Willie. [*Pause. Eyes front.*] May one still speak of time? [*Pause.*] Say it is a long time now, Willie, since I saw you. [*Pause.*] Since I heard you. [*Pause.*] May one? [*Pause.*] One does. [*Smile.*] The old style! [*Smile off.*] There is so little one can speak of. [*Pause.*] One speaks of it all. [*Pause.*] All one can. [*Pause.*] I used to think . . . [*Pause.*] . . . I say I used to think that I would learn to talk alone. [*Pause.*] By that I mean to myself, the wilderness. [*Smile.*] But no. [*Smile broader.*] No no. [*Smile off.*] Ergo you are there. [*Pause.*] Oh no doubt you are dead, like the others, no doubt you have died, or gone away and left me, like the others, it doesn't matter, you are there. [*Pause. Eyes left.*] The bag too is there, the same as ever, I can see it. [*Pause. Eyes right. Louder.*] The bag is there, Willie, as good as ever, the one you gave me that day . . . to go to market. [*Pause. Eyes front.*] That day. [*Pause.*] What day? [*Pause.*] I used to pray. [*Pause.*] I say I used to pray. [*Pause.*] Yes, I must confess I did. [*Smile.*] Not now. [*Smile broader.*] No no. [*Smile off. Pause.*] Then . . . now . . . what difficulties here, for the mind. [*Pause.*] To have been always what I am — and so changed from what I was. [*Pause.*] I am the one, I say the one, then the other. [*Pause.*] Now the one, then the other. [*Pause.*] Now the one, then the other. [*Pause.*] There is so little one can say, one says it all. [*Pause.*] All one can. [*Pause.*] And no truth in it anywhere. [*Pause.*] My arms. [*Pause.*] My breasts. [*Pause.*] What arms? [*Pause.*] What breasts? [*Pause.*] Willie. [*Pause.*] What Willie? [*Sudden vehement affirmation.*] My Willie! [*Eyes right, calling.*] Willie! [*Pause. Louder.*] Willie! [*Pause. Eyes front.*] Ah well, not to know, not to know for sure, great mercy, all I ask. [*Pause.*] Ah yes . . . then . . . now . . . beechen green . . . this . . . Charlie . . . kisses . . . this . . . all that . . . deep trouble for the mind. [*Pause.*] But it does not trouble mine. [*Smile.*] Not now. [*Smile broader.*] No no. [*Smile off. Long pause. She closes eyes. Bell rings loudly. She opens eyes. Pause.*] Eyes float up that seem to close in peace . . . to see . . . in peace. [*Pause.*] Not mine. [*Smile.*] Not now. [*Smile broader.*] No no. [*Smile off. Long pause.*] Willie. [*Pause.*] Do you think the earth has lost its atmosphere, Willie? [*Pause.*] Do you, Willie? [*Pause.*] You have no opinion? [*Pause.*] Well that is like you, you never had any opinion about anything. [*Pause.*] It's understandable. [*Pause.*] Most. [*Pause.*] The earth-ball. [*Pause.*] I sometimes wonder. [*Pause.*] Perhaps not quite all. [*Pause.*] There always remains something. [*Pause.*] Of everything. [*Pause.*] Some remains. [*Pause.*] If the mind were to go. [*Pause.*] It won't of course. [*Pause.*] Not quite. [*Pause.*] Not mine. [*Smile.*] Not now. [*Smile broader.*] No no. [*Smile off. Long pause.*] It might be the eternal cold. [*Pause.*] Everlasting perishing cold. [*Pause.*] Just chance, I take it, happy chance. [*Pause.*] Oh yes, great mercies, great mercies. [*Pause.*] And now? [*Long pause.*] The face. [*Pause.*] The nose. [*She squints down.*] I can see it . . . [*squinting down*] . . . the tip . . . the nostrils . . . breath of life . . . that curve you so admired . . . [*pouts*] . . . a hint of lip . . . [*pouts again*] . . . if I pout them out . . . [*sticks out tongue*] . . . the tongue of course . . . you so admired . . . if I stick it out . . . [*sticks it out again*] . . . the tip . . . [*eyes up*] . . . suspicion of brow . . . eyebrow . . . imagination possibly . . . [*eyes left*] . . . cheek . . . no . . . [*eyes right*] . . . no . . . [*distends cheeks*] . . . even if I puff them out . . . [*eyes left, distends cheeks again*] . . . no . . . no damask. [*Eyes front.*] That is all. [*Pause.*] The bag of course . . . [*eyes left*] . . . a little blurred perhaps . . . but the bag. [*Eyes front. Offhand.*] The earth of course and sky. [*Eyes right.*] The sunshade you gave me . . .

that day . . . [*Pause.*] . . . that day . . . the lake . . . the reeds. [*Eyes front. Pause.*] What day? [*Pause.*] What reeds? [*Long pause. Eyes close. Bell rings loudly. Eyes open. Pause. Eyes right.*] Brownie of course. [*Pause.*] You remember Brownie, Willie, I can see him. [*Pause.*] Brownie is there, Willie, beside me. [*Pause. Eyes front.*] That is all. [*Pause.*] What would I do without them? [*Pause.*] What would I do without them, when words fail? [*Pause.*] Gaze before me, with compressed lips. [*Long pause while she does so.*] I cannot. [*Pause.*] Ah yes, great mercies, great mercies. [*Long pause. Low.*] Sometimes I hear sounds. [*Listening expression. Normal voice.*] But not often. [*Pause.*] They are a boon, sounds are a boon, they help me . . . through the day. [*Smile.*] The old style! [*Smile off.*] Yes, those are happy days, when there are sounds. [*Pause.*] When I hear sounds. [*Pause.*] I used to think . . . [*Pause.*] . . . I say I used to think they were in my head. [*Smile.*] But no. [*Smile broader.*] No no. [*Smile off.*] That was just logic. [*Pause.*] Reason. [*Pause.*] I have not lost my reason. [*Pause.*] No yet. [*Pause.*] Not all. [*Pause.*] Some remains. [*Pause.*] Sounds. [*Pause.*] Like little . . . sunderings, little falls . . . apart. [*Pause. Low.*] It's things, Willie. [*Pause. Normal voice.*] In the bag, outside the bag. [*Pause.*] Ah yes, things have their life, that is what I always say, *things* have a life. [*Pause.*] Take my looking-glass, it doesn't need me. [*Pause.*] The bell. [*Pause.*] It hurts like a knife. [*Pause.*] A gouge. [*Pause.*] One cannot ignore it. [*Pause.*] How often . . . [*Pause.*] . . . I say how often I have said, Ignore it, Winnie, ignore the bell, pay no heed, just sleep and wake, sleep and wake, as you please, open and close the eyes, as you please, or in the way you find most helpful. [*Pause.*] Open and close the eyes, Winnie, open and close, always that. [*Pause.*] But no. [*Smile.*] Not now. [*Smile broader.*] No no. [*Smile off. Pause.*] What now? [*Pause.*] What now, Willie? [*Long pause.*] There is my story of course, when all else fails. [*Pause.*] A life. [*Smile.*] A long life. [*Smile off.*] Beginning in the womb, where life used to begin, Mildred has memories, she will have memories, of the womb, before she dies, the mother's womb. [*Pause.*] She is now four or five already and has recently been given a big waxen dolly. [*Pause.*] Fully clothed, complete outfit. [*Pause.*] Shoes, socks, undies, complete set, frilly frock, gloves. [*Pause.*] White mesh. [*Pause.*] A little white straw hat with a chin elastic. [*Pause.*] Pearly necklet. [*Pause.*] A little picture-book with legends in real print to go under her arm when she takes her walk. [*Pause.*] China blue eyes that open and shut. [*Pause. Narrative.*] The sun was not well up when Milly rose, descended the steep . . . [*Pause.*] . . . slipped on her nightgown, descended all along the steep wooden stairs, backwards on all fours, though she had been forbidden to do so, entered the . . . [*Pause.*] . . . tiptoed down the silent passage, entered the nursery and began to undress Dolly. [*Pause.*] Crept under the table and began to undress Dolly. [*Pause.*] Scolding her . . . the while. [*Pause.*] Suddenly a mouse — [*Long pause.*] Gently, Winnie. [*Long pause. Calling.*] Willie! [*Pause. Louder.*] Willie! [*Pause. Mild reproach.*] I sometimes find your attitude a little strange, Willie, all this time, it is not like you to be wantonly cruel. [*Pause.*] Strange? [*Pause.*] No. [*Smile.*] Not here. [*Smile broader.*] Not now. [*Smile off.*] And yet . . . [*Suddenly anxious.*] I do hope nothing is amiss. [*Eyes right, loud.*] Is all well, dear? [*Pause. Eyes front. To herself.*] God grant he did not go in head foremost! [*Eyes right, loud.*] You're not stuck, Willie? [*Pause. Do.*] You're not jammed, Willie? [*Eyes front, distressed.*] Perhaps he is crying out for help all this time and I do not hear him! [*Pause.*] I do of course hear cries. [*Pause.*] But they are in my head surely. [*Pause.*] Is it possible that . . . [*Pause. With finality.*] No no, my head was always full of cries. [*Pause.*] Faint confused cries. [*Pause.*] They come. [*Pause.*] Then go. [*Pause.*] As on a wind. [*Pause.*] That is what I find so wonderful. [*Pause.*] They cease. [*Pause.*] Ah yes, great mercies, great mercies. [*Pause.*] The day is now well advanced. [*Smile. Smile off.*] And yet it is perhaps a little soon for my song. [*Pause.*] To sing too soon is fatal, I always find. [*Pause.*] On the other hand it is possible to leave it too late. [*Pause.*] The bell goes for sleep and one has not sung. [*Pause.*] The whole day has flown — [*smile, smile off*] — flown by, quite by, and no song of any class, kind or description. [*Pause.*] There is a problem here. [*Pause.*] One cannot sing . . . just like that, no. [*Pause.*] It bubbles up, for some unknown reason, the time is ill chosen, one chokes it back. [*Pause.*] One says, Now is the time, it is now or never, and one cannot. [*Pause.*] Simply cannot sing. [*Pause.*] Not a note. [*Pause.*] Another thing, Willie, while we are on this subject. [*Pause.*] The sadness after song. [*Pause.*] Have you run across that, Willie? [*Pause.*] In the course of your experience. [*Pause.*] No? [*Pause.*] Sadness after intimate sexual intercourse one is familiar with of course. [*Pause.*] You would concur with Aristotle there, Willie, I fancy. [*Pause.*] Yes, that one knows and is prepared to face. [*Pause.*] But after song . . . [*Pause.*] It does not last of course. [*Pause.*] That is what I find so wonderful. [*Pause.*] It wears away. [*Pause.*] What are those exquisite lines? [*Pause.*] Go forget me why should something o'er that something shadow fling . . . go forget me . . . why should sorrow . . . brightly smile . . . go forget me . . . never hear me . . . sweetly smile . . . brightly sing . . . [*Pause. With a sigh.*] One loses one's classics. [*Pause.*] Oh not all. [*Pause.*] A part. [*Pause.*] A part remains. [*Pause.*] That is what I find so wonderful, a part remains, of one's classics, to help one through the day. [*Pause.*] Oh yes, many mercies, many mercies. [*Pause.*] And now? [*Pause.*] And now, Willie? [*Long pause.*] I call to the eye of the mind . . . Mr Shower — or Cooker. [*She closes her eyes. Bell rings loudly. She opens her eyes. Pause.*] Hand in hand, in the other hands bags. [*Pause.*] Getting on . . . in life. [*Pause.*] No longer young, not yet old. [*Pause.*] Standing there gaping at me. [*Pause.*] Can't have been a bad bosom, he says, in its day. [*Pause.*] Seen worse shoulders, he says, in my time. [*Pause.*] Does she feel her legs? he says. [*Pause.*] Is there any life in her legs? he says. [*Pause.*] Has she anything on underneath? he says. [*Pause.*] Ask her, he says, I'm shy. [*Pause.*] Ask her what? she says. [*Pause.*] Is there any life in her legs. [*Pause.*] Has she anything on underneath. [*Pause.*] Ask her yourself, she says. [*Pause. With sudden violence.*] Let go of me for Christ sake and drop! [*Pause. Do.*] Drop dead! [*Smile.*] But no. [*Smile broader.*] No no. [*Smile off.*] I watch them recede. [*Pause.*] Hand in hand — and the bags. [*Pause.*] Dim. [*Pause.*] Then gone. [*Pause.*] Last human kind — to stray this way. [*Pause.*] Up to date. [*Pause.*] And now? [*Pause. Low.*] Help. [*Pause. Do.*] Help, Willie. [*Pause. Do.*] No? [*Long pause. Narrative.*] Suddenly a mouse . . . [*Pause.*] Suddenly a mouse ran up her little thigh and Mildred, dropping Dolly in her fright, began to scream — [WINNIE *gives a sudden piercing scream*] — and screamed and screamed — [WINNIE *screams twice*] — screamed and screamed and screamed and screamed till all came running, in their night attire, papa, mamma, Bibby and . . . old Annie, to see what was the matter . . . [*Pause.*] . . . what on earth could possibly be the matter. [*Pause.*] Too late. [*Pause.*] Too late. [*Long pause. Just audible.*] Willie. [*Pause. Normal voice.*] Ah well, not long now, Winnie, can't be long now, until the bell for sleep. [*Pause.*] Then you may close your eyes, then you must close your eyes — and keep them closed. [*Pause.*] Why say that again? [*Pause.*] I used to think . . . [*Pause.*] . . . I say I used to think there was no difference between one fraction of a second and the next. [*Pause.*] I used to say . . . [*pause*] . . . I say I used to say, Winnie, you are changeless, there is never any difference between one fraction of a second and the next. [*Pause.*] Why bring that up again? [*Pause.*] There is so little one can bring up, one brings up all. [*Pause.*] All one can. [*Pause.*] My neck is hurting me! [*Pause.*] Ah that's better. [*With mild irritation.*] Everything within reason. [*Long pause.*] I can do no more. [*Pause.*] Say no more. [*Pause.*] But I must say more. [*Pause.*] Problem here. [*Pause.*] No, something must move, in the world, I can't any more. [*Pause.*] A zephyr. [*Pause.*] A breath. [*Pause.*] What are those immortal lines? [*Pause.*] It might be the eternal dark. [*Pause.*] Black night without end. [*Pause.*] Just chance, I take it, happy chance. [*Pause.*] Oh yes, abounding mercies. [*Long pause.*] And now? [*Pause.*] And now, Willie? [*Long pause.*] That day. [*Pause.*] The pink fizz. [*Pause.*] The flute glasses. [*Pause.*] The last guest gone. [*Pause.*] The last bumper with the bodies nearly touching. [*Pause.*] The look. [*Long pause.*] I hear cries. [*Pause.*] Sing. [*Pause.*] Sing your old song, Winnie.

[*Long pause. Suddenly alert expression. Eyes switch right.* WILLIE'*s head appears to her right round corner of mound. He is on all fours, dressed to kill — top hat, morning coat, striped trousers, etc., white gloves in hand. Very long bushy white Battle of Britain moustache. He halts, gazes front, smooths moustache. He emerges completely from behind mound, turns to his left, halts, looks up at* WINNIE. *He advances on all fours towards centre, halts, turns head front, gazes front, strokes moustache, straightens tie, adjusts hat, advances a little further, halts, takes off hat and looks up at* WINNIE. *He is now not far from centre and within her field of vision. Unable to sustain effort of looking up he sinks head to ground.*]

WINNIE: [*mondaine*] Well this is an unexpected pleasure! [*Pause.*] Reminds me of the day you came whining for my hand. [*Pause.*] I worship you, Winnie, be mine. [*He looks up.*] Life a mockery without Win. [*She goes off into a giggle.*] What a get up, you do look a sight! [*Giggles.*] Where are the flowers? [*Pause.*] That smile today. [WILLIE *sinks head.*] What's that on your neck, an anthrax? [*Pause.*] Want to watch that, Willie, before it gets a hold on you. [*Pause.*] Where were you all this time? [*Pause.*] What were you doing all this time? [*Pause.*] Changing? [*Pause.*] Did you not hear me screaming for you? [*Pause.*] Did you get stuck in your hole? [*Pause. He looks up.*] That's right, Willie, look at me. [*Pause.*] Feast your old eyes, Willie. [*Pause.*] Does anything remain? [*Pause.*] Any remains? [*Pause.*] No? [*Pause.*] I haven't been able to look after it, you know. [*He sinks his head.*] You are still recognizable, in a way. [*Pause.*]

Are you thinking of coming to live this side now . . . for a bit maybe? [*Pause.*] No? [*Pause.*] Just a brief call? [*Pause.*] Have you gone deaf, Willie? [*Pause.*] Dumb? [*Pause.*] Oh I know you were never one to talk, I worship you Winnie be mine and then nothing from that day forth only titbits from Reynolds' News. [*Eyes front. Pause.*] Ah well, what matter, that's what I always say, it will have been a happy day, after all, another happy day. [*Pause.*] Not long now, Winnie. [*Pause.*] I hear cries. [*Pause.*] Do you ever hear cries, Willie? [*Pause.*] No? [*Eyes back on* WILLIE.] [*Pause.*] Look at me again, Willie. [*Pause.*] Once more, Willie. [*He looks up. Happily.*] Ah! [*Pause. Shocked.*] What ails you, Willie, I never saw such an expression! [*Pause.*] Put on your hat, dear, it's the sun, don't stand on ceremony, I won't mind. [*He drops hat and gloves and starts to crawl up mound towards her. Gleeful.*] Oh I say, this is terrific! [*He halts, clinging to mound with one hand, reaching up with the other.*] Come on, dear, put a bit of jizz into it, I'll cheer you on. [*Pause.*] Is it me you're after, Willie . . . or is it something else? [*Pause.*] Do you want to touch my face . . . again? [*Pause.*] Is it a kiss you're after, Willie . . . or is it something else? [*Pause.*] There was a time when I could have given you a hand. [*Pause.*] And then a time before that again when I did give you a hand. [*Pause.*] You were always in dire need of a hand, Willie. [*He slithers back to foot of mound and lies with face to ground.*] Brrum! [*Pause. He rises to hands and knees, raises his face towards her.*] Have another go, Willie, I'll cheer you on. [*Pause.*] Don't look at me like that! [*Pause. Vehement.*] Don't look at me like that! [*Pause. Low.*] Have you gone off your head, Willie? [*Pause. Do.*] Out of your poor old wits, Willie?
     [*Pause.*]
WILLIE: [*just audible*] Win.
     [*Pause.* WINNIE's *eyes front. Happy expression appears, grows.*]
WINNIE:  Win! [*Pause.*] Oh this *is* a happy day, this will have been another happy day! [*Pause.*] After all. [*Pause.*] So far.
     [*Pause. She hums tentatively beginning of song, then sings softly, musical-box tune.*]
Though I say not
What I may not
Let you hear,
Yet the swaying
Dance is saying,
Love me dear!
Every touch of fingers
Tells me what I know,
Says for you,
It's true, it's true,
You love me so!
     [*Pause. Happy expression off. She closes her eyes. Bell rings loudly. She opens her eyes. She smiles, gazing front. She turns her eyes, smiling, to* WILLIE, *still on his hands and knees looking up at her. Smile off. They look at each other. Long pause.*]

CURTAIN

# Lorraine Hansberry

# A Raisin in the Sun

## CHARACTERS

RUTH YOUNGER
TRAVIS YOUNGER
WALTER YOUNGER, "BROTHER"
BENEATHA YOUNGER
LENA YOUNGER, "MAMA"
JOSEPH ASAGAI
GEORGE MURCHISON
KARL LINDNER
BOBO
MOVING MEN

*The action of the play is set in Chicago's Southside, sometime between World War II and the present.*

## ACT ONE

*Scene I.* Friday morning.
*Scene II.* The following morning.

## ACT TWO

*Scene I.* Later, the same day.
*Scene II.* Friday night, a few weeks later.
*Scene III.* Moving day, one week later.

## ACT THREE

An hour later.

## ACT I

SCENE I———*The* YOUNGER *living room would be a comfortable and well-ordered room if it were not for a number of indestructible contradictions to this state of being. Its furnishings are typical and undistinguished and their primary feature now is that they have clearly had to accommodate the living of too many people for too many years — and they are tired. Still, we can see that at some time, a time probably no longer remembered by the family (except perhaps for* MAMA*) the furnishings of this room were actually selected with care and love and even hope — and brought to this apartment and arranged with taste and pride.*

*That was a long time ago. Now the once loved pattern of the couch upholstery*

529

has to fight to show itself from under acres of crocheted doilies and couch covers which have themselves finally come to be more important than the upholstery. And here a table or a chair has been moved to disguise the worn places in the carpet; but the carpet has fought back by showing its weariness, with depressing uniformity, elsewhere on its surface.

Weariness has, in fact, won in this room. Everything has been polished, washed, sat on, used, scrubbed too often. All pretenses but living itself have long since vanished from the very atmosphere of this room.

Moreover, a section of this room, for it is not really a room unto itself, though the landlord's lease would make it seem so, slopes backward to provide a small kitchen area, where the family prepares the meals that are eaten in the living room proper, which must also serve as dining room. The single window that has been provided for these "two" rooms is located in this kitchen area. The sole natural light the family may enjoy in the course of a day is only that which fights its way through this little window.

At left, a door leads to a bedroom which is shared by MAMA and her daughter, BENEATHA. At right, opposite, is a second room (which in the beginning of the life of this apartment was probably a breakfast room) which serves as a bedroom for WALTER and his wife, RUTH.

[At Rise: It is morning dark in the living room. TRAVIS is asleep on the make-down bed at center. An alarm clock sounds from within the bedroom at right, and presently RUTH enters from that room and closes the door behind her. She crosses sleepily toward the window. As she passes her sleeping son she reaches down and shakes him a little. At the window she raises the shade and a dusky Southside morning light comes in feebly. She fills a pot with water and puts it on to boil. She calls to the boy, between yawns, in a slightly muffled voice.

RUTH is about thirty. We can see that she was a pretty girl, even exceptionally so, but now it is apparent that life has been little that she expected, and disappointment has already begun to hang in her face. In a few years, before thirty-five even, she will be known among her people as a "settled woman."

She crosses to her son and gives him a good, final, rousing shake.]
RUTH: Come on now, boy, it's seven thirty! [Her son sits up at last, in a stupor of sleepiness.] I say hurry up, Travis! You ain't the only person in the world got to use a bathroom! [The child, a sturdy, handsome little boy of ten or eleven, drags himself out of the bed and almost blindly takes his towels and "today's clothes" from drawers and a closet and goes out to the bathroom, which is in an outside hall and which is shared by another family or families on the same floor. RUTH crosses to the bedroom door at right and opens it and calls in to her husband] Walter Lee! . . . It's after seven thirty! Lemme see you do some waking up in there now! [she waits] You better get up from there, man! It's after seven thirty I tell you. [She waits again.] All right, you just go ahead and lay there and next thing you know Travis be finished and Mr. Johnson'll be in there and you'll be fussing and cussing round here like a mad man! And be late too! [She waits, at the end of patience.] Walter Lee — it's time for you to get up!
[She waits another second and then starts to go into the bedroom, but is

*apparently satisfied that her husband has begun to get up. She stops, pulls the door to, and returns to the kitchen area. She wipes her face with a moist cloth and runs her fingers through her sleep-disheveled hair in a vain effort and ties an apron around her housecoat. The bedroom door at right opens and her husband stands in the doorway in his pajamas, which are rumpled and mismated. He is a lean, intense young man in his middle thirties, inclined to quick nervous movements and erratic speech habits — and always in his voice there is a quality of indictment.]*

WALTER: Is he out yet?

RUTH: What you mean *out*? He ain't hardly got in there good yet.

WALTER: [*wandering in, still more oriented to sleep than to a new day*] Well, what was you doing all that yelling for if I can't even get in there yet? [*stopping and thinking*] Check coming today?

RUTH: They *said* Saturday and this is just Friday and I hopes to God you ain't going to get up here first thing this morning and start talking to me 'bout no money — 'cause I 'bout don't want to hear it.

WALTER: Something the matter with you this morning?

RUTH: No — I'm just sleepy as the devil. What kind of eggs you want?

WALTER: Not scrambled. [RUTH *starts to scramble eggs.*] Paper come? [RUTH *points impatiently to the rolled up* Tribune *on the table, and he gets it and spreads it out and vaguely reads the front page.*] Set off another bomb yesterday.

RUTH: [*maximum indifference*] Did they?

WALTER: [*looking up*] What's the matter with you?

RUTH: Ain't nothing the matter with me. And don't keep asking me that this morning.

WALTER: Ain't nobody bothering you. [*reading the news of the day absently again*] Say Colonel McCormick is sick.

RUTH: [*affecting tea-party interest*] Is he now? Poor thing.

WALTER: [*sighing and looking at his watch*] Oh, me. [*He waits.*] Now what is that boy doing in the bathroom all this time? He just going to have to start getting up earlier. I can't be being late to work on account of him fooling around in here.

RUTH: [*turning on him*] Oh, no he ain't going to be getting up no earlier no such thing! It ain't his fault that he can't get to bed no earlier nights 'cause he got a bunch of crazy good-for-nothing clowns sitting up running their mouths in what is supposed to be his bedroom after ten o'clock at night . . .

WALTER: That's what you mad about, ain't it? The things I want to talk about with my friends just couldn't be important in your mind, could they?

[*He rises and finds a cigarette in her handbag on the table and crosses to the little window and looks out, smoking and deeply enjoying this first one.*]

RUTH: [*almost matter of factly, a complaint too automatic to deserve emphasis*] Why you always got to smoke before you eat in the morning?

WALTER: [*at the window*] Just look at 'em down there . . . Running and racing to work . . . [*he turns and faces his wife and watches her a moment at the stove, and then, suddenly*] You look young this morning, baby.

RUTH: [*indifferently*] Yeah?

WALTER: Just for a second — stirring them eggs. It's gone now — just for a second it was — you looked real young again. [*then, drily*] It's gone now — you look like yourself again.

RUTH: Man, if you don't shut up and leave me alone.

WALTER: [*looking out to the street again*] First thing a man ought to learn in life is not to make love to no colored woman first thing in the morning. You all some evil people at eight o'clock in the morning.

> [TRAVIS *appears in the hall doorway, almost fully dressed and quite wide awake now, his towels and pajamas across his shoulders. He opens the door and signals for his father to make the bathroom in a hurry.*]

TRAVIS: [*watching the bathroom*] Daddy, come on!

> [WALTER *gets his bathroom utensils and flies out to the bathroom.*]

RUTH: Sit down and have your breakfast, Travis.

TRAVIS: Mama, this is Friday. [*gleefully*] Check coming tomorrow, huh?

RUTH: You get your mind off money and eat your breakfast.

TRAVIS: [*eating*] This is the morning we supposed to bring the fifty cents to school.

RUTH: Well, I ain't got no fifty cents this morning.

TRAVIS: Teacher say we have to.

RUTH: I don't care what teacher say. I ain't got it. Eat your breakfast, Travis.

TRAVIS: I *am* eating.

RUTH: Hush up now and just eat!

> [*The boy gives her an exasperated look for her lack of understanding, and eats grudgingly.*]

TRAVIS: You think Grandmama would have it?

RUTH: No! And I want you to stop asking your grandmother for money, you hear me?

TRAVIS: [*outraged*] Gaaaleee! I don't ask her , she just gimme it sometimes!

RUTH: Travis Willard Younger — I got too much on me this morning to be . . .

TRAVIS: Maybe Daddy . . .

RUTH: *Travis!*

> [*The boy hushes abruptly. They are both quiet and tense for several seconds.*]

TRAVIS: [*presently*] Could I maybe go carry some groceries in front of the supermarket for a little while after school then?

RUTH: Just hush, I said. [*Travis jabs his spoon into his cereal bowl viciously, and rests his head in anger upon his fists.*] If you through eating, you can get over there and make up your bed.

> [*The boy obeys stiffly and crosses the room, almost mechanically, to the bed and more or less carefully folds the covering. He carries the bedding into his mother's room and returns with his books and cap.*]

TRAVIS: [*sulking and standing apart from her unnaturally*] I'm gone.

RUTH: [*looking up from the stove to inspect him automatically*] Come here. [*He crosses to her and she studies his head.*] If you don't take this comb and fix this here head, you better! [TRAVIS *puts down his books with a great sigh of oppression, and crosses to the mirror. His mother mutters under her breath about his "stubbornness."*] 'Bout to march out of here with that head looking just like chickens slept in it! I just don't know where you get your stubborn ways . . . And get your jacket, too. Looks chilly out this morning.

TRAVIS: [*with conspicuously brushed hair and jacket*] I'm gone.

RUTH: Get carfare and milk money — [*waving one finger*] — and not a single penny for no caps, you hear me?

TRAVIS: [*with sullen politeness*] Yes'm.

> [*He turns in outrage to leave. His mother watches after him as in his frustration he approaches the door almost comically. When she speaks to him, her voice has become a very gentle tease.*]

RUTH: [*mocking; as she thinks he would say it*] Oh, Mama makes me so mad sometimes, I don't know what to do! [*She waits and continues to his back as he stands stock-still in front of the door.*] I wouldn't kiss that woman good-bye for nothing in this world this morning! [*The boy finally turns around and rolls his eyes at her, knowing the mood has changed and he is vindicated; he does not, however, move toward her yet.*] Not for nothing in this world! [*She finally laughs aloud at him and holds out her arms to him and we see that it is a way between them, very old and practiced. He crosses to her and allows her to embrace him warmly but keeps his face fixed with masculine rigidity. She holds him back from her presently and looks at him and runs her fingers over the features of his face. With utter gentleness —*] Now — whose little old angry man are you?

TRAVIS: [*The masculinity and gruffness start to fade at last.*] Aw gaalee — Mama . . .

RUTH: [*mimicking*] Aw — gaaaaalleeeee, Mama! [*She pushes him, with rough playfulness and finality, toward the door.*] Get on out of here or you going to be late.

TRAVIS: [*in the face of love, new aggressiveness*] Mama, could I *please* go carry groceries?

RUTH: Honey, it's starting to get so cold evenings.

WALTER: [*coming in from the bathroom and drawing a make-believe gun from a make-believe holster and shooting at his son.*] What is it he wants to do?

RUTH: Go carry groceries after school at the supermarket.

WALTER: Well, let him go . . .

TRAVIS: [*quickly, to the ally*] I *have* to — she won't gimme the fifty cents . . .

WALTER: [*to his wife only*] Why not?

RUTH: [*simply, and with flavor*] 'Cause we don't have it.

WALTER: [*to* RUTH *only*] What you tell the boy things like that for? [*Reaching down into his pants with a rather important gesture*] Here, son —

> [*He hands the boy the coin, but his eyes are directed to his wife's.* TRAVIS *takes the money happily.*]

TRAVIS: Thanks, Daddy.

> [*He starts out.* RUTH *watches both of them with murder in her eyes.* WALTER *stands and stares back at her with defiance, and suddenly reaches into his pocket again on an afterthought.*]

WALTER: [*without even looking at his son, still staring hard at his wife*] In fact, here's another fifty cents . . . Buy yourself some fruit today — or take a taxicab to school or something!

TRAVIS: Whoopee —

> [*He leaps up and clasps his father around the middle with his legs, and they face each other in mutual appreciation; slowly* WALTER LEE *peeks*]

*around the boy to catch the violent rays from his wife's eyes and draws his
head back as if shot.*]

WALTER: You better get down now — and get to school, man.

TRAVIS: [*at the door*] O.K. Good-bye. [*He exits.*]

WALTER: [*after him, pointing with pride*] That's my boy. [*She looks at him in disgust
and turns back to her work.*] You know what I was thinking 'bout in the
bathroom this morning?

RUTH: No.

WALTER: How come you always try to be so pleasant!

RUTH: What is there to be pleasant 'bout!

WALTER: You want to know what I was thinking 'bout in the bathroom or not!

RUTH: I know what you thinking 'bout.

WALTER: [*ignoring her*] 'Bout what me and Willy Harris was talking about last night.

RUTH: [*immediately — a refrain*] Willy Harris is a good-for-nothing loud mouth.

WALTER: Anybody who talks to me has got to be a good-for-nothing loud mouth,
ain't he? And what you know about who is just a good-for-nothing loud
mouth? Charlie Atkins was just a "good-for-nothing loud mouth" too, wasn't
he! When he wanted me to go in the dry-cleaning business with him. And
now — he's grossing a hundred thousand a year. A hundred thousand dollars a
year! You still call *him* a loud mouth!

RUTH: [*bitterly*] Oh, Walter Lee . . .

[*She folds her head on her arms over the table.*]

WALTER: [*rising and coming to her and standing over her*] You tired, ain't you? Tired
of everything. Me, the boy, the way we live — this beat-up hole — everything.
Ain't you? [*She doesn't look up, doesn't answer.*] So tired — moaning and
groaning all the time, but you wouldn't do nothing to help, would you? You
couldn't be on my side that long for nothing, could you?

RUTH: Walter, please leave me alone.

WALTER: A man needs for a woman to back him up . . .

RUTH: Walter —

WALTER: Mama would listen to you. You know she listen to you more than she do
me and Bennie. She think more of you. All you have to do is just sit down with
her when you drinking your coffee one morning and talking 'bout things like
you do and — [*He sits down beside her and demonstrates graphically what he
thinks her methods and tone should be.*] — you just sip your coffee, see, and say
easy like that you been thinking 'bout that deal Walter Lee is so interested in,
'bout the store and all, and sip some more coffee, like what you saying ain't
really that important to you — And the next thing you know, she be listening
good and asking you questions and when I come home — I can tell her the
details. This ain't no fly-by-night proposition, baby. I mean we figured it out,
me and Willy and Bobo.

RUTH: [*with a frown*] Bobo?

WALTER: Yeah. You see, this little liquor store we got in mind cost seventy-five
thousand and we figured the initial investment on the place be 'bout thirty
thousand, see. That be ten thousand each. Course, there's a couple of hundred
you got to pay so's you don't spend your life just waiting for them clowns to let
your license get approved —

RUTH: You mean graft?

WALTER: [*frowning impatiently*] Don't call it that. See there, that just goes to show you what women understand about the world. Baby, don't *nothing* happen for you in this world 'less you pay *somebody* off!

RUTH: Walter, leave me alone! [*She raises her head and stares at him vigorously — then says, more quietly.*] Eat your eggs, they gonna be cold.

WALTER: [*straightening up from her and looking off*] That's it. There you are. Man say to his woman: I got me a dream. His woman say: Eat your eggs. [*sadly, but gaining in power*] Man says: I got to take hold of this here world, baby! And a woman will say: Eat your eggs and go to work. [*passionately now*] Man say: I got to change my life. I'm choking to death, baby! And his woman say — [*in utter anguish as he brings his fists down on his thighs*] — Your eggs is getting cold!

RUTH: [*softly*] Walter, that ain't none of our money.

WALTER: [*not listening at all or even looking at her*] This morning, I was lookin' in the mirror and thinking about it . . . I'm thirty-five years old; I been married eleven years and I got a boy who sleeps in the living room — [*very, very quietly*] — and all I got to give him is stories about how rich white people live . . .

RUTH: Eat your eggs, Walter.

WALTER: *Damn my eggs . . . damn all the eggs that ever was!*

RUTH: Then go to work.

WALTER: [*looking up at her*] See — I'm trying to talk to you 'bout myself — [*shaking his head with the repetition*] — and all you can say is eat them eggs and go to work.

RUTH: [*wearily*] Honey, you never say nothing new. I listen to you every day, every night and every morning, and you never say nothing new. [*shrugging*] So you would rather *be* Mr. Arnold than be his chauffeur. So — I would *rather* be living in Buckingham Palace.

WALTER: That is just what is wrong with the colored woman in this world . . . Don't understand about building their men up and making 'em feel like they somebody. Like they can do something.

RUTH: [*drily, but to hurt*] There *are* colored men who do things.

WALTER: No thanks to the colored woman.

RUTH: Well, being a colored woman, I guess I can't help myself none.

[*She rises and gets the ironing board and sets it up and attacks a huge pile of rough-dried clothes, sprinkling them in preparation for the ironing and then rolling them into tight fat balls.*]

WALTER: [*mumbling*] We one group of men tied to a race of women with small minds.

[*His sister BENEATHA enters. She is about twenty, as slim and intense as her brother. She is not as pretty as her sister-in-law, but her lean almost intellectual face has a handsomeness of its own. She wears a bright-red flannel nightie, and her thick hair stands wildly about her head. Her speech is a mixture of many things; it is different from the rest of the family's insofar as education has permeated her sense of English — and perhaps the Midwest rather than the South has finally — at last — won out in her inflection; but not altogether, because over all of it is a soft slurring and transformed use of vowels which is the decided influence of*]

*the Southside. She passes through the room without looking at either* RUTH
*or* WALTER *and goes to the outside door and looks, a little blindly, out to the
bathroom. She sees that it has been lost to the Johnsons. She closes the
door with a sleepy vengeance and crosses to the table and sits down a little
defeated.*]

WALTER: You should get up earlier.

BENEATHA: [*Her face in her hands. She is still fighting the urge to go back to bed.*]
Really — would you suggest dawn? Where's the paper?

WALTER: [*pushing the paper across the table to her as he studies her almost clini-
cally, as though he has never seen her before*] You a horrible-looking chick at
this hour.

BENEATHA: [*drily*] Good morning, everybody.

WALTER: [*senselessly*] How is school coming?

BENEATHA: [*in the same spirit*] Lovely. Lovely. And you know, biology is the
greatest. [*looking up at him*] I dissected something that looked like you yesterday.

WALTER: I just wondered if you've made up your mind and everything.

BENEATHA: [*gaining in sharpness and impatience*] And what did I answer yesterday
morning — and the day before that?

RUTH: [*from the ironing board, like someone disinterested and old*] Don't be so nasty,
Bennie.

BENEATHA: [*still to her brother*] And the day before that and the day before that!

WALTER: [*defensively*] I'm interested in you. Something wrong with that? Ain't
many girls who decide —

WALTER: *and* BENEATHA: [*in unison*] — "to be a doctor."
[*Silence.*]

WALTER: Have we figured out yet just exactly how much medical school is going to
cost?

RUTH: Walter Lee, why don't you leave that girl alone and get out of here to work?

BENEATHA: [*exits to the bathroom and bangs on the door*] Come on out of there,
please!
[*She comes back into the room.*]

WALTER: [*looking at his sister intently*] You know the check is coming tomorrow.

BENEATHA: [*turning on him with a sharpness all her own*] That money belongs to
Mama, Walter, and it's for her to decide how she wants to use it. I don't care if
she wants to buy a house or a rocket ship or just nail it up somewhere and look
at it. It's hers. Not ours — *hers*.

WALTER: [*bitterly*] Now ain't that fine! You just got your mother's interest at heart,
ain't you, girl? You such a nice girl — but if Mama got that money she can
always take a few thousand and help you through school too — can't she?

BENEATHA: I have never asked anyone around here to do anything for me!

WALTER: No! And the line between asking and just accepting when the times comes
is big and wide — ain't it!

BENEATHA: [*with fury*] What do you want from me, Brother — that I quit school or
just drop dead, which!

WALTER: I don't want nothing but for you to stop acting holy 'round here. Me and
Ruth done made some sacrifices for you — why can't you do something for the
family?

RUTH: Walter, don't be dragging me in it.

WALTER: You are in it — Don't you get up and go work in somebody's kitchen for the last three years to help put clothes on her back?

RUTH: Oh, Walter — that's not fair . . .

WALTER: It ain't that nobody expects you to get on your knees and say thank you, Brother; thank you, Ruth; thank you, Mama — and thank you, Travis, for wearing the same pair of shoes for two semesters —

BENEATHA: [*dropping to her knees*] Well — I *do* — al right? — thank everybody . . . and forgive me for ever wanting to be anything at all . . . forgive me, forgive me!

RUTH: Please stop it! Your mama'll hear you.

WALTER: Who the hell told you you had to be a doctor? If you so crazy 'bout messing 'round with sick people — then go be a nurse like other women — or just get married and be quiet . . .

BENEATHA: Well — you finelly got it said . . . It took you three years but you finally got it said. Walter, give up; leave me alone — it's Mama's money.

WALTER: *He was my father, too!*

BENEATHA: So what? He was mine, too — and Travis' grandfather — but the insurance money belongs to Mama. Picking on me is not going to make her give it to you to invest in any liquor stores — [*underbreath, dropping into a chair*] — and I for one say, God bless Mama for that!

WALTER: [*to* RUTH] See — did you hear? Did you hear!

RUTH: Honey, please go to work.

WALTER: Nobody in this house is ever going to understand me.

BENEATHA: Because you're a nut.

WALTER: Who's a nut?

BENEATHA: You — you are a nut. Thee is mad, boy.

WALTER: [*looking at his wife and his sister from the door, very sadly*] The world's most backward race of people, and that's a fact.

BENEATHA: [*turning slowly in her chair*] And then there are all those prophets who would lead us out of the wilderness — [WALTER *slams out of the house*] — into the swamps!

RUTH: Bennie, why you always gotta be pickin' on your brother? Can't you be a little sweeter sometimes? [*Door opens.* WALTER *walks in.*]

WALTER: [*to* RUTH] I need some money for carfare.

RUTH: [*looks at him, then warms; teasing, but tenderly*] Fifty cents? [*She goes to her bag and gets money.*] Here, take a taxi.

> [WALTER *exits.* MAMA *enters. She is a woman in her early sixties, full-bodied and strong. She is one of those women of a certain grace and beauty who wear it so unobstrusively that it takes a while to notice. Her dark-brown face is surrounded by the total whiteness of her hair, and, being a woman who has adjusted to many things in life and overcome many more, her face is full of strength. She has, we can see, wit and faith of a kind that keeps her eyes lit and full of interest and expectancy. She is, in a word, a beautiful woman. Her bearing is perhaps most like the noble bearing of the women of the Hereros of Southwest Africa — rather as if she imagines that as she walks she still bears a basket or a vessel upon her head. Her speech, on the other hand, is as careless as her carriage is precise — she is*

*inclined to slur everything — but her voice is perhaps not so much quiet as simply soft.*]

MAMA: Who that 'round here slamming doors at this hour?
   [*She crosses through the room, goes to the window, opens it, and brings in a feeble little plant growing doggedly in a small pot on the window sill. She feels the dirt and puts it back out.*]

RUTH: That was Walter Lee. He and Bennie was at it again.

MAMA: My children and they tempers. Lord, if this little old plant don't get more sun than it's been getting it ain't never going to see spring again. [*She turns from the window.*] What's the matter with you this morning, Ruth? You looks right peaked. You aiming to iron all them things? Leave some for me. I'll get to 'em this afternoon. Bennie honey, it's too drafty for you to be sitting 'round half dressed. Where's your robe?

BENEATHA: In the cleaners.

MAMA: Well, go get mine and put it on.

BENEATHA: I'm not cold, Mama, honest.

MAMA: I know — but you so thin . . .

BENEATHA: [*irritably*] Mama, I'm not cold.

MAMA: [*seeing the make-down bed as* TRAVIS *has left it*] Lord have mercy, look at that poor bed. Bless his heart — he tries, don't he?
   [*She moves to the bed* TRAVIS *has sloppily made up.*]

RUTH: No — he don't half try at all 'cause he knows you going to come along behind him and fix everything. That's just how come he don't know how to do nothing right now — you done spoiled that boy so.

MAMA: Well — he's a little boy. Ain't supposed to know 'bout housekeeping. My baby, that's what he is. What you fix for his breakfast this morning?

RUTH: [*angrily*] I feed my son, Lena!

MAMA: I ain't meddling — [*underbreath; busy-bodish*] I just noticed all last week he had cold cereal, and when it starts getting this chilly in the fall a child ought to have some hot grits or something when he goes out in the cold —

RUTH: [*furious*] I gave him hot oats — is that all right!

MAMA: I ain't meddling. [*pause*] Put a lot of nice butter on it? [RUTH *shoots her an angry look and does not reply.*] He likes lots of butter.

RUTH: [*exasperated*] Lena —

MAMA: [*to* BENEATHA. MAMA *is inclined to wander conversationally sometimes.*] What was you and your brother fussing 'bout this morning?

BENEATHA: It's not important, Mama.
   [*She gets up and goes to look out at the bathroom, which is apparently free, and she picks up her towels and rushes out.*]

MAMA: What was they fighting about?

RUTH: Now you know as well as I do.

MAMA: [*shaking her head*] Brother still worrying hisself sick about that money?

RUTH: You know he is.

MAMA: You had breakfast?

RUTH: Some coffee.

MAMA: Girl, you better start eating and looking after yourself better. You almost thin as Travis.

RUTH: Lena —

MAMA: Un-hunh?

RUTH: What are you going to do with it?

MAMA: Now don't you start, child. It's too early in the morning to be talking about money. It ain't Christian.

RUTH: It's just that he got his heart set on that store —

MAMA: You mean that liquor store that Willy Harris want him to invest in?

RUTH: Yes —

MAMA: We ain't no business people, Ruth. We just plain working folks.

RUTH: Ain't nobody business people till they go into business. Walter Lee say colored people ain't never going to start getting ahead till they start gambling on some different kinds of things in the world — investments and things.

MAMA: What done got into you, girl? Walter Lee done finally sold you on investing.

RUTH: No, Mama, something is happening between Walter and me. I don't know what it is — but he needs something — something I can't give him any more. He needs this chance, Lena.

MAMA: [*frowning deeply*] But liquor, honey —

RUTH: Well — like Walter say — I spec people going to always be drinking themselves some liquor.

MAMA: Well — whether they drinks it or not ain't none of my business. But whether I go into business selling it to 'em *is*, and I don't want that on my ledger this late in life. [*stopping suddenly and studying her daughter-in-law*] Ruth Younger, what's the matter with you today? You look like you could fall over right there.

RUTH: I'm tired.

MAMA: Then you better stay home from work today.

RUTH: I can't stay home. She'd be calling up the agency and screaming at them, "My girl didn't come in today — send me somebody! My girl didn't come in!" Oh, she just have a fit . . .

MAMA: Well, let her have it. I'll just call her up and say you got the flu —

RUTH: [*laughing*] Why the flu?

MAMA: 'Cause it sounds respectable to 'em. Something white people get, too. They know 'bout the flu. Otherwise they think you been cut up or something when you tell 'em you sick.

RUTH: I got to go in. We need the money.

MAMA: Somebody would of thought my children done all but starved to death the way they talk about money here late. Child, we got a great big old check coming tomorrow.

RUTH: [*sincerely, but also self-righteously*] Now that's your money. It ain't got nothing to do with me. We all feel like that — Walter and Bennie and me — even Travis.

MAMA: [*thoughtfully, and suddenly very far away*] Ten thousand dollars —

RUTH: Sure is wonderful.

MAMA: Ten thousand dollars.

RUTH: You know what you should do, Miss Lena? You should take yourself a trip somewhere. To Europe or South America or someplace —

MAMA: [*throwing up her hands at the thought*] Oh, child!

RUTH: I'm serious. Just pack up and leave! Go on away and enjoy yourself some. Forget about the family and have yourself a ball for once in your life —

MAMA: [*drily*] You sound like I'm just about ready to die. Who'd go with me? What I look like wandering 'round Europe by myself?

RUTH: Shoot — these here rich white women do it all the time. They don't think nothing of packing up their suitcases and piling on one of them big steamships and — swoosh! — they gone, child.

MAMA: Something always told me I wasn't no rich white woman.

RUTH: Well — what are you going to do with it them?

MAMA: I ain't rightly decided. [*Thinking. She speaks now with emphasis.*] Some of it got to be put away for Beneatha and her schoolin' — and ain't nothing going to touch that part of it. Nothing. [*She waits several seconds, trying to make up her mind about something, and looks at* RUTH *a little tentatively before going on.*] Been thinking that we maybe could meet the notes on a little old two-story somewhere, with a yard where Travis could play in the summertime, if we use part of the insurance for a downpayment and everybody kind of pitch in. I could maybe take on a little day work again, few days a week —

RUTH: [*studying her mother-in-law furtively and concentrating on her ironing, anxious to encourage without seeming to.*] Well, Lord knows, we've put enough rent into this here rat trap to pay for four houses by now . . .

MAMA: [*looking up at the words "rat trap" and then looking around and leaning back and sighing — in a suddenly reflective mood —*]"Rat trap" — yes, that's all it is. [*smiling*] I remember just as well as the day me and Big Walter moved in here. Hadn't been married but two weeks and wasn't planning on living here no more than a year. [*She shakes her head at the dissolved dream.*] We was going to set away, little by little, don't you know, and buy a little place out in Morgan Park. We had even picked out the house. [*chuckling a little*] Looks right dumpy today. But Lord, child, you should know all the dreams I had 'bout buying that house and fixing it up and making me a little garden in the back — [*She waits and stops smiling.*] And didn't none of it happen. [*dropping her hands in a futile gesture*]

RUTH: [*keeps her head down, ironing*] Yes, life can be a barrel of disappointments, sometimes.

MAMA: Honey, Big Walter would come in here some nights back then and slump down on that couch there and just look at the rug, and look at me and look at the rug and then back at me — and I'd know he was down then . . . really down. [*after a second very long and thoughtful pause; she is seeing back to times that only she can see*] And then, Lord, when I lost that baby — little Claude — I almost thought I was going to lose Big Walter too. Oh, that man grieved hisself! He was one man to love his children.

RUTH: Ain't nothin' can tear at you like losin' your baby.

MAMA: I guess that's how come that man finally worked hisself to death like he done. Like he was fighting his own war with this here world that took his baby from him.

RUTH: He was sure a fine man, all right. I always liked Mr. Younger.

MAMA: Crazy 'bout his children! God knows there was plenty wrong with Walter Younger — hard-headed, mean, kind of wild with women — plenty wrong with him. But he sure loved his children. Always wanted them to have something — be something. That's where Brother gets all his notions, I reckon. Big Walter used to say, he'd get right wet in the eyes sometimes, lean his head back with the water standing in his eyes and say, "Seem like God didn't see fit to give the black man nothing but dreams — but He did give us children to make them dreams seem worth while." [*She smiles.*] He could talk like that, don't you know.

RUTH: Yes, he sure could. He was a good man, Mr. Younger.

MAMA: Yes, a fine man — just couldn't never catch up with his dreams, that's all.
[BENEATHA *comes in, brushing her hair and looking up to the ceiling, where the sound of a vacuum cleaner has started up.*]

BENEATHA: What could be so dirty on that woman's rugs that she has to vacuum them every single day?

RUTH: I wish certain young women 'round here who I could name would take inspiration about certain rugs in a certain apartment I could also mention.

BENEATHA: [*shrugging*] How much cleaning can a house need, for Christ's sakes.

MAMA: [*not liking the Lord's name used thus*] Bennie!

RUTH: Just listen to her — just listen!

BENEATHA: Oh, God!

MAMA: If you use the Lord's name just one more time —

BENEATHA: [*a bit of a whine*] Oh, Mama —

RUTH: Fresh — just fresh as salt, this girl!

BENEATHA: [*drily*] Well — if the salt loses its savor —

MAMA: Now that will do. I just ain't going to have you 'round here reciting the scriptures in vain — you hear me?

BENEATHA: How did I manage to get on everybody's wrong side by just walking into a room?

RUTH: If you weren't so fresh —

BENEATHA: Ruth, I'm twenty years old.

MAMA: What time you be home from school today?

BENEATHA: Kind of late. [*with enthusiasm*] Madeline is going to start my guitar lessons today.
[MAMA *and* RUTH *look up with the same expression.*]

MAMA: Your *what* kind of lessons?

BENEATHA: Guitar.

RUTH: Oh, Father!

MAMA: How come you done taken it in your mind to learn to play the guitar?

BENEATHA: I just want to, that's all.

MAMA: [*smiling*] Lord, child, don't you know what to do with yourself? How long it going to be before you get tired of this now — like you got tired of that little play-acting group you joined last year? [*looking at* RUTH] And what was it the year before that?

RUTH: The horseback-riding club for which she bought that fifty-five-dollar riding habit that's been hanging in the closet ever since!

MAMA: [*to* BENEATHA] Why you got to flit so from one thing to another, baby?

BENEATHA: [*sharply*] I just want to learn to play the guitar. Is there anything wrong with that?

MAMA: Ain't nobody trying to stop you. I just wonders sometimes why you has to flit so from one thing to another all the time. You ain't never done nothing with all that camera equipment you brought home —

BENEATHA: I don't flit I — I experiment with different forms of expression —

RUTH: Like riding a horse?

BENEATHA: — People have to express themselves one way or another.

MAMA: What is it you want to express?

BENEATHA: [*angrily*] Me! [MAMA *and* RUTH *look at each other and burst into raucous laughter.*] Don't worry — I don't expect you to understand.

MAMA: [*to change the subject*] Who you going out with tomorrow night?

BENEATHA: [*with displeasure*] George Murchison again.

MAMA: [*pleased*] Oh — you getting a little sweet on him?

RUTH: You ask me, this child ain't sweet on nobody but herself — [*underbreath*] Express herself!

      [*They laugh.*]

BENEATHA: Oh — I like George all right, Mama. I mean I like him enough to go out with him and stuff, but —

RUTH: [*for devilment*]] What does *and stuff* mean?

BENEATHA: Mind your own business.

MAMA: Stop picking at her now, Ruth. [*a thoughtful pause, and then a suspicious sudden look at her daughter as she turns in her chair for emphasis*] What *does* it mean?

BENEATHA: [*wearily*] Oh, I just mean I couldn't ever really be serious about George. He's — he's so shallow.

RUTH: Shallow — what do you mean he's shallow? He's *Rich!*

MAMA: Hush, Ruth.

BENEATHA: I know he's rich. He knows he's rich, too.

RUTH: Well — what other qualities a man got to have to satisfy you, little girl?

BENEATHA: You wouldn't even begin to understand. Anybody who married Walter could not possibly understand.

MAMA: [*outraged*] What kind of way is that to talk about your brother?

BENEATHA: Brother is a flip — let's face it.

MAMA: [*to* RUTH, *helplessly*] What's a flip?

RUTH: [*glad to add kindling*] She's saying he's crazy.

BENEATHA: Not crazy. Brother isn't really crazy yet — he — he's an elaborate neurotic.

MAMA: Hush your mouth!

BENEATHA: As for George. Well. George looks good — he's got a beautiful car and he takes me to nice places and, as my sister-in-law says, he is probably the richest boy I will ever get to know and I even like him sometimes — but if the Youngers are sitting around waiting to see if their little Bennie is going to tie up the family with the Murchisons, they are wasting their time.

RUTH: You mean you wouldn't marry George Murchison if he asked you someday? That pretty, rich thing? Honey, I knew you was odd —

BENEATHA: No I would not marry him if all I felt for him was what I feel now. Besides, George's family wouldn't really like it.

MAMA: Why not?

BENEATHA: Oh, Mama — The Murchisons are honest-to-God-real-*live*-rich colored people, and the only people in the world who are more snobbish than rich white people are rich colored people. I thought everybody knew that. I've met Mrs. Murchison. She's a scene!

MAMA: You must not dislike people 'cause they well off, honey.

BENEATHA: Why not? It makes just as much sense as disliking people 'cause they are poor, and lots of people do that.

RUTH: [*a wisdom-of-the-ages manner. To* MAMA] Well, she'll get over some of this —

BENEATHA: Get over it? What are you talking about, Ruth? Listen, I'm going to be a doctor. I'm not worried about who I'm going to marry yet — if I ever get married.

MAMA *and* RUTH: *If!*

MAMA: Now, Bennie—

BENEATHA: Oh, I probably will . . . but first I'm going to be a doctor, and George, for one, still thinks that's pretty funny. I couldn't be bothered with that. I am going to be a doctor and everybody around here better understand that!

MAMA: [*kindly*] 'Course you going to be a doctor, honey, God willing.

BENEATHA: [*drily*] God hasn't got a thing to do with it.

MAMA: Beneatha—that just wasn't necessary.

BENEATHA: Well—neither is God. I get sick of hearing about God.

MAMA: Beneatha!

BENEATHA: I mean it! I'm just tired of hearing about God all the time. What has He got to do with anything? Does he pay tuition?

MAMA: You 'bout to get your fresh little jaw slapped!

RUTH: That's just what she needs, all right!

BENEATHA: Why? Why can't I say what I want to around here like everybody else?

MAMA: It don't sound nice for a young girl to say things like that—you wasn't brought up that way. Me and your father went to trouble to get you and Brother to church every Sunday.

BENEATHA: Mama, you don't understand. It's all a matter of ideas, and God is just one idea I don't accept. It's not important. I am not going out and be immoral or commit crimes because I don't believe in God. I don't even think about it. It's just that I get tired of Him getting credit for all the things the human race achieves through its own stubborn effort. There simply is no blasted God— there is only man and it is he who makes miracles!

> [MAMA *absorbs this speech, studies her daughter and rises slowly and crosses to* BENEATHA *and slaps her powerfully across the face. After, there is only silence and the daughter drops her eyes from her mother's face, and* MAMA *is very tall before her.*

MAMA: Now—you say after me, in my mother's house there is still God. [*There is a long pause and* BENEATHA *stares at the floor wordlessly.* MAMA *repeats the phrase with precision and cool emotion.*] In my mother's house there is still God.

BENEATHA: In my mother's house there is still God.

> [*A long pause.*]

MAMA: [*walking away from* BENEATHA, *too disturbed for triumphant posture. Stopping and turning back to her daughter*] There are some ideas we ain't going to have in this house. Not long as I am at the head of this family.

BENEATHA: Yes, Ma'am.

> [MAMA *walks out of the room.*]

RUTH: [*almost gently, with profound understanding*] You think you a woman, Bennie—but you still a little girl. What you did was childish—so you got treated like a child.

BENEATHA: I see. [*quietly*] I also see that everybody thinks it's all right for Mama to be a tyrant. But all the tyranny in the world will never put a God in the heavens!

> [*She picks up her books and goes out.*]

RUTH: [*goes to* MAMA's *door*] She said she was sorry.

MAMA: [*coming out, going to her plant*] They frightens me, Ruth. My children.

RUTH: You got good children, Lena. They just a little off sometimes—but they're good.

MAMA: No—there's something come down between me and them that don't let us understand each other and I don't know what it is. One done almost lost his mind thinking 'bout money all the time and the other done commence to talk about things I can't seem to understand in no form or fashion. What is it that's changing, Ruth?

RUTH: [*soothingly, older than her years*] Now . . . you taking it all too seriously. You just got strong-willed children and it takes a strong woman like you to keep 'em in hand.

MAMA: [*looking at her plant and sprinkling a little water on it*] They spirited all right, my children. Got to admit they got spirit—Bennie and Walter. Like this little old plant that ain't never had enough sunshine or nothing—and look at it . . .
[*She has her back to* RUTH, *who has had to stop ironing and lean against something and put the back of her hand to her forehead.*]

RUTH: [*trying to keep* MAMA *from noticing*] You . . . sure . . . loves that little old thing, don't you? . . .

MAMA: Well, I always wanted me a garden like I used to see sometimes at the back of the houses down home. This plant is close as I ever got to having one. [*She looks out of the window as she replaces the plant.*] Lord, ain't nothing as dreary as the view from this window on a dreary day, is there? Why ain't you singing this morning, Ruth? Sing that "No Ways Tired." That song always lifts me up so—[*She turns at last to see that* RUTH *has slipped quietly into a chair, in a state of semiconsciousness.*] Ruth! Ruth honey—what's the matter with you . . . Ruth!

SCENE II———*It is the following morning; a Saturday morning, and house cleaning is in progress at the* YOUNGERS. *Furniture has been shoved hither and yon and* MAMA *is giving the kitchen-area walls a washing down.* BENEATHA, *in dungarees, with a handkerchief tied around her face, is spraying insecticide into the cracks in the walls. As they work, the radio is on and a Southside disk-jockey program is inappropriately filling the house with a rather exotic saxophone blues.* TRAVIS, *the sole idle one, is leaning on his arms, looking out of the window.*

TRAVIS: Grandmama, that stuff Bennie is using smells awful. Can I go downstairs, please?

MAMA: Did you get all them chores done already? I ain't seen you doing much.

TRAVIS: Yes'm—finished early. Where did Mama go this morning?

MAMA: [*looking at* BENEATHA] She had to go on a little errand.

TRAVIS: Where?

MAMA: To tend to her business.

TRAVIS: Can I go outside then?

MAMA: Oh, I guess so. You better stay right in front of the house, though . . . and keep a good lookout for the postman.

TRAVIS: Yes'm. [*He starts out and decides to give his* AUNT BENEATHA *a good swat on the legs as he passes her.*] Leave them poor little old cockroaches alone, they ain't bothering you none.
[*He runs as she swings the spray gun at him both viciously and playfully.* WALTER *enters from the bedroom and goes to the phone.*]

MAMA: Look out there, girl, before you be spilling some of that stuff on that child!

TRAVIS: [*teasing*] That's right — look out now!

    [*He exits.*]

BENEATHA: [*drily*] I can't imagine that it would hurt him — it has never hurt the roaches.

MAMA: Well, little boys' hides ain't as tough as Southside roaches.

WALTER: [*into phone*] Hello — Let me talk to Willy Harris.

MAMA: You better get over there behind the bureau. I seen one marching out of there like Napoleon yesterday.

WALTER: Hello, Willy? It ain't come yet. It'll be here in a few minutes. Did the lawyer give you the papers?

BENEATHA: There's really only one way to get rid of them, Mama —

MAMA: How?

BENEATHA: Set fire to this building.

WALTER: Good. Good. I'll be right over.

BENEATHA: Where did Ruth go, Walter?

WALTER: I don't know.

    [*He exits abruptly.*]

BENEATHA: Mama, where did Ruth go?

MAMA: [*looking at her with meaning*] To the doctor, I think.

BENEATHA: The doctor? What's the matter? [*They exchange glances.*] You don't think —

MAMA: [*with her sense of drama*] Now I ain't saying what I think. But I ain't never been wrong 'bout a woman neither.

    [*The phone rings.*]

BENEATHA: Hay-lo . . . [*pause, and a moment of recognition*]Well — when did you get back! . . . And how was it? . . . Of course I've missed you — in my way . . . This morning? No . . . house cleaning and all that and Mama hates it if I let people come over when the house is like this . . . You *have*? Well, that's different . . . What is it — Oh, what the hell, come on over . . . Right, see you then.

    [*She hangs up.*]

MAMA: [*who has listened vigorously, as is her habit*] Who is that you inviting over here with this house looking like this? You ain't got the pride you was born with!

BENEATHA: Asagai doesn't care how houses look, Mama — he's an intellectual.

MAMA: *Who?*

BENEATHA: Asagai — Joseph Asagai. He's an African boy I met on campus. He's been studying in Canada all summer.

MAMA: What's his name?

BENEATHA: Asagai, Joseph. Ah-sah-guy . . . He's from Nigeria.

MAMA: Oh, that's the little country that was founded by slaves way back . . .

BENEATHA: No, Mama — that's Liberia.

MAMA: I don't think I never met an African before.

BENEATHA: Well, do me a favor and don't ask him a whole lot of ignorant questions about Africans. I mean, do they wear clothes and all that —

MAMA: Well, now, I guess if you think we so ignorant 'round here maybe you shouldn't bring your friends here —

BENEATHA: It's just that people ask such crazy things. All anyone seems to know about when it comes to Africa is Tarzan—

MAMA: [*indignantly*] Why should I know anything about Africa?

BENEATHA: Why do you give money at church for the missionary work?

MAMA: Well, that's to help save people.

BENEATHA: You mean save them from *heathenism*—

MAMA: [*innocently*] Yes.

BENEATHA: I'm afraid they need more salvation from the British and the French.
  [RUTH *comes in forlornly and pulls off her coat with dejection. They both turn to look at her.*]

RUTH: [*dispiritedly*] Well, I guess from all the happy faces—everybody knows.

BENEATHA: You pregnant?

MAMA: Lord have mercy, I sure hope it's a little old girl. Travis ought to have a sister.
  [BENEATHA *and* RUTH *give her a hopeless look for this grandmotherly enthusiasm.*]

BENEATHA: How far along are you?

RUTH: Two months.

BENEATHA: Did you mean to? I mean did you plan it or was it an accident?

MAMA: What do you know about planning or not planning?

BENEATHA: Oh, Mama.

RUTH: [*wearily*] She's twenty years old, Lena.

BENEATHA: Did you plan it, Ruth?

RUTH: Mind your own business.

BENEATHA: It is my business—where is he going to live, on the *roof?* [*There is silence following the remark as the three women react to the sense of it.*] Gee—I didn't mean that, Ruth, honest. Gee, I don't feel like that at all. I—I think it is wonderful.

RUTH: [*dully*] Wonderful.

BENEATHA: Yes—really.

MAMA: [*looking at* RUTH *worried*] Doctor say everything going to be all right?

RUTH: [*far away*] Yes—she says everything is going to be fine . . .

MAMA: [*immediately suspicious*] "She"—What doctor you went to?
  [RUTH *folds over, near hysteria.*]

MAMA: [*worriedly hovering over* RUTH] Ruth honey—what's the matter with you—you sick?
  [RUTH *has her fists clenched on her thighs and is fighting hard to suppress a scream that seems to be rising in her.*]

BENEATHA: What's the matter with her, Mama?

MAMA: [*working her fingers in* RUTH's *shoulder to relax her*] She be all right. Women gets right depressed sometimes when they get her way. [*speaking softly, expertly, rapidly*] Now you just relax. That's right . . . just lean back, don't think 'bout nothing at all . . . nothing at all—

RUTH: I'm all right—
  [*The glassy-eyed look melts and then she collapses into a fit of heavy sobbing. The bell rings.*]

BENEATHA: Oh, my God—that must be Asagai.

MAMA: [*to* RUTH] Come on now, honey. You need to lie down and rest awhile . . . then have some nice hot food.

[*They exit,* RUTH's *weight on her mother-in-law.* BENEATHA, *herself profoundly disturbed, opens the door to admit a rather dramatic-looking young man with a large package.*]

ASAGAI: Hello, Alaiyo —

BENEATHA: [*holding the door open and regarding him with pleasure*] Hello . . . [*long pause*] Well — come in. And please excuse everything. My mother was very upset about my letting anyone come here with the place like this.

ASAGAI: [*coming into the room*] You look disturbed too . . . Is something wrong?

BENEATHA: [*still at the door, absently*] Yes . . . we've all got acute ghetto-itus. [*She smiles and comes toward him, finding a cigarette and sitting.*] So — sit down! How was Canada?

ASAGAI: [*a sophisticate*] Canadian.

BENEATHA: [*looking at him*] I'm very glad you are back.

ASAGAI: [*looking back at her in turn*] Are you really?

BENEATHA: Yes — very.

ASAGAI: Why — you were quite glad when I went away. What happened?

BENEATHA: You went away.

ASAGAI: Ahhhhhhhh.

BENEATHA: Before — you wanted to be so serious before there was time.

ASAGAI: How much time must there be before one knows what one feels?

BENEATHA: [*stalling this particular conversation. Her hands pressed together, in a deliberately childish gesture*] What did you bring me?

ASAGAI: [*handing her the package*] Open it and see.

BENEATHA: [*eagerly opening the package and drawing out some records and the colorful robes of a Nigerian woman*] Oh, Asagai! . . . You got them for me! . . . How beautiful . . . and the records too! [*She lifts out the robes and runs to the mirror with them and holds the drapery up in front of herself.*]

ASAGAI: [*coming to her at the mirror*] I shall have to teach you how to drape it properly. [*He flings the material about her for a moment and stands back to look at her.*] Ah — Oh-pay-gay-day, oh-ghah-mu-shay. [*a Yoruba exclamation for admiration*] You wear it well . . . very well . . . mutilated hair and all.

BENEATHA: [*turning suddenly*] My hair — what's wrong with my hair?

ASAGAI: [*shrugging*] Were you born with it like that?

BENEATHA: *reaching up to touch it*] No . . . of course not. [*She turns back to the mirror, disturbed.*]

ASAGAI: [*smiling*] How then?

BENEATHA: You know perfectly well how . . . as crinkly as yours . . . that's how.

ASAGAI: And it is ugly to you that way?

BENEATHA: [*quickly*] Oh, no — not ugly . . . [*more slowly, apologetically*] But it's so hard to manage when it's, well — raw.

ASAGAI: And so to accommodate that — you mutilate it every week?

BENEATHA: It's not mutilation!

ASAGAI: [*laughing aloud at her seriousness*] Oh . . . please! I am only teasing you because you are so very serious about these things. [*He stands back from her and folds his arms across his chest as he watches her pulling at her hair and frowning in the mirror.*] Do you remember the first time you met me at

school? . . . [*He laughs.*] You came up to me and you said—and I thought
you were the most serious little thing I had ever seen—you said: [*He imitates
her.*] "Mr. Asagai—I want very much to talk with you. About Africa. You see,
Mr. Asagai, I am looking for my *identity!*"
    [*He laughs.*]
BENEATHA: [*turning to him, not laughing*] Yes—
    [*Her face is quizzical, profoundly disturbed.*]
ASAGAI: [*still teasing and reaching out and taking her face in his hands and turning
    her profile to him*] Well . . . it is true that this is not so much a profile of a
    Hollywood queen as perhaps a queen of the Nile—[*a mock dismissal of the
    importance of the question*] But what does it matter? Assimilationism is so
    popular in your country.
BENEATHA: [*wheeling, passionately, sharply*] I am not an assimilationist!
ASAGAI: [*The protest hangs in the room for a moment and* ASAGAI *studies her, his
    laughter fading.*] Such a serious one. [*There is a pause.*] So—you like the
    robes? You must take excellent care of them—they are from my sister's
    personal wardrobe.
BENEATHA: [*with incredulity*] You—you sent all the way home—for me?
ASAGAI: [*with charm*] For you—I would do much more . . . Well, that is what I
    came for. I must go.
BENEATHA: Will you call me Monday?
ASAGAI: Yes . . . We have a great deal to talk about. I mean about identity and
    time and all that.
BENEATHA: Time?
ASAGAI: Yes. About how much time one needs to know what one feels.
BENEATHA: You never understood that there is more than one kind of feeling which
    can exist between a man and a woman—or, at least, there should be.
ASAGAI: [*shaking his head negatively but gently*] No. Between a man and a woman
    there need be only one kind of feeling. I have that for you . . . Now
    even . . . right this moment . . .
BENEATHA: I know—and by itself—it won't do. I can find that anywhere.
ASAGAI: For a woman it should be enough.
BENEATHA: I know—because that's what it says in all the novels that men write. But
    it isn't. Go ahead and laugh—but I'm not interested in being someone's little
    episode in America or—[*with feminine vengeance*]—one of them! [ASAGAI
    *has burst into laughter again.*] That's funny as hell, huh!
ASAGAI: It's just that every American girl I have known has said that to me. White—
    black—in this you are all the same. And the same speech, too!
BENEATHA: [*angrily*] Yuk, yuk, yuk!
ASAGAI: It's how you can be sure that the world's most liberated women are not
    liberated at all. You all talk about it too much!
    [MAMA *enters and is immediately all social charm because of the presence
    of a guest.*]
BENEATHA: Oh—Mama—this is Mr. Asagai.
MAMA: How do you do?
ASAGAI: [*total politeness to an elder*] How do you do, Mrs. Younger. Please forgive
    me for coming at such an outrageous hour on a Saturday.
MAMA: Well, you are quite welcome. I just hope you understand that our house

don't always look like this. [*chatterish*] You must come again. I would love to hear all about — [*not sure of the name*] — your country. I think it's so sad the way our American Negroes don't know nothing about Africa 'cept Tarzan and all that. And all that money they pour into these churches when they ought to be helping you people over there drive out them French and Englishmen done taken away your land.

> [*The mother flashes a slightly superior look at her daughter upon completion of the recitation.*]

ASAGAI: [*taken aback by this sudden and acutely unrelated expression of sympathy*] Yes . . . yes . . .

MAMA: [*smiling at him suddenly and relaxing and looking him over*] How many miles is it from here to where you come from?

ASAGAI: Many thousands.

MAMA: [*looking at him as she would* WALTER] I bet you don't half look after yourself, being away from your mama either. I spec you better come 'round here from time to time to get yourself decent homecooked meals . . .

ASAGAI: [*moved*] Thank you. Thank you very much. [*They are all quiet, then —*] Well . . . I must go. I will call you Monday, Alaiyo.

MAMA: What's that he call you?

ASAGAI: Oh — "Alaiyo." I hope you don't mind. It is what you would call a nickname, I think. It is a Yoruba word. I am a Yoruba.

MAMA: [*looking at* BENEATHA] I — I thought he was from —

ASAGAI: [*understanding*] Nigeria is my country. Yoruba is my tribal origin —

BENEATHA: You didn't tell us what Alaiyo means . . . for all I know, you might be calling me Little Idiot or something . . .

ASAGAI: Well . . . let me see . . . I do not know how just to explain it . . . The sense of a thing can be so different when it changes languages.

BENEATHA: You'r evading.

ASAGAI: No — really it is difficult . . . [*thinking*] It means . . . it means One for Whom Bread — Food — Is Not Enough. [*He looks at her.*] Is that all right?

BENEATHA: [*understanding, softly*] Thank you.

MAMA: [*looking from one to the other and not understanding part of it*] Well . . . that's nice . . . You must come see us again — Mr. —

ASAGAI: Ah-say-guy . . .

MAMA: Yes . . . Do come again.

ASAGAI: Good-bye.

> [*He exits.*]

MAMA: [*after him*] Lord, that's a pretty thing just went out here! [*insinuatingly, to her daughter*] Yes, I guess I see why we done commence to get so interested in Africa 'round here. Missionaries my aunt Jenny!

> [*She exits.*]

BENEATHA: Oh, Mama! . . .

> [*She picks up the Nigerian dress and holds it up to her in front of the mirror again. She sets the headdress on haphazardly and then notices her hair again and clutches at it and then replaces the headdress and frowns at herself. Then she starts to wriggle in front of the mirror as she thinks a Nigerian woman might.* TRAVIS *enters and regards her.*]

TRAVIS: You cracking up?

BENEATHA: Shut up.

> [*She pulls the headdress off and looks at herself in the mirror and clutches at her hair again and squinches her eyes as if trying to imagine something. Then, suddenly, she gets her raincoat and kerchief and hurriedly prepares for going out.*]

MAMA: [*coming back into the room*] She's resting now. Travis, baby, run next door and ask Miss Johnson to please let me have a little kitchen cleanser. This here can is empty as Jacob's kettle.

TRAVIS: I just came in.

MAMA: Do as you told. [*He exits and she looks at her daughter.*] Where you going?

BENEATHA: [*halting at the door*] To become a queen of the Nile!

> [*She exits in a breathless blaze of glory.* RUTH *appears in the bedroom doorway.*]

MAMA: Who told you to get up?

RUTH: Ain't nothing wrong with me to be lying in no bed for. Where did Bennie go?

MAMA: [*drumming her fingers*] Far as I could make out — to Egypt. [RUTH *just looks at her.*] What time is it getting to?

RUTH: Ten twenty. And the mailman going to ring that bell this morning just like he done every morning for the last umpteen years.

> [TRAVIS *comes in with the cleanser can.*]

TRAVIS: She say to tell you that she don't have much.

MAMA: [*angrily*] Lord, some people I could name sure is tight-fisted! [*directing her grandson*] Mark two cans of cleanser down on the list there. If she that hard up for kitchen cleanser, I sure don't want to forget to get her none!

RUTH: Lena — maybe the woman is just short on cleanser —

MAMA: [*not listening*] — Much baking powder as she done borrowed from me all these years, she could of done gone into the baking business!

> [*The bell sounds suddenly and sharply and all three are stunned — serious and silent — mid-speech. In spite of all the other conversations and distractions of the morning, this is what they have been waiting for, even* TRAVIS, *who looks helplessly from his mother to his grandmother.* RUTH *is the first to come to life again.*]

RUTH: [*to* TRAVIS] Get down them steps, boy!

> [TRAVIS *snaps to life and flies out to get the mail*]

MAMA: [*her eyes wide, her hand to her breast*] You mean it done really come?

RUTH: [*excited*] Oh, Miss Lena!

MAMA: [*collecting herself*] Well . . . I don't know what we all so excited about 'round here for. We known it was coming for months.

RUTH: That's a whole lot different from having it come and being able to hold it in your hands . . . a piece of paper worth ten thousand dollars . . . [TRAVIS *bursts back into the room. He holds the envelope high above his head, like a little dancer, his face is radiant and he is breathless. He moves to his grandmother with sudden slow ceremony and puts the envelope into her hands. She accepts it, and then merely holds it and looks at it.*] Come on! Open it . . . Lord have mercy, I wish Walter Lee was here!

TRAVIS: Open it, Grandmama!

MAMA: [*staring at it*] Now you all be quiet. It's just a check.

RUTH: Open it . . .

MAMA: [*still staring at it*] Now don't act silly . . . We ain't never been no people to act silly 'bout no money —

RUTH: [*swiftly*] We ain't never had none before — open it!

> [MAMA *finally makes a good strong tear and pulls out the thin blue slice of paper and inspects it closely. The boy and his mother study it raptly over* MAMA's *shoulders.*]

MAMA: *Travis!* [*She is counting off with doubt.*] Is that the right number of zeros.

TRAVIS: Yes'm . . . ten thousand dollars. Gaalee, Grandmama, you rich.

MAMA: [*She holds the check away from her, still looking at it. Slowly her face sobers into a mask of unhappiness.*] Ten thousand dollars. [*She hands it to* RUTH.] Put it away somewhere, Ruth. [*She does not look at* RUTH; *her eyes seem to be seeing something somewhere very far off.*] Ten thousand dollars they give you. Ten thousand dollars.

TRAVIS: [*to his mother, sincerely*] What's the matter with Grandmama — don't she want to be rich?

RUTH: [*distractedly*] You go on out and play now, baby. [TRAVIS *exits.* MAMA *starts wiping dishes absently, humming intently to herself.* RUTH *turns to her, with kind exasperation.*] You've gone and got yourself upset.

MAMA: [*not looking at her*] I spec if it wasn't for you all . . . I would just put that money away or give it to the church or something.

RUTH: Now what kind of talk is that. Mr. Younger would just be plain mad if he could hear you talking foolish like that.

MAMA: [*stopping and staring off*] Yes . . . he sure would. [*sighing*] We got enough to do with that money, all right. [*She halts then, and turns and looks at her daughter-in-law hard;* RUTH *avoids her eyes and* MAMA *wipes her hands with finality and starts to speak firmly to* RUTH.] Where did you go today, girl?

RUTH: To the doctor.

MAMA: [*impatiently*] Now, Ruth . . . you know better than that. Old Doctor Jones is strange enough in his way but there ain't nothing 'bout him make somebody slip and call him "she" — like you done this morning.

RUTH: Well, that's what happened — my tongue slipped.

MAMA: You went to see that woman, didn't you?

RUTH: [*defensively, giving herself away*] What woman you talking about?

MAMA: [*angrily*] That woman who —

> [WALTER *enters in great excitement.*]

WALTER: Did it come?

MAMA: [*quietly*] Can't you give people a Christian greeting before you start asking about money?

WALTER: [*to* RUTH] Did it come? [RUTH *unfolds the check and lays it quietly before him, watching him intently with thoughts of her own.* WALTER *sits down and grasps it close and counts off the zeros.*] Ten thousand dollars — [*He turns suddenly, frantically to his mother and draws some papers out of his breast pocket.*] Mama — look. Old Willy Harris put everything on paper —

MAMA: Son — I think you ought to talk to your wife . . . I'll go on out and leave you alone if you want —

WALTER: I can talk to her later — Mama, look —

MAMA: Son —

WALTER: WILL SOMEBODY PLEASE LISTEN TO ME TODAY!

MAMA: [*quietly*] I don't 'low no yellin' in this house, Walter Lee, and you know it — [WALTER *stares at them in frustration and starts to speak several times.*] And there ain't going to be no investing in no liquor stores. I don't aim to have to speak on that again.

    [*A long pause.*]

WALTER: Oh — so you don't aim to have to speak on that again? So *you* have decided . . . [*crumpling his papers*] Well, *you* tell that to my boy tonight when you put him to sleep on the living-room couch . . . [*turning to* MAMA *and speaking directly to her*] Yeah — and tell it to my wife, Mama, tomorrow when she has to go out of here to look after somebody else's kids. And tell it to *me*, Mama, every time we need a new pair of curtains and I have to watch *you* go out and work in somebody's kitchen. Yeah, you tell me then!

    [WALTER *starts out.*]

RUTH: Where you going?

WALTER: I'm going out!

RUTH: Where?

WALTER: Just out of this house somewhere —

RUTH: [*getting her coat*] I'll come too.

WALTER: I don't want you to come!

RUTH: I got something to talk to you about, Walter.

WALTER: That's too bad.

MAMA: [*still quietly*] Walter Lee — [*She waits and he finally turns and looks at her.*] Sit down.

WALTER: I'm a grown man, Mama.

MAMA: Ain't nobody said you wasn't grown. But you still in my house and my presence. And as long as you are — you'll talk to your wife civil. Now sit down.

RUTH: [*suddenly*] Oh, let him go on out and drink himself to death! He makes me sick to my stomach! [*She flings her coat against him.*]

WALTER: [*violently*] And you turn mine too, baby! [RUTH *goes into their bedroom and slams the door behind her.*] That was my greatest mistake —

MAMA: [*still quietly*] Walter, what is the matter with you?

WALTER: Matter with me? Ain't nothing the matter with *me!*

MAMA: Yes there is. Something eating you up like a crazy man. Something more than me not giving you this money. The past few years I been watching it happen to you. You get all nervous acting and kind of wild in the eyes — [WALTER *jumps up impatiently at her words.*] I said sit there now, I'm talking to you!

WALTER: Mama — I don't need no nagging at me today.

MAMA: Seem like you getting to a place where you always tied up in some kind of knot about something. But if anybody ask you 'bout it you just yell at 'em and bust out the house and go out and drink somewheres. Walter Lee, people can't live like that. Ruth's a good, patient girl in her way — but you getting to be too much. Boy, don't make the mistake of driving that girl away from you.

WALTER: Why — what she do for me?

MAMA: She loves you.

WALTER: Mama — I'm going out. I want to go off somewhere and be by myself for a while.

MAMA: I'm sorry 'bout your liquor store, son. It just wasn't the thing for us to do. That's what I want to tell you about —

WALTER: I got to go out, Mama —
  [*He rises.*]
MAMA: It's dangerous, son.
WALTER: What's dangerous?
MAMA: When a man goes outside his home to look for peace.
WALTER: [*beseechingly*] Then why can't there never be no peace in this house then?
MAMA: You done found it in some other house?
WALTER: No — there ain't no woman! Why do women always think there's a woman somewhere when a man gets restless. [*coming to her*] Mama — Mama — I want so many things . . .
MAMA: Yes, son —
WALTER: I want so many things that they are driving me kind of crazy . . . Mama — look at me.
MAMA: I'm looking at you. You a good-looking boy. You got a job, a nice wife, a fine boy and —
WALTER: A job. [*looks at her*] Mama, a job? I open and close car doors all day long. I drive a man around in his limousine and I say, "Yes, sir; no sir; very good, sir; shall I take the Drive, sir?" Mama, that ain't no kind of job . . . that ain't nothing at all. [*very quietly*] Mama, I don't know if I can make you understand.
MAMA: Understand what, baby?
WALTER: [*quietly*] Sometimes it's like I can see the future stretched out in front of me — just plain as day. The future, Mama. Hanging over there at the edge of my days. Just waiting for me — a big, looming blank space — full of *nothing*. Just waiting for *me*. [*pause*] Mama — sometimes when I'm downtown and I pass them cool, quiet-looking restaurants where them white boys are sitting back and talking 'bout things . . . sitting there turning deals worth millions of dollars . . . sometimes I see guys don't look much older than me —
MAMA: Son — how come you talk so much 'bout money?
WALTER: [*with immense passion*] Because it is life, Mama!
MAMA: [*quietly*] Oh — [*very quietly*] So now it's life. Money is life. Once upon a time freedom used to be life — now it's money. I guess the world really do change . . .
WALTER: No — it was always money, Mama. We just didn't know about it.
MAMA: No . . . something has changed. [*She looks at him.*] You something new, boy. In my time we was worried about not being lynched and getting to the North if we could and how to stay alive and still have a pinch of dignity too . . . Now here come you and Beneatha — talking 'bout things we ain't never even thought about hardly, me and your daddy. You ain't satisfied or proud of nothing we done. I mean that you had a home; that we kept you out of trouble till you was grown; that you don't have to ride to work on the back of nobody's streetcar — You my children — but how different we done become.
WALTER: You just don't understand, Mama, you just don't understand.
MAMA: Son — do you know your wife is expecting another baby? [WALTER *stands, stunned, and absorbs what his mother has said.*] That's what she wanted to talk to you about. [WALTER *sinks down into a chair.*] This ain't for me to be telling — but you ought to know. [*She waits.*] I think Ruth is thinking 'bout getting rid of that child.
WALTER: [*slowly understanding*] No — no — Ruth wouldn't do that.

MAMA: When the world gets ugly enough—a woman will do anything for her family. *The part that's already living.*

WALTER: You don't know Ruth, Mama, if you think she would do that.

[RUTH *opens the bedroom door and stands there a little limp.*]

RUTH: [*beaten*] Yes I would too, Walter. [*pause*] I gave her a five-dollar down payment.

[*There is a total silence as the man stares at his wife and the mother stares at her son.*]

MAMA: [*presently*] Well—[*tightly*] Well—son, I'm waiting to hear you say something . . . I'm waiting to hear how you be your father's son. Be the man he was . . . [*pause*] Your wife say she going to destroy your child. And I'm waiting to hear you talk like him and say we a people who give children life, not who destroys them—[*She rises.*] I'm waiting to see you stand up and look like your daddy and say we done give up one baby to poverty and that we ain't going to give up nary another one . . . I'm waiting.

WALTER: Ruth—

MAMA: If you a son of mine, tell her! [WALTER *turns, looks at her and can say nothing. She continues, bitterly.*] You . . . you are a disgrace to your father's memory. Somebody get me my hat.

# ACT II

SCENE I———*Time: Later, the same day.*

[*At rise:* RUTH *is ironing again. She has the radio going. Presently* BE-NEATHA'*s bedroom door opens and* RUTH'*s mouth falls and she puts down the iron in fascination.*

RUTH: What have we got on tonight!

BENEATHA: [*emerging grandly from the doorway so that we can see her thoroughly robed in the costume Asagai brought.*] You are looking at what a well-dressed Nigerian woman wears—[*She parades for* RUTH, *her hair completely hidden by the headdress; she is coquettishly fanning herself with an ornate oriental fan, mistakenly more like Butterfly than any Nigerian that ever was.*] Isn't it beautiful? [*She promenades to the radio and, with an arrogant flourish, turns off the good loud blues that is playing.*] Enough of this assimilationist junk! [RUTH *follows her with her eyes as she goes to the phonograph and puts on a record and turns and waits ceremoniously for the music to come up. Then, with a shout*—] O COMOGOSIAY!

[RUTH *jumps. The music comes up, a lovely Nigerian melody.* BENEATHA *listens, enraptured, her eyes far away*—"*back to the past.*" *She begins to dance.* RUTH *is dumfounded.*]

RUTH: What kind of dance is that?

BENEATHA: A folk dance.

RUTH: [*Pearl Bailey*] What kind of folks do that, honey?

BENEATHA: It's from Nigeria. It's a dance of welcome.

RUTH: Who you welcoming?

BENEATHA: The men back to the village.

RUTH: Where they been?

BENEATHA: How should I know—out hunting or something. Anyway, they are coming back now . . .

RUTH: Well, that's good.

BENEATHA: [*with the record*]
Alundi, alundi
Alundi alunya
Jop pu a jeepua
Ang gu soooooooooo

Ai yai yae . . .
Ayehaye—alundi . . .
[WALTER *comes in during this performance; he has obviously been drinking. He leans against the door heavily and watches his sister, at first with distaste. Then his eyes look off—"back to the past"—as he lifts both his fists to the roof, screaming*]

WALTER: YEAH . . . AND ETHIOPIA STRETCH FORTH HER HANDS AGAIN! . . .

RUTH: [*drily, looking at him*] Yes—and Africa sure is claiming her own tonight. [*She gives them both up and starts ironing again.*]

WALTER: [*all in a drunken, dramatic shout*] Shut up! . . . I'm digging them drums . . . them drums move me! . . . [*He makes his weaving way to his wife's face and leans in close to her.*] In my *heart of hearts—*[*He thumps his chest.*]—I am much warrior!

RUTH: [*without even looking up*] In your heart of hearts you are much drunkard.

WALTER: [*coming away from her and starting to wander around the room, shouting*] Me and Jomo . . . [*Intently, in his sister's face. She has stopped dancing to watch him in this unknown mood*] That's my man, Kenyatta. [*shouting and thumping his chest*] FLAMING SPEAR! HOT DAMN! [*He is suddenly in possession of an imaginary spear and actively spearing enemies all over the room.*] OCOMOGOSIAY . . . THE LION IS WAKING . . . OWI-MOWEH! [*He pulls his shirt open and leaps up on a table and gestures with his spear. The bell rings.* RUTH *goes to answer.*]

BENEATHA: [*to encourage* WALTER, *thoroughly caught up with this side of him*] OCOMOGOSIAY, FLAMING SPEAR!

WALTER: [*On the table, very far gone, his eyes pure glass sheets. He sees what we cannot, that he is a leader of his people, a great chief, a descendant of Chaka, and that the hour to march has come.*] Listen, my black brothers—

BENEATHA: OCOMOGOSIAY!

WALTER: —Do you hear the waters rushing against the shores of the coastlands—

BENEATHA: OCOMOGOSIAY!

WALTER: —Do you hear the screeching of the cocks in yonder hills beyond where the chiefs meet in council for the coming of the mighty war—

BENEATHA: OCOMOGOSIAY!

WALTER: —Do you hear the beating of the wings of the birds flying low over the mountains and the low places of our land—
[RUTH *opens the door.* GEORGE MURCHISON *enters.*]

BENEATHA: OCOMOGOSIAY!

WALTER: Do you hear the singing of the women, singing the war songs of our fathers

to the babies in the great houses . . . singing the sweet war songs? OH, DO
YOU HEAR, MY BLACK BROTHERS!

BENEATHA: [*completely gone*] We hear you, Flaming Spear —

WALTER: Telling us to prepare for the greatness of the time — [*to* GEORGE] Black
Brother!

> [*He extends his hand for the fraternal clasp.*]

GEORGE: Black Brother, hell!

RUTH: [*having had enough, and embarrassed for the family*] Beneatha, you got
company — what's the matter with you? Walter Lee Younger, get down off
that table and stop acting like a fool . . .

> [WALTER *comes down off the table suddenly and makes a quick exit to the*
> *bathroom.*]

RUTH: He's had a little to drink . . . I don't know what her excuse is.

GEORGE: [*to* BENEATHA] Look honey, we're going *to* the theatre — we're not going to
be *in* it . . . so go change, huh?

RUTH: You expect this boy to go out with you looking like that?

BENEATHA: [*looking at* GEORGE] That's up to George. If he's ashamed of his heritage
—

GEORGE: Oh, don't be so proud of yourself, Bennie — just because you look eccentric.

BENEATHA: How can something that's natural be eccentric?

GEORGE: That's what being eccentric means — being natural. Get dressed.

BENEATHA: I don't like that, George.

RUTH: Why must you and your brother make an argument out of everything people
say?

BENEATHA: Because I hate assimilationist Negroes!

RUTH: Will somebody please tell me what assimila-whoever means!

GEORGE: Oh, it's just a college girl's way of calling people Uncle Toms — but that
isn't what it means at all.

RUTH: Well, what does it mean?

BENEATHA: [*cutting* GEORGE *off and staring at him as she replies to* RUTH] It means
someone who is willing to give up his own culture and submerge himself
completely in the dominant, and in this case, *oppressive* culture!

GEORGE: Oh, dear, dear, dear! Here we go! A lecture on the African past! On our
Great West African Heritage! In one second we will hear all about the great
Ashanti empires; the great Songhay civilizations; and the great sculpture of
Benin — and then some poetry in the Bantu — and the whole monologue will
end with the word *heritage!* [*nastily*] Let's face it, baby, your heritage is
nothing but a bunch of raggedy-assed spirituals and some grass huts!

BENEATHA: *Grass huts!* [RUTH *crosses to her and forcibly pushes her toward the*
*bedroom.*] See there . . . you are standing there in your splendid ignorance
talking about people who were the first to smelt iron on the face of the earth!
[RUTH *is pushing her through the door.*] The Ashanti were performing surgical
operations when the English — [RUTH *pulls the door to, with* BENEATHA *on the*
*other side, and smiles graciously at* GEORGE. BENEATHA *opens the door and*
*shouts the end of the sentence defiantly at* GEORGE] — were still tattooing
themselves with blue dragons . . . [*She goes back inside.*]

RUTH: Have a seat, George. [*They both sit.* RUTH *folds her hands primly on her lap, determined to demonstrate the civilization of the family.*] Warm, ain't it? I mean for September. [*pause*] Just like they always say about Chicago weather: If it's too hot or cold for you, just wait a minute and it'll change. [*She smiles happily at this cliché of clichés.*] Everybody say it's got to do with them bombs and things they keep setting off. [*pause*] Would you like a nice cold beer?

GEORGE: No, thank you. I don't care for beer. [*He looks at his watch.*] I hope she hurries up.

RUTH: What time is the show?

GEORGE: It's an eight-thirty curtain. That's just Chicago, though. In New York standard curtain time is eight forty.

[*He is rather proud of his knowledge.*]

RUTH: [*properly appreciating it*] You get to New York a lot?

GEORGE: [*offhand*] Few times a year.

RUTH: Oh — that's nice. I've never been to New York.

[WALTER *enters. We feel he has relieved himself, but the edge of unreality is still with him.*]

WALTER: New York ain't got nothing Chicago ain't. Just a bunch of hustling people all squeezed up together — being "Eastern."

[*He turns his face into a screw of displeasure.*]

GEORGE: Oh — you've been?

WALTER: *Plenty* of times.

RUTH: [*shocked at the lie*] Walter Lee Younger!

WALTER: [*staring her down*] Plenty! [*pause*] What we got to drink in this house? Why don't you offer this man some refreshment. [*to* GEORGE] They don't know how to entertain in this house, man.

GEORGE: Thank you — I don't really care for anything.

WALTER: [*feeling his head; sobriety coming*] Where's Mama?

RUTH: She ain't come back yet.

WALTER: [*Looking* MURCHISON *over from head to toe, scrutinizing his carefully casual tweed sports jacket over cashmere V-neck sweater over soft eyelet shirt and tie, and soft slacks, finished off with white buckskin shoes.*] Why all you college boys wear them fairyish-looking white shoes?

RUTH: Walter Lee!

[GEORGE MURCHISON *ignores the remark.*]

WALTER: [*to* RUTH] Well, they look crazy as hell — white shoes, cold as it is.

RUTH: [*crushed*] You have to excuse him —

WALTER: No he don't! Excuse me for what? What you always excusing me for! I'll excuse myself when I needs to be excused! [*a pause*] They look as funny as them black knee socks Beneatha wears out of here all the time.

RUTH: It's the college *style*, Walter.

WALTER: Style, hell. She looks like she got burnt legs or something!

RUTH: Oh, Walter —

WALTER: [*an irritable mimic*] Oh, Walter! Oh, Walter! [*to* MURCHISON] How's your old man making out? I understand you all going to buy that big hotel on the Drive? [*He finds a beer in the refrigerator, wanders over to* MURCHISON, *sipping and wiping his lips with the back of his hand, and straddling a chair backwards to talk to the other man.*] Shrewd move. Your old man is all right, man. [*tapping his head and half winking for emphasis*] I mean he knows how to operate. I mean he thinks *big,* you know what I mean, I mean for a *home,* you know? But I think he's kind of running out of ideas now. I'd like to talk to him. Listen, man, I got some plans that could turn this city upside down. I mean I think like he does. *Big.* Invest big, gamble big, hell, lose *big* if you have to, you know what I mean. It's hard to find a man on this whole Southside who understands my kind of thinking — you dig? [*He scrutinizes* MURCHISON *again, drinks his beer, squints his eyes and leans in close, confidential, man to man.*] Me and you ought to sit down and talk sometimes, man. Man, I got me some ideas . . .

GEORGE: [*with boredom*] Yeah — sometimes we'll have to do that, Walter.

WALTER: [*understanding the indifference, and offended*] Yeah — well, when you get the time, man. I know you a busy little boy.

RUTH: Walter, please —

WALTER: [*bitterly, hurt*] I know ain't nothing in this world as busy as you colored college boys with your fraternity pins and white shoes . . .

RUTH: [*covering her face with humiliation*] Oh, Walter Lee —

WALTER: I see you all all the time — with the books tucked under your arms — going to your [*British A — a mimic*] "clahsses." And for what! What the hell you learning over there? Filling up your heads — [*counting off on his fingers*] — with the sociology and the psychology — but they teaching you how to be a man? How to take over and run the world? They teaching you how to run a rubber plantation or a steel mill? Naw — just to talk proper and read books and wear white shoes —

GEORGE: [*looking at him with distaste, a little above it all*] You're all wacked up with bitterness, man.

WALTER: [*intently, almost quietly, between the teeth, glaring at the boy*] And you — ain't you bitter, man? Ain't you just about had it yet? Don't you see no stars gleaming that you can't reach out and grab? You happy? — You contented son-of-a-bitch — you happy? You got it made? Bitter? Man, I'm a volcano. Bitter? Here I am a giant — surrounded by ants! Ants who can't even understand what it is the giant is talking about.

RUTH: [*passionately and suddenly*] Oh, Walter — ain't you with nobody!

WALTER: [*violently*] No! 'Cause ain't nobody with me! Not even my own mother!

RUTH: Walter, that's a terrible thing to say!

[BENEATHA *enters, dressed for the evening in a cocktail dress and earrings.*]

GEORGE: Well — hey, you look great.

BENEATHA: Let's go, George. See you all later.

RUTH: Have a nice time.

GEORGE: Thanks. Good night. [*to* WALTER *sarcastically*] Good night, *Prometheus.*

[BENEATHA *and* GEORGE *exit.*]

WALTER: [*to* RUTH] Who is Prometheus?

RUTH: I don't know. Don't worry about it.

WALTER: [*in fury, pointing after* GEORGE] See there — they get to a point where they can't insult you man to man — they got to talk about something ain't nobody never heard of!

RUTH: How do you know it was an insult? [*to humor him*] Maybe Prometheus is a nice fellow.

WALTER: Prometheus! I bet there ain't even no such thing! I bet that simple-minded clown —
RUTH: Walter —
　　　　[*She stops what she is doing and looks at him.*]
WALTER: [*yelling*] Don't start!
RUTH: Start what?
WALTER: Your nagging! Where was I? Who was I with? How much money did I spend?
RUTH: [*plaintively*] Walter Lee — why don't we just try to talk about it . . .
WALTER: [*not listening*] I been out talking to people who understand me. People who care about the things I got on my mind.
RUTH: [*wearily*] I guess that means people like Willy Harris.
WALTER: Yes, people like Willy Harris.
RUTH: [*with a sudden flash of impatience*] Why don't you all just hurry up and go into the banking business and stop talking about it!
WALTER: Why? You want to know why? 'Cause we all tied up in a race of people that don't know how to do nothing but moan, pray and have babies!
　　　　[*The line is too bitter even for him and he looks at her and sits down.*]
RUTH: Oh, Walter . . . [*softly*] Honey, why can't you stop fighting me?
WALTER: [*without thinking*] Who's fighting you? Who even cares about you?
　　　　[*This line begins the retardation of his mood.*]
RUTH: Well — [*She waits a long time, and then with resignation starts to put away her things.*] I guess I might as well go to bed . . . [*more or less to herself*] I don't know where we lost it . . . but we have . . . [*then, to him*] I — I'm sorry about this new baby, Walter. I guess maybe I better go on and do what I started . . . I guess I just didn't realize how bad things was with us . . . I guess I just didn't really realize — [*She starts out to the bedroom and stops.*] You want some hot milk?
WALTER: Hot milk?
RUTH: Yes — hot milk.
WALTER: Why hot milk?
RUTH: 'Cause after all that liquor you come home with you ought to have something hot in your stomach.
WALTER: I don't want no milk.
RUTH: You want some coffee then?
WALTER: No, I don't want no coffee. I don't want nothing hot to drink. [*almost plaintively*] Why you always trying to give me something to eat?
RUTH: [*standing and looking at him helplessly*] What else can I give you, Walter Lee Younger?
　　　　[*She stands and looks at him and presently turns to go out again. He lifts his head and watches her going away from him in a new mood which began to emerge when he asked her "Who cares about you?"*]
WALTER: It's been rough, ain't it, baby? [*She hears and stops but does not turn around and he continues to her back.*] I guess between two people there ain't never as much understood as folks generally think there is. I mean like between me and you — [*She turns to face him.*] How we gets to the place where we scared to talk softness to each other. [*He waits, thinking hard himself.*] Why

you think it got to be like that? [*He is thoughtful, almost as a child would be.*] Ruth, what is it gets into people ought to be close?

RUTH: I don't know, honey. I think about it a lot.

WALTER: On account of you and me, you mean? The way things are with us. The way something done come down between us.

RUTH: There ain't so much between us, Walter . . . Not when you come to me and try to talk to me. Try to be with me . . . a little even.

WALTER: [*total honesty*] Sometimes . . . sometimes . . . I don't even know how to try.

RUTH: Walter—

WALTER: Yes?

RUTH: [*coming to him, gently and with misgiving, but coming to him*] Honey . . . life don't have to be like this. I mean sometimes people can do things so that things are better . . . You remember how we used to talk when Travis was born . . . about the way we were going to live . . . the kind of house . . . [*She is stroking his head.*] Well, it's all starting to slip away from us . . .

[MAMA *enters, and* WALTER *jumps up and shouts at her.*]

WALTER: Mama, where have you been?

MAMA: My—them steps is longer than they used to be. Whew! [*She sits down and ignores him.*] How you feeling this evening, Ruth?

[RUTH *shrugs, disturbed some at having been prematurely interrupted and watching her husband knowingly.*]

WALTER: Mama, where have you been all day?

MAMA: [*still ignoring him and leaning on the table and changing to more comfortable shoes*] Where's Travis?

RUTH: I let him go out earlier and he ain't come back yet. Boy, is he going to get it!

WALTER: Mama!

MAMA: [*as if she has heard him for the first time*] Yes, son?

WALTER: Where did you go this afternoon?

MAMA: I went downtown to tend to some business that I had to tend to.

WALTER: What kind of business?

MAMA: You know better than to question me like a child, Brother.

WALTER: [*rising and bending over the table*] Where were you, Mama? [*bringing his fists down and shouting*]Mama, you didn't go do something with that insurance money, something crazy?

[*The front door opens slowly, interrupting him, and* TRAVIS *peeks his head in, less than hopefully.*]

TRAVIS: [*to his mother*] Mama, I—

RUTH: "Mama I" nothing! You're going to get it boy! Get on in that bedroom and get yourself ready!

TRAVIS: But I—

MAMA: Why don't you all never let the child explain hisself.

RUTH: Keep out of it now, Lena.

[MAMA *clamps her lips together, and* RUTH *advances toward her son menacingly.*]

RUTH: A thousand times I have told you not to go off like that—

MAMA: [*holding out her arms to her grandson*] Well—at least let me tell him something. I want him to be the first one to hear . . . Come here, Travis. [*The boy obeys, gladly.*] Travis — [*She takes him by the shoulder and looks into his face.*] — you know that money we got in the mail this morning?

TRAVIS: Yes'm —

MAMA: Well — what you think your grandmama gone and done with that money?

TRAVIS: I don't know, Grandmama.

MAMA: [*putting her finger on his nose for emphasis*] She went out and she bought you a house! [*The explosion comes from* WALTER *at the end of the revelation and he jumps up and turns away from all of them in a fury.* MAMA *continues, to* TRAVIS.] You glad about the house? It's going to be yours when you get to be a man.

TRAVIS: Yeah — I always wanted to live in a house.

MAMA: All right, gimme some sugar then — [TRAVIS *puts his arms around her neck as she watches her son over the boy's shoulder. Then, to* TRAVIS, *after the embrace*] Now when you say your prayers tonight, you thank God and your grandfather — 'cause it was him who give you the house — in his way.

RUTH: [*taking the boy from* MAMA *and pushing him toward the bedroom*] Now you get out of here and get ready for your beating.

TRAVIS: Aw, Mama —

RUTH: Get on in there — [*closing the door behind him and turning radiantly to her mother-in-law*] So you went and did it!

MAMA: [*quietly, looking at her son with pain*] Yes, I did.

RUTH: [*raising both arms classically*] Praise God! [*Looks at* WALTER *a moment, who says nothing. She crosses rapidly to her husband.*] Please, honey — let me be glad . . . you be glad too. [*She has laid her hands on his shoulders, but he shakes himself free of her roughly, without turning to face her.*] Oh, Walter . . . a home . . . a home. [*She comes back to* MAMA.] Well — where is it? How big is it? How much it going to cost?

MAMA: Well —

RUTH: When we moving?

MAMA: [*smiling at her*] First of the month.

RUTH: [*throwing back her head with jubilance*] Praise God!

MAMA: [*tentatively, still looking at her son's back turned against her and* RUTH] It's — it's a nice house too . . . [*She cannot help speaking directly to him. An imploring quality in her voice, her manner, makes her almost like a girl now.*] Three bedrooms — nice big one for you and Ruth . . . Me and Beneatha still have to share our room, but Travis have one of his own — and [*with difficulty*] I figure if the — new baby — is a boy, we could get one of them double-decker outfits . . . And there's a yard with a little patch of dirt where I could maybe get to grow me a few flowers . . . And a nice big basement . . .

RUTH: Walter honey, be glad —

MAMA: [*still to his back, fingering things on the table*] 'Course I don't want to make it sound fancier than it is . . . It's just a plain little old house — but it's made good and solid — and it will be *ours*. Walter Lee — it makes a difference in a man when he can walk on floors that belong to *him* . . .

RUTH: Where is it?

MAMA: [*frightened at this telling*] Well — well — it's out there in Clybourne Park —

[RUTH'S *radiance fades abruptly, and* WALTER *finally turns slowly to face his mother with incredulity and hostility.*]

RUTH: Where?

MAMA: [*matter-of-factly*] Four o six Clybourne Street, Clybourne Park.

RUTH: Clybourne Park? Mama, there ain't no colored people living in Clybourne Park.

MAMA: [*almost idiotically*] Well, I guess there's going to be some now.

WALTER: [*bitterly*] So that's the peace and comfort you went out and bought for us today!

MAMA: [*raising her eyes to meet his finally*] Son — I just tried to find the nicest place for the least amount of money for my family.

RUTH: [*trying to recover from the shock*] Well — well — 'course I ain't one never been 'fraid of no crackers, mind you — but — well, wasn't there no other houses nowhere?

MAMA: Them houses they put up for colored in them areas way out all seem to cost twice as much as other houses. I did the best I could.

RUTH: [*Struck senseless with the news, in its various degrees of goodness and trouble, she sits a moment, her fists propping her chin in thought, and then she starts to rise, bring her fists down with vigor, the radiance spreading from cheek to cheek again.*] Well — well! — All I can say is — if this is my time in life — *my time* — to say good-bye [*and she builds with momentum as she starts to circle the room with an exuberant, almost tearfully happy release*] — to these God-damned cracking walls! — [*She pounds the walls.*] — and these marching roaches! — [*She wipes at an imaginary army of marching roaches.*] — and this cramped little closet which ain't now or never was no kitchen! . . . then I say it loud and good, *Hallelujah! and goodbye misery* . . . *I don't never want to see your ugly face again!* [*She laughs joyously, having practically destroyed the apartment, and flings her arms up and lets them come down happily, slowly, reflectively, over her abdomen, aware for the first time perhaps that the life therein pulses with happiness and not despair.*] Lena?

MAMA: [*moved, watching her happiness*] Yes, honey?

RUTH: [*looking off*] Is there — is there a whole lot of sunlight?

MAMA: [*understanding*] Yes, child, there's a whole lot of sunlight.

[*Long pause.*]

RUTH: [*collecting herself and going to the door of the room* TRAVIS *is in*] Well — I guess I better see 'bout Travis. [*to* MAMA] Lord, I sure don't feel like whipping nobody today!

[*She exits.*]

MAMA: [*The mother and son are left alone now and the mother waits a long time, considering deeply, before she speaks.*] Son — you — you understand what I done, don't you? [WALTER *is silent and sullen.*] I — I just seen my family falling apart today . . . just falling to pieces in front of my eyes . . . We couldn't of gone on like we was today. We was going backwards 'stead of forwards — talking 'bout killing babies and wishing each other was dead . . . When it gets like that in life — you just got to do something different, push on out and do something bigger . . . [*She waits.*] I wish you say something, son . . . I wish you'd say how deep inside you you think I done the right thing —

WALTER: [*crossing slowly to his bedroom door and finally turning there and speaking measuredly*] What you need me to say you done right for? *You* the head of this family. You run our lives like you want to. It was your money and you did what you wanted with it. So what you need for me to say it was all right for? [*bitterly, to hurt her as deeply as he knows is possible*] So you butchered up a dream of mine — you — who always talking 'bout your children's dreams . . .

MAMA: Walter Lee —

[*He just closes the door behind him.* MAMA *sits alone, thinking heavily.*]


SCENE II ———— *Time: Friday night. A few weeks later. At rise: Packing crates mark the intention of the family to move.* BENEATHA *and* GEORGE *come in, presumably from an evening out again.*

GEORGE: O.K. . . . O.K., whatever you say . . . [*They both sit on the couch. He tries to kiss her. She moves away.*] Look, we've had a nice evening; let's not spoil it, huh? . . .

[*He again turns her head and tries to nuzzle in and she turns away from him, not with distaste but with momentary lack of interest; in a mood to pursue what they were talking about.*]

BENEATHA: I'm *trying* to talk to you.

GEORGE: We always talk.

BENEATHA: Yes — and I love to talk.

GEORGE: [*exasperated; rising*] I know it and I don't mind it sometimes . . . I want you to cut it out, see — The moody stuff, I mean. I don't like it. You're a nice-looking girl . . . all over. That's all you need, honey, forget the atmosphere. Guys aren't going to go for the atmosphere — they're going to go for what they see. Be glad for that. Drop the Garbo routine. It doesn't go with you. As for myself, I want a nice — [*groping*] — simple [*thoughtfully*] — sophisticated girl . . . not a poet — O.K.?

[*She rebuffs him again and he starts to leave.*]

BENEATHA: Why are you angry?

GEORGE: Because this is stupid! I don't go out with you to discuss the nature of "quiet desperation" or to hear all about your thoughts — because the world will go on thinking what it thinks regardless —

BENEATHA: Then why read books? Why go to school?

GEORGE: [*with artificial patience, counting on his fingers*] It's simple. You read books — to learn facts — to get grades — to pass the course — to get a degree. That's all — it has nothing to do with thoughts.

[*A long pause.*]

BENEATHA: I see. [*a longer pause as she looks at him*] Good night, George.

[GEORGE *looks at her a little oddly, and starts to exit. He meets* MAMA *coming in.*]

GEORGE: Oh — hello, Mrs. Younger.

MAMA: Hello, George, how you feeling?

GEORGE: Fine — fine, how are you?

MAMA: Oh, a little tired. You know them steps can get you after a day's work. You all have a nice time tonight?

GEORGE: Yes — a fine time. Well, good night.

MAMA: Good night. [*He exits.* MAMA *closes the door behind her.*] Hello, honey. What you sitting like that for?

BENEATHA: I'm just sitting.

MAMA: Didn't you have a nice time?

BENEATHA: No.

MAMA: No? What's the matter?

BENEATHA: Mama, George is a fool — honest. [*She rises.*]

MAMA: [*Hustling around unloading the packages she has entered with. She stops.*] Is he, baby?

BENEATHA: Yes.

[BENEATHA *makes up* TRAVIS' *bed as she talks.*]

MAMA: You sure?

BENEATHA: Yes.

MAMA: Well — I guess you better not waste your time with no fools.

[BENEATHA *looks up at her mother, watching her put groceries in the refrigerator. Finally she gathers up her things and starts into the bedroom. At the door she stops and looks back at her mother.*]

BENEATHA: Mama —

MAMA: Yes, baby —

BENEATHA: Thank you.

MAMA: For what?

BENEATHA: For understanding me this time.

[*She exits quickly and the mother stands, smiling a little, looking at the place where* BENEATHA *just stood.* RUTH *enters.*]

RUTH: Now don't you fool with any of the stuff, Lena —

MAMA: Oh, I just thought I'd sort a few things out.

[*The phone rings.* RUTH *answers.*]

RUTH: [*at the phone*] Hello — Just a minute. [*goes to door*] Walter, it's Mrs. Arnold. [*Waits. Goes back to the phone. Tense*] Hello. Yes, this is his wife speaking . . . He's lying down now. Yes . . . well, he'll be in tomorrow. He's been very sick. Yes — I know we should have called, but we were so sure he'd be able to come in today. Yes — yes, I'm very sorry. Yes . . . Thank you very much. [*She hangs up.* WALTER *is standing in the doorway of the bedroom behind her.*] That was Mrs. Arnold.

WALTER: [*indifferently*] Was it?

RUTH: She said if you don't come in tomorrow that they are getting a new man . . .

WALTER: Ain't that sad — ain't that crying sad.

RUTH: She said Mr. Arnold has had to take a cab for three days . . . Walter, you ain't been to work for three days! [*This is a revelation to her.*] Where you been, Walter Lee Younger? [WALTER *looks at her and starts to laugh.*] You're going to lose your job.

WALTER: That's right . . .

RUTH: Oh, Walter, and with your mother working like a dog every day —

WALTER: That's sad too — Everything is sad.

MAMA: What you been doing for these three days, son?

WALTER: Mama — you don't know all the things a man what got leisure can find to do in this city . . . What's this — Friday night? Well — Wednesday I bor-

rowed Willy Harris' car and I went for a drive . . . just me and myself and I
drove and drove . . . Way out . . . way past South Chicago, and I parked
the car and I sat and looked at the steel mills all day long. I just sat in the car and
looked at them big black chimneys for hours. Then I drove back and I went to
the Green Hat. [*pause*] And Thursday — Thursday I borrowed the car again
and I got in it and I pointed it the other way and I drove the other way — for
hours — way, way up to Wisconsin, and I looked at the farms, O just drove and
looked at the farms. Then I drove back and I went to the Green Hat. [*pause*]
And today — today I didn't get the car. Today I just walked. All over the
Southside. And I looked at the Negroes and they looked at me and finally I just
sat down on the curb at Thirty-ninth and South Parkway and I just sat there
and watched the Negroes go by. And then I went to the Green Hat. You all
sad? You all depressed? And you know where I am going right now —

    [RUTH *goes out quickly.*]

MAMA: Oh, Big Walter, is this the harvest of our days?

WALTER: You know what I like about the Green Hat? [*He turns the radio on and a
steamy, deep blues pours into the room.*] I like this little cat they got there who
blows a sax . . . He blows. He talks to me. He ain't but 'bout five feet tall and
he's got a conked head and his eyes is always closed and he's all music —

MAMA: [*rising and getting some papers out of her handbag*] Walter —

WALTER: And there's this other guy who plays the piano . . . and they got a sound.
I mean they can work on some music . . . They got the best little combo in
the world in the Green Hat . . . You can just sit there and drink and listen to
them three men play and you realize that don't nothing matter worth a damn,
but just being there —

MAMA: I've helped do it to you, haven't I, son? Walter, I been wrong.

WALTER: Naw — you ain't never been wrong about nothing, Mama.

MAMA: Listen to me, now. I say I been wrong, son. That I been doing to you what the
rest of the world been doing to you. [*She stops and he looks up slowly at her
and she meets his eyes pleadingly.*] Walter — what you ain't never understood
is that I ain't got nothing, don't own nothing, ain't never really wanted nothing
that wasn't for you. There ain't nothing as precious to me . . . There ain't
nothing worth holding on to, money, dreams, nothing else — if it means — if it
means it's going to destroy my boy. [*She puts her papers in front of him and he
watches her without speaking or moving.*] I paid the man thirty-five hundred
dollars down on the house. That leaves sixty-five hundred dollars. Monday
morning I want you to take this money and take three thousand dollars and put
it in a savings account for Beneatha's medical schooling. The rest you put in a
checking account — with your name on it, and from now on any penny that
come out of it or that go in it is for you to look after. For you to decide. [*She
drops her hands a little helplessly.*] It ain't much, but it's all I got in the world
and I'm putting it in your hands. I'm telling you to be the head of this family
from now on like you supposed to be.

WALTER: [*stares at the money*] You trust me like that, Mama?

MAMA: I ain't never stop trusting you. Like I ain't never stop loving you.

    [*She goes out, and* WALTER *sits looking at the money on the table as the
music continues in its idiom, he gets up, and, in mingled joy and desperation, picks up the money. At the same moment,* TRAVIS *enters for bed.*]

TRAVIS: What's the matter, Daddy? You drunk?

WALTER: [*sweetly, more sweetly than we have ever known him*] No, Daddy ain't drunk. Daddy ain't going to never be drunk again. . . .

TRAVIS: Well, good night, Daddy.

[*The* FATHER *has come from behind the couch and leans over, embracing his son.*]

WALTER: Son, I feel like talking to you tonight.

TRAVIS: About what?

WALTER: Oh, about a lot of things. About you and what kind of man you going to be when you grow up . . . Son — son, what do you want to be when you grow up?

TRAVIS: A bus driver.

WALTER: [*laughing a little*] A what? Man, that ain't nothing to want to be!

TRAVIS: Why not?

WALTER: 'Cause, man — it ain't big enough — you know what I mean.

TRAVIS: I don't know then. I can't make up my mind. Sometimes Mama asks me that too. And sometimes when I tell her I just want to be like you — she says she don't want me to be like that and sometimes she says she does. . . .

WALTER: [*gathering him up in his arms*] You know what, Travis? In seven years you going to be seventeen years old. And things are going to be very different with us in seven years, Travis. . . . One day when you are seventeen I'll come home — home from my office downtown somewhere —

TRAVIS: You don't work in no office, Daddy.

WALTER: No — but after tonight. After what your daddy gonna do tonight, there's going to be offices — a whole lot of offices. . . .

TRAVIS: What you gonna do tonight, Daddy?

WALTER: You wouldn't understand yet, son, but your daddy's gonna make a transaction . . . a business transaction that's going to change our lives. . . . That's how come one day when you 'bout seventeen years old I'll come home and I'll be pretty tired, you know what I mean, after a day of conferences and secretaries getting things wrong the way they do . . . 'cause an executive's life is hell, man — [*The more he talks the farther away he gets.*] And I'll pull the car up on the driveway . . . just a plain black Chrysler, I think, with white walls — no — black tires. More elegant. Rich people don't have to be flashy . . . though I'll have to get something a little sportier for Ruth — maybe a Cadillac convertible to do her shopping in . . . And I'll come up the steps to the house and the gardener will be clipping away at the hedges and he'll say, "Good evening, Mr. Younger." And I'll say, "Hello, Jefferson, how are you this evening?" And I'll go inside and Ruth will come downstairs and meet me at the door and we'll kiss each other and she'll take my arm and we'll go up to your room to see you sitting on the floor with the catalogues of all the great schools in America around you . . . All the great schools in the world! And — and I'll say, all right son — it's your seventeenth birthday, what is it you've decided? . . . Just tell me where you want to go to school and you'll go. Just tell me, what is it you want to be — and you'll *be* it . . . Whatever you want to be — Yessir! [*He holds his arms open for* TRAVIS.] You just name it son . . . [TRAVIS *leaps into them.*] and I hand you the world!

[WALTER'S *voice has risen in pitch and hysterical promise and on the last line he lifts* TRAVIS *high.*]

SCENE III——— *Time: Saturday, moving day, one week later. Before the curtain rises.*
RUTH'S *voice, a strident, dramatic church alto, cuts through the silence.*

> [*It is, in the darkness, a triumphant surge, a penetrating statement of expectation: "Oh, Lord, I don't feel no ways tired! Children, oh, glory hallelujay!"*
>
>> *As the curtain rises we see that* RUTH *is alone in the living room, finishing up the family's packing. It is moving day. She is nailing crates and tying cartons.* BENEATHA *enters, carrying a guitar case, and watches her exuberant sister-in-law.*]

RUTH: Hey!

BENEATHA: [*putting away the case*] Hi.

RUTH: [*pointing at a package*] Honey — look in that package there and see what I found on sale this morning at the South Center. [RUTH *gets up and moves to the package and draws out some curtains*] Lookahere — hand-turned hems!

BENEATHA: How do you know the window size out there?

RUTH: [*who hadn't thought of that*] Oh — Well, they bound to fit something in the whole house. Anyhow, they was too good a bargain to pass up. [RUTH *slaps her head, suddenly remembering something.*] Oh, Bennie — I meant to put a special note on that carton over there. That's your mama's good china and she wants 'em to be very careful with it.

BENEATHA: I'll do it.

> [BENEATHA *finds a piece of paper and starts to draw large letters on it.*]

RUTH: You know what I'm going to do soon as I get in that new house?

BENEATHA: What?

RUTH: Honey — I'm going to run me a tub of water up to here . . . [*with her fingers practically up to her nostrils*] And I'm going to get in it — and I am going to sit . . . and sit . . . and sit in that hot water and the first person who knocks to tell *me* to hurry up and come out —

BENEATHA: Gets shot at sunrise.

RUTH: [*laughing happily*] You said it, sister! [*noticing how large* BENEATHA *is absent-mindedly making the note*] Honey, they ain't going to read that from no airplane.

BENEATHA: [*laughing herself*] I guess I always think things have more emphasis if they are big, somehow.

RUTH: [*looking up at her and smiling*] You and your brother seem to have that as a philosophy of life. Lord, that man — done changed so 'round here. You know — you know what we did last night? Me and Walter Lee?

BENEATHA: What?

RUTH: [*smiling to herself*] We went to the movies. [*looking at* BENEATHA *to see if she understands*] We went to the movies. You know the last time me and Walter went to the movies together?

BENEATHA: No.

RUTH: Me neither. That's how long it been. [*smiling again*] But we went last night. The picture wasn't much good, but that didn't seem to matter. We went — and we held hands.

BENEATHA: Oh, Lord!

RUTH: We held hands — and you know what.

BENEATHA: What?

RUTH: When we come out of the show it was late and dark and all the stores and things was closed up . . . and it was kind of chilly and there wasn't many people on the streets . . . and we was still holding hands, me and Walter.

BENEATHA: You're killing me.

[WALTER *enters with a large package. His happiness is deep in him; he cannot keep still with his new-found exuberance. He is singing and wiggling and snapping his fingers. He puts his package in a corner and puts a phonograph record, which he has just brought in with him, on the record player. As the music comes up he dances over to* RUTH *and tries to get her to dance with him. She gives in at last to his raunchiness and in a fit of giggling allows herself to be drawn into his mood and together they deliberately burlesque an old social dance of their youth.*]

BENEATHA: [*regarding them a long time as they dance, then drawing in her breath for a deeply exaggerated comment which she does not particularly mean*] Talk about — olddddddddddd-fashionedddddddd — Negroes!

WALTER: [*stopping momentarily*] What kind of Negroes?

[*He says this in fun. He is not angry with her today, nor with anyone. He starts to dance with his wife again.*]

BENEATHA: Old-fashioned.

WALTER: [*as he dances with* RUTH] You know, when these *New Negroes* have their convention — [*pointing at his sister*] — that is going to be the chairman of the Committee on Unending Agitation. [*He goes on dancing, then stops.*] Race, race, race! . . . Girl, I do believe you are the first person in the history of the entire human race to successfully brainwash yourself. [BENEATHA *breaks up and he goes on dancing. He stops again, enjoying his tease.*] Damn, even the N double A C P takes a holiday sometimes! [BENEATHA *and* RUTH *laugh. He dances with* RUTH *some more and starts to laugh and stops and pantomimes someone over an operating table.*] I can just see that chick someday looking down at some poor cat on an operating table before she starts to slice him, saying . . . [*pulling his sleeves back maliciously*] "By the way, what are your views on civil rights down there? . . ."

[*He laughs at her again and starts to dance happily. The bell sounds.*]

BENEATHA: Sticks and stones may break my bones but . . . words will never hurt me!

[BENEATHA *goes to the door and opens it as* WALTER *and* RUTH *go on with the clowning.* BENEATHA *is somewhat surprised to see a quiet-looking middle-aged white man in a business suit holding his hat and a briefcase in his hand and consulting a small piece of paper.*]

MAN: Uh — how do you do, miss. I am looking for a Mrs. — [*he looks at the slip of paper.*] Mrs. Lena Younger?

BENEATHA: [*smoothing her hair with slight embarrassment*] Oh — yes, that's my mother. Excuse me. [*She closes the door and turns to quiet the other two.*] Ruth! Brother! Somebody's here. [*Then she opens the door. The man casts a curious quick glance at all of them.*] Uh — come in please.

MAN: [*coming in*] Thank you.

BENEATHA: My mother isn't here now. Is it business?

MAN: Yes . . . well, sort of.

WALTER: [*freely, the Man of the House*] Have a seat. I'm Mrs. Younger's son. I look after most of her business matters.

[RUTH *and* BENEATHA *exchange amused glances.*]

MAN: [*regarding* WALTER, *and sitting*] Well — My name is Karl Lindner . . .

WALTER: [*stretching out his hand*] Walter Younger. This is my wife — [RUTH *nods politely.*] — and my sister.

LINDNER: How do you do.

WALTER: [*amiably, as he sits himself easily on a chair, leaning with interest forward on his knees and looking expectantly into the newcomer's face*] What can we do for you, Mr. Lindner!

LINDNER: [*some minor shuffling of the hat and briefcase on his knees*] Well — I am a representative of the Clybourne Park Improvement Association —

WALTER: [*pointing*] Why don't you sit your things on the floor?

LINDNER: Oh — yes. Thank you. [*He slides the briefcase and hat under the chair.*] And as I was saying — I am from the Clybourne Park Improvement Association and we have had it brought to our attention at the last meeting that you people — or at least your mother — has bought a piece of residential property at — [*He digs for the slip of paper again.*] — four o six Clybourne Street . . .

WALTER: That's right. Care for something to drink? Ruth, get Mr. Lindner a beer.

LINDNER: [*upset for some reason*] Oh — no, really. I mean thank you very much, but no thank you.

RUTH: [*innocently*] Some coffee?

LINDNER: Thank you, nothing at all.

[BENEATHA *is watching the man carefully.*]

LINDNER: Well, I don't know how much you folks know about our organization. [*He is a gentle man; thoughtful and somewhat labored in his manner.*] It is one of these community organizations set up to look after — oh, you know, things like block upkeep and special projects and we also have what we call our New Neighbors Orientation Committee . . .

BENEATHA: [*grily*] Yes — and what do they do?

LINDNER: [*turning a little to her and then returning the main force to* WALTER] Well — it's what you might call a sort of welcoming committee, I guess. I mean they, we, I'm the chairman of the committee — go around and see the new people who move into the neighborhood and sort of give them the lowdown on the way we do things out in Clybourne Park.

BENEATHA: [*with appreciation of the two meanings, which escape* RUTH *and* WALTER] Uh-huh.

LINDNER: And we also have the category of what the association calls — [*He looks elsewhere.*] — uh — special community problems . . .

BENEATHA: Yes — and what are some of those?

WALTER: Girl, let the man talk.

LINDNER: [*with understated relief*] Thank you. I would sort of like to explain this thing in my own way. I mean I want to explain to you in a certain way.

WALTER: Go ahead.

LINDNER: Yes. Well. I'm going to try to get right to the point. I'm sure we'll all appreciate that in the long run.

BENEATHA: Yes.

WALTER: Be still now!

LINDNER: Well —

RUTH: [*still innocently*] Would you like another chair — you don't look comfortable.

LINDNER: [*more frustrated than annoyed*] No, thank you very much. Please. Well

— to get right to the point I — [*a great breath, and he is off at last*] I am sure
you people must be aware of some of the incidents which have happened in
various parts of the city when colored people have moved into certain areas —
[BENEATHA *exhales heavily and starts tossing a piece of fruit up and down in the
air.*] Well — because we have what I think is going to be a unique type of
organization in American community life — not only do we deplore that kind
of thing — but we are trying to do something about it. [BENEATHA *stops tossing
and turns with a new and quizzical interest to the man.*] We feel — [*gaining
confidence in his mission because of the interest in the faces of the people he is
talking to*] — we feel that most of the trouble in this world, when you come
right down to it — [*He hits his knee for emphasis.*] — most of the trouble exists
because people just don't sit down and talk to each other.

RUTH: [*nodding as she might in church, pleased with the remark*] You can say that
again, mister.

LINDNER: [*more encouraged by such affirmation*] That we don't try hard enough in
this world to understand the other fellow's problem. The other guy's point of
view.

RUTH: Now that's right.

[BENEATHA *and* WALTER *merely watch and listen with genuine interest.*]

LINDNER: Yes — that's the way we feel out in Clybourne Park. And that's why I was
elected to come here this afternoon and talk to you people. Friendly like, you
know, the way people should talk to each other and see if we couldn't find
some way to work this thing out. As I say, the whole business is a matter of
*caring* about the other fellow. Anybody can see that you are a nice family of
folks, hard working and honest I'm sure. [BENEATHA *frowns slightly, quizzi-
cally, her head tilted regarding him.*] Today everybody knows what it means to
be on the outside of *something.* And of course, there is always somebody who is
out to take advantage of people who don't always understand.

WALTER: What do you mean?

LINDNER: Well — you see our community is made up of people who've worked hard
as the dickens for years to build up that little community. They're not rich and
fancy people; just hard-working, honest people who don't really have much
but those little homes and a dream of the kind of community they want to raise
their children in. Now, I don't say we are perfect and there is a lot wrong in
some of the things they want. But you've got to admit that a man, right or
wrong, has the right to want to have the neighborhood he lives in a certain kind
of way. And at the moment the overwhelming majority of our people out there
feel that people get along better, take more of a common interest in the life of
the community, when they share a common background. I want you to believe
me when I tell you that race prejudice simply doesn't enter into it. It is a matter
of the people of Clybourne Park believing, rightly or wrongly, as I say, that for
the happiness of all concerned that our Negro families are happier when they
live in their *own* communities.

BENEATHA: [*with a grand and bitter gesture*] This, friends, is the Welcoming Committee!

WALTER: [*dumbfounded, looking at* LINDNER] Is this what you came marching all the
way over here to tell us?

LINDNER: Well, now we've been having a fine conversation. I hope you'll hear me all
the way through.

WALTER: [*tightly*] Go ahead, man.

LINDNER: You see — in the face of all things I have said, we are prepared to make your family a very generous offer . . .

BENEATHA: Thirty pieces and not a coin less!

WALTER: Yeah?

LINDNER: [*putting on his glasses and drawing a form out of the briefcase*] Our association is prepared, through the collective effort of our people, to buy the house from you at a financial gain to your family.

RUTH: Lord have mercy, ain't this the living gall!

WALTER: All right, you through?

LINDNER: Well, I want to give you the exact terms of the financial arrangement —

WALTER: We don't want to hear no exact terms of no arrangements. I want to know if you got any more to tell us 'bout getting together?

LINDNER: [*taking off his glasses*] Well — I don't suppose that you feel . . .

WALTER: Never mind how I feel — you got any more to say 'bout how people ought to sit down and talk to each other? . . . Get out of my house, man.

[*He turns his back and walks to the door.*]

LINDNER: [*looking around at the hostile faces and reaching and assembling his hat and briefcase*] Well — I don't understand why you people are reacting this way. What do you think you are going to gain by moving into a neighborhood where you just aren't wanted and where some elements — well — people can get awful worked up when they feel that their whole way of life and everything they've ever worked for is threatened.

WALTER: Get out.

LINDNER: [*at the door, holding a small card*] Well — I'm sorry it went like this.

WALTER: Get out.

LINDNER: [*almost sadly regarding* WALTER] You just can't force people to change their hearts, son.

[*He turns and put his card on a table and exits.* WALTER *pushes the door to with stinging hatred, and stands looking at it.* RUTH *just sits and* BENEATHA *just stands. They say nothing.* MAMA *and* TRAVIS *enter.*]

MAMA: Well — this all the packing got done since I left out of here this morning. I testify before God that my children got all the energy of the dead. What time the moving men due?

BENEATHA: Four o'clock. You had a caller, Mama.

[*She is smiling, teasingly.*]

MAMA: Sure enough — who?

BENEATHA: [*her arms folded saucily*] The Welcoming Committee.

[WALTER *and* RUTH *giggle.*]

MAMA: [*innocently*] Who?

BENEATHA: The Welcoming Committee. They said they're sure going to be glad to see you when you get there.

WALTER: [*devilishly*] Yeah, they said they can't hardly wait to see your face.

[*laughter*]

MAMA: [*sensing their facetiousness*] What's the matter with you all?

WALTER: Ain't nothing the matter with us. We just telling you 'bout the gentleman who came to see you this afternoon. From the Clybourne Park Improvement Association.

MAMA: What he want?

RUTH: [*in the same mood as* BENEATHA *and* WALTER] To welcome you, honey.

WALTER: He said they can't hardly wait. He said the one thing they don't have, that they just *dying* to have out there is a fine family of colored people! [*to* RUTH *and* BENEATHA] Ain't that right!

RUTH *and* BENEATHA: [*mockingly*] Yeah! He left his card in case —
    [*They indicate the card, and* MAMA *picks it up and throws it on the floor — understanding and looking off as she draws her chair up to the table on which she has put her plant and some sticks and some cord.*]

MAMA: Father, give us strength. [*knowingly — and without fun*] Did he threaten us?

BENEATHA: Oh — Mama — they don't do it like that any more. He talked Brother-hood. He said everybody ought to learn how to sit down and hate each other with good Christian fellowship.
    [*She and* WALTER *shake hands to ridicule the remark.*]

MAMA: [*sadly*] Lord, protect us . . .

RUTH: You should hear the money those folks raised to buy the house from us. All we paid and then some.

BENEATHA: What they think we going to do — eat 'em?

RUTH: No, honey, marry 'em.

MAMA: [*shaking her head*] Lord, Lord, Lord . . .

RUTH: Well — that's the way the crackers crumble. Joke.

BENEATHA: [*laughingly noticing what her mother is doing*] Mama, what are you doing?

MAMA: Fixing my plant so it won't get hurt none on the way.

BENEATHA: Mama, you going to take *that* to the new house?

MAMA: Un-huh —

BENEATHA: That raggedy-looking old thing?

MAMA: [*stopping and looking at her*] It expresses *me*.

RUTH: [*with delight, to* BENEATHA] So there, Miss Thing!
    [WALTER *comes to* MAMA *suddenly and bends down behind her and squeezes her in his arms with all his strength. She is overwhelmed by the suddenness of it and, though delighted, her manner is like that of* RUTH *and* TRAVIS.]

MAMA: Look out now, boy! You make me mess up my thing here!

WALTER: [*His face lit, he slips down on his knees beside her, his arms still about her.*] Mama . . . you know what it means to climb up in the chariot?

MAMA: [*gruffly, very happy*] Get on away from me now . . .

RUTH: [*near the gift-wrapped package, trying to catch* WALTER's *eye*] Psst —

WALTER: What the old song say, Mama . . .

RUTH: Walter — Now?
    [*She is pointing at the package.*]

WALTER: [*Speaking the lines, sweetly, playfully, in his mother's face*]
    I got wings . . . you got wings . . .
    All God's Children got wings . . .

MAMA: Boy — get out of my face and do some work . . .

WALTER: When I get to heaven gonna put on my wings,
    Gonna fly all over God's heaven . . .

BENEATHA: [*teasingly, from across the room*] Everybody talking 'bout heaven ain't going there!

WALTER: [*to* RUTH, *who is carrying the box across to them*] I don't know, you think we ought to give her that . . . Seems to me she ain't been very appreciative around here.

MAMA: [*eyeing the box, which is obviously a gift*] What is that?

WALTER: [*taking it from* RUTH *and putting it on the table in front of* MAMA] Well — what do you think? Should we give it to her?

RUTH: Oh — she was pretty good today.

MAMA: I'll good you —
[*She turns her eyes to the box again.*]

BENEATHA: Open it, Mama.
[*She stands up, looks at it, turns and looks at all of them, and then presses her hands together and does not open the package.*]

WALTER: [*sweetly*] Open it, Mama. It's for you. [MAMA *looks in his eyes. It is the first present in her life without it being Christmas. Slowly she opens her package and lifts out, one by one, a brand-new sparkling set of gardening tools.* WALTER *continues, prodding.*] Ruth made up the note — read it . . .

MAMA: [*picking up the card and adjusting her glasses*] "To our own Mrs. Miniver — Love from Brother, Ruth and Beneatha." Ain't that lovely . . .

TRAVIS: [*tugging at his father's sleeve*] Daddy, can I give her mine now?

WALTER: All right son. [TRAVIS *flies to get his gift.*] Travis didn't want to go in with the rest of us, Mama. He got his own. [*somewhat amused*] We don't know what it is . . .

TRAVIS: [*racing back in the room with a large hatbox and putting it in front of his grandmother*] Here!

MAMA: Lord have mercy, baby. You done gone and bought your grandmother a hat?

TRAVIS: [*very proud*] Open it!
[*She does and lifts out an elaborate, but very elaborate, wide gardening hat, and all the adults break up at the sight of it.*]

RUTH: Travis, honey, what is that?

TRAVIS: [*who thinks it is beautiful and appropriate*] It's a gardening hat! Like the ladies always have on in the magazines when they work in their gardens.

BENEATHA: [*giggling fiercely*] Travis — we were trying to make Mama Mrs. Miniver — not Scarlett O'Hara!

MAMA: [*indignantly*] What's the matter with you all! This here is a beautiful hat! [*absurdly*] I always wanted me one just like it!
[*She pops it on her head to prove it to her grandson, and the hat is ludicrous and considerably oversized.*]

RUTH: Hot dog! Go, Mama!

WALTER: [*doubled over with laughter*] I'm sorry, Mama — but you look like you ready to go out and chop you some cotton sure enough!
[*They all laugh except* MAMA, *out of deference to* TRAVIS' *feelings.*]

MAMA: [*gathering the boy up to her*] Bless your heart — this is the prettiest hat I ever owned — [WALTER, RUTH *and* BENEATHA *chime in-noisily, festively and insincerely congratulating* TRAVIS *on his gift.*] What are we all standing here for? We ain't finished packin' yet. Bennie, you ain't packed one book.
[*The bell rings.*]

BENEATHA: That couldn't be the movers . . . it's not hardly two good yet —
[BENEATHA *goes into her room,* MAMA *starts for the door.*]

WALTER: [*turning, stiffening*] Wait — wait — I'll get it.
> [*He stands and looks at the door.*]
MAMA: You expecting company, son?
WALTER: [*just looking at the door*] Yeah — yeah . . .
> [MAMA *looks at* RUTH, *and they exchange innocent and unfrightened glances.*]
MAMA: [*not understanding*] Well, let them in, son.
BENEATHA: [*from her room*] We need some more string.
MAMA: Travis — you run to the hardware and get me some string cord.
> [MAMA *goes out and* WALTER *turns and looks at* RUTH. TRAVIS *goes to a dish for money.*]
RUTH: Why don't you answer the door, man?
WALTER: [*suddenly bounding across the floor to her*] 'Cause sometimes it hard to let the future begin! [*stooping down in her face*]
> I got wings! You got wings!
> All God's children got wings!
> [*He crosses to the door and throws it open. Standing there is a very slight little man in a not too prosperous business suit and with haunted frightened eyes and a hat pulled down tightly, brim up, around his forehead.* TRAVIS *passes between the men and exits.* WALTER *leans deep in the man's face, still in his jubilance.*]
> When I get to heaven gonna put on my wings,
> Gonna fly all over God's heaven . . .
> [*The little man just stares at him*]
> Heaven — [*Suddenly he stops and looks past the little man into the empty hallway.*] Where's Willy, man?
BOBO: He ain't with me.
WALTER: [*not disturbed*] Oh — come on in. You know my wife.
BOBO: [*dumbly, taking off his hat*] Yes — h'you, Miss Ruth.
RUTH: [*quietly, a mood apart from her husband already, seeing* BOBO] Hello, Bobo.
WALTER: You right on time today . . . Right on time. That's the way! [*He slaps* BOBO *on his back.*] Sit down . . . lemme hear.
> [RUTH *stands stiffly and quietly in back of them, as though somehow she senses death, her eyes fixed on her husband.*]
BOBO: [*his frightened eyes on the floor, his hat in his hands*] Could I please get a drink of water, before I tell you about it, Walter Lee?
> [WALTER *does not take his eyes off the man.* RUTH *goes blindly to the tap and gets a glass of water and brings it to* BOBO.]
WALTER: There ain't nothing wrong, is there?
BOBO: Lemme tell you —
WALTER: Man — didn't nothing go wrong?
BOBO: Lemme tell you — Walter Lee. [*looking at* RUTH *and talking to her more than to* WALTER] You know how it was. I got to tell you how it was. I mean first I got to tell you how it was all the way . . . I mean about the money I put in, Walter Lee . . .
WALTER: [*with taut agitation now*] What about the money you put in?
BOBO: Well — it wasn't much as we told you — me and Willy — [*He stops.*] I'm sorry, Walter. I got a bad feeling about it. I got a real bad feeling about it . . .

WALTER: Man, what you telling me about all this for? . . . Tell me what happened in Springfield . . .

BOBO: Springfield.

RUTH: [*like a dead woman*] What was supposed to happen in Springfield?

BOBO: [*to her*] This deal that me and Walter went into with Willy — Me and Willy was going to go down to Springfield and spread some money 'round so's we wouldn't have to wait so long for the liquor licence . . . That's what we were going to do. Everybody said that was the way you had to do, you understand, Miss Ruth?

WALTER: Man — what happened down there?

BOBO: [*a pitiful man, near tears*] I'm trying to tell you, Walter.

WALTER: [*screaming at him suddenly*] THEN TELL ME, GODDAM- MIT . . . WHAT'S THE MATTER WITH YOU?

BOBO: Man . . . I didn't go to no Springfield, yesterday.

WALTER: [*halted, life hanging in the moment*] Why not?

BOBO: [*the long way, the hard way to tell*] 'Cause I didn't have no reasons to . . .

WALTER: Man, what are you talking about!

BOBO: I'm talking about the fact that when I got to the train station yesterday morning — eight o'clock like we planned . . . Man — *Willy didn't never show up.*

WALTER: Why . . . where was he . . . where is he?

BOBO: That's what I'm trying to tell you . . . I don't know . . . I waited six hours . . . I called his house . . . and I waited . . . six hours . . . I waited in that train station six hours . . . [*breaking into tears*] That was all the extra money I had in the world . . . [*looking up at* WALTER *with tears running down his face*] Man, *Willy is gone.*

WALTER: Gone, what you mean Willy is gone? Gone where? You mean he went by himself. You mean he went off to Springfield by himself — to take care of getting the license — [*turns and looks anxiously at* RUTH] You mean maybe he didn't want too many people in on the business down there? [*looks to* RUTH *again, as before*] You know Willy got his own ways. [*looks back to* BOBO] Maybe you was late yesterday and he just went on down there without you. Maybe — maybe — he's been callin' you at home tryin' to tell you what happened or something. Maybe — maybe — he just got sick. He's some- where — he's got to be somewhere. We just got to find him — me and you got to find him. [*grabs* BOBO *senselessly by the collar and starts to shake him*] We got to!

BOBO: [*in sudden angry, frightened agony*] What's the matter with you, Walter! *When a cat take off with your money he don't leave you no maps!*

WALTER: [*turning madly, as though he is looking for* WILLY *in the very room*] Willy! . . . Willy . . . don't do it . . . Please don't do it . . . Man, not with that money . . . Man, please, not with that money . . . Oh, God . . . Don't let it be true . . . [*He is wandering around, crying out for* WILLY *and looking for him or perhaps for help from God.*] Man . . . I trusted you . . . Man, I put my life in your hands . . . [*He starts to crumple down on the floor as* RUTH *just covers her face in horror.* MAMA *opens the door and comes into the room, with* BENEATHA *behind her.*] Man . . . [*He starts to pound the floor with his fists, sobbing wildly.*] That money is made out of my father's flesh . . .

BOBO: [*standing over him helplessly*] I'm sorry, Walter . . . [*Only* WALTER'S *sobs reply.* BOBO *puts on his hat.*] I had my life staked on the this deal, too . . . [*He exits.*]

MAMA: [*to* WALTER] Son — [*She goes to him, bends down to him, talks to his bent head.*] Son . . . Is it gone? Son, I gave you sixty-five hundred dollars. Is it gone? All of it? Beneatha's money too?

WALTER: [*lifting his head slowly*] Mama . . . I never . . . went to the bank at all . . .

MAMA: [*not wanting to believe him*] You mean . . . your sister's school money . . . you used that too . . . Walter? . . .

WALTER: Yessss! . . . All of it . . . It's all gone . . .

> [*There is total silence.* RUTH *stands with her face covered with her hands;* BENEATHA *leans forlornly against a wall, fingering a piece of red ribbon from the mother's gift.* MAMA *stops and looks at her son without recognition and then, quite without thinking about it, starts to beat him senselessly in the face.* BENEATHA *goes to them to stop it.*]

BENEATHA: Mama!

> [MAMA *stops and looks at both of her children and rises slowly and wanders vaguely, aimlessly away from them.*]

MAMA: I seen . . . him . . . night after night . . . come in . . . and look at that rug . . . and then look at me . . . the red showing in his eyes . . . the veins moving in his head . . . I seen him grow thin and old before he was forty . . . working and working and working like somebody's old horse . . . killing himself . . . and you — you give it all away in a day . . .

BENEATHA: Mama —

MAMA: Oh, God . . . [*She looks up to Him.*] Look down here — and show me the strength.

BENEATHA: Mama —

MAMA: [*folding over*] Strength . . .

BENEATHA: [*plaintively*] Mama . . .

MAMA: Strength!

# ACT III

*An hour later.*

> At curtain, there is a sullen light of gloom in the living room, gray light not unlike that which began the first scene of Act One. At left we can see WALTER within his room, alone with himself. He is stretched out on the bed, his shirt out and open, his arms under his head. He does not smoke, he does not cry out, he merely lies there, looking up at the ceiling, much as if he were alone in the world.
> In the living room BENEATHA sits at the table, still surrounded by the now almost ominous packing crates. She sits looking off. We feel that this is a mood struck perhaps an hour before, and it lingers now, full of the empty sound of profound disappointment. We see on a line from her brother's bedroom the sameness of their attitudes. Presently the bell rings and BENEATHA rises without ambition or interest in answering. It is ASAGAI, smiling broadly, striding into the room with energy and happy expectation and conversation.

ASAGAI: I came over . . . I had some free time. I thought I might help with the packing. Ah, I like the look of packing crates! A household in preparation for a journey! It depresses some people . . . but for me . . . it is another feeling. Something full of the flow of life, do you understand? Movement, progress . . . It makes me think of Africa.

BENEATHA: Africa!

ASAGAI: What kind of a mood is this? Have I told you how deeply you move me?

BENEATHA: He gave away the money, Asagai . . .

ASAGAI: Who gave away what money?

BENEATHA: The insurance money. My brother gave it away.

ASAGAI: Gave it away?

BENEATHA: He made an investment! With a man even Travis wouldn't have trusted.

ASAGAI: And it's gone?

BENEATHA: Gone!

ASAGAI: I'm very sorry . . . And you, now?

BENEATHA: Me? . . . Me? . . . Me I'm nothing . . . Me. When I was very small . . . we used to take our sleds out in the wintertime and the only hills we had were ice-covered stone steps of some houses down the street. And we used to fill them in with snow and make them smooth and slide down them all day . . . and it was very dangerous you know . . . far too steep . . . and sure enough one day a kid named Rufus came down too fast and hit the sidewalk . . . and we saw his face just split open right there in front of us . . . And I remember standing there looking at his bloody open face thinking that was the end of Rufus. But the ambulance came and they took him to the hospital and they fixed the broken bones and they sewed it all up . . . and the next time I saw Rufus he just had a little line down the middle of his face . . . I never got over that . . .

> [WALTER *sits up, listening on the bed. Throughout this scene it is important that we feel his reaction at all times, that he visibly respond to the words of his sister and* ASAGAI.]

ASAGAI: What?

BENEATHA: That that was what one person could do for another, fix him up — sew up the problem, make him all right again. That was the most marvelous thing in the world . . . I wanted to do that. I always thought it was the one concrete thing in the world that a human being could do. Fix up the sick, you know — and make them whole again. This was truly being God . . .

ASAGAI: You wanted to be God?

BENEATHA: No — I wanted to cure. It used to be so important to me. I wanted to cure. It used to matter. I used to care. I mean about people and how their bodies hurt . . .

ASAGAI: And you've stopped caring?

BENEATHA: Yes — I think so.

ASAGAI: Why?

> [WALTER *rises, goes to the door of his room and is about to open it, then stops and stands listening, leaning on the door jamb.*]

BENEATHA: Because it doesn't seem deep enough, close enough to what ails mankind — I mean this thing of sewing up bodies or administering drugs. Don't you understand? It was a child's reaction to the world. I thought that doctors had the secret to all the hurts . . . That's the way a child sees things — or an idealist.

ASAGAI: Children see things very well sometimes — and idealists even better.

BENEATHA: I know that's what you think. Because you are still where I left off — you still care. This is what you see for the world, for Africa. You with the dreams of the future will patch up all Africa — you are going to cure the Great Sore of colonialism with Independence —

ASAGAI: Yes!

BENEATHA: Yes — and you think that one word is the penicillin of the human spirit: "Independence!" But then what?

ASAGAI: That will be the problem for another time. First we must get there.

BENEATHA: And where does it end?

ASAGAI: End? Who even spoke of an end? To life? To Living?

BENEATHA: An end to misery!

ASAGAI: [*smiling*] You sound like a French intellectual.

BENEATHA: No! I sound like a human being who just had her future taken right out of her hands! While I was sleeping in my bed in there, things were happening in this world that directly concerned me — and nobody asked me, consulted me — they just went out and did things — and changed my life. Don't you see there isn't any real progress, Asagai, there is only one large circle that we march in, around and around, each of us with our own little picture — in front of us — our own little mirage that we think is the future.

ASAGAI: That is the mistake.

BENEATH: What?

ASAGAI: What you just said — about the circle. It isn't a circle — it is simply a long line — as in geometry, you know, one that reaches into infinity. And because we cannot see the end — we also cannot see how it changes. And it is very odd but those who see the changes are called "idealists" — and those who cannot, or refuse to think, they are the "realists." It is very strange, and amusing too, I think.

BENEATHA: You — you are almost religious.

ASAGAI: Yes . . . I think I have the religion of doing what is necessary in the world — and of worshipping man — because he is so marvelous, you see.

BENEATHA: Man is foul! And the human race deserves its misery!

ASAGAI: You see: *you* have become the religious one in the old sense. Already, and after such a small defeat, you are worshipping despair.

BENEATHA: From now on, I worship the truth — and the truth is that people are puny, small and selfish . . .

ASAGAI: Truth? Why is it that you despairing ones always think that only you have the truth? I never thought to see *you* like that. You! Your brother made a stupid, childish mistake — and you are grateful to him. So that now you can give up the ailing human race on account of it. You talk about what good is struggle; what good is anything? Where are we all going? And why are we bothering?

BENEATHA: *And you cannot answer it!* All your talk and dreams about Africa and Independence. Independence and then what? What about all the crooks and petty thieves and just plain idiots who will come into power to steal and plunder the same as before — only now they will be black and do it in the name of the new Independence — You cannot answer that.

ASAGAI: [*shouting over her*] *I live the answer!* [*pause*] In my village at home it is the exceptional man who can even read a newspaper . . . or who ever *sees* a book at all. I will go home and much of what I will have to say will seem strange to the people of my village . . . But I will teach and work and things will happen, slowly and swiftly. At times it will seem that nothing changes at all . . . and then again . . . the sudden dramatic events which make history leap into the future. And then quiet again. Retrogression even. Guns, murder, revolution. And I even will have moments when I wonder if the quiet was not better than all that death and hatred. But I will look about my village at the illiteracy and disease and ignorance and I will not wonder long. And perhaps . . . perhaps I will be a great man . . . I mean perhaps I will hold on to the substance of truth and find my way always with the right course . . . and perhaps for it I will be butchered in my bed some night by the servants of empire . . .

BENEATHA: *The martyr!*

ASAGAI: . . . or perhaps I shall live to be a very old man, respected and esteemed in my new nation . . . And perhaps I shall hold office and this is what I'm trying to tell you, Alaiyo; perhaps the things I believe now for my country will be wrong and outmoded, and I will not understand and do terrible things to have things my way or merely to keep my power. Don't you see that there will be young men and women, not British soldiers then, but my own black countrymen . . . to step out of the shadows some evening and slit my then useless throat? Don't you see they have always been there . . . that they always will be. And that such a thing as my own death will be an advance? They who might kill me even . . . actually replenish me!

BENEATHA: Oh, Asagai, I know all that.

ASAGAI: Good! Then stop moaning and groaning and tell me what you plan to do.

BENEATHA: Do?

ASAGAI: I have a bit of a suggestion.

BENEATHA: What?

ASAGAI: [*rather quietly for him*] That when it is all over — that you come home with me —

BENEATHA: [*slapping herself on the forehead with exasperation born of misunderstanding*] Oh — Asagai — at this moment you decide to be romantic!

ASAGAI: [*quickly understanding the misunderstanding*] My dear, young creature of the New World — I do not mean across the city — I mean across the ocean; home — to Africa.

BENEATHA: [*slowly understanding and turning to him with murmured amazement*] To — to Nigeria?

ASAGAI: Yes! . . . [*smiling and lifting his arms playfully*] Three hundred years later the African Prince rose up out of the seas and swept the maiden back across the middle passage over which her ancestors had come —

BENEATHA: [*unable to play*] Nigeria?

ASAGAI: Nigeria. Home. [*coming to her with genuine romantic flippancy*] I will show you our mountains and our stars; and give you cool drinks from gourds and

teach you the old songs and the ways of our people — and, in time, we will
pretend that — [*very softly*] — you have only been away for a day —
  [*She turns her back to him, thinking. He swings her around and takes her
  full in his arms in a long embrace which proceeds to passion.*]
BENEATHA: [*pulling away*] You're getting me all mixed up —
ASAGAI: Why?
BENEATHA: Too many things — too many things have happened today. I must sit
  down and think. I don't know what I feel about anything right this minute.
  [*She promptly sits down and props her chin on her fist.*]
ASAGAI: [*charmed*] All right, I shall leave you. No — don't get up. [*touching her,
  gently, sweetly*] Just sit awhile and think . . . Never be afraid to sit awhile and
  think. [*He goes to the door and looks at her.*] How often I have looked at you
  and said, "Ah — so this is what the New World hath finally wrought . . ."
  [*He exits.* BENEATHA *sits on alone. Presently* WALTER *enters from his room
  and starts to rummage through things, feverishly looking for something.
  She looks up and turns in her seat.*]
BENEATHA: [*hissingly*] Yes — just look at what the New World hath wrought! . . .
  Just look! [*She gestures with bitter disgust.*] There he is! *Monsieur le petit
  bourgeois noir* — himself! There he is — Symbol of a Rising Class! Entrepre-
  neur! Titan of the system! [WALTER *ignores her completely and continues
  frantically and destructively looking for something and hurling things to floor
  and tearing things out of their place in his search.* BENEATHA *ignores the
  eccentricity of his actions and goes on with the monologue of insult.*] Did you
  dream of yachts on Lake Michigan, Brother? Did you see yourself on that
  Great Day sitting down at the Conference Table, surrounded by all the mighty
  bald-headed men in America? All halted, waiting, breathless, waiting for your
  pronouncements on industry? Waiting for you — Chairman of the Board?
  [WALTER *finds what he is looking for — a small piece of white paper — and
  pushes it in his pocket and puts on his coat and rushes out without ever having
  looked at her. She shouts after him.*] I look at you and I see the final triumph of
  stupidity in the world!
  [*The door slams and she returns to just sitting again.* RUTH *comes quickly
  out of* MAMA'S *room.*]
RUTH: Who was that?
BENEATHA: Your husband.
RUTH: Where did he go?
BENEATHA: Who knows — maybe he has an appointment at U.S. Steel.
RUTH: [*anxiously, with frightened eyes*] You didn't say nothing bad to him, did you?
BENEATHA: Bad? Say anything bad to him? No — I told him he was a sweet boy and
  full of dreams and everything is strictly peachy keen, as the ofay kids say!
  [MAMA *enters from her bedroom. She is lost, vague, trying to catch hold, to
  make some sense of her former command of the world, but it still eludes
  her. A sense of waste overwhelms her gait; a measure of apology rides on
  her shoulders. She goes to her plant, which has remained on the table,
  looks at it, picks it up and takes it to the window sill and sits it outside, and
  she stands and looks at it a long moment. Then she closes the window,
  straightens her body with effort and turns around to her children.*]
MAMA: Well — ain't it a mess in here, though? [*a false cheerfulness, a beginning of*

*something*] I guess we all better stop moping around and get some work done. All this unpacking and everything we got to do. [RUTH *raises her head slowly in response to the sense of the line; and* BENEATHA *in similar manner turns very slowly to look at her mother.*] One of you all better call the moving people and tell 'em not to come.

RUTH: Tell 'em not to come?

MAMA: Of course, baby. Ain't no need in 'em coming all the way here and having to go back. They charge for that too. [*She sits down, fingers to her brow, thinking.*] Lord, ever since I was a little girl, I always remembers people saying, "Lena — Lena Eggleston, you aims too high all the time. You needs to slow down and see life a little more like it is. Just slow down some." That's what they always used to say down home — "Lord, that Lena Eggleston is a high-minded thing. She'll get her due one day!"

RUTH: No, Lena . . .

MAMA: Me and Big Walter just didn't never learn right.

RUTH: Lena, no! We gotta go. Bennie — tell her . . . [*She rises and crosses to* BENEATHA *with her arms outstretched.* BENEATHA *doesn't respond.*] Tell her we can still move . . . the notes ain't but a hundred and twenty-five a month. We got four grown people in the house — we can work . . .

MAMA: [*to herself*] Just aimed too high all the time —

RUTH: [*turning and going to* MAMA *fast — the words pouring out with urgency and desperation*] Lena — I'll work . . . I'll work twenty hours a day in all the kitchens in Chicago . . . I'll strap my baby on my back if I have to and scrub all the floors in America and wash all the sheets in America if I have to — but we got to move . . . We got to get out of here . . .

[MAMA *reaches out absently and pats* RUTH's *hand.*]

MAMA: No — I see things differently now. Been thinking 'bout some of the things we could do to fix this place up some. I seen a second-hand bureau over on Maxwell Street just the other day that could fit right here. [*She points to where the new furniture might go.* RUTH *wanders away from her.*] Would need some new handles on it and then a little varnish and then it look like something brand-new. And — we can put up them new curtains in the kitchen . . . Why this place be looking fine. Cheer us all up so that we forget trouble ever came . . . [*to* RUTH] And you could get some nice screens to put up in your room round the baby's bassinet . . . [*She looks at both of them, pleadingly.*] Sometimes you just got to know when to give up some things . . . and hold on to what you got.

[WALTER *enters from the outside, looking spent and leaning against the door, his coat hanging from him.*]

MAMA: Where you been, son?

WALTER: [*breathing hard*] Made a call.

MAMA: To who, son?

WALTER: To The Man.

MAMA: What man, baby?

WALTER: The Man, Mama. Don't you know who The Man is?

RUTH: Walter Lee?

WALTER: *The Man.* Like the guys in the streets say — The Man. Captain Boss — Mistuh Charley . . . Old Captain Please Mr. Bossman . . .

BENEATHA: [*suddenly*] Lindner!

WALTER: That's right! That's good. I told him to come right over.

BENEATHA: [*fiercely, understanding*] For what? What do you want to see him for!

WALTER: [*looking at his sister*] We going to do business with him.

MAMA: What you talking 'bout, son?

WALTER: Talking 'bout life, Mama. You all always telling me to see life like it is. Well — I laid in there on my back today . . . and I figured it out. Life just like it is. Who gets and who don't get. [*He sits down with his coat on and laughs.*] Mama, you know it's all divided up. Life is. Sure enough. Between the takers and the "tooken." [*He laughs.*] I've figured it out finally. [*He looks around at them.*] Yeah. Some of us always getting "tooken." [*He laughs.*] People like Willy Harris, they don't never get "tooken." And you know why the rest of us do? 'Cause we all mixed up. Mixed up bad. We get to looking 'round for the right and the wrong; and we worry about it and cry about it and stay up nights trying to figure out 'bout the wrong and the right of things all the time . . . And all the time, man, them takers is out there operating, just taking and taking. Willy Harris? Shoot — Willy Harris don't even count. He don't even count in the big scheme of things. But I'll say one thing for old Willy Harris . . . he's taught me something. He's taught me to keep my eye on what counts in this world. Yeah — [*shouting out a little*] Thanks, Willie!

RUTH: What did you call that man for, Walter Lee?

WALTER: Called him to tell him to come over to the show. Gonna put on a show for the man. Just what he wants to see. You see, Mama, the man came here today and he told us that them people out there where you want us to move — well they so upset they willing to pay us not to move out there. [*He laughs again.*] And — and oh, Mama — you would of been proud of the way me and Ruth and Bennie acted. We told him to get out . . . Lord have mercy! We told the man to get out. Oh, we was some proud folks this afternoon, yeah. [*He lights a cigarette.*] We were still full of that old-time stuff . . .

RUTH: [*coming toward him slowly*] You talking 'bout taking them people's money to keep us from moving in that house?

WALTER: I ain't just talking 'bout it, baby — I'm telling you that's what's going to happen.

BENEATHA: Oh, God! Where is the bottom! Where is the real honest-to-God bottom so he can't go any further.

WALTER: See — that's the old stuff. You and that boy that was here today. You all want everybody to carry a flag and a spear and sing some marching songs, huh? You wanna spend your life looking into things and trying to find the right and the wrong part, huh? Yeah. You know what's going to happen to that boy someday — he'll find himself sitting in a dungeon, locked in forever — and the takers will have the key! Forget it, baby! There ain't no causes — there ain't nothing but taking in this world, and he who takes most is smartest — and it don't make a damn bit of difference *how*.

MAMA: You making something inside me cry, son. Some awful pain inside me.

WALTER: Don't cry, Mama. Understand. That white man is going to walk in that door able to write checks for more money than we ever had. It's important to him and I'm going to help him . . . I'm going to put on the show, Mama.

MAMA: Son — I come from five generations of people who was slaves and sharecroppers — but ain't nobody in my family never let nobody pay 'em no money that was a way of telling us we wasn't fit to walk the earth. We ain't never been that poor. [*raising her eyes and looking at him*] We ain't never been that dead inside.

BENEATHA: Well — we are dead now. All the talk about dreams and sunlight that goes on in this house. All dead.

WALTER: What's the matter with you all! I didn't make the world! It was give to me this way! Hell, yes, I want me some yachts someday! Yes, I want to hang some real pearls 'round my wife's neck. Ain't she supposed to wear no pearls? Somebody tell me — tell me, who decides which women is supposed to wear pearls in this world. I tell you I am a *man* — and I think my wife should wear some pearls in this world!

> [*This last line hangs a good while and* WALTER *begins to move about the room. The word "Man" has penetrated his consciousness; he mumbles it to himself repeatedly between strange agitated pauses as he moves about.*]

MAMA: Baby, how you going to feel on the inside?

WALTER: Fine! . . . Going to feel fine . . . a man . . .

MAMA: You won't have nothing left then, Walter Lee.

WALTER: [*coming to her*] I'm going to feel fine, Mama. I'm going to look that son-of-a-bitch in the eyes and say — [*He falters.*] — and say, "All right, Mr. Lindner — [*He falters even more.*] — that's your neighborhood out there. You got the right to keep it like you want. You got the right to have it like you want. Just write the check and — the house is yours." And, and I am going to say — [*His voice almost breaks.*] And you — you people just put the money in my hand and you won't have to live next to this bunch of stinking niggers! . . . [*He straightens up and moves away from his mother, walking around the room.*] Maybe — maybe I'll just get down on my black knees . . . [*He does so;* RUTH *and* BENNIE *and* MAMA *watch him in frozen horror.*] Captain, Mistuh, Bossman. [*He starts crying.*] A-hee-hee-hee! [*wringing his hands in profoundly anguished imitation*] Yasssssuh! Great White Father, just gi' ussen de money, fo' God's sake, and we's ain't gwine come out deh and dirty up yo' white folks neighborhood . . .

> [*He breaks down completely, then gets up and goes into the bedroom.*]

BENEATHA: That is not a man. That is nothing but a toothless rat.

MAMA: Yes — death done come in this here house. [*She is nodding, slowly, reflectively.*] Done come walking in my house. On the lips of my children. You what supposed to be my beginning again. You — what supposed to be my harvest. [*to* BENEATHA] You — you mourning your brother?

BENEATHA: He's no brother of mine.

MAMA: What you say?

BENEATHA: I said that individual in that room is no brother of mine.

MAMA: That's what I thought you said. You feeling like you better than he is today? [BENEATHA *does not answer.*] Yes? What you tell him a minute ago? That he wasn't a man? Yes? You give him up for me? You done wrote his epitaph too — like the rest of the world? Well, who give you the privilege?

BENEATHA: Be on my side for once! You saw what he just did, Mama! You saw him — down on his knees. Wasn't it you who taught me — to despise any man who would do that. Do what he's going to do.

MAMA: Yes—I taught you that. Me and your daddy. But I thought I taught you something else too . . . I thought I taught you to love him.

BENEATHA: Love him? There is nothing left to love.

MAMA: There is always something left to love. And if you ain't learned that, you ain't learned nothing. [*looking at her*] Have you cried for that boy today? I don't mean for yourself and for the family 'cause we lost the money. I mean for him; what he been through and what it done to him. Child, when do you think is the time to love somebody the most; when they done good and made things easy for everybody? Well then, you ain't through learning—because that ain't the time at all. It's when he's at his lowest and can't believe in hissself 'cause the world done whipped him so. When you starts measuring somebody, measure him right, child, measure him right. Make sure you done taken into account what hills and valleys he come through before he got to wherever he is.

[TRAVIS *bursts into the room at the end of the speech, leaving the door open.*]

TRAVIS: Grandmama—the moving men are downstairs! The truck just pulled up.

MAMA: [*turning and looking at him*] Are they, baby? They downstairs?

[*She sighs and sits.* LINDNER *appears in the doorway. He peers in and knocks lightly, to gain attention, and comes in. All turn to look at him.*]

LINDNER: [*hat and briefcase in hand*] Uh—hello . . . [RUTH *crosses mechanically to the bedroom door and opens it and lets it swing open freely and slowly as the lights come up on* WALTER *within, still in his coat, sitting at the far corner of the room. He looks up and out through the room to* LINDNER.]

RUTH: He's here.

[*A long minute passes and* WALTER *slowly gets up.*]

LINDNER: [*coming to the table with efficiency, putting his briefcase on the table and starting to unfold papers and unscrew fountain pens*] Well, I certainly was glad to hear from you people. [WALTER *has begun the trek out of the room, slowly and awkwardly, rather like a small boy, passing the back of his sleeve across his mouth from time to time.*] Life can really be so much simpler than people let it be most of the time. Well—with whom do I negotiate? You, Mrs. Younger, or your son here? [MAMA *sits with her hands folded on her lap and her eyes closed as* WALTER *advances.* TRAVIS *goes close to* LINDNER *and looks at the papers curiously.*] Just some official papers, sonny.

RUTH: Travis, you go downstairs.

MAMA: [*opening her eyes and looking into* WALTER'S] No. Travis, you stay right here. And you make him understand what you doing, Walter Lee. You teach him good. Like Willy Harris taught you. You show where our five generations done come to. Go ahead, son—

WALTER: [*looks down into his boy's eyes.* TRAVIS *grins at him merrily and* WALTER *draws him beside him with his arm lightly around his shoulders.*] Well, Mr. Lindner. [BENEATHA *turns away.*] We called you—[*There is a profound, simple groping quality in his speech.*]—because, well, me and my family [*He looks around and shifts from one foot to the other.*] Well—we are very plain people . . .

LINDNER: Yes—

WALTER: I mean—I have worked as a chauffeur most of my life—and my wife here, she does domestic work in people's kitchens. So does my mother. I mean—we are plain people . . .

LINDNER: Yes, Mr. Younger—

WALTER: [*really like a small boy, looking down at his shoes and then up at the man*] And—uh—well, my father, well, he was a laborer most of his life.

LINDNER: [*absolutely confused*] Uh, yes—

WALTER: [*looking down at his toes once again*] My father almost beat a man to death once because this man called him a bad name or something, you know what I mean?

LINDNER: No, I'm afraid I don't.

WALTER: [*finally straightening up*] Well, what I mean is that we come from people who had a lot of pride. I mean — we are very proud people. And that's my sister over there and she's going to be a doctor—and we are very proud—

LINDNER: Well—I am sure that is very nice, but—

WALTER: [*starting to cry and facing the man eye to eye*] What I am telling you is that we called you over here to tell you that we are very proud and that this is — this is my son, who makes the sixth generation of our family in this country, and that we have all thought about your offer and we have decided to move into our house because my father—my father—he earned it. [MAMA *has her eyes closed and is rocking back and forth as though she were in church, with her head nodding the amen yes.*] We don't want to make no trouble for nobody or fight no causes — but we will try to be good neighbors. That's all we got to say. [*He looks the man absolutely in the eyes.*] We don't want your money.

[*He turns and walks away from the man.*]

LINDNER: [*looking around at all of them*] I take it then that you have decided to occupy.

BENEATHA: That's what the man said.

LINDNER: [*to* MAMA *in her reverie*] Then I would like to appeal to you, Mrs. Younger. You are older and wiser and understanding things better I am sure . . .

MAMA: [*rising*] I am afraid you don't understand. My son said we was going to move and there ain't nothing left for me to say. [*shaking her head with double meaning*] You know how these young folks is nowadays, mister. Can't do a thing with 'em. Good-bye.

LINDNER: [*folding up his materials*] Well—if you are that final about it . . . There is nothing left for me to say. [*He finishes. He is almost ignored by the family, who are concentrating on* WALTER LEE. *At the door* LINDNER *halts and looks around.*] I sure hope you people know what you're doing.

[*He shakes his head and exits.*]

RUTH: [*looking around and coming to life*] Well, for God's sake — if the moving men are here—LET'S GET THE HELL OUT OF HERE!

MAMA: [*into action*] Ain't it the truth! Look at all this here mess. Ruth, put Travis' good jacket on him . . . Walter Lee, fix your tie and tuck your shirt in, you look just like somebody's hoodlum. Lord have mercy, where is my plant? [*She flies to get it amid the general bustling of the family, who are deliberately trying to ignore the nobility of the past moment.*] You all start on down . . . Travis child, don't go empty-handed . . . Ruth, where did I put that box with my skillets in it? I want to be in charge of it myself. . . . I'm going to make us the biggest dinner we ever ate tonight . . . Beneatha, what's the matter with them stockings? Pull them things up, girl . . .

[*The family starts to file out as two moving men appear and begin to carry out the heavier pieces of furniture, bumping into the family as they move about.*]

BENEATHA: Mama, Asagai — asked me to marry him today and go to Africa —

MAMA: [*in the middle of her getting-ready activity*] He did? You ain't old enough to marry nobody — [*seeing the moving men lifting one of her chairs precariously*] Darling, that ain't no bale of cotton, please handle it so we can sit in it again. I had that chair twenty-five years . . .

[*The movers sigh with exasperation and go on with their work.*]

BENEATHA: [*girlishly and unreasonably trying to pursue the conversation*] To go to Africa, Mama — be a doctor in Africa . . .

MAMA: [*distracted*] Yes, baby —

WALTER: Africa! What he want you to go to Africa for?

BENEATHA: To practice there . . .

WALTER: Girl, if you don't get all them silly ideas out your head! You better marry yourself a man with some loot . . .

BENEATHA: [*angrily, precisely as in the first scene of the play*] What have you got to do with who I marry!

WALTER: Plenty. Now I think George Murchison —

[*He and* BENEATHA *go out yelling at each other vigorously;* BENEATHA *is heard saying that she would not marry* GEORGE MURCHISON *if he were Adam and she were Eve, etc. The anger is loud and real till their voices diminish.* RUTH *stands at the door and turns to* MAMA *and smiles knowingly.*]

MAMA: [*fixing her hat at last*] Yeah — they something all right, my children . . .

RUTH: Yeah — they're something. Let's go, Lena.

MAMA: [*stalling, starting to look around the house*] Yes — I'm coming. Ruth —

RUTH: Yes?

MAMA: [*quietly, woman to woman*] He finally come into his manhood today, didn't he? Kind of like a rainbow after the rain . . .

RUTH: [*biting her lip lest her own pride explode in front of* MAMA] Yes, Lena.

[WALTER'S *voice calls for them raucously.*]

MAMA: [*waving* RUTH *out vaguely*] All right, honey — go on down. I be down directly.

[RUTH *hesitates, then exits.* MAMA *stands, at last alone in the living room, her plant on the table before her as the lights start to come down. She looks around at all the walls and ceilings and suddenly, despite herself, while the children call below, a great heaving thing rises in her and she puts her fist to her mouth, takes a final desperate look, pulls her coat about her, pats her hat and goes out. The lights dim down. The door opens and she comes back in, grabs her plant, and goes for the last time.*]

# Sam Shepard

# Fool For Love

## This play is to be performed relentlessly without a break

### SCENE

SCENE———*Stark, low-rent motel room on the edge of the Mojave Desert. Faded green plaster walls. Dark brown linoleum floor. No rugs. Cast iron four poster single bed, slightly off center favoring stage right, set horizontally to audience. Bed covered with faded blue chenille bedspread. Metal table with well-worn yellow formica top. Two matching metal chairs in the 50s "S" shape design with yellow plastic seats and backs, also well-worn. Table set extreme down left (from actor's p.o.v.). Chairs set upstage and down right of table. Nothing on the table. Faded yellow exterior door in the center of the stage left wall. When this door is opened, a small orange porch light shines into room. Yellow bathroom door up right of the stage right wall. This door slightly ajar to begin with, revealing part of an old style porcelain sink, white towels, a general clutter of female belongings and allowing a yellow light to bleed onto stage. Large picture window dead center of upstage wall, framed by dirty, long, dark green plastic curtains. Yellow-orange light from a street lamp shines thru window.*

*Extreme down left, next to the table and chairs is a small extended platform on the same level as the stage. The floor is black and it's framed by black curtains. The only object on the platform is an old maple rocking chair facing upstage right. A pillow with no slipcover rests on the seat. An old horse blanket with holes is laced to the back of the rocker. The color of the blanket should be subdued—grays and blacks.*

*Lights fade to black on set. In the dark, Merle Haggard's tune, "Wake Up" from his "The Way I Am" album is heard. Lights begin to rise slowly on stage in the tempo of the song. Volume swells slightly with the lights until they arrive at their mark. The platform remains in darkness with only a slight spill from the stage lights. Three actors are revealed.*

### CHARACTERS

THE OLD MAN *sits in the rocker facing up right so he's just slightly profile to the audience. A bottle of whiskey sits on the floor beside him. He picks up bottle and pours whiskey into a styrofoam cup and drinks. He has a scraggly red beard, wears an old stained "open-road" Stetson hat (the kind with the short brim), a sun-bleached, dark quilted jacket with the stuffing coming out at the elbows, black and white checkered slacks that are too short in the legs, beat up, dark Western boots, an old vest and a pale green shirt. He exists only in the minds of* MAY *and* EDDIE, *even though they might talk to him directly and acknowledge his physical presence.* THE OLD MAN *treats them as though they all existed in the same time and place.*

587

MAY *sits on edge of bed facing audience, feet on floor, legs apart, elbows on knees, hands hanging limp and crossed between her knees, head hanging forward, face staring at floor. She is absolutely still and maintains this attitude until she speaks. She wears a blue denim full skirt, baggy white t-shirt and bare feet with a silver ankle bracelet. She's in her early thirties.*

EDDIE *sits in the upstage chair by the table, facing* MAY. *He wears muddy, broken down cowboy boots with silver gaffer's tape wrapped around them at the toe and instep, well-worn, faded, dirty jeans that smell like horse sweat. Brown western shirt with snaps. A pair of spurs dangles from his belt. When he walks, he limps slightly and gives the impression he's rarely off a horse. There's a peculiar broken-down quality about his body in general, as though he's aged long before his time. He's in his late thirties.*

*On the floor, between his feet, is a leather bucking strap like bronc riders use. He wears a bucking glove on his right hand and works resin into the glove from a small white bag. He stares at* MAY *as he does this and ignores* THE OLD MAN. *As the song nears the end of its fade, he leans over, sticks his gloved hand into the handle of the bucking strap and twists it so that it makes a weird stretching sound from the friction of the resin and leather. The song ends, lights up full. He pulls his hand out and removes gloves.*

EDDIE: [*seated, tossing glove on the table*] [*short pause*] May, look. May? I'm not goin' anywhere. See? I'm right here. I'm not gone. Look. [*She won't.*] I don't know why you won't just look at me. You know it's me. Who else do you think it is. [*Pause*] You want some water or somethin'? Huh? [*He gets up slowly, goes cautiously to her, strokes her head softly, she stays still.*] May? Come on. You can't just sit around here like this. How long you been sittin' here anyway? You want me to go outside and get you something? Some potato chips or something? [*She suddenly grabs his closest leg with both arms and holds tight burying her head between his knees.*] I'm not gonna' leave. Don't worry. I'm not gonna' leave. I'm stayin' right here. I already told ya' that. [*She squeezes tighter to his leg, he just stands there, strokes her head softly.*] May? Let go, okay? Honey? I'll put you back in bed. Okay? [*She grabs his other leg and holds on tight to both.*] Come on. I'll put you in bed and make you some hot tea or somethin'. You want some tea? [*She shakes her head violently, keeps holding on.*] With lemon? Some Ovaltine? May, you gotta' let go of me now, okay? [*Pause, then she pushes him away and returns to her original position.*] Now just lay back and try to relax. [*He starts to try to push her back gently on the bed as he pulls back the blankets. She erupts furiously, leaping off bed and lashing out at him with her fists. He backs off. She returns to bed and stares at him wild-eyed and angry, faces him squarely.*]

EDDIE: [*after pause*] You want me to go? [*She shakes her head.*]

MAY: No!

EDDIE: Well, what do you want then?

MAY: You smell.

EDDIE: I smell.

MAY: You do.

EDDIE: I been drivin' for days.

MAY: Your fingers smell.

EDDIE: Horses.

MAY: Pussy.

EDDIE: Come on, May.

MAY: They smell like metal.

EDDIE: I'm not gonna' start this shit.

MAY: Rich pussy. Very clean.

EDDIE: Yeah, sure.

MAY: You know it's true.

EDDIE: I came to see if you were all right.

MAY: I don't need you!

EDDIE: Okay. [*Turns to go, collects his glove and bucking strap.*] Fine.

MAY: Don't go!

EDDIE: I'm goin'.

[*He exits stage left door, slamming it behind him; the door booms.*]

MAY: [*agonized scream*] Don't go!!!

[*She grabs pillow, clutching it to her chest then throws herself face down on bed, moaning and moving from one end of bed to the other on her elbows and knees.* EDDIE *is heard returning to stage left door outside. She leaps off bed clutching pillow, stands upstage right of bed, facing stage left door.* EDDIE *enters stage left door, banging it behind him. He's left the glove and bucking strap off stage. They stand there facing each other for a second. He makes a move toward her.* MAY *retreats to extreme upstage right corner of room clutching pillow to her chest.* EDDIE *stays against left wall, facing her.*]

EDDIE: What am I gonna' do? Huh? What am I supposed to do?

MAY: You know.

EDDIE: What.

MAY: You're gonna' erase me.

EDDIE: What're you talkin' about?

MAY: You're either gonna' erase me or have me erased.

EDDIE: Why would I want that? Are you kidding?

MAY: Because I'm in the way.

EDDIE: Don't be stupid.

MAY: I'm smarter than you are and you know it. I can smell your thoughts before you even think 'em.

[EDDIE *moves along wall to upstage left corner.* MAY *holds her ground in opposite corner.*]

EDDIE: May, I'm tryin' to take care of you. All right?

MAY: No, you're not. You're just guilty. Gutless and guilty.

EDDIE: Great.

[*He moves down left to table, sticking close to wall.*] [*Pause*]

MAY: [*quietly, staying in corner*] I'm gonna' kill her ya' know.

EDDIE: Who?

MAY: Who.

EDDIE: Don't talk like that.

[MAY *slowly begins to move down stage right as* EDDIE *simultaneously moves up left. Both of them press the walls as they move.*]

MAY: I am. I'm gonna' kill her and then I'm gonna' kill you. Systematically. With sharp knives. Two separate knives. One for her and one for you. [*She slams wall with her elbow. Wall resonates.*] So the blood doesn't mix. I'm gonna' torture her first though. Not you. I'm just gonna' let you have it. Probably in the midst of a kiss. Right when you think everything's been healed up. Right in the moment when you're sure you've got me buffaloed. That's when you'll die.

> [*She arrives extreme down right at the very limits of the set.* EDDIE *in the extreme up left corner. Pause*]

EDDIE: You know how many miles I went outa' my way just to come here and see you? You got any idea?

MAY: Nobody asked you to come.

EDDIE: Two thousand, four hundred and eighty.

MAY: Yeah? Where were you, Katmandu or something?

EDDIE: Two thousand, four hundred and eighty miles.

MAY: So what!

> [*He drops his head, stares at floor. Pause. She stares at him. He begins to move slowly down left, sticking close to wall as he speaks.*]

EDDIE: I missed you. I did. I missed you more than anything I ever missed in my whole life. I kept thinkin' about you the whole time I was driving. Kept seeing you. Sometimes just a part of you.

MAY: Which part?

EDDIE: Your neck.

MAY: My neck?

EDDIE: Yeah.

MAY: You missed my neck?

EDDIE: I missed all of you but your neck kept coming up for some reason. I kept crying about your neck.

MAY: Crying?

EDDIE: [*He stops by stage left door. She stays down right.*] Yeah. Weeping. Like a little baby. Uncontrollable. It would just start up and stop and then start up all over again. For miles. I couldn't stop it. Cars would pass me on the road. People would stare at me. My face was all twisted up. I couldn't stop my face.

MAY: Was this before or after your little fling with the Countess?

EDDIE: [*He bangs his head into wall. Wall booms.*] There wasn't any fling with any Countess!

MAY: You're a liar.

EDDIE: I took her out to dinner once, okay?

MAY: Ha!

> [*She moves upstage right wall.*]

EDDIE: Twice.

MAY: You were bumping her on a regular basis! Don't gimme that shit.

EDDIE: You can believe whatever you want.

MAY: [*She stops by bathroom door, opposite Eddie.*] I'll believe the truth! It's less confusing.

> [*Pause*]

EDDIE: I'm takin' you back, May.

> [*She tosses pillow on bed and moves to upstage right corner.*]

MAY: I'm not going back to that idiot trailer if that's what you think.

EDDIE: I'm movin' it. I got a piece of ground up in Wyoming.

MAY: Wyoming? Are you crazy? I'm not moving to Wyoming. What's up there? Marlboro Men?

EDDIE: You can't stay here.

MAY: Why not? I got a job. I'm a regular citizen here now.

EDDIE: You got a job?

MAY: [*she moves back down to head of bed*] Yeah. What'd you think, I was helpless?

EDDIE: No. I mean — it's been a long time since you had a job.

MAY: I'm a cook.

EDDIE: A cook? You can't even flip an egg, can you?

MAY: I'm not talkin' to you anymore!

> [*She turns away from him, runs into bathroom, slams door behind her.*
> EDDIE *goes after her, tries door but she's locked it.*]

EDDIE: [*at bathroom door*] May, I got everything worked out. I been thinkin' about this for weeks. I'm gonna' move the trailer. Build a little pipe corral to keep the horses. Have a big vegetable garden. Some chickens maybe.

MAY'S VOICE: [*unseen, behind bathroom door*] I hate chickens! I hate horses! I hate all that shit! You know that. You got me confused with somebody else. You keep comin' up here with this lame country dream life with chickens and vegetables and I can't stand any of it. It makes me puke to even think about it.

EDDIE: [EDDIE *has crossed stage left during this, stops at table.*] You'll get used to it.

MAY: [*enters from bathroom*] You're unbelievable!

> [*She slams bathroom door, crosses upstage to window.*]

EDDIE: I'm not lettin' go of you this time, May.

> [*He sits in chair upstage of table.*]

MAY: You never had a hold of me to begin with. [*pause*] How many times have you done this to me?

EDDIE: What.

MAY: Suckered me into some dumb little fantasy and then dropped me like a hot rock. How many times has that happened?

EDDIE: It's no fantasy.

MAY: It's all a fantasy.

EDDIE: And I never dropped you either.

MAY: No, you just disappeared!

EDDIE: I'm here now aren't I?

MAY: Well, praise Jesus God!

EDDIE: I'm gonna take care of you, May. I am. I'm gonna' stick with you no matter what. I promise.

MAY: Get outa' here.

> [*Pause*]

EDDIE: What'd you have to go and run off for anyway?

MAY: Run off? Me?

EDDIE: Yeah. Why couldn't you just stay put? You knew I was comin' back to get you.

MAY: [*crossing down to head of bed*] What do you think it's like sittin' in a tin trailer for weeks on end with the wind ripping through it? Waitin' around for the Butane to arrive. Hiking down to the laundromat in the rain. Do you think that's thrilling or somethin'?

EDDIE: [*still sitting*] I bought you all those magazines.

MAY: What magazines?

EDDIE: I bought you a whole stack of those fashion magazines before I left. I thought you liked those. Those French kind.

MAY: Yeah, I especially liked the one with the Countess on the cover. That was real cute.

    [*Pause*]

EDDIE: All right.

    [*He stands.*]

MAY: All right, what.

    [*He turns to go out stage left door.*]

MAY: Where are you going?

EDDIE: Just to get my stuff outa' the truck. I'll be right back.

MAY: What're you movin' in now or something?

EDDIE: Well, I thought I'd spend the night if that's okay.

MAY: Are you kidding?

EDDIE: [*opens door*] Then I'll just leave, I guess.

MAY: [*she stands*] Wait.

    [*He closes door. They stand there facing each other for a while. She crosses slowly to him. She stops. He takes a few steps toward her. Stops. They both move closer. Stop. Pause as they look at each other. They embrace. Long, tender kiss. They are very soft with each other. She pulls away from him slightly. Smiles. She looks him straight in the eyes, then suddenly knees him in the groin with tremendous force.* EDDIE *doubles over and drops like a rock. She stands over him. Pause.*]

MAY: You can take it, right. You're a stuntman.

    [*She exits into bathroom, stage right, slams the door behind her. The door is amplified with microphones and a bass drum hidden in the frame so that each time an actor slams it, the door booms loud and long. Same is true for the stage left door.* EDDIE *remains on the floor holding his stomach in pain. Stage lights drop to half their intensity as a spot rises softly on* THE OLD MAN. *He speaks directly to* EDDIE.]

THE OLD MAN: I thought you were supposed to be a fantasist, right? Isn't that basically the deal with you? You dream things up. Isn't that true?

EDDIE: [*stays on floor*] I don't know.

THE OLD MAN: You don't know. Well, if you don't know I don't know who the hell else does. I wanna' show you somethin'. Somethin' real, okay? Somethin' actual.

EDDIE: Sure.

THE OLD MAN: Take a look at that picture on the wall over there. [*He points at wall stage right. There is no picture but* EDDIE *stares at the wall.*] Ya' see that? Take a good look at that. Ya' see it?

EDDIE: [*staring at wall*] Yeah.

THE OLD MAN: Ya' know who that is?

EDDIE: I'm not sure.

THE OLD MAN: Barbara Mandrell. That's who that is. Barbara Mandrell. You heard a' her?

EDDIE: Sure.

THE OLD MAN: Well, would you believe me if I told ya' I was married to her?

EDDIE: [*pause*] No.

THE OLD MAN: Well, see, now that's the difference right there. That's realism. I am
actually married to Barbara Mandrell in my mind. Can you understand that?

EDDIE: Sure.

THE OLD MAN: Good. I'm glad we have an understanding.

> [THE OLD MAN *drinks from his cup. Spot slowly fades to black as stage
> lights come back up full. These light changes are cued to the opening and
> closing of doors.* MAY *enters from bathroom, closes door quietly. She is
> carrying a sleek red dress, panty hose, a pair of black high heels, a black
> shoulder purse and a hair brush. She crosses to foot of bed and throws the
> clothes on it. Hangs the purse on a bed post, sits on foot of bed her back to*
> EDDIE *and starts brushing her hair.* EDDIE *remains on floor. She finishes
> brushing her hair, throws brush on bed, then starts taking off her clothes
> and changing into the clothes she brought on stage. As she speaks to* EDDIE
> *and changes into the new clothes, she gradually transforms from her
> former tough drabness into a very sexy woman. This occurs almost unno-
> ticeably in the course of her speech.*]

MAY: [*very cold, quick, almost monotone voice like she's writing him a letter*] I don't
understand my feelings. I really don't. I don't understand how I could hate you
so much after so much time. How, no matter how much I'd like to not hate
you, I hate you even more. It grows. I can't even see you now. All I see is a
picture of you. You and her. I don't even know if the picture's real anymore. I
don't even care. It's a made-up picture. It invades my head. The two of you.
And this picture stings even more than if I'd actually seen you with her. It cuts
me. It cuts me so deep I'll never get over it. And I can't get rid of this picture
either. It just comes. Uninvited. Kinda' like a little torture. And I blame you
more for this little torture than I do for what you did.

EDDIE: [*standing slowly*] I'll go.

MAY: You better.

EDDIE: Why?

MAY: You just better.

EDDIE: I thought you wanted me to stay.

MAY: I got somebody coming to get me.

EDDIE: [*short pause, on his feet*] Here?

MAY: Yeah, here. Where else?

EDDIE: [*makes a move toward her upstage*] You been seeing somebody?

MAY: [*She moves quickly down left, crosses right.*] When was the last time we were
together, Eddie? Huh? Can you remember that far back?

EDDIE: Who've you been seeing?

> [*He moves violently toward her.*]

MAY: Don't you touch me! Don't you even think about it.

EDDIE: How long have you been seeing him!

MAY: What difference does it make!

> [*Short pause. He stares at her, then turns suddenly and exits out the stage
> left door and slams it behind him. Door booms.*]

MAY: Eddie! Where are you going? Eddie!

> [*Short pause. She looks after* EDDIE, *then turns fast, moves upstage to*

*window. She parts the Venetian blinds, looks out window, turns back into room. She rushes to upstage side of bed, gets down on hands and knees, pulls a suitcase out from under bed, throws it on top of bed, opens it. She rushes into bathroom, disappears, leaving door open. She comes back on with various items of clothing, throws stuff into suitcase, turns as if to go back into bathroom. Stops. She hears* EDDIE *off left. She quickly shuts suitcase, slides it under bed again, rushes around to downstage side of bed. Sits on bed. Stands again. Rushes back into bathroom, returns with hairbrush, slams bathroom door. Starts brushing her hair as though that's what she's been doing all along. She sits on bed brushing her hair.* EDDIE *enters stage left, slams door behind him, door booms. He stands there holding a ten gauge shotgun in one hand and a bottle of tequila in the other. He moves toward bed, tosses shotgun on bed beside her.*]

MAY: [*she stands, moves upstage, stops brushing her hair*] Oh, wonderful. What're you gonna' do with that?

EDDIE: Clean it.

[*He opens the bottle.*]

EDDIE: You got any glasses?

MAY: In the bathroom.

EDDIE: What're they doin' in the bathroom?

[EDDIE *crosses toward bathroom door with bottle.*]

MAY: I keep everything in the bathroom. It's safer.

EDDIE: You want some a' this?

MAY: I'm on the wagon.

EDDIE: Good. 'Bout time.

[*He exits into bathroom.* MAY *moves back to bed, stares at shotgun.*]

MAY: Eddie, this is a very friendly person who's coming over here. He's not malicious in any way. [*pause*] Eddie?

EDDIE'S VOICE: [*off right*] Where's the damn glasses?

MAY: In the medicine cabinet!

EDDIE'S VOICE: What the hell're they doin' in the medicine cabinet!

[*Sound of medicine cabinet being opened and slammed shut off right*]

MAY: There's no germs in the medicine cabinet!

EDDIE'S VOICE: Germs.

MAY: Eddie, did you hear me?

[EDDIE *enters with a glass, pouring tequila into it slowly until it's full as he crosses to table down left.*]

MAY: Did you hear what I said, Eddie?

EDDIE: About what?

MAY: About the man who's coming over here.

EDDIE: What man?

MAY: Oh, brother.

[EDDIE *sets bottle of tequila on table then sits in upstage chair. Takes a long drink from glass. He ignores* THE OLD MAN.]

EDDIE: First off, it can't be very serious.

MAY: Oh, really? And why is that?

EDDIE: Because you call him a "man."

MAY: What am I supposed to call him?

EDDIE: A "guy" or something. If you called him a "guy", I'd be worried about it but since you call him a "man" you give yourself away. You're in a dumb situation with this guy by calling him a "man". You put yourself below him.

MAY: What in the hell do you know about it.

EDDIE: This guy's gotta' be a twerp. He's gotta' be a punk chump in a two dollar suit or somethin'.

MAY: Anybody who doesn't half kill themselves falling off horses or jumping on steers is a twerp in your book.

EDDIE: That's right.

MAY: And what're you supposed to be, a "guy" or a "man"?

[EDDIE *lowers his glass slowly. Stares at her. Pause. He smiles then speaks low and deliberately.*]

EDDIE: I'll tell you what. We'll just wait for this "man" to come over here. The two of us. We'll just set right here and wait. Then I'll let you be the judge.

MAY: Why is everything a big contest with you? He's not competing with you. He doesn't even know you exist.

EDDIE: You can introduce me.

MAY: I'm not introducing you. I am definitely not introducing you. He'd be very embarrassed to find me here with somebody else. Besides, I've only just met him.

EDDIE: Embarrassed?

MAY: Yes! Embarrassed. He's a very gentle person.

EDDIE: Is that right? Well, I'm a very gentle person myself. My feelings get easily damaged.

MAY: What feelings?

[EDDIE *falls silent, takes a drink, then gets up slowly with glass, leaves bottle on table, crosses to bed, sits on bed, sets glass on floor, picks up shotgun and starts dismantling it.* MAY *watches him closely.*]

MAY: You can't keep messing me around like this. It's been going on too long. I can't take it anymore. I get sick everytime you come around. Then I get sick when you leave. You're like a disease to me. Besides, you got no right being jealous of me after all the bullshit I've been through with you.

[*Pause.* EDDIE *keeps his attention on shotgun as he talks to her.*]

EDDIE: We've got a pact.

MAY: Oh, God.

EDDIE: We made a pact.

MAY: There's nothing between us now!

EDDIE: Then what're you so excited about?

MAY: I'm not excited.

EDDIE: You're beside yourself.

MAY: You're driving me crazy. You're driving me totally crazy!

EDDIE: You know we're connected, May. We'll always be connected. That was decided a long time ago.

MAY: Nothing was decided! You made all that up.

EDDIE: You know what happened.

MAY: You promised me that was finished. You can't start that up all over again. You promised me.

EDDIE: A promise can't stop something like that. It happened.

MAY: Nothing happened! Nothing ever happened!

EDDIE: Innocent to the last drop.

MAY: [*pause, controlled*] Eddie—will you please leave? Now.

EDDIE: You're gonna' find out one way or the other.

MAY: I want you to leave.

EDDIE: You didn't want me to leave before.

MAY: I want you to leave now. And it's not because of this man. It's just—

EDDIE: What.

MAY: Stupid. You oughta' know that by now.

EDDIE: You think so, huh?

MAY: It'll be the same thing over and over again. We'll be together for a little while and then you'll be gone.

EDDIE: I'll be gone.

MAY: You will. You know it. You just want me now because I'm seeing somebody else. As soon as that's over, you'll be gone again.

EDDIE: I didn't come here because you were seein' somebody else! I don't give a damn who you're seeing! You'll never replace me and you know it!

MAY: Get outa' here!

> [*Long silence.* EDDIE *lifts his glass and toasts her, then slowly drinks it dry. He sets glass down softly on floor.*]

EDDIE: [*smiles at her*] All right.

> [*He rises slowly, picks up the sections of his shotgun. He stands there looking down at the shotgun pieces for a second.* MAY *moves slightly toward him.*]

MAY: Eddie—

> [*His head jerks up and stares at her. She stops cold.*]

EDDIE: You're a traitor.

> [*He exits left with shotgun. Slams door. Door booms.* MAY *runs toward door.*]

MAY: Eddie!!

> [*She throws herself against stage left door. Her arms reach out and hug the walls. She weeps and slowly begins to move along the stage left wall upstage to the corner, embracing the wall as she moves and weeps.* THE OLD MAN *begins to tell his story as* MAY *moves slowly along the wall. He tells it directly to her as though she's a child.* MAY *remains involved with her emotion of loss and keeps moving clear around the room, hugging the walls during the course of the story until she arrives in the extreme downstage right corner of the room. She sinks to her knees.*]

> [*Slowly, in the course of* MAY's *mourning, the spotlight softly rises on* THE OLD MAN *and the stage lights decrease to half again.*]

THE OLD MAN: Ya' know, one thing I'll never forget. I'll never forget this as long as I live—and I don't even know why I remember it exactly. We were drivin' through Southern Utah once, I think it was. Me, you and your mother—in that old Plymouth we had. You remember that Plymouth? Had a white plastic hood ornament on it. Replica of the Mayflower I think it was. Some kind a' ship. Anyway, we'd been drivin' all night and you were sound asleep in the front. And all of a sudden you woke up crying. Just bustin' a gut over somethin'. I don't know what it was. Nightmare or somethin'. Woke your Mom right up and she climbed over the seat in back there with you to try to get you settled down. But you wouldn't shut up for hell or high water. Just kept wailing away. So I stopped the Plymouth by the side of the road. Middle a' nowhere. I can't even remember where it was exactly. Pitch black. I picked you up outa' the back seat there and carried you into this field. Thought the cold air might quiet you down a little bit. But you just kept on howling away. Then, all of a sudden, I saw somethin' move out there. Somethin' bigger than both of us put together. And it started to move toward us kinda' slow.

[MAY *begins to crawl slowly on her hands and knees from down right corner toward bed. When she reaches bed, she grabs pillow and embraces it, still on her knees. She rocks back and forth embracing pillow as* THE OLD MAN *continues.*]

And then it started to get joined up by some other things just like it. Same shape and everything. It was so black out there I could hardly make out my own hand. But these things started to kinda' move in on us from all directions in a big circle. And I stopped dead still and turned back to the car to see if your mother was all right. But I couldn't see the car anymore. So I called out to her. I called her name loud and clear. And she answered me back from outa' the darkness. She yelled back to me. And just then these things started to "moo". They all started "mooing" away.

[*He makes the sound of a cow.*]

And it turns out, there we were, standin' smack in the middle of a goddamn herd of cattle. Well, you never heard a baby pipe down so fast in your life. You never made a peep after that. The whole rest of the trip.

[MAY *stops rocking abruptly. Suddenly* MAY *hears* EDDIE *off left. Stage lights pop back up. Spot on* THE OLD MAN *cuts to black. She leaps to her feet, completely dropping her grief, hesitates a second, then rushes to chair upstage of table and sits. She takes a drink straight from the bottle, slams bottle down on table, leans back in the chair and stares at the bottle as though she's been sitting like that the whole time since he left.* EDDIE *enters fast from stage left door carrying two steer ropes. He slams door. Door booms. He completely ignores* MAY. *She completely ignores him and keeps staring at the bottle. He crosses upstage of bed, throws one of the ropes on bed and starts building a loop in the other rope, feeding it with the left hand so that it makes a snake-like zipping sound as it passes through the honda. Now he begins to pay attention to* MAY *as he continues fooling with the rope. She remains staring at the bottle of tequila.*]

EDDIE: Decided to jump off the wagon, huh?

[*He spins the rope above his head in a flat horn-loop, then ropes one of the bedposts, taking up the slack with a sharp snap of the right hand. He takes the loop off the bedpost, rebuilds it, swings and ropes another bedpost. He continues this right around the bed, roping every post and never missing.* MAY *takes another drink and sets bottle down quietly.*]

MAY: [*still not looking at him*] What're you doing?

EDDIE: Little practice. Gotta' stay in practice these days. There's kids out there ropin' calves in six seconds dead. Can you believe that? Six and no change. Flyin' off the saddle on the right hand side like a bunch a' Spider Monkeys. I'm tellin' ya', they got it down to a science.

[*He continues roping bedposts, making his way around the bed in a circle.*]

MAY: [*flatly, staring at bottle*] I thought you were leaving. Didn't you say you were leaving?

EDDIE: [*as he ropes*] Well, yeah, I was gonna'. But then it suddenly occurred to me in the middle of the parking lot out there that there probably isn't any man comin' over here at all. There probably isn't any "guy" or any "man" or anybody comin' over here. You just made all that up.

MAY: Why would I do that?

EDDIE: Just to get even.

[*She turns to him slowly in chair, takes a drink, stares at him, then sets bottle on table.*]

MAY: I'll never get even with you.

[*He laughs, crosses to table, takes a deep drink from bottle, cocks his head back, gargles, swallows, then does a back flip across stage and crashes into stage right wall.*]

MAY: So, now we're gonna' get real mean and sloppy, is that it? Just like old times.

EDDIE: Well, I haven't dropped the reins in quite a while ya' know. I've been real good. I have. No hooch. No slammer. No women. No nothin'. I been a pretty boring kind of a guy actually. I figure I owe it to myself. Once a once.

[*He returns to roping the bedposts. She just stares at him from the chair.*]

MAY: Why are you doing this?

EDDIE: I already told ya'. I need the practice.

MAY: I don't mean that.

EDDIE: Well, say what ya' mean then, honey.

MAY: Why are you going through this whole thing again like you're trying to impress me or something. Like we just met. This is the same crap you laid on me in High School.

EDDIE: [*still roping*] Well, it's just a little testimony of my love, see baby. I mean if I stopped trying to impress you, that'd mean it was all over, wouldn't it?

MAY: It *is* all over.

EDDIE: You're trying to impress me, too, aren't you?

MAY: You know me inside and out. I got nothing new to show you.

EDDIE: You got this guy comin' over. This new guy. That's very impressive. I woulda' thought you'd be hung out to dry by now.

MAY: Oh, thanks a lot.

EDDIE: What is he, a "younger man" or something?

MAY: It's none of your damn business.

EDDIE: Have you balled him yet?

[*She throws him a mean glare and just pins him with her eyes.*]

EDDIE: Have you? I'm just curious. [*pause*] You don't have to tell me. I already know.

MAY: You're just like a little kid, you know that? A jealous, little snot-nosed kid.

[EDDIE *laughs, spits, makes a 'snot-nosed-kid' face, keeps roping bedposts.*]

EDDIE: I hope this guy comes over. I really hope he does. I wanna' see him walk through that door.

MAY: What're you gonna' do?

[*He stops roping, turns to her. He smiles.*]

EDDIE: I'm gonna nail his ass to the floor. Directly.

      [*He suddenly ropes chair downstage, right next to* MAY. *He takes up slack and drags chair violently back toward bed. Pause. They stare at each other.* MAY *suddenly stands, goes to bedpost, grabs her purse, slings it on her shoulder and heads for stage left door.*]

MAY: I'm not sticking around for this.

      [*She exits stage left door leaving it open.* EDDIE *runs off stage after her.*]

EDDIE: Where're you goin'?

MAY: [*off left*] Take your hands off a' me!

EDDIE: [*off left*] Wait a second, wait a second. Just a second, okay?

      [MAY *screams.* EDDIE *carries her back on stage screaming and kicking. He sets her down, slams door shut. She walks away from him stage right, straightening her dress.*]

EDDIE: Tell ya' what. I'll back off. I'll be real nice. I will. I promise. I'll be just like a little ole pussy cat, okay? You can introduce me to him as your brother or something. Well — maybe not your brother.

MAY: Maybe not.

EDDIE: Your cousin. Okay? I'll be your cousin. I just wanna' meet him is all. Then I'll leave. Promise.

MAY: Why do you want to meet him? He's just a friend.

EDDIE: Just to see where you stand these days. You can tell a lot about a person by the company they keep.

MAY: Look. I'm going outside. I'm going to the pay phone across the street. I'm calling him up and I'm telling him to forget about the whole thing. Okay?

EDDIE: Good. I'll pack up your stuff while you're gone.

MAY: I'm not going with you Eddie!

      [*Suddenly headlights arc across the stage from upstage right, through window. They slash across the audience, then dissolve off left. These should be two intense beams of piercing white light and not 'realistic' headlights.*]

MAY: Oh, great.

      [*She rushes upstage to window, looks out.* EDDIE *laughs, takes a drink.*]

EDDIE: Why don't ya' run on out there. Go ahead. Run on out. Throw yourself into his arms or somethin'. Blow kisses in the moonlight.

      [EDDIE *laughs, moves to bed, pulls a pair of old spurs off his belt. Sits. Starts putting spurs on his boots. It's important these spurs look old and used, with small rowels — not cartoon "cowboy" spurs.* MAY *goes into bathroom leaving door open.*]

MAY: [*off right*] What're you doing?

EDDIE: Puttin' my hooks on. I wanna' look good for this "man". Give him the right impression. I'm yer cousin after all.

MAY: [*entering from bathroom*] If you hurt him, Eddie —

EDDIE: I'm not gonna' hurt him. I'm a nice guy. Very sensitive, too. Very civilized.

MAY: He's just a date, you know. Just an ordinary date.

EDDIE: Yeah? Well, I'm gonna' turn him into a fig.

      [*He starts laughing so hard at his own joke that he rolls off the bed and*

crashes to the floor. He goes into a fit of laughter, pounding his fists into
the floor. MAY  makes a move toward the door, then stops and turns to
EDDIE.]

MAY: Eddie! Do me a favor. Just this once, okay?

EDDIE: [laughing hard] Anything you want, honey. Anything you want.
        [He goes on laughing hysterically.]

MAY: [turning away from him] Shit.
        [She goes to stage left door and throws it open. Pitch black outside with
        only the porch light glowing. She stands in the doorway, staring out. Pause
        as EDDIE slowly gains control of himself and stops laughing. He stares at
        MAY.]

EDDIE: [still on floor] What're you doing? [Pause. MAY keeps looking out.] May?

MAY: [staring out open door] It's not him.

EDDIE: It's not, huh?

MAY: No, it's not.

EDDIE: Well, who is it then?

MAY: Somebody else.

EDDIE: [slowly getting up and sitting on bed] Yeah. It's probably not ever gonna' be
        "him". What're you tryin' to make me jealous for? I know you've been livin'
        alone.

MAY: It's a big, huge, extra-long, black Mercedes Benz.

EDDIE: [pause] Well, this is a motel, isn't it? People are allowed to park in front of a
        motel if they're stayin' here.

MAY: People who stay here don't drive a big, huge, extra-long, black, Mercedes
        Benz.

EDDIE: You don't, but somebody else might.

MAY: [still at door] This is not a black Mercedes Benz type of motel.

EDDIE: Well, close the damn door then and get back inside.

MAY: Somebody's sitting out there in that car looking straight at me.

EDDIE: [stands fast] What're they doing?

MAY: It's not a "they". It's a "she".
        [EDDIE drops to floor behind bed.]

EDDIE: Well what's she doing, then?

MAY: Just sitting there. Staring at me.

EDDIE: Get away from the door, May.

MAY: [turning toward him slowly] You don't know anybody with a black Mercedes
        Benz by any chance, do you?

EDDIE: Get away from the door!
        [Suddenly the white headlight beams slash across the stage through the
        open door. EDDIE rushes to door, slams it shut and pushes MAY aside. Just
        as he slams the door the sound of a large caliber magnum pistol explodes
        off left, followed immediately by the sound of shattering glass then a car
        horn blares and continues on one relentless note.]

MAY: [yelling over the sound of horn] Who is that! Who in the hell is that out there!

EDDIE: How should I know.
        [EDDIE flips the light switch off by the stage left door. Stage lights go black.
        Bathroom light stays on.]

MAY: Eddie!

EDDIE: Just get down will ya'! Get down on the floor!

[EDDIE *grabs her and tries to pull her down on the floor beside the bed.* MAY *struggles in the dark with him. Car horn keeps blaring. Headlights start popping back and forth from high beam to low beam, slashing across stage through the window now.*]

MAY: Who is that? Did you bring her with you! You sonofabitch!

[*She starts lashing out at* EDDIE, *fighting with him as he tries to drag her down on the floor.*]

EDDIE: I didn't bring anybody with me! I don't know who she is! I don't know where she came from! Just get down on the floor will ya'!

MAY: She followed you here! Didn't she! You told her where you were going and she followed you.

EDDIE: I didn't tell anybody where I was going. I didn't know where I was going 'til I got here.

MAY: You are gonna' pay for this! I swear to God. You are gonna' pay.

[EDDIE *finally pulls her down and rolls over on top of her so she can't get up. She slowly gives up struggling as he keeps her pinned to the floor. Car horn suddenly stops. Headlights snap off. Long pause. They listen in the dark.*]

MAY: What do you think she's doing?

EDDIE: How should I know?

MAY: Don't pretend you don't know her. That's the kind of car a Countess drives. That's the kind of car I always pictured her in. [*She starts struggling again.*]

EDDIE: [*holding her down*] Just stay put.

MAY: I'm not gonna' lay here on my back with you on top of me and get shot by some dumb rich twat. Now lemme up, Eddie!

[*Sound of tires burning rubber off left. Headlights arc back across the stage again from left to right. A car drives off. Sound fades.*]

EDDIE: Just stay down!

MAY: I'm down!

[*Long pause in the dark. They listen.*]

MAY: How crazy is this chick anyway?

EDDIE: She's pretty crazy.

MAY: Have you balled her yet? [*pause*]

[EDDIE *gets up slowly, hunched over crosses upstage to window cautiously, parts Venetian blinds and peeks outside.*]

EDDIE: [*looking out*] Shit, she's blown the windshield outa' my truck. Goddamnit.

MAY: [*still on floor*] Eddie?

EDDIE: [*still looking out window*] What?

MAY: Is she gone?

EDDIE: I don't know. I can't see any headlights. [*pause*] I don't believe it.

MAY: [*gets up, crosses to light switch*] Yeah, you shoulda' thought of the consequences before you got in her pants.

[*She switches the lights back on.* EDDIE *whirls around toward her. He stands.*]

EDDIE: [*moving toward her*] Turn the lights off! Keep the lights off! [*He rushes to *light switch and turns lights back off. Stage goes back to darkness.* MAY *shoves past him and turns the lights back on again. Stage lit.*]

MAY: This is my place!

EDDIE: Look, she's gonna' come back here. I know she's gonna' come back. We either have to get outa' here now or you have to keep the fuckin' lights off.

MAY: I thought you said you didn't know her!

EDDIE: Get your stuff! We're gettin' outa' here.

MAY: I'm not leaving! This is your mess, not mine.

EDDIE: I came here to get you! Whatsa' matter with you! I came all this way to get you! Do you think I'd do that if I didn't love you! Huh? That bitch doesn't mean anything to me! Nuthin'. I got no reason to be here but you.

MAY: I'm not goin', Eddie.

> [*Pause.* EDDIE *stares at her.*]
>
> [*Spot rises on* OLD MAN. *Stage lights stay the same.* EDDIE *and* MAY *just stand there staring at each other through the duration of* THE OLD MAN'S *words. They are not 'frozen', they just stand there and face each other in a suspended moment of recognition.*]

THE OLD MAN: Amazing thing is, neither one a' you look a bit familiar to me. Can't figure that one out. I don't recognize myself in either one a' you. Never did. 'Course your mothers both put their stamp on ya'. That's plain to see. But my whole side a' the issue is absent, in my opinion. Totally unrecognizable. You could be anybody's. Probably are. I can't even remember the original circumstances. Been so long. Probably a lot a' things I forgot. Good thing I got out when I did though. Best thing I ever did.

> [*Spot fades on* OLD MAN. *Stage lights come back up.* EDDIE *picks up his rope and starts to coil it up.* MAY *watches him.*]

EDDIE: I'm not leavin'. I don't care what you think anymore. I don't care what you feel. None a' that matters. I'm not leavin'. I'm stayin' right here. I don't care if a hundred "dates" walk through that door — I'll take every one of 'em on. I don't care if you hate my guts. I don't care if you can't stand the sight of me or the sound of me or the smell of me. I'm never leavin'. You'll never get rid of me. You'll never escape me either. I'll track you down no matter where you go. I know exactly how your mind works. I've been right every time. Every single time.

MAY: You've gotta' give this up, Eddie.

EDDIE: I'm not giving it up!

> [*Pause*]

MAY: [*calm*] Okay. Look. I don't understand what you've got in your head anymore. I really don't. I don't get it. *Now*, you desperately need me. *Now*, you can't live without me. NOW, you'll do anything for me. Why should I believe it this time?

EDDIE: Because it's true.

MAY: It was supposed to have been true every time before. Every other time. Now it's true again. You've been jerking me off like this for fifteen years. Fifteen years I've been a yo-yo for you. I've never been split. I've never been two ways about you. I've either loved you or not loved you. And now I just plain don't love you. Understand? Do you understand that? I don't love you. I don't need you. I don't want you. Do you get that? Now if you can still stay then you're either crazy or pathetic.

> [*She crosses down left to table, sits in upstage chair facing audience, takes slug of tequila from bottle, slams it down on table. Headlights again come slashing across the stage from up right, across audience then disappear off left.* EDDIE *rushes to light switch, flips it off. Stage goes black. Exterior lights shine through.*]

EDDIE: [*taking her by shoulder*] Get in the bathroom!

MAY: [*pulls away*] I'm not going in the bathroom! I'm not gonna' hide in my own house! I'm gonna' go out there. I'm gonna' go out there and tear her damn head off! I'm gonna' wipe her out!

> [*She moves toward stage left door.* EDDIE *stops her. She screams. They struggle as* MAY *yells at stage left door.*]

MAY: [*yelling at door*] Come on in here! Come on in here and bring your dumb gun! You hear me? Bring all your weapons and your skinny silly self! I'll eat you alive!

> [*Suddenly the stage left door bursts open and* MARTIN *crashes onstage in the darkness. He's in his mid-thirties, solidly built, wears a green plaid shirt, baggy work pants with suspenders, heavy work boots.* MAY *and* EDDIE *pull apart.* MARTIN *tackles* EDDIE *around the waist and the two of them go crashing into the stage right bathroom door. The door booms.* MAY *rushes to light switch, flips it on. Lights come back up on stage.* MARTIN *stands over* EDDIE *who's crumpled up against the wall on the floor.* MARTIN *is about to smash* EDDIE *in the face with his fist.* MAY *stops him with her voice.*]

MAY: Martin, wait!

> [*Pause.* MARTIN *turns and looks at* MAY. EDDIE *is dazed, remains on floor.* MAY *goes to* MARTIN *and pulls him away from* EDDIE.]

MAY: It's okay, Martin. It's uh — It's okay. We were just having a kind of an argument. Really. Just take it easy. All right?

> [MARTIN *moves back away from* EDDIE. EDDIE *stays on floor. Pause.*]

MARTIN: Oh, I heard you screaming when I drove up and then all the lights went off. I thought somebody was trying to —

MAY: It's okay. This is my uh — cousin. Eddie.

MARTIN: [*stares at* EDDIE] Oh. I'm sorry.

EDDIE: [*grins at* MARTIN] She's lying.

MARTIN: [*looks at* MAY] Oh.

MAY: [*moving to table*] Everything's okay, Martin. You want a drink or something? Why don't you have a drink?

MARTIN: Yeah. Sure.

EDDIE: [*stays on floor*] She's lying through her teeth.

MAY: I gotta' get some glasses.

> [MAY *exits quickly into bathroom, stepping over* EDDIE. MARTIN *stares at* EDDIE. EDDIE *grins back. Pause.*]

EDDIE: She keeps the glasses in the bathroom. Isn't that weird?

> [MAY *comes back on with two glasses. She goes to table, pours two drinks from bottle.*]

MAY: I was starting to think you weren't going to show up, Martin.

MARTIN: Yeah, I'm sorry. I had to water the football field down at the High School. Forgot all about it.

EDDIE: Forgot all about what?

MARTIN: I mean I forgot all about watering. I was halfway here when I remembered. Had to go back.

EDDIE: Oh, I thought you meant you forgot all about her.

MARTIN: Oh, no.

EDDIE: How far was halfway?

MARTIN: Excuse me?

EDDIE: How far were you when it was halfway here?

MARTIN: Oh — uh — I don't know. I guess a couple miles or so.

EDDIE: Couple miles? That's all? Couple a' lousy little miles? You wanna' know how many miles I came? Huh?

MAY: We've been drinking a little bit, Martin.

EDDIE: She hasn't touched a drop.

        [*Pause*]

MAY: [*offering drink to* MARTIN] Here.

EDDIE: Yeah, that's my tequilla, Martin.

MARTIN: Oh.

EDDIE: I don't care if you drink it. I just want you to know where it comes from.

MARTIN: Thanks.

EDDIE: You don't have to thank me. Thank the Mexicans. They made it.

MARTIN: Oh.

EDDIE: You should thank the entire Mexican nation in fact. We owe everything to Mexico down here. Do you realize that? You probably don't realize that do ya'. We're sittin' on Mexican ground right now. It's only by chance that you and me aren't Mexican ourselves. What kinda' people do you hail from anyway, Martin?

MARTIN: Me? Uh — I don't know. I was adopted.

EDDIE: Oh. You must have a lota' problems then, huh?

MARTIN: Well — not really, no.

EDDIE: No? You orphans are supposed to steal a lot aren't ya'? Shoplifting and stuff. You're also supposed to be the main group responsible for bumping off our Presidents.

MARTIN: Really? I never heard that.

EDDIE: Well, you oughta' read the papers, Martin.

        [*Pause*]

MARTIN: I'm really sorry I knocked you over. I mean, I thought she was in trouble or something.

EDDIE: She is in trouble.

MARTIN: [*looks at* MAY] Oh.

EDDIE: She's in big trouble.

MARTIN: What's the matter, May?

MAY: [*moves to bed with drink, sits*] Nothing.

MARTIN: How come you had the lights off?

MAY: We were uh — just about to go out.

MARTIN: You were?

MAY: Yeah—well, I mean, we were going to come back.

> [MARTIN *stands there between them. He looks at* EDDIE, *then back to* MAY. *Pause.*]

EDDIE: [*laughs*] No, no, no. That's not what we were gonna' do. Your name's Martin, right?

MARTIN: Yeah, right.

EDDIE: That's not what we were gonna' do, Marty.

MARTIN: Oh.

EDDIE: Could you hand me that bottle, please?

MARTIN: [*crossing to bottle at table*] Sure.

EDDIE: Thanks.

> [MARTIN *moves back to* EDDIE *with bottle and hands it to him.* EDDIE *drinks.*]

EDDIE: [*after drink*] We were actually having an argument about you. That's what we were doin'.

MARTIN: About me?

EDDIE: Yeah. We were actually in the middle of a big huge argument about you. It got so heated up we had to turn the lights off.

MARTIN: What was it about?

EDDIE: It was about whether or not you're actually a man or not. Ya' know? Whether you're a "man" or just a "guy".

> [*Pause.* MARTIN *looks at* MAY. MAY *smiles politely.* MARTIN *looks back to* EDDIE.]

EDDIE: See, she says you're a man. That's what she calls you. A "man". Did you know that? That's what she calls you.

MARTIN: [*looks back to* MAY] No.

MAY: I never called you a man, Martin. Don't worry about it.

MARTIN: It's okay. I don't mind or anything.

EDDIE: No, but see I uh—told her she was fulla' shit. I mean I told her that way before I even saw you. And now that I see you I can't exactly take it back. Ya' see what I mean, Martin?

> [*Pause,* MAY *stands.*]

MAY: Martin, do you want to go to the movies?

MARTIN: Well, yeah—I mean, that's what I thought we were going to do.

MAY: So let's go to the movies.

> [*She crosses fast to bathroom, steps over* EDDIE, *goes into bathroom, slams door, door booms. Pause as* MARTIN *stares at bathroom door.* EDDIE *stays on floor, grins at* MARTIN.]

MARTIN: She's not mad or anything is she?

EDDIE: You got me, buddy.

MARTIN: I didn't mean to make her mad.

> [*Pause*]

EDDIE: What're you gonna' go see. Martin?

MARTIN: I can't decide.

EDDIE: What d'ya' mean you can't decide? You're supposed to have all that worked out ahead of time aren't ya?

MARTIN: Yeah, but I'm not sure what she likes.

EDDIE: What's that got to do with it? You're takin' her out to the movies, right?

MARTIN: Yeah.

EDDIE: So you pick the movie, right? The guy picks the movie. The guy's always supposed to pick the movie.

MARTIN: Yeah, but I don't want to take her to see something she doesn't want to see.

EDDIE: How do you know what she wants to see?

MARTIN: I don't. That's the reason I can't decide. I mean what if I take her to something she's already seen before?

EDDIE: You miss the whole point, Martin. The reason you're taking her out to the movies isn't to see something she hasn't seen before.

MARTIN: Oh.

EDDIE: The reason you're taking her out to the movies is because you just want to be with her. Right? You just wanna' be close to her. I mean you could take her just about anywhere.

MARTIN: I guess.

EDDIE: I mean after a while you probably wouldn't have to take her out at all. You could just hang around here.

MARTIN: What would we do here?

EDDIE: Well, you could uh — tell each other stories.

MARTIN: Stories?

EDDIE: Yeah.

MARTIN: I don't know any stories.

EDDIE: Make 'em up.

MARTIN: That'd be lying wouldn't it?

EDDIE: No, no. Lying's when you believe it's true. If you already know it's a lie, then it's not lying.

MARTIN: [*after pause*] Do you want some help getting up off the floor?

EDDIE: I like it down here. Less tension. You notice how when you're standing up, there's a lot more tension?

MARTIN: Yeah. I've noticed that. A lot of times when I'm working, you know, I'm down on my hands and knees.

EDDIE: What line a' work do you follow, Martin?

MARTIN: Yard work mostly. Maintenance.

EDDIE: Oh, lawns and stuff?

MARTIN: Yeah.

EDDIE: You do lawns on your hands and knees?

MARTIN: Well — edging. You know, trimming around the edges.

EDDIE: Oh.

MARTIN: And weeding around the sprinkler heads. Stuff like that.

EDDIE: I get ya'.

MARTIN: But I've always noticed how much more relaxed I get when I'm down low to the ground like that.

EDDIE: Yeah. Well, you could get down on your hands and knees right now if you want to. I don't mind.

MARTIN: [*grins, gets embarrassed, looks at bathroom door*] Naw, I'll stand. Thanks.

EDDIE: Suit yourself. You're just gonna' get more and more tense.
        [*Pause*]

MARTIN: You're uh — May's cousin, huh?

EDDIE:  See now, right there. Askin' me that. Right there. That's a result of tension. See what I mean?

MARTIN:  What?

EDDIE:  Askin' me if I'm her cousin. That's because you're tense you're askin' me that. You already know I'm not her cousin.

MARTIN:  Well, how would I know that?

EDDIE:  Do I look like her cousin?

MARTIN:  Well, she said that you were.

EDDIE:  [*grins*] She's lying.

       [*Pause*]

MARTIN:  Well—what are you then?

EDDIE:  [*laughs*] Now you're really gettin' tense, huh?

MARTIN:  Look, maybe I should just go or something. I mean—

       [MARTIN *makes a move to exit stage left.* EDDIE *rushes to stage left door and beats* MARTIN *to it.* MARTIN *freezes then runs to window upstage, opens it and tries to escape.* EDDIE *runs to him and catches him by the back of the pants, pulls him out of the window, slams him up against stage right wall then pulls him slowly down the wall as he speaks. They arrive at down right corner.*]

EDDIE:  No, no. Don't go, Martin. Don't go. You'll just get all blue and lonely out there in the black night. I know. I've wandered around lonely like that myself. Awful. Just eats away at ya'. [*He puts his arm around* MARTIN'S *shoulder and leads him to table down left.*] Now just come on over here and sit down and we'll have us a little drink. Okay?

MARTIN:  [*as he goes with* EDDIE] Uh—do you think she's okay in there?

EDDIE:  Sure she's okay. She's always okay. She just likes to take her time. Just to torture you.

MARTIN:  Well—we were supposed to go to the movies.

EDDIE:  She'll be out. Don't worry about it. She likes the movies.

       [*They sit at table, down left.* EDDIE *pulls out the down right chair and seats* MARTIN *in it, then he goes to the upstage chair and sits so that he's now partially facing* THE OLD MAN. *Spot rises softly on* THE OLD MAN *but* MARTIN *does not acknowledge his presence. Stage lights stay the same.* MARTIN *sets his glass on table.* EDDIE *fills it up with the bottle.* THE OLD MAN'S *left arm slowly descends and reaches across the table holding out his empty styrofoam cup for a drink.* EDDIE *looks* THE OLD MAN *in the eye for a second then pours him a drink, too. All three of them drink.* EDDIE *takes his from the bottle.*]

MARTIN:  What exactly's the matter with her anyway?

EDDIE:  She's in a state a' shock.

       [THE OLD MAN *chuckles to himself. Drinks.*]

MARTIN:  Shock? How come?

EDDIE:  Well, we haven't seen each other in a long time. I mean—me and her, we go back quite a ways, see. High School.

MARTIN:  Oh. I didn't know that.

EDDIE:  Yeah. Lota' miles.

MARTIN:  And you're not really cousins?

EDDIE: No. Not really. No.

MARTIN: You're — her husband?

EDDIE: No. She's my sister. [*He and* THE OLD MAN *look at each other then he turns back to* MARTIN.] My half-sister.

> [*Pause.* EDDIE *and* OLD MAN *drink.*]

MARTIN: Your sister?

EDDIE: Yeah.

MARTIN: Oh. So — you knew each other even before High School then, huh?

EDDIE: No, see, I never even knew I had a sister until it was too late.

MARTIN: How do you mean?

EDDIE: Well, by the time I found out we'd already — you know — fooled around.

> [OLD MAN *shakes his head, drinks. Long pause.* MARTIN *just stares at* EDDIE.]

EDDIE: [*grins*] Whatsa' matter, Martin?

MARTIN: You fooled around?

EDDIE: Yeah.

MARTIN: Well — um — that's illegal, isn't it?

EDDIE: I suppose so.

THE OLD MAN: [*to* EDDIE] Who is this guy?

MARTIN: I mean — is that true? She's really your sister?

EDDIE: Half. Only half.

MARTIN: Which half?

EDDIE: Top half. In horses we call that the "topside".

THE OLD MAN: Yeah, and the mare's what? The mare's uh — "distaff", isn't it? Isn't that the bottom half? "Distaff." Funny I should remember that.

MARTIN: And you fooled around in High School together?

EDDIE: Yeah. Sure. Everybody fooled around in High School. Didn't you?

MARTIN: No. I never did.

EDDIE: Maybe you should have, Martin.

MARTIN: Well, not with my sister.

EDDIE: No, I wouldn't recommend that.

MARTIN: How could that happen? I mean —

EDDIE: Well, see — [*pause, he stares at* OLD MAN] — our Daddy fell in love twice. That's basically how it happened. Once with my mother and once with her mother.

THE OLD MAN: It was the same love. Just got split in two, that's all.

MARTIN: Well, how come you didn't know each other until High School, then?

EDDIE: He had two separate lives. That's how come. Two completely separate lives. He'd live with me and my mother for a while and then he'd disappear and go live with her and her mother for a while.

THE OLD MAN: Now don't be too hard on me, boy. It can happen to the best of us.

MARTIN: And you never knew what was going on?

EDDIE: Nope. Neither did my mother.

THE OLD MAN: She knew.

EDDIE: [*to* MARTIN] She never knew.

MARTIN: She must've suspected something was going on.

EDDIE: Well, if she did she never let on to me. Maybe she was afraid of finding out. Or maybe she just loved him. I don't know. He'd disappear for months at a time and she never once asked him where he went. She was always glad to see him when he came back. The two of us used to go running out of the house to meet him as soon as we saw the Studebaker coming across the field.

THE OLD MAN: [*to* EDDIE] That was no Studebaker, that was a Plymouth. I never owned a goddamn Studebaker.

EDDIE: This went on for years. He kept disappearing and reappearing. For years that went on. Then, suddenly, one day it stopped. He stayed home for a while. Just stayed in the house. Never went outside. Just sat in his chair. Staring. Then he started going on these long walks. He'd walk all day. Then he'd walk all night. He'd walk out across the fields. In the dark. I used to watch him from my bedroom window. He'd disappear in the dark with his overcoat on.

MARTIN: Where was he going?

EDDIE: Just walking.

THE OLD MAN: I was making a decision.

> [EDDIE *gets* MARTIN *to his feet and takes him on a walk around the entire stage as he tells the story.* MARTIN *is reluctant but* EDDIE *keeps pulling him along.*]

EDDIE: But one night I asked him if I could go with him. And he took me. We walked straight out across the fields together. In the dark. And I remember it was just plowed and our feet sank down in the powder and the dirt came up over the tops of my shoes and weighed me down. I wanted to stop and empty my shoes out but he wouldn't stop. He kept walking straight ahead and I was afraid of losing him in the dark so I just kept up as best I could. And we were completely silent the whole time. Never said a word to each other. We could barely see a foot in front of us, it was so dark. And these white owls kept swooping down out of nowhere, hunting for jackrabbits. Diving right past our heads, then disappearing. And we just kept walking silent like that for miles until we got to town. I could see the drive-in movie way off in the distance. That was the first thing I saw. Just square patches of color shifting. Then vague faces began to appear. And, as we got closer, I could recognize one of the faces. It was Spencer Tracy. Spencer Tracy moving his mouth. Speaking without words. Speaking to a woman in a red dress. Then we stopped at a liquor store and he made me wait outside in the parking lot while he bought a bottle. And there were all these Mexican migrant workers standing around a pick-up truck with red mud all over the tires. They were drinking beer and laughing and I remember being jealous of them and I didn't know why. And I remember seeing the old man through the glass door of the liquor store as he paid for the bottle. And I remember feeling sorry for him and I didn't know why. Then he came outside with the bottle wrapped in a brown paper sack and as soon as he came out, all the Mexican men stopped laughing. They just stared at us as we walked away.

> [*During the course of the story the lights shift down very slowly into blues and greens — moonlight.*]

EDDIE: And we walked right through town. Past the donut shop, past the miniature golf course, past the Chevron station. And he opened the bottle up and offered it to me. Before he even took a drink, he offered it to me first. And I took it and drank it and handed it back to him. And we just kept passing it back and forth like that as we walked until we drank the whole thing dry. And we never said a word the whole time. Then, finally, we reached this little white house with a red awning, on the far side of town. I'll never forget the red awning because it flapped in the night breeze and the porch light made it glow. It was a hot, desert breeze and the air smelled like new cut alfalfa. We walked right up to the front porch and he rang the bell and I remember getting real nervous because I wasn't expecting to visit anybody. I thought we were just out for a walk. And then this woman comes to the door. This real pretty woman with red hair. And she throws herself into his arms. And he starts crying. He just breaks down right there in front of me. And she's kissing him all over the face and holding him real tight and he's just crying like a baby. And then through the doorway, behind them both, I see this girl.[*The bathroom door very slowly and silently swings open revealing* MAY, *standing in the door frame back-lit with yellow light in her red dress. She just watches* EDDIE *as he keeps telling story. He and* MARTIN *are unaware of her presence.*] She just appears. She's just standing there, staring at me and I'm staring back at her and we can't take our eyes off each other. It was like we knew each other from somewhere but we couldn't place where. But the second we saw each other, that very second, we knew we'd never stop being in love.

    [MAY *slams bathroom door behind her. Door booms. Lights bang back up to their previous setting.*]

MAY: [*to* EDDIE] Boy, you really are incredible! You're unbelievable! Martin comes over here. He doesn't know you from Adam and you start telling him a story like that. Are you crazy? None of it's true, Martin. He's had this weird, sick idea for years now and it's totally made up. He's nuts. I don't know where he got it from. He's completely nuts.

EDDIE: [*to* MARTIN] She's kinda embarrassed about the whole deal, see. You can't blame her really.

MARTIN: I didn't even know you could hear us out here, May. I—

MAY: I heard every word. I followed it very carefully. He's told me that story a thousand times and it always changes.

EDDIE: I never repeat myself.

MAY: You do nothing but repeat yourself. That's all you do. You just go in a big circle.

MARTIN: [*standing*] Well, maybe I should leave.

EDDIE: NO! You sit down.

    [*Silence.* MARTIN *slowly sits again.*]

EDDIE: [*quietly to* MARTIN, *leaning toward him*] Did you think that was a story, Martin? Did you think I made that whole thing up?

MARTIN: No. I mean, at the time you were telling it, it seemed real.

EDDIE: But now you're doubting it because she says it's a lie?

MARTIN: Well—

EDDIE: She suggests it's a lie to you and all of a sudden you change your mind? Is that it? You go from true to false like that, in a second?

MARTIN: I don't know.

MAY: Let's go to the movies, Martin.

    [MARTIN *stands again.*]

EDDIE: Sit down!

    [MARTIN *sits back down. Long pause.*]

MAY: Eddie—

[*Pause*]

EDDIE: What?

MAY: We want to go to the movies. [*Pause.* EDDIE *just stares at her.*] I want to go to the movies with Martin. Right now.

EDDIE: Nobody's going to the movies. There's not a movie in this town that can match the story I'm gonna tell. I'm gonna finish this story.

MAY: Eddie —

EDDIE: You wanna' hear the rest of the story, don't ya', Martin?

MARTIN: [*Pause. He looks at* MAY *then back to* EDDIE] Sure.

MAY: Martin, let's go. Please.

MARTIN: I —

[*Long pause.* EDDIE *and* MARTIN *stare at each other.*]

EDDIE: You what?

MARTIN: I don't mind hearing the rest of it if you want to tell the rest of it.

THE OLD MAN: [*to himself*] I'm dyin' to hear it myself.

[EDDIE *leans back in his chair. Grins.*]

MAY: [*to* EDDIE] What do you think this is going to do? Do you think this is going to change something?

EDDIE: No.

MAY: Then what's the point?

EDDIE: It's absolutely pointless.

MAY: Then why put everybody through this? Martin doesn't want to hear this bullshit. *I* don't want to hear it.

EDDIE: I know *you* don't wanna' hear it.

MAY: Don't try to pass it off on me! You got it all turned around, Eddie. You got it all turned around. You don't even know which end is up anymore. Okay. Okay. I don't need either of you. I don't need any of it because I already know the rest of the story. I know the whole rest of the story, see. [*She speaks directly to* EDDIE, *who remains sitting.*] I know it just exactly the way it happened. Without any little tricks added on to it.

[THE OLD MAN *leans over to* EDDIE, *confidentially.*]

THE OLD MAN: What does she know?

EDDIE: [*to* OLD MAN[ She's lying.

[*Lights begin to shift down again in the course of* MAY's *story. She moves very slowly downstage then crosses toward* OLD MAN *as she tells it.*]

MAY: You want me to finish the story for you, Eddie? Huh? You want me to finish this story? [*Pause as* MARTIN *sits again*] See, my mother — the pretty red-haired woman in the little white house with the red awning, was desperately in love with the old man. Wasn't she, Eddie? You could tell that right away. You could see it in her eyes. She was obsessed with him to the point where she couldn't stand being without him for even a second. She kept hunting for him from town to town. Following little clues that he left behind, like a postcard maybe, or a motel on the back of a matchbook. [*To* MARTIN] He never left her a phone number or an address or anything as simple as that because my mother was his secret, see. She hounded him for years and he kept trying to keep her at a distance because the closer these two separate lives drew together, these two separate women, these two separate kids, the more nervous he got. The more filled with terror that the two lives would find out about each other and devour

him whole. That his secret would take him by the throat. But finally she caught
up with him. Just by a process of elimination she dogged him down. I remember the day we discovered the town. She was on fire. "This is it!" she kept
saying; "this is the place!" Her whole body was trembling as we walked
through the streets, looking for the house where he lived. She kept squeezing
my hand to the point where I thought she'd crush the bones in my fingers. She
was terrified she'd come across him by accident on the street because she knew
she was trespassing. She knew she was crossing this forbidden zone but she
couldn't help herself. We walked all day through that stupid hick town. All day
long. We went through every neighborhood, peering through every open
window, looking in at every dumb family, until finally we found him.
  [Rest]
  It was just exactly supper time and they were all sitting down at the table and
they were having fried chicken. That's how close we were to the window. We
could see what they were eating. We could hear their voices but we couldn't
make out what they were saying. Eddie and his mother were talking but the old
man never said a word. Did he, Eddie? Just sat there eating his chicken in
silence.

THE OLD MAN: [to EDDIE] Boy, is she ever off the wall with this one. You gotta' do
  somethin' about this.

MAY: The funny thing was, that almost as soon as we'd found him — he disappeared.
  She was only with him about two weeks before he just vanished. Nobody saw
  him after that. Ever. And my mother — just turned herself inside out. I never
  could understand that. I kept watching her grieve, as though somebody'd died.
  She'd pull herself up into a ball and just stare at the floor. And I couldn't
  understand that because I was feeling the exact opposite feeling. I was in love,
  see. I'd come home after school, after being with Eddie, and I was filled with
  this joy and there she'd be — standing in the middle of the kitchen staring at
  the sink. Her eyes looked like a funeral. And I didn't know what to say. I didn't
  even feel sorry for her. All I could think of was him.

THE OLD MAN: [to EDDIE] She's gettin' way outa' line, here.

MAY: And all he could think of was me. Isn't that right, Eddie? We couldn't take a
  breath without thinking of each other. We couldn't eat if we weren't together.
  We couldn't sleep. We got sick at night when we were apart. Violently sick.
  And my mother even took me to see a doctor. And Eddie's mother took him to
  see the same doctor but the doctor had no idea what was wrong with us. He
  thought it was the flu or something. And Eddie's mother had no idea what was
  wrong with him. But my mother — my mother knew exactly what was wrong.
  She knew it clear down to her bones. She recognized every symptom. And she
  begged me not to see him but I wouldn't listen. Then she begged Eddie not to
  see me but he wouldn't listen. Then she went to Eddie's mother and begged
  her. And Eddie's mother — [Pause. She looks straight at EDDIE] — Eddie's
  mother blew her brains out. Didn't she, Eddie? Blew her brains right out.

THE OLD MAN: [standing, he moves from the platform onto the stage, between EDDIE
  and MAY] Now, wait a second! Wait a second. Just a goddamn second here.
  This story doesn't hold water. [To EDDIE who stays seated.] You're not gonna'
  let her off the hook with that one are ya'? That's the dumbest version I ever
  heard in my whole life. She never blew her brains out. Nobody ever told me

that. Where the hell did that come from? [*To* EDDIE *who remains seated*] Stand up! Get on yer feet now goddamn it! I wanna' hear the male side a' this thing. You gotta' represent me now. Speak on my behalf. There's no one to speak for me now! Stand up!

> [EDDIE *stands slowly. Stares at* OLD MAN.]

Now tell her. Tell her the way it happened. We've got a pact. Don't forget that.

EDDIE: [*calmly to* OLD MAN] It was your shotgun. Same one we used to duck hunt with. Browning. She never fired a gun before in her life. That was her first time.

THE OLD MAN: Nobody told me any a' that. I was left completely in the dark.

EDDIE: You were gone.

THE OLD MAN: Somebody could've found me! Somebody could've hunted me down. I wasn't that impossible to find.

EDDIE: You were gone.

THE OLD MAN: That's right, I was gone! I was gone! You're right. But I wasn't disconnected. There was nothing cut off in me. Everything went on just the same as though I'd never left. [*to* MAY] But *your* mother—your mother wouldn't give it up, would she?

> [THE OLD MAN *moves toward* MAY *and speaks directly to her.* MAY *keeps her eyes on* EDDIE *who very slowly turns toward her in the course of* THE OLD MAN's *speech. Once their eyes meet they never leave each other's gaze.*]

THE OLD MAN: [*to* MAY] She drew me to her. She went out of her way to draw me in. She was a force. I told her I'd never come across for her. I told her that right from the very start. But she opened up to me. She wouldn't listen. She kept opening up her heart to me. How could I turn her down when she loved me like that? How could I turn away from her? We were completely whole.

> [EDDIE *and* MAY *just stand there staring at each other.* THE OLD MAN *moves back to* EDDIE. *Speaks to him directly.*]

THE OLD MAN: [*to* EDDIE] What're you doin'? Speak to her. Bring her around to our side. You gotta' make her see this thing in a clear light.

> [*Very slowly* EDDIE *and* MAY *move toward each other.*]

THE OLD MAN: [*to* EDDIE] Stay away from her! What the hell are you doin'! Keep away from her! You two can't come together! You gotta hold up my end a' this deal. I got nobody now! Nobody! You can't betray me! You gotta' represent me now! You're my son!

> [EDDIE *and* MAY *come together center stage. They embrace. They kiss each other tenderly. Headlights suddenly arc across stage again from upright, cutting across the stage through window then disappearing off left. Sound of loud collision, shattering glass, an explosion. Bright orange and blue light of a gasoline fire suddenly illuminates upstage window. Then sounds of horses screaming wildly, hooves galloping on pavement, fading, then total silence. Light of gas fire continues now to end of play.* EDDIE *and* MAY *never stop holding each other through all this. Long pause. No one moves. Then* MARTIN *stands and moves upstage to window, peers out through Venetian blinds. Pause.*]

MARTIN: [*upstage at window, looking out into flames*] Is that your truck with the horse trailer out there?

EDDIE: [*stays with* MAY] Yeah.

MARTIN: It's on fire.

EDDIE: Yeah.

MARTIN: All the horses are loose.

EDDIE: [*steps back away from* MAY] Yeah, I figured.

MAY: Eddie —

EDDIE: [*to* MAY] I'm just gonna' go out and take a look. I gotta' at least take a look, don't I?

MAY: What difference does it make?

EDDIE: Well, I can't just let her get away with that. What am I supposed to do? [*moves toward stage left door*] I'll just be a second.

MAY: Eddie —

EDDIE: I'm only gonna' be a second. I'll just take a look at it and I'll come right back. Okay?

> [EDDIE *exits stage left door.* MAY *stares at door, stays where she is.* MARTIN *stays upstage.* MARTIN *turns slowly from window upstage and looks at* MAY. *Pause.* MAY *moves to bed, pulls suitcase out from underneath, throws it on bed and opens it. She goes into bathroom and comes out with clothes. She packs the clothes in suitcase.* MARTIN *watches her for a while then moves slowly downstage to her as she continues.*]

MARTIN: May —

> [MAY *goes back into bathroom and comes back out with more clothes. She packs them.*]

MARTIN: Do you need some help or anything? I got a car. I could drive you somewhere if you want. [*Pause.* MAY *just keeps packing her clothes.*] Are you going to go with him?

> [*She stops. Straightens up. Stares at* MARTIN. *Pause.*]

MAY: He's gone.

MARTIN: He said he'd be back in a second.

MAY: [*Pause*] He's gone.

> [MAY *exits with suitcase out stage left door. She leaves the door open behind her.* MARTIN *just stands there staring at open door for a while.* THE OLD MAN *looks stage left at his rocking chair then a little above it, in blank space. Pause.* OLD MAN *starts moving slowly back to the platform.*]

THE OLD MAN: [*pointing into space, stage left*] Ya' see that picture over there? Ya' see that? Ya' know who that is? That's the woman of my dreams. That's who that is. And she's mine. She's all mine. Forever.

> [*He reaches rocking chair, sits, but keeps staring at imaginary picture. He begins to rock very slowly in the chair. After* OLD MAN *sits in rocker, Merle Haggard's "I'm the One who Loves You" starts playing as lights begin a very slow fade.* MARTIN *moves slowly upstage to window and stops. He stares out with his back to audience. The fire glows through window as stage lights fade.* OLD MAN *keeps rocking slowly. Stage lights keep fading slowly to black. Fire glows for a while in the dark then cuts to black. Song continues in dark and swells in volume.*]

END